More Praise for
Being Thomas Jefferson

"Noted Jefferson scholar Andrew Burstein has produced an elegantly written exploration of our third president's inner life. *Being Thomas Jefferson* is a thought-provoking and timely addition to the literature on Jefferson."

—Annette Gordon-Reed, author of *The Hemingses of Monticello: An American Family* and *On Juneteenth*

"An exciting, sensitive, and perceptive probe into the hidden Jefferson. It is a touchingly personal and succinct book that complements and culminates Burstein's lifelong contribution to understanding Jefferson. Those new to Jefferson literature will find it comprehensive and engaging. Scholars will appreciate its insights and speculations about its mysterious subject."

—Fred Kaplan, author of *John Quincy Adams: American Visionary* and *His Masterly Pen: A Biography of Jefferson the Writer*

"Fresh and persuasive, *Being Thomas Jefferson* helps reinterpret this immensely complex man for the modern reader. Through enormous and wide-ranging research, Andrew Burstein intervenes at critical moments in Thomas Jefferson's long life to offer penetrating analytical insights."

—John B. Boles, author of *Jefferson: Architect of American Liberty*

"There is no finer scholar of the inner life of Thomas Jefferson than Andrew Burstein. In this brilliant, provocative new book, Burstein picks up where Fawn Brodie left off fifty years ago and shows us a Jefferson who was torn between his powerful desire to achieve fame and leave his mark on history, and the impulse to retreat from public life. The result is a beautifully written study that shows Jefferson in a new light, calling us to reconsider what we thought we knew about the Sage of Monticello."

—Francis D. Cogliano, author of *A Revolutionary Friendship: Washington, Jefferson, and the American Republic*

"I thought I knew Thomas Jefferson. I've read the hagiographies, the political philosophers, the learned biographies, the psychologists, the muckrakers. I'm familiar with the facts and speculations about his secret life with Sally Hemings. I've studied the marble statue on the Tidal Basin and the arguments for taking that statue down. It turns out I didn't know Jefferson half so well as I thought. This 'intimate history' is neither gossip nor psychoanalysis. It's not hero worship or iconoclasm. Burstein has an encyclopedic knowledge of Jefferson's world—which vegetables came to table in Virginia, which philosophers could be found in Philadelphia bookstores, and what pornography one might access in Paris. He also has that genius quality of telling us what we could have known all along, if only we were sensible enough to see what was in plain sight. It turns out that Thomas Jefferson, like you and me, was a human being."

—Joseph Kelly, author of *Marooned* and *The Biggest Lie*

BEING THOMAS JEFFERSON

BY THE SAME AUTHOR

*Longing for Connection: Entangled Memories and Emotional
Loss in Early America* (2024)

*Democracy's Muse: How Thomas Jefferson Became an FDR Liberal, a Reagan
Republican, and a Tea Party Fanatic, All the While Being Dead* (2015)

*Lincoln Dreamt He Died: The Midnight Visions of Remarkable
Americans from Colonial Times to Freud* (2013)

The Original Knickerbocker: The Life of Washington Irving (2007)

Jefferson's Secrets: Death and Desire at Monticello (2005)

The Passions of Andrew Jackson (2003)

Letters from the Head and Heart: Writings of Thomas Jefferson (2002)

*America's Jubilee: How in 1826 a Generation Remembered
Fifty Years of Independence* (2001)

Sentimental Democracy: The Evolution of America's Romantic Self-Image (1999)

The Inner Jefferson: Portrait of a Grieving Optimist (1995)

CO-AUTHORED WITH NANCY ISENBERG

*The Problem of Democracy: The Presidents Adams Confront the
Cult of Personality* (2019)

Madison and Jefferson (2010)

CO-EDITED WITH NANCY ISENBERG

Rip Van Winkle's Republic: Washington Irving in History and Memory (2022)

Mortal Remains: Death in Early America (2003)

Miniature portrait of Thomas Jefferson by Connecticut artist John Trumbull, 1788. This oil painting on wood was presented by the artist to Jefferson's then sixteen-year-old daughter Martha ("Patsy"). (Courtesy Thomas Jefferson Foundation)

BEING THOMAS JEFFERSON

An Intimate History

ANDREW BURSTEIN

BLOOMSBURY PUBLISHING
NEW YORK · LONDON · OXFORD · NEW DELHI · SYDNEY

BLOOMSBURY PUBLISHING
Bloomsbury Publishing Inc.
1359 Broadway, New York, NY 10018, USA
50 Bedford Square, London, WC1B 3DP, UK
Bloomsbury Publishing Ireland Limited,
29 Earlsfort Terrace, Dublin 2, D02 AY28, Ireland

BLOOMSBURY, BLOOMSBURY PUBLISHING, and the Diana logo are trademarks
of Bloomsbury Publishing Plc

First published in the United States 2026

Copyright © Andrew Burstein, 2026

All rights reserved. No part of this publication may be: i) reproduced or transmitted in any form, electronic or mechanical, including photocopying, recording, or by means of any information storage or retrieval system without prior permission in writing from the publishers; or ii) used or reproduced in any way for the training, development, or operation of artificial intelligence (AI) technologies, including generative AI technologies. The rights holders expressly reserve this publication from the text and data mining exception as per Article 4(3) of the Digital Single Market Directive (EU) 2019/790.

Bloomsbury Publishing Plc does not have any control over, or responsibility for, any third-party websites referred to or in this book. All internet addresses given in this book were correct at the time of going to press. The author and publisher regret any inconvenience caused if addresses have changed or sites have ceased to exist, but can accept no responsibility for any such changes.

ISBN: HB: 978-1-63973-768-0; EBOOK: 978-1-63973-769-7

LIBRARY OF CONGRESS CATALOGING-IN-PUBLICATION DATA IS AVAILABLE

2 4 6 8 10 9 7 5 3 1

Typeset by Westchester Publishing Services
Printed in the United States at Lakeside Book Company

To find out more about our authors and books visit www.bloomsbury.com
and sign up for our newsletters.

Bloomsbury books may be purchased for business or promotional use. For information on bulk purchases please contact Macmillan Corporate and Premium Sales Department at specialmarkets@macmillan.com.

For product safety–related questions contact productsafety@bloomsbury.com.

In memory of Daniel P. Jordan (1938–2024)

There was a sympathy between his heart and the great popular heart, which nothing ever did, ever can, shake.

—HENRY S. RANDALL, *LIFE OF THOMAS JEFFERSON* (1858)

He indulged himself like a prince, confident that such was his right as an aristocrat of the spirit and valued servant to the state. It is likely that this habit of indulgence began as a child.

—FAWN M. BRODIE, *THOMAS JEFFERSON: AN INTIMATE HISTORY* (1974)

CONTENTS

List of Illustrations — xv
Introduction: Jefferson Seen and Unseen — xvii

PART I: PERSONAL GROWTH

1. "Savage Enough": His Ruptured Childhood — 3
2. "Sukey at Smith": Sexual Secrets of a Young Lawyer — 29
3. "Till Harmony Rouse Ev'ry Gentle Passion": Mountain Paradise — 53

PART II: PASSIONATE YEARS

4. "Thrown into a Reverie": From Romance to Revolution — 67
5. "Every Fibre of That Passion": A Declaration and an Adieu — 93
6. "Gazing Like a Lover at His Mistress": French Women — 123
7. "An Abuse of Strength": Condorcet's Challenge, Maria's Maid — 145

PART III: POLITICAL HAZARDS

8. "Open Mouthed Against Me": An Age of Contempt — 169
9. "The Late Political Paroxysm": Fever, Delirium, and Calumny — 195
10. "The Campaign of Slander Is Opening": Adams vs. Jefferson vs. Burr — 227
11. "Bloody Teeth & Fangs": Sentimental Rage, Presidential Power — 245
12. "I Feel No Passion, I Take No Part": Second Term Schisms — 269

PART IV: IMPERILED LEGACY

13. "Suspicions & Certainties, Rumors & Realities": Exorcising Washington's Ghost — 295

Appendix A: Jefferson-Wayles-Hemings Family Tree — 325
Appendix B: A Note on Sources, and Sources of Inspiration — 327
Acknowledgments — 333
Notes — 337
Index — 415

LIST OF ILLUSTRATIONS

Frontispiece: Thomas Jefferson, miniature by John Trumbull, 1788

Fig. 1	The Cherokee warrior Outassetè	2
Fig. 2	Title page, Lieut. Henry Timberlake's 1765 memoir	25
Fig. 3	Monticello layout, ca. 1768	28
Fig. 4	George Wythe	35
Fig. 5	Page from Jefferson's library record, 1783	52
Fig. 6	Title page, *Fingal, An Ancient Epic Poem*, 1762	66
Fig. 7	Title page, Jefferson's *A Summary View*, 1774	76
Fig. 8	Jefferson's original draft, Declaration of Independence	92
Fig. 9	Letter, Jefferson to Elizabeth Wayles Eppes, 1782	117
Fig. 10	Maria Cosway	122
Fig. 11	Letter, Jefferson to Maria Cosway, 1787	141
Fig. 12	The Marquis de Condorcet	144
Fig. 13	Alexander Hamilton	168
Fig. 14	"Congressional Pugilists," 1798	194
Fig. 15	President Jefferson	226
Fig. 16	The President's House, 1807	244
Fig. 17	"Thomas Jefferson, the Pride of America," 1809	268
Fig. 18	Jefferson's opinion of Aaron Burr	278
Fig. 19	Monticello	294
Fig. 20	Jefferson's polygraph	314
Fig. 21	Jefferson's grave, ca. 1866	322

INTRODUCTION

Jefferson Seen and Unseen

WHAT MIGHT IT HAVE been like to be Thomas Jefferson? Just weighing such a question raises questions anew, implicitly demanding a rationale for reopening the locked box of agitated memory that an intimate history entails. As one of the most polarizing figures in all of American history, Jefferson bequeathed a strong heartbeat in the form of an extensive, often impassioned, correspondence. He dreamt big and made himself known, advertising himself as a man of wholesome public aims who marveled endlessly at the natural world, cherished hearth and home, and, when pressures built, valued his solitude. He wrote constantly, lyrically, affectingly.

In his mid-twenties, this completely self-taught architect decided to level a mountain and undertake construction of a unique residence, his awe-inspiring Palladian villa, Monticello. From this breathtaking location he collected thousands of books on every topic imaginable, from ancient history to modern medical practices. He looked out at the world with eagerness and readiness. In doing so, the occasional philosopher and steadfast correspondent was periodically tripped up by secrets he could not keep hidden and words that went too far. Navigating the "rocks and shoals" of a life beset by emotional challenges, he lurched for safe harbor.[1]

This book is about the extraordinary drama that punctuated the life of a famous man who had an unusual need to control his environment. As much as his creative imagination led to memorable achievements, the capaciousness of his intellect exacted a price. When enticed by nature's mysteries, his eyes were wide open to new possibilities. But when it came to the clash of egos in public venues, he was acutely sensitive to slights. He rarely admitted error and, as a sensualist, rationalized the indulgences he allowed himself. Jefferson was a complicated man.

There is a good explanation for his vacillating moods when under pressure. The Age of Enlightenment that shaped his critical mind was also an age of nervous sensibility. The brain was seen as "the seat of sensations." It exalted ethical deliberation and led a thinker to prize individual freedom. It promoted sociability while cautioning against wanton gratification of the natural passions. And it pronounced rigid expectations from men of letters, who were to guard against an incapacitating "irritability" of nerves that improper diet and agitated sleep brought on. An explosion of thought and theory—this new science of man—placed demands on both body and spirit. To be of the Enlightenment was to study desires and appetites, not just ways of knowing.[2]

In this world, Jefferson contracted personal friendships that were marked by an intense resolve and that grew to encompass great names on both sides of the Atlantic. In the danger zone of politics, he deployed his personal relationships much as a battlefield commander would, aware that he had enemies who could never be won over. He convinced himself that they would destroy everything he valued if he remained passive.

Yet Thomas Jefferson was essentially an introvert, a bookish individual whose "alone time" was precious to him. He internalized a great deal of what sat on his bookshelves, and ordered his private world accordingly. As a student of science who experimented regularly, he approached situations with due deliberation. As a romantic, he imagined it possible to change the world for the better and wrote with high-flown expectancy. It was the latter trait that led the more critical among his peers to label him a "philosopher," which was their way of saying "dreamer."

To write an intimate history is a formidable summons, because any approach to historical biography is autopsy, not a two-sided conversation. I have spent a sizable chunk of my career with Jefferson and have at length arrived at a place where I feel I can tackle the largest questions that have hamstrung a slew of professional historians. *Being Thomas Jefferson* emphasizes the drive for public celebrity that the subject scrupulously hid. As a study of inner life, the book's central drama is the negotiation going on in his mind as he wavers between involvement and retreat, between conviction and irresolution.

Here was a family man, a gentleman scholar, a political actor. These three distinct layers to his personality—which is not to say that his identity lacked additional layers—fell out of alignment each time the serene farmer ("a son of nature," he once called himself) surrendered to partisan combat. He bristled at the irritants that beset a politician's life. More often than not, though he felt the friction of going against his stated desire, he couldn't resist national office.

"Public" versus "private" are convenient terms for what this book examines, although people are more complex than that. One does not carry around a private and a public self and opt to deploy one or the other in a given situation. The private Jefferson lived in areas set apart: the bedroom, the *unseen* room where strong feelings emerge, where sex occurs, where a woman gives birth surrounded by other women (midwife, servants), and where the waiting for death occurs, as it too often did at Monticello. Then there is the *seen* though still private realm, intimate settings where Jefferson performs as entertainer over food and drink, where the self is exposed to people; or, in writing a letter, where he lets his mind range with a single recipient in mind.

Jefferson's instinct to guard his privacy was strong. As soon as he moved into the building that stands at 1600 Pennsylvania Avenue, which was less than a year old in 1801, he ordered the outhouse removed and an indoor water closet built to his specifications. He then set out to introduce adornments to the public spaces, adding decorative molding to the walls, colorful upholstery to the furnishings, and glass doors. He shaped environments with the same care he gave to written compositions.[3]

A second theme, integrally related to private versus public, concerns Jefferson's expectations from citizens of the republic, as he envisioned it and them. He believed that the character of a nation mirrored its people's sensibilities. His outlook on intimate connections, pledges of commitment, and historically formed affinities played a role in most of what he wrote for public consumption. He made everything personal. So it's no accident that his original draft of the Declaration of Independence decried "the last stab to agonizing affection," compelling the former colonies to "renounce for ever these unfeeling brethren." It is no less intriguing that the art of expression that made him a future-directed idealist merged with a presidential agenda that was methodically pursued. He wrote intuitively and unreservedly, and he held forth alertly on real-world problems without reneging on his idealistic pronouncements.[4]

Jefferson's powers of concentration were extraordinary. In advancing his vision of representative democracy, he knew precisely the message he wanted to deliver, and he invariably found the rhetorical framing that best supported it. Language was an intoxicating field of study in his day, known for its ability to move a nation. Modern Americans insufficiently grasp how much Jefferson did to shape a new national vocabulary and give birth to an American cultural identity.

As he seeks to persuade or seduce or selectively reveal, he tells us something about himself. That "something" speaks directly to the probative purpose of this book: how to read intent in the words he chooses, how to detect angst in the novel ways he tries to control his image. His story becomes something of a psychological reckoning when he reveals a hidden agenda in this manner.

Part of that psychological reckoning must involve Jefferson's participation in—one might say attachment to—the institution of slavery. Scholars of slavery and antislavery have, from various angles, exposed his weak rationalizations, his sophistry, his selfish choices. We know why he receives this kind of coverage: the powerful, enduring statement about human dignity and equality that he penned in 1776 grants him symbolic importance in America's story and makes him an obvious target. In this book, Jefferson's activities as an enslaver and timidity as a would-be abolitionist belong to a discussion of both his public and his private character—they are an integral component part, but not the centerpiece, of his moral identity. I am scrutinizing a many-sided individual whose emotional makeup was shaped by a wide range of influences, the sum of which carries both negative and positive weight.[5]

I hold that the private-public disjunction is as much a cause of frustration for biographers who have offered competing interpretations of his impulses as it was for the historical Jefferson who scrambled to find the right tools to survive in a problematic social environment. In either case, this man of private needs and public objectives carried on a pitched battle that is not covered in our history texts. He fought what he saw as agitation emanating from unfriendly sources; yet his own actions fed unrest, which he then had to undo. This is another reason why this complicated man, who died two hundred years ago, continues to command our attention.

∼

MOST AMERICANS HAVE FORMED some idea of who Jefferson was. They might think of the domed memorial in Washington, D.C., lit up brilliantly as night descends, the founder's exquisite words circling the inside of the open-air structure: I HAVE SWORN UPON THE ALTAR OF GOD ETERNAL HOSTILITY AGAINST EVERY FORM OF TYRANNY OVER THE MIND OF MAN. To step onto the lawn of the university he founded in Charlottesville, Virginia, as a retired ex-president is to realize that his architectural designs and ardent desire to grow an educated citizenry live on. He would not die before he'd made that gift to the cause of human knowledge. A bold thinker. A humane philosopher. A champion of freedom who embodies the American ideal.[6]

That's one Jefferson. But he was also stubborn and reactive, unwilling to reconsider a prejudice when good contradictory evidence was presented to him. Gratuitous insults toward Black individuals may be the clearest example of this failing, but there are other unsettling examples of his misjudgment as a public figure, enough to establish a larger pattern of distortion in his thinking.

He was, notably, the first chief executive to occupy the White House for two terms, defeating the opposition party and marking the first peaceful transition of power. His most conspicuous achievement, of course, is the Declaration of Independence, which he drafted in Philadelphia at the age of thirty-three. The worn parchment remains on display in the National Archives, a sacred relic encased in glass. The mind of Jefferson is unquestionably embedded in its words, though the Continental Congress, when it adopted the Declaration in early July 1776, toned it down somewhat. The pride of its penman led Jefferson, in his late seventies, to make certain that posterity would have his original draft to place alongside the finished text.

So, who was the "real" Thomas Jefferson? Can that person be credibly reconstituted? I am bold enough to suggest that a map of social engagement can be drawn, that intimate relations are discoverable, and that a modest amount of psychic penetration is possible.

From the Virginia Piedmont that was imprinted on him at birth, through the particular education he was afforded and the accidents of fortune that brought him celebrity, Jefferson presents a somewhat muddled picture to the historian. One sees a man of strong social purposes, and also a man of extreme reserve. What motivated him? What was his endgame? Others have posed these kinds of questions. In order to set my work apart, I enter untrodden areas of inquiry and revisit relationships that have been undervalued. These will be previewed below.

~

How language worked on people of the past matters greatly. One cannot fully appreciate the Declaration, Jefferson's five years as U.S. minister to France (1784–1789), his subsequent role in George Washington's cabinet (1790–1793), or the willfulness he brought to the presidency (1801–1809) without intelligently encountering an emotional reality that is at odds with modern sensibilities.

I find this subject at once daunting and invigorating. The only way to legitimize a work of history—an intimate history, especially—is to cross the threshold into the past with great care, sensitive to "us" versus "them." It means sketching the contours of life among the learned, reading correspondence for implications in what is said or left unsaid. It also means looking at manifestations of privacy (or "interiority") in physical spaces and in literary prose, reproducing a perceptual environment now lost. How the five senses cooperated in that world, how words on a page provoked adoration or outrage, speak volumes. As the differences are taken into account, one begins to reorient enough to operate within boundaries of emotional expression closer to what was available to Jefferson and his peers.[7]

Despite the seemingly endless Jefferson studies that adorn library shelves, few tease out truths about his inner life. Some of our best historians, after years of analyzing the ins and outs of his career, admitted defeat in plumbing Jefferson's personality. He was "impenetrable," "the hardest to sound to the depths of being," confessed the erudite Merrill D. Peterson in the preface to his thousand-page biography. For some scholars, it is enough to contrast Jefferson with a mindful minority who were exponents of antislavery, and thus to label the self-styled humanist a hypocrite. That's too easy. One must know more.[8]

It has been fifty years since the controversial Jefferson biographer and UCLA historian Fawn Brodie sent shock waves through the historical profession by claiming insight into his psyche—and, most sensationally, his libido. Her *Thomas Jefferson: An Intimate History* (1974) remains popular. It reveals Brodie as a dyed-in-the-wool Freudian, bold and unflinching in her speculations. The alluring portrait she painted merits a proper update.

Professor Brodie set academia on fire when she relaunched the long-dismissed tabloid tale of Thomas Jefferson and the biracial Sally Hemings, which DNA effectively verified in 1997, long after Brodie's death. Those who persist in dismissing the importance of Jefferson's private life have generally treated such inquiries as displays of peeping-Tom prurience. An intimate history, as I conceive the matter, cannot just be a single-minded quest to expose bad behavior or deceit. Biographers' attempts to decode Jefferson's political positions and reckon with his occasionally deficient way of governing himself have tended not to view expansively enough the ways in which intimacy played out across early American society.[9]

Intimacy, as presented here, encompasses sex but is not confined to sex. It extends to emotional relationships shaped by culture: meaningful friendships, mentors in early adulthood, even personal enemies. Freud saw sex everywhere—this is not that. I am interested only in examining the eighteenth-century mode of treating sexuality and intimacy. Ideas about human anatomy, common medical conditions, and mental health are part of that. Older perceptions of sex are also critical to an understanding of Jefferson's experience of intimacy. He was a keen student of private life and sexual instincts as these were expressed in works of literature, dating to classical antiquity, that he owned and studied, reread and quoted.[10]

I open the book by examining the sensations that greeted colonial Virginians, body and mind. There are the obvious facts: Jefferson's America was an unsanitary, slow-moving, candlelit domain. Then there are matters of personal comportment and social concerns that place him at a distance from our century. Marriages were most often contracted at an early age, though few husbands and wives grew old together; divorce was rare and remarriage extremely common after the death of a spouse. Social rank was intuited, respect for age implicit, continuity pursued through inheritance, and personal psychology arranged in few categories we would recognize—which is to say that members of Jefferson's social class perceived the separation between vital essence and public façade less as camouflage and more a matter of decency and propriety. For the same reason, they did not write historical biography to penetrate: it was meant to convey civic lessons.

Domestic life was alluded to indirectly and presented superficially. As a courtly representative of Virginia's elite class, Jefferson was expected to let down his guard with close male friends and tailor his behavior when in mixed company. He adopted a gentle, comforting manner with female acquaintances, an easygoing air that preserved masculine confidence while subtly reflecting his sensitivity to gender differences. We might perceive this not as refinement (the way they did), but as artifice. Some of the same posturing takes place in eighteenth-century correspondence and requires careful parsing—a task that is central to this book and to all history writing.[11]

Among this peerless book collector's well-thumbed leather-bound volumes, I find a significant number that were designated "philosophical medicine," and these presented male and female biological nature in ways that played into male privilege and male dominance (as the law also directed). The same code stigmatized an ambitious woman, who was said to "unsex" herself by striving to compete, even intellectually. In some quarters, misogyny was mainstream, and gender-specific humor, like racist humor, wholly admissible.

Fawn Brodie had a great deal to say about Jefferson's social skills and conversation that squares with my own view. He was not a misogynist in the way we think of it today. He disapproved of a "liberated" female in theory, yet respected the minds of numerous women of his acquaintance. Then again, he expressed blatantly misogynistic feelings about particular women whose outspokenness rubbed him the wrong way. As a privileged son of the South, bound to custom, he periodically showed signs of anxiety lest female intellectualism should go too far and upset gender norms. Thus, in matters of intimacy, he was not a liberal thinker in ways we might imagine. He was not modern.[12]

Despite a famously calm outward presentation—the enslaved at Monticello never saw him lose his temper—he satisfied a complex set of urges over the course of his life. This book represents Jefferson's behavior within a sexualized world. It shows that he was not too moral to seek an adulterous connection, risking long-term complications. On paper, he plainly objected to young men's predisposition to visit prostitutes, yet at the same time he accepted that men could not be expected to lock themselves away from all temptation. He does what he can to leave history guessing.[13]

On the strength of occasional musings in letters to friends, and the books he owned that prescribed healthful, regular sex for men like him, it is fair to conclude that he subscribed to the mainstream belief that the postpubescent female was biologically endowed with organs of pleasure in the service of conception. Like her male counterpart, she lacked an impulse to remain chaste. A gentlewoman could not rely on men to temper their lustful ways. She had to be determinedly taught to restrain libidinous thoughts, and to be removed from so-called "promiscuous" (that is, random, indiscriminately formed) settings where young people might be tempted to transgress on societal norms. The choice of a marital partner tended to be a complicated dance that involved family name, property, dowry, and kinship alliances. Curiously, while his peers married women who were presumptive virgins, Jefferson, at twenty-eight, chose for his spouse a young widow with a child.

Romantic life receives its due treatment in these pages, not because sex sells but because it matters that Jefferson loses at love more than he succeeds. Ten years of what he termed "unchequered happiness" with Martha Wayles Jefferson (he called his wife Patty) end with her death at thirty-three. Instead of remarrying someone from his social class, as his bereaved peers did, he took an enslaved domestic, Sally Hemings, as his concubine when she was quite young and, by all existing standards, a less than suitable companion. She was not a partner in the way his wife had been, but a woman who met the needs of a master, one who, by law, could exploit his human property. She was Patty Jefferson's half sister, which meant that in a roundabout way their connection mimicked an accepted pattern among eighteenth-century Virginians who married within family bloodlines. These facts reveal only so much: intimate spheres were disguised.

In both private and public ways, Jefferson suffers for his choices, or so it would appear. The ultimate love of his life may have been Monticello, which he lost to creditors and could not even pass on to family members. His intimate world becomes almost Shakespearean in how he brings about his own misfortunes.

The timing of his statements about love and lust matter. From 1772, when he married, Jefferson claimed to value companionate marriage. In the 1780s, after Patty's death, and while posted to Paris, he touted American cultural norms over the libertine practices among the upper classes in Europe. Yet he did not expect monogamy to remain secure in America either. Well into retirement, he was still musing (here to John Adams) that as much as society wished for the best specimens of male and female to breed, human nature proved that the best that could be hoped for was "the accidental *aristoi* produced by the fortuitous concourse of breeders." His "fortuitous concourse" was another way of saying that sexual desire ruled the day, that the "natural aristocracy" of proven talents his politics hoped for was, in that sense, a pipe dream. It bears mentioning that while Adams, his wife, and their eldest son were highly critical of white masters and their sexual activities with enslaved women, the elder Adams was apparently unwilling to buy in to the rumors, in circulation since 1802, of Jefferson's liaison with Hemings.[14]

Issues of private sexual behavior, like matters of race, have weight because they attach to day-to-day experience. It is no less the case that throughout his years as a political operative, the strategies Jefferson adopts are a direct outgrowth of an inner state that relates to his sense of dignity and authority. Who and how Jefferson hates matters as much as who and how he loves. All of this is intimacy.

In the external world, reputations rose and fell, some by gradual descent, some with catastrophic suddenness, typically owing to measures of public honor. As an eldest son from a good family, with the substantial expectations that this entailed, Jefferson was under pressure to perform. To warrant the public's trust, to serve as a model of right conduct, any Virginia gentleman had to be seen among others of his social set. He had to exhibit the studied conviviality of the age. As one entered eighteenth-century society, being seen was nearly synonymous with belonging.

JEFFERSON WAS A SECRETIVE individual, for the most part. As a product of his culture, he almost had to be. What self-revelation occurred was not done casually. It, too, was performative, and it generally came about through letter writing, a mannerly occupation whose conventions were not limited by geography. A letter bore a dignified face, which unfolded into something both refined and personal. Enough personality emerged that a letter-based friendship might endure for decades. More than a routine conveyor of information, the familiar letter (as these penned testaments are known) was treated as a keepsake, periodically reread, almost like a favorite poem.

Theirs was an age of typography. The penned or printed word directed both reason and imagination. For this reason, a skilled writer's collected letters were published and circulated. No one understood this fact better than the unusually well-read Thomas Jefferson, an enlightened practitioner within the justly named "republic of letters." He recognized the converse of the pen as the lifeblood of educated men and women, abounding in possibilities for practical instruction and psychological well-being. A polished, discriminating style was valued as a manifestation of one's identity, a way of sharing while adroitly establishing public credentials. When done well, it delivered personal advantage. Jefferson was famously artful in this manner, to the delight of most and to the dismay of those who saw him as duplicitous and were gleeful whenever a leaked letter caused him political embarrassment. Letters carried personal power and therefore invited judgment. They were barometers of emotion.

Untranslated, out of context, eighteenth-century letters can appear technical and unfeeling compared to what we now consider conversational writing. But as the practice evolved, eager writers like Jefferson and John Adams (but not George

Washington or James Madison, for instance), gravitated to a richer, sympathy-bearing idiom, which no doubt bled into intimate speech, now lost. Soft-spoken in person, Jefferson was extraordinarily adept at communicating emotion on the page. He designed his letters with the recipient's unique sensibility in mind and at times took real chances with what he left on the page. No matter what prompted a letter, he considered the exercise pointless if he did not at the same time convey an unmitigated spirit of elevated humanity—his true calling card.

Still, his words require considerable decoding. Within one letter, he'll transition from serious matters to local gossip with witty references to history or popular literature sandwiched in between. Often, his philosophy of life, his vaunted pursuit of happiness, anchored his letter. That optimistic spirit he delivered on was a supple tool of the trade, especially when he came to pair refined behavior with affectionate social bonds—initially denoted as "republican," and later "democratic," feeling. This was the beginning of America's comforting (albeit mythic) ideal of national greatness: selling the nation, and then the wider world, on the image of a young country that was the home of a do-good, upright, generous-hearted, *exceptional* people.

Notwithstanding a temperament ill-suited for hand-to-hand combat, Jefferson was unable to restrain himself from pushing his grand recipe for public happiness. Opposing those who excited (in the idiom of the day) "unhealthy passions," he put forward a galvanizing concept, "affectionate sympathy," which helped grow a popular fascination with the American idea of enlightened commonness—which, once again, translated as "democracy." The most hopeful voices of every subsequent generation have chosen to define democracy Jefferson's way. While by no means entirely of his invention, the rhetoric of the American Revolution has forever attached to the idea of *Jeffersonian* democracy. Jefferson is thus a fixture in both the birth of the United States and in the moral identity it claims.

∼

AS THE READER WILL shortly come to understand, Jefferson may have been the firstborn son in a land-rich lineage, but he did not have it easy. His was a fractured family, and he suffered profound losses. His private character came under fire at key moments in his nation's early history, conditioning his attitude toward political enemies. Inaction on the subject of race enslavement, which stains his modern reputation, was already a subject of mockery when he was president. And though he did not react, allegations of his sexual attraction to Sally Hemings, a woman he'd inherited from his father-in-law, rendered him a cartoonish figure in those places where he had more detractors than supporters. Indeed, sordid unauthorized histories detailing the sexual lives of the titled and the privileged were nothing new—they went back centuries and were to be expected.[15]

Yet it is important to note that neither race nor sex, important as they may now be in exploring who Jefferson was, caused him to lose sleep. Rather, it was the scandals he could not hide from involving personal hatreds that he struggled with until the end of his days. These were the ones that threatened his entire legacy as the patriot who strove to save his nation from devolving from sovereign republic into an overcentralized, antirepublican tyranny of the few.[16]

He wanted to let go of ambition, to retreat, but he was egged on by those in politics who regularly pleaded with him to return to the field of action when he wanted only to retire to the protected mountaintop where he'd carved out an idyllic (if economically insecure) family seat. He tried retirement more than once, but it did not stick. His close confidants knew, even though he and they never acknowledged it publicly, that he thrived on being designated a "man of the people," and so they let his private impulses play out.

Public and private combined to disrupt his personal quest for peace. The exercise of power, not surprisingly, contributed to the restlessness of a busy mind that waged battles against a committed opposition. Recurring headaches at pivotal moments in Jefferson's political life, sometimes lasting weeks, tell a story of frustration, overexpectation, and hidden angst. A fastidious man of unspoken, but very real, ambition, he lived with chronic bowel issues and could not tolerate disorder or derangement of a ritualized, lifelong system of health-conscious self-governance. There was no rest for the famous—except when he lived surrounded by family at the mountain refuge of his own design. His ideals were ever at home at Monticello.

∽

FAME IS A FACET of culture and needs to be viewed through a historical lens. Something no Jefferson scholar, myself included, has previously reckoned with until now is this beguiling writer's pursuit, not just of happiness, but of celebrity.[17] He *needed* to publicize his thoughts, both to achieve a feeling of concordance (that all was right in the world) and to assert his vision for state and nation. It was through a passive-aggressive urge to shape the literal, as well as political, landscape that he became an iconic force in the larger story of continental empire. He crafted the laws of Virginia after independence was declared, planned state and federal buildings in the grand classical manner, and longed to preside over an America that would awe Europeans by its embrace of individual freedom.

The word "fame" had multiple meanings in eighteenth-century America. Depending on context, it was akin to "rumor" (as in "common fame," word on the street); or it meant character, respectability, reputation; or it meant just what it means today: public eminence, a name. The fame Jefferson sought was the second one, closer to honor and the acceptance of one's ideas, credit for possession of a desirable character and a favorable reputation that would outlive him. Of course, he couldn't have the second meaning of "fame" without the third as well.

The fame (respect for his ideas) that Jefferson feared losing was that which he tied to a vibrant localized democracy. He worried about his political vision dissolving into one that moved governmental power from periphery to center, potentially leading back to monarchical forms. This became an extreme fear at the end of his life, though his prescriptive writing tried to deny it. What tends to be lost in the record is how stubbornly Jefferson resisted change. At identifiable moments over a long public career he prophesied ruinous consequences if his personal vision for a healthy republic was ignored. As a result, he made enemies, and he came up with behind-the-scenes plans to get the best of them.[18]

He did not experience fame as it is typically thought of today. He lived decades before photography, at a time when having a name meant recognition in print, and being talked about as a result. For much of his life, Jefferson enjoyed anonymity when he traveled. His manner of dress—shabby, his critics said mockingly—was largely a performance, symbolic of the lack of ostentation he deemed appropriate for elected leaders in a republic. In most other respects, he spent lavishly; for example, in maintaining a wine cellar from the earliest iteration of his home, and in making his family seat a showpiece of architectural splendor. Monticello is stunningly beautiful. It has been a National Historical Landmark since 1960, and it is now a UNESCO World Heritage site—one of only twelve in the United States.[19]

The larger point is that whatever his underlying reasons, Jefferson from a fairly early age wanted to make a difference. That mission to stand out grew by the decade until he could not have it any other way: to preserve the republic, and the vaunted spirit of 1776, America's historical consciousness required that his name and fame endure. This is not what is conventionally termed "vanity," and he was the very opposite of flamboyance. Yet his passion became a rare species of idealistic extremism. Jefferson the visionary came to regard himself as a rescuer, the preserver of a creative, dynamic spirit without which American political culture could not progress to its destiny.

∼

IN HIS ROLE AS a legislator, and much later as the nation's third chief executive, Jefferson did not doubt himself nor reverse an opinion. Writing to a firm friend in the middle of his first presidential term and claiming to act on behalf of all the people, he congratulated the citizenry (who spoke through him) with a resolve that was characteristic of him: "We are acting under obligations not confined to the limits of our own society," he pronounced. "It is impossible not to be sensible that we are acting for all mankind." If representative democracy could have a savior, that was who Thomas Jefferson aspired to be.[20]

The evidence presented in the chapters on Jefferson's late-career political struggles shows, in the stamina he exhibited and the imperative language that poured forth from his pen, that he indeed cast himself in this way: as the preeminent deliverer of enlightened republicanism. Among the problems he created for himself was wishing away challenges he considered too difficult to remediate. With his shaky rationalizations in furtherance of the institution of slavery or the dispossession of Native lands, for instance, he made allowances for himself while judging others' imperfections with considerably less sympathy.

I devote a fair amount of space in the book to how Jefferson got to a place in his own mind where a diagnosis of "republican savior" makes sense. But that's not where he started out. Prior to assuming his earliest public role as a legislator in the colonial capital of Williamsburg, he was already recognized as mindful, inventive, and adaptive; physically energetic, self-sufficient, yet eager to belong. As a learner, he respected his elders. He was patient and pliable.

From his early twenties to early thirties, great books did much to shape his outlook on history as it applied to the fortunes of nations. His philosophy told him that a nation, or a man who assumed a social position, should be strong in morals and conscientious in manners. Yet, as the Librarian of Congress Daniel Boorstin wrote, early in his own career, of the Jeffersonian mindset, it "combined a realistic and rather uncomplimentary view of the nature of man with a general hopefulness about society." Jefferson expected plentiful argument from his contentious fellows, but he summoned up a far more optimistic perspective on the composite functioning of elective government. Elected to the American Philosophical Society in 1780, he served as its president from 1797 through his post-presidency. Here is one of many places where Jefferson's self-image was amplified.[21]

He acquired his faith from a number of sources. John Locke's philosophy lit the lamp of Reason, lifting up the political idea of consent of the governed. Sir Isaac Newton's ordered, mechanistic universe provided the comforts of a material science that promised to progressively enlarge upon existing knowledge. Even the quashing of religious dogma still left open a world of sensation that could be better understood through experimental psychology. These conceptions of the European Enlightenment profoundly affected Jefferson as a young scholar. He read voraciously on the human condition, which brought him to doctrines of natural law and natural rights—the idea that one's resort to Reason took natural law and applied it to human government to produce the greatest good. Shortly before he assumed the presidency, the lawyer-politician provided a definition of "that fundamental law of nature, by which alone self government can be exercised by a society, I mean the *lex majoris partis* [majority rule]." No less important to his intellectual outlook than the right of self-government was Jefferson's love of natural wonders. His mind at all times juggled the practicable and the sublime.[22]

His political education as a son of the Virginia gentry did not complete the race to the top of state governance; it merely started the engine. To make everything he wanted from public life fit his temperament required more. It required community. The meaning of friendship was critical to Jefferson's emotional well-being throughout life. One example is his repeated effort to draw select friends physically close to him, practically begging them to move to the neighborhood of Monticello. The most important of these, his good-humored, independent-minded political alter ego James Madison, was unwilling to provide Jefferson the total communion he yearned for. He resisted the allure that was to entrap so many younger men—some famous in their own right, like James Monroe—who went on to do Jefferson's bidding uncritically.

Both as a promoter of his native county of Albemarle, and because he knew he could not change the complexion of political life on his own, he felt a need to bring his friends closer. In the hypermasculine world of political speech, he was construed by those he thought of as rivals to be a coward who, in his hidden bitterness, adopted stealth tactics to achieve his aims. His detractors were not entirely mistaken. He held grudges.

In this book, the reader encounters a reluctant campaigner whose public display of imperturbability masked what he actually felt when his pride was being assailed. How he fought back in aggressive letters to supporters and trusted friends is a revealing part of the story, and it goes far in explaining how he eventually came to regard himself as the republic's savior.

◡

WHAT ACCORDS POWER TO words? Clearly, Jefferson knew. It was the work of his pen that made him, and it is his words that enshrine him in national lore. The best Jefferson is foundational, his words far-reaching, and no biographical study of him is complete without a careful analysis of how he rose to prominence on this basis.

Fortunately, for students of history, he bequeathed to posterity an immense written record. He did so by design, because he hoped that a determined preservation of documents would stand him in good stead with future historians. Naturally, he could not forecast what our passions, our concerns, would lead us to emphasize in evaluating that record. Since the 1960s, the pendulum has swung forcefully, and scholarly works critical of his political personality and personal decisions have registered more significantly than ever before. The number of hagiographic treatments of the third president has receded, to the point where it is at least equaled by the number of hypercritical ones.[23]

To a great extent, Jefferson set himself up for such treatment. Sensitive and suspicious, he was an inveterate saver of scraps and errant scribblings, a habitual cataloger of details who swore by his professedly faithful, unprejudiced notes, created "in the moment," no more dramatically deployed than those he took down during Washington administration cabinet meetings while he was serving as secretary of state. Relying on these notes, he repackaged his own past in order to cleanse it of negative press. He couldn't help himself. With an intense need for exoneration, he was prone to reframing a narrative and shaving the truth. Chapter 1 shows him engaged in a self-serving exercise to smooth out rough edges in his autobiography when describing his near-religious ecstasy in the presence of a Native American orator.

Yet no one was his equal in defining what Americans stood for, such that the idealized national identity he constructed still resonates. Chapter 5 dissects the rich humanist idiom[24] he brought to the Declaration of Independence, a spellbinding testament to justice made possible by its author's creativity. The rolling, rhythmical cadence Jefferson brought to the page was extraordinary for its time. It is not just the sound of the words; it's how they combine.

From the opening line of the Declaration—"in the course of human events"—the reader is situated on a grand historical stage. The challenge embedded in this part of the document—that "governments long established should not be changed for light and transient causes"—is presented with breathtaking earnestness. With percussive insistence, Jefferson goes on to list the abuses a respectful people have suffered: "neglected" by the king tasked with protecting them, repeatedly mocked, their rights usurped, and patience tested, they were left exposed to the combined "dangers of invasions from without and convulsions within." What resort was left them but lifesaving resistance? The irresistible longing of a community of minds to secure "safety and happiness" for all demanded the radical act of separation.

Speaking for the assembled representatives of thirteen forlorn colonies in an almost funereal tone, Jefferson chastised "our British brethren" for being unresponsive when the American colonists had begged for their "native justice and magnanimity." Like the tyrant king, "they too have been deaf to the voice of justice and of consanguinity." They covered their ears and refused to hear. As a result of willful ignorance, as the severed body of America bled out, presumptive ties of blood (consanguinity) were lost. Metaphors can be highly emotive; none of Jefferson's colleagues in Congress were so well armed with pulsating phrases.

Even his less routinely cited words display the same vivacity. From his 1801 First Inaugural: "During the throes and convulsions of the ancient world, during the agonizing spasms of infuriated man seeking through blood and slaughter his long-lost liberty . . ." Agonizing spasms? Infuriated man? This went well beyond political theory.

The nervous symptoms implied in Jefferson's later writing are as potent as the attack on King George in the Declaration for having dispatched royal officers in "swarms . . . to harrass [sic] our people & eat out their substance." ("Harass," at that time, meant to physically exhaust, to enfeeble, or, in a military sense, to repeatedly attack and wear down.[25]) Jefferson's genius with language rests on his ability to validate his side as the one exercising self-control while implicating the other in censurable acts or deviousness. He externalizes anxieties by enticing the reader to feel. His long-sustained popularity owes much to the community of interests he creates with sensation-producing phrases.

Hyperbole had a place in the best writing of the eighteenth century—something we frown upon now. When Jefferson wrote to a female friend that he was "violently smitten" in his encounter with a Parisian building, he was saying more than that he was impressed by the design. He was saying that he was capable of heart-pounding passion himself, but without transgressing.

Whether public or private in orientation, Jefferson's deft writing style felt intimate, while at the same time properly restrained. Among his generally unremarked upon writing habits, it is also notable that he adopted an idiosyncratic manner of spelling. While many of his well-educated peers continued, for example, to capitalize nouns in the old style and write the long *s* that looks like an *f,* Jefferson went in the opposite direction, beginning sentences with a lowercase letter. He always put an apostrophe in "it's" as a modifier; he left the *w* out of "knowledge" for no apparent reason. He did not often follow the "i before e" rule, and a word he used momentously, he routinely spelled "independance." A Jefferson-authored document is readily distinguishable.[26]

~

THE TENSION BETWEEN A people's passion for the preservation of history and the real fear of what collective memory loss means to nationhood is yet another reason for the appearance of this book at this moment. America on the eve of the 250th anniversary of the Declaration of Independence unfailingly associates the document's now faded ink with the once vibrant mind of its penman. Thomas Jefferson communicates the drama of the founding in a very tangible way.

His attachment to all kinds of tactile objects is of more than passing interest. The exalted designer of Monticello, an inveterate collector, took an abiding interest in invention. Style, appearance, and usefulness mattered immensely to Jefferson. He surrounded himself with both imported and homemade furniture, oversaw installation of an inlaid beech and red cherry parquet floor in the mansion's parlor, purchased musical instruments, mechanical timepieces, porcelain tableware, paintings, busts. He hung Indian artifacts and oil paintings.

The diversified gentleman's library, one of the finest and most exhaustive in America, was more than a sign of material abundance; it was a register of elite taste that disclosed a fierce commitment to preservation. Jefferson took his vocation to an unprecedented level of care and attention when he set up his private rooms, into which few were ever admitted. Here he maintained his workstation and kept to meticulous habits of organization. He looked far and wide for time-saving conveniences such as a specially constructed swivel or "whirligig" chair (with attached candleholders), and the revolving bookstand that sat on the writing table before him. His comfort mattered as much to him as his privacy.[27]

The sense of touch has been called the deepest sense, with good reason. The intimate nature of taking an object in hand opens up a world beyond what the eye takes in. Material comfort relates to personal hospitality, which was very much the case in Jefferson's museum-like home. Visitors rarely failed to write of the experience. He strove to be unusual, exceptional.[28]

If his personality emerges in material culture, it is most apparent in his collected letters. These give us insight into everything from the how and why of his book purchases to his attitudes about power. He was hands-on about everything. His habits as a writer bear a historic weight, as demonstrated by the modern *Papers of Thomas Jefferson*, a project begun at Princeton University after World War II, which has been publishing nonstop since 1950. Three-quarters of a century and some seventy volumes later, that mission is only now nearing its completion. Editor J. Jefferson Looney estimates the total number of letters Jefferson received at twenty-eight thousand and the total he wrote at nineteen thousand.[29]

From the conclusion of the Revolutionary War through the final year of his long life, Jefferson made annotations in a "Summary Journal of Letters." No matter where he was, at home or abroad, he took pains to preserve copies of his outgoing correspondence, including drafts. Letters sent and received were scrupulously filed at Monticello, organized chronologically; a separate section of the journal cross-referenced each correspondent by name, listing dates of prior correspondence. Jefferson recurred to this epistolary record whenever he revisited a subject he'd earlier discussed. Amazingly, in a five-mile-an-hour world, a horse-drawn and seafaring world, his conversation reached across the globe. Until he tired of answering his mail in his later years, he delighted in maintaining his connections. He would respond with long, meaningful letters to people young and old whom he expected he'd never meet.

~

THE SHREWD, SEDUCTIVE, SELF-EXPRESSIVE writer was relentless in putting out ideas. Jefferson aimed to be read in a certain way, to convince others, at a distance, of his reasonableness. In person, in the way he imparted his own life experience and told entertaining stories over dinner, one gleans a largely undocumented desire to draw others close.[30]

His conduct behind closed doors is something else. When he made repeated attempts to seduce the wife of a close friend, he put to the test a "way with words" quite apart from the irresistible script that has come down through the ages as brilliant propaganda on behalf of a nation declaring itself to the world. The private Jefferson was, at times, a bit too artful for his own good. He put pressure on others, urging and cajoling, effectively prompting a legislator, "Don't you think it would be a good idea if someone . . ." Seduction was his brand.

The dysfunction is apparent when he goes to lengths to present to the public an image of moral purity, at the same time imploring recipients of letters to keep his secrets. He did not always succeed. Disclosures of private intelligence blew up in his face. The partisan press of 1800 was no less determined to tear down national figures than it has been in the twenty-first century. Even George Washington bristled at the bad press he received. It wasn't just a noble gesture that he chose to retire at the end of his second term, setting the precedent for honorable exits from public life.

Within Jefferson resides an eerie duality that today's America still struggles to resolve. As an embodiment of the American Enlightenment, he stated peerless propositions for humanity while living by a different set of rules at home. We can either throw up our hands at his willful blindness on subjects that are tender today (race and gender), or we can find a useful workaround by showing that such issues aren't always black-and-white. In this case, a partial answer can be found in the relationship Jefferson maintained with the Marquis de Condorcet.

In Chapter 7, the reader meets Condorcet, a forceful antislavery thinker and protofeminist. His long-overlooked association with Jefferson was profound. Their connection exposes what was realistically possible for Jefferson to have done if he had mustered the courage to rethink his stated positions and preach justice for Black Americans, free and enslaved. The point is that he came closer than most think to imagining a different path, and a different outcome.

Condorcet was Voltaire's protégé and literary executor, the so-called "last of the philosophes." He was the same age as Jefferson, with a faith in the human spirit that rivaled the Virginian's. In the late 1780s, as the two communed in Paris, Jefferson undertook to translate the Frenchman's daring book on the evils of slavery. He would allow himself to speak to resistant slave owners through Condorcet—at least, that was the plan until he returned home and gave it up. The Condorcet connection is critically important and is, I contend, a missing piece to the puzzle of Jefferson and what held him back, before he finally retreated into the hardened position of all whose racial "science" became a major determinant in Southern conservatism.

～

Professional historians rarely go out on a limb and claim psychological insight. The danger is obvious, as Fawn Brodie discovered. In assembling the materials needed for what might be called a psychological reckoning on Jefferson, I embrace the obvious: life registered differently for him. Modern cultural conditioning is unrelatable to that of 250 years ago, when sudden early death afflicted virtually every household and medical options were few, when communication across distance was slow and handwritten and competed with word of mouth in ways that are hard for us to assess. It is easier to describe the power of the subject's mind than to isolate what exerted power over his mind. The only recourse is to focus on evidence of emotional patterns that are peculiar to him.

To interpret a man known, as Jefferson was, for his resourcefulness and concentration of energy requires that we relate personal motives to public designs. We will not be effective, otherwise, in demonstrating how and why a planter-aristocrat allowed himself to be thought a workingman's hero. It bears repeating that over time, his politically charged correspondence grew increasingly defensive, when not still framed to disarm or coax or charm. Believing in the rightness of his vision, Jefferson stiffened his resolve, repeatedly pressing his case for how democracy ought to be. Absorbing the lessons of two thousand years, he extracted a history of the world that suited his optimistic personality while feeding a political timetable. The very concept of American exceptionalism, though the phrase was adopted only in the twentieth century, arguably begins with the mind of Jefferson.

He restlessly, and perhaps fervently, wished for future generations to see him as an enlightened, compassionate friend of humanity. Nearly everything he set down on the page was intended to point to the man he wished to be—honest to the core. So the temptation to judge him is strong.

From the age of twenty-four, he almost obsessively maintained records of daily life. One of the most representative publications from the *Papers of Thomas Jefferson* is known today as the *Memorandum Books*. In them a researcher can immediately access Jefferson's every purchase: stationery (an essential for him); horses (names included) and oats to feed them; building materials, brooms, candles, knitting needles; wines and whiskey; medicines and midwives; firewood for the President's House and a pet mockingbird and cage to keep him company there; the cost of a haircut, a shave. He recorded expenditures, no matter how insignificant, in a compact, perfectly legible hand: the sum won or lost at backgammon; the cost of a ferry ride, clock repairs, a toothpick case; the gratuity given to an enslaved person on a plantation he visited.[31]

Throughout these records, it must be stated, his attachment to an odious system of economy, maximizing profits by enslaving others, is as plain as day. With his well-honed pose as a steady, sympathy-dispensing patriot, he did not realize that his "philosophic" treatment of racial differences would be regarded as a virulent and repugnant ideology when later Americans came to pass judgment on the racism of his age. Jefferson felt certain it would be his role in the advent of the two-party system that alone hung over his legacy. He obviously misjudged.

The unsteady course of his posthumous reputation is itself a fascinating story, a shortcut to an understanding of America's invented identity.[32] One failure of Jefferson's that is rarely spoken of is his reluctance to confront the incongruities that exist in his political philosophy. He forged ahead with blatantly unfounded optimism, fantasizing a country in which both poverty and impoverished minds were already on the way to disappearing. He prophesied an America that could not be.

Yet it was his fantasy that made him a model messenger for the liberal creed that Franklin Roosevelt's New Deal was eager to sell. The larger-than-life Virginian was cast as a nineteen-foot statue in the Tidal Basin memorial, dedicated on Jefferson's two hundredth birthday, April 13, 1943. In the midst of a war to defeat tyranny, FDR reenshrined Jefferson as the Revolutionary thinker who only wanted what was best for democracy. Today, the historical record yields an abundance of evidence in support of the argument that Jefferson grossly overestimated the good that democratic individualism would achieve.[33]

As if we need further reminder that historical memory is unstable, we have learned that even lifeless statues can become the focus of public angst. In 2021, after considerable debate, a full-size 1833 Jefferson likeness—he stood holding the Declaration of Independence—was removed from New York City Hall to erase an "eyesore," symbolically expunging a lifelong slaveholder whose beautiful words about liberty and human dignity were challenged by his way of life.[34]

Being Thomas Jefferson is an attempt to exit that debate, advancing historical knowledge without prescriptive politics. This book aims not to promote or dethrone, but to explain the talented Jefferson with the tools of the archive. Scrupulously examining the dramas and the traumas he faced, along with the triumphs he enjoyed, is stimulating enough work. The book's conclusion will not shy from judgment, because the evidence leads somewhere very specific.

America's first "man of the people" was not heroic, and he did not act alone. He was nevertheless a good example of what we admiringly style a "Renaissance man." He honored the cause of democracy by introducing a stirring vocabulary of individual rights, social justice, and the collective good before ceding control of his life's meaning to successive generations. Thomas Jefferson made himself worth noticing, and history has repeatedly remade him. It's what we do.[35]

PART I

Personal Growth

Our inner life is what counts most for each of us and yet we have to pretend to live it as if we paid no attention to it.

—ALBA DE CÉSPEDES, *FORBIDDEN NOTEBOOK*

The only efficient way to guarantee the darkness of what needs to be hidden against the light of publicity is private property, a privately owned place to hide in.

—HANNAH ARENDT, *THE HUMAN CONDITION*

Figure 1. The Cherokee warrior/orator whom Jefferson designated "Outassetè." A frequent visitor to the Jeffersons' home, Shadwell, in the years before a teenaged Thomas lost his father, Outassetè (also spelled "Outacity" or "Ostenaco") had yet another, more ferocious name: Man Killer. Engraving by unknown artist, after Joshua Reynolds's 1762 portrait. (Courtesy National Portrait Gallery, Smithsonian Institution)

CHAPTER 1

"Savage Enough"
His Ruptured Childhood

JEFFERSON'S MOST CHERISHED WORLD was a private world of his own design, where he loved and where he bore the losses of the ones he loved. And yes, where he dominated a workforce that came to him as human property. For eighty-three years, Thomas Jefferson (1743–1826) associated his identity with a physical location to which he attached his fondest hopes and where he faced considerable obstacles to happiness.

We enter Jefferson's mind, unconventionally, through the graveyard he laid out at Monticello. Its design—quite unintentionally, I hold—is a psychic map of an intense, if also remarkably self-possessed and otherwise emotionally hidden, landscape architect's life. Many have remarked on Jefferson's humble choice in composing his own epitaph: his decision to lead with the obvious, his authorship of the immortal Declaration, but to omit his public service as president of the United States in favor of his work to advance religious freedom and higher education in Virginia. It is easy to reach a conclusion about that conspicuous excision of his occupancy of the highest elective office: it's the same conclusion everyone else has drawn since the nineteenth century. Which is just what Jefferson wanted. Humble servant of the people.

I find it far more interesting that in the cemetery he so carefully conceived, he has placed his mother, who died in 1776, at a fair distance from him. The only company he would provide her with in death were relatives she never knew in life who were not especially important to her son either. In the case of his father, who died in 1757, long before the mountaintop was leveled, one must presume that Jefferson was content for him to remain beside the ruins of Shadwell, the house he built, where Thomas was born; that structure succumbed to fire in 1770, and the farmland was later leased out, so that Jefferson's actual birthplace most likely held less and less emotional attachment for him as time passed. The exact location of his father's grave is unknown.

Jefferson chose to be buried next to the best friend of his youth, Dabney Carr (1743–1773). The twenty-nine-year-old father of six was initially interred on the Shadwell farm, his coffin disinterred on Jefferson's orders only days later and carted up the mountain. The unfortunate young attorney was the first to be laid to rest at Monticello, before the mansion itself was truly habitable. The two had formed a sentimental pact, promising each other that the one who outlived his friend would see to it that they were buried close together. Dabney Carr lies beside his wife, the woman he left behind, Thomas Jefferson's younger sister.[1]

In the Monticello cemetery, no one comes between Dabney Carr and Thomas Jefferson except the young widow Jefferson married in 1772, Martha ("Patty") Wayles Jefferson (1748–1782). Her early death made him a widower after they'd lived ten years on the mountaintop: "ten years of unchequered happiness," as he termed it in a truncated autobiographical sketch drawn up in the last decade of his life.

Notice the geometry of the most intimate grouping. Four sides. A virtual square. Jefferson's married younger daughter, Mary ("Maria") Jefferson Eppes (1778–1804), lies on the other side of him. She resembled her mother and died as her mother did, failing to recover from a difficult childbirth—and at an even younger age. At that point in the story of the Monticello graveyard, in the fourth year of his presidency, the space Jefferson set aside for his own mortal remains was properly framed, awaiting him. The two who would be added after 1826, his elder daughter, Martha ("Patsy") Jefferson Randolph (1772–1836), and her husband and third cousin, Thomas Mann Randolph (1768–1828), complete the square.

We find another rather telling example of Jefferson's associating a square with intimate and enduring friendship. After his wife died, he sought to restore himself by bringing the men he knew best and cared for most to the neighborhood of Monticello. To James Madison, James Monroe, and William Short (the last of whom studied law with Jefferson and became his private secretary), he fantasized a mathematically formed foursome, adapting the French *partie carrée*, which more typically

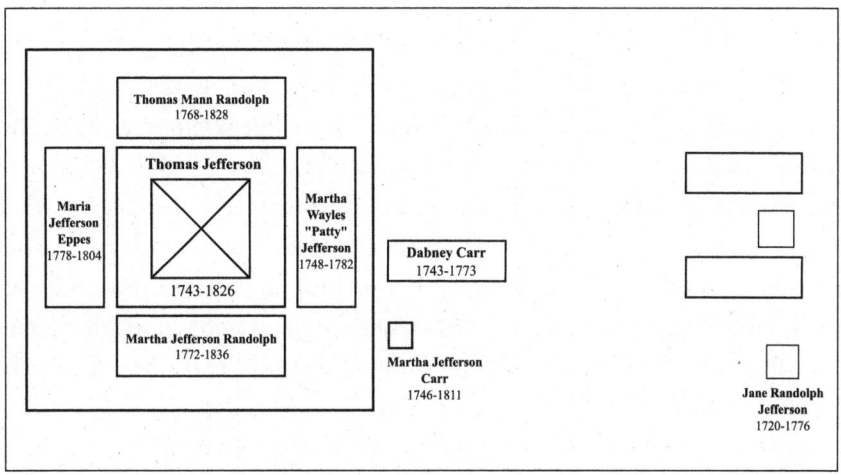

consisted of two men and two women. Having Monroe and, he thought, Short on board with his orchestrated land purchase, Jefferson wrote to the last holdout: "Would you but make it a 'partie quarree' I should believe that life still had some happiness in store for me," he coaxed Madison. "Agreeable society is the first essential in constituting the happiness and of course the value of our existence: and it is a circumstance worth a great attention when we are making first our choice of a residence."[2]

A residence, but also a final resting place. When Jefferson sensed that his own end was near, he sketched the modest monument of "coarse stone" that would most gratify him: a three-foot cube "surmounted by an Obelisk." He directed that the epitaph should say "Here was buried / Thomas Jefferson / author of the Declaration of American Independence / of the Statute of Virginia for religious freedom / & Father of the University of Virginia." Just that, "& not a word more." The image I have in mind, though, is another. I picture the micromanaging executive showing the gravediggers where he wished to locate each of the nine individuals he buried between 1773 and 1826.[3]

The Monticello cemetery is only one indication of the meanings contained in friendship, love, and loss in the private world of Thomas Jefferson.

STARTING FROM SHADWELL

There is no better way to make sense of Jefferson's time on this planet than to survey the Piedmont of Virginia, the vistas he so often praised, the rich, yielding land where he was born, where he died. He hailed from a place where Nature dwarfed everything else. Until he traveled to the colonial capital of Williamsburg to attend college, he did not often experience daily life in a market town. Later, when he came to advertise to distant correspondents the charms of his "little mountain," he would fix on the value of self-sufficiency and on the feelings inspired by his bucolic surroundings. He advanced a homespun image of himself, which Alexander Hamilton, the most bitter of his public enemies, would turn on its head as he sneered at "plain Thomas J."

The polished image of the cosmopolitan who returned from five lavish years as U.S. minister to France and added a stately dome to his mansion erases some of the earthiness of his actual roots. The erasure leaves history in a perpetual fog. We want solid ground, yet the grounding of this particular "Founding Father" has been cleansed of the deprivation he experienced. So that's where this is going: while he was socially privileged, Jefferson was not born into an enchanted world, nor is it even known whether his was a loving family.

There was not yet a Charlottesville, Virginia, when Jefferson was born. The surrounding County of Albemarle was created in 1744, several years after his father arrived there; but the city associated with the university he designed and devoted his best efforts to in post-presidential retirement was not formally established until 1762, when he was away at college, some five days distant. Until then, when he wasn't living apart from his family with a hired tutor (in the absence of an established school system), he was at home with his mother, Jane Randolph Jefferson, whose husband, Peter, died of natural causes in 1757, just shy of fifty. She'd endured nine pregnancies over fifteen years and still outlived him by nineteen years.

As was customary, Peter Jefferson willed the "use and profits" of the property to his "Dear & Well beloved Wife Jane Jefferson for and Dureing her Natural Life or Widdowhood." This is to say that she was subsidized: she could not inherit landed property in the way it is done today because she was a woman, a wife. Power was patrilineal, which meant that Thomas, at fourteen, the elder of their two sons, would come into his full inheritance as an adult and would provide for his mother. Until then, widowed at thirty-seven, Jane Jefferson was left with eight children to raise, a working plantation, and approximately sixty enslaved men and women. The couple's daughters received enslaved body servants in the will, while Thomas was bequeathed "my mulatto fellow Tawny, my books, my mathematical instruments, and my cherry tree desk and bookcase."[4]

In all, Peter Jefferson owned forty-nine volumes. In addition to titles relating to history, geography, and global exploration, he had multivolume sets of the *Tatler* and *Spectator*, greatly admired periodical essays published in London from 1709 to 1714, which commented wryly on town and country manners. This frontiersman was no rube.

Almost from the start of their nineteen-year marriage, Peter and Jane Jefferson resided in the Virginia Piedmont. Their home, on a four-hundred-acre tract, was named Shadwell after the London parish where she was born. It sat in the immediate shadow of the Southwest Mountains, some distance from the visible, more imposing Blue Ridge. Despite its isolation, the original plantation house appears to have been well stocked with foodstuffs and spices available in the colonial capital. The family kept cattle, sheep, and hogs. Thomas learned to hunt at a young age, telling his eldest grandson that his father put a gun into his hands at the age of ten and sent him "into the forest alone" to learn self-reliance. There was probably venison, turkey, and fish at the family table. Berries were grown, and an early record in Thomas's hand shows that the garden produced asparagus, peas (at Monticello he would cultivate thirty-nine varieties), onions, broccoli, and cauliflower. Chinaware, kitchen paraphernalia, and silver spoons recovered from the site suggest that dining in style mattered to this family.[5]

The house sat on a small prominence, bounded on one side by the Rivanna, a northern tributary of the James River. The James was Virginia's lifeline, on whose banks the earliest residents built their brick mansions. On the other side of the Jefferson plantation ran the east-west Three-Notch'd Road, a major artery that led more than a hundred miles from Richmond to the far side of the Blue Ridge; it intersected with the even earlier constructed Secretary's Road (meant mainly for the transport of tobacco), foreordaining the settlement of Charlottesville at the crossroads. Three-Notch'd Road was a heavily wooded hunting trail originally marked out by Indian peoples, and travelers unfamiliar with the route received needed assurances by taking note of notches carved into trees. At least forty-six mile markers were conveyed in this manner by the year Thomas Jefferson was born.[6]

Land and its productivity dominated daily life. Peter Jefferson was a surveyor and a member of the Loyal Land Company, which was the beneficiary of grants in the hundreds of thousands of acres. Land speculation was an appetite easily whetted across the colonies, and especially in Virginia. Two of Thomas's guardians after his father's death, John Harvie and Dr. Thomas Walker, were key players in the Loyal Land Company; so was Edmund Pendleton, one of the most respected attorneys in Virginia and a political mentor to Jefferson when he sat in the Continental Congress. In short, the Loyal Company bound the interests of those who cared about political power.

It should already be apparent that despite their living at a tremendous distance from the seat of power, Peter and Jane Jefferson were not common people. Both belonged to the colonial gentry. Her father was Isham Randolph, a colonial official and noted horticulturalist. It has been more than once suggested that Thomas Jefferson's love of the garden was a family inheritance. One of Isham's brothers married the great-granddaughter of Pocahontas, which says two things: that the colony's crude beginnings were not yet ancient history; and that the Randolph clan kept track of the several branches of a genealogical tree that connected it to every corner of the colonial power elite. Rather than being regarded a rustic, young Thomas Jefferson was considered of good stock on the strength of his mother's bloodline alone.[7]

In their prime, both father and son held the position of Albemarle County surveyor. In one "Land Roll," the son of Peter Jefferson recorded that in 1737, Shadwell was "purchased by P. Jefferson of William Randolph," his best friend and Jane Randolph Jefferson's first cousin. Thomas listed his own home, Monticello, with the precision he is known for: "acres 1052 3/4 . . . patented by Peter Jefferson. 1735. July 19." He came into more than five thousand acres acquired by his father, and he would add to them over time.

Whether or not he inherited his penchant for mathematics from his surveyor father, as an adult Thomas Jefferson was very much a numbers man, clear about dates, meticulous with expense records, ready to provide builders with measurements down to a fraction of an inch. Monticello, his signature architectural triumph, became so emblematic of the United States that it has been reproduced on the U.S. five-cent coin since 1938. But his landscape design, as architectural scholars have noted, did not adhere to regular geometry, following instead the "undulating lines of his Piedmont landscape"; his plowing followed "the curves of nature." He challenged conformity in his spatial understanding.[8]

Jane Randolph was nineteen, fully a dozen years younger than Peter Jefferson, when they wedded in 1738. He was a militia colonel, a title that was not merely honorific. He took charge of preparedness along a frontier that expected armed engagements with French forces in the 1750s. Jane bore ten children, eight of whom survived infancy. Thomas, the eldest son, came third. The only other son to live a full life was Randolph, her last, a twin who was twelve years younger than Thomas, with more modest expectations from life. The eldest Jefferson child, named after her mother, was three years older than Thomas and a cherished sister.

Jane's death at twenty-five fell hard on Thomas. We know by his own testimony that he cherished the memory of her musical voice. That his sister's remains, like his father's, were left undisturbed at the time of Dabney Carr's reinterment at Monticello seems to indicate that Jefferson was reacting to the shock of an unexpected loss, acting out of an impulse as well as honoring their pact. Carr's removal from the Shadwell plot was but a minor disturbance to the landscape. It may say nothing of Jefferson's feelings of intimacy or emotional distance from his father, though mystery persists, insofar as no marker for either Peter Jefferson or his daughter Jane has yet been found on the property.[9]

Losing his father at fourteen could not have been easy, though the son did not put into writing the nature of the unease he felt. It should be said that Peter Jefferson spent a good amount of time away from home; his son was left in the care of a private tutor for the better part of the five years leading to Peter's death. None of this was uncommon. Thomas grew up more accepting of tragic circumstances than we do today. Letters of a lifetime make that clear.

Nineteenth-century descriptions and family traditions are hard to take at face value, because they are burnished and brightened. Peter Jefferson was said to have been something of a physical specimen, hardier in build than his trim, reddish-haired, long-lived son. One imagines Peter on horseback by habit; his son, when grown, rode for exercise religiously but was conducted over distances by carriage almost as often. If Thomas's personality borrowed from his father's (or mother's, for that matter), there is little hard evidence: the cursive script of Peter and Thomas Jefferson bear some resemblance. We can't know whether the son believed his allotted span was tied in any way to that of his father, though a certain fatalism comes through in his forty-second year, when he confided in Abigail Adams during their time together in Paris that "he expects not to live above a Dozen years," which would have had Jefferson projecting his own death in his early fifties.[10]

He outlived his own expectations and, with John Adams, outlived all but one of the fifty-six signers of the Declaration of Independence.[11] As far as is known, no one in the Jefferson-Randolph line, going back to the seventeenth century, lived anywhere near as long as Thomas Jefferson, who passed his eighty-third birthday before his final illness set in; Adams was past ninety when the two "conspired" to die on the fiftieth anniversary of the first Fourth of July. In their world, the tenuousness of life was reflected in the pathos of poetry and literature, ancient and modern, which Jefferson collected in abundance.

The Jefferson genealogy includes three previous Thomases, the last of whom died in 1723, having barely attained his majority. Jane Randolph Jefferson's direct line was no more fortunate. Thomas Jefferson sometimes quoted the line in the Anglican *Book of Common Prayer* that expressed the resignation everyone felt: "In the midst of life we are in death." Only two of his nine siblings accompanied him into his post-presidency. They were his brother Randolph, twelve years his junior, who died ahead of his seventieth birthday, in 1815; and Dabney Carr's widow, Martha, who died at sixty-five, in 1811.[12]

FEELINGS FOR THE INDIAN

Peter Jefferson's importance as a surveyor was enhanced by his intimate association with a former professor of mathematics, Joshua Fry, who moved out west from Williamsburg and took the lead in pressing for official authorization to survey the Virginia–North Carolina boundary. The result of their collaboration came to be known as the Fry-Jefferson map, printed in 1751. It was formally titled "Map of the Inhabited Part of Virginia," and it was Peter's most tangible accomplishment on behalf of the colonial government. His son, an avid collector of atlases and travel narratives, would bring up the Fry-Jefferson map repeatedly in letters over the years. He was justly proud of it.[13]

The Virginia Piedmont was home to few Native Americans when Peter Jefferson moved there. The Monacan deliberately kept their distance, having moved to higher elevations. Young Thomas Jefferson at least once encountered Monacan people paying tribute at a burial mound near Shadwell and was keenly aware that living Indians knew who now resided on land they'd enjoyed for centuries. Growing up, Jefferson was not shielded from the sight of Indians any more than he was kept apart from white squatters and the rural poor. How often he was in contact with Indians is impossible to gauge, though a range of Indian artifacts have been unearthed at what remains of Shadwell. One unusual title in Peter Jefferson's inventory of books was dedicated to instructing Indians in Christianity.

It is a fact that Cherokees from the Tennessee River area were familiar with the Jefferson plantation and were at times made welcome there while journeying to and from Williamsburg on diplomatic missions. A warrior chief who bore several names, including the rather imposing Man Killer, was among these. One of early America's most distinguished Indian allies during a time of war, he was known to a young Thomas Jefferson by the name Jefferson spelled Outassetè.

The Cherokee chief was a storied individual. In the 1750s, he came to the attention of an ambitious young militia officer named George Washington, who was charged by the colonial government with the defense of an impossibly long frontier, in the face of French Canadian incursions. Troops under Washington's command openly preferred the advantages offered by the use of Indian fighting tactics, so he approved the assignment of Indian instructors to his men. In Jefferson's later accounting, Outassetè was a "frequent guest" of his father at Shadwell. He and his party may have stayed inside the house, though it is equally possible that they camped outdoors.[14]

In the recently formed Albemarle County, communications were unpredictable. News traveled slowly, and communication failures in the Southern colonies led to otherwise preventable misunderstandings. An Anglo-Cherokee war erupted in the Carolinas in 1758 and raged sporadically for three years. The Cherokees, like the Virginians, were spread about and suffered for it. Maintaining the friendship of one as important to the colony as Outassetè was critical. As it turned out, the Cherokee chief would side with the British during the American Revolution, after trade with their former American allies slowed markedly and backcountry whites committed acts of violence against his people.

While the county was thinly populated in Jefferson's youth, Albemarle was a stable, nonviolent territory, less a backcountry and more distinguished by its cultural connection to the eastern counties. Its country seats remained spread about, and it had not been subject to conflict with Indigenous tribes for some time. Not too much farther west there were lands where poorer Virginians were described casually as "white Savages." This means that Jefferson had enough familiarity with Indians while growing up that he could appreciate the porous character of backcountry culture. It was inevitable that as Americans ventured west, the northern and southern branches of the Cherokees would be effectively cut off from each other. Frustrated tribes came up with derogatory stereotypes of their own for those who trespassed on their lands: "the white nothings," "white ugly people."[15]

The Proclamation Line of 1763, decreed in London, prohibited white settlement west of the Appalachians. It was virtually unenforceable. The land-hungry kept coming. Young Jefferson had to be sufficiently aware of frontier conditions to recognize Indians as primary players in a constant drama of land-intense politics. No such sentiment appears in Jefferson's voluminous writings, leaving us in the dark about his early impressions.

Here is why that matters. As his intellectual style evolved, Jefferson relegated thoughts about Indian cultures to an ethereal realm. He analyzed the Indian in a way that is disturbingly similar to his infamous remarks on African Americans: as specimens observed in Nature. Though many native attributes appealed to Jefferson, after enough time passed and white-Indian conflict was occurring farther and farther from the Virginia settlements, his conversion of Indigenous tribes into exhibits was total. In textual terms, he led the way in mourning their loss to history. Unlike those whose physical remains rested in the cemetery alongside Dabney Carr, Indians, in Jefferson's hands, were a vanishing race. They belonged to a largely primitive world that existed before white inhabitants crammed into forts and built towns.

The more rapturous that Jefferson's writing about his home turf became, the more he tuned out real sensations of the past. As he pursued worldly connections, he found himself driven to dissolve time by shelving memories. Once his mind entered the enlightened republic of letters, he wrote about Indians as clinical subjects, part of a taxonomy he'd devised. Whatever actual emotions the real Indian had previously sparked in him came out on the page as processed emotion. Though Indians were still very much alive and active on the continent, they were not quite present in Jefferson's conception of national development.

The most enduring example of this Jeffersonian conversion of the Indian is his popularization of a story presented in the *Virginia Gazette* in 1774. The protagonist in the piece is an Indian chief in western Virginia who went by the Anglicized name Logan. He had suffered the loss of his entire family in a brutal attack conducted by frontier Virginians. In the decade that followed, Jefferson retrieved the newspaper record and made Logan his prime example of the depth of feeling that he insisted ran counter to the popular stereotype of the "stoic," impassive Indian, a breed with less native intelligence or civilized feeling than whites. The episode appears in the one influential book he authored, *Notes on the State of Virginia* (1785),[16] in which he writes: "I may challenge the whole orations of Demosthenes and Cicero, and of any more eminent orator, if Europe has furnished more eminent, to produce a single passage, superior to the speech of Logan." With intended hyperbole, Jefferson moves to the heart of his appeal, citing Logan's own words: "Such was my love for the whites, that my countrymen pointed as they passed, and said, 'Logan is the friend of white men.'" Logan's is a story of betrayal, just as the Declaration of Independence is a story of betrayal.

The grammatically polished speech that Jefferson's *Notes* extracted and repurposed reaches its crescendo with a clear justification for violence in response to whites' aggression. This is followed by the resounding plaint of a bereaved husband and father: "There runs not one drop of my blood in the veins of any living creature," cries Logan. "This called on me for revenge. I have sought it: I have killed many: I have fully glutted my vengeance... Who is there to mourn for Logan?—Not one." Jefferson's parable reaches an inevitable conclusion: but for the lack of civilized culture in the form of a written tradition, the Native American is the white man's equal in moral faculties.

We now know Jefferson's belletristic calling card. The Indian's "vivacity and activity of mind" is equal to the white's, "his friendships are strong and faithful to the uttermost extremity." But who is Jefferson really speaking for here, the Indian or himself? He has conceived the Logan script as he conceived his immortal Declaration, with funereal remorse at being backed into a corner where resistance was the final recourse of good souls. The sentimental assumptions are all Jefferson's when he sides with Logan, who has no descendants and owns no private cemetery where he can properly mourn his losses. Logan does not "save" any family in the sense that Jefferson "saves" his family by interring them—selectively, as we've seen—in the patriarchal recomposition of land he makes sacred.[17]

Let us not be overly judgmental, but let us also be clear. To subject any race to scientific analysis is an act of depersonalization, whether it be the Indians Jefferson largely esteems or the African Americans he presents as physically unappealing and mentally inferior. When he slices off the Indian world from the white world, Jefferson is simultaneously denying any earthier heritage for himself in central Virginia.

The division between savagery and civilization is unnuanced for him and would remain so from this time forward. The region's Indians were, of course, not theoretical, or philosophically drawn sons of the forest; yet as the War for Independence ended, Jefferson already felt himself far enough removed from his youthful experiences that he could deliberately turn living Indians into romantic artifacts.

The framing of Logan's lament gives it a purpose beyond its mournful aspect. It marks Virginia itself as a place of historic grandeur where dramas are readily staged, while subtly justifying Jefferson's personal ambition to be classed with the versatile scholars of Europe. *Notes on Virginia* did not emerge in a vacuum. The book was undertaken in response to queries from the secretary of the French legation in

Philadelphia during the Revolutionary War. François Barbé-Marbois represented the ally most instrumental in helping Americans secure their independence. While Jefferson brought a sense of order to every creative project he undertook, this one was especially meaningful. He was defending a new nation, as he had in the Declaration of Independence; and he was, in the same breath, pronouncing for the movers and shakers in Europe Virginia's vastness and political importance. The chapter headings range from geographical features and geological formations to vegetable production and the system of justice. But no subject is so painstakingly researched and self-consciously, taxonomically wrought as Query XI, the section titled "Aborigines."

Jefferson registered his strong desire to record as much as was known of Native peoples, including tribes that effectively became extinct in his century. The effort was more than most of his generation were doing to give Indians a contoured history. Natives were having to share the land with aggressors who chose to delimit it, reducing it to grids through formal surveys. That would be Jefferson's policy, too. The most he would do to "save" the Indian at any time was to lift a commiserating pen. Few among his peers would do anything more. As he immersed himself in public life, he increasingly adopted the perspective of those who occupied the hub of political power with him. As president, he'd have plenty of occasions to hear from government appointees and others who lived among the western tribes. They acted with genuine compassion, the same compassion Jefferson claimed he'd never stopped feeling.

Jefferson is inclined to write in a benevolent vein. In 1812, his seventieth year, he maintained in a letter to John Adams that "impressions of attachment & commiseration" felt for Indians "in the very early part of my life... have never been obliterated." Here he was recalling the Albemarle County of his father. Living abroad in 1785, he objected to the received wisdom shared among Europeans as to the supposed inferiority of American Indians, and said abstractly, almost boastfully: "I have seen some thousands myself, and conversed much with them, and have found in them a male, sound understanding." Some thousands? This was not conventional hyperbole. He was claiming wealth of insight as a witness, a nearly bicultural one.

Because he leaves us a limited amount of first-person testimony, we must make do with accounts like these. In the 1812 letter to Adams, it was not Logan he mentioned by name, but the "Man Killer" Outassetè. By then, five decades had passed since his last encounter with the Cherokee chief. His late father's Indian friend was addressing fellow tribesmen in Williamsburg before embarking for England and an audience with George III. We do not know how much of the Cherokee tongue Peter Jefferson understood—some, no doubt. His son reports only on Outassetè's group as he observed them in 1762. "I was in his camp," he told Adams, implying more than idle observance, if not intimacy. His memory had come to bathe the event in warm hues.

Jefferson could not even begin to decipher Outassetè's farewell appeal, so he employed a kind of verbal stagecraft to recreate the scene for his correspondent. "The moon was in full splendor," he recalls of that night, "and to her he seemed to address himself in his prayers for his own safety on the voyage, and that of his people during his absence. His sounding voice, distinct articulation, animated action, and the solemn silence of his people at their several fires, filled me with awe & veneration, altho' I did not understand a word he uttered."[18]

In trying to convey the sublimity he attached to this snapshot in time, Jefferson registers his capacity to marvel at an emotional performance, but he provides no clue as to whether there was personal contact or mutual recognition at the encampment in Williamsburg. All he says is "I knew much the great Outassetè." Adams had asked for book suggestions on North American Indians. In response, Jefferson privileged his own experience over the best-known treatments of the day, which he found lacking. "Reading" the Indian while touting his own powers of perception, Jefferson expressed admiration for the orator's subordination of technique to pure feeling. He genuinely believed that an Indian's proximity to nature brought out an arcadian simplicity that bespoke an ancient strength. To him, Outassetè's delivery gave voice to a universality of heart and excited a devotional response.[19]

We can do little more than this in assessing Jefferson's state of mind. Old Adams was especially interested in religious ceremony among the Indians. Maybe that is why Jefferson opted for "awe & veneration." Self-presentation in a familiar letter allowed for embroidery when it was meant to be received as a sign of feeling. So what we have in this rehearsal is an effect that Jefferson constantly reaches for in writing about the productions of nature: he advertises his attraction to its imposing grandeur in such a way that no one would doubt the sincerity of his expression. Unfortunately, what we don't learn in the letter to Adams is the writer's sense of how, before he left Albemarle for Williamsburg at the age of seventeen, he was taught to think about the Indian. We can't even picture Man Killer at Shadwell.

There is more for us to learn, from a separate source, about the warrior Peter Jefferson befriended and his son encountered in the flesh. According to the Virginia military officer who traveled with Outassetè during Jefferson's youth, to and from his base in eastern Tennessee, he was a formidable presence in the forest. Lieutenant Henry Timberlake was regularly at the Cherokee chief's side, dodging Outassetè's tribal enemy when warriors strayed from their hunting grounds to the north. Notably, Timberlake accompanied the party of Cherokees on that voyage from Williamsburg to England. He writes of a backcountry, circa 1761, where Indians traveled with both muskets and bows and arrows, where scalps were displayed and prisoners of war were tortured by the women of the camp. Virginia soldiers took Cherokee wives, travelers slept on bearskins, and the existence of spirits and apparitions was a meaningful element in the mind's eye.

The ways of Indians were respected by gentry families, and maybe that is what Jefferson was getting at. Any violence that was still occurring happened far from Jefferson's world. The child at Shadwell was brought up in the gentry manner. But was he stretching the truth about his early feelings of "attachment & commiseration" in the letter to Adams? Memories that are psychologically valid may be factually false. Perhaps Jefferson's memories and feelings were just real enough to return in a rhetorical guise.[20]

His father hosted the Cherokee party, which is very different from young Jefferson's encountering "thousands" of Indians while traveling. He was not the pathfinder his father was, let alone Timberlake, who lived for a time in the Indian manner and married the warrior chief's daughter. Through his close associations with real frontiersmen, Jefferson collected stories that he'd have shared with dinner companions as the years went by. While few particulars were ever recorded of his recitation of colonial conditions, the more he saw of the wider world, the more he would have been queried about his home province. It is not inconceivable that he saw fit to dress up stories by borrowing knowledge from his frontier-crossing father's generation of Virginians. It was his direct inheritance, after all. He became an expert on the history of his colony during the war years, collecting an immense amount of data for his ethnographically precise, geographically comprehensive *Notes on Virginia*. Much of what he translated onto the page derived from those intrepid men, one generation removed, whose ambitious lives melted into his own.

We accept that memory displaces, but sometimes historical truth is without disguise. Thomas Jefferson came of age at midcentury, knowing that the Cherokees who passed along the Three-Notch'd Road were a commanding people, tactically advanced in wartime, and a greatly desirable ally to have and keep happy. He knew, too, that backcountry whites were more likely to be trespassers than happy traders, and a constant annoyance to the Cherokees of Kentucky and eastern Tennessee. And though an older Jefferson "declaws" Outassetè by privileging the orator over the warrior in the story of what took place in 1762, the chief was not done fighting then, or even in 1779, when he made his peace with America's enemy. Indian removal had to be put on pause, and borders, whether natural or cultural, remained porous.[21]

A FAMILY'S EMOTIONAL AMBIVALENCE

If the Jeffersons lived in a world where Indians occasionally appeared from out of nowhere on the Three-Notch'd Road, the Shadwell home was also a place where the marks of literate culture were regularly maintained. Their spatial knowledge guided them, which may ultimately explain why both Peter and Thomas Jefferson were adroit mathematicians. The father was not schooled in the classical languages, but he enjoyed Shakespeare and knew what a superior education consisted of. He did what he could, while alive, to ensure that Thomas was pointed in that direction. The lad's first tutor, a Scottish cleric named William Douglas, turned out to be a mediocre Latin scholar. He'd have better luck going forward.

The choice of Douglas appears to have been one of convenience. The growing Jefferson clan left Shadwell in 1745, when Thomas was two, for a place near Richmond called Tuckahoe, some sixty miles to the east. They would not return full-time for seven years. Peter Jefferson's closest friend, William Randolph, had died, and Peter, at his friend's behest, combined their families by uprooting his own. The Tuckahoe Randolph home was a large brick structure that accommodated the extra family without difficulty. By the time the Jeffersons finally moved back to Albemarle, four more children had been added to the family. They relieved themselves of one, Thomas, who boarded with the Tuckahoe-area clergyman Douglas. It meant that he did not see his father for long stretches of time; and then, in August 1757, after an illness of some duration, Peter Jefferson met his own end.

There has been considerable speculation over the years as to the level of warmth or coolness in Jefferson's relationship with his mother. She died at fifty-seven, in 1776, by which time her son, as every American knows, was engaged in important business. No less a Jefferson authority than Merrill Peterson, the Thomas Jefferson Memorial Foundation Professor of History at the University of Virginia, proposed in his 1970 biography that Jane Randolph Jefferson was "a zero quantity in his life." That seems harsh, given the paucity of evidence: there does not even appear to be a sample of her handwriting preserved. At some point after Shadwell was destroyed in a fire, she moved up to Monticello, where she lived out her days.

It may mean something or it may mean nothing that the Monticello cemetery, laid out by her son, places her grave at some distance from where Jefferson's wife, children, and brother-in-law Carr are buried. On the other hand, Jefferson's favorite granddaughter described the great-grandmother she never met as "a person of sweet temper." Amid the historical confusion over Thomas Jefferson's relationship with his mother, no one has ever suggested that he felt anything but warmth, respect, and admiration for the father who was off mapping wilderness when Thomas was six and seven, and on his return placed him in the care of a tutor. From 1752 to 1757, as the youth entered his teens, Thomas and Peter were under the same roof only sporadically. In the son's plentiful correspondence with family members over the course of his life, he tells no heartwarming stories nor makes any reference of personal significance regarding his father.[22]

We know this much: Peter Jefferson was an informed reader and a respected member of the colony's legislative body, the House of Burgesses. He was all those things traditionalists have admired who celebrate the lure of the West and the so-called pioneer spirit: surveyor, mapmaker, land investor, settler, achiever. His nineteenth-century descendants repeated stories about the adventurer's physical feats that strain credibility. However, his coverage of a great expanse of their sprawling colony, the largest of the thirteen, cannot be doubted, nor the fact that he made himself known far and wide.[23]

Here is something else to consider: before the privately tutored Thomas attended college, he did not know the geometry of a settled town of any size. He would not venture beyond Virginia's borders until the age of twenty-three, in 1766, when he took in Philadelphia and New York. The images Thomas retained of his parents' world at Shadwell and Tuckahoe were dominated by slow patterns, interrupted only by a fast-moving horse. His famously inventive mind as yet knew no agricultural equipment more complex, more mechanical, than what was forged by a smith. Along with tobacco production, milling was the most common enterprise at Shadwell and farms like it. To keep carts operational, a wheelwright would have to be found. Cabinetry or furniture making was one of the artisanal skills taught to the enslaved. Imported goods were few. The family owned imported goods, offsetting the other outward signs of rusticity.[24]

Everyday life in the Virginia colony was a delicate affair for one who lived at a distance from any commercial hub. Maintaining a household was especially strained whenever a father or mother suffered from physical incapacity, or a father left for an extended period while his wife was pregnant—an ever-present concern for these Jeffersons. Population increase in western Virginia was occurring at a slower pace than in older parts of the colonies. Wives might spend half their lives pregnant, aware that the odds of recovering full health after childbirth were only slightly better than the odds of a child surviving to school age.

WITH JAMES MAURY AND DABNEY CARR

At the age of fourteen, after a false start with Reverend Douglas that dragged on for two years, a fatherless Thomas Jefferson struck pay dirt with the Reverend James Maury. He arrived at Maury's home for his further education directly after Peter Jefferson's death. Maury was one of the luckier men of the age: his long-lived wife produced thirteen children over twenty-five years, all but one surviving to adulthood.

The Anglican clergyman resided fourteen miles from Shadwell, and he knew Peter Jefferson in consequence of his own involvement in the Loyal Land Company. Thirty-eight years old when he took in fourteen-year-old Thomas, James Maury had a reputation for entering public debate. He'd written to colonial authorities the year before, urging them to be more proactive in fending off Virginia's frontier enemies. With the French and Indian War looming, he heard tales of woe in encountering the flow of refugees from beyond the Blue Ridge. As survivors of terror, they were, Maury warned, the first of many, obviously panicked by an "unhappy Concurrence of various sinister Events & untoward Circumstances" and apprehensive of "Bloody Tragedies," "Havoc & Desolation," beyond what they'd already witnessed. He castigated those in charge of the colony for not doing more to secure its backcountry.

The force of his words should seem familiar. Here is his pupil twenty years later, in the Declaration of Independence, warning of a worsening invasion from abroad and painting the unfolding disaster in apocalyptic terms: ". . . large Armies of foreign Mercenaries to compleat the works of death, desolation, and tyranny, already begun with circumstances of Cruelty & Perfidy scarcely paralleled in the most barbarous ages."

Maury evoked what the people of the West feared most: "Cruelties & Depredations of the Savages," and again, "Acts of Cruelty and Outrage." Good folks as far away as Maryland and Pennsylvania might "fall a Sacrifice to the butchering Hands of the Savages." He worried that friendly Cherokees might decide to abandon their Virginia allies.

Jefferson, in 1776, wrote with even less subtlety. Exaggerating the Indians' impulses for effect, he called out the king: "He has excited domestic insurrections amongst us, and has endeavoured to bring on the inhabitants of our frontiers, the merciless Indian Savages whose known rule of warfare, is an undistinguished destruction of all ages, sexes and conditions." The word choices and emotional content of the two texts are strikingly similar.

In his impassioned appeal of 1756, Maury described Virginia's social order in a way that informs us of its apparent divisions. For him there were two kinds of whites in the backcountry: "Scarce do I know a Neighbourhood, but what has lost some Families, & expects quickly to lose more. And, what aggravates the Misfortune, is, that many of these are, not the Idler & the Vagrant, Pests of Society, whom 'tis ever salutary to a Body politic to purge off, but the honest & industrious, Men of Worth & Property." We can plainly see who was meant to be protected by government.[25]

Though clearly a man of his times, bearing purposes suited to an elite sensibility, James Maury was not a doctrinaire cleric. His intellect had tremendous range, and he possessed an excellent library. In later years, Jefferson, though a deist, would serve as vestryman at the same Anglican church where Peter Jefferson had earlier served, because in Virginia, traditions held. Maury had a penetrating mind and an incisive quality about him, which explains how he produced scholars who could think for themselves while dutifully defending their colony—and later, the newly formed nation. What made this Irish-born Anglican different from those religious leaders Jefferson distrusted and consistently deplored over the course of his career was Maury's practical understanding, his desire to comprehend how language and history interacted.

Biographers Dumas Malone and Fawn Brodie both characterized the man Jefferson remembered as "a correct classical scholar" less charitably. She called him "self-righteous and bigoted," insisting that the adolescent Jefferson "recklessly concentrated" on his teacher the deep frustration he felt after having lost his father. There is scant evidence of that, and to her credit, Brodie did not neglect Maury's positive influence on Jefferson: she commended the teacher's love of languages and his facility for them. Malone, focusing on the religious disputes of the time, generalizes Maury as "intolerant." Most other historians note Maury's role in Jefferson's intellectual development but appear less interested in fathoming his personality.[26]

Jefferson was at a most teachable age during his two years at Maury's home. The teacher set the stage for Jefferson's lifelong fascination with the natural world, and he encouraged his charge to think historically about the human condition. As a classicist, James Maury recognized that when one teased a knowledge of culture from the history of language, the return on investment was deeply satisfying.

Importantly, too, the clergyman-educator was a major advocate of continental expansion. This viewpoint might or might not have been imparted to Jefferson, but it should not be overlooked. Maury was married to a daughter of the land-rich Dr. Thomas Walker of Albemarle, the head of the Loyal Land Company. Walker was granted some 800,000 acres in Kentucky and surveyed it himself years before Daniel Boone arrived on the scene. Maury himself was keen on enlisting a Virginia adventurer to explore the Missouri River and seek out a path to the Pacific. The outbreak of the French and Indian War put an end to all that. It was President Thomas Jefferson, a half century later, who fulfilled his teacher's dream when he orchestrated the Lewis and Clark expedition.[27]

Jefferson formed sturdy friendships at Maury's with the four other, all younger, students. James Madison, six years younger, was a future Anglican bishop and president of the College of William and Mary; he was the slightly older second cousin of the famed constitutionalist and U.S. president of the same name. Then there was James Maury Jr., the teacher's second-oldest child, three years younger than Jefferson, who would go on to serve for decades as a U.S. consul in England. Another of the boys in Maury's household was John ("Jack") Walker, eldest son of the all-important Dr. Thomas Walker. Jack was one year younger than Jefferson and would attend college with him. His "fame," at least in Jefferson lore, would attach to the later animosity he harbored toward his Monticello neighbor, a combination of political disagreements and a personal affront caused by Jefferson alone.

But none of the other boys meant as much to Jefferson as good-natured Dabney Carr, the closest to him in age and, as time would tell, an irreplaceable bosom friend. Life changed when he met Carr, the fifth child born to a couple whose nearby country seat was known as Bear Castle. Indicative of life's fragility in this era, Dabney's parents eventually surrendered half of their twelve offspring to the grave as infants. Maury's created a surrogate family.

Friendships formed among pubescent youth can be quite intense, with the rapid growth of body and mind taking place concurrent with the emergence of socialization needs and skills. That Jefferson recognized the sensations attached to this period of life is evident in many letters he wrote to old friends as the years passed, expressing sentiments such as "The friendships contracted earliest in life, are those which stand by us the longest" and "Those of our earliest years stand nearest in our affections." He attested to the trustworthiness of a neighbor's sons in a letter of introduction, by assuring that they were "of an antient [sic] and respectable family of this state" and "sons of two brothers with whom I have from my infancy been in habits of the most intimate friendship and affection." These "ancient" bonds mattered. In 1811, after retiring from the presidency, he wrote charmingly, by way of an imaginative metaphor: "I find friendship to be like wine, raw when new, ripened with age, the true old man's milk & restorative cordial." And the year following, to James Maury Jr.: "All my old friends are nearly gone. Of those in my neighborhood mr Divers, & mr Lindsay alone remain. If you could make it a partie quarrée, it would be a comfort indeed. We would beguile our lingering hours with talking over our youthful exploits, our hunts on Peter's mountain [the highest peak in the area], . . . and feel, by recollection at least, a momentary flash of youth. Reviewing the course of a long & sufficiently succesful [sic] life, I find in no portion of it, happier moments than those were." His imagined "partie quarrée" of good friends, a fantasy pursued over a lifetime, began at Maury's.[28]

Owing to the expectations that family and society placed on them, Dabney Carr and Thomas Jefferson were meant to become publicly prominent men. When these inseparable companions broke from their studies, they carried hunting guns on long walks through surrounding woodlands and up Peter's Mountain. That was how the most confidential friendship in Thomas Jefferson's life began.

Maury schooled them in natural history and geology as well as the classical languages that were an absolute requirement for Virginia gentlemen. When college beckoned, the inseparable pair matriculated at William and Mary and took classes together—where all but one member of the faculty were, like Maury, Anglican ministers. Once their Williamsburg years were behind them, Carr married Jefferson's younger sister Martha; they produced six children in eight years. In the fifth year of a marriage that would be cut short by tragedy, Jefferson wrote to his second-closest college classmate, John Page of Rosewell, that his companion Carr, "in a very small house, with a table, half a dozen chairs, and one or two servants, is the happiest man in the universe." We must understand that Jefferson developed his attachment to creative hyperbole early on, and that Dabney and Martha Carr were not struggling. Carr was by then a successful attorney, and his father owned considerably more land than Peter Jefferson's heirs. Dabney Carr's "one or two servants," of course, were enslaved people. He was financially secure.[29]

Jefferson and Carr sat together in the Virginia House of Burgesses in the lead-up to the Revolution, until Carr succumbed to a fever in his thirtieth year just as Jefferson's Revolutionary light began to shine. The surviving best friend and brother-in-law underwrote the education of Dabney Carr's sons and served as their surrogate father. For these and surely other reasons, Thomas Jefferson retained strong memories of his time at Maury's.

Nor did his matriculation at the College of William and Mary separate him from his sylvan past. He returned to Shadwell during holidays. There were moments when reminders of the backcountry greeted him in Williamsburg. The memorable appearance of the Cherokee chief Outassetè in 1762 that he brought up to John Adams a half century later was but one such occasion. The obsession that colonial leaders shared regarding land issues made life and death on the western frontier a constant news item.

By the second decade of the nineteenth century, Jefferson was a longtime collector of Indian vocabularies and had, as president, met personally with delegations from the distant reaches of his fast-expanding nation. From Washington, D.C., he expressed scant concern with the process of buying off Indians and pushing tribes farther west, yet he said the following in his Second Inaugural Address with regard to the dispersed nations: "I have regarded [them] with the commiseration their history inspires."

It is sometimes hard to know what part of a political composition is not contrived. But here, Jefferson seems to be hoping that the cynicism he conveys proves wrong. "Endowed with the faculties and the rights of men, breathing an ardent love of liberty and independence, and occupying a country which left them no desire but to be undisturbed, the stream of overflowing population from other regions directed itself on these shores."

His solution in 1805 was to supply the tribes with a stock of agricultural implements, that they might become more industrious while improving "minds and morals." It all sounds like a cop-out, but the states' push westward into Indian territories was unrelenting, and no early American president could imagine stopping it. Twenty years later, as Jefferson and Adams neared the end of their lives, President John Quincy Adams and Secretary of State Henry Clay would concur that the Indigenous peoples of North America were on an irreversible path to extinction and no one could save them from their sad destiny.

How genuinely Jefferson commiserated with the Indians and their fate is hard to determine. All one can do is to regard his consistency across the years in humanizing the ancient "race," as he and everyone else labeled them, along with his culpability as one of the political class that privileged the nation's expansionism over all else. The Indians' manners bespoke a cultural distance, feeding the conventional belief that they existed on an observable scale that ranged from "savagery," symbolized by the tomahawk, to "civilized" (or possessing the capacity for it).

In his 1812 letter to Adams, rationalizing the Madison administration's resort to war in the same spirit employed by James Maury on the eve of the French and Indian War, Jefferson hoped for an American takeover of Canada. His stated objective was a popular one: to defend settlements in the Great Lakes region (and American expansion more generally) and in so doing protect "our women & children forever from the tomahawk & scalping knife, by removing those who excite them." Those who "excited" Indians to commit atrocities were their handlers, British military commanders.

Still, Jefferson's claim to "impressions of attachment & commiseration" is less than determinative. Marveling at the Outassetè farewell speech that he had no way of understanding beyond tone and gesture was meant to exemplify an outsider's liberal sense of compassionate engagement. Aware of the public's interest in seeing the Adams-Jefferson correspondence published in its entirety before too many more years passed, Jefferson wanted posterity to remember him this way. He expected Adams to take him at his word, and us to lap up a well-crafted story.

But was any part of it fictional? Two decades before he became president himself, as a U.S. senator during Jefferson's presidency, John Quincy Adams rolled his eyes at the "large stories" Jefferson would pull out when he entertained guests at the President's House. The younger Adams gave credit to Jefferson's ingenuity but grew annoyed listening to what he knew firsthand to be falsifications.[30]

RETURN TO THE GRAVE

Jefferson did not feel an overpowering desire to reconstitute the Shadwell family in his cemetery, nor did he include his enslaved "family" that lived and labored at Monticello in his budding plan. Rather, he orchestrated an arrangement that expressed what he felt more deeply. Each individual buried at Monticello occupies a place that mirrors their placement in Jefferson's heart and memory. He preserves his "partie quarrée."

He could not have thought very much about the souls of area Indians. They were not to be repatriated on the land they had inhabited for millennia, in Albemarle or elsewhere. We have seen how, from his writing desk, Jefferson converted the corporeal Native into words on a page, allowing an Indian speech to float serenely with the movement of mountain air. He rationalized Indian erasure in Virginia because the concept of private property invited it. Previously independent tribal villages were broken up and their people relocated, so that Indian warriors could pose no threat to Albemarle property. In keeping with this reality, Jefferson generates his strongest feelings of compassion for the remote, not the present, Indian. He utters a plea to let Logan's story live on, and he assures us that Outassetè, the Cherokee Demosthenes, was a sublime communicator. Jefferson knows how to convey the Indian's resilience, humanity, and worth.

A reality check is in order. Jefferson is principally known for his bookish preoccupation, his literary genius, his political savvy; there is no disputing that he excelled at his solitary pursuits. He was effective in verbal engagement one-on-one or in small gatherings. But as a notoriously poor public speaker, he admired Outassetè's oratory as something he himself could not achieve. And yet it turns out that the Cherokee chief of his reconstructed imagination did not actually live up to the standard Jefferson set for him.

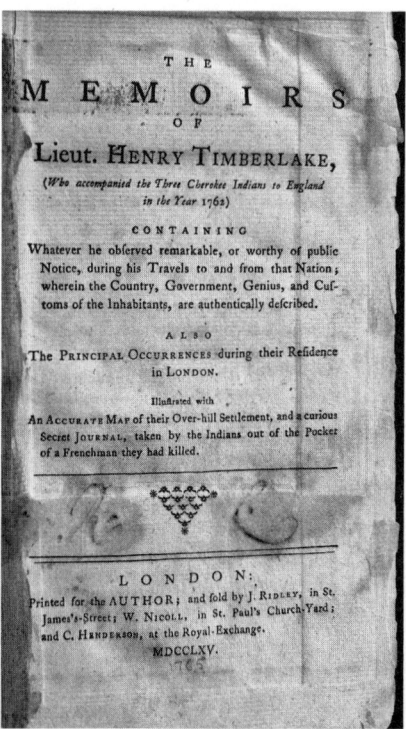

Figure 2. Title page of the 1765 memoir by Lieutenant Henry Timberlake, who lived among the Cherokees, married the daughter of Outassetè, and accompanied him to England. (Courtesy Special Collections, University of Virginia Library)

The final word on this subject must go to Lieutenant Henry Timberlake. In his highly detailed memoir, published soon after Jefferson completed the William and Mary curriculum, the Virginia-born soldier, who traveled with the Cherokee chief for months on end, gives a clinical view of what happened in London later in the same year that Jefferson experienced rapture in the chief's presence. Timberlake informs us that Outassetè, in advance of his return to America, gave a speech before the one individual he truly hoped to impress, the young King George III. The lieutenant's comprehension of Cherokee, serviceable but limited, was enough that he could admit he was unimpressed by the oratorical quality of the Indian's farewell address before the king. It contained "nothing more than protestations of friendship, faithful alliance, &c."

In the older Jefferson's reconstructed memory, the "awe & veneration" that washed over him on hearing the chief speak caused him to retain an unabated "attachment & commiseration" for Indian people. As he took in the Williamsburg spectacle, his mind banked its sumptuous sentiment. That the sensations of the moment were immediately imprinted is a bit odd when one considers that Jefferson did not comprehend a word of the speech. Meanwhile, Henry Timberlake, the white soldier who knew the Indian best and who cared for him most directly, saw far less sublimity in his address and none of the grandeur in Outassetè's untutored nature that a spellbound Jefferson contrived for himself, for his friend Adams, and for us.[31]

When he was in Paris in the mid-1780s, Jefferson, like his associate Benjamin Franklin, sought to play up his rusticity as a red-blooded American. "I am savage enough to prefer the woods, the wilds, and the independance [sic] of Monticello, to all the brilliant pleasures of this gay capital," he wrote to a Prussian acquaintance, a nobleman who'd been housed near Monticello after the Hessians surrendered to the Continental Army at Saratoga. Around the same time, to an Italian friend, he quaintly represented himself as "a savage of the mountains of America." Jefferson played upon stereotypes then current, by which an Anglo-American borrowed something from Indian character. He was both spiritually redeemed through his proximity to wilderness, where the Indian flourished, and, by comparison to European stock, uncultivated because of that same environment.[32]

The irony of a senior diplomat, an Enlightenment intellect, describing himself as "savage" was mitigated by the pride Jefferson could not resist expressing for the panoramic situation of his rural seat. Old World cityscapes caught his architect's eye as he contemplated the improvements he would make there on his return. Although perfectly at ease among the upper crust of an exquisite European capital, the lands of central Virginia had cast a spell on him. The loved ones buried there marked Monticello mountain as the only place that was truly home.

We know, in a rudimentary way, what the young Jefferson learned from Maury, but we possess less information about the skills he learned at Shadwell. As the eldest son of a planter, he was duty-bound to become one; yet a large gap remains in our understanding of how that process began. In the years from his father's death to his embarkation for college, the culture of the earth is unremarked upon, either because he learned by watching or perhaps because there is no extant correspondence from Jefferson in this period.

Jefferson's attachment to the red soil of central Virginia is legend. His earliest sketches of the grounds at Monticello, in the late 1760s, show him already laying out the flowering trees (Virginia catalpa and sweet-smelling Persian jasmine) that he intended to plant outside a house that was as yet unbuilt.[33] In 1790, soon after his return from Paris, he invented a moldboard plow "of least resistance," of which he was justly proud. Agriculture, he wrote, was "the most useful of the occupations of man"; and "ploughing deep . . . the recipe for almost every good thing in farming." Yet, as he entered retirement, he wrote cryptically, with studied modesty, to a fellow Virginia planter: "I am only an amateur, having only that knoledge [*sic*] which may be got from books. In the field I am entirely ignorant, & am now too old to learn." One suspects that the ignorance, if he was being literal, was owing to the fact that enslaved men and women did the fieldwork, while he spent an hour here and there working in his garden. All in all, we must accept that major gaps exist in his personal history, and that we do not in fact know how much Jefferson learned from watching his father's Shadwell farm produce from season to season.[34]

Beginning in 1760, when he removed to Williamsburg, one can finally read his thoughts as they are presented on the page. Only then is Thomas Jefferson's voice heard.

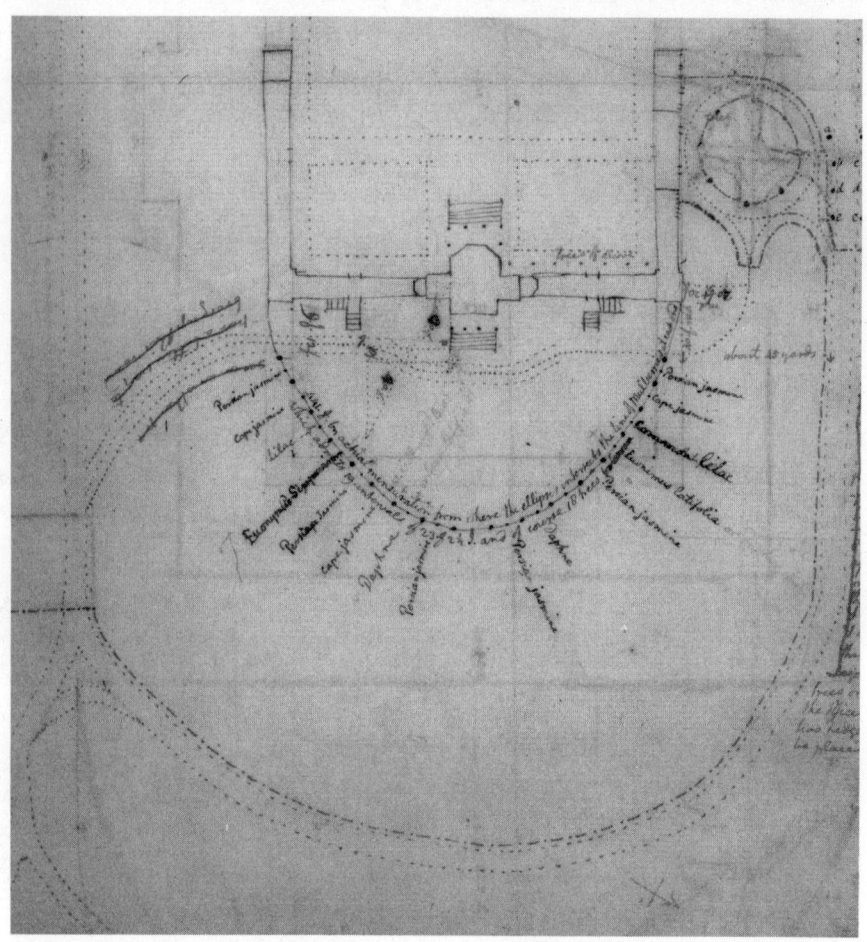

Figure 3. Monticello layout, ca. 1768. Jefferson's earliest plan for his mountaintop estate, showing its walking paths and naming the varieties of flowering trees he was going to plant. (Courtesy Coolidge Collection of Thomas Jefferson Manuscripts, Massachusetts Historical Society)

CHAPTER 2

"Sukey at Smith"

Sexual Secrets of a Young Lawyer

THE COLLEGE OF WILLIAM and Mary was founded in 1693. When Jefferson arrived there, at seventeen, he became acclimated to a social environment that forever changed him. Bearing a recognizable surname, though not an ostentatious one, he was accepted without question into the society of the colony's elite. Invited into the company of his elders, he behaved deferentially, openly appreciative of the interest they took in him. He was eager to make friends, and succeeded at it. Being without pretense, by all accounts, he participated but did not take the lead in their social activities. He studied harder than any of his mates, and he exercised moderation, while witnessing the overindulgence of peers in the vices of that era: drinking and gambling.

His day would have begun with prayers at the school chapel. Everyone knew the Anglican prayer book, because the colony's law required that it be studied. Much of the college library of three thousand volumes consisted of theological works. Unimpressed with the main building of the college during the years he lived there, Jefferson happened upon a book about architecture from an unlikely source, "an old drunken Cabinetmaker." No syllabus is extant to inform us of the specific coursework assigned in 1761–62, but it is almost enough to know that his teachers were not interested in Anglicanism; instead, they were steeped in the most famous texts of the Age of Enlightenment. They taught rational authors and scientific works, rhetoric, logic, ethics, and natural history.[1]

One gleans from letters that at college, Jefferson was a bit stiff, or, to put a positive gloss on it, he considered it important to maintain self-control. In a didactic letter to his eldest grandson, the temperamental Thomas Jefferson Randolph, written near the end of his presidency when "Jeff" was sixteen, he recalled his Williamsburg associations this way: "I was often thrown into the society of horse racers, cardplayers, foxhunters, scientific & professional men, and of dignified men." Naming the temptations he faced, he said he looked inward and posed a rhetorical question: "Which of these kinds of reputation should I prefer?" In a conventional script, he explained that he chose the "prudent" path to a happiness in which "good humor" produced "peace & tranquility" (the reward of constancy); his less principled peers pursued wealth and artifice (the flimsier path to expedience).

He sternly criticized his fellow Virginians for their gambling habits, yet for all his self-righteous talk, Jefferson turned out to be a poor money manager himself, naïvely counting on the next harvest, and the next after that, to pay down his debts to bankers. As a full-time student, though, he had no time to dwell on a future in farming. Not yet. Nor, it would appear, did his less industrious classmates. They were minors. Their priority was to become worthy of their family names.

Even if he had wanted to, Jefferson could never have been Patrick Henry, his elder by a scant few years, whom he met and befriended around this time. Brimming with self-confidence, a happy fiddler and partier, the future Revolutionary orator had a bluff manner that made him the envy of all. Dressed, we are informed, in "backwoods" mode, with an accent to match, he told stories with the air of a natural entertainer. In later years, after friendship turned to enmity, after Henry was dead, Jefferson would almost giddily detract from Henry's fame: he was a "rottenhearted," money-grubbing rube, a phony, too lazy to read a book from cover to cover. A decade before Alexander Hamilton entered the picture, Patrick Henry got in the way of Jefferson's growing self-directedness, his dawning ambition.

Jefferson was to acquire some of the same useful social skills as the charismatic Henry, though he was unable to command attention the way Henry could in any gathering where he happened to show up. Even as Jefferson came to excel at the art of storytelling, Henry-like oratory was a talent he would never master. He regarded the Indian's skill at speechmaking as a cultural attribute, but Patrick Henry's appeal was something else altogether, and to Jefferson, inevitably, a reflection of his own incompleteness. Jefferson's natural voice was thin and understated, though in intellectual comprehension and written expression his abilities were matched by few. He held in reserve any criticism he might have harbored of unrecorded speech, and only deemed it of lesser importance for a statesman when Henry came to represent his strongest competition for popularity in their native state. Under those circumstances, both he and his friend John Page represented Patrick Henry's pronunciation as common and rusticated.[2]

If Thomas Jefferson was privately jealous of men whose social success came to them naturally, he appears to have felt more self-doubt in realizing that he was unable to match his mates' early success in finding wives. Henry's appeal to the masses was primarily what is now referred to as a function of "alpha male" behavior; but Jefferson's frustration with women went deeper, at least in these years, if for no other reason than because adulthood was attained by a Virginia gentleman when he put down roots, when he rose to the position of head of family. A home life, enriched by the presence of a wife and children, was the essence of belonging.

In their world, a lady was, euphemistically put, of "the fair sex," an "ornament," whose propriety gave a worthy man his due stature among social equals. (In its various applications, the word "ornament" was often paired with words denoting happiness, or a similar sentiment.) The wife of a patriarch fulfilled her role by breeding. Jefferson, while unmarried, saw the wives of those closest to him dutifully bear sons and daughters every year or two.[3]

To get started on life, then, he required a wife, just as he required a home that would impress visitors—Shadwell, his widowed mother's place, was not it. One cannot treat Jefferson's loving attention to the construction and constant improvement of Monticello without relating it to the outward attributes of the compleat gentleman. Home and the growth of family was everything in colonial Virginia. To be a manor lord, even at so distinguished an architectural achievement as Monticello, meant little without the patriarchal element. As he navigated Williamsburg, a son of the outlying country of Albemarle needed to lure a planter's wife west, someone who could bear his children. Bachelorhood was meant to be a phase, a time for self-cultivation amid experiment. But it was supposed to end sooner than it did for Jefferson. To be surrounded by a family of one's making was vital to any pursuit of happiness. Pressure to obtain that family was real.

These facts of life help us evaluate the early examples of Jefferson's disparaging remarks about women during his extended years of study prior to marriage. Among the sayings he quotes from the classics by Euripides, Homer, Horace, and Virgil, he singles out lines that some have described as outright misogyny. Copying in Greek, Jefferson penned, for instance, this lament of a husband who contracts an unhappy marriage: " 'Tis clear from this, how great a curse a woman is." It goes on: "For he is in this dilemma; say his marriage has brought him good connections, he is glad then to keep the wife he loathes; or, if he gets a good wife but useless relations, he tries to stifle the bad luck with the good. But it is easiest for him who has settled in his house as wife a mere nobody . . ." From Virgil's *Aeneid*, he copies out "Tyrant Love, to what dost thou not drive the hearts of men!" and "A fickle and changeful thing is woman ever."[4]

There are plentiful descriptions of troublemaking women in Jefferson's quotations from the works of John Milton as well, including cautionary passages from his 1671 poem *Samson Agonistes*. In the familiar Old Testament story of Samson and Delilah, the hero is brought down because of his lover's betrayal. She exhibits all the weakness of womanhood, "outward Ornament" having been "lavish'd on their Sex," and "inward Gifts . . . left for Haste unfinished, judgment scant." Jefferson's long excerpt from Milton, dating to his early twenties, stressed a concern with female inconstancy, her seductive charms, her tendency toward "Mischeif." One was meant to understand that "God's universal Law / Gave to Man despotic Power / Over his Female," lest he fall prey to her wiles as Samson did.[5]

But there is more to this than a woman-hating spirit. Without practicing psychoanalysis on an eighteenth-century Virginian, even one as profuse in his writings as Jefferson, the evidence apart from such distinctive note-taking shows him expressing an understandable anxiety as he contemplates the future while comparing himself to other men. He is troubled, throughout his twenties, when he sees that he cannot exercise his claim to manhood at the time his friends have already begun to do so. His insecurity, though it comes across as misogynistic, is not misogyny but an expression of the inability to control his own growth process in a timely way. He feels stunted, unfinished. Occasionally, panic, if it may be called that, emerges in a jealous kind of acting out, most strikingly in the attempted seduction of the wife of one of his closest friends.

THE WORTH OF WYTHE

At first encounter, the slender, indrawn Jefferson was said to come across as unexpressive, even icy. His hazel-gray eyes complemented a placid countenance, and he was commonly credited with the enviable quality of unflappability. Fully grown, he attained the impressive height of six feet two and a half inches. One notable description of him that would continue into old age was the impressive erectness of his posture.

Once the surface frigidity was penetrated, he had a sunny disposition. But something within generated considerable stress, because he was prone to debilitating migraines. They first occurred when he was in his early twenties. He called them his "periodical head-achs," and they sent him into isolation and utter darkness. Head pain persisted for hours each day, for up to two weeks at a time. He accepted each episode as a separate physiological event, unconnected to any other, and he was unable or unwilling to attribute a psychological component to it.[6]

He appeared unprepossessing, courteous, and well informed—an eighteenth-century gentleman's bearing. That is, until he balanced a goose quill between his fingers. The man the public saw was unflappable, but he also had a testy side, which grew in intensity and severity as the years progressed. Young Jefferson had yet to aspire to dominate. Beginning in his thirties, thrust forward as a visionary in politics, he would become easily provoked and exhibit peevishness. With some rivals, he was callous and malicious, wishing injury.

The contrast between magnanimous feeling and vengeful thought remained constant over the course of his public life. He saw the written word as potential energy, a tactile instrument of personal power. If his writing desk was a place where learned conversation began, it was also an outlet for emotional unease. In Williamsburg, at least, he was surrounded by like-minded young men; they compared notes, socialized, shared confidences, and faced the future with collective purpose. If Jefferson ranked his friends and held suspicions about others, his early letters do not suggest it.

At twenty, he was an intense student who aimed to please his professors. The two who mattered most, who carried forward where James Maury left off, were William Small (1734–1775), another Scotsman, who taught mathematics, ethics, and rhetoric at the College; and George Wythe (1726–1806), regarded as Virginia's paramount legal scholar, who would join his star pupil in signing the Declaration of Independence.

Small was nine years older than his devoted charge and, judging by Jefferson's later tribute, cast a spell on the teenager. He was a benign authority figure, a model of urbanity. When Jefferson reflected on his past, he was sure to credit the Scotsman's wisdom and encouragement. Teacher and student carried on their conversation beyond the classroom. Small's capacious reach brought texts to Jefferson's attention that he might not otherwise have known, which fed his passion for astronomy, mechanical drawing, and invention—helping him conceive his award-winning plow. It could only have been Dr. Small that he was thinking of a half century after they parted company, when he wrote to a friendly newspaper editor: "When I was young, mathematics was the passion of my life."[7]

Small returned to England in 1764, where he set up a medical practice and communed with scientists. Student and professor stayed in touch until the latter's death on the eve of the Revolution. Jefferson was ever thankful for the *partie carrée* that Dr. Small made possible when he brought his prized student to the dinner table of the colonial governor. Small introduced Jefferson to the friend and colleague who would shape his professional life more than any other single person: George Wythe. At the governor's table, listening to these men converse, the student savored high-level conversation. He contributed to the tenor of the occasion with his correct violin in concert with other young musicians.

These were the "dignified men" Jefferson named in the instructive letter to eldest grandson Jefferson ("Jeff") Randolph nearly a half century later. Small was a master of multiple subjects. Wythe taught the law. In Jefferson's words, the first possessed a "large and liberal mind," and the second, generous to a fault, was "my faithful and beloved Mentor in youth, and my most affectionate friend through life." Evidence bears out Jefferson biographer Dumas Malone's statement "His friendship with older men is one of many signs of the essential seriousness of his nature."[8]

That is not all there was to Wythe. Personality tends to be reduced in the eulogistic tribute that guides most conventional biography. Henry Clay remarked that Wythe bade adieu to visitors with "the courtliest bow" he'd ever seen; but the famously serene scholar was not without a sense of humor, either, to judge by the poetic battle he sustained (while he and Jefferson were together in Philadelphia) with a Rhode Island delegate to the Second Continental Congress whose ideas differed from his own. In keeping with the mock grandeur that an amateur poet deployed as a way to stay humble, Wythe's verses brought the Greek gods into the picture: "I flatter'd myself that Apollo / Had told me the Muses to follow." The legal scholar also shared his amused sensibility with Samuel Adams, and no doubt with his colleague Jefferson as well.[9]

The persevering student was only nineteen when he finished at the college and was apprenticed to Wythe, who was then in his late thirties, married and childless. He readied Jefferson for the bar and saw to it that he attained standing in the colony's elite General Court. Only the very select argued before the General Court, demonstrating the level of confidence the legal scholar and former attorney general of Virginia reposed in his protégé.

Figure 4. George Wythe. No one was as instrumental in Jefferson's preparation for public service as his college law instructor, lifelong friend, and fellow signer of the Declaration of Independence. Noted for his gentle manner as well as his erudition, Wythe willed his library to the bibliophile Jefferson. Drawing by James B. Longacre, ca. 1825. (Courtesy National Portrait Gallery, Smithsonian Institution)

Jefferson and Wythe enjoyed a unique relationship. Sharing a passionate love for the power of the printed word, they discussed book culture and the preservation of libraries. It is possible that Wythe taught others before Jefferson, but if he did, there is no record of it. He would go on to educate, among others, the long-serving chief justice (and Jefferson hater) John Marshall, the master politician Henry Clay, and several justices of Virginia's Supreme Court.

As the Revolutionary War dragged on, Wythe and Jefferson jointly redesigned the code of laws of Virginia. After the end of fighting, Wythe expressed his strong conviction that Virginians needed to act to end slavery. He himself held individuals in bondage, but he saw to it that they were educated. His prized student and eager collaborator proved incapable of taking meaningful steps in the direction his mentor was urging, though Wythe did not argue the case with him, convinced that Jefferson's patriotism would lead him in the right direction.

Here we start to encounter the nature of Jefferson's confused sentiment. Married to the strong, unbending prejudices of his class and loath to see Blacks as full citizens, he nevertheless could not ignore the ethical model he had before him in this judicious elder who was to take "all men are created equal" literally and wish for it to be applied across racial lines. Jefferson tried, but briefly, to test the waters to see whether a consensus might form among Virginia's planter aristocracy to accept emancipation as a near-term goal. Wythe stuck to his guns. Jefferson did not. His heart wasn't in it, and he evidently felt too little guilt about his slave owning. That said, he was constrained in ways Wythe was not, having come into a considerable amount of land and, with it, an enslaved workforce and debts to London bankers. Wythe, residing in town, was reliant on the practice of law and teaching for his income.[10]

Named chancellor of Virginia in 1788, George Wythe continued practicing what he preached till the end of his days. He heard a slavery case as a Court of Appeals judge during Jefferson's second term as president. Three generations of an enslaved Virginia family of mixed heritage and varying skin pigmentation were facing sale beyond the boundaries of the state, and they petitioned for their freedom on the basis of their descent from a free Indian woman. Their master insisted that their maternal lineage was through an enslaved woman and an Indian man. The truth was unprovable, and Wythe ruled in favor of the enslaved, stating that the burden of proof lay with the master, thereby treating the petitioners as full human beings rather than someone else's property. The decision was met with disapproval from those in the Virginia legal community who shuddered at the idea of applying the Bill of Rights to the enslaved.

That same year, 1806, Wythe was teaching the classics to a biracial youth ("Michael the Mulatto Boy") who lived with him—whom he had freed—when both were tragically done in by Wythe's grandnephew. Forging a bank note wasn't enough for George Wythe Sweeney, who couldn't wait for his inheritance. The method he employed was arsenic-laced coffee—using a poison widely available in Virginia as a rat killer. Three days before he died, Wythe, past eighty, called out: "I am murdered!" On learning the facts, Jefferson wrote: "Such an instance of depravity has been hitherto known to us only in the fables of the poets." The slowly murdered judge had the presence of mind to disinherit the accused once Michael, having also drunk the coffee, was already dead. Sweeney was acquitted of the murder charge, in large measure because testimony from African American witnesses was deemed inadmissible. George Wythe, Jefferson's faithful friend of a lifetime, willed his private library to the sitting president.[11]

Dignity. Conscience. Rectitude. Wythe was a levelheaded advocate for justice and humane causes who stood against encroachments upon rights and retained his scholarly persona no matter how emotion-filled the moment was. As an intellectual father figure to Jefferson and many others who went on to distinguish themselves, he was nothing less than a symbol of enlightened humanity. Yet for Jefferson, he was more, because his own short-lived father was not the emotional center of his early life.

That George Wythe is not generally regarded as a member of America's pantheon of founding giants reminds us of a problematic feature of historical memory: the standards history uses to immortalize leaders will often grant moral authority to the morally flawed, so long as they performed *ceremonially* as moral exemplars. In a highly contentious age in which tales of glory abounded and genealogies counted, where one who married into a powerful family might attain a position of public trust through artifice or the power of persuasion, the deserving George Wythe was destined to be relegated to second-tier status in the annals of American achievement. Quiet deeds rarely stand up to the forgetfulness of memory. The fact remains that Jefferson's wise mentor was uniformly celebrated for the "purity" and "integrity" of his private character, as exhibited in his generosity of spirit toward those without power. It speaks well of Thomas Jefferson that Wythe was a hero to him.

The law established Jefferson as a rising member of the gentry, lifting him within a few years to a position of influence within Virginia's constellation of political actors. Wythe imparted to him the calm self-confidence necessary to propose major changes to the laws, taking aim at the colonial mind and remolding it to give greater definition to *American* ideals. The Wythe model was in this way integrated into Jefferson's emergent worldview. He understood how, when personal humility combined with rational argument, a leading individual might be positioned to earn acceptance as a secular moral authority. Jefferson was not George Wythe, though. His radical ambition outpaced the teacher's. There could be no compromise when Jefferson found a cause.[12]

If Wythe was a source, as I contend he was, of Jefferson's philosophic zealotry, then it is worth further noting the elder's attainments as the first faculty member in U.S. history officially denoted "Professor of Law" (1779). The book collection he bequeathed to his apprentice was rich in legal philosophy and works of classical antiquity and included three separate editions of Shakespeare's works. His bookplate featured the Latin motto "Secundus Dubiisque Rectus" (Upright in Prosperity and Peril).[13]

Interestingly, Wythe grew up with a mother who taught him Latin and Greek at home, when theirs was a world in which young ladies were not encouraged to study the classics. Jefferson at one point sent him the gift of a nuanced treatise on "the use of the middle voice in Greek," writing with unfeigned admiration: "If it gives you half the pleasure it did me, mine will be doubled still." Their relationship can be summed up in that one line.[14]

Wythe was elected to the governing House of Burgesses when he was in his late twenties; Jefferson would be seated in the same body in 1769, at the age of twenty-six. But unlike his self-possessed mentor in the law, Jefferson only ever achieved his lifelong pursuit of tranquil "felicity" and inner calm in short stretches. With his debilitating "head-achs" erupting in 1764 and continuing through the end of his career, there is obviously more to the story. As bookish as he was, the multifaceted man did not stay put.

The curriculum that obliged him to study history and moral philosophy did not prevent him from turning to less demanding fare. Pocketing what he reaped from his formal education, Jefferson sharpened his outlook by studying the interplay of public opportunities and private pitfalls through the lens of popular literature. Americans in the eighteenth and early nineteenth centuries gravitated to novels that featured sentimental themes, marriage scenarios, and excitable characters whose inner torment leads them to fateful choices. In these books, passivity is unproductive, and the impulsive resort to subversive tactics inevitably backfires. Everyone aims for personal peace and calm (the morally desirable result), but almost no one reaches that goal. Tragedy is unavoidable.

The imagination is rebellious in this literature, but even more so in the remarkable novels Jefferson made a point of praising. In the 1760s, he leaned in the direction of clever and satirical authors—escapist literature—far more than the long, moralizing epistolary novels that were no less popular, if female-centered. In 1771, recommending works of literature to a Virginian of his own generation, Jefferson could not resist the picaresque: the immortal *Don Quixote* along with the ingenious *Gil Blas* (by Alain-René Lesage), whose eponymous hero triumphs in a devious world on the basis of his quick wit. Jefferson approved of the comic novels of Henry Fielding (*Tom Jones* and others) and applauded the prolific Tobias Smollett, translator of *Don Quixote* and *Gil Blas* and himself the author of *The Adventures of Roderick Random* and *The Adventures of Peregrine Pickle*. In later life, Jefferson largely gave up on fiction, as well as poetry, but in these years he was clearly a big fan. The takeaway is simple: if outwardly unassuming and resistant to youthful acts of disobedience, Jefferson was by no means humorless.[15]

"AN AFFAIR OF THAT KIND"

Studious and sociable. These are the two, admittedly bland, characterizations of Jefferson given by those who knew him at this time. He claimed he studied as many as fifteen hours a day. The seemingly playful, self-denying correspondence with his lifelong friend John Page of Rosewell, inheritor of a commodious estate, provides us with precious hints of Jefferson's awkwardness in particular settings. The Page letters reveal him looking for a wife to bring home to Albemarle after only his second year in the colonial capital. He aimed high with Rebecca Burwell, whose brother was a fellow student. The family was well-established and politically connected. Hers was a surname loaded with honors. They were Virginia nobility.

In describing how it felt to be around her, he sounds impatient, insecure, tongue-tied—not a good combination. Writing to Page about their common desire to find a mate within the closed circle of the planter set, Jefferson exaggerates the degree of his "suffering" both as a student under pressure and a suitor with little to boast. He prays that Page will speak for him in his absence. Afraid to mention Rebecca's name lest his confessional letter should fall into the hands of a stealthy prankster out to embarrass him, he renames his love interest "Belinda"—which, whether or not he meant anything by it, was also the name of an enslaved twenty-four-year-old at Shadwell whom he'd known all his life.[16]

Keeping busy at Shadwell in the summer of 1763, Jefferson rejected his friend's advice, which was to "go immediately and lay siege." Page expected him to confess his love to Rebecca's guardian (she'd lost her parents) so as to learn where he stood. Evidently, the would-be suitor was not just tormented but obsessive, talking in maudlin terms about his chances. Unwilling to see things through, he weaseled out with the claim of a half-formed plan to go to England, with an open-ended return date. Were he to do so, it would be imprudent to act prematurely. "To begin an affair of that kind now, and carry it on so long a time in form is by no means a proper plan," Jefferson justified. "No, no, Page, whatever assurances I may give her in private of my esteem for her, or whatever assurances I may ask in return from her, depend on it they must be kept in private." He was not about to appear before the elders, opting instead to wait for credible proof that his intended's feelings approximated his own. "I say necessity will oblige me to it, because I never can bear to remain in suspence so long a time."[17]

Impatience to know whether one's feelings are reciprocated is understandable, especially among the young. While biographers have used these juvenile messages as a way to point to his early ineptness as a lover, I find young Jefferson's words revealing for two very different reasons: first, he is loath to make his case in person, that is, to be physically present and immediately accountable; second, he displays a penchant for secrecy that will have long-term consequences.

Self-protection is a perfectly normal human trait, of course. Adolescence is a time in personality development when rejection can trigger lifelong responses, when a snub is especially hurtful and promptly internalized, and when peer acceptance becomes critically helpful in a person's recovery. While early marriage was fairly standard in colonial Virginia, modern science in this case tracks with a slew of evidence in Jefferson's letters from his student days to his years in the public eye. More than most, he cannot handle loss of control.[18]

Here as well we begin to grasp Jefferson's fascination with the unseen, how he used mystery to quietly maneuver. It gave him power where he otherwise had none. To use time and invisibility in this manner is more than an expression of self-protectiveness for a reserved individual. The aggressiveness that placidity hides would make Jefferson an adept poker player.

Something was already building in him that intensifies later on with a failure to confront head-on the anxiety he feels. After setbacks or unwanted exposure, he'll want to flee to Monticello and retire from public affairs. In those instances, returning to the relative isolation of his private mountain allows Jefferson to retreat into himself, to become reimmersed in his ever-expanding library, where he is able to control whom he sees and under what conditions.

Facing rejection from the Burwells, Jefferson bowed out—how gracefully is debatable, for he remained smitten with "Belinda" for some months more. This fatherless young man from the more recently settled piedmont west lacked the requisite nerve to present a winning argument before one of the First Families of Tidewater Virginia. With his romantic ambition stymied, it could hardly have added to his self-confidence that his friend Page was successfully courting another of the same lineage: Frances Burwell. "How does your pulse beat?" Jefferson lightly taunted him after a Page visit to the Burwell family seat.[19]

Clearly, Jefferson's pride suffered when Rebecca Burwell chose instead Jaquelin (Jack) Ambler. But he might also have rationalized that Jack was a slightly older, socially well positioned William and Mary graduate from nearby Yorktown. Seventeen years later, when she was only sixteen, the second of their five daughters, Mary, married future chief justice John Marshall, himself one of fifteen children, and ultimately a greater nemesis to Jefferson than even Alexander Hamilton. The respectable Jack Ambler died in 1798, and his Rebecca survived just one decade more. The Marshalls, John and Mary, were among the fortunate few in that their marriage endured nearly a half century; yet tragedies piled up for them, too: only four of their ten children lived to adulthood. Mary herself proved frail; during the second half of the Marshalls' marriage, she was mostly bedridden.

As the nineteenth century arrived, Chief Justice Marshall and President Thomas Jefferson were sworn enemies. Their problems were irreversible, but entirely unrelated to private life. In the world they shared, lines of affinity, once established, tended to be sharply drawn. Close family members tended to join forces, as suspicions about those outside the fold curdled. Among Northerners, Virginia as a whole appeared clannish; and Jefferson's attachment to his fellow Virginians was so pronounced that the political party he, together with James Madison, brought into being would be known elsewhere, in adversarial terms, as the "Virginia party." After leaning heavily on John Page and Dabney Carr during and after college, he would have Madison, Monroe, and other Virginians to serve as emotional sounding boards and a firm support network going into the next century.

Virginia always weighed heavily in Jefferson's thinking. It is a long trajectory that carries his story from Williamsburg to the White House, but some key markings are already suggested. A surrogate family—that *partie carrée* idea—took the place of family since his own lacked the political clout of Pages, Burwells, Amblers, and others with Williamsburg-area riverfront plantations. Here, as well, is where the Randolph bond failed to cohere. While Thomas Jefferson and John Marshall were both of Randolph stock, some scholars believe that a rift between their respective Randolph branches going back a couple of generations is one part of what set them at odds.[20]

The nature of Virginia's interfamilial machinations opens up an even bigger conundrum in the co-signing of loans and balancing of debt payments—in simply staying afloat. Large extended families and marriages that joined different First Families in socially prescribed pairings were important elements of a strategy to stave off financial dissolution. Co-signing a loan taken out by his grandson's father-in-law would ultimately dash an aged Jefferson's hope of getting himself out of debt.

Large planter families speculated, and not always responsibly. Besides the Loyal Land Company that gave the Walkers, Peter Jefferson, and others in Albemarle and environs a common goal, the Northern Neck Lee and Washington families, along with neighbor George Mason, owned shares in the Ohio Company. Even Thomas Jefferson, who avoided land speculation ventures for the most part, for a time joined Washington, one of the Lees, and Patrick Henry in the doomed Mississippi Company.

If Virginia surnames shared fortunes, few were truly secure. The gradual downfall of one or another branch of a lineage caused reverberations. Gentleman planters of the late colonial period, mocked as provincials in the British metropolis, kept their heads above water just well enough that their post-Revolutionary offspring looked back on them as noble progenitors. But hard times left the debtor class scrambling for a solution that would never come. Some legitimately worried about the fate of their most valued inheritance: the social order that qualified them as gentlefolk.[21]

CROSSING THE LINE

The gentry were privileged, but not all-powerful. No one with this background went through life without personal dramas of one kind or another. The experience of John Page of Rosewell was widely shared. An inheritor of First Family status, he became a member of the First Congress of the United States concurrent with Jefferson's service as secretary of state, and he was governor of Virginia while Jefferson was president. The Pages' marriage was by all accounts a harmonious one. Frances bore ten children, though few survived to adulthood. She herself died young, in

1784, when Jefferson was himself two years a widower. Seen from this perspective, losing Rebecca Burwell to Jack Ambler could not have been as traumatic as the loss, in the fall of 1765, of his sister Jane, three years Thomas's elder. Jefferson was robbed of friends and loved ones by death, and so was everyone he knew. It's what they all expected.[22]

Jefferson's path to celebrity was far from predictable. He certainly did not act as one who believed himself destined for a life of ease and contentment—not at this time, anyway. Rather, he behaved the way a privileged youth let loose in a far-flung country did. Here is where his story takes a turn.

Fated to remain single for seven years after the Page-Burwell union took place, Thomas Jefferson made sexual advances on the wife of one of his most intimate friends as the two of them were just starting their careers. Jack Walker, whose 1764 wedding he attended, never suspected. Jefferson's behavior toward Betsy Walker remained a secret from Jack until sometime after 1784, when the offender went to France. Only when the two men were entering their sixties and Jefferson was the occupant of the President's House was the indiscretion publicized and Jefferson forced to endure public shaming. Sullying his name in the press ("the antagonist presses," as he put it to Walker at that time) was something he expected from a virulent political opposition suddenly aware that they had lucked into an ancient smear they could make stick to their mild-mannered presidential piñata.[23]

After marriage, Jack and Betsy Walker settled at Belvoir, six miles from Monticello. Jefferson occasionally transacted business with Jack Walker as well as with his father, the prestigious Dr. Thomas Walker, who was placed in charge of disposing of town lots in the new settlement of Charlottesville. Jefferson cultivated Dr. Walker and cared what that gentleman thought of him. In the summer or early autumn of 1768, as Jefferson was following his schedule for construction on the mountain where he would make his home, he had his hands full with legal cases. Jack was dispatched to central New York as an Indian negotiator (for four months, as it turned out), and Jefferson stopped by Belvoir, as a good friend did, out of concern for the well-being of his friend's wife. Nor would Jack have expected otherwise, for just as his father had stood up for the legal interests of Peter Jefferson's surviving children, the younger Walker, before embarking on his journey to New York, had named his friend Jefferson an executor of his will.

Jefferson, now twenty-five, and Mrs. Walker, a twenty-two-year-old recent mother, were accustomed to a degree of intimacy that makes it almost a cliché that her single friend found the nerve to attempt a seduction. He did so on more than one occasion, and if the gossipy record is to be believed, he didn't stop after he was married. The evidence is tantalizing, though considerably less than the law (and law of historians) requires for conviction.

Mysterious hints that connect him to another married woman appear in Jefferson's daily account books for 1770. Molly Dudley was the wife of George Dudley, a local landowner who was paid to make bricks used in Monticello's construction. She is mentioned by name in his accounts, and mentioned in code elsewhere. In fact, Jefferson departs from his distinct rounded hand in the notebook he carried on the road only where he deploys a secret script that combines letters in a way that resembles nothing so much as Japanese hiragana. The source he uses for the code is Thomas Shelton's *Tachygraphy, or Short-Writing the Most Easie Exact and Speedie*, a guide that dates to the first half of the seventeenth century.

Jefferson was intrigued by Shelton's system. He had thought of teaching it to Page during the "Belinda" period in his as yet unfulfilling romantic career, writing that friend: "We must fall on some scheme of communicating our thoughts to each other, which shall be totally unintelligible to everyone but to ourselves. I will send you some of these days Shelton's Tachygraphical Alphabet." What makes all of this doubly curious is that his appeal to Page that they devise an impenetrable private language is followed directly by a sentence that reads hauntingly in context. He writes: "Jack Walker is engaged to Betsy Moore, and desired all his brethren might be made acquainted with his happiness." A few short years later, Jefferson would be interfering with the couple's happiness.[24]

If Shelton's shorthand was not phonetically sounding out Molly Dudley's name so that Jefferson could recall a conquest, what else could it have been? It is hard to come up with an innocent explanation. Molly didn't press her case so that history would notice, but Betsy Walker did—or, rather, the affronted Jack Walker did, a decade and a half after he learned of his once trusted neighbor's indiscreet moves. Fawn Brodie speculates that the Walker affair, as it became known, marked an important stage in Jefferson's harboring of secrets and the "separation of chastity and morality."[25]

Something is clearly going on here. Jefferson's first recorded meeting with his future wife at her father's estate southeast of Richmond took place one month after the second of his coded references to Molly Dudley. In the weeks following, two more tachygraphical squiggles appear in the notebook, this time naming "Sukey at Smith"; and some months after that, a "Sukey at Stith." In the eighteenth century, Sukey was a fairly common diminutive for Susan, and here most likely refers to an enslaved woman; a precise location for Smith and/or Stith is unverifiable. It certainly seems meaningful that women's names are the only names Jefferson opts to enter into his traveling books in the form of coded graphs.[26]

COMMONPLACING

At least some of the disappearing dots can be connected. The decision to build at Monticello appears to have had some relationship to his setbacks in Williamsburg. In one of many moments when he was weaving fantasies for the eyes of his levelheaded classmate Page, Jefferson vowed that if Rebecca Burwell were to accept him as a husband, he would establish himself in the colonial capital. After being jilted, and back home with his mother in Albemarle, the forlorn bachelor found a new romantic vision for himself: a country seat that low-lying Williamsburg could not replicate, where he made the rules and where the natural beauty of his surroundings captivated the senses and advertised the inventiveness of the exceptional man who had conceived it all.

Owing to the impracticality of building on the scale Jefferson intended, it was an emotional decision to give structure to his vision of a life at the top of his own private mountain. In the process of accumulating what was then viewed as an inconceivable number of books, he would install himself in a scenic situation, serene and secluded, luring friends great distances to partake of the invigorating air and feed off the tranquil spirit the place produced in a visitor. The woods were dense all the way up the mountain, and it was going to require an immense amount of work to construct roads and transport materials up its incline. If he built it, they would come. And he'd have Molly Dudley's husband, George, supply the bricks.[27]

Work started in 1767 and would continue apace for the next dozen years. Jefferson, as one might expect, supervised all aspects of the clearing and construction that year and the next. To earn a living, he rode to and from Williamsburg, with occasional forays across the Blue Ridge Mountains to Augusta County, paying for "entertainments" and meeting many people for the first time.[28] Solitary travel evidently contributed to whatever spirit of adventure he felt as he ruminated on the dreamscape of the eventual Monticello. It cannot be stated with any conviction that he found a way to compartmentalize his misstep(s) with his friend Jack Walker's wife—if indeed she was in fact wholly indifferent to his advances. Nor can we speculate as to whether at that time he resolved what he might someday have to say to Jack if word got out.

His college friends were important to him. The memories they shared belonged to an impressionable time in life when all were building toward positions they would inevitably assume as members of the governing class. Their bond was fortified in the mid- to late 1760s, because they had an inkling that change was coming to Virginia, even before there was the least talk of revolution.

Jefferson belonged to two neighborhoods now. Williamsburg was the center of colonial authority, where appearances mattered and conversation had immediacy. The welcoming estate of John Page, Rosewell, was nearby when companionship was needed. The other neighborhood, of course, was where his patrimony, his future, lay. The two who lived closest to him in Albemarle were the two he communed with most: Jack Walker, privileged son of the imposing Dr. Thomas Walker; and Dabney Carr, the cherished friend he could always confide in, and for the past three years his brother-in-law. Carr had already supplied Jefferson with three nieces (three nephews were yet to come). Before very much longer, though, Dabney Carr would live on in memory alone, while Jack Walker remained ignorant of his friend's betrayal. Once their personal lives became public fodder, any true reconciliation would be impossible.

Fortunately for Jefferson, John Page was to remain a stalwart among his college friends. They'd endure the pain of loss and offer their condolences in turn. After the death of his wife, Page would remarry and go on to father many more children who took his name. And while Jefferson outlived him by nearly two decades, these two proud planters, born two weeks apart, would alike face financial ruin at the end of their lives. Page saw it coming and was scared. Jefferson lived in denial much of the time, justifying to his creditors every delay and capitalizing on his political position to keep the wolves at bay. The downfall of John Page was the more catastrophic. He'd inherited one of the most impressive tracts on the York River, just opposite Williamsburg; its reduction was historic.

As it was for many Virginia planters besides them, the cause of collapse was a cruel combination of factors: a declining tobacco economy, imprudently negotiated loans, and reliance on a slave-based economy in which the perverse idea of breeding human property for sale increasingly became the resort of large landowners. They'd all been taught that the land would save them—not commerce, not paper money, but what they produced. Jefferson, in decrying the pestilential city, never stopped believing that land ownership fed health, stability, rootedness, moral purpose—happiness. And while he abhorred all forms of gambling, he ended up gambling away his patrimony on a beautiful vision of agrarian independence. By allowing the Northern states to modernize fast, fostering a capital-intensive infrastructure, the South isolated itself. Bills came due. Jefferson lived out his fantasy and paid the price.[29]

None of this was foreseeable in the mid-1760s, when the bonds between Jefferson and his fellows were set. In combination, they represented the future of Virginia, the colony with the greatest expanse of territory. Their governors were well liked, and Jefferson, as a student, was recognized by Governor Francis Fauquier and invited to his dinner table.

He resided at Shadwell in the summer months but spent the greater portion of the year in Williamsburg with George Wythe, preparing to practice law. Reading intensively in legal history, classical literature, philosophy, and poetry, he looked for ways to assist his memory. The commonplace book, into which an eager student transcribed memorable passages from respected authors, was not a new invention in the mid-eighteenth century. Like the diary form, it was known but not everywhere kept, even by advanced scholars. After he went to France in the mid-1780s, Jefferson discovered there that the renowned French political philosopher Montesquieu, author of the compendious *Spirit of the Laws* (1748), was an inveterate practitioner. He learned that "Montesquieu was a man of immense reading, that he had commonplaced all his reading, and that his object was to throw the whole contents of his commonplace book into systematical order, and to shew his ingenuity by reconciling the contradictory facts it presented."[30]

In Jefferson's case, commonplacing marked the beginning of a lifelong passion to maintain daily accounting records, to compile seasonal reports on agricultural productivity, and to list the requirements, as he saw them, of providing for the enslaved people he'd inherited. He started his "Garden Book" in 1766 at Shadwell, charting when seeds were sown and the harvested produce "came to table." At home and away, from the close of the Revolution through his last days on earth, he rigorously preserved a "Summary Journal of Letters," listing by date, correspondent, and content each letter he wrote or received. That record alone eventually amounted to 656 pages.

He retained among his papers a Literary Commonplace Book, some of its entries dating to his time with Maury (1758 or so), and a Legal Commonplace Book, which he began at the end of his apprenticeship with Wythe, around the time he passed the bar (1765–66). The two commonplace books allow us to establish what writings mattered most to him, what framed his mental outlook in those formative years, as he conceived a public role for himself among the Virginia elite. "I cannot live without books," he famously proclaimed in a letter to John Adams after selling 6,487 volumes to the Library of Congress to replenish what was lost during the War of 1812. Being Thomas Jefferson, he didn't take much time before ordering titles anew.[31]

The Literary Commonplace Book consists of 123 manuscript pages, which he cared enough for to have bound in leather in Philadelphia. Now in safekeeping at the Library of Congress, it informs history of what its owner, constantly surrounded by books, wanted to keep close in the years before he gained renown. He recorded, in the original Greek, excerpts from the historian Herodotus, the playwright Euripides, and the *Iliad* of Homer. In Latin: Virgil, Horace, Cicero. In English: the incomparable Shakespeare, Milton's *Paradise Lost*, and, from the generation just preceding his own, James Thompson's paean to rural life, *The Seasons*, along with Alexander Pope's constantly quoted *Essay on Man* and Edward Young's lugubrious *Night-Thoughts*. All of these continued to move the hearts of readers into the next century. The most extensively cited author in the commonplace book was Henry St. John, Viscount Bolingbroke, the early-eighteenth-century materialist philosopher whose critique of religious dogma Jefferson assiduously adopted. In case he needed any help, Bolingbroke led him to the stark realization that the scriptures were not to be fetishized as "the word of God" but regarded purely as texts belonging to human history. Bolingbroke liberated young Jefferson.

It is especially curious that during the most active of his Williamsburg years, 1762–1766, Jefferson posted in his Literary Commonplace Book more entries in Greek than in English. The law was his chosen profession, as it was for all of his college friends, but his fascination with the ethereal, with the Athenian heart, appears to have been paramount in his mind—a counterweight to the determinative character of a law practice dominated by land and inheritance matters.[32]

It was, to an extent not precisely measurable, the standard set by Wythe that sparked Jefferson's translation of classical humanism (beginning with the Greeks) into a government's devotion to the betterment of humanity. His signature attachment to Epicurus, for whom tranquility of mind was life's main pursuit, appears throughout Jefferson's public and private writings. This is where he obtained his intuitive guide to conscience and his acceptance that reason cannot be easily detached from the passion of self-love. The objective, then, was to find a "noble" nature that lifted one above "common" nature.[33]

To Jefferson's Epicurean foundation was added the relatable Renaissance discovery of individuality. From a humanist tradition writ large, Jefferson discovered forms of "genius" and an aesthetic opposed to artificiality that combined well with a proto-Romantic appreciation for sublimity in grand Nature. That is what Monticello's diverseness increasingly came to mean, as the manor lord found an expression of his own uniqueness in an impressionistic architecture, in a lofty home where he might cohabit harmoniously with the natural world, and where, in the same breath, the spirits of ancient Greece and Rome were captured.

If the memoir of an English-born stage actor is to be believed (the author has an eyebrow-raising exuberance in his writing style), John Bernard recounts a conversation with Jefferson during a visit to Monticello in 1798, in which the host explained that having been "bred to the law," he was exposed to "the dark side of humanity"; to offset its effect, he turned to poetry as a means to locate more of humanity's "bright side," and in the process learned a valuable lesson: "Between the two extremes I have contrived through life to draw the due medium." If the quote is accurate, these sentiments match what is known of Jefferson's reading in the 1760s, when he resided with his teacher in the colonial capital.[34]

Besides the Greeks and Romans, another author he eagerly accepted into the Literary Commonplace Book as an ancient was the Celtic Ossian. In this the impressionable student was one of many who were duped. He could not accept that "Ossian" was actually a modern poet named Macpherson who'd defrauded the public by claiming to have unearthed the tattered oeuvre of a warrior-bard of the third century A.D. Also of tremendous significance was the one author in the Literary Commonplace Book whom Jefferson did recognize as modern when he included an extended quotation, namely, the Anglican minister turned comic giant Laurence Sterne. His novel of the 1760s, *Tristram Shandy*, was decidedly absurd, delightfully mischievous, and emotionally enticing. Sterne's idealization of passion spoke to the Virginian, who may also be said to have profited from the author in developing an almost ethereal skill with inventive metaphor and hyperbole. Jefferson was eclectic in his reading choices and not averse to lighter, edgier fare as he journeyed in his mind beyond what the law demanded of him.[35]

The modern editors of Jefferson's Legal Commonplace Book note that he was more wide-ranging than his peers in his extractions from authors, especially in joining philosophy and history to standard legal texts. Though he is well known to history as a collector of books and artifacts, this was not something he was directly taught so much as it can be designated a personality trait. In a very real sense, Jefferson's library defined him.

Wythe's prized protégé passed the bar in 1765, but he took longer than most to start practicing law. The only reason for this delay that makes any sense is that he chose to read and ruminate, watch and learn, in order to gain in confidence. (Perhaps he was wife hunting, too.) Most likely with Wythe's encouragement, he learned Anglo-Saxon, a language in which many legal concepts were set. The impact of this extra effort should not be passed over lightly. Jefferson's study of Britain's early history would become a critical point of departure in the following decade as he adopted a revolutionary argument: that Saxon independence of thought and courageous action took the Germanic tribes to England, where they reinvented themselves—precisely what the British colonists of North America were in the process of doing.[36]

The key takeaway here is that while he was under George Wythe's roof, Jefferson shifted gears, acquiring a new, more critical perspective on the world and his purpose in it. At the same time that he was identifying as nonsensical (owing to Bolingbroke) historically suspect Christian beliefs that hinged on revelation, he was privately calling out what was to him another farcical notion: that the American colonies should exist for the commercial benefit of England.[37]

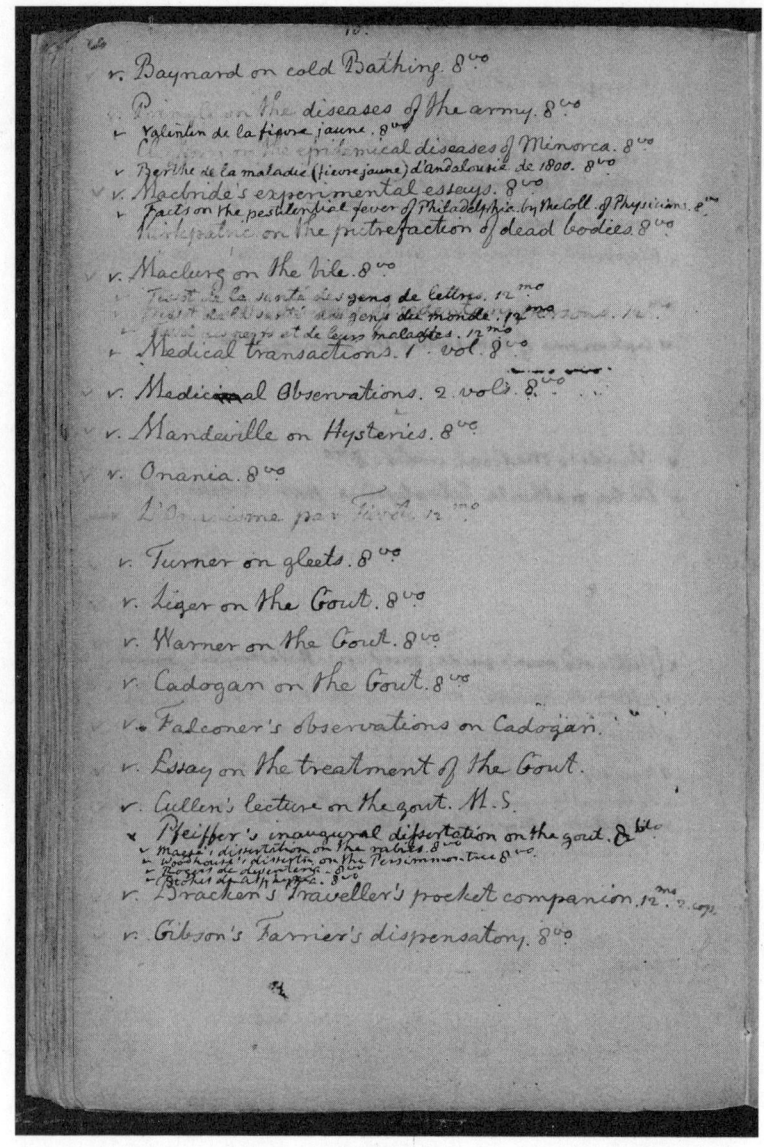

Figure 5. Jefferson's record of the contents of his library in 1783 contains the works of leading medical theorists. Hysteria was a nervous disorder thought to afflict females most, sometimes causing nymphomania; it could only be remediated by the restoration of "tranquility of mind." Jefferson also owned, in English and French, *Onania* or *L'Onanisme*, by the Swiss physician Samuel-Auguste Tissot, on the nature of male and female lust. Onanism refers to masturbation, which Tissot insisted was the source of a number of diseases, typically caused by "hard study." For a man of letters, regular sex with a "fruitful" female was the ideal remedy for solitary sex. "Turner on gleets" is a treatise on gonorrhea. (Courtesy Coolidge Collection of Thomas Jefferson Manuscripts, Massachusetts Historical Society)

CHAPTER 3

"Till Harmony Rouse Ev'ry Gentle Passion"

Mountain Paradise

IN THE SPRING OF 1766, Jefferson traveled to Philadelphia to be inoculated against smallpox (a procedure not yet performed in Williamsburg) and continued from there to New York. There he connected with non-Virginians who would become close political associates. In Philadelphia he met Charles Thomson; in New York, Elbridge Gerry. The first, Irish-born and orphaned young, was on his way to establishing himself, like Jefferson, as a man of science and philosophy. Thomson was to become a key figure in each of the congresses that led from the Revolution to the presidency of George Washington. Gerry, a Boston-reared merchant at the time of their first meeting, was to sign the Declaration of Independence and conclude his career as Madison's vice president. All that this meant was that Thomas Jefferson, still just twenty-three, was becoming a little less provincial.

Something else of interest was taking place. In the mid-1760s, as he began preparing for the bar, Jefferson's handwriting gradually evolved from an angular, right-slanted presentation typical of the majority of writers of the time into a rounder, pleasingly balanced vertical script. While both styles were tightly controlled, he stuck with the round style ever after. He must have moved his pen in a slow and measured way: every production of his appears to have been patiently wrought and is plainly readable.[1]

In 1767, he began the law practice he would abandon seven years later when he opted for Revolutionary politics. The prominent Jefferson scholar Merrill Peterson put it neatly: "The law was not his mistress but a profession of service and, incidentally, of livelihood." That is, it was incidental to how he saw himself. He divided his time between tending, in some manner, to his mother's farm at Shadwell and taking on clients—who were not hard to find.

Land issues and estate resolution dominated the practice. Handling cases, Jefferson encountered a variety of human passions: character assassination, assault, tax evasion, horse, cow, and hog stealing, destruction of property, and yes, inappropriate sexual contact. He was called in on one occasion to use his professional influence to get rid of a morally compromised Albemarle pastor who drank excessively and attempted to seduce one of his parishioners.[2]

Although his practice centered on the General Court at Williamsburg, he no doubt felt the rarity of a mind like his own, because most members of the county courts were not particularly learned—in a moment of elitist pique, he demeaned them as unworthy "insects." His detailed appreciation for English legal traditions worked to his benefit, yet Jefferson still lacked the advantages Patrick Henry had through his ability to mesmerize juries despite his inferior legal erudition and, relative to Jefferson, aversion to hard study.[3]

As dutiful an attorney as Jefferson was, he was a soft touch, and a good many clients stiffed him. The law provided, but it did not make him rich. More important for him in the long run was that he represented the interests of Williamsburg's oldest surnames; the work he did gained him their trust and won him prestige. They knew him as conscientious and exceedingly well mannered. They also knew he could sometimes be a little daring in conceiving arguments. That was a good thing.

In 1770, Jefferson took a philosophic turn in legal strategy when he attempted to apply the law of nature ("we are all born free") in a case where the client was a biracial man suing for freedom. Taking the case pro bono, he argued that his client's descent from a white woman—one grandmother—precluded his being held in bondage. (Its premise was not dissimilar from that of the case involving Indian-descended slaves that George Wythe was to adjudicate in 1806.) Unlike Patrick Henry, to whom Jefferson would defer for some years yet, his formalistic presentation and lack of a strong voice put him at a disadvantage when speaking in open court. In small groups, Jefferson was comfortable enough, but the more clamorous the company, the more his naturally taciturn bearing was on display. In this instance, he lost the nonwhite client's case.[4]

Losses were inevitable. One in January 1770 was especially jarring—tragic, he would say—though no lives were sacrificed other than those that lived in books.

The house at Shadwell burned to the ground, incinerating Jefferson's library in the process. His college friends knew what this meant and commiserated from afar. One wonders how much, at such times, Jefferson confided in Jupiter, an enslaved man he'd known all his life, who accompanied him most everywhere as body servant. Born at Shadwell the same year, Jefferson and Jupiter were as intimate as brothers, if unequal companions. In Williamsburg, the demands of the student at law were, we can be sure, accommodated without protest. On the road, Jefferson entrusted Jupiter with cash and asked his "servant" to purchase violin strings, hair ointment, and sundry household staples, or to travel distances on specific business-related errands.

Jupiter was with Jefferson in the fall of 1770, on the specific days when the coded references to "Sukey at Smith" appear in Jefferson's daily account book. Jupiter understood his master in ways we cannot. Regrettably, he does not speak to history. Jefferson, famed for his visible reserve, literally held the reins in this relationship. He often drove his carriage while Jupiter rode behind on one of the horses. It should already be clear that Jefferson was what pop psychology these days recognizes as a common personality type: the control freak. His servant/groom was entrusted to carry out personal missions that were more than errands, yet precious little documentation survives of a relationship that lasted more than fifty years.

The best we can do here is to interpolate. The relationship between Jupiter's son Phil Evans and Jefferson's eldest grandson, Thomas Jefferson Randolph, was true friendship, punctuated by fraternal concern for the other's happiness and little emotional distance, though in formal terms they were still master and servant. In his memoir, late in life, T. J. Randolph wrote of his early abolitionist feelings: "Fourteen years older than my oldest brother; having no companion of my own age, I associated entirely with slaves and formed for them early and strong attachments." Here he termed Phil Evans his "friend through life."[5]

MARTHA WAYLES SKELTON BECOMES MRS. JEFFERSON

On New Year's Day 1772, twenty-nine-year-old Thomas Jefferson wedded the widow Martha Wayles Skelton, five and half years his junior. Known familiarly as Patty, she'd married another of Jefferson's college classmates, Bathurst Skelton (1744–1768), five years before, and had a son, a toddler named John, when Jefferson began courting her. The record is not entirely clear whether the child whom

Jefferson would have helped raise died at the Wayles estate, called the Forest, months before their wedding or months after.[6]

Beginning in 1770, Jefferson made periodic visits to the Forest. He more likely than not learned of John's death by letter. As the Jeffersons' intimate correspondence was deliberately destroyed, no record exists of the emotional toll the boy's death took upon the mother and prospective stepfather, though it was never surprising in those days when a little one succumbed to illness. As a rule, young people grew up quickly and rarely waited to start a family once a compatible, socially suitable mate was introduced. Jefferson, the last of his friends to marry, courted the widow Skelton for a good year; the son's death, whenever it occurred, would not have altered their plans to embark on a future together.

Patty's father, John Wayles, was in his fifty-seventh year, "a lawyer of much practice," as Jefferson characterized him. He had already buried three wives. Patty's mother, Martha Eppes, was herself a widow when she married Wayles in 1746; she died in the fall of 1748, at the age of twenty-seven, only days after delivering her one daughter. Patty grew up with three half sisters by her father's second marriage. His third wife lived only one year into the marriage. After losing three wives, John Wayles entered into a relationship with a biracial woman he owned named Elizabeth (Betty) Hemings, who was herself a mother several times over when that relationship began.

All of this underscores again just how foreign their world is from ours. By eighteenth-century Virginia standards it was not at all unusual for a white plantation owner to fulfill his procreative desire without legalizing the union. Wayles and Hemings went on to have six children together, the youngest of whom was Sally (no doubt Sarah, officially). As the daughter of an enslaved woman, she retained her mother's surname.

During the period of their courtship, Jefferson assuredly prepared Patty for the unusual situation of Monticello in painstaking detail, because that was how he thought. He'd have shared his drawings, his creative logic, his long-term fantasies. Most Virginia gentry built their homes, as Peter Jefferson did, near a river where their hogsheads of tobacco could easily be loaded onto flat-bottom boats and floated to market; and as a practical matter, Jefferson invested much time and energy clearing the Rivanna of debris and improving its navigability.

Monticello, of course, was otherwise conceived. Jefferson never described its arcadian vista to someone who hadn't been to the top in words that were not rapturous. As to the mountaintop mansion and the graded fields heading downslope, he would have shown his betrothed sketches of something that resembled a Roman villa. Already collecting and experimenting with seeds, he was planning plentiful fruit orchards (apple, pear, cherry, peach, apricot, nectarine, and fig—the last a particular favorite). Soil-destructive tobacco would be grown at a lower elevation. As time went on, Jefferson would set about eliminating tobacco cultivation at Monticello.[7]

Two years after work at the site began—and if its placement in his memorandum book accurately reflects the date, just days before Patty became his wife—Jefferson set forth a powerful romantic vision. He was thinking in part of his sister Jane, interred at Shadwell, when he poeticized the future site of a burial ground on the mountaintop where loved ones would lie. The young man who not so long before could not keep himself from propositioning the wife of one of his closest friends was in a state of exalted anticipation, expressing soulful desires.

Borrowing a concept of landscape design from the English garden authority and poet laureate William Shenstone, while citing the language of a staged drama by the Englishman Nicholas Rowe, *The Fair Penitent* (1703), Jefferson penned these words: "Chuse out a Burying place some unfrequented vale in the park where"—and here the quote from Rowe's play picks up—"'No sound to break the silence but a brook, That bubbling winds among the weeds: no mark of any human shape that had been there, Unless a skeleton of some poor wretch Who sought that place out to despair and die in.' Let it be among antient and venerable oaks." Beneath these lines he sketched a crude drawing of this vision, in the middle of which stood "a small Gothic temple of antique appearance."

He carried notebooks wherever he traveled, recording every expense incurred plus brief notations about cases before the court. This particular notebook was 8 x 4 inches, 124 pages, and bound in sheepskin. Anticipating the reburial of his beloved older sister on the mountaintop (which apparently never took place), he added a Latin inscription that translates as "Ah! Joanna [i.e., Jane], best of girls. Ah! Torn away from the bloom of vigorous age." The fantasy continues to unfold with lines from Shenstone on "an African slave" who is to be interred there as well. A spring, a series of terraces, and a gentle cascade would spill down from one terrace to the next, landing on a stone floor. Jefferson was filtering history and leafing through an ever-growing library, undeterred by the Shadwell fire, in a bid to create at Monticello a compleat garden where friendship held and love endured.[8]

Rowe's famous play *The Fair Penitent* has still more to say to us. Apart from its evocation of musically inspired love in Jefferson's Literary Commonplace Book

("The Sprightly string, & softly breathing Lute / Till Harmony rouse ev'ry gentle Passion"), it spoke in an uncensored way of male lust. It was in *The Fair Penitent* that the world met the unprincipled Lothario, whose very name is to this day a synonym for debauchery. Lothario was rejected as a suitor by the father of Calista, and he reaped his vengeance by successfully seducing Calista while she was engaged to Altamont, a good man who truly loved her. After lowering her resistance with a "soothing Tale," the shameless libertine boasted, "her easy Heart was mine." Once she realized that her seducer had no interest in a marital connection, Calista yelled "Villain! Monster!" in his face; but the best he would offer in return was to be "Keeper of her Secrets."

Yet as the play proceeds, the shamed woman reconsiders, allowing that her "relenting heart" might be able to "pardon all, and quite forget that 'twas he undone me." Altamont's intimate friend Horatio is far less generous-minded, warning Calista that unless she would risk trading her "rare Beauty" for "Infamy, Diseases, Prostitution," her "Fame"—her reputation—would be jeopardized if she should even be seen talking to the despised Lothario. When Horatio has to tell Altamont that his betrothed had yielded to Lothario, the betrayed lover is unbelieving, until he catches Lothario with Calista. This prompts a duel, in which Lothario is slain. Calista tries to turn the sword on herself, but Altamont stays her hand. At the end of the play, she finally succeeds, upon hearing that a mob in mourning for Lothario had mortally wounded her father.

Happiness eludes all in a tragedy that can also be read as farce, given the ambiguities in Calista's feelings toward the unlovable Lothario. However Jefferson may have interpreted it, Nicholas Rowe's infidelity drama was well known to him at the time he propositioned his neighbor's wife in 1767, when he did all he could to keep his betrayal of a friendship secret.[9]

In the summer of 1771, in a much different frame of mind, Jefferson exchanged letters with Robert Skipwith, who had married Patty Jefferson's younger half sister Tabitha and was interested in assembling a private library. The prospect of the two couples enjoying the mountain air together is an early example of the young builder's vision of community. Inviting Skipwith (who humbly described himself as "a common reader") to scour the shelves at Monticello, "a library formed on a more extensive plan" than what the young gentleman could as yet afford, Jefferson advertised more than a book collection: "A spring, centrically situated, might be the scene of every evening's joy. There we should talk over the lessons of the day, or lose them in Musick, Chess, or the merriments of our family companions. The heart thus lightened, our pillows would be soft, and health and long life would attend the happy scene." Before building had commenced, Jefferson had called his future home the Hermitage, for which he substituted the more clever "Monticello," or "little mountain," as he was teaching himself Italian.[10]

While maintaining a flourishing law practice, the first-time architect was especially busy in the years 1769–1771, dealing at once with the partial restoration of Shadwell and the complicated logistics of hauling materials up an 867-foot mountain. An immense amount of enslaved labor was needed to level the summit, remove tree stumps, and part the forest with winding roads suitable for horse and carriage. His mother leased out Shadwell's slaves as he needed them.

Constructing an enclosure for deer, providing food to attract "hares, squirrels, pheasants, partridges," and seeking to keep at bay animals of prey, Jefferson would ever describe the managed setting with authorial pride, an idyllic combination of nature and art. He acquired from the Wayles plantation what may have been his first pet mockingbirds, whose song so delighted him that years later, in France, he claimed the American species superior to Europe's vaunted nightingale—"a superior being in the form of a bird," he giddily told family members. A warbling mockingbird followed him upstairs when he went to bed at the President's House in Washington. As much as he was sketching out ideas and crunching numbers, he was thinking about ways to provide amusement to himself and others.[11]

And then there were the grim realities of eighteenth-century life. Martha Wayles Skelton Jefferson had to have steeled herself to life's emotional struggles by the start of her second marriage. Married for the first time at eighteen, having known only stepmothers, she was a widow at twenty who, at twenty-three, buried her toddler, removing to her new husband's as yet modest mountaintop habitation with only the image he painted for her of the future Monticello. Mrs. Jefferson began life at a Monticello that was as far as one can imagine from its refined appearance today.

While much of the family's lore is protective of the patriarch, some facts can be taken at face value. Thomas and Patty Jefferson shared a love of music. He played the violin and she the harpsichord. During the period of their engagement, he ordered for her a pianoforte from England, a wedding gift for which he spared no expense. One cherished story told from generation to generation within the family was how she and her new husband arrived at the unfinished Monticello with few belongings after trudging through heavy snow in darkness. The "horrible dreariness" of that moment became a storied memory, a counterpoint to what was in the end, as Jefferson lovingly described it in his truncated 1821 autobiography, "ten years of unchequered happiness." Jupiter had accompanied Jefferson from Monticello to the Wayles estate. One wonders whether he accompanied the newlyweds home, whether he, too, contended with the snow. Or did Jefferson wish to travel without his body servant on this special occasion?[12]

No images exist of Patty Jefferson. While her precise height is not known, she is said to have been fair-haired and petite, dwarfed by her six-foot-two-and-a-half-inch husband. According to grandchildren who never knew her, she possessed "large expressive eyes" and "a frank, warm-hearted, and somewhat impulsive disposition." At one point in the marriage, she was overheard berating her husband for his excessive generosity, evidently viewing herself as the more savvy in avoiding being taken in by others. Patty left behind precious few examples of her handwriting, but it has been well established that she was a skilled household manager. She became pregnant immediately after beginning her life at Monticello, giving birth in September 1772 to another Martha. Her newborn ushered in the third consecutive generation of Marthas in her lineage: Eppes, Wayles, and now Jefferson.[13]

Jefferson had sketched out a spacious wine cellar before he'd even begun the main house. He and his bride shared a bottle on that first snowy night on the partially sculpted mountain. By September 1772, when the baby was born, the inventory consisted of "72 bottles of Madeira, 37 bottles of Lisbon wine," plus port and rum. They were getting an early taste of the elegance and abundance Monticello would be celebrated for in coming years.

Having anointed himself not just his own building architect but also landscape architect and general contractor, Jefferson left the toilsome work to those, white or Black, enslaved or free, who sawed wood, dug wells, mixed chemicals, and laid bricks. Fruit was harvested in the first year of the marriage; the following year, still active as an attorney, Jefferson purchased a small limestone quarry to the east, north of the Three-Notch'd Road, where he burned lime for mortar, as the ancient Romans did. At the same time, he was chiseling out the first of the "roundabouts," a level-by-level sectioning of the little mountain into ringlike paths, walking and riding trails, that eventually reached four miles in length.[14]

If the first year was taken up with pregnancy and the elaborate business of construction at Monticello, the second year was punctuated by yet more tragedy. John Wayles died a slow death in May 1773, while, twelve days earlier, Dabney Carr's death at Shadwell came suddenly. With no idea of what was to occur below Monticello, Patty—it was she, no longer his mother, who was now designated "Mrs. Jefferson" in his account books—had traveled three days to be by her ailing father's side. She was with him in his final hours. What shock she endured in losing a father had to have been amplified on her return to Albemarle to find her husband's best friend gone as well. Dabney Carr was just shy of thirty.

The epitaph Jefferson composed for him was effusive and concluded with a very personal statement: TO HIS VIRTUE, GOOD SENSE, LEARNING AND FRIENDSHIP, / THIS STONE IS DEDICATED BY / THOMAS JEFFERSON, / WHO OF ALL MEN LOVED HIM MOST. Until he contracted a deadly "bilious" fever, Carr's was, if we recur to his best friend's telling in the earlier-cited letter to Page in 1770, a short but secure, hopeful, and happy life. It was up to Jefferson to keep that memory alive, which he did, confident in his claim that Carr was about to emerge as a Revolutionary leader when he expired.

More prosaically, adhering to eighteenth-century custom and feeling no need to speak from the heart, Jefferson wrote to Will Fleming, a William and Mary classmate with whom Jefferson and Carr had been intimate. He wrote before Carr's reburial on the mountaintop, while at his grieving sister's side: "You have before this heard and lamented the death of our good friend Carr. Some steps are necessary to be immediately taken on behalf of his clients." Open cases apparently could not wait. If Fleming would agree to step in, Jefferson said, he'd convey their late friend's legal notes. "They would put you in possession of a valuable business." Life went on somehow.[15]

To Judge Dabney Carr, who had been only a few weeks old when his father died, Jefferson outdid the epitaph in a letter he wrote in 1816: "His character was of a high order. A spotless integrity, sound judgment[,] handsome [then meaning moral and admirable] imagination, ... of correct & ready elocution, impressing every hearer with the sincerity of the heart from which it flowed." It is hard to find a more effusive statement from him on a man's character, save perhaps for his later tribute to Wythe. It continues: "Never had man more of the milk of human kindness, of indulgence, of softness, of pleasantry in conversation & conduct. The number of his friends, & the warmth of their affection were proofs of his worth." Remembrance was everything. It was crucial to Jefferson that he leave the family with sentiments they could pass down through ensuing generations of Carrs.[16]

∼

AS A RESULT OF marriages and frequent early deaths, many planters acquired property that was at a considerable distance from their own country seat. At this early stage of his career, with his father-in-law's passing, Jefferson, turning thirty, came into possession of acreage roughly equal to what his father had left him. Some of it was conveniently situated on the James, but it also included a pleasingly productive tract in Bedford County, seventy miles southwest of Monticello, where Jefferson would grow tobacco and, as president, build his octagonal Poplar Forest retreat. When British troops tore through Albemarle in 1781, he fled to Bedford; in the next century, he would bring his granddaughters there when he wanted to escape the bustle of Monticello and the unwanted visitors who hiked to the top for a glimpse of the famous man.

The Wayles inheritance "doubled the ease of our circumstances," Jefferson attested in his handwritten autobiography. These words overlook the fact that the land came to him with an immense amount of debt, and that debt became Jefferson's undoing. Taking possession of a rich acreage, he agreed to repay what his father-in-law owed a British merchant house. In 1773, that already amounted to more than ten times Jefferson's annual income as a lawyer. No bumper crop would make a dent in what was owed, though Jefferson consistently maintained that he would someday satisfy the creditors—even as he came to condemn them for their punishing persistence. John Wayles had lived large, thinking he could get out from under by paying in tobacco.[17]

The marriage of the Wayles and Jefferson estates had more consequences than those determined by legal instrument. When the estate was settled in 1774, it was not simply the "ease" of circumstances that was doubled; the number of enslaved people for whom Thomas Jefferson was responsible rose from 52 to 187 souls. Over his lifetime, while he purchased fewer than twenty slaves on his own account, he may have been responsible for the lives of as many as six hundred enslaved human beings. Among those brought over from the Wayles estate was a sixteen-year-old cook named Suck, who shortly thereafter became Jupiter's wife. Twelve-year-old Robert (Bob) Hemings, John Wayles's light-skinned son, took over Jupiter's position as traveling companion. Jefferson would free Bob in the 1790s, though not without feeling somehow cheated of services he felt were still owed him.[18]

And then there was the last of John Wayles's children. Sally Hemings arrived as an infant. When she was nine, she saw Mrs. Jefferson during her final pregnancy and postpartum decline. Her place in Jefferson's life as a widower's "concubine"—the same role her still living mother had assumed with respect to John Wayles—has led, of course, to centuries of controversy and speculation.

The present study promises only partial answers to lingering questions about the character of the relationship. There are elements to be considered apart from

Jefferson's stale remarks about race and slavery, which scholars have weighed in on at great length. These include not only his sexual history, but also emotional factors that bear upon his choice of a partner and Sally Hemings's acquiescence—a more neutral word than either "capitulation" or "submission"—to an arrangement that spanned decades.

This is the problem, post-DNA, for scholars trying to evaluate the likely feelings on the part of both parties to this relationship. While the truth remains elusive, the possibilities can still be narrowed through an improved understanding of cultural norms that applied, the nature of privilege in their world, the Wayles-Hemings-Jefferson dynamic broadly viewed, and the particular impulses of Thomas Jefferson. At this point in the narrative, he is a new husband and his future "concubine" a baby. We shall return to the story in due course.

The "little mountain" would never be empty. Before marriage, Jefferson had to consider the numbers of enslaved men, women, and children who would be living and dying in close proximity, much as he had imaginatively incorporated Shenstone's "African Slave" into his otherwise dry account book. They would be buried somewhere on the mountain, but not, as it turned out, in the area where white Jeffersons came to rest. One might suppose that as a feeling person, he would feel the loss of these people too. But the deaths of men and women who were neither intimate friends nor blood relatives tended to be conveyed in letters with matter-of-factness, saying less about any deeper struggle with feelings of remorse.

That said, Jefferson could hardly engage with those who shared his life on the mountain without some sentiment and conviction. In time, he took in six nieces and nephews, the children of his brother-in-law Carr, who joined the three Marthas—Jefferson's wife, daughter, and sister (Mrs. Carr). Theirs was a world in which women, as breeders, passed down family names.

In 1773 and 1774, as engaged as he was in Albemarle, Jefferson was a rising member within the colony's self-governing body, the House of Burgesses, which was still under genial royal governors. He spent a considerable amount of time in Williamsburg. In between trips, Patty became pregnant with their second child. Jane Randolph Jefferson was born on April 3, 1774, and died sometime in September 1775. Given the scrupulousness with which Jefferson noted births and deaths in the account books he carried with him, it is highly unusual that the date of his baby's death is nowhere noted. It probably occurred near the end of the month. On the twenty-fifth, he writes: "Set out from Monticello to Philadelphia." The Continental Congress beckoned. Patty would mourn this child without him.[19]

PART II

Passionate Years

If your passion in love is too powerful, disperse it, they say; and they say true, for I have often tried it with profit. Break it up into various desires, of which one may be ruler and master, if you will; but for fear it may dominate and tyrannize you, weaken it, check it, by dividing and diverting it.

—MICHEL DE MONTAIGNE, "OF DIVERSION" (1585–88)

If you wish to do battle with the will of nature, you might just as well try poking a hole in water with a stick.

—DENIS DIDEROT, *JACQUES THE FATALIST* (1796)

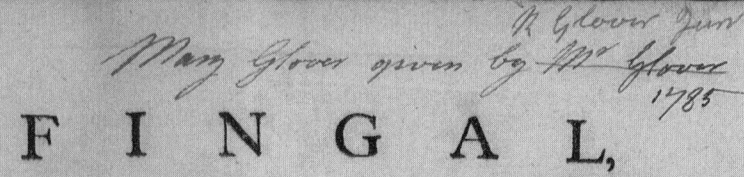

FINGAL,
AN
ANCIENT EPIC POEM,
In SIX BOOKS:

Together with several other POEMS, composed by

OSSIAN the Son of FINGAL.

Translated from the GALIC LANGUAGE,

By JAMES MACPHERSON.

Fortia facta patrum. VIRGIL.

LONDON;
Printed for T. BECKET and P. A. DE HONDT, in the Strand.
M DCC LXII.

Figure 6. *Fingal, An Ancient Epic Poem* (1762). Jefferson had a lifelong fascination with the third-century Celtic bard Ossian, "the greatest poet that has ever existed," and refused to accept that the "translator" of the newly unearthed Gaelic texts was, in fact, a fraud. The independent spirit of the ancients fed Jefferson's historically framed critique of modern British policy toward the American colonies. (Courtesy Special Collections, University of Virginia Library)

CHAPTER 4

"Thrown into a Reverie"

From Romance to Revolution

THE STIMULATION JEFFERSON OBTAINED from works of literature and philosophy asks the modern reader to develop an affinity for an intricate language that is less evocative today; yet that idiom conditioned everything from the power of Nature to the power of historical example. In the absence of electronic stimuli, the very act of reading fed sensory experience and intimate communication. Mental pictures gleaned from fiction and nonfiction alike fed an urge. So, if we are to discover more about Jefferson's qualities, the language that spoke to him has to be better understood. Fortunately, the existing record makes it possible to understand what led to his euphoric ideas about individual liberty and his deep anxiety about its deprivation.[1]

There is a direct correlation between Jefferson's appraisal of the books he read and the texts he penned that yielded his most memorable ideas about America. After spending crucial months in Philadelphia in 1775 and 1776, where he significantly enlarged his national profile, he returned to Virginia in the hope of changing his state for the better. Despite the exigencies of wartime, he was leading a life of private and public fulfillment.

In the years that followed, however, he found himself facing the kind of damage to reputation that no elected executive could surmount, as a governor accused of cowardice as the British overran his state. Shortly thereafter, he endured the greatest personal loss a loving husband could know. As America celebrated the winning of its independence, Jefferson suffered enormous anguish. The combination of these jarring changes in his life caused him to turn inward and beg for release. The Revolutionary years, taken together, chart a rise and fall in his willpower. As the young up-and-comers Madison and Monroe entered his circle of friends, he weighed the amount of self-exposure he was comfortable with, what chances he was willing to take, and how open he was to change.

THE POLITICAL CAREER OF Thomas Jefferson began amid hopeful signs. The right people respected him. In 1774, as he entered the third year of a strong marriage, he was known in Williamsburg and beyond for both mental discipline and cordiality. He was a conciliator, good-humored—"sanguine in temperament" was a phrase used then, rarely these days—but nowhere was it suggested that he charmed his fellows. Whatever else he was in the company of friends, he was a serious person with serious ideas.

During the winter months, he was mostly at home, as he was when, in February 1774, his mentally challenged sister Elizabeth, a year and a half younger, drowned, along with her enslaved maid Sall, Jupiter's younger sister. Jefferson recorded the discovery of the bodies impersonally. Aided by his legal adviser George Wythe, he continued to deal with the estates of Bathurst Skelton and John Wayles. In May, he traveled to Williamsburg.

These were trying times for Virginia's political leadership. Tobacco prices had been in decline for several years. Ever since Patrick Henry, with his accustomed fervor, had seized the attention of nervous Virginians during the 1765 Stamp Act protests, taxation-related issues had wafted in the air. Jefferson signed on to the nonimportation resolution, a boycott of British imports, as a new member of the House of Burgesses in 1769. When he began a life with Patty, his commitment to colonial affairs receded somewhat; but in the spring of 1773, one notable exception occurred: Dabney Carr introduced the Revolutionary instrument known as Committees of Correspondence, meant to support cross-colonial unity. It was his moment in the sun, never to be forgotten by his friend Jefferson.

In June 1774, the gentry of the colony found their conflict intensifying with the increasingly imperious Lord Dunmore, now in his third year as royal governor. On his way home from Williamsburg, Jefferson sold a horse with the conspicuous name of Fingal to someone he'd known since childhood, Thomas Mann Randolph of Tuckahoe (son of Peter Jefferson's dearest friend), whose five-year-old son and namesake would later marry the Jeffersons' eldest, Martha (Patsy).[2]

OSSIANIC PHANTOMS

Fingal, A Poem in Six Books, by Ossian: Translated from the Original Galic by Mr. Macpherson. That's how Jefferson might have seen it first advertised. In February 1773, having by then copied lines from a 1763 edition of the poem into his Literary Commonplace Book, he'd somewhat innocently written to a kinsman of said Macpherson, the force behind the third-century A.D. epic poem. Might the gentleman, a London merchant Jefferson had met in Virginia, secure for him a copy of the Gaelic originals that he might teach himself to read the ancient language? "I am not ashamed to own," the supplicant wrote, "that I think this rude bard of the North the greatest poet that has ever existed."

Attempting to sweeten what was clearly an imposition on a man he did not know well, Jefferson said he would gladly pay whatever its cost for a bound manuscript copy, if a printed one could not be had: "I would chuse it in a fair, round, hand, on fine paper, with a good margin, bound in parchment as elegantly as possible, lettered on the back and marbled or gilt on the edges of the leaves. I should not regard expence in doing this. I would further beg the favor of you to give me a catalogue of books written in that language, and to send me such of them as may be necessary for learning it." In his instructions alone, we learn much about Jefferson's passion for historical knowledge, his desire to surround himself with objects of beauty, and his penchant for precision and aesthetic control.

He received his answer a half year later, though not the one he was hoping for. "I should be glad to accommodate any friend of yours," James Macpherson had written to his relation, "especially one of Mr. Jefferson's taste and character. But I cannot, having [re]fused them to so many, give a copy of the Gaëlic poems with any decency out of my hands. The labour, besides, would be great. I know of none, that could copy them ... Make my humble respects to your American friend." Enclosing the letter, Charles McPherson (as he spelled the family name) added his personal regards, recalling with pleasure his brief visit to Monticello, "your sweet retreat," while lamenting that "a few religious Books excepted, we have no publication in the Gaelic Language, no dictionary, no grammar."[3]

As we take note of his hyperbole in complimenting a fraud as "the greatest poet that has ever existed," it must be stressed that Jefferson was not alone in excitedly seeking more from Ossian. In England and Scotland, from the moment he began publishing in 1761, a number of scholars had been asking James Macpherson for permission to inspect the ancient texts. They were variously told that the cherished pages would be revealed in due time, were under review elsewhere, or were in too poor a condition to be viewed.

The challenge persisted, and Macpherson kept everyone hanging on. As his fame grew—he eventually entered Parliament in 1780—he became increasingly resistant, even pugnacious. Jefferson had to have expressed at least some interest in this debate, because by the time he met up with a teenage John Quincy Adams in Paris in the mid-1780s, he still said he had no doubt about the authenticity of Ossian, son of Fingal.

To eighteenth-century Scots, Macpherson's Ossian represented the Caledonia known to Rome, where the warrior Fingal and his battle-ready grandson Oscar sought greatness on the windswept grounds. While the tales featured no intervening gods such as existed in Homer, upon publication, Ossianic lore was immediately compared to the Greek epics; the descriptive language was altogether similar. In *Fingal*, Ossian is "king of songs" more than he is a fighter, though he is never far from the war that forms the substance of the work. The cries he records are louder than those in Homer, the tears weepier.

Fingal tells of "helmets of steel" and "dark-brown shields," "stormy nights" and "angry ghosts," personal combat interrupted only by friends grieving friends and lovers parting. These are heroes who do not choose war from bloodlust but from necessity. They sit beside streams and meditate on their fate before resolve sets in, when they must lock swords with a respected foe, even a former friend. They are nostalgic for earlier times, when the prospect of war was a distant thought. "Mournful is thy tale," Ossian narrates in Book II. "It sends my soul back to ages of old, and to the days of other years." As one trained to hunt, who'd roamed the hills with the friends of his youth, Jefferson related to the esprit de corps that permeates Ossianic verse: "We moved to the chace together; and one was our bed in the heath."

The reason all this matters is twofold. In the Declaration of Independence, Jefferson will make it a point to contrast colonial feelings of "common kindred" with the tragic necessity of war once the British grow "deaf to the voice of justice and of consanguinity." He will be sad to separate from respected elders, when such goodhearted royalists chose to leave Virginia for England in 1775. Of more immediate importance to him, when Dabney Carr died, Jefferson first thought of composing his friend's epitaph by merging his own words with lines from one of the Ossianic tales. The intended inscription was doleful in its opening: "This stone shall rise with all it's moss and speak to other years 'here lies gentle Carr within the dark and narrow house where no morning comes...'"[4]

Jefferson would regularly confront grief—no one of his time was immune. The words "mourn" and "mournful" are repeated constantly in Ossian as blood mixes with pride. As in Homer, time and again a youth falls in battle and repercussions are felt: "His gray dogs are howling at home, and see his passing ghost." Macpherson adds an enticing footnote: "It was the opinion of the times, that the souls of heroes went immediately after death to the hills of their country, and the scenes they frequented the most happy time of their life. It was thought too that dogs and horses saw the ghosts of the deceased." The Scot's interpretations of Celtic culture were peppered with observations on the similarities between Ossian's style and select passages in the *Iliad*. Jefferson was hooked.[5]

Like the Homeric epic, Ossianic tragedy represented a form of cultural therapy for its fans by poeticizing human agency through models of noble character who must confront mortality. Choice overshadows fate. Already a lover of all things Greek, Jefferson was transported to this other heroic world, one closer to his own genealogical roots. Among the titles he recommended to Robert Skipwith was the two-volume *Ossian with Blair's Criticisms*. Jefferson did not doubt the assessment of Ossian offered by one as distinguished as the Professor of Rhetoric and Belles Lettres at the University of Edinburgh.

The Scottish minister and rhetorician Hugh Blair (1718–1800) did not know Gaelic, yet he had no problem embracing his countryman's text as the genuine article. Macpherson was just twenty-three when the scholar-clergyman met and spoke with him and bought his explanation. Once Blair signed on, Edinburgh's literary community responded en masse to the Gaelic Homer. Giving their oft-maligned people firmer roots in antiquity helped the cause of Scotland. Blair applauded the moral message in Ossian: unlike Homer or Shakespeare, the bard of their people offered sublimity and melancholy without combining them with ribaldry or indelicacy.[6]

The bardic tradition of poetic storytelling went far back, each of the clans relying on its own bard to repeat generally unrecorded histories. But how far back was the question. Other than wispy fragments, no known text existed that was more than a few hundred years old. Macpherson was claiming to have taken a trip to the west of Scotland, flitting across the islands and returning with manuscripts of the most ancient provenance.

In retrospect, it seems odd that James Macpherson's scam took so many decades to be exposed. Though a modern Gaelic speaker, he was in no way a scholar of a long-lost vernacular. When a fourteenth-century Gaelic text was placed before him, he admitted he could not read it. He was not known for learned conversation, and even Blair referred to Macpherson as "irritable and morose." According to the English historian Hugh Trevor-Roper, who made a career of embracing historical controversy, Macpherson was not savvy enough to have produced *Fingal* alone. There was in fact a well-educated cousin in whose handwriting one chapter from *Fingal* was found.[7]

Other questions obviously arise: How did descriptions of late medieval structures and ideas of gallantry creep into Macpherson's translation? How could a careful reader such as Jefferson have overlooked these incongruities?

The answer to the latter question is that Jefferson was a romantic who resisted self-correction. Blair, though no romantic, was also undeterred, supporting Macpherson for decades even as doubts circulated in public. One English critic with unimpeachable credentials felt no such compunction: upon its publication, the lexicographer Samuel Johnson wasted no time in proclaiming Ossian an "unconnected rhapsody" of recent vintage. As the cult of Ossian grew—around the time when Jefferson wrote to the merchant Charles Macpherson—Dr. Johnson proved he was serious about getting things right. He traveled to the same places in the west of Scotland and spoke to some of the same people as Macpherson. On his return to London, he was doubly certain that, as he put it, the Ossianic poems "never existed in any other form" than that of Macpherson's invented text. Macpherson's refusal to show any legitimate scholar his so-called originals was tantamount to an admission of fraud.[8]

Aside from the horse Fingal that he sold, Jefferson gave names taken from Ossianic characters to several other horses in the early 1770s. In 1787, recommending a course in poetry to his nephew, Dabney Carr's son Peter, Jefferson placed Ossian in select company: "Homer—Milton—Ossian—Sophocles—Aeschylus—Eurip.—Metastasio—Shakesp."

Jefferson did not doubt his judgment or admit error. The "rude bard" remained a giant among poets for him. In time he would introduce his daughters and granddaughters to Ossianic poetry: in 1802, 1803, and 1807, as president, he purchased new editions. In 1813, in a book of poetry dedicated to Jefferson, the author and family friend Judith Lomax headed one poem, which contained unambiguous Ossianic allusions, "Written at Monticello, Albemarle county, and composed while viewing the Clouds gathering and rolling about the Mountain." It was not hard to think of the Celtic scenery here: "These forms fantastic, bring along, / To Fancy's mental eye, / Those times when Ossian, 'Son of Song...'"[9]

Macpherson died in 1796 without producing any evidence of the existence of the *Fingal* epic he claimed he had translated. The controversy over Ossian continued into the next century, a controversy Jefferson wanted no part in.

What was it about Jefferson that drew him to Ossian? Why would poetry centered on warfare suit the unmartial Revolutionary? Napoleon was an Ossian fan, which is more understandable. But Jefferson? The preface to an early edition of *Fingal* provides clues. With suspicions circulating, Macpherson had to defend himself against the likes of Samuel Johnson. He supposed that the insults aimed at him flowed from "prejudices of the present age against the ancient inhabitants of Britain, who are thought incapable of the generous sentiments to be met with in the poems of Ossian." This was a sentiment Jefferson completely understood: it supplied serious moral justification when he composed the Declaration of Independence.[10]

The English privileged their way of life, and the Scots (as inheritors of Celtic traditions), like America's colonists, were sensitive to the power and critical judgments emanating from London. As a subject of the king with rarely discussed Welsh paternal roots, Jefferson grew to deplore the supercilious manner of those in London who deemed his brethren an inferior breed and openly denied the possibility of genius emerging from the peripheries of the empire. English deprecation of Scottish culture did not go unnoticed in the American colonies either.

In what they wrote, both the poet Macpherson and the proto-Romantic Jefferson foraged through history for literary luster, choosing themes that linked manly independence with native dignity. Jefferson, with backcountry credentials, adapted well to life in the populous communities of Williamsburg, Philadelphia, and Paris, but we know he did not abandon his taste for the primitive either. "Rudeness" did not bother Jefferson. Haughtiness did.[11]

He was attracted to stories that combined the human spirit with the raw power of nature. When he recommended Ossian to Robert Skipwith, he explained what he looked for as a reader. With Shakespeare serving as a prime example, he wrote, "We never reflect whether the story we read be truth or fiction. If the painting be lively, and a tolerable picture of nature, we are thrown into a reverie, from which if we awaken it is the fault of the writer." In this single sentence, Jefferson is claiming for himself a poetic consciousness.[12]

A decade later, in the waning days of the War for Independence, he welcomed a titled visitor to Monticello, François-Jean de Beauvoir, Marquis de Chastellux. They became fast friends. One night after dinner on the mountaintop the pair found an almost spiritual communion over an epic they both admired. "We happened to speak of the poetry of Ossian," the somewhat older Frenchman recorded. "It was a spark of electricity which passed rapidly from one to the other; we recalled the passages of those sublime poems which had particularly struck us, and we recited them for the benefit of my traveling companions." When Jefferson brought out the book, the two principals, between toasts of an alcoholic punch, entertained themselves at length. To hear the Frenchman tell it, they were indeed thrown into a reverie.[13]

THE SAXON PRECEDENT

In late July 1774, Jefferson and Jack Walker (as yet unaware of his friend's betrayal) were both elected as Albemarle's delegates to the Virginia Convention, which had been called to meet in Williamsburg in place of the Burgesses, which body Lord Dunmore had disbanded. Delegate Jefferson, though unable to travel because of a gastrointestinal complaint, increased his visibility dramatically when, in his stead, Jupiter delivered to Williamsburg a statement from his master titled *A Summary View of the Rights of British America*. The full text was published and distributed through the colonies, and copies found their way to London. Drawing on his study of history, Jefferson found a coequal to the American colonists in the Saxon tribes that had long before migrated from northern Europe to England. He maintained that voluntary resettlement was determinative in both cases.

Sometime in the latter years of the Western Roman Empire, in the fourth or fifth century, a people later called Saxon left northern Europe for the south of England. Along with the Gaels and Picts and others in the north of Britain, these faceless Germanic tribes combined with those earlier present in the British Isles, including the Celts, forging the culture that became British. It is curious, at the very least, that Jefferson added to his Legal Commonplace Book, sometime around 1773, a good many pages from a history of the Celts written in French, and he went out of his way to acquire his own copy in 1776. This book, *Histoire des Celtes*, by Simon Pelloutier (1694–1757), dug deep into the geography of Europe, starting in ancient Gaul. It traced how a group of languages distinguished the tribal confederations that spread through France, Belgium, the Netherlands, Germany, and Switzerland

and would eventually migrate to England. According to the author, "the Celtic religion was preserved in great purity in England," while being greatly altered on the Continent. Something about this vital culture retained its spiritual form over time. It could not be conquered.[14]

The theory he came up with may not have been perfect, but Jefferson was convinced of its logical consistency. He and Macpherson were working with comparable linguistic tools when they cast the distant past into a new light and imbued it with a vital radiance. Primitive yet accessible, evocatively appealing to popular tastes, Jefferson's Saxon predecessors shaped the destiny of the country people of the northern climes and branched out over time, eventually coming to intermingle in North America. It was an ingenious ploy on Jefferson's part: like the Saxons whose history he'd reconstructed, Americans were wholly unassisted by London in their hardy adventures in settlement; they were employed in a long-term nation-building project, questioning cultural hierarchies and cherishing a spirit of independence.

From Macpherson's perspective, something momentous was in the wind as he conceived the Ossianic saga. He had the "senachies" to draw on, musical storytellers of the Scots-Irish tradition. They tended not to be from the upper echelons of society, lending authority to the democratic origins of the historical narrative he pretended was real. Back in the Celtic era, or so Macpherson held, the Scottish and Irish, despite their known differences in modern times, were "almost the same people," until those of the more remote Scottish Highlands adopted distinctive patterns.

What Macpherson did under the pretense of being the bard's "translator" was a bit like what Jefferson undertook with far less guile in conceiving his Saxon proposition. The ornery Scot and the Welsh-English Virginian each walked a fine line in demonstrating their common conviction that history is necessarily built on uncertain traditions. And hidden passions.

There was something else about the "rude bard" that tapped into Jefferson's preferences and prejudices: Macpherson insisted that Ossian's people, living beyond the pale of Roman influence, possessed no knowledge of Christians anywhere. His heroic ancestors, so often accused of "barbarism," could be thought, on the strength of their humanity, an advanced people. Jefferson couldn't have been happier.

A Summary View of the Rights of British America, published in Williamsburg in September 1774, surely gave Jefferson more exposure than he intended when he wrote it, placing his political career on a trajectory that might even be characterized as fate. His work was taken up first in Williamsburg, then redirected to the

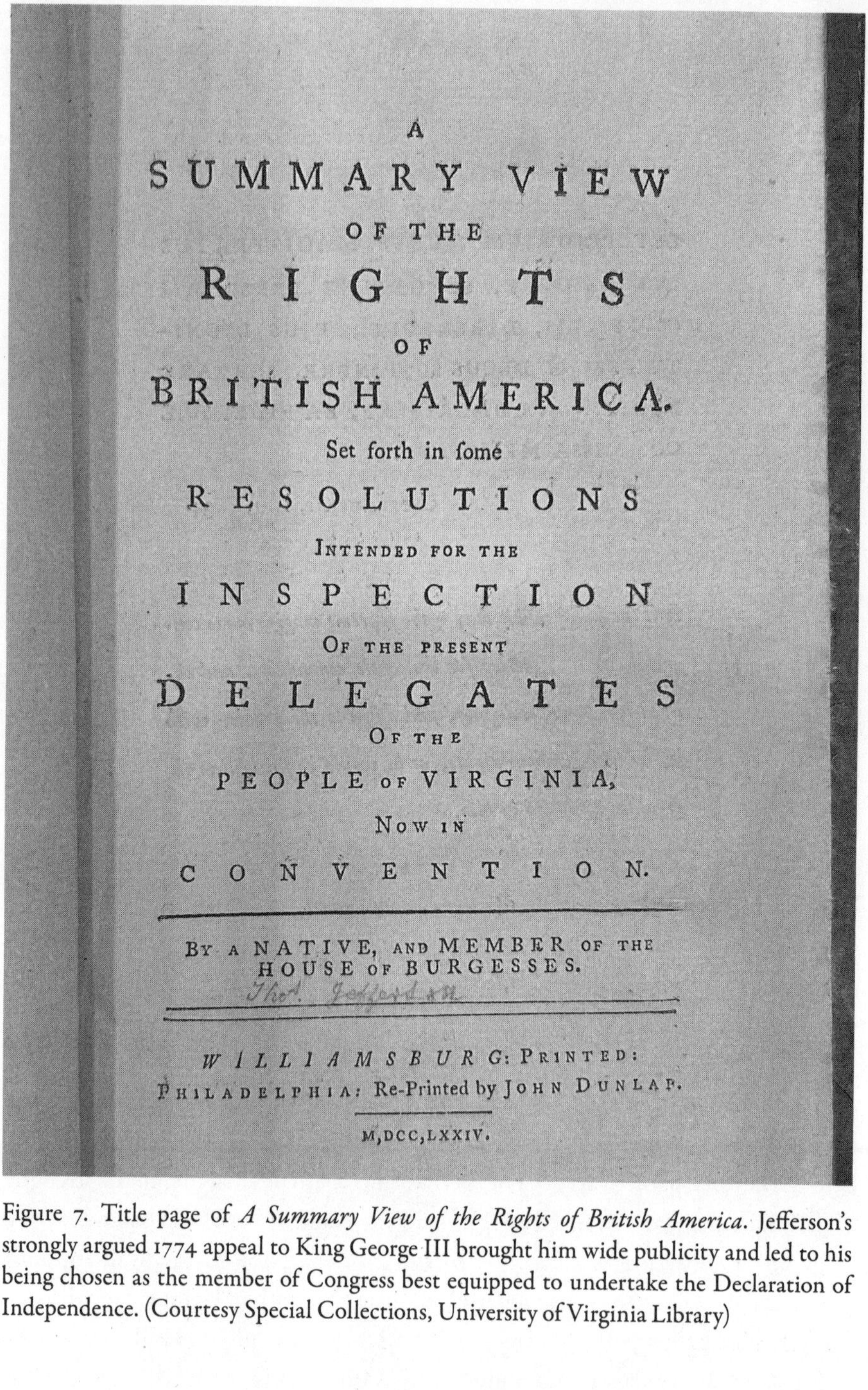

> A
> SUMMARY VIEW
> OF THE
> RIGHTS
> OF
> BRITISH AMERICA.
> Set forth in some
> RESOLUTIONS
> INTENDED FOR THE
> INSPECTION
> OF THE PRESENT
> DELEGATES
> OF THE
> PEOPLE OF VIRGINIA,
> NOW IN
> CONVENTION.
>
> BY A NATIVE, AND MEMBER OF THE
> HOUSE OF BURGESSES.
> *Thos. Jefferson*
>
> WILLIAMSBURG: PRINTED:
> PHILADELPHIA: Re-Printed by JOHN DUNLAP.
> M,DCC,LXXIV.

Figure 7. Title page of *A Summary View of the Rights of British America.* Jefferson's strongly argued 1774 appeal to King George III brought him wide publicity and led to his being chosen as the member of Congress best equipped to undertake the Declaration of Independence. (Courtesy Special Collections, University of Virginia Library)

First Continental Congress, which had just convened in Philadelphia. Not every colony was as fired up as Massachusetts and Virginia, given the fear among members of the merchant class in New York and Pennsylvania for whom a disruption in Anglo-American trade did not seem worth whatever might otherwise be gained in adopting a common agenda. Semiautonomous entities with provincial patterns and prejudices, even their own currencies, the colonies could not easily abandon the one thing they had always had in common: an attachment to Britain. These Americans were by no means "one people" when the Continental Congress convened, let alone Revolutionaries.[15]

Virginia sent seven delegates to Congress, all of them Jefferson's elders. They included George Washington, Patrick Henry, Edmund Pendleton, and Peyton Randolph. Henry and Pendleton rode together to Mount Vernon, picking up Washington as they embarked on a five-day carriage ride, accompanied by enslaved men who tended to their needs. Peyton Randolph, exceedingly rotund and unhealthy, was chosen president of the First Continental Congress, an instant recognition of Virginia's centrality—though Boston was the physical site of the most notorious of confrontations between Crown and colonies.

Randolph was London-educated, a barrister on the basis of his study at the Inns of Court. His father and Jefferson's maternal grandfather were brothers. "A most excellent man," Jefferson said in his autobiography; "and none was ever more beloved and respected by his friends." In language that echoed what others would later write about Jefferson in his political prime, he noted that Peyton Randolph was "somewhat cold and coy toward strangers, but of the sweetest affability when ripened into acquaintance." Eminence did not have to be self-assertive.

Edmund Pendleton's role in Jefferson's story increased in importance that year, when this "most virtuous & benevolent of men" served as a sounding board. It hardly mattered whether Jefferson's concern was of a private or public nature, he regarded Pendleton as a thoughtful and reliable friend. Fatherless, with an overburdened mother, Pendleton lacked privileges that others who argued in the General Court grew up with. In his midfifties when Jefferson drew close, he had reached the pinnacle of political life on the strength of a keen legal mind and judicious views. He was generally described as a man of good cheer and polite bearing. Which makes it especially odd that while they were equally supportive of, and beloved by, the rising generation of lawyers, Edmund Pendleton and George Wythe, near contemporaries (Pendleton was five years older), disliked each other. They tangled often in the courtroom, which may have been what initially set them off.

Jefferson harbored great respect for the standard-bearers of the colony. He saw Pendleton and Wythe as examples of intellectual rigor and republican manhood and continued to rely heavily on both in the critical years to come. He did not leave behind any comment on their squabbles, though he was incapable of perceiving, let alone breathing a word of, any flaw in Wythe. If the famously mild jurist and teacher was capable of open hatred, as it appears he was, and as Jefferson got on well with Wythe's courtroom antagonist, then history has been shortchanged. For all his sunny optimism, there were many truths that Jefferson refused to acknowledge—and this is one of them. He clearly knew more than he let on regarding the Wythe-Pendleton feud. We are left with the obvious conclusion: that then as now, politics made for clashing egos, not just strange bedfellows.

In 1774, after he finished writing *A Summary View*, Jefferson made two copies, one directed to Peyton Randolph, the second to Patrick Henry. As he correctly assumed, Randolph shied from its more forceful language, while Henry, full of fire, embraced its content. Before long, though, Jefferson's relationship with Henry would come to mirror the situation that left Pendleton and Wythe in a zero-sum contest with each other.[16]

The main philosophical point of *A Summary View* was to assert that nothing in history is wholly independent of past occurrences or the basic human desire to be free of unwarranted control. "No circumstance has occurred to distinguish materially the British from the Saxon emigration," Jefferson explained. "America was conquered, and her settlements made, and firmly established, at the expence of individuals, and not of the British public." That "conquering" did not necessarily imply the displacement of Indigenous communities; in this context, it chiefly demanded the surmounting of natural obstacles. The "expence" Jefferson referred to was an outlay of resources and personal effort. No one helped the Saxons cross the English Channel. Those who settled the American colonies took all the risks.

An ability to use the long sweep of history to advance a proposition is what gives *A Summary View* its power. Exactly who the Saxons once were is far hazier than who they became over time. For Jefferson, what mattered was how their migration set a precedent for transatlantic migrations later on. The common trait between peoples centuries removed was hardiness of commitment: "Their own blood was spilt in acquiring lands for their settlement, their own fortunes expended in making that settlement effectual." It was not only Virginians, but by clear imputation New Englanders and the rest. "No shilling was ever issued from the public treasures of his majesty or his ancestors, for their assistance, till of very late times, after the colonies had become established on a firm and permanent footing."

The Declaration of Independence borrows from *A Summary View* in both its tenor and its content. The historical element in Jefferson's 1774 political pamphlet is fundamentally a story of royal neglect, leading to increasingly greater ills. Outlining errors of judgment by King George III's father and "exercises of usurped power" resulting in "parliamentary tyranny," Jefferson comes to the defense of the people of Boston who had recently resorted to the destruction of East India Company tea. On this very tender subject he writes: "There are extraordinary situations which require extraordinary interposition. An exasperated people... are not easily restrained within limits strictly regular." Bostonians, acting out of moral indignation, had confined themselves to the one target, following which they "dispersed without doing any other act of violence." This was Jefferson's friendly interpretation of what came to be known colloquially, many years later, as the Boston Tea Party.

Turning back to the specific issues confronting Virginians, he related a collective desire to establish contiguous western counties on their own terms, without constraint from abroad. In this, he adopts a stern prosecutorial mode: the British monarch repeatedly failed to understand the stakes, choosing to interfere in colonial affairs "for the most trifling reasons, and sometimes for no conceivable reason"— generally, just to say no to reasonable requests. Here Jefferson is previewing the expunged paragraph in his extant first draft of the Declaration with regard to London's responsibility for the African slave trade: "The abolition of domestic slavery is the great object of desire in those colonies, where it was unhappily introduced in their infant state."

Of course, this is nowhere close to an honest or thorough explanation of the thorny matter of slavery's persistence in the colonies. Nevertheless, *A Summary View* holds that moving in an antislavery direction requires first the cessation of "further importations from Africa," which the king had vetoed. "Our repeated attempts to effect this by prohibitions, and by imposing duties which might amount to a prohibition, have been hitherto defeated by his Majesty's negative." With Parliament an unrecognized authority, George III alone was left to exercise his options to prevent a final breach between his government and his colonies: "Or does his majesty seriously wish, and publish it to the world, that his subjects should give up the glorious right of representation, with all the benefits derived from that, and submit themselves the absolute slaves of his sovereign will?" Jefferson's voice (on the page, at least) is devastatingly bold for 1774.

But even this does not represent the crescendo in Jefferson's composition. He still has more to say about the Saxons and their legacy by linking the discussion to what he terms the "fictitious principle that all lands belonged originally to the king." Reminding George III that the early-seventeenth-century North American colonists were "farmers, not lawyers," and thus easily taken in by this royal fiction, they "accordingly took grants of their own lands from the crown." The error was never corrected, and the time had come to change all that: "These are our grievances which we have thus laid before his majesty, with that freedom of language and sentiment which becomes a free people claiming their rights, as derived from the laws of nature, and not as the gift of their chief magistrate: Let those flatter who fear; it is not an American art."

As an American art, *A Summary View* is a masterpiece of prosecutorial art, and the very reason Jefferson was selected, when the time came, to draft a declaration of American independence. It is abundantly clear in the 1774 text, even as he affects a restrained pose, that he has chosen to personalize his attack on the monarch, precisely as he would do in 1776: "Open your breast, sire, to liberal and expanded thought," he commands the king. "Let not the name of George the third be a blot in the page of history." A blot is a stain. It was a derogatory, condemnatory, demonizing synonym, as the writer intended it to be. It was revolutionary.[17]

JEFFERSON AND THE SCOTTISH ENLIGHTENMENT

One wonders whether, had he been aware that the contentious James Macpherson had a reputation in London as a nouveau riche bore, Jefferson would have been quite as charitable toward him. It is richly ironic that when Macpherson turned to politics, he was hired to write a tract titled *The Rights of Great Britain Asserted Against the Claims of America*, which could not have been more subversive of Jefferson's interests. It was published in 1776 (in Philadelphia!) by Robert Bell, the same printer who brought out Thomas Paine's intoxicating Revolutionary pamphlet *Common Sense* a short time before. *The Rights of Great Britain* was not "equal time" or "freedom of the press," however. Bell had had a falling-out with Paine over money. This was payback.

Macpherson's title reads as a direct response to Jefferson's 1774 *Summary View*, though it was in fact a response to the "strange" (as he calls it) Declaration of Independence and the years of protest against Parliamentary taxation that led up to it. In Macpherson's text, the Continental Congress demanded that the king give them what he was constitutionally unable to grant, so they systematically pursued "their plan of deception" by petitioning in a language of peace while forcing Britain's hand with their consistent "misrepresentation of facts." Of Jefferson's emotion-laden final paragraphs, *The Rights of Great Britain* is entirely dismissive: "The conclusion of the Declaration, though laboured, contains nothing but empty declamation, and therefore merits little notice." Macpherson's entire argument is framed around the distinction between an "indulgent Parent" and an "undutiful Child."[18]

What are we to make of all this? It was, by this time, three years since Jefferson's unsuccessful appeal to Charles Macpherson. With so many Loyalists about and pressing issues commanding his pen, and as a member of the Second Continental Congress, Jefferson the Virginian was too preoccupied with what lay ahead to regard this one publication as a personal affront. As it was, Virginia Loyalists who chose to return to Britain were accorded respect, unlike those from elsewhere in the rebellious former colonies. Girding for war was all that mattered.

Macpherson's name did not appear on his pamphlet. When *The Rights of Great Britain* was first published in London, its title page read: "Said to be Written by Lord GEORGE GERMAINE"—secretary of state for the Colonies since November 1775. Germaine was a notorious hard-liner when it came to the colonies, desperate to preserve his nation's power across the Atlantic; before he assumed office, he'd thought his government should have leaned harder on the misbehaving Bostonians. "By a manly and steady perseverance," he said, "things may be restored from a state of anarchy and confusion, to peace, quietude, and due obedience." Germaine was a prominent, if scandal-prone, minister, lampooned in the press for his reported same-sex relationships. As for Jefferson's "manly" thoughts on James Macpherson's politics, the record is silent. (More than simply "masculine," the adjective meant "proudly, maturely conceived"; in his initial draft of the Declaration, Jefferson asserted that "manly spirit" commanded Americans "to renounce for ever these unfeeling brethren!")[19]

The thinking of other Scots was far friendlier to Jefferson's political agenda. Indeed, Scottish moral philosophy did much to strengthen the already spirited rhetoric that Americans published in setting forth their Revolutionary agenda; and Jefferson was one of the most pronounced beneficiaries of Scottish Enlightenment ideas.

Foremost among the Scots was Henry Home, Lord Kames. While under George Wythe's tutelage, Jefferson spent a fair amount of time with *Historical Law Tracts* by Kames. In his Legal Commonplace Book, this text occupies more space than just about any other work. Like Jefferson and others among the philosophically inclined Revolutionaries, Kames liberally took his inspiration from historical example. He went as far back as ancient Egypt while privileging Athens and the Roman Empire, as one might expect.

First, Kames's remarks on the evolution of royal authority made a clear impression on Jefferson. The interposition of the sovereign authority to punish crimes was an uncommon practice but became regularized over time, willingly accepted. This was the historical nature of law, of precedent; it was the way in which, Kames explains, "common practice was reckoned a branch of the common law." As "moral duties, originally weak and feeble, acquire[d] great strength by refinement of manners," so most Americans continued to recognize the king's "prerogative to interpose" until 1776. Altogether, as a guide to custom, *Historical Law Tracts* spoke to Jefferson's legal understanding of conflict resolution, which subtly influenced his political writings.[20]

Jefferson appreciated the tension between Scottish and English ways of seeing the human condition, and he generally found himself predisposed in the Scots' favor. Thirty of the titles (twenty percent) on Jefferson's 1771 list of recommendations for a well-established gentleman's library (the Skipwith list) were by Scottish authors—including David Hume's multivolume *History of England*. Under the subject heading "Criticism on the Fine Arts," Jefferson listed Thomas Reid's 1764 *Inquiry into the Human Mind*, Lord Kames's 1751 *Essays on the Principles of Morality and Natural Religion*, and Adam Smith's 1759 *Theory of Moral Sentiments*.

All of these titles are important. They went to the heart of human nature. Note, again, that in Jefferson's self-fashioning there was a good deal more poetry and fiction than politics. When he conceived the Skipwith list, his political ambition still lay, as his father's had, exclusively within Virginia.

Scottish thought was everywhere (at least within Jefferson's orbit) in the 1760s and 1770s. The Scots probed deep into causes that mattered. Several of Jefferson's Revolutionary peers studied with Edinburgh-trained John Witherspoon, president of Princeton (then the College of New Jersey) since 1768. Witherspoon embraced a moral philosophy that sanctioned resistance to political tyranny; he would join Jefferson in Philadelphia in 1776, in time to sign the Declaration. His students at Princeton included James Madison and Aaron Burr. Though Jefferson clutched his personal commitment of Virginia so close to his chest that it would occasionally interfere with his national obligations, his thoughts extended a great distance from his provincial roots.[21]

The Scots-Irish, as scholars now refer to them, were the largest non-English Protestant group within the white population of late colonial America. Most came from Ulster and settled in the interior, from western Pennsylvania to the Carolinas. A fair number arrived as indentured servants, and their reputed ruggedness became the stuff of legend. On the other hand, the highly educated, more polished Edinburgh and Glasgow Scots came to dominance through print culture. From William Buchan's indispensable *Domestic Medicine* to Henry Mackenzie's paean to selfless giving, *The Man of Feeling*, private libraries were well stocked with Scottish-authored volumes published in Edinburgh, Dublin, London, and, before too much longer, in Philadelphia. As Revolutionary sentiment rose and the "enslavement" metaphor infused Patriot propaganda, the radical voices of Scots and Irish—whose sense of "despotism," "oppression," and "enslavement" to England preceded Americans'—buttressed the cause Jefferson championed.[22]

Jefferson was quite specific about the Scottish moral philosophy he embraced. One he favored, though no longer well known, is Thomas Reid (1710–1796), who explored nature-given sensations and what they meant in social life. He stated his case emphatically and, we might say, democratically: that philosophy had "no other root but the principles of Common Sense." He meant that humans should trust their mental faculties even though they know that they will be proved wrong in many instances. Philosophy flowed from reasonable beliefs, from reflection. Overdoing skepticism gets you nowhere.

Humans are not natural mind readers, Reid goes on. A would-be "anatomist of the mind" can know only his own with any accuracy at all. "He may, from outward signs, collect the operations of other minds; but these signs are for the most part ambiguous, and must be interpreted by what he sees within himself." In spending a lifetime collecting data, conducting experiments, and philosophizing, Jefferson may be classed as a "Common Sense" thinker.[23]

Reid studied under Lord Kames, who was an esteemed moral philosopher in addition to being a jurist whom Jefferson extensively commonplaced. At seventy-seven, he had just published *Gentleman Farmer* (1772), which Jefferson recommended to fellow Virginians and others for many years. On a less earthbound subject, from at least 1798, Jefferson began suggesting to younger scholars that they study Kames's *Natural Religion* (1751) as part of a broad-based education. That work dealt with self-awareness, morality, and justice, while providing an explanation for belief in a deity rooted in the senses (so-called "natural theology").[24]

The authority of the five external senses fed, but did not require, belief in God, according to Kames. The "law of our nature," to use Jefferson's term in the context of his reading of Kames, was Nature allowing for refinement in taste or behavior. Kames saw "a marvelous harmony betwixt our inward feelings, and the course of external events." He had what Jefferson apparently felt was a lovely way of looking at the possibilities of human perfectibility. Nature instructed, and man performed actions by taking instruction.

Late in *Natural Religion*, Kames introduced the idea that *sense* had more to do with belief than *reason* did, and that humans were equipped to perceive how the deity existed as a benevolent force in the world: "A very slight view of human nature is sufficient to convince us, that we were not dropt here by accident." Praising the "instinctive faculties" and "intuitive knowledge of the things that surround us," he recognized at the same time that "the dread of unknown objects is apt to fire the imagination, so as to magnify their supposed evil qualities . . . , as if those qualities were real and not imaginary." The philosopher concludes with the very Jeffersonian maxim, "The more of nature is explored and known, the less of evil appears."

At the end of *Natural Religion*, Kames exclaims: "*O Eternal Mind!* Sovereign Architect of all!" With a vocabulary unlike Jefferson's, but in keeping with Jefferson's known conviction that the moral sense was an endowment from birth, Kames says, "If in the verdure of the fields, and the azure of the skies, the ignorant rustic admires thy creative power; how blind must that man be, who, looking into his own nature, contemplating this living structure, this moral frame, discerns not thy forming hand?" Monticello's sovereign architect was himself encouraged by the power of a Creator who created creators like himself.[25]

Kames is Jeffersonian, or Jefferson Kamesian, when he delights in a mind that has been given the capacity to discover truths. In praising *Natural Religion*, Jefferson is as confident in Kames as Kames is in himself: "A man owes no duty to which he is not urged by some impulsive feeling," he wrote in 1814 to the son of an Anglican bishop who'd become a Washington insider. Having recommended Kames with regularity over the years, he confessed here that he'd not opened the book in fifty years, but that the Kames he'd read in the 1760s never ceased to impress his mind.[26]

Adam Smith's *Theory of Moral Sentiments* (1759) went beyond the ideas of Lord Kames. In *Natural Religion*, Kames discoursed on passion and compassion, friendship and gratitude—the "social affections," as they were known. Smith started with the first human impulse, self-preservation, from which he derived the powerful forces of friendship: sympathy and good fellowship. In Kames, it was "Grief, compassion and sympathy, are strong connecting principles, by which every particular man is made subservient to the general good of the whole species." In Smith, it became "The man of the most perfect virtue, the man whom we naturally love and review the most, is he who joins, to the most perfect command of his only original and selfish feelings, the most exquisite sensibility, both to the original, and sympathetic feelings of others." Affection, he says, is nothing but "habitual sympathy."[27]

Throughout *Theory of Moral Sentiments*, Smith shows that a person needs to attend to the opinions of others in order to judge his own worth. But just how introspective was Jefferson? How honest with himself was he over the course over a long career? Was he as fair-minded as he claimed? This is the trickiest part of addressing Jefferson's personal psychology. He vowed a hatred for contention, and, on becoming president, swore he would treat the opposition with magnanimity. Yet he remained a symbol of disreputability in the hands of vengeful politicians and mercenary journalists, testing his stated resolve. Scottish moral theory infused his thought; but in the hyperpartisan arena of American politics, it did not bear up well, as subsequent chapters will reveal.

Smith's hopeful assessment of human potentiality had obvious appeal. His remarks on vanity and ambition themselves sound Jeffersonian: "Humanity does not desire to be great, but to be beloved," Smith writes. "It is not in being rich, that truth and justice would rejoice, but in being trusted, and believed." Jefferson sought the "inward tranquility and self-satisfaction" that Smith writes about; but still, splitting headaches came on when he descended from his mountain sanctuary. He was fighting for a cause, at the same time masking his passion. Which means there was more going on in him.[28]

On the subject of the passions, Smith is expansive from the start of his book. He regards lustful sex as the "most furious of all the passions," which explains why he says men must exude sympathy when speaking with women: "Their company should inspire us with more gaiety, more pleasantry, and more attention," so that those appetites that arise from the body appear less like the "brute" nature that humans share with the animal kingdom.

Smith's less physiologically drawn taxonomy separates the "social" and "unsocial" passions. Imagination or temperament being "ductile" (capable of yielding to persuasion), as passion becomes more of the mind than of the body, it takes on its social or unsocial character; in personal terms, one's dignity is often at the center of this calculus. Yet no passion arising from the imagination is as uniformly appreciated as love is: "There is in love a strong mixture of humanity, generosity, kindness, friendship, esteem; passions with which, of all others, ... we have the greatest propensity to sympathize." Every being understands and will react with sympathetic feeling to another's loss of heartfelt love and the "expectations of romantic happiness" that sink with such a loss.

In political terms, Smith outlines "unsocial" passions that can be made "agreeable," and as such appealing to social sympathies: "A person becomes contemptible who tamely sits still and submits to insults, without attempting either to repel or to revenge them." This is how the American Revolutionaries, and Jefferson in particular, regarded inaction in the face of "unfeeling" treatment by the authorities in London. Toward an avowed enemy, sympathy becomes an emotion that is out of place, once that enemy's attitude and intent prove self-seeking and dishonorable and are cruelly acted upon. The counterpositioning of "feeling" and "unfeeling" not only resonates in the Declaration of Independence; it is a staple of Jefferson's moralism more broadly.[29]

The philosopher generally considered first in the pantheon of Scots is Francis Hutcheson (1694–1746). Though Irish by birth, he was Scottish-educated. Jefferson owned his seminal *An Inquiry into the Origin of Our Ideas of Beauty and Virtue* (1725), the substance of which accords with Jefferson's semantics. Hutcheson associates the aesthetic sense of "beauty" with the interior sensation of "harmony." The sound of language exerts effect beyond the ordinary understood function of the five "external" senses; there's a world of perception beyond the most literal. One can appreciate Hutcheson's formula in Jefferson's recurrence to musicality in the cadence of his political script: not only is he himself euphonic in his written presentation, he idealizes "harmony" as productive of social "affection." As it is with the saying "it's music to my ears," so it is that to care about others is to receive pleasure.[30]

Hutcheson's name is associated with those who followed the path he'd laid out: Thomas Reid and Adam Smith, plus David Hume; he was favored as well by John Witherspoon at Princeton. All of these thinkers recurred to the same language of sensation, moral imagination, and critical examination that found their way into Jefferson's familiar letters. His instruction to Peter Carr is the most literal example of the Scots' way of seeing the human being:

> The moral sense, or conscience, is as much a part of man as his leg or arm. It is given to all human beings in a stronger or weaker degree ... It may

be strengthened by exercise, as may any particular limb of the body. This sense is submitted indeed in some degree to the guidance of reason; but it is a small stock which is required for this: even a less one than what we call Common sense.

The message to his nephew is democratically drawn in the example he uses:

> State a moral case to a ploughman and a professor. The former will decide it as well, and often better than the latter, because he has not been led astray by artificial rules. In this branch therefore read good books because they will encourage as well as direct your feelings.[31]

Before he had traveled much beyond Williamsburg, Jefferson already knew how to get his hands on Scottish books. He advised Robert Skipwith in 1771 to purchase the above-cited titles from a London bookseller, Thomas Waller. Not until the 1790s would it be possible to obtain such books in the United States. When Jefferson was acquiring the books he suggested to Skipwith, Britain was exporting more books to its American colonies than to the continent of Europe. The trade paused during the Revolution but picked up again afterward. Scottish titles continued strong.[32]

SUSPENSE

As the year 1775 began, following similar actions taken in the eastern Virginia counties, Albemarle established its Committee of Safety, a popular organ complementing the Committee of Correspondence and furthering collective action. When the votes of freeholders were counted, Jefferson had the most (of the fifteen nominated), followed by Jack Walker. The two neighbors took charge, although—presumably for reasons of safety—no records were kept.[33]

Jefferson's path to the Second Continental Congress went through Richmond, where the Second Virginia Convention met in March 1775. Richmond was a small inland town, nothing like a city. British regulars had not yet fired on militiamen at Lexington and Concord, but Lord Dunmore's show of indifference to legislators' concerns was fast growing into a direct opposition.

Richmond was therefore chosen, being a site where resistance views could be safely aired. Insults flew. Dunmore's unfriendly behavior had led the *Virginia*

Gazette to publicize long-standing rumors about the royal governor's habit of debauchery. Supposed to have taken as his mistress the daughter of the king's long-serving attorney general of Virginia, he was now alleged to display a particular fancy for African American females.[34]

Also in Richmond, Patrick Henry urged greater preparedness on his colleagues—"a well regulated Militia composed of Gentlemen and Yeomen"—and incited those assembled with his clarion call for liberty at all costs. Richard Henry Lee, another strong orator, followed on Henry's heels, these two respective leaders hailed as America's Demosthenes and Cicero respectively. Jefferson shared their unyielding purpose, adding robust if less inflammatory sentiments to theirs.

Jefferson waged his war of words with dignity, while Henry was impatient to advance to the next stage. As soon as news of the fighting in and around Boston reached him, he took charge of a company of men and marched on Williamsburg with a dramatic sense of resolve, prompting the governor to put a target on Henry's back. (At that point, Jefferson was away from the capital.) Having made his show of force, Henry left Williamsburg, as Dunmore, temporizing, called for the Burgesses to reassemble in order to weigh London's latest proposals in a final effort to salvage peace. Jefferson was among those who showed up, but no meaningful words of conciliation were spoken by either side.

After a six-month hiatus, a Second Continental Congress had been called in Philadelphia, opening its doors on May 10, 1775. Henry, as Virginia's most celebrated activist, rejoined his colleagues, and the erudite Peyton Randolph was reelected as president of the solemn body. But Randolph spent only four days in Philadelphia before hastening back to Williamsburg to resume his position of Speaker of the House of Burgesses for Dunmore's emergency session. Boston's John Hancock was elected to succeed him.

As first alternate, Jefferson was called upon to relieve Randolph in Congress. But as he, too, cared most about his home colony, he took his time before heading north. Dunmore, in turn, gave up on face-to-face communication, moving with his family to a warship anchored offshore. With no further business to conduct in Williamsburg, Jefferson purchased the services of an enslaved man known only as Richard, outfitting him in clean clothes so as to arrive in the City of Brotherly Love with a respectable-looking manservant. He took to the road in an open carriage (he called it a "phaeton"), in no particular hurry, purchasing books along the way. Thus, his seat in Congress remained vacant for another ten days. Because their letters are no longer extant, nothing is known about his conversations with Patty prior to departure, but one must assume that his sense of duty in a time of peril was perfectly understood between them.³⁵

Right away, the new recruit was plunged into the business of drawing up a "Declaration of the Causes and Necessity of Taking Up Arms." When not at work, Jefferson shopped, finding sheet music and violin strings, a tomahawk (no explanation given), and of course more books. He remained in Philadelphia until the beginning of August, returning home by way of Richmond, where, once again, political meetings beckoned. After barely a month back at Monticello he was obliged to go north again. With one daughter, Patsy, now a healthy toddler, Patty had a respite from pregnancy. She would not conceive again until her husband's stint in Philadelphia was over and the Declaration of Independence signed.³⁶

In the fall of 1775, Jefferson boarded with others of the Virginia delegation, including Peyton Randolph and Randolph's wife. On October 22, Jefferson and Randolph dined together at the home of a Pennsylvania wine merchant, six miles outside the city, where the corpulent fifty-four-year-old Randolph suddenly collapsed. In his daily account book Jefferson wrote: "This evening the amiable Peyton Randolph, esq. our Speaker died about 9. o'clock of an apoplexy." Nine days later, he penned an anxious letter to John Page, having received no word from Patty since he left her. "I have set apart nearly one day in every week since I came here to write letters. Notwithstanding this I have never received the scrip of a pen from any mortal breathing." A week after that, to Francis Eppes, the husband of Patty's half sister Elizabeth, he was all the more fraught: "The suspense under which I am is too terrible to be endured. If any thing has happened, for god's sake let me know it."

Patty was fine. The mails could be slow, but in this case it was she who had failed to reckon with his overactive imagination. Jefferson remained in Philadelphia through the end of the year, making the pleasurable acquaintance of Dr. Benjamin Franklin in the process.³⁷

Before proceeding to the year 1776, a brief detour is in order to recapture a moment in Jefferson's history that combines levity with the very serious business of revolution. Back in 1771, two lawyers concluded a comical pact. Attorney General John Randolph (one of several notables of that name), a younger brother of Peyton, was, like Jefferson, a better than average violinist, whose instrument Jefferson openly admired. With Patrick Henry and George Wythe as witnesses, Randolph and Jefferson made a macabre sort of bargain that, given the considerable difference in their ages, granted the younger man a decided advantage: if Randolph should die first, Jefferson would get the prized violin, and if Jefferson predeceased him, the elder would get his entire library.[38]

In 1775, Peyton and John came down on opposite sides in what Jefferson now termed "this unnatural contest" between Britain and her colonies. The Loyalist brother resolved to leave his American life behind and, in settling his affairs, sell Jefferson the violin, thus nullifying their earlier agreement. When Peyton died, it fell to Jefferson to inform his brother in London of the "melancholy intelligence." Turning to the subject they would never see eye to eye on, Jefferson respectfully but determinedly laid out the future—more than six months before the Declaration and two months before the publication of Paine's *Common Sense*, which history has tended to grant emotive priority for having pointed Congress toward independence. "By the god that made me," wrote Jefferson to John Randolph, "I will cease to exist before I yeild [*sic*] to a connection on such terms as the British parliament propose and in this I think I speak the sentiments of America. We want neither inducement nor power to declare and assert a separation." After predicting that "one bloody campaign will probably decide everlastingly our future course," he resorted to an immodest reproach of King George that this Randolph might not have appreciated: "We must drub you soundly before the sceptered tyrant will know we are not mere brutes, to crouch under his hand and kiss the rod with which he deigns to scourge us."

Once again, as in *A Summary View*, Jefferson's radicalism lay on the page. He did not hear from Randolph for another four years, at which time the lapsed Virginian referred to the earlier letter as one he'd treated less as a personal affront than as an attempt at publicity abroad. Randolph understood ambition, and he understood Jefferson's style of presentation in the letter as a sign that it had been drawn up to be discussed publicly.

So, in his animated reply, Randolph turned the tyrant charge around. He did it not in a bid for public dissemination of his argument, and not to call out Jefferson either, but to recall to Jefferson's mind the enlightened conception that differing views—even on the political destiny of a continent—rose from judgments that were best reasoned through, all passion set aside. "If a Difference in opinion, was a good Ground for an Intermission of Friendship," Randolph opined, "Mankind might justly be said, to live in a State of Warfare." That is, if you condemn someone for possessing a sentiment unlike your own, you claim your judgment to be the only conceivable standard; this not only "wounds the great Liberty we enjoy, of thinking for ourselves," but also "tyrannizes over the Mind, which Nature intended should be free and unconfin'd." He hit back at Jefferson's polemic with language that one could quite easily have mistaken for Jefferson's.

By the time he had his long-delayed reply from John Randolph, Jefferson was Virginia's sitting governor. The letter writer's son, Edmund Randolph, had completed his service as an aide to General Washington and, in an ironic twist of epic proportions, now occupied the same post his father had held under the colonial regime: attorney general of Virginia.[39]

Jefferson spent the early months of 1776 at Monticello. The death of his mother on March 31 was followed by an extended period during which he suffered, on a daily basis, his "periodical head ach," delaying his return to Congress. On arrival in Philadelphia in mid-May, he plunged back in, apparently without a relapse. Rather than hint at momentous happenings, though, his account book reveals the ordinariness of his days: the purchases of toothbrushes, "wash balls" (soap), "scissars & pencils," watch repair, a visit to the barber, meals at taverns, and, on June 1, "Pd. seeing a monkey."[40]

Independence was a foregone conclusion when, one week after Jefferson's monkey viewing, Congress named a committee of five to the task of making it official. For years afterward, Congress, as a body, would be celebrated annually as the party responsible for the "immortal" Declaration. Transfer of credit to a singular penman would come about only years later, when Jefferson challenged his fellow committee member, John Adams, for the office of president of the United States. For now, Jefferson was perfectly content to be a team player.

Adams of Massachusetts, Roger Sherman of Connecticut, Benjamin Franklin of Philadelphia, and Robert Livingston of New York (at thirty the youngest member) placed the weight of the committee's work on the bony shoulders of the thirty-three-year-old Jefferson. No one realized at the time that the parchment they and their colleagues were to sign would serve as a symbol more potent than a simple certificate of birth. A compelling explanation for that outcome was Jefferson's extraordinary gift, the ability to reach deep with a language of honorable passion, sentimental attachment, and moral assertiveness, giving a proud identity to a new nation no less ambitious than he was.

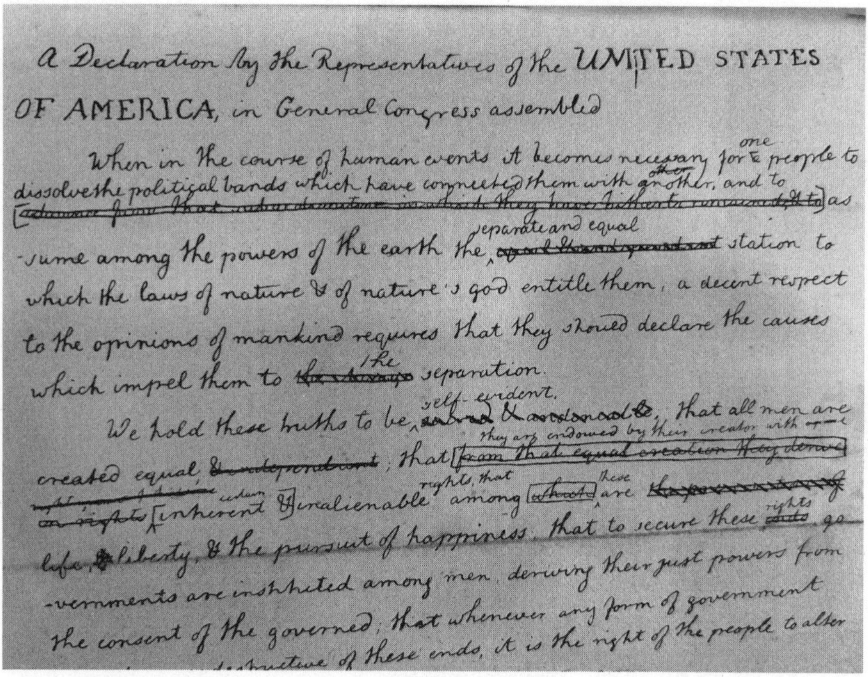

Figure 8. Facsimile of Jefferson's original draft of the Declaration of Independence, from the accordion foldout leaf in Volume 1 of Henry S. Randall's *Life of Thomas Jefferson* (1858), the three-volume biography authorized by Jefferson's living descendants prior to the Civil War.

CHAPTER 5

"Every Fibre of That Passion"

A Declaration and an Adieu

THE GIFTED SCOTTISH AUTHORS, interpreters of the world of perception and sensation, had exerted real influence on Jefferson. Their arguments with regard to the power of human connections in establishing social purposes may well have been the deadliest arrow in Jefferson's quiver. When he said to the Loyalist John Randolph, "I think I speak the sentiments of America," he was really saying that he felt he knew how to draw out those sentiments. The uncompromising belief he held, the ethical justifications he offered, the phrases he wove together, spelled inevitability. This is what led Garry Wills to argue in the last century that Jefferson's opening, "When in the course of human events, it becomes *necessary* . . . ," came from the Scots.[1]

But it was not only the Scots. Moral sense and the natural rights doctrines of John Locke fuse in the text. Though a rejection of monarchical power dominates the Declaration, the underlying legal theory is still English. What Locke provides, above all, is a guide to political justice: *the consent of the governed*. Jefferson's legal scholarship and his years of experience guaranteed that British common law would remain the foundation of whatever he recommended for his state going forward. It was a settled matter. The common law, under his eye, and with the assistance of his mentor George Wythe, would be replicated in Virginia during and after the war without waiving the requirement of projecting independent America as a truly new idea.[2]

Also involved in Jefferson's construction of the Declaration's arguments, if not explicitly so, were the Greeks and Romans, from whom he acquired much of his creativity with language. On matters that involve the imagination, freedom of thought, and human destiny, he communed with antiquity even as he relied on the reigning thinkers of the eighteenth century. The ancients, like the Scots, contributed to his composition an intangible yet animating spirit—not a theory of government, but a moral take on history (Tacitus) and the channeling of passion into a deeper appreciation for the cause of human happiness (Epicurus).[3]

"NATURE'S GOD"

The first few sentences of the Declaration of Independence are familiar to all who have made it through elementary school in the United States. But can the Declaration be read in the context of its time, delivering the fullness of feeling that it brought to the readers and hearers Jefferson was writing for? Let's try.

The opening, a solemn exhortation ("When in the course of human events, it becomes necessary . . ."), is an appeal to good sense, set forth with frankness in order to make the ensuing list of grievances part of what is "necessary" and just. Jefferson is previewing the case for rejection of a distant ruler, promising to enumerate the causes (twenty-seven in all) that justify political separation.

Prosecuting his case against an unfeeling king and conniving ministers, he invokes the "Laws of Nature and of Nature's God" to give American independence a universal justness that is hard to argue against. If *A Summary View* found its point of departure in Jefferson's Saxon analogy, the Declaration finds its essential strength as an idea in Jefferson's applications of lessons from Nature. A key tenet of his eclectic philosophy is a people's legitimate right to "dissolve the political bands" binding them to a despot.

To explain "the Laws of Nature and of Nature's God," we must first accept the premises that Jefferson's intended (elite) readership already found convincing: that the language of Nature is unrestricted; that the Law of Nature is beneficent. Inherent limitations attach to human knowledge, by which Nature may be misunderstood. Having inconstant motives, people are prone to deceive. But Nature does not lie. Nature transcends. It possesses, for example, healing powers that, when understood, help a person survive a contracted disease. To imitate Nature through education is to preserve health and potentially rescue the future from what threatens. This explains the primacy of experimental science in the Enlightenment. All improvement is in human hands.

Nature's God is synonymous with the Law of Nature: it is God manifest in Nature. How does humanity fit into the picture? In brief, the living profit from experience. Nature's law is a power of mind to be fed, just as the senses, including the moral sense, are tools that enable individuals to find community. So it is with "pursuit of happiness," equally an individual and community pursuit. Without collective happiness, individual happiness cannot truly be realized; by implication, a humanely directed government that aims to maximize shared interests among its citizens is what, in Jefferson's mind, constitutes the happiness that in later times would be embellished as "the American Dream." This is the best I can do to convey, in brief, to a twenty-first-century reader what "Nature," a term lacking philosophical association now, meant in 1776.[4]

In the study of Nature, the philosophes explained, reason guides morality. For Jefferson, this meant a decisive rejection of what he and like-minded critics deemed "mysticism" (he as often wrote "mystery" or "superstition"). Nature's God is unaffiliated with conventional religious practice. When Jefferson refers to the Creator as the "author" of the universe, it is the God in Nature, not the Judeo-Christian God, that is meant. Similarly, the "gift of God," a phrase one of Jefferson's persuasion might well use, was acceptable as another way to say the "gift of Nature," as the only visible expression of God. In his 1775 letter to the Tory attorney general Randolph, Jefferson's expression "By the god that made me" was no more Judeo-Christian-specific than was "Nature's God."

In his brilliant, exhaustive study titled *Nature's God*, Matthew Stewart finds "the anti-theology of the age" in the climax of Epistle 1 of Alexander Pope's *Essay on Man* (1733): "All are but parts of one stupendous Whole, / Whose body Nature is, and God the soul." The fourth and final Epistle, which begins "O happiness, our being's end and aim!," states near the end: "Slave to no sect, who takes no private road, / But looks through Nature up to Nature's God." These quoted lines are anything but obscure: if any eighteenth-century poet was "worshipped" by literate Americans in 1776, it was Pope, his *Essay on Man* above all. Pope sought to make sense, philosophically, of individual morality in a world where the ultimate purpose of the Giver of Life remained unknowable.

In Stewart's analysis, Nature's God (already so-named by midcentury) owed more to Newtonian physics than to Christianity, which was just how Jefferson thought. Along with Jefferson, the English poet embraced mysteries only to the degree that science was applied in an effort to solve them. In setting forth what was to become the spirit of the age, Baruch Spinoza, a philosopher residing in Amsterdam (and a contemporary of Sir Isaac Newton), wrote: "The greater our knowledge of natural phenomena, the more perfect is our knowledge of God's essence." For such thinkers as these, whose works added much to Enlightenment thought, God's only revelation was in and of Nature.[5]

A revolutionary reaches for certainty. Line by line, Jefferson's approach in the Declaration allows no room for questioning or readjustment. Before it was edited by the committee to read "We hold these truths to be self-evident," he'd written, "We hold these truths to be sacred and undeniable." The word "self-evident" is strong enough, but it is emotionally empty; "sacred" is stronger, because it says that what follows is "undeniable" and morally incontestable. Though Jefferson's "sacred and undeniable" was removed and replaced, American history has effectively restored its meaning. The truth Jefferson is touting is what we now label "human rights" and see as the gift of God, that is, a superior truth that resides in Nature and is not only discoverable but can also be intelligently defined.[6]

In matters of religion, Jefferson was far more circumspect than he was in the realm of confrontational politics. Personally, he would come to welcome Unitarianism when it reached America's shores, for it largely coincided with what he called "rational" religion. Though loath to describe his faith on the page, he unfailingly made allowances for the conventionally religious and graciously responded to clergymen who sent him their religious pamphlets. He honored John Page's strong attachment to the Episcopalian Church in hopeful language and by offering prayers, a pattern he continued to observe in his correspondence of later years. That is not to say that he prayed. He attended Episcopal services from time to time in the neighborhood of Monticello, both as a social obligation and out of respect for the principle of freedom of worship. He accepted phrases into public documents that he knew would soothe the many who went to church every week. His principle would reincarnate in the mid-twentieth century as "nonsectarian monotheism," a safe means of embracing God's Providence without getting into the weeds of sectarian debate.[7]

Richard Henry Lee, an astute member of an illustrious line in Virginia political circles, served in both the First and Second Continental Congresses. It was Lee who formally introduced the resolution to declare independence in the first week of June, and it was to this colleague that Jefferson wrote one month later—in a nonreligious way—that "the finger of providence has as yet saved us" on the battlefield. Lee may well have shared his colleague's tolerance of religious difference, but he would later oppose Jefferson's effort to end religious establishment in Virginia.

In a number of other instances, Jefferson opted for "the hand of providence," still using body parts to render "providence" less godlike than something under human control. When he used the verb "pray," it was a synonym for "please" ("Pray let me know whether...") unless he was communicating with a religious individual. To Madison, when Patrick Henry became a formidable political opponent of theirs, he put it cruelly (but not literally): "What we have to do I think is devoutly to pray for his death." In the same letter, he gave "teeth & fangs" to the active Episcopalians of Virginia, though his friend Page was one of them. Here, he took care to encode key words so that if intercepted, the letter could not be used against him. Ultimately, it didn't matter how much stealth Jefferson employed: his personal beliefs would become fodder in electoral politics ever after.[8]

His formulation was, to put in the simplest terms, and as most historians have concluded, deistic. Without challenging the existence of a life-giving God, Jefferson found personal sustenance not in church, or in an active deity, but in the reproducible life found in the natural world where all the God he needed was manifest. Much later in life, he would say that the Jesus of the Gospels never once claimed divinity. He took umbrage at the arrogance of clerics (especially those from New England) who, he said, misled their congregations in the interest of personal power—in other words, exhibited the sin of pride. They called him out when he sought the presidency, tossing around words like "atheist" to stoke fear. In *Notes on Virginia*, well before he'd engaged in party politics, Jefferson wrote preciously: "It does no injury for my neighbor to say there are twenty gods or no god. It neither picks my pocket nor breaks my leg." This statement was often quoted back to him by trolling letter writers who'd been convinced by his clerical enemies. In a letter to Dr. Benjamin Rush, a man of faith whom he counted among his close friends, Jefferson said that if his actual views were known, only a religious bigot would regard him as an atheist.[9]

Here is where Jefferson's dispute with the power-engrossing clergy of New England lay, and why he wrote to Rush in the manner he did. Piety was one thing, blind obedience to power another. Once a believer judged that a providential God meted out rewards and punishments, religious authority could easily exploit their susceptibility. That was the "tyranny over the mind of man" Jefferson openly despised. In Revolutionary politics, he saw "toryism" through the same lens. And in the decades to follow, he'd tar his Federalist opposition as "monarchists" as well as "tories," who disparaged ordinary people and cared only to retain their social privileges.

Where he saw weakness in an acquiescence before symbols of power, Jefferson looked for political avenues to effect change. His first project upon reentering public life at the end of the Revolution was to honor the commitment to the right of conscience that is implied in the Declaration. In this he would team with James Madison to urge legislation upon the Virginia Assembly. The change they sought together was enacted in the Virginia Statute for Religious Freedom, precursor to the First Amendment. The first, in 1785, separated church and state in the Commonwealth, the second, in 1790, across the nation. Jefferson saw an indissoluble connection between politics and Nature: God had created the mind free. It was up to conscientious legislators to arrest the perversion of Nature's Law and Nature's God by any self-interested faction.[10]

DIVORCE

Religious politics was not the issue when Jefferson invoked "Nature's God" in the Declaration. The term was simply a way to acknowledge an essential truth about a people yearning for freedom. The right to life and liberty had to transcend politics. Even Jefferson's unpalatable racist logic, as fiercely as he clung to it, was not so overwhelming in his mind as to lead him to rationalize denying to Africa-descended Americans the same liberty, the same self-determinative power, as whites. The solution he came up with, as we know, was to deport them, to divorce Black from white and give the former "their own country," where their color would not offend their neighbors.[11]

Disconnection had multiple meanings in 1776. Where physical closeness and long familiarity subsisted between the enslavers and those they enslaved, matters of intimacy were impossible to ignore. The same held for Anglo-American relations writ large. In the first year of the war, the Continental Congress weighed existential matters that superseded the moral imperative to mitigate or abolish the slave system, but it's obvious why the language of kinship, affinity, and familiarity remained inextricable from the content and purpose of the Declaration. When Jefferson announced the causes justifying white Americans' craving for "their own country," he expressed the colonists' hurt in decidedly intimate terms.

The Declaration is best understood as a divorce petition. King George III (already the father of eleven in 1776) is treated by Jefferson as an abusive husband rather than as an absent father. He refers to England as the "mother country" in *A Summary View* ("Nor was ever any claim of superiority or dependence asserted over them by that mother country from which they had migrated"), but he does not use that term in the Declaration; in fact he does not use it at all in his correspondence for the duration of the war.[12]

The divorce analogy makes sense for a number of reasons. In 1772, at the high point of his career as a practicing attorney, Jefferson took extensive notes in preparing the case of a client who wished to divorce his wife. At the time, it was virtually unheard of for a husband or wife to succeed in a divorce suit as we understand it, even in cases of adultery. The colonial legislature would have to vote in favor, and the royal governor would then have the final say. Except that King George III had recently forbidden royal governors to approve legislative divorces. Jefferson was seeking to effect a divorce by appeal to the Burgesses, which was quite unlikely, barring the overturn of British authority in the colonies.[13]

The 1772 case was a complicated one. Jefferson was called in to protect the estate of Dr. John Blair, a Williamsburg physician, married over a year, with medical problems of his own. He resented rumors about his inability to perform sexually, and he died at the end of that same year, without a will; his sexual reputation remained "he said, she said." Jefferson claimed that the wife had refused her husband his conjugal rights, that the marriage was never consummated, but he came to acknowledge that Dr. Blair had been physically unable to have sex with his wife. In effect, Jefferson was retroactively (posthumously) seeking an annulment. Here he was adopting the strategy preferred by the other counsel for Blair and his estate, Edmund Pendleton.

Attorney Jefferson's objective was, in any event, to deny the widow life interest in the late Dr. Blair's property. So it did not matter which party was right about the dead man's sexual reputation. Or, for that matter, whether there was any truth to the charge that during the brief marriage, the wife had engaged in an adulterous liaison with the last colonial governor, Lord Dunmore. To make matters even more complicated, Patrick Henry was part of the widow's legal team, and thus on the side of Dunmore, who ruled the only way the law permitted: no annulment occurred while Dr. Blair lived, and despite the deceased's hatred for the woman he married, she was granted a widow's right, life interest in a portion of his property. She later remarried.[14]

In preparation for so challenging a case, Jefferson did what a diligent student of the law would do: he went to his library and conducted a search of all the historical precedent he could dig up, from the Hebrew Bible to the Gospels of Matthew and

Mark, from John Milton to John Locke to David Hume. But the expert on marriage and divorce whom he most often cited was the German jurist Samuel von Pufendorf, whose *Of the Law of Nature and Nations* (1672) was praised by eighteenth-century thinkers for its breadth and humanity. It ranged across every conceivable philosophic tradition: the nature of the moral conscience, free will, consent, the legality of suicide, civil obligation, and "the Dictates of Right Reason." Notably, one of the subjects Pufendorf took on was "That all Men are to be accounted by *Nature Equal.*"

"Of Matrimony," part of the sixth book of the *Law of Nature and Nations*, gets to the heart of marriage and divorce. Pufendorf titles his categories unabashedly: "*Loose and random Amours are repugnant to the Law of Nature*," "Mankind ought to be propagated by the Marriage Covenant only," "*Irregular* or Amazonian *Marriages*" (in which the female bears a child to satisfy her own desire, wanting no man to help her raise it), "The Husband's Authority *over the* Wife, *whence derived*," "*Whether* Consent, *and not* Bedding, *makes a proper Marriage*" (why a marriage contract must precede "the Ceremony of the *Bed*"). None of these century-old themes would have appeared out of place in pre-Revolutionary Virginia.

Jefferson consulted the sections headed "*Marriage dissolved by* Adultery, *and by* Wicked Desertion," and "*Whether* Intolerable Manners and Humour *are a just Reason of* Divorce." Pufendorf regarded them as human issues, answerable to the Law of Nature. He held the view that divorce, as a rule, "shock[ed] the Strength, and Credit of Families; and the Grace and good Order of the whole Common-wealth."[15]

Jefferson's original draft of the Declaration was composed as a legal instrument. With the extensive note-taking on equity law that he undertook while under George Wythe's roof, he privileged fairness (natural law) over legal technicalities and drew a sharp line when it came to the conditions under which a complete and final separation from England could be granted. Thus it is instructive that the first entry in Jefferson's notes from 1772, arguing in favor of divorce, reads that it is "cruel to continue by violence an union made at first by mutual love, but now dissolved by hatred." A few lines later, reflecting the culture he was reared in, he stated—and this cannot be stressed enough—that the purpose of marriage is to breed ("Propagation & Happiness") and that "where can be neither, should be dissolved."

Jefferson's approach to the Declaration mirrors the foregoing principles. He is saying that "propagation" was curtailed when the king turned a blind eye to Parliament's denial of the colonies' freedom to expand west; that "happiness" was undermined by routine demands and threats and the imposition of unjust laws; that "violence" was inflicted when British redcoats and Hessian mercenaries mercilessly invaded and rampaged.[16]

As his list of the king's abuses lengthens, it becomes increasingly clear why the injured colonies were so urgently compelled to stand and fight. George III had "plundered our seas, ravaged our Coasts, burnt our towns, and destroyed the lives of our people." The verbs spell devastation, threaten extinction. In 1776, "ravage" and "plunder" were synonymous, meaning to lay waste to the land. The accused tyrant was "transporting large Armies of foreign Mercenaries to compleat the works of death, desolation and tyranny." Here, "desolation" doubles down on the image of invaders despoiling land that becomes uninhabitable as a result of thoughtless cruelty; "desolation" works because it is visceral, even more felt than the generalized nouns "death" and "tyranny."[17]

The language in Jefferson's original draft is gut-wrenching, purposefully so. He means to establish America as a victim of "repeated injuries" administered by her erstwhile protector. Having declared the colonies "out of his allegiance & protection" (which is a husband's duty), George III had gone so far as to dispatch foreign troops to "deluge us in blood." Leading to his evocation of the likely fatal consequence, Jefferson frames the Declaration—again, as a legal brief—around enumerated charges. The active verbs define a tyrant: "he has refused . . . ," "he has forbidden . . . ," and so on, each entry supplying an example of the king's callous disregard for Americans' "safety & happiness."

Jefferson lays into the royal transgressor's repeated pattern of abuse, doing so in terms of a consistent denial of "affection" for those who showed him only patience and conciliation. When he is done stating his case, and in view of overwhelming evidence, the divorce petitioner sees no alternative: "These facts have given the last stab to agonizing affection." *The last stab*—a violent summoning. Congress removed that resonant phrase, rejecting Jefferson's preferred imagery of an intentional deadly blow that ended any hope of a resumption of affectionate ties. It was an "agonizing" decision, he is saying, yet an unavoidable, lifesaving decision for the all too patient colonies.

Jefferson's rhythmic inflections create an almost musical composition. With sadness, with emotional clarity, he lets out one additional sigh, one more blue note: the British people who remain subject to this king were no longer within Americans' family circle: "We must forget our former love for them." This one sentence expresses the larger consequence of the divorce. Yet the word "love" appears only in Jefferson's draft, not in the final version Congress approved. Jefferson is alone in privileging the divorce analogy.

THE STATE OF MRS. JEFFERSON'S HEALTH

But how sensitive was he to implications that involved his own behavior? In his reading of Pufendorf, Jefferson set his eyes squarely on a series of unblushing statements that might have given him some slight pause. Treating virginity, animal lust, premarital sex, and a host of other situations that preoccupied the ancient world, the German related social concerns past to the ethical concerns of his present. This was a habit of the classicist Jefferson, too, whose bookshelves were lined with texts that treated human passions. His collection embraced the Greeks, whose sexual appetites were indulged, while also featuring the latest medical theorists of Europe, who recommended balance and an avoidance of the "irritants" that caused "agitations" in one's nervous constitution.

Adultery is a major theme of Pufendorf's divorce chapter, with detailed discussions of who the aggrieved party is in this or that circumstance. It is precisely where Jefferson cites Pufendorf's stricture that "Propagation & Happiness" are interrelated features of an ideal marital union that he would have encountered the scenario in which a faithful wife is taken advantage of suddenly: "If she be overcome by the Usurper, . . . we can on no pretence call her Virtue in Question. And though it be commonly reckoned a more Heinous Crime, to assault her Chastity thus, by main Strength and Power, than to ensnare or betray it by Flattery and Charm; yet the Truth is, the former offers the more grievous Injury to the Wife, but the latter to the Husband." Husband and wife each had a right over the other's body.[18]

Prior to meeting Patty, Jefferson had clearly taken a chance that he might destroy the marriage of Jack and Betsy Walker by way of seduction. In terms of the jurist-ethicist Pufendorf, the "more grievous" insult was to the husband, his old and dear friend. Had Jefferson found some way to apologize to Betsy? Did Patty have any inkling? Or did Jefferson simply press on, trusting that Betsy would never tell?

Perhaps he'd buried the memory of his transgressions. By 1776, it had been more than five years since he'd started courting Patty at the Forest, and the lawyer-legislator had adopted a plainly sentimental perspective on marriage. Once the Declaration had been signed by fifty-six men from thirteen former colonies, he did not care who knew how anxious he felt, or that his feelings for his wife were profound. He wanted badly to leave Congress and return home.

If the Virginia delegation was to preserve its quorum, Richard Henry Lee would have to return to Philadelphia. At the end of July, Jefferson wrote to him, pleading: "For god's sake, for your country's sake, and for my sake, come. I receive by every post such accounts of the state of Mrs. Jefferson's health, that it will be impossible for me to disappoint her expectation of seeing me at the time I have promised, which supposed my leaving this place on the 11th. of next month."[19]

He had also expressed his fears for Patty to Edmund Pendleton, who was heading the effort to shape a constitution for the new state of Virginia. Despite the transformative effect of Jefferson's words and stances, something at his core rebelled against ambition. Pendleton knew him well and sensitively acknowledged his colleague's priority: "I am extreamly concerned [by] . . . the indisposition of Mrs. Jefferson; May heaven restore her health and grant you a joyful meeting." The patriotic Pendleton was as convinced that Virginia needed Jefferson as Jefferson was that Congress needed Lee. "I hope you'l [sic] get cured of your wish to retire so early in life from the memory of man" was how Pendleton put it.[20]

In an idiom common at the time, happiness was said to lie in pursuing the quiet path—not in the chase for wealth or honors. Alexander Pope's phrase from *Essay on Man*, "the soul's calm sunshine and the heart-felt joy," could have been Jefferson's motto in praise of the Monticellian vision, where, as he'd written Robert Skipwith, couples might sit together, enjoy the background sound of gently flowing water at night, and savor the "merriments" of music and companionship with "lightened" hearts and the healthful feeling it produced. He knew the comfort of family and understood the physical frailty of a wife whose experience in bearing children was attended with real danger. He was of two minds when government beckoned.

His increasingly frequent absences meant that Patty was managing the mountain on her own and probably not getting as much rest as she needed. Where his account records concern her, they show payments between April and August 1776 for whiskey, cotton cloth, thread, gloves, "powder blue" (a cobalt compound used to brighten the appearance of linen); a loan of ten pounds to her husband's brother, Randolph Jefferson; and regular transactions with enslaved people who independently raised poultry and other food essentials.[21]

Finally granted the freedom to travel south, Jefferson arrived back at Monticello on September 9, 1776. While Patty still required doctor visits, she nevertheless became pregnant immediately. After his first month back, Jefferson returned to his legislative seat in Williamsburg, Dunmore having fled the country. Pendleton's ambition for Jefferson had won out; or perhaps it was a joint effort, because the legislator brought Patty and little Patsy with him, and they lodged for a time at the Williamsburg home of George Wythe, who had since joined the Philadelphia delegation.

Meanwhile, the leaders in the Continental Congress had apparently misread Jefferson's intentions, because he learned in Williamsburg that he been named to the U.S. delegation to France, along with Benjamin Franklin and Silas Deane of Connecticut. Franklin would become a hit among the French; Deane, despite his part in securing the French alliance, was shunned in consequence of his being accused of unsavory practices that included wartime profiteering. Jefferson did not need time to consider: he promptly answered John Hancock, the president of Congress, declining the appointment due to "circumstances very peculiar in the situation of my family." Either he did not wish to risk his wife's health on a perilous ocean crossing (or go abroad without her), or, just as likely, he did not want to abandon to others the work he was embarked upon in charting a future for Virginia's government. It was crucial to his self-worth and sense of purpose that his imprint should be on the state's new system of laws. He had used, for the first time, the words "United States of America," at the end of the Declaration; but his identity as a Virginian was the stronger identity at this juncture. His priority as a legislator lay at home.[22]

Patty gave birth to a son at the end of May 1777, but the nameless child—the only male child she would bear for Jefferson—died two weeks later. While large families were the norm, it is quite possible that the desire for a son made it even less likely that Jefferson thought about sexual restraint in the bedroom. Pufendorf, for one, cites Euripides (a decided favorite of Jefferson's in the 1760s) in his chapter "On Matrimony," to remind his readers what hardly needed to be said: *Male Children are the Pillars of great Families.*

WARTIME TRAVAILS

One of the ways to determine where Jefferson was at any given time is to inspect his daily weather observations, maintained through most of his life. His passion for data collection was almost an obsession. No matter where he was, he took temperature measurements in the early morning, then either in the evening or midafternoon or both—he aimed for four o'clock, because, he said, he wanted to capture each day's high temperature.

He rose between five and six most mornings, retiring sometime after nine o'clock at night. Especially when traveling, he liked to add notations: whether the day was fair or rainy, the first appearance of frost, the singing of bluebirds, wrens, and mockingbirds. As it happens, Jefferson's earliest surviving temperature record dates to July 1776, when he was in Philadelphia. It indicates that on July 4, he was not otherwise engaged at nine in the morning, one in the afternoon, or nine at night, with temperatures consistently in the low- to mid-seventies. To be sure, the delegate had business to attend to in the intervening hours.[23]

From the moment of his return from Philadelphia through 1779, he had the best of two worlds, working on what he loved to think about in his library at Monticello when not being called to Williamsburg. After Dunmore's departure, the war left Virginia untouched for more than three years. "Matters in our part of the continent are too much in quiet to send you news from hence," Jefferson wrote from Williamsburg to John Adams in May 1777, the earliest example of their five decades of an on-and-off, but always dynamic, correspondence. Adams replied immediately in what was becoming an increasingly familiar refrain, praising Jefferson and imploring him to return to Congress: "We want your Industry and Abilities," coaxed Adams. "Your Country is not yet, quite secure enough, to excuse your retreat to the delights of domestic life." They would next meet in Paris in 1784, after Adams had replaced the shady Silas Deane and Jefferson arrived to fill in for Dr. Franklin.[24]

Jefferson was a fixture in Williamsburg during long legislative sessions. The Burgesses having disbanded, the capital now had in place a House and a Senate. Its popular first governor was Patrick Henry. For two years, Jefferson was present for up to several months at a time, in close communion with his confidant George Wythe. The accomplished Edmund Pendleton was a sparring partner, yet, even in disagreement, Jefferson's friend. At times, Pendleton wanted to take it slow when Jefferson took the initiative.

Because they generally agreed that British statutes should remain unchanged, Jefferson confined his innovations to subjects that mattered most to him. The two bills he authored that were closest to his heart were the one for establishing religious freedom and ending special privileges for the Episcopal Church, and another "for the more general diffusion of knowledge." The first took the better part of a decade before it finally passed; the second never succeeded, largely because the state legislature was too cheap to support public education in the manner Jefferson prescribed. Yet Jefferson's commitment to this bill was unsurpassed: "Preach, my dear Sir," he exhorted George Wythe from Paris in 1786, "a crusade against ignorance; establish and improve the law for educating the common people." Jefferson would not let go of his dream of an informed citizenry, beginning with early education at public expense.[25]

He sought to democratize inheritance practices and to open up education to more non-elites. His attempts to deal with slavery do not sound like "reforms" to us, representing at best a tentative step in the direction of emancipation. He recommended outlawing the importation of enslaved individuals from other states, as well as from overseas; but he also specified that those men and women, on earning their freedom, had to leave the state.

In August 1778, the Jeffersons' daughter Mary was born, known in the family as Polly, and in adulthood as Maria. Other than her elder sister, the long-lived Patsy, she would be the only one of Patty Jefferson's children to survive to adulthood. Jefferson gave Patsy responsibility and judged her; he indulged the more sensitive Polly and sought to keep her happy and entertained.

Despite all that was on the commanding general's mind militarily, Washington was distraught to learn that Jefferson, Wythe, and Pendleton were devoting their energies to Virginia instead of the affairs of Congress in Philadelphia. But Jefferson was exactly where he wanted to be. In the fall of 1777, after the American capture of several thousand British and Hessians at the Battle of Saratoga, the prisoners were herded south and eventually arrived at prison barracks in Charlottesville. Jefferson warmed up to the cultured German generals among them who were permitted to lodge with their families at superior accommodations in the neighborhood of Monticello while awaiting repatriation. He played music with these gentlemen as they gathered to discuss philosophy.

Once again, little in the psychological environment of Thomas Jefferson is comparable to the present day. As bitter as he remained toward the British soldiery, and despite his choice words in the Declaration about foreign mercenaries sent "to deluge us in blood," he was quite keen on these Germans. They were men of standing, men with ethical standards he agreed with, so that he and they communed easily. They'd come to America with their wives. This was not an enemy who would attempt to flee. Jefferson was fond enough of one, Baron von Geismar, that he went out of his way to meet him in Frankfurt a decade later, visiting with several other former officers "stationed in Albemarle while in captivity." Traveling together through the Rhine region, Geismar became his cicerone, his teacher and guide.[26]

As committed as Jefferson was to his charming mountain dreamscape where he was importing books and experimenting with seeds, he was intensely interested in enlarging his transatlantic network of sympathetic scholars. Four years before the Germans arrived in his neighborhood, he had talked the Florentine Philip Mazzei into settling on land adjacent to Monticello, where he grew grapes and tried to produce wine, while Jefferson started growing Italian vegetables, all the while honing his book-taught Italian. This was the world Thomas Jefferson wanted to inhabit: the republic of letters. Even as he was monitoring the ups and mostly downs of the ongoing struggle to win independence, his bliss was locatable in scholarly engagement, of which he could never get enough. Political life could not match that.

He had achieved quite a reputation in Williamsburg. Jefferson had been a legislator since his election to the House of Burgesses in 1769, a whole decade earlier. He had not sought an executive position until he was elected governor of the state in 1779. On seeing the vote tally, he made unnecessary apologies to runner-up John Page, who'd served to that point as an active lieutenant governor under Patrick Henry. Victory over his bosom friend was a mixed blessing, to say the least; the governorship would prove ruinous to Jefferson's reputation once the British launched their southern campaign and invaded Virginia full-on.

He did not wish to be a forceful executive. (The presidency would be of a different order.) The structure of the Virginia state government gave the legislature a weightier role than the governor possessed. But in one illustrative instance, he took the reins in a revealingly punitive way. The incident warrants attention because it coincides with a breach between Virginia's first two governors that was never repaired.

Patrick Henry had been intent on prolonging Virginia's presence in its frontier territories, which extended all the way to the Mississippi River. Both he and Jefferson cultivated George Rogers Clark, whose hardy band performed brilliantly against the British in Kentucky and Illinois. But once the army of Cornwallis sliced its way through the Carolinas, not all of Virginia's legislators remained eager to underwrite the western contingent, and eventually former governor Henry's commitment wavered too. Jefferson held firm, lavishing praise on the fighting man he'd promoted to general. Maintaining a strategic correspondence despite the seven hundred miles or so that separated them, he eventually revealed his spiteful side when it came to Henry, using prickly language to complain about "one person hostile to you as far as he has personal courage to shew hostility to any man. Who he is, you will probably have heard, or may know him by this description, as being all tongue without either head or heart."[27]

The unproven accusation that Henry lacked courage shows a mean-spiritedness that does not jibe with the genteel, conciliatory letter writer who'd imbibed the humane message of the Scottish philosophes. Jefferson the politician had a rich capacity to hate, and time would exhibit a stubborn refusal to let go of such feelings. Without mentioning Patrick Henry by name, he described his rival as a blabberer who was not very bright. He would say the same and worse during his presidency when supplying facts and impressions to Henry's first biographer, the Jefferson admirer and future U.S. attorney general William Wirt. Alive or dead, he wanted to see Henry humiliated.

Governor Jefferson was exceedingly vengeful in another instance when he vented his spleen against the British whom he detested by willfully singling out one particular official, who was under Jefferson's control, for the strictest punishment. Henry Hamilton, the lieutenant governor of British-held Detroit, was captured by George Rogers Clark in a daring operation. One of Hamilton's nicknames was "scalp-buyer"; he was known for inducing Indians to behave mercilessly, even toward American women and children, by inviting Indian warriors to present American scalps to him. He was led in shackles to Richmond, where, for strategic reasons, Jefferson had relocated the state capital. For the duration of his governorship, he kept Hamilton in a small, dank cell, denying him the right to have visitors.

General Clark had given his prisoner every assurance of fair treatment. Jefferson ignored the promise. A British general whose character he respected, one of those kept in Charlottesville along with their German allies, appealed for leniency, and again Jefferson would not hear of it. His anger would not abate. It was only through the intercession of General Washington himself that Henry Hamilton, who denied paying for scalps or controlling how Indians at war conducted themselves, was sent to New York and then permitted to return to England.[28]

It is worth noting here that, until 1779, confiscation of Loyalist property in Virginia lagged behind most of the other former colonies. Before Jefferson became governor, those properties were kept in limbo, expected to be returned to their owners eventually; in the meantime, profits earned from Loyalists' lands went into the state treasury. However, after a year of drought, with the threat of invasion increasing, and financial burdens mounting, confiscation became expedient. Some British subjects sold their land to friends, but the toll the war had already taken on the public mind resulted in a hardening of hearts. Jefferson was on board with confiscation just prior to his election as governor; after assuming the executive role, he ordered all British subjects to "depart the Commonwealth in such manner as shall be prescribed to them," or else face "the ultimate peril." Militiamen were instructed to arrest and jail the miscreants. It was Jefferson's hope, as he wrote to his college pal

Will Fleming, that the new policy would "put our finances into a better way and enable us to cooperate with our sister states." To which he added, "Every other remedy is nonsensical quackery."²⁹

This outwardly reserved man who could quickly turn vindictive had an impressive facility for constituting a network of like-minded friends when it aided him politically. Just as the cabinet officers in his presidential administration would prove an unusually compatible and communicative group, Governor Jefferson's inner circle, his formal Council of Advisors, included trusted friends Page and Walker and his newest ally, the twenty-six-year-old Princeton graduate James Madison Jr. They'd met in the autumn of 1776, though their partnership, built on a shared reform agenda, did not truly jell until 1779.

Despite these advantages, Jefferson's governorship slowly unraveled. After he moved the capital from the more vulnerable Williamsburg, the war crept closer, and in the spring of 1780, an all-out British invasion opened. General Charles Cornwallis took the city of Charleston, South Carolina, capturing thousands of American fighters, hundreds of them Virginians. He humiliated General Horatio Gates, a national hero since the Saratoga campaign. Though subsequent battles across the Carolinas were not without impressive American victories, Washington was tied up in New Jersey and Pennsylvania. Nothing could stop the British from pushing their way into Virginia.³⁰

The French had recently entered the war on America's side, resulting in premature expressions of optimism among those who expected the tide to turn quickly. In reality, the majority of Virginia's home-grown defenders were deployed elsewhere, the enlistment effort was not going at all well, essential supplies were lacking, and tobacco exports were shut down. With the depreciation of currency and citizens' resistance to taxation, the state treasury was nearly exhausted. Jefferson himself went to the coast to meet the French naval command, but it did not change much. The French could not be expected to save the day—yet.

Despite Jefferson's appeals, Congress did precious little for Virginia. With means to alleviate his problems seemingly out of reach, the frustrated governor made time to take under his wing a lawyer in training. He was a hungry twenty-two-year-old Continental Army veteran named James Monroe, who had suffered a serious wound at the Battle of Trenton in December 1776. While only the second-best of Jefferson's two protégés who had the law and a future in political office in mind, Monroe bonded with Jefferson as Jefferson had bonded with Wythe, and eagerly served as the governor's confidential courier to the southern theater. Then, a second, brighter student entered Jefferson's circle. William Short was a nephew of Robert Skipwith who had studied with George Wythe in Williamsburg. Beyond the relationship of law tutor and law student, Short would serve Jefferson in a very different, and rather more intimate, way as his principal aide in France.[31]

In the late fall of 1780, Jefferson expected a concerted attack on the state, though neither he nor anyone else could anticipate precisely how it would unfold—only that Cornwallis's men were on their way up from North Carolina. Jefferson was not a student of war, and in early December, he let John Page know that he did not feel up the task of governing anymore and wished to yield the office to someone who could do better. He made arguments that had a familiar ring to Page, who immediately dismissed his self-contradicting friend's oft-stated craving for a tranquil life away from contention: "I know your Love of Study and Retirement must strongly solicit you to leave the Hurry, Bustle, and Nonsense your station daily exposes you to," Page wrote in early December. War was hardly "Nonsense," of course, as Page well knew. He advised Jefferson to put all thoughts of quitting out of his head for the months that remained in his term. "Deny yourself your darling Pleasures for th[at] Space of Time," he coaxed, "and then you may despise not only now, but forever, the Impertinence of the silly World." It was his choice of "silly" that was nonsensical—the juvenile banter seems a strange reversion to their college days. But Page knew this side of Jefferson, the heart that wished it could achieve its goals painlessly. The former lieutenant governor felt he needed to give his pal a pat on the back. "All who know y[ou] know how eminently qualified you are to fill the s[tation] you hold." All in all, a disturbing letter.[32]

Jefferson's lamentation has been used as proof of his cowardice, but if it is, it surely isn't as simple as that. It was Jefferson the legislative innovator, the constitutional thinker, who rose to be governor. His elevation had taken place when the war was being fought elsewhere. Even if he can sound sensitive to hurt (which he demonstrated, over time, that he was), Jefferson was always clear about his priorities. He knew where his talents lay, and mobilizing a durable defense was not a talent of his. For weeks if not months leading up to this moment of indecision, when legislative concerns were subsumed into wartime exigencies, he kept up regular correspondence with militia commanders and probably thought it was in his state's best interest to have a leader with greater background in military tactics to succeed him before the looming threat became truly dire. His proposal of a premature exit from the governorship was emotionally driven but rationally drawn, and not necessarily a cowardly reflex.

Jefferson's behavior does reveal a wavering quality about him. The same man who refused to display the least humanity toward the "scalp-buyer," who wanted Hamilton to suffer deprivation, could not see himself rising to the occasion and finding means to organize resistance to the invader. Sit out the war he had helped as much as anyone to bring about?

He was a compulsive organizer bent on bringing order to his world. Yet as an unmartial character, he felt impotent. He hinted that he thought Page, who had served in the militia, should take the reins. While it is difficult to make a certain judgment here, it can be said with some assurance that Jefferson cared too much about succeeding at what he was good at to permit himself to "go down with the ship," to become any kind of martyr. To dread a degradation in his status as a public authority is not exactly the definition of cowardice, but it's not a definition of courage either.

The traitorous General Benedict Arnold, formerly a favorite of Washington's, led British troops ashore in January 1781, but instead of targeting Williamsburg, as all anticipated, he took full advantage of good winds and launched a series of inland raids along the James River, torching plantations before setting fire to a largely undefended Richmond. Jefferson had to abandon the young town he'd made the state's capital, and he did about all anyone could have done in the crisis to alert the county militias. Blame did not fall entirely on him, but as events continued to unfold, Arnold's invasion would be treated as a reminder of Jefferson's alleged failures as governor. He would have to fight for himself, for his reputation.

In March, he wrote a letter of welcome, as it were, to the Marquis de Lafayette, a youth scarcely older than Monroe, whom Washington had named a major general. The French volunteer had already acquitted himself well on the battlefield when Washington sent him to Virginia to coordinate with French naval commanders and hopefully capture Arnold. As they had yet to meet face-to-face, Jefferson apologized to Lafayette, in his way, that the citizens of his state (as he collectively imagined them) were "a People not used to war and prompt obedience." He meant it as a clue to the difficulties that lay ahead. In retrospect, it sounds as though he was rationalizing his own inability to mobilize Virginians. Even Jefferson's nineteenth-century biographer Henry S. Randall, generally his staunchest defender, made excuses for the "yeomanry" who would not turn out and fight in the wake of Arnold's raid: "Are there not natural duties to mothers, to wives, and to daughters, which take precedence even of duty to one's country?" he wrote.

Wasn't Jefferson's frustration warranted? The lack of resources at his command is uncontested historical fact. The number of men of militia age was not very considerable (less than one per square mile), and their meager store of arms ("less than one serviceable gun to five militiamen") did not bode well for them. A handful of Continental regulars were left to guard the prisoners at Charlottesville. Until General Cornwallis hunkered down and made his fatal blunder along the coast, Virginia settlements remained ripe for assault from his overwhelming numbers.[33]

"SUSPECTED AND SUSPENDED"

The enemy returned to the James River in April 1781. This time Jefferson had advance intelligence. Lafayette led his troops to Richmond and helped stave off an incursion. Arnold had been dispatched north, but in view of the modest numbers of defenders, Cornwallis still had a plan to reduce Virginia, certain that one Frenchman, no matter how committed, could not stop the numbers of armed infantry and cavalry the British general had at his disposal. At this point, Jefferson wrote to Washington, urging him, as a native son, to come to Virginia. Convinced that Washington alone could lift spirits and supply the manpower needed to save the state, Jefferson asked him to "lend us your personal aid." He made sure the commander understood that his own governorship was to end soon and that he, true to form, wanted to leave the state in "abler" hands than his own.

Jefferson's last act as governor, in late May, was to call the legislature into session, this time in Charlottesville. Ballots were to be cast for a new governor. But before the election could take place, fate intervened in the form of a militiaman with good hearing and expert intuition. Captain Jack Jouett caught wind of a British plot to capture the outgoing governor and make an example of him. He raced forty miles to Jefferson's mountaintop to alert him, then rode into the town below to give the same intelligence to the assembled legislators, several of whom did not get the message in time and were seized.

Hunted by mounted infantry and quite nearly taken by them, Jefferson made haste through the woods to a neighbor's property. But he stopped in the town below first rather than simply head for the hills. Patty, who had lost another infant earlier that spring, was sent off first with daughters Patsy and Polly in tow. The family reunited later in the day, riding south to the greater safety of the Poplar Forest property Jefferson had inherited from John Wayles. They were accompanied by Jefferson's protégé William Short, whose increasing devotion to the well-being of the family would be amply rewarded. The little clan did not return to Monticello for nearly two months, owing, Jefferson reported, to a fall from his horse.

In October 1781, Cornwallis was cornered by French and American forces at Yorktown, his surrender effectively ending British military operations in North America. But Jefferson did not have the luxury of removing himself from contention even then. What hounded him from June forward began in the legislature as a political attack and grew into scurrilous jokes at the failed governor's expense that would not go away. His term ended before a successor could be elected, and Jefferson stewed as George Nicholas, a legislator allied with the ever popular once and future governor Patrick Henry, introduced a resolution inquiring into Jefferson's conduct in office. Certain that Henry was the source of his problem (and he may have been mistaken), Jefferson wrote to Nicholas immediately on his return to Monticello from Poplar Forest, demanding from that gentleman a precise explanation of the "ill conduct" he meant "to adduce against me." It was a short letter, and Jefferson's pique was undisguised. He wanted chapter and verse that the "inquiry" was owing to "some particular instance or instances of ill conduct" and not intended just as a stab at his reputation. In his reply, Nicholas sought to save face by insisting that his fact-finding inquiry was simply a means to learn what had gone so wrong that the British had had an easy time of ravaging the state. "You consider me in a wrong point of view when you speak of me as an accuser," the accuser weakly contested. He said he personally knew of no particular instance of misconduct.[34]

Although he was fully exonerated, Jefferson would spend the rest of his life having to defend his record as governor. He enlisted a series of writers to get his side of the story out, to put the charge to rest. He could not take any chance that posterity would revive the accusation of cowardice. His earliest effort was the most anguished: a carefully drawn letter to James Monroe in May 1782, which Jefferson no doubt intended for circulation (and inclusion in the historical record). Here he stated his personal outlook in absolute terms. "Before I ventured to declare to my countrymen my determination to retire from public employment, I examined well my heart to know whether it were thoroughly cured of every principle of political ambition, whether no lurking particle remained which might leave me uneasy when reduced within the limits of mere private life. I became satisfied that every fibre of that passion was thoroughly eradicated." He had suffered grievous mistreatment. His reputation had been impaired.

The letter is crafted with the same lyricism he put into the Declaration of Independence, but with far less nobility: "I stood arraigned for treasons of the heart, and not mere weaknesses of the head. And I felt that these injuries, for such they have been since acknowledged, had inflicted wound on my spirit which will only be cured by the all-healing grave." In spite of the "exculpatory declaration" belatedly offered him, he was for a considerable time—note here the doubling of emotion through alliteration—"suspected and suspended in the eyes of the world." It was a distasteful memory he did not expect he could ever truly banish from his mind. Writing from abroad, he'd admit to a Philadelphia friend seven years later: "I find the pain of a little censure, even when it is unfounded, is more acute than the pleasure of much praise." No, he didn't forget.[35]

In fact, the psychological drama became more interesting just six months after the letter to Monroe as Jefferson tried to turn the tables on Patrick Henry. It appears he had been waiting for the opportunity, for this was when the words spill from Jefferson's pen to George Rogers Clark, accusing Patrick Henry ("all tongue without either head or heart") of political cowardice in denying support to Virginians fighting in the area of the Mississippi River.

A disillusioned Jefferson, at the age of thirty-nine, was determined never again to step into the cesspool of politics. The life he wanted was that of gentleman farmer and gentleman scientist. He was productively engaged in the all-embracing *Notes on Virginia*, communicating with record keepers in other parts who could supply him with the data he required. In the same letter in which he tried stirring up trouble for Patrick Henry, he segued from peevishness to cordiality, politely petitioning George Rogers Clark to find natural history specimens for him to study: "Descriptions of animals, vegetables, minerals, or other curious things, notes as to the Indians, information of the country between the Missisipi [sic] and waters of the South sea &c. &c." His ambitious designs were being channeled into projects for which he needed only his Monticello library, pen, and ink.

In the partial autobiography he penned in his late seventies, rather than comment on a two-year governorship he'd rather forget, he directs readers to a history of Virginia in wartime, drawn from his personal papers. Louis Girardin, its French-born author, tells the story as Jefferson would have told it, emphasizing the need for a military man to seize the initiative and finding that hero in the Marquis de Lafayette. Girardin's narrative shows it to have been impossible for Jefferson to have done anything more than he did.[36]

The closest Jefferson gets to reliving the governorship in the 1821 autobiography are these brief lines: "From a belief that under the pressure of the invasion under which we were then laboring the public would have more confidence in a Military chief, and that the Military commander, being invested with the Civil power also, both might be wielded with more energy promptitude and effect for the defence of the state, I resigned the administration at the end of my 2d. year."37

"TORN FROM HIM BY DEATH"

Patty became pregnant for the sixth time in nine years during the summer of 1781, shortly after their return from Poplar Forest. In her ninth month, the Marquis de Chastellux visited the mountain for four enchanted days, when he and Jefferson bonded over their love of Ossian. May 8, 1782, saw the birth of Lucy Elizabeth, given the same name as the couple's last daughter, who had survived but a few months. No one knows how the ill-fated mother reacted to the trials of her husband over the two years prior, how they discussed it—he wrote his profuse letter to Monroe when Lucy was twelve days old—but his priority quickly became Mrs. Jefferson, as her recovery from childbirth became increasingly uncertain.

She languished for four months. It was not the first time Patty Jefferson was "brought to bed" (in the parlance of the time) and fared poorly. This time was different. The notation in her husband's daily account book for September 6, 1782, is as terse as the entry on the day his mother passed away: "My dear wife died this day at 11H–45' A.M."38

In her final days and weeks, Patty Jefferson was cared for by her husband, by his sister Martha Carr (Dabney Carr's widow), and by the Hemingses she'd known as a girl. Patsy was ten years old, Polly four, when they lost their mother. Once she'd come of age and had children of her own, then grandchildren, Patsy prepared a memoir of her life and said of her father that he "was never out of calling" when her mother was struggling, that he was most often at his writing desk a few feet from the bed. "A moment before the closing scene, he was led from the room in a state of insensibility by his sister."

The ten-year-old became his "constant companion" in the weeks following, attesting that she observed "the violence of his emotion, when, almost by stealth, I entered his room by night." After the initial "fainting fit," he had a difficult time functioning normally. He "walked almost incessantly night and day" until he finally exhausted himself. During the next stage of recovery, he rode on horseback through the woods, accompanied by Patsy, without venturing to any place where they might encounter other people.

As time fell out of sync for those many weeks, his correspondence stalled, though he had the presence of mind, two weeks after burying his wife, to address the present governor on an outstanding matter of legal liability dating to his own governorship. Nearly two more weeks went by before he was able to write to his late wife's half sister with assurances that Patsy and Polly were coping. As for himself, the future could not be salvaged: "All my plans of comfort and happiness reversed by a single event and nothing answering in prospect before me but a gloom unbrightened with one cheerful expectation." His daughters, at best, were "temporary abstractions from wretchedness," allowing him to imagine only that "there is one angel at least who views these attentions with pleasure and wishes continuance of them." Patty was now an angel.[39]

He had not experienced anything remotely comparable since the death of Dabney Carr, forced to adapt to a world he couldn't control. As he had when his closest friend died too young, Jefferson gave much consideration to what he wanted inscribed in the stone that marked his wife's grave. In the end, between the lines indicating date of birth and date of death, it reads: TORN FROM HIM BY DEATH. *Torn.* A violent image from an anguished man prone to debilitating headaches, who wrote so often and elusively of "tranquil felicity," "tranquil happiness," "tranquil pleasures," "tranquil joys," and "tranquil amusements" but found the desired state of peace and tranquility woefully impermanent. Below her date of death are the words THIS MONUMENT OF HIS LOVE IS INSCRIBED; below that, in Greek, are lines from the *Iliad* about a companionship that can never be lost to remembrance. Jefferson went further than most of his contemporaries in materially preserving the memory of his marriage.[40]

That impulse, along with the impermanence of human connections, is present in the exquisite keepsake found by his one surviving daughter in the private drawer beside his bed at the close of his own life more than four decades later. The paper is written in two hands—the wife's, then the husband's—on a scrap of ordinary paper, four and a half inches square, its creases and folds indicating that it was repeatedly consulted over the years. Tucked inside was a lock of Patty's hair as well. The lovers' message begins: "Time wastes too fast: every letter I trace tells me with what rapidity life follows my pen. the days and hours of it are flying over our heads like clouds of windy day never to return." The surviving spouse added to the sentiment, spelling out the certainty of their parting: "And every time I kiss thy hand to bid adieu, every absence which follows it are preludes to that eternal separation which we are shortly to make!" She knew. They knew. It is horrible to imagine what the waiting must have been like.

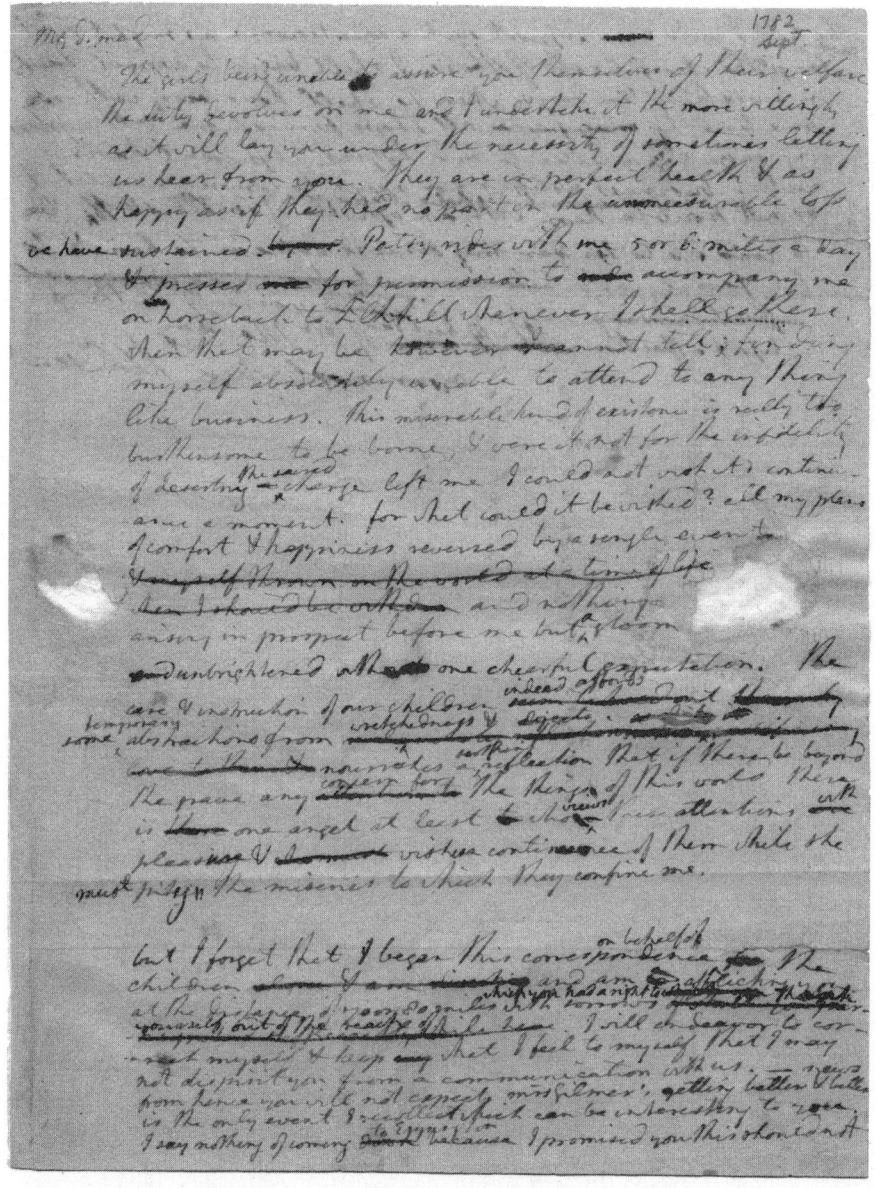

Figure 9. "This miserable kind of existence is really too burthensome to be borne... all my plans for comfort & happiness reversed by a single event." Letter, Jefferson to Elizabeth Wayles Eppes, October 3[?], 1782, with cross-outs and interlining. The bereaved husband pours his heart out to his late wife's half sister. (Courtesy Massachusetts Historical Society)

The lines are from Laurence Sterne's *Tristram Shandy*. They appear near the end of a book that is without order or a linear plotline, a semiserious stream-of-consciousness tale of longing. The passage chosen as a deathbed adieu was cribbed from Jefferson's Literary Commonplace Book. While the entry was undated, it is reliably estimated to have been written in the months or year after the two were married, around the same time as the Ossian entries. How close to death she was when she and he copied out their final statement of love and commitment is not knowable, but it's the only significant text (household accounts don't qualify) in which Patty's handwriting has been preserved. None of the correspondence husband and wife exchanged exists now. It is enough to know that theirs was an eighteenth-century tale that countless others are known to have experienced. After reverie came ruin.[41]

Everything points to a marriage marked by passion. Love is about shared identities and shared interests, as well as admiration for a partner's character and personal charms. Trust is a constant requirement in human relations, but especially so between spouses. The emotional breakdown Jefferson suffered upon her death can only be evidence of how much Patty meant to him, and he to her. But these features are universals, and can be understood only in the context of the world they lived in.

A planter's wife fully expected to spend the greater part of her marriage pregnant. Her power, given by Nature, was reproduction and nurture. In all other respects, she was not meant to stand up to her husband and deny him his "rights." Though her husband was a difficult man, daughter Patsy Jefferson would bear twelve children between the years 1791 and 1818, that is, from age nineteen to forty-five. She accepted her lot as a breeder of the next generation, even after having witnessed her young mother's decline, almost up to "the closing scene," at an impressionable time in her own life. She was dutiful, dependent, traditional, and, as it turned out, a survivor.

The literature available to a Southern woman typically stressed self-regard and the dictate that she fashion herself so as to thrive as a fit companion to her husband. She should bend when necessary for the sake of domestic harmony. It was generally assumed, objectionable though it sounds today, that when a husband sought company elsewhere, his wife was in some measure responsible. The idea that a woman might wish to avoid becoming a mortality statistic was repudiated in most published literature. Women who remained single were thought selfish and destined for a life of loneliness. Motherhood and female virtue—the "soft and tender passions"—were synonymous.

Even without childbirth complications, acceptance was already part of this age of untreatable pathologies, and mourning was a facet of every life. "Death is deaf to love," wrote the early-eighteenth-century English minister and poet Isaac Watts. What, then, should be made of Jefferson's apparent refusal to take measures to safeguard his wife's health? Who is to judge him for observing her unsteady constitution, yet failing to curtail his procreative activity? It is quite likely that he wanted to keep trying for sons; but was that the prime motivator?

It would have been unusual for an elite Virginia husband to sacrifice a lineage at the altar of conjugal happiness, though it is also possible that he and Patty did try to time her pregnancies, avoiding contact during fertile times of the month as some were doing in the last quarter of their century. Regardless, Jefferson gambled with her life.

"The suspense under which I am is too terrible to be endured," he'd said to Patty's relations in the fall of 1775, when she had failed to write in a timely way during a stint in Philadelphia. "If any thing has happened, for god's sake let me know it." Seven years later, the husband who felt such panic when she was not even pregnant may well have been left feeling extreme guilt. His broken-heartedness in the fall of 1782 is explainable: had he chosen to practice withdrawal when satisfying the lust he felt—Adam Smith's "most furious of all the passions"—he might have protected her life. In theory, at least, he understood that. Of course, we cannot know what Patty's thoughts were when they spoke of childbearing. Did she express caution, or did she encourage him? Either way, guilt piled on the reality of his loss seems a plausible explanation for the depth of his grief.

Four years later, Jefferson expressed a cavalier attitude toward pregnancy when writing in a jocular way to John and Abigail Adams's son-in-law, shortly after he and their daughter Nabby had wed. To the new husband, Jefferson ended a letter that contained language hinting at ongoing romantic "follies" of his own in Paris. He was hopeful, he said, that Nabby was "very sick, otherwise I would observe that is high time." He was referring, of course, to morning sickness.

Studies have shown that for most wives of this era, fertility and family building figured in the image they had of themselves. Often, their friends took part in the birthing process, and it was common for married women to comment on the state of health of one of the sisterhood when discussing how they rebounded from childbirth. To be "fruitful" was to be doing right. While something like thirty percent of women died before the age of forty-five, stoicism (or was it perhaps indoctrination?)

was an attitude widely shared by Southern women of childbearing years. Thomas Jefferson was not one to imagine anything different.[42]

Word spread. The hopelessness of Patty's condition had to have been known for some time, based on sentiments Edmund Randolph expressed to James Madison two weeks after her passing: "Mrs. Jefferson has at last shaken off her tormenting pains by yielding to them, and has left our friend inconsolable." Randolph and Madison, close in age, had become fast friends in Congress the year before. This letter was sent from Richmond, which meant that Jefferson's extreme reaction had escaped the mountain, probably by way of an attending physician, or the clergyman who spoke at her funeral. Randolph's language precisely matches the information Patsy much later passed on to her children. "I ever thought him to rank domestic happiness in the first class of the chief good," Randolph told Madison, "but I scarcely supposed, that his grief would be so violent, as to justify the circulating report, of his swooning away, whenever he sees his children."[43]

Figure 10. Engraving of Maria Cosway, by Luigi Schiavonetti, 1791, after a 1785 portrait by Richard Cosway. Jefferson romantically pursued the married Anglo-Italian artist in Paris in 1786. (Courtesy Royal Academy of Arts, London)

CHAPTER 6

"Gazing Like a Lover at His Mistress"
French Women

THE WIDOWER EMERGED FROM his self-imposed isolation at the urging of his friends Randolph and Madison. They valued his legal mind and wished for his return to public life. Conditions were improved markedly when Richmond rescinded the charges earlier made with regard to Governor Jefferson's negligence at the time of Arnold's invasion, restating "in the strongest manner . . . Mr. Jefferson's ability, rectitude and integrity, as Chief Magistrate of this Commonwealth."

He no longer "stood arraigned for treasons of the heart," as he dramatized in the letter to the young Monroe. So he could not employ the rationale he'd often turned to, his ailing wife's condition, when he'd refused to join diplomats Adams and Franklin in France. He agreed to join them now, two and a half months after the loss of his wife: Monticello held only memories of a life that had ended. The Confederation Congress, successor to the Second Continental Congress, was a central government lacking either an executive or a judicial branch, but it at least supported a secretary of foreign affairs. Without objection, Congress renewed Jefferson's dormant appointment as peace commissioner.

Prior to Patty's death, he had convinced himself that he was going to abandon politics forever. But, as he wrote a few years later to a Virginia-bred woman who had moved away, "all the favors of fortune have been embittered by domestic losses. Of six children I have lost four, and finally their mother. This happened too in the moment when I had retired from all public business, determined to enjoy the remainder of life in the bosom of my family." Bred to public service, he accepted the guidance of friends who insisted that at this moment, there was no better place for him.[1]

On to Philadelphia once more, where he shared accommodations with Madison. Discretion was essential in the event that their future correspondence fell into the wrong hands, so the two worked out a system of ciphers.[2] The plan was for Jefferson to proceed to France, with daughter Patsy as his main companion on the voyage. The younger daughters, Maria (Polly) and baby Lucy, would stay with their maternal relations until he called for them. Jefferson was no less reluctant to be abandoning Monticello and its library, with already more than twenty-six hundred volumes.

It was fifteen months since Cornwallis's surrender. As Jefferson was ready to set sail, word arrived that the Treaty of Paris had at last been signed, securing British recognition of American independence. Initially, Congress determined that he should still join the American contingent in Paris. But as weather moved in and the father-daughter adventurers found themselves stuck in port, Congress reversed itself. Await further instructions, it said.

He renewed his contacts in Richmond, and in early June 1783, two years (almost to the day) since his precipitous departure from the governorship, the General Assembly, reconstituted as Senate and House of Delegates (the former House of Burgesses), elected him to Congress. He had recently turned forty. Paris would have to wait.

WIDOWER AT WORK

From November 1783 through May 1784, Jefferson was given a lead role in several enterprises. He superintended ratification of the Treaty of Paris, which, despite its importance, had to await a quorum in an inconstant, somewhat aimless legislature that alternated between Annapolis and Philadelphia. "Our body was little numerous, but very contentious," he reflected years later. He argued decisively for a national coinage system based on the Spanish dollar, given the simplicity of its decimal standard; in this, he went up against the nation's senior financier, Robert Morris, whose system was convoluted. The capacious mind of Jefferson prevailed.[3]

The most critical work he did in the postwar Congress concerned the organization of the massive amount of territory Great Britain acknowledged, at least on paper, as subject to the new national government. Jefferson was named to head the committee recommending the means to govern the Northwest Territory, with an eye toward the eventual incorporation of new states into the Union. He influenced his native state's cession of distant and unsettled lands (extending to the Mississippi), setting forth the 1784 Land Ordinance, an important step in establishing a workable means of preparing newly settled areas north of the Ohio River for statehood, with fixed boundaries agreed upon in advance and with slavery prohibited. Owing to the existing states' competing claims and unresolved separatist movements, the final ordinance would not be codified until 1787.[4]

These activities further advanced Jefferson's stature as a national figure. His colleagues were all aware of his heartfelt personal tragedy—his manner showed it as he spoke of his loss. One testament to his unsettled emotional state comes by way of a Dutch observer in Congress, who wrote that "his mind, accustomed to the unalloyed pleasure of a lovable wife, was impervious since her loss to the feeble attractions of common society." The widower came across as "cool and reserved," not outwardly friendly (something akin to shyness). However, one didn't require much time to recover from the mistaken first impression and find him attentive and obliging, brimming with information and eager to learn from conversation.[5]

Jefferson left his two youngest daughters with his late wife's sister and her family and settled Patsy in a good Philadelphia home while he traveled on business. To the eleven-year-old, under the constant care of a tutor, he wrote from Annapolis in December 1783, a letter worth noting for its rigorous approach to parenting, a policy he stuck with throughout her teen years. In setting up a weekly schedule, he demanded she keep him updated on all she read and the music she played:

> from 8. to 10 o'clock practice music.
> from 10. to 1. dance one day and draw another.
> from 1. to 2. draw on the day you dance, and write a letter next day.
> from 3. to 4. read French.
> from 4. to 5. exercise yourself in music.
> from 5. till bedtime read English, write, &c.

Two weeks after writing this letter, Jefferson found himself addressing a tender subject with his daughter: death writ large. In some way, not made clear, Patsy had either heard or gotten into her head that the apocalypse would come to pass at a not distant date. "I hope you will have good sense enough to disregard those foolish predictions that the world is to be at an end soon," her father wrote back. "The almighty has never made known to anybody at what time he created it, nor will he tell anybody when he means to put an end to it." (The foregoing is a good example of Jefferson's wry wit.) He advised that the best preparation, if the world really *was* to end, was to be always on one's best behavior. Her own death, he wrote assuredly, was "a much more certain event" than the possibility of all life being destroyed at once.

Having required of his daughter that she save all of his letters as permanent reminders of the expectations he placed upon her, he cautioned that she had already failed to comply in several particulars. "I do not wish you to be gayly clothed at this time of life," he said, each of his strictures applying to the proper comportment of a female: "Nothing is so disgusting to our sex as a want of cleanliness and delicacy in yours." Neatness mattered. His aim was to develop a sense of shame in her—whether or not the planet was fated to explode within her lifetime.[6]

Father and daughter saw each other only irregularly during the period when Congress sat. That changed when he answered the call to replace Treaty of Paris signatory John Jay and join Franklin and Adams in France. Father and daughter were in close quarters for nineteen summery days, a quick and unusually trouble-free passage aboard a vessel called the *Ceres*, which had made only one previous transit. It was not entirely a matter of luck, either. Jefferson took care not to risk their lives on a ship's maiden voyage or on one with too much history and too many possibilities of things going wrong. The day they docked in England, Patsy had a fever. It passed, and they crossed into France. Their coach arrived in Paris on August 6, 1784.[7]

"DREAMS AND SPECULATIONS"

During his five years in Europe, the shy-on-first-meeting Virginia gentleman was decidedly more social than he'd been before, though his long sojourn began with colds and agues. He called this time of uncertain health, of adjustment to a new environment, a "seasoning." He was finally relieved of it by the more regular appearance of the sun—"my almighty physician," he wrote to James Monroe.[8]

Once he'd immersed himself in the society of the liberal nobility and improved his admittedly imperfect facility for spoken French, he became privy to more detailed conversations where his input was sought after. He became a connoisseur of wines and visited vineyards not just in France, but in Germany and Italy as well. He complained about the insufficient funds allotted by the government that had dispatched him, but he made do. The student of Epicurus wanted to entertain his—that is, America's—French friends.

He was delighted to see his Ossian-loving friend the Marquis de Chastellux. Through Dr. Franklin he met the learned *salonnières*, women who entertained the literati and who were accomplished in their own right. In 1785, once Franklin had returned to Philadelphia and John Adams had taken up his post in London, Jefferson was left in charge of U.S. diplomacy with the French. By all accounts, he came alive in Paris. Parisians understood beauty. He wanted to be of them, to live in a certain style—not ostentatious, but à la mode. "I had rather be ruined in my fortune, than in their esteem," he told Monroe.⁹

One of those he met through Franklin, the Comtesse d'Houdetot, stood out, though she lived at a greater distance and Jefferson saw less of her than he did several others. He wrote to Abigail Adams of a fruitful visit to her country seat at Sannois, which "opened a door of admission" to her impressive circle. The Comtesse had been described by Jean-Jacques Rousseau in his *Confessions* as "the first and only love in all my life." Thirty years younger at the time Rousseau became so enraptured, she was now disfigured by smallpox and "not in the least beautiful"; but she possessed "a very natural and very pleasant wit" and was so generous and sweet-tempered that she became a mainstay among the key figures of the French Enlightenment. The Comtesse d'Houdetot took a special interest in America, had studied its plants and trees, and maintained a regular correspondence with Jefferson. In her letters to him, she invariably praised his country, convinced that its virtues mirrored those of Washington, Franklin ("he will never leave my mind or my heart"), and Jefferson, whose amiable character she termed "sage et humain" (wise and humane).¹⁰

M. et Mme de Corny were the couple he saw most regularly. The husband, Louis-Éthis de Corny, was a career soldier and, like Chastellux, had been present at the decisive Battle of Yorktown along with Major General Lafayette. In 1785, Corny became an adviser to the king and assisted Jefferson in arranging for the purchase of American grain. But it was Madame de Corny whom Jefferson bonded with most. Gilbert Chinard, the French scholar known for his studies of Jefferson's intimate friendships in France, described their relationship: "Young, pretty, witty, and married to a husband much older than herself, she enjoyed Jefferson's company, took with him many walks in the Bois de Boulogne and perhaps, secretly, found him too scrupulously polite." Reading backward, there's a letter she wrote just after Jefferson was elected president, a dozen years after she had last set eyes on him, in reply to a lost letter from him, and it suggests how close they were at one time: "Since you have awakened all my feelings of friendship for you," she wrote, "for pity's sake write to me. It provides an interest to spread through my life." And then, "it is no longer permitted for you to abandon a correspondence that you yourself have renewed. Nothing wears down friendship like alternating hope and abandon." She alludes to his frequent reflections on Monticello while in Paris and even hints at her willingness to trade Napoleonic France for a new life in the United States, if her old friend would only help facilitate it.

Madame de Corny, who was especially fond of Jefferson's daughters, held back little when she communicated with him. In a letter of 1789, after remarking on Lafayette's levelheadedness amid the turmoil of the unfolding French Revolution, she could not restrain herself, even then, from weighing in on what she considered Rousseau's questionable depiction of the Comtesse d'Houdetot. Yet Mme de Corny was not the most gossipy of Jefferson's French acquaintances—that title goes to Madame Sophie de Tott, an impoverished artist of Greek extraction and protégée of Adrienne-Catherine de Noailles, Comtesse de Tessé. It seems the effusive Tott especially enjoyed communicating scandalous information about men's and women's private lives. In 1786 and 1787, Jefferson sent her books he thought she'd like, including that of her "countryman" Homer, in response to which she unreservedly flattered him: "how proud I would be if I could believe that I deserved for a moment this interest from a man such as You!"

Though she wrote in French and Jefferson responded in English, his tone was comparable to hers: "That your road, through life, may be covered with roses, is the sincere prayer of him who has the honour to mingle his Adieus with sentiments of the most affectionate esteem and respect." In a long, flirtatious letter he wrote while traveling in the south of France, he fantasized that she was by his side, admiring the scenes of Marseilles along with him: "You have been in Paris and it's neighborhood, constantly since I had the pleasure of seeing you there: yet I declare you have been with me above half my journey. I could repeat to you long conversations, word for word, and on a variety of subjects."

This letter is unusually novelistic and overflowing in sentiment. He deliberately imitates Laurence Sterne's *A Sentimental Journey*: "A traveller, sais I, retired at night to his chamber in an Inn, all his effects contained in a single trunk, all his cares circumscribed by the walls of his apartment, unknown to all, unheeded, and undisturbed, writes, reads, thinks, sleeps, just in the moments when nature and the movements of his body and mind require."

Like Sterne, but in his own voice, he elaborates:

> I should go on, Madam, detailing to you my dreams and speculations; but that my present situation is most unfriendly to speculation. Four thousand three hundred and fifty market-women (I have counted them one by one) brawling, squabbling, and jabbering Patois, three hundred asses braying and bewailing to each other, and to the world, their cruel oppressions, four files of mule-carts passing in constant succession, with as many bells to every mule as can be hung about him, all this in the street under my window, and the weather too hot to shut it. Judge whether in such a situation it is easy to hang one's ideas together.

In the midst of all this, he starts one sentence, "The plan of my journey, as well as of my life, being to take things by the smooth handle . . ." Here is a claim that bears little resemblance to Jefferson's familiar pattern of striving, at all costs, to micromanage his environment, to write down every minor expense, record daily temperatures and weather conditions, and list in his "Summary Journal of Letters" every piece of mail sent and received. He did so in France, too.[11]

Letters to Patsy during this period are not comparable, not playful in the least. They are as demanding as when she was in Philadelphia. He makes strict demands on her time and occupation, with chastisement when, for instance, she wished an advance on her allowance to purchase a garment the same week she and her father were to dine with the Marquis de Lafayette: "This is a departure from that rule which I wish to see you governed by, thro' your whole life," he insisted, "of never buying anything which you have not money in your pocket to pay for." This was a clear case of "Do as I say, not as I do."

The "outer" Jefferson was levelheaded. He projected a habit of chasteness and frugality that his sensualist mode belied. In truth, there was no "smooth handle" in the life of the migraine-prone bibliophile who had manic bursts of mental energy and a healthy libido. Yet on his European travels, he certainly seemed open to new experiences. When he was invited to sup at the exquisite Château Chaville of M. et Mme de Tessé, where he communed with a devoted, impressionable Mme de Tott, he opened up to something more than conventional politesse.

As usual with Jefferson, though, the written record contains as many disguises as revelations. One wonders how well Sophie de Tott understood the imagery he offered in his richly adorned letters, and whether sparks flew at all. Chinard does not suggest anything unusual in his relations with the unmarried Greek, and

Brodie ignores her completely; but the twenty-seven-year-old was unabashed, to say the least, exposing her breast for an erotic portrait in 1785 by the successful, scandal-prone painter Élisabeth Vigée Le Brun, in which the sitter is shown with lips parted.[12]

Château Chaville was near Versailles. Mme de Tessé, the aunt of Lafayette's wife, was a woman of enlarged mind who maintained an intellectually and politically progressive salon. In her, the American minister found extraordinary generosity and a kindred spirit. To her, he was capable of writing of emotion, as in the memorable opening to a letter he penned from Nîmes, giving testament to his adoration of great architecture:

> Here I am, Madam, gazing whole hours at the Maison quarrée, like a lover at his mistress ... This is the second time I have been in love since I left Paris. The first was with a Diana at the Chateau de Laye Epinaye in the Beaujolois [near Lyon], a delicious morsel of sculpture, by Michael Angelo Slodtz. This, you will say, was in rule, to fall in love with a fine woman: but, with a house! It is out of all precedent! No, madam, it is not without a precedent in my own history.

Jefferson was introduced to her by the Marquis de Lafayette himself. She was a year and a half older than Jefferson and adored nature as he did. In his retirement, the two of them were still exchanging seeds and cuttings to plant in their respective gardens.[13]

Of special interest, too, is Louis Alexandre, duc de La Rochefoucauld, a man in his mid-fifties whose very young wife, the duchesse Rosalie, became the lover (with La Rochefoucauld's full knowledge) of Jefferson's "adoptive son," as he himself referred to his loyal, hardworking, and ever charming personal secretary, William Short. Lafayette made appearances at the Hôtel de La Rochefoucauld and was still reminiscing with Jefferson two decades later. Mourning the death of Mme de Tessé, the marquis wrote: "You Remember our Happy Hours, and Animated Conversations at Chaville—How far from us those times, and those of the venerable Hôtel de La Rochefoucauld!"[14]

Many of his French friends came into Jefferson's life by way of the vivacious Dr. Franklin and constituted a lively crowd. Beyond their penchant for entertaining, they showed him tremendous warmth. And yet, in the company of elite men and women who married into wealth, took lovers, and were open about all such matters, Jefferson found himself at something of an impasse. He came from a place where women of elite backgrounds were expected to defer to their husbands, a place where sexual standards always favored men's interests. The outspokenness of French women, in that sense, disturbed him. Virginia women certainly did not assert their sexual rights as French women did; in a Virginia context, male sexual conquests were understandable, but a sexually active woman was looked upon as dissolute. In "Of Polygamy and Divorce," while acknowledging that he understood the female mind but little, David Hume averred that men as tyrants were responsible for undoing "that nearness of rank, not to say equality, which nature has established between the sexes." Jefferson loved the French, but he could never import their social conventions as he did their cuisine and wines.[15]

One of the ways he dealt with his inability to treat women and men on an equal basis was to imbue his letters to women with a kind of wink-wink humor, what the historian Maurizio Valsania terms a "slightly naughty" affectation—this is what his playful letters to Mesdames de Tott and Tessé reveal. He found an outlet by contending with women lightheartedly. He had a much harder time doing so with Abigail Adams, whose directness and sternness he was obliged to respect and whose incontrovertible feminism did not leave him much of an opening.[16]

What the modern reader must understand is that the so-called "culture of sensibility" that many associate with the novels of Jane Austen placed conjugal happiness within reach. Such writings lavished attention on the delicacy of manners in gentry families, but were written to entertain and not to preach. Though they addressed conventions, they did not place the kinds of limits on female independence or pursuit of pleasure that surface readings might suggest. Nor did the language of sensibility that permeated Jefferson's script, especially in letters to women, and especially in what he wrote from France, dissociate emotion from physicality or even the sexual impulse. The language of sensibility was, indeed, a bodily language, especially among the French, whose philosophers of medicine (their titles were well known to Jefferson) regarded the brain as a sexual organ and sensibility's inner workings (stopping short of Freud) as inherently sexual. The tone carried by Jefferson's witty expressions in his letters to women cannot be read in any other way. Every sensitive soul knew passion.[17]

In his world, it was not unknown for a wealthy widower of sixty to marry a woman barely twenty. He does not appear to have ever asked himself whether this practice in some way violated the woman's rights. It was a custom he simply accepted. Though far distant from Monticello, he remained indelibly attached to the Virginia planter tradition, convinced that American youths sent to France to experience an alternate worldview would learn the wrong things. They would be poisoned by the lax rules that prevailed with regard to sex and marriage, unable to appreciate female chastity once they'd sailed home.

It is not clear whether Jefferson was at all reflecting his own premarital angst. He was trying to come across as prudent, not prudish, and he was saying less than he could have were he to be completely honest. He is not prepared to interrogate social conditions in the dysfunctional state of Virginia, treating French elites less charitably than his fellows who experimented sexually with enslaved women. Otherwise—and unless he paid visits to white prostitutes in Williamsburg and Philadelphia—one would have to believe that Jefferson was sexually inexperienced when he married Patty, and that his friend Madison, unmarried until the age of forty-one, was a virgin when he tied the knot with the widowed mother Dolley Payne Todd. Neither of these conjectures would appear credible.

In his letter to an older Italian who had spent time in Virginia, Jefferson wrote with unconvincing primness of his aversion to the French manner: "Intrigues of love occupy the younger, and those of ambition the more elderly part of the great. Conjugal love having no existence among them, domestic happiness, of which that is the basis, is utterly unknown." Here he is claiming for himself a strength of moral character that his later admission in the Walker affair effectively belies, in which case one may assume that he internalized his "ten years of unchequered happiness" with Patty as the "real" Jefferson.

His language is explicit, though. It is "female intrigue" that he professes to fear in this scenario, which he couples with the allure of extravagant living, aristocratic manners, and monarchy. Two weeks after dispatching the letter to his Italian friend, in a similar frame of mind, Jefferson issued an injunction to John Banister Jr., the son and namesake of a distinguished Virginia friend. The youth had been sent to France for his health, for it was then thought that an ocean voyage could restore a sickly young person. In this paternalistic letter, Jefferson strongly recommends that Banister continue his studies back home at the College of William and Mary (he mentions George Wythe by name), rather than lose in Europe all that stands to make a man happy as he advances in life. The wary surrogate parent warns that the allure of "European luxury and dissipation" is too strong a temptation for any American youth, and that if Jack Banister chose incorrectly, he would return home with "a contempt for the simplicity of his own country." By the end of the long letter, Jefferson admits to having penned a sermon. Yet he does not apologize for leaning so heavily on young Jack, who, despite his precarious health, had given Jefferson the impression that he was very much attracted to the French ladies.

In another section of the same lecture, Jefferson's hyperbole magnifies with his claim that "the lovely equality which the poor enjoys with the rich" in Virginia does not exist abroad (it did not exist in Virginia either); that a suggestible youth "forms foreign friendships which will never be useful to him" (an indefensible argument); and that the same youth "is led by the strongest of all the human passions into a spirit for female intrigue destructive of his own and others happiness, or a passion for whores destructive of his health, and in both cases learns to consider fidelity to the marriage bed as an ungentlemanly practice and inconsistent with happiness." This last is where the letter has been aiming all along.

Jefferson must have thought a good deal about this subject, because after only a year in France he is already presuming that once back on American soil, a corrupted Jack Banister would discover to his chagrin that "he recollects the voluptuary dress and arts of the European women and pities and despises the chaste affections and simplicity of those of his own country." Annette Gordon-Reed and Peter S. Onuf argue even more forcefully that as Jefferson's fondness for the French and their culture rubbed up against his Virginia leanings, he did more than project an inner conflict. Perhaps his avowed love for the French was either a "sham" or a "delusion," they write, because why else would he fix upon the "dissolute pleasures of French society" as a dangerous kind of allure for a susceptible visitor from abroad?[18]

Jefferson takes effort to interpret. He was acquiring an expensive taste in wines and purchasing superior fabric for his female family and friends in Virginia. So, even if Jack was sufficiently familiar with Jefferson's manner to recognize his language as literary license, we still have to accept that Jefferson's strange preoccupation with European manners was not a temporary phenomenon, but something of an ingrained system. History wrongly assumes a sturdy "revolutionariness" in Thomas Jefferson, based on his political writings. Seeing moral decay in the relaxation of boundaries between men's and women's lives marks a level of fear in him that on occasion rises to a state of panic.

There is yet another lesson to draw here. Whether or not he could ever have admitted it, Jefferson had something in common with the dukes and duchesses, marquis and marquises. On his side of the Atlantic, men of privilege made their own rules. He himself commanded an inherited workforce at Monticello, where he held court. No moral constraint or law could penetrate his remote, self-constituted world. He was king of his mountain.

Having bonded with the liberal French aristocracy in modes unrelated to gender roles, Jefferson would have to rationalize the deprivation these same people were forced to endure in the tumult that was coming in 1789. Biding his time as the French Revolution went through painful gyrations, he was to show less compassion for the victims than he perhaps ought to have; the extant record does not reveal him mourning the premature deaths of his former companions in any significant way. In pronouncements as a president and ex-president, while repeating his optimism that educable voters would make sound choices in selecting candidates for office, he could never dislodge the recurring fear that attraction to aristocracy and monarchy was a latent virus that had yet to be eliminated from American minds.

Knowing these things about him, we must ask: When does Jefferson ever appear to judge himself? Does he ever admit to have gone too far in his attachment to a theory? One is hard-pressed to isolate an instance of any significance in which he does so.

MARIA HADFIELD COSWAY

In Jefferson biography, the second half of 1786 is generally depicted as a "romantic interlude," when the cerebral single parent fell for a beautiful young Anglo-Italian artist. It used to be thought that he quickly got over her and returned, desexualized, to his important diplomatic duties. Once Fawn Brodie published her bestselling biography in 1974, since bolstered by the DNA revelation of 1998, all that changed; and a suspicion lingers that it was the fourteen-year-old Sally Hemings who turned his head and made him forget the lovely, highly successful Englishwoman whose Italian far exceeded any facility with her father's native tongue. What's missing is the detail needed to fill in the blanks regarding Maria Cosway's world, that explains her "availability," if the word can be set down without too much suggestiveness. The historical record up to now has not shown much nuance in depicting her personality or speculating about what she might have meant to Thomas Jefferson.

Maria Luisa Caterina Cecilia Hadfield Cosway (1760–1838) entered Jefferson's life in August 1786, introduced, along with her husband, by the Connecticut artist John Trumbull. She was twenty-six, close in age to Sophie de Tott. Jefferson was forty-three. Born near Florence to a successful English innkeeper and an Italian mother, she was raised Catholic and had plans to abandon a career and take her vows, were it not for her precocious talent as a painter. At only eighteen, she was elected to the Florentine Academy of Drawing, arriving in London the following year. At twenty-one, Maria Hadfield was married to the well-connected artist Richard Cosway. In addition to her celebrity as an artist (she exhibited at the Louvre), she played the harp quite well. The practiced violinist Jefferson talked music with her, as well as architecture and sculpture. Nor should it be lost on the reader that he knew enough Italian to make an impression.

No record exists of their having touched on the subjects of race or slavery, yet prior to her arrival in Paris, Maria had become intimately associated with a West African named Quobna Ottobah Cugoano. Formerly enslaved in the Caribbean, he was three years her elder and resided with the Cosways in their London home. Ostensibly employed as their household servant, "John Stuart," as he was by then known, fared quite differently than did any free Black man in America. He'd received an education in England before getting involved in antislavery advocacy. In 1787, during his time with the Cosways, he published *Thoughts and Sentiments on the Evil and Wicked Traffic of the Slavery and Commerce of the Human Species*, which was considered radical at the time. Richard and Maria Cosway introduced Cugoano to British royalty and facilitated his work with leaders of the abolition movement; in 1786, he played a key role in rescuing a Black man who was about to be transported to the West Indies. Cugoano was in fact the first Black writer in the English language to assert that the enslaved had not just the right, but also the moral duty, to resist their enslavers.[19]

Maria Cosway was clearly more than a pretty face. The celebrated artist had depth, and she had admirers besides the accomplished widower from America. Jefferson would have been aware of her reputation when he met her. Fawn Brodie describes Maria as "languorously feminine..., with luminous blue eyes, exquisite skin, and a halo of golden curls." She did not appear at all suited to her husband of five years. Richard Cosway, although a renowned portrait painter and a sought-after miniaturist, was by all accounts odd (*outré*, to use a borrowed French word), and in his dress and bearing, decidedly eccentric. Theirs was not in the least a love match, and Richard was not anyone's idea of a good husband.

Jefferson's infatuation with Maria Cosway is fairly well known and has even been chronicled in modern cinema.[20] But scant attention has been given to Richard Cosway's position in the art world and the nature of the marriage beyond vague suppositions about the husband's extramarital dalliances, his possible bisexuality, and his wife's later choice to live apart from him. At their residence in London, the Cosways were something of a power couple throughout the decade of the 1780s.

The bulk of Jefferson scholarship misses the social chatter: everyone in the art world knew about Richard, and many had thoughts about Maria, too.

She was not without agency. I would suggest that her independence ultimately helped convince Jefferson to drop any fantasy he had of a longer-term romance. Her Catholicism was another barrier to deeper affinity, yet the two appear to have had a spiritual connection in their shared appreciation for beauty in nature and in architecture. It was this same quality that brought Jefferson closer to the well-established French women whose animated salons he visited. If he was not conventionally handsome, he possessed a certain near-feminine quality that put women at ease. His studies of the natural world served him well; he entertained Mme de Tessé at length in this regard. His love of the arts gave him a bearing unlike that of the more businesslike husbands of these elite Europeans.

Whether or not it was predominantly in the realm of the physical, something about Maria Cosway allowed him to fantasize easily. In reflecting on Monticello's relative isolation and its architect's enduring passion to establish a university within its view, it adds interest to know that in her later years, the incompletely understood Maria settled into a convent in northern Italy, where she founded a college for promising girls. Correspondence within European art circles and among gentlemen collectors casts the sexuality of Maria in a somewhat different light than she has been shown in most scholarship. The woman who appealed to Thomas Jefferson did not flaunt her sex so much as her husband sexualized her for his own ill-defined ends.[21]

Richard Cosway (1742–1821) was born in the southwest of England a few months before Jefferson. Given opportunity through the efforts of his schoolteacher father, he attended the Society of Arts in London. He was seen as a man on the make, finding his first patrons in a pair of Italian émigrés around the time Jefferson was busy establishing himself in Williamsburg. According to a scholar who has studied Parisian art circles, in the 1760s, Richard "was not above pandering to the demand for mildly erotic subjects." He happily painted pornographic lids on snuff boxes for aristocrats.

The prominent German painter Johan Zoffany, who taught Maria Hadfield in Italy, encountered Richard often. He subtly mocked the peculiar, self-important Cosway by depicting him awkwardly in a 1773 group portrait of members of the Royal Academy; and in a letter to the established art collector Charles Townley, Zoffany called out the upstart miniaturist's "rakish boasting." Cosway is quoted as saying, "If the Italian women fuck as well in Italy as they do here, you must be happy indeed—I am such a zealot for them that I'll be damned if I ever fuck an English woman again." While the bohemian art world has long been known for its excesses and irregularities, it is hard to find a sympathetic portrait of the offbeat yet gifted Richard Cosway.[22]

In the late 1770s, when her mother took her to London, Maria Hadfield found a friend in the collector Townley, who introduced the young artist around. Through Townley, she met Francesco Bartolozzi, one of the Italians who had taken an interest in Richard Cosway at a time when he was still obscure. A foppish dresser and known flirt, Richard was never able to exhibit the grace of his social betters, even as he purchased the well-appointed home where, after their 1781 marriage, he and Maria maintained an elegant lifestyle. In 1785, the year before he and his wife met Jefferson in Paris, Richard was lauded by a royal patron, the Prince of Wales. As his career reached its high point, his wife's independent career profited in turn.[23]

The reason they came to Paris in 1786 was Richard's commission to paint portraits of family members of the duc d'Orléans. He evidently did not mind that his wife went off with the American minister on private excursions along the Seine during September. She and Jefferson visited art museums, inspected Parisian architecture, and sought inspiration in the natural landscape outside the city center. They had time to themselves in romantic vistas, and in one instance that he immediately regretted, Jefferson attempted an act of physical prowess, stumbled, and fractured his right wrist. He admitted to John Adams's London-based son-in-law that the painful injury was the result of "one of those follies from which good cannot come, but ill may." Poorly set by the French physicians who attended him, the wrist would cause trouble for the habitual writer for many months and reemerge as an issue in later years.[24]

The subsequent correspondence between Jefferson and Mrs. Cosway is laden with fond, even titillating, references to the days they spent together, the sum of which still leaves uncertain how much sex their feelings led to. But this much is known: the widower related to her in detail his life with Patty on their mountaintop seat that he invariably described in exalted language. By narrating the sorrows he'd endured after his wife's death, he clearly conveyed the impression that he was open to intimacy with the young beauty whose husband was insufficiently attentive and who, at the start of their marriage, out of arrogance, sought to discourage her from painting for commercial purposes. She owed Richard her lifestyle—but not enough to surrender her freedom. In fact, back in London after she and Jefferson parted, Maria is alleged to have become the lover of a man who was nearly the same age as Jefferson, and whose position at Court was "Master of the King's Musick." Jefferson fell for her in Paris. How hard he fell remains open to conjecture.²⁵

When he met the Cosways, Jefferson had had four years in which to mourn Patty's loss. An attraction to married (sexually experienced) women had preceded his married life, a fact that would seem relevant here. If something stood in the way of consummation during the first two months of their acquaintance, it would not have been a sense of fidelity to her unloved husband on Maria's part. To make things even clearer, the Cosways' marriage had been deftly engineered from the start by a pair of strong women: Maria's ambitious mother, in financial peril since the death of her husband, and the wildly popular Swiss-born portrait painter Angelica Kauffman, who was eager to undertake responsibility for Maria's professional advancement. The miniature of Jefferson that Maria kept with her in Italy until her death was painted by the New Englander Trumbull, who served as a courier of their most private letters. Judged to be a good likeness of him, it is an image that suggests a reserved, dignified physiognomy. For his part, Jefferson hung an engraving of Maria, by Bartolozzi, at Monticello.²⁶

Jefferson's painstakingly wrought dialogue between his Head and Heart was dated October 12, 1786, one week to the day after he had seen off the Cosways when they started back to London. The twelve-page letter, undoubtedly the longest he wrote to any woman, was penned with his left hand, because he could not use the right without significant pain. The handwriting is nevertheless careful and balanced, indicating the intense hours he devoted to its composition.

Jefferson proclaimed himself a man of sentiment in staging a mock battle between his rational and compassionate parts. "You kindle," the constraining Head charges, selecting a verb that connotes the fire that ignites in the Heart; "you were imprudently engaging your affections" with a "lady" of "modesty, beauty, and that softness of disposition which is the ornament of her sex and charm of ours." How wrong it is to do those things that "increase the pang of separation." Better to remain cool and detached, avoiding potentially hurtful feelings.

But the Heart cannot be contained. Nor should it be. It wins the argument in Jefferson's afflicted mind by embracing everything that lends itself to an appreciation of beauty and commitment, that acknowledges the sensations that generate hope, that gives up calm in favor of a life-affirming participation in the affairs of the world. To feel for humanity is to live. "And what more sublime delight than to mingle tears with one whom the hand of heaven hath smitten! To watch over the bed of sickness, and to beguile it's tedious and it's painful moments! To share our bread with one to whom misfortune has left none! The world abounds indeed with misery: to lighten its burthen we must divide it with one another."

The exclamation points have the same impact as Jefferson's final release—"the eternal separation we are shortly to make!"—in the deathbed adieu he and Patty composed, in sequence, in 1782. There are no greater examples of rhapsodic torment among Jefferson's preserved letters than the deathbed conversation of Thomas and Patty Jefferson and this riveting letter, four years later, to Maria Cosway.

The Head and Heart letter is a love letter. It is a plea for communion, an ironic cry of delight in the agony of separation. The Heart's ability to feel is celebrated in its dismissal of any value the Head places on a monkish retreat from emotional life. Underscoring the Heart's power over body as well as mind, Jefferson contests the foolish monks he has dreamt up as proxies of the feeling-phobic Head, and he makes the point in a most visceral way: "Had they ever felt the solid pleasure of one generous spasm of the heart, they would exchange for it all the frigid speculations of their lives." Jefferson's soulful appeal to Maria, its seemingly involuntary energy, is no contrivance; nor are his feelings for her superficial in the least—at that moment, anyway. Is it love? No historian can claim to have the answer.

As clever and as artful as Jefferson's familiar letter writing is, Head vs. Heart is as long as it is (close to five thousand words) because of his more than spiritual desire for the addressee. For hours, perhaps an entire day, the unpracticed left hand pulsated as it painted its picture of a communion that cannot occur outside the imagination. She is married, and he, despite what his Heart commands, is bent on avoiding too many complications. He wants what he cannot have.[27]

Diplomatic life offered diversion, as did travel to the south of France and northern Italy. As time passed, their correspondence became less and less frequent. But occasionally, Jefferson slipped back into a mode of appealing to her as he had done to other young female artists. As he did with Sophie de Tott, he did with Mrs. Cosway, mimicking Laurence Sterne in flirtatious letters. "With none to do I converse more fondly than with my good Maria," he began a sentiment, before contrasting her vivaciousness with another by that name, the emotional Maria of *A Sentimental Journey*, who sits, lovelorn, beneath a poplar. Sterne's journeying narrator wipes her tears and says: "I am positive I have a soul." This was Jefferson, less soulful than he was teasing and self-indulgent. Above his signature, he bade his Maria adieu with the words "Love me much, and love me always."[28]

As it was, he worried a good deal about the heart of fellow Virginian William Short, his invaluable and devoted personal secretary, who mastered the French language in order to make up for Jefferson's lack of fluency. Short was attractive to and attracted by the ladies. In his early thirties, he was in every respect a member of Jefferson's Paris family. He was close to Patsy, and close enough to Jefferson to read the emotions of that hidden man.

William Short became so enamored with the young wife of the duc de La Rochefoucauld that he opposed the strictures of Jefferson's Head. He would ultimately choose to remain behind in Paris after Jefferson and his daughters sailed home in 1789. He would spend the tumultuous years that lay ahead dodging trouble and protecting his beloved duchesse, Rosalie, while serving in a string of diplomatic capacities and remaining Jefferson's eyes and ears in Europe. He was also strong-minded enough to contest his mentor and ostensible protector when Jefferson voiced opinions that he found cause to dispute. In most respects, Short outgrew Jefferson.[29]

Lafayette noted certain parallels between Jefferson and Short, characterizing the two for George Washington in a letter of 1788. He wrote: "Nothing Can Excell M. Jefferson's abilities, virtues, pleasing temper, and Every thing in Him that Constitutes the Great States man, zealous Citizen, and Amiable friend. He Has a Young Gentleman with Him, Mr Short, a Virginian, who is a very able, Engaging, and Honest Man." Lafayette unfailingly worked to promote and publicize Jefferson and his interests, impressed by the fact that Short spoke for Jefferson and often took his place at official meetings.[30]

Short was willing to take the kinds of risks Jefferson turned away from. While Jefferson was smitten with Maria Cosway, he was neither young nor unencumbered enough to hazard the future he was planning as a gentleman farmer for an unlikely ideal. Yet he adored Maria's native Italy—"a peep into Elysium," he wrote to her on his return, while at the same time lamenting, "I am born to lose every thing I love." He had to have realized long before now that Maria could never be happy in the quiet domesticity of a Monticello wife. Or perhaps he never once fantasized the possibility. While only so much can be known of their understanding, she was far more than a passing fancy or an object of his lust. He wanted to bring her close, even if it was just to watch her mix paints and capture the panoramic view from his mountain.[31]

In "My Head and My Heart," the Heart's outpouring is most enchanted in the passage about Monticello, as the letter writer lingers at the site he has only his words to describe now:

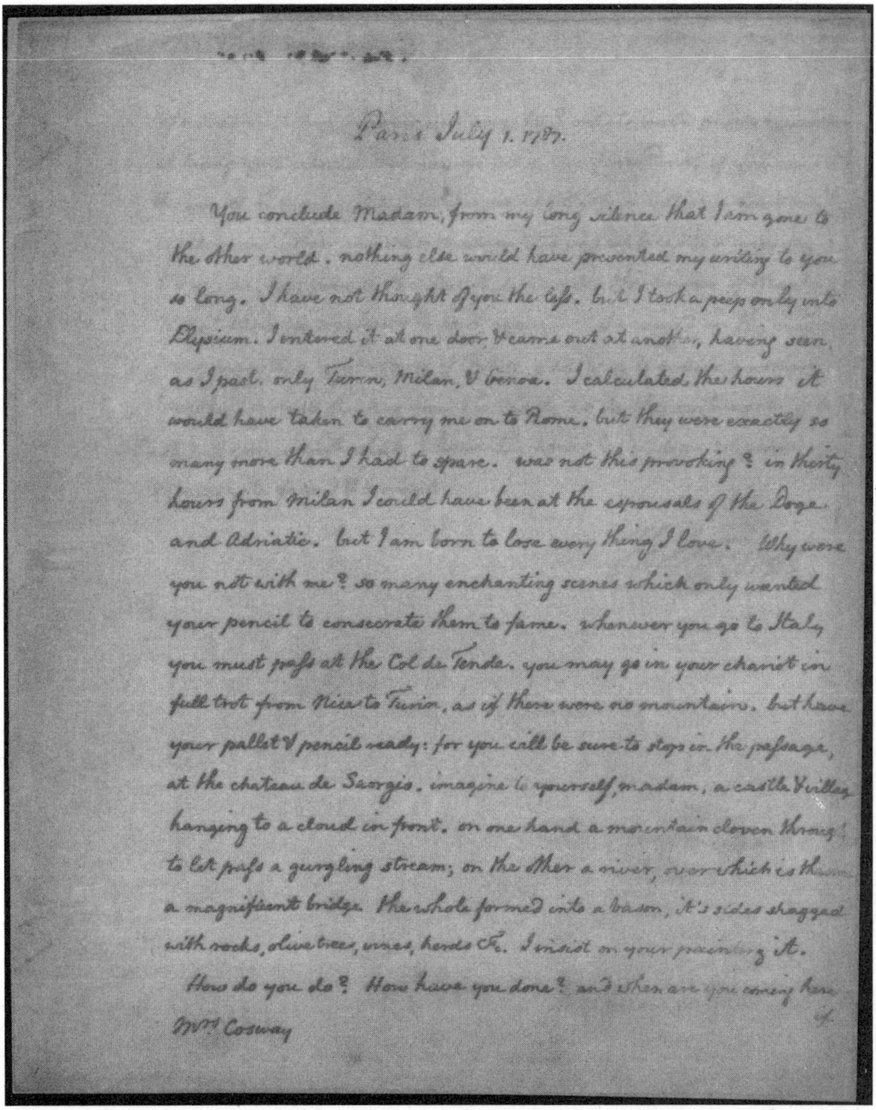

Paris July 1. 1787.

You conclude Madam, from my long silence that I am gone to the other world. nothing else would have prevented my writing to you so long. I have not thought of you the less. but I took a peep only into Elysium. I entered it at one door & came out at another, having seen as I past, only Turin, Milan, & Genoa. I calculated the hours it would have taken to carry me on to Rome. but they were exactly so many more than I had to spare. was not this provoking? in thirty hours from Milan I could have been at the espousals of the Doge and Adriatic. but I am born to lose every thing I love. Why were you not with me? so many enchanting scenes which only wanted your pencil to consecrate them to fame. whenever you go to Italy you must pass at the Col de Tende. you may go in your chariot in full trot from Nice to Turin, as if there were no mountain. but have your pallet & pencil ready: for you will be sure to stop in the passage, at the chateau de Saorgio. imagine to yourself, madam, a castle & village hanging to a cloud in front. on one hand a mountain cloven through to let pass a gurgling stream; on the other a river, over which is thrown a magnificent bridge. the whole formed into a bason, it's sides shagged with rocks, olive trees, vines, herds &c. I insist on your painting it.

How do you do? How have you done? and when are you coming here?

Mrs. Cosway

Figure 11. "But I am born to lose every thing I love." Letter, Jefferson to Maria Cosway, 1787. (Courtesy Special Collections, University of Virginia Library)

And our own dear Monticello, where has nature spread so rich a mantle under the eye? mountains, forests, rocks, rivers. With what majesty do we there ride above the storms! How sublime to look down into the work-house of nature, to see her clouds, hail, snow, rain, thunder, all fabricated at our feet! And the glorious Sun, when rising as if out of a distant water, just gilding the tops of the mountains, and giving life to all nature!

The repetition of exclamation marks is more than an effort to convince her of his sincere conviction. He rarely shares his feelings in so poetic a style or at such extraordinary length. The appeal for her to capture Monticello in oil expresses his desire to share what means the most to him, what constitutes *his* canvas. The cognate "Monticello" is a musical combination, and a reminder that, long before they met, he appreciated the flow of the language Maria Hadfield spoke. He liked to pepper his letters to her with conversational Italian.

The plan of return to "our own dear Monticello" enlarged after 1787, when he sought, from afar, to persuade Madison and Monroe, as well as Short, to move to his neighborhood and constitute a "partie quarrée." To Monroe, newly wedded with a baby daughter, he put it this way: "I sincerely take part with you in your domestic felicity. There is no other in this world worth living for. The loss of it alone can make us know it's full worth. It would indeed be a most pleasing circumstance to me to see you settle in the neighborhood of Monticello, for thither all my views tend, and not a day passes over my head without looking forward to my return. This would be much hastened could I see such a society forming there as yourself, Madison, and Short." In the end, only one of the three, Monroe, complied.[32]

To Short, Jefferson projected his angst when he wrote not long before returning to Virginia: "A young man indeed may do without marriage in a great city. In the beginning it is pleasant enough; but take what course he will[,] whether that of rambling, or of a fixed attachment, he will become miserable as he advances in years. It is then he will feel the want of that friendship which can be formed during the enthusiasm of youth alone, and formed without reproach. It is then too he will want the amusement and comfort of children." Jefferson could not envision true contentment other than as he'd constituted "ten years of unchequered happiness" with his wife and daughters at Monticello. It was perfectly understood at this time that Short could not marry Rosalie. It was equally understood that Jefferson was not rendering a moral judgment. He was simply saying that a romance with an Anglo-Italian artist or a French duchesse could last only so long.[33]

His letters to Maria Cosway in London were almost never consigned to the prying post, but were instead hand-delivered by trusted travelers who crossed the Channel. As he put it in one of these, "the breathings of a pure affection" were too sensitive to be delivered by any other means. By the time he began to envisage his return to America, he took the pressure off himself and resumed with Maria the mode of expression in which he corresponded with women with whom there was no sexual tension: artful and clever, but safe.

After 1790, the letters were few in number. A perceptible fondness revived late in Jefferson's retirement years, when he expressed nostalgia for the times they'd shared and went so far as to fantasize a postcorporeal reunion: "Such is the present state of our former coterie, dead, diseased & dispersed. But 'tout ce qui est différé n'est pas perdu' [not all that is deferred is lost], says the French proverb, and the religion you so sincerely profess, tells us we shall meet again." After his death, when his eldest grandson, Thomas Jefferson Randolph, arranged for publication of Jefferson's correspondence, he included the Head and Heart letter, because he felt it could be presented as a philosophical essay on enlightened friendship. He withheld those others that breathed passion.[34]

Gaps necessarily exist in the historical record, yet the above assessment makes it obvious that Jefferson was in a relationship marked by tenderness and moments of poignancy. The subjects Maria chose for her canvases—curiously, one was a scene from Macpherson's Ossianic tales—were consciously moral and at odds with the uncertain character her exhibitionist husband Richard showed the world. She retained her Catholicism, bore a daughter in 1789, and returned to Italy with her (and without Richard). The child died at the age of six; the bereaved mother refused to see her husband for a good many years after that. It is known that he suffered from mental issues, and some of her letters to him are bitter and accusatory. At the end of his life, she returned to tend to him, though she appears to have found solace when separated from the pleasure-taking world she inhabited as young Mrs. Cosway.[35]

Figure 12. The Marquis de Condorcet, known to history as the "last of the philosophes." He and Jefferson spent many productive hours together in Paris, though Condorcet's progressive ideas lost out to Virginia provincialism after Jefferson's return to the United States in 1789. (Engraving in author's possession)

CHAPTER 7

"An Abuse of Strength"
Condorcet's Challenge, Maria's Maid

T HE PARIS ART WORLD greatly appealed to Jefferson. Whether or not Maria Cosway intentionally drew such men to her, it was while in her company that the American minister became well acquainted with a couple of men in their sixties whose checkered careers did not appear to disturb either him or her. The man who shared Jefferson's carriage when he accompanied the Cosways on their departure from Paris in October was an old friend of theirs, an artist and antiquarian who traded in erotic art. "Danquerville promised to visit me, but has not done it as yet," Jefferson writes in the final paragraph of the twelve-page Head and Heart letter. "De latude comes sometimes to take family soupe with me." It is the lives and characters of these two unusual gentlemen that compel a slight detour in the story of Jefferson's residence in France.

Pierre-François Hugues Hancarville (1719–1805) knew the inside of debtor's prison. In the 1780s, he was something of a hanger-on who sought out well-respected aesthetes like the Cosways and denoted Maria "l'aimable" (the good-natured one) in a note he wrote to Jefferson. Hancarville, who called himself the Baron d'Hancarville, had been expelled from Italy. An Italian friend wrote of this teller of tales: "His penetrating, voracious eyes, his flaring nostrils, his lips which barely touch each other are the outward signs of his longing to see everything." In 1780, he published a pornographic book on "the secret cult of Roman ladies," which was followed by another, in 1787, on "the private lives of the Caesars." He had a particular interest in phallic cults and saw art very much in tactile terms. Curiously, a 1781 Zoffany painting is of the collector Charles Townley surrounded by pieces he owned while in conversation with Hancarville and two other men—this time, Richard Cosway is not among them. Maria's friendship with the long-lived Hancarville continued in the years after Jefferson returned to America.[1]

The other celebrity hound who "comes sometimes to take family soupe with me" was the even more colorful Jean Danry (1725–1805). The inscrutable Danry became a popular subject of melodrama in France in his later years, under the name of Latude. With little formal education, he served for a time as an assistant army surgeon before being implicated in an alleged scheme to poison Madame de Pompadour, mistress of King Louis XV. He came to Jefferson's attention after obtaining his freedom, when he was, for a brief period, the toast of the town. For thirty-five years, from 1749 to 1784, the year Jefferson arrived in France, Latude had been imprisoned in the Bastille and other fortresses. His notoriety derived from his multiple escapes over those three and a half decades.

His mother, a seamstress and weaver, was unmarried when she became pregnant by the vicomte Vissec de Latude. In his midtwenties and down on his luck, Danry (unacknowledged by Latude) thought up a plan to appear the hero by warning the king's favorite about those who wished her ill. Things spun out of control and he was adjudicated a plotter, possibly a madman, in either case best removed from society.

From the Bastille, Danry/Latude was sent to the castle at Vincennes, where his stature was confirmed by his proximity to a distinguished fellow prisoner, Denis Diderot, a philosophe and religious heretic who, like Latude, was subject to internment because of a royal *lettre de cachet*, or writ of incarceration. It was from Vincennes that Latude staged his first escape, aided along the route by young females he was able to charm. Instead of melting into low society, he behaved as an upright patriot would and wrote to Mme de Pompadour, reiterating his apology and leaving a return address. The law came and rearrested the escapee. He ended up back in the dreaded Bastille, shackled and left to rot in a dungeon. Five and a half years later, in the dead of winter, he staged the second of his three daring escapes, with the help of a makeshift ladder fashioned from discarded clothes.

After three and a half months of life on the run, he exposed himself again by asking his mother for funds—her mail was being monitored. Once again, he staged an escape from the Bastille, this time disarming a guard. By now, he claimed the title of vicomte de Latude from the recently deceased nobleman who had sired him, and he penned further appeals to officialdom as Latude.

The notorious convict became the poster child for resistance to abusive authority. Ten years after the death of Louis XV, twenty after the death of Pompadour, acclaimed names came to adopt his cause, with the result that the court finally released him. Men and women were suddenly inviting Latude into their homes, saluting his dogged determination. Wined and dined, the longest-surviving prisoner in France was compassionately attended wherever he went.

Unfortunately, he overstayed his welcome. A refusal to accept life on a modest scale brought an end to the charmed existence he'd found after prison. He complained loudly when he received a smaller pension than expected for all he'd suffered. Former groupies found him distasteful, and Latude lost his star quality.[2]

His appeal to Jefferson in 1786 is easy to imagine. The American minister was himself a great storyteller (more markedly so as he aged), and he was attracted to unusual characters who shared that talent. The French escape artist was a truth embroiderer (to some, a mythomaniac) who savored his fame, and one suspects that the convivial Jefferson, curious about oddities and well disposed toward relative strangers, was taken in by him. No doubt he empathized, as much as he got a charge from hearing the ex-prisoner's perspective on life, even as Parisians found Latude's grandiosity too much to take. For his part, the celebrated escapee remembered Jefferson with personal fondness, and on two occasions (1798 and 1804) transmitted copies of his memoir to American diplomats in France, requesting of both that they convey his respects to Jefferson—in the latter instance, he included a print of a recent portrait.[3]

THE CONSCIENCE OF CONDORCET

The people who mattered day to day in the lives of historical actors are not always the ones who help tell an electrifying story. In that respect, the most consequential relationship Jefferson had in France was not with either Maria Cosway, with whom he interacted during a relatively brief period, or with the mother of his unacknowledged children, Sally Hemings, a young teen when she arrived in Paris in 1787, accompanying an even younger Maria Jefferson. Despite an abundance of evidence, Jefferson biographers have grossly undervalued the enduring impression made on him by Marie-Jean-Antoine-Nicolas Caritat, Marquis de Condorcet, often referred to as the "last of the philosophes." He and Jefferson had a great deal in common. They were prodigious learners, accomplished writers, and personal friends; and their public lives followed similar trajectories.[4]

Condorcet and Jefferson were both born in 1743. The Virginian lost his prominent father as a young teen, but the Frenchman never even knew his titled father, who died in battle just weeks after he was born. Raised by his commoner mother, he proved a mathematical prodigy and was admitted to the prestigious Académie des Sciences at twenty-two, where he was welcomed into the distinguished society of French scholars who orbited Voltaire. As Jefferson was gaining traction in Williamsburg and obtaining wider notice with his powerful *Summary View of the Rights of British America*, Condorcet was on the receiving end of Voltaire's urgent appeals on behalf of the unjustly prosecuted critics of established authority in France. Voltaire was a prolific poet and philosophe, best loved at the time, though no longer, for his work as a dramatist. To the end of his iconoclastic life, he appreciated Condorcet's scrupulous honesty in telling him things others would not say about his creations for fear of upsetting him. Nor should it be overlooked that Condorcet was one of Voltaire's chief literary executors.[5]

Condorcet and Jefferson were in their mid-forties when they became acquainted, traveling in the same social circles throughout Jefferson's tenure. They were at the height of their intellectual powers and had attained massive political reputations at a time when the American minister was particularly open to French influence. They shared a love for applied mathematics and championed the decimalization of standard weights and measures. Condorcet's 1785 *Essay on the Application of Analysis to the Probability of Majority Decisions* introduced an argument in support of majority rule, known as social choice theory. Jefferson's strongly held conviction on the subject of inherited debt, presented to Madison in 1789, averred "that the Earth belongs in usufruct to the living"; this view was, at the very minimum, stimulated by Condorcet's calculations. Jefferson's proviso that one generation should not be contractually bound to the last, that constitutions should be revised after nineteen years, borrowed from Condorcet, who'd put the number at twenty.

These commonalities may not sound sexy, but they provided fodder for long conversations, drew the two men close, and ought to be considered as important as their common passion to realize Enlightenment values in the political world. As an influential author on political and economic topics, Condorcet strove to give the French people a coherent national identity, which Jefferson did as adamantly, of course, in his own country. At the outbreak of revolution in 1789, the Marquis de Condorcet was as important to France as the more famous, longer-lived Marquis de Lafayette. And Jefferson, sympathizing, was in the thick of it.[6]

There can be no doubt but that theirs was a true meeting of the minds. Both Condorcet and Jefferson directed their philosophical commitment to the cause of human dignity and the application of Enlightenment rationalism to constitutional law. They struggled against the automatic acceptance of mediocre monarchs and vice-ridden aristocrats who infiltrated the inner circles of power in the Old World. They were disillusioned by social stagnation and could not see the triumph of liberty apart from awarding positions of power to individuals of exemplary character who worked for the public good. They were distinguished as idealists in a time of strife.

As his friendship and understanding with Jefferson grew, Condorcet published a tract on the influence of the American Revolution and declared it a fit model for enlightened Europe. In July 1788, at the height of their collaboration and precisely one year before the storming of the Bastille, he creatively took on the persona of a foreign observer in the anonymously authored *Lettres d'un citoyen des États-Unis* (Letters of a Citizen of the United States), in which he called "parliamentary aristocracy" the enemy of freedom as he directly compared colonial Americans' protests against unfair parliamentary taxation to the situation he saw in France, where taxation "weighs heavily on the poor in order to spare the rich." His fictional American citizen sounds particularly Jeffersonian in asserting, "I believe that the more free nations there are, the more assured everyone's freedom is." The like-minded pair concurred that a genuine renewal of the human spirit was to be achieved through good and mild government and an expansion of civic education among the populace.[7]

Six months before the outbreak of the French Revolution, Jefferson sent Madison two related publications, each a Declaration of Rights. One was by Lafayette—"our friend"—who was expressing his opinions in the open: "You will see that it contains the essential principles of ours accomodated [*sic*] as much as could be to the actual state of things here." The other was authored by Condorcet, whose name was in this instance disguised, and rendered by Jefferson as "a very sensible man, a pure theorist, of the sect called the economists." Condorcet's went further than Lafayette's, not merely in addressing current abuses, but planting seeds of previously undreamed-of rights as well. As an enthusiastic apostle of the grand Enlightenment, Condorcet was the same kind of inspired optimist as Jefferson. Let us underscore that point.[8]

They were both algebraically inclined social theorists and social planners, though it is fair to say that Condorcet was the less inflexible of the two. His intellectualism resembled Madison's in its inherent moderation. On one key subject, though, he and Jefferson agreed wholeheartedly: a vehemence in their demand that secular authority prevail over the false pose and outright artificiality they attributed to aristocratic pretense and religious dogma. In a very real sense, their intellectual partnership served Jefferson as a substitute for the physical absence of Madison.

Though Jefferson and Condorcet were regarded, in life and ever since, as visionaries who subscribed to a basic goodness in human nature, we must state plainly the key differences that separated their governing philosophies. One was Condorcet's embrace of a unicameral legislative branch, a position he'd imbibed from his mentor and late minister to Louis XVI, Anne-Robert-Jacques Turgot. He sought to convince Jefferson that with a strictly calculated measure to ensure an acceptable character in those granted the franchise, there was no need for a counterbalancing lower chamber; that is, as long as there was no ambiguity in voting rules and procedures, a reliable, emotionally restrained expression of the popular will was achievable. Their second difference was more ethereal: both wished to privilege the popular voice in affairs of state, but Condorcet's abject refusal to condone mob action distinguished him from the looser stylings of Jefferson.

The Frenchman felt that the rights of the people were best preserved by calming class resentments. He preferred a strong "counterpropaganda" to offset the radicalism of writers ("maniacs") who enjoyed stirring up trouble. He abjured an idiom that used imagery of war and bloodshed, lest the public be less horrified by actual bloodshed. By contrast, Jefferson was prone to hyperbole and seemed always to minimize the possibility of mob rule arising from popular agitation. His December 1786 letter to Yale's president, Ezra Stiles, offers a pertinent example. Speaking to the nervous standoff amid Shays's Rebellion, a foreclosure protest staged by disgruntled former soldiers in western Massachusetts, Jefferson said: "If the happiness of the mass of the people can be secured at the expence of a little tempest now and then, or even of a little blood, it will be a precious purchase."[9]

Even better known is Jefferson's restless remark to John Adams's son-in-law, William Stephens Smith, as news of the Constitutional Convention reached him. Reflecting again on Shays's Rebellion, he wrote: "We have had 13. states indepedant [sic] 11. years. There has been one rebellion. That comes to one rebellion in a century and a half for each state. What country before ever existed a century and half without a rebellion? . . . What signify a few lives lost in a century or two?" On the very same subject, as the Condorcet scholar Iain McLean notes, the French thinker had already done the math, providing Jefferson with the precise calculation of 143 years (rendered by Jefferson as "in a century or two"). "Dans quels autres gouvernements les soulèvements ont-ils été aussi rares?" Condorcet posed. "In what other governments have uprisings been so rare?" And, of course, it was not Condorcet but Jefferson who supplied the coup de grâce with an agrarian metaphor that so many commentators have harped on: "The tree of liberty must be refreshed from time to time with the blood of patriots and tyrants," Jefferson illustrated. "It is it's natural manure."[10]

Jefferson's choice of words in this instance has been too often decontextualized and used to make him appear more bloodthirsty than he was. His idealism as a theorist might be said to have predisposed him to be a tad insensitive to the real lives of people with whom he had no contact. Still, his reaction to Shays's Rebellion says something about his not entirely theoretical acceptance of a modicum of political violence. To put a point on it, a few years on, as Jefferson was struggling to accommodate the Jacobins' infamous Reign of Terror, his esteemed friend Condorcet would be meeting a cruel fate in a dank prison cell. One sees, then, how Jefferson's imagery highlights a real distinction between the two otherwise agreeable men. In expressing his faith that "the people" would safely self-correct, a rationale he laid out in several letters around this time, Jefferson showed little understanding of the dangers of mob violence.[11]

Condorcet soared past Jefferson in those matters of social injustice that appeal most to us today. He proposed plain legislative solutions to deficiencies he saw in society that have yet to be adequately remediated in our own time, assuring equal rights to Blacks and women in a world meant to be remade according to Enlightenment principles. Here, Condorcet and Jefferson were clearly at odds. Jefferson could not conceive that those deemed Black or mulatto could be assimilated into the mainstream of any republican future without the loss of that Anglo-American essence he favored. And the idea of women participating in political life was utter anathema to him.

Condorcet first weighed in on slavery in the French colony of Saint-Domingue (modern Haiti) in 1773, fifteen years before he published his remarkable *Réflexions sur l'esclavage des nègres* (Reflections on Negro Slavery). He doubtless heard from Jefferson how the paragraph decrying the African slave trade was expunged by Congress from his draft of the Declaration of Independence. They must also have discussed at some length Jefferson's "practical" suggestion in *Notes on Virginia* that whites' refusal to live as equals with emancipated slaves, plus Black resentment built up over two centuries, left an imbalance between Black and white that could be settled only through a permanent separation of the races. There is no record of how or whether Condorcet pressed a differing opinion on Jefferson; for he projected the means to develop harmonious biracial living through short-term monitoring of postenslavement working conditions, meant to guide the transition and preserve public order.

To be clear, Condorcet's stand against the "barbaric" practice of race enslavement (first put forward in 1781, revised in 1788) was unforgiving. To him, human rights were not race-specific. To enslave, he said, was to steal a person's right to self-ownership. By 1788, he turned from the moral question to the mechanics of changing economic conditions so that privileging human rights (natural law) over property rights was not controversial. "The interests of the powerful and the rich must fade before the rights of any one man," he boldly wrote.[12]

Condorcet was not urging immediate abolition, nor leaning on Jefferson to the degree that Lafayette would persist in doing in years to come. Condorcet was a gradualist who proposed that all plantation-born Blacks be freed at age thirty-five. He might, under the right conditions, have nudged Jefferson in a different direction than the one he took in refusing to reconsider colonization of America's nonwhite population "beyond the reach of mixture." But unstoppable political events in the streets of Paris made all such considerations secondary at best. In 1789, prior to his recall, Jefferson put his head to the task of translating *Réflexions sur l'esclavage des nègres* into English. After returning to the United States, however, with the French Revolution in motion, he discontinued that work, partly, one must assume, in view of Southern politics and partly owing to his own inertia and lack of leadership on issues of race. It was a lost opportunity, to say the least.

As balm for the soul of the liberal philosophe, Jefferson made a point in 1791 of presenting Condorcet with new evidence of his openness to a reconsideration of the racist pronouncements he'd made in *Notes on Virginia*. How genuine he was being is another question. The subject was Benjamin Banneker of Maryland, whom Jefferson, as secretary of state, had named to the commission planning the future city of Washington, D.C. Proudly, he wrote to the French philosophe: "I am happy to be able to inform you that we have now in the United States a negro, the son of a black man born in Africa, and of a black woman born in the United States, who is a very respectable Mathematician." He had single-handedly "procured" this important job for Banneker, a free man, and it gave him hope that this "very worthy and respectable member of society" would prove to be more than an anomaly. "I shall be delighted," Jefferson wrote, "to see these instances of moral eminence so multiplied as to prove that the want of talents observed in them is merely the effect of their degraded condition, and not proceeding from any difference in the structure of the parts on which intellect depends." Jefferson obviously expected Condorcet to take at face value his claim of sincerity.[13]

Flash forward to 1809. Entering retirement, Jefferson gave a less generous and decidedly self-serving explanation of his racial views to a fellow Francophile, the Connecticut-born, Yale-educated poet Joel Barlow (1754–1812). Barlow, a trusted Jeffersonian Republican, had resided in France during the 1790s. As Jefferson read the back-and-forth between the Abbé Henri Grégoire (1750–1831) and Barlow, two old acquaintances, he sympathized with the American for reasons all his own.

The bishop was criticizing Barlow's work, publicly accusing him of having "renounced Christianity." Barlow responded in print, insisting that Grégoire greatly mistook his "principles and feelings." Jefferson was impressed by Barlow's response to the "diatribe," though he also thought his friend's "sugary" public letter was too restrained, and better than his critic deserved. By the time of his presidency, Jefferson knew well what it felt like to be publicly accused of atheism. Yet it wasn't Jefferson's religion but his thoughts on race that he brought to mind in relating to Barlow what the Abbé had written to him after reading *Notes on Virginia*. He had his own problem with the "credulity" of Grégoire about the innate capacity of Blacks.

Jefferson had retained the antiracist writings of the Abbé, and he now told Barlow that the "doubts" he expressed in his *Notes* "as to the grade of understanding of the negroes" had led Grégoire to "gather up every story he could find of men of colour (without distinguishing whether black, or of what degree of mixture) however slight the mention." He had written back to Grégoire politely—"as you have done, a soft answer."

Smugness is a Jefferson trait little remarked upon. He clearly does not believe he can be taught anything about racial differences. It was his published opinion that Black inferiority was plainly observable, that African Americans were shallow thinkers, unreflective, their minds improved after one generation in bearing the child of a white—which he insisted was "proof of their inferiority." Covering his tracks (but poorly), he claimed he meant these views to be understood not as a final determination, but "as a suspicion only."

Obviously expecting Barlow to agree that he'd been more than fair in his assessment of Blacks' capacities, Jefferson took full credit for his largesse: "It was impossible for doubt to have been more tenderly or hesitatingly expressed than that was in the Notes of Virginia." Dismissive of the Abbé's research methods, he could not resist the example of Banneker, telling Barlow: "He had spherical trigonometry enough to make almanacs, but not without the suspicion of aid from" a white neighbor and friend. (Once again, a "suspicion.") The next line in the letter to Barlow finds him undercutting what he had told Condorcet to demonstrate his hopefulness and open-mindedness: "I have a long letter from Banneker, which shows him to have had a mind of very common stature indeed." Then, more waffling language: "Nothing was or is farther from my intentions than to enlist myself as the champion of a fixed opinion." By 1809, Jefferson (he of fixed opinions) had long since abandoned the wondrous possibilities he saw in the writings of the now deceased Frenchman whose approval he had previously sought.[14]

He cannot, then, be classed with Condorcet, whose progressive posture was especially remarkable when he persisted in working toward a realizable measure of gender equality. Even before Mary Wollstonecraft published her groundbreaking *Vindication of the Rights of Women*, the marquis took aim at inequality in education. In the latter decades of the eighteenth century, the myth persisted that men were formed to reason and render judgment, women to feel and react emotionally. Though Jefferson maintained close relationships with learned women (Patty Jefferson should be counted among them), he would not abandon the view that daughters should be reared to become dutiful wives first and foremost. In contrast, Condorcet wrote of the stereotypical view of women that "it is true that they are not led by men's reason, but they are led by their own." He resisted that biological essentialism to which Jefferson, like most, succumbed. He insisted that observed differences between the sexes lay in social pressure put upon women—in nurture more than in nature—and he decried the age-old stigma placed on female sexual independence. Whereas Jefferson maintained an outward primness, Condorcet did not shy from exploring all such concerns with an open mind.[15]

In 1786, as Jefferson found himself enchanted by the much younger Maria Cosway, Condorcet married Sophie de Grouchy, a twenty-three-year-old of impeccable aristocratic pedigree who was noted for her intelligence and wit. Among her many accomplishments, she translated Adam Smith's *Theory of Moral Sentiments*, and she made their home into a center for philosophical and political conversation, continuing to do so for years after her husband's needless death. Despite the age difference, theirs was a happy marriage, of the sort Jefferson assumed rare among the nobility. Hopes of marital bliss were cut short after only seven years, when the revolution Sophie and her husband looked forward to turned against the philosophe.

PROGRESS OF THE HUMAN MIND

At the time he and Jefferson met, Condorcet had already attained national stature as a political economist and served as perpetual secretary of the Académie des Sciences. Unlike Jefferson, who would not publish under his own name and who politicked by disseminating his letters among a select group of legislators and other influencers, Condorcet published regularly (at times identified by name), and he let his ideas circulate openly despite the risks. He and Jefferson had many of the same friends. Both were intimates and consistent supporters of the political gadfly Thomas Paine and the entrepreneurial Florentine Philip Mazzei, Jefferson's neighbor for a period of years in the 1770s, whose wife lay buried at Monticello.[16]

Like Jefferson, Condorcet was known for his pleasing temperament. He made friends easily, but he came down hard on all forms of social injustice. His most comprehensive, most progressive study was the posthumously printed *Esquisse d'un tableau historique des progrès de l'esprit humain* (Sketch for a Historical Picture of the Progress of the Human Mind). He gleaned from his talks with Jefferson an at once humane and nationalistic perspective on the American Revolution, reciting his trusted friend's assessment in confident strains. "Simple common sense taught the inhabitants of the British colonies that Englishmen born beyond the Atlantic Ocean had been endowed by nature with exactly the same rights as other Englishmen born under the meridian of Greenwich," Condorcet wrote. "The British government affected to believe that God had created America, as he had created Asia, for the pleasure of the inhabitants of London; for it wanted to have in its power a vassal nation beyond the seas ... We see then for the first time, a great people delivered from all its chains, giving itself in peace the laws and the constitution that it believed most likely to bring it happiness."[17]

Three thousand copies of *Esquisse* were issued in 1795, nine years before the publication of Condorcet's Collected Writings in twenty-one volumes. As a systematic compendium of the philosophe's outlook on all matters of human invention and the "perfectibility" of the species, the book advances through the stages of social development from early times in order to address the need for liberation of the progressive spirit through all available means of encouragement. He applauds every perceptible advance toward closing the economic gap between the wealthy and everyone else, as well as equality under the law, rights of conscience, decolonization, and universal suffrage. It is difficult to find another Enlightenment figure who went as far as Condorcet in envisioning a just society.

He deplored those at the head of society, in any age, who reduced the likelihood of progress in science, the arts, and political life by acting to protect their own high status. In limiting access to discoveries, these powerful families and powerful sects, monopolists of information, holy men, pedants, and their ilk, deprived others of useful knowledge. He noted the opening of the historic "war between philosophy and superstition" upon the death of Socrates, and its amelioration beginning in the seventeenth century with the invention of the printing press, a reduction of religious bigotry, and recognition that rights needed to be extended to more people. The consensus, since John Locke, was that it was improper "to divide humanity into two races, the one fated to rule, the other to obey."[18]

It is easy to see Jeffersonian political logic here, for Condorcet was restating the tenets of Enlightenment doctrine as the American Revolutionaries drank it in. To this he added something new, however: his "doctrine of the indefinite perfectibility of the human race." Condorcet did not claim credit for introducing this doctrine, an extension of rights discourse; he gave all credit to the writings of three individuals—all of them, it should be noted, intimates of Benjamin Franklin. The three were Condorcet's mentor, Turgot, along with two of Jefferson's staunch friends, the moral philosopher Richard Price, a Welsh minister, and the chemist-theologian Joseph Priestley, who would be hounded for his pro-French views and forced to flee England for America in the early 1790s.[19]

Richard Price shared his strong political feelings with Jefferson in early 1785, when his hopes for post-Revolutionary America began to sink on account of Southern planters' refusal to consider dismantling the institution of slavery. Like Condorcet, Price had idealistically projected a future America where concerted efforts to treat the existing "inequality of property" would go hand in hand with the gradual eradication of slavery. He shared his writings with proslavery Americans, whose "affronted" reaction took him aback. "Should Such a disposition prevail," he told Jefferson, "I shall have reason to fear that I have made myself ridiculous" by heaping praise on the new republic. How, he appealed to Jefferson, could "the people who have been Struggling so earnestly to save *themselves* from Slavery [be] ready to enslave *others*?"[20]

The publication in question was unambiguously titled *Observations on the Importance of the American Revolution*. "The Negro Trade cannot be censured in language too severe," he wrote. Because it was "shocking to humanity, cruel, wicked, and diabolical," it could hardly endure; as it was, an enslaved person became free simply by setting foot in England. All too optimistically, he proceeded: "I am happy to find that the united [sic] States are entering into measures for discountenancing" the slave trade. Price did not mince his words: " 'Till they have done this, it will not appear they deserve the liberty for which they have been contending. For it is self-evident, that if there are any men whom they have a right to hold in slavery, there may be *others* who have had a right to hold *them* in slavery."

On receipt of his personal copy of *Observations,* before Price learned of its mixed reception, Jefferson commended the author, characteristically anticipating no adverse publicity: "The spirit which it breathes is as affectionate as the observations themselves are wise and just. I have no doubt it will be reprinted in America and produce much good there." Jefferson was just then awaiting the publication of his own *Notes on the State of Virginia,* which was, of course, to pronounce upon race and slavery in an unsatisfying way, ambiguous at best. It was only Jefferson's indictment of the slave trade that was uncompromising, and that gave those like Price and Condorcet some comfort.[21]

Yet before we dismiss out of hand Jefferson's inability to reconsider the Southern way, we have to assess his ardent response to Price's follow-up letter, in the summer of 1785, which complicates matters we have seemingly put to rest. Jefferson as a man with debts who enslaved others still wished he could get out from under that moral burden. Increasingly reluctant to call out his fellow planters, he wanted influential men such as the pro-American Price to do that work for him, assuring this liberal-minded Englishman that younger minds in America were malleable and that Maryland was not South Carolina. And as far as Virginia was concerned, he held up the virtuous educator George Wythe as a proper model, "whose sentiments on the subject of slavery are unequivocal." Urging Price not to give up—"I wish you would do more"—Jefferson promised him that Price's further antislavery writings would bolster the likes of Wythe and have a pronounced effect on the rising generation, leading to the end of slavery in America.[22]

It is undeniable that Jefferson's favored correspondents gave him real and plentiful encouragement. While the active legislator Madison kept their common hopes alive back home, he had Condorcet near at hand for a reinforcement of his ideals. Jefferson had grown immeasurably through his European connections. Having succeeded Franklin as his nation's senior diplomat in France, he envisioned himself as a connector of Old and New World humanism. The fearless Condorcet, who appreciated the assertive character of Jefferson's language of rights, gave him greater focus and helped center him. Like Richard Price, and before long Joseph Priestley and Thomas Paine, Condorcet provided means for the further advance of the Revolutionary views Jefferson had summarized in the Declaration a dozen years before.

If his name is not on the tips of tongues, the Marquis de Condorcet can be said to have mattered more than almost anyone else in the France that Jefferson embraced. At the end of a life cut short, he compared Revolutionary America to Revolutionary France, and allowed (with tragic irony) that the French version "was more far-reaching than that in America and therefore more violent." The Americans, Condorcet argued, did not have to contend with the great distinctions in wealth that existed in Europe; they did not have to dismantle an established aristocracy or crush a "system of religious intolerance." These observations echoed Jefferson.

Like Jefferson in *Notes on Virginia*, Condorcet links politics and manners directly in his *Esquisse*. At the end of the book, he returns to the justice being denied women: "Among the causes of the progress of the human mind that are of the utmost importance to the general happiness, we must number the complete annihilation of the prejudices that have brought about an inequality of rights between the sexes, an inequality fatal even to the party in whose favor it works... This inequality has its origin solely in an abuse of strength, and all later sophistical attempts that have been made to excuse it are vain." Others decried slavery and the slave trade, but Condorcet was clearly ahead of his time in his uncompromising feminism.[23]

No less than Jefferson, Condorcet symbolizes Enlightenment speculation on America's potential to launch a desirable global transformation in politics and manners. A "science of morality" animated his political vision. The optimism the two men shared drew from historical examples, from a distinctive faith in progress and "universal philanthropy"; but it must be repeated that Condorcet conceived of progress through a broadening of public education that was far more modern and far more determined than anything Jefferson projected. Condorcet would not hesitate to reward excluded groups. He saw no reason to confine opportunity to white males. And again, unlike the timid abolitionist Jefferson, Condorcet boldly refused to consider what blowback he might get from traditionalists when he contested the majority that feared the kinds of compassionate change he proposed.

Along with his championing of women's rights, Condorcet includes in the final section of the *Esquisse* a remarkable scenario in which he advocates for a government that ensures the lifetime care of widows, orphans, and farmworkers, "guaranteeing people in old age a means of livelihood produced partly by their own savings and partly by the savings of others who make the same outlay, but who die before they need to reap the reward." He who began as a mathematician ended as a proponent of what eventually became Social Security.[24]

While Condorcet was open to more new ideas than Jefferson, their colleagues in political life described their personalities and inherent contradictions in surprisingly similar language. Jefferson was perennially good-tempered, yet unmistakably stubborn in his opinions and able to check his choler only so long. Condorcet was called "an enraged sheep" by his patron Turgot, "a snow-covered volcano" by the scientist-encyclopedist Jean le Rond d'Alembert, and a "timid conspirator" by his Jacobin enemy Maximilien Robespierre.[25]

SALLY HEMINGS ENTERS THE PICTURE

Given what we know about his friendship and admiration for those with whom he could expect emotionally satisfying conversation, how is one to imagine that Jefferson felt deep affection for an enslaved servant, whose children he would not acknowledge as his own, that is in any way comparable to what he felt for Sally Hemings's much older half sister, the late Patty Wayles Jefferson, or even the charming and talented Maria Cosway? There must be a better explanation than companionate love for the position she assumed in Thomas Jefferson's life.[26]

Fawn Brodie, who helped make the Sally Hemings of Jefferson's household a household name in modern times, sees her as a nonvoting conspirator in the cruel trick played on Maria (Polly) Jefferson that separated her from her maternal relatives in order to satisfy her father's demand that she cross the Atlantic to be with him. In 1784, at age six, she had been considered too young to join her father and older sister on the *Ceres* voyage. Three years had passed, and she barely remembered what her father looked like.

"Maria's maid" (as Jefferson referred to Sally in correspondence as late as 1799) could not but have looked at Jefferson as a man of commanding stature. As a member of his Paris household, unable at first to understand any French, she no doubt, says Brodie, felt lonely. The psychobiographer makes her case for Jefferson's early physical attraction to the teenager—or, at least, an obsessive interest—by focusing on Jefferson's repeated use of the adjective "mulatto" in 1788, when he is describing landscapes. Considering the fact that Sally Hemings was "mighty near white,... long straight hair down her back," in the later words of the enslaved Isaac Jefferson, who knew her at Monticello, his use of "mulatto" hardly counts as evidence of anything here. Brodie reads decision into a letter from Jefferson to Maria Cosway in which he adopts a carefree pose, as he had in his earlier "taking life by the smooth handle" pose to Sophie de Tott. In this instance, he rhapsodizes: "I am but a son of nature, loving what I see and feel, without being able to give a reason, nor caring much whether there be one." Not caring? Again, it's something of a stretch to accept, as easily as Brodie did, that the smooth-talking "son of nature" moved quickly from Maria to the teenage maid who was legally recognized, at least in the United States, as his property. Precisely what his feelings toward her (or hers toward him) were at any stage in their lives is simply not ascertainable, though it is hard to argue that Hemings exercised free will.[27]

The first opinion of "Maria's maid" that history receives comes courtesy of Abigail Adams, whose husband, John, had his hands full as America's inaugural minister to Great Britain. A year after the couple moved from Paris to London, she made it abundantly clear to her friend Jefferson that she had tired of life abroad—"surfeited with Europe," she told him, identifying with the caged starling in Sterne's *A Sentimental Journey* that cries pathetically, "I can't get out!" Her husband, duty-bound and more accepting, left it to his outspoken wife to express her concerns about the two girls who showed up at their door in June 1787.

Both the ship's captain who carried them across the ocean and the hypercritical Mrs. Adams took an immediate liking to the fragile Polly and scoffed at the servant's immaturity and uselessness. "The Girl who is with her is quite a child," she wrote, "and Captain Ramsay is of the opinion will be of so little service that he had better carry her back with him. But of this you will be a judge. She seems fond of the child and appears good-natured." Without even supplying her name, Abigail informed Jefferson that she was "the Sister of the Servant you have with you." James Hemings, then twenty-two, trained as a French chef and was becoming worldly. Jefferson profited from his chef's creativity and skill, but proved unjustifiably slow to sacrifice his personal comfort in favor of James's freedom. Sally might have been lonely, as Brodie surmises, but she had a benefactor and teacher in James.[28]

In successive letters, Mrs. Adams made it clear that the sensitive, impressionable Maria Jefferson was quite fragile and needed to bond with her father and her older sister, Martha (Patsy). Abigail looked forward to witnessing a family reunion and was shocked when a stranger, Jefferson's French butler, was sent from Paris to collect the girls. Jefferson's seemingly unfeeling reaction to his child's emotional health stands in stark contrast to the writer of the Head and Heart letter who had seen a tremendous amount of suffering, trembled as an intimate faced an affliction, and professed joy in commitment to those under his care.

He had lost his wife and four of their six offspring. The year after her father had left her and her baby sister, Lucy, with their late mother's relatives, Polly was present for the little one's death from whooping cough and nearly succumbed to it herself. At the time he learned of Lucy's death, Jefferson wallowed in anger, confusion, and disgust with a world he couldn't control. And yet, at this moment of anticipation of Maria's arrival in Europe, he wavered and chose a man who spoke practically no English to fetch his child.

There is more. Just a few months earlier, at the urging of his doctor, Jefferson had traveled a far greater distance to the south of France to test the healing powers of the waters in Aix. His failure to sacrifice a few days to bring joy to his own child is hard to rationalize—especially in view of how Abigail Adams described Maria months afterward: "I never felt so attached to a child in my Life on so short an acquaintance." In similar fashion, his dear friend Madame de Corny, in England at the time the child arrived, taunted Jefferson by letter, at once begging for an update on the condition of his wrist and allowing that had it been Madame, not Mrs. Adams, who took charge of the adorable Maria, "qui scait sil ne vous eut pas ete bien difficile de la ravoir" (Who knows what difficulty you'd have had in getting her back).[29]

These, then, were the circumstances under which Jefferson was reintroduced to Sally, who was just old enough and near enough in 1782 to register the final days of her mistress / half sister at Monticello. Jefferson had not requested her as a companion for his daughter, though he made sure she was well taken care of in Paris. Initially, anyway, she presented as childlike.

If a sexual relationship began before they departed France, as their son Madison Hemings stated in 1873, and if she became pregnant at sixteen with a child who did not survive long and whose birth went unrecorded, no certain documentary evidence exists. It is not an unreasonable assumption, however. The son reported that his mother told of a negotiation with her master and sexual partner in Paris, trading her own freedom for that of her prospective children.

In advance of sailing to America, Jefferson spent what Brodie notes is "a surprising amount" on clothes for Sally—a meaningful gesture, one supposes, but not necessarily indicative of a romantic tie. He could have been moved to see her dressed attractively because he saw a meaningful resemblance between his late wife and her young half sister—it's impossible to know whether his motivation was that she carried his child or something else. Whatever sensibility and commitment to Sally he might have come to exhibit in later years, when she lived at Monticello as a seamstress and chambermaid, there is no smoking gun as of 1789. What warmth did he feel toward her then? William Short wasn't talking.[30]

Statements by the once enslaved indicate that Sally Hemings, with few choices in life, became Thomas Jefferson's "concubine," acquiescing to her role as one who satisfied his urges. In Paris, she was by law entitled to personal freedom; in Virginia, she became his personal property again. This effectively presents Jefferson as one who eroticized dominance over the female. By modern standards, it's not a pretty picture, and yet in Jefferson's (pre-Victorian) lifetime it was treated less as a moral matter than as a subject of satire: the philosopher who lowered himself to mate with a not-even-white servant.

It was a time when coarse caricature and bawdy songs delighted in what is called "phallic narcissism," as the historian Vic Gatrell writes of the peculiarities of male culture: "Sexual pleasure was justified by the urgent promptings of 'Nature.'" Publications by Hancarville were well known in the European culture Jefferson was now immersed in: one could write without self-censoring about races and cultures from a standpoint of biological urges and the perception of pleasure. Jefferson demonstrated as much in *Notes on Virginia* as well as in letters. Intellectualization of sex did not mean the writer was a prude.[31]

And then there is this: Prior to his arrival in France, Jefferson had had mixed success as a suitor. Lagging behind his fellows when he attained marriageable age, he was unable to check his sex drive in the attempted seduction of his close friend's wife, and he evidently indulged himself with those in a social class below his (free and unfree alike). The moral laxity of the French and the wide availability of prostitutes in Paris troubled him only when he contemplated the likely effects on the sons of planters who found multiple partners while abroad.

Posing as immune in his letters to fellow Virginians, Jefferson does not reveal all that he thought on the subject of sexual activity. It should not come as a shock, then, that as a widower in his forties, he might feel impelled to cross another barrier and engage in procreative sex with his late wife's half sister—a life of privilege corresponding with his own emotional self-awareness. With less of an attachment to his partner than had grown over his ten years of marriage, were the concubine to die young, as his wife did, he would not have to endure the same degree of anguish. This is, of course, pure speculation, but it is not out of line with the lack of pain or heartache exhibited by Jefferson when confronted with the deaths of some of his closest French friends during the Terror of 1793. He was, in a word, accepting of these losses. Sally Hemings was someone familiar to him, yet owing to her station in life he would not draw so close to her as to be capable of worrying about her when they were apart, as he had done while Patty lived. This does not preclude feelings of fondness for his concubine, though it does limit his exposure to pain.[32]

Of immediate concern to Jefferson in 1789 was the future of his daughter Martha (Patsy), who was giving thought to becoming a nun, just as Maria Cosway had contemplated at a similar age. Jefferson had enrolled Patsy as a boarding student at the Abbaye Royale de Panthémont, a convent school, where she was afforded the best education in Paris for a female. There she found friends and a comfortable situation, which obliged Jefferson to erase Catholicism from her thoughts by returning her to Virginia and seeing that she found a husband acceptable to him.

That is what occurred soon after the three Jeffersons and two Hemingses returned to Monticello. Thomas Mann Randolph Jr. was a distant cousin and the son of a close friend of Jefferson's, whose studies in Edinburgh coincided with the Jeffersons' time in Paris. The marriage was performed at Monticello by an Episcopal minister. The bride was seventeen, the groom twenty-two. It bears repeating that Patsy Jefferson and Sally Hemings were born within months of each other, and here it was that Jefferson was fully prepared to release his daughter into the arms of a man who desired her sexually. This says something about how Jefferson might have perceived Sally, Patsy's "mighty near white" relative.

The teenager's persistently controlling father arranged for the very young couple to settle a short distance from Monticello rather than days away at the Randolphs' seat. Among family members in the extended Randolph lineage there was an unusual amount of friction, and Jefferson's new son-in-law was to prove a prime example of aberrant behavior, for which Martha, as a mother many times over, would suffer grievously. Increasingly aware of Tom Randolph's volatility, Jefferson advised his dutiful daughter to put up with as much as she could withstand. He gave her no chance to fashion any life outside that of a traditional Virginia gentry wife who accepted her familial role as a breeder of the next generation.[33]

In the years to come, in the writings of a good many people intimately associated with life at Monticello, white men would be said to associate openly with enslaved females; mixed-race people were numerous and remarked upon by visitors. Annette Gordon-Reed points out that "practically every adult Jefferson male" was named as the sexual partner of a Hemings female. "In a way it seems at once astounding and unsurprising," she writes. "Monticello seems to have resembled a mini-version of the stereotypical view of New Orleans—a place where white males pursued and attached themselves to light-skinned black women."[34]

One of the great mysteries in the life of Martha Jefferson Randolph is how she felt about and acted toward "Maria's maid," her enslaved "aunt" Sally Hemings. Maria herself was fated to die as her mother had, as a consequence of childbirth, in 1804. Martha, the only one of Patty Jefferson's children who outlived her father, intentionally left posterity in the dark while quietly orchestrating the later family denial that Sally had meant anything special to the master of Monticello.

THE FRENCH REVOLUTION

In 1788, Jefferson petitioned Congress to recall him temporarily in order to get his business affairs in order and resettle his daughters. Official permission to return arrived in his hands on August 26, 1789, six weeks after revolution erupted with the storming of the Bastille. He received regular reports from his French friends during his final weeks in Paris. Lafayette sent him a draft of his proposed constitution for a French republic.

On the eve of departure, Jefferson hosted a dinner for three liberal noblemen: Condorcet, Lafayette, and La Rochefoucauld. He left his books and furniture behind, expecting to return to France after a few months to complete his tour. He looked forward to monitoring a revolution against monarchy whose present leaders were all well known to him and about which he was therefore entirely hopeful.[35]

It was before the end of his first year in Paris that Jefferson wrote the letter to Baron Geismar in which he said, "I am savage enough to prefer the woods, the wilds and independance of Monticello, to all the pleasures of this gay capital." Whether or not he had any inkling by then that his Paris circle would present outlets for his own "savage" lust, he was now heading home to his private mountain much changed. His taste in art, architecture, cuisine, and hospitality itself were all French-accented now. He arrived at the port of Norfolk on November 23, bearing the books and wines he'd packed for the voyage, along with a stock of new ideas gleaned from five years abroad.[36]

He did not know that James Madison and George Washington had a different course in mind for him than a brief turnaround before resuming his work in Paris. And the prediction of Mme de Corny, in personal terms, was no closer to what life had in store. "Je vais vous prédire votre sort," she wrote. (I am foretelling your future.) "Vous vous remarierez, oui, c'est sûr, et votre femme sera heureuse." (You will remarry, yes, it's certain, and your wife will be happy.)

Mme de Corny may have blown one prediction, but the desperation she expressed in the same letter would prove justified. Jefferson was leaving France at a perilous time, she insisted. "La vie calme et heureuse" was over. There was nothing left for her, she said, but her sweet memories: to love and miss her friends. She would lose her husband and home to the anxiety and trauma of Revolutionary politics.[37]

Of the three liberal noblemen to whom Jefferson had just bidden farewell, none would fare well in the Revolution. After radical forces took over and ordered his arrest, Lafayette fled the country only to be captured by the Austrians, who incarcerated him for five years. An even worse fate belonged to the generous nobleman La Rochefoucauld, who was stoned to death before the eyes of his immediate family. Condorcet remained outspoken and was forced into hiding, where he hammered out his *Esquisse* over several months. Then, on March 27, 1794, the man known as "the last of the philosophes" was located and dispatched to prison. Two days later, he was found dead in his cell. And Jefferson, as George Washington's secretary of state during the French Terror, had little if any power to alter the course of these inhuman events.[38]

PART III

Political Hazards

I wish the Gods had nothing else to do,
But to confirm my Curses.

—SHAKESPEARE, *CORIOLANUS*
(AS COPIED BY JEFFERSON INTO HIS LITERARY COMMONPLACE BOOK)

Figure 13. Portrait of Alexander Hamilton, by John Trumbull, 1805. The Jefferson-Hamilton feud over the direction of the federal government devolved into a competition for influence over President Washington, which Hamilton won, hands down. (Courtesy Library of Congress)

CHAPTER 8

"Open Mouthed Against Me"
An Age of Contempt

Alexander Hamilton didn't just frustrate Jefferson. He was the better Machiavellian.[1] He circumvented Jefferson at critical junctures and ultimately forced his rival out of the Washington administration. He succeeded in turning the president against Jefferson and anyone allied with him, installing a crew that was loyal to Hamilton alone. He infiltrated the cabinet of President John Adams, too, before Adams saw the light and fought back, at which point the hellbent Hamilton published a long, scathing pamphlet bludgeoning Adams's character and doing all he could to deny the second president four more years. Clear enough?

Nor is it an exercise in hyperbole to assess Jefferson's feelings toward Hamilton and Hamiltonianism as a compound of contempt and disgust, using the categorical definitions provided by the legal scholar and cultural historian William Ian Miller. "Disgust helps define boundaries between us and them and me and you," Miller writes. "It helps prevent *our* way from being subsumed into *their* way."

Like disgust, the emotion of contempt requires that one rank the other below oneself, and find justification for doing so. This describes Jefferson when he alludes to Hamilton's lack of appreciation for the welcome America gave him as a humble immigrant; or when he diagnoses the Hamiltonian ("monocrat") threat to republican principles as a kind of nervous disorder manifest as weak-mindedness. As he framed his political creed, Jefferson philosophized, psychologized, and personalized the threat posed to the nation by a new breed of Tory.[2]

Here, the antecedents are instructive. Before Hamilton threatened his position and interfered with his broader vision, we know that Jefferson suffered hurtful attacks on his good name in his home state. He was quite sensitive to the menace of the ever-popular Patrick Henry, and expressed his repugnance by categorizing Henry as a fraud, a dull mind worsened by distinct character flaws. Even a decade after Henry's death, he would not let go of his resentment.

When Jefferson warned off George Rogers Clark from Henry in 1782, he went so far as to accuse him of personal cowardice. He was equally unrestrained in his post-presidential correspondence thirty years later in successive letters to Henry's acclaimed biographer William Wirt. In the first, he attributed to Henry the attorney a "ravenous avarice"—"ravenous" not by accident being the same adjective he applied to Napoleon's appetite for power. Alluding to Henry and moneymaking in the second instance (while declaring for himself an unblemished "love of peace and tranquility"), he replaced "ravenous" with "insatiable."

This gut-level criticism smacks not of envy so much as a form of denial. Jefferson was definitely not one to strong-arm clients after providing legal services, but he did keep precise records, down to the penny. He always knew what he was owed and, increasingly, what he owed. He did not treat the acquisition of wealth as a badge of honor, but he was a collector of valuable objects who spent lavishly—one might say irresponsibly—in keeping up the lifestyle of a manor lord. As the U.S. president, out of a sense of duty, he spent personal funds on entertainment, but that did not make Henry unjustifiably committed to earning a good living.

Was Henry a hoarder of hard currency? No such evidence exists. He was paid a good deal more for his legal services than Jefferson and others were, based on the perceived value of his advocacy, and there is anecdotal evidence to suggest that he could be persuaded to take on an otherwise unpromising case if the price was right. Granted, too, that despite his popularity as a state executive who identified with regular people, Henry was not Jefferson's intellectual equal. But the historical record does not bear out the charge of avarice simply on the basis of the courtroom performer's ability to entrance audiences and command greater fees. Patrick Henry understood the system, framed passionate arguments, and peppered them with humor at the behest of thankful clients.[3]

"Rotten-hearted" avarice, though? Words don't get much harsher than that. On the surface, it seems odd that Jefferson was inclined to level this criticism. He himself was not the most virtuous or most efficient of money managers. Maybe he thought he was. He had a complicated relationship with bankers for most of his adult life, eternally haunted by unpaid debts. One obvious cost of his five years in France was that minimal production occurred on his plantations. In the months before he joined Washington's cabinet, when he staged his daughter's wedding and reestablished himself at Monticello, he was painfully aware that he owed his late father-in-law's British creditors more than the annual revenue on his tobacco crop could ever hope to raise. Had enough of the Wayles land been sold back in 1773, his lifelong burden of debt could have been resolved without too much difficulty. Yet he wasn't doing any soul-searching, at least as far as the record shows.

Throughout the 1790s, when he was as often away as he was in Albemarle, Jefferson lagged behind even recently agreed-upon annual payments on his mounting debt. He drafted self-righteous letters to his multiple creditors, in each instance comforting himself by adopting the position that it was not he, but the less prudent John Wayles, who had created the situation he found himself in; nor could he be held morally accountable for a poor crop or price fixing: "None of these things depended on me," he protested to a demanding creditor in 1792. Patrick Henry did not live as large as Jefferson, did not spend as freely. It's possible that in dwelling on Henry's smallness, Jefferson was saying something about his own anxieties.[4]

Again, according to Jefferson, Henry's money worship was second only to his "love of popularity." That observation may well have been true, though it bears notice that Henry resisted President Washington's offer of a cabinet post, where he would have had power and visibility. It could be argued that Jefferson was not quite as thin-skinned about criticism as Washington was, but he did court popularity when he urged others to prop up his political interests in the press. He wanted to see his most powerful enemies fall from favor, so as to justify his claims about them.

Countervailing evidence didn't interest Jefferson. Henry's suspicious nature regarding corruption and consolidation of power was pretty close to Jefferson's at the time Hamilton was pushing his agenda at Treasury. But this convergence did not produce a thaw in relations between the two Virginians. And when Washington sought unsuccessfully to lure Henry into the cabinet in 1794–95, Henry confessed that he had bought in to hearsay that Washington distrusted him as "a factional, seditious character." The truth is that all of these founding "greats" were easily caught up in callow gossip, and Jefferson, though he routinely denied it, sometimes permitted flimsy forms of personal discomfort to grow into the kind of animosity that could and did linger for decades.[5]

As Jefferson's desire to mete out posthumous justice applied to the multiterm Virginia governor who never held national office, he reaped pleasure from his "realization" that Henry could not perform when his skill at declamation was valued less than actual legislative specifics, when mere voice came across as empty of substance. It is curious, too, that one with Jefferson's timidity of voice when putting forth an argument in a legislative body—that is, when not writing—would observe that Henry's eloquence carried "no weight" in an assembly of "cool-headed, reflecting, judicious men" among whom "sober reasoning" was called for in place of dramatic flourishes. Jefferson's biased portrait of Patrick Henry was that of an intellectual lightweight, routinely confused in his judgments. Though once he had been a worthy asset to the Revolution, he did not appreciate the demands of the post-Revolutionary age. With malice aforethought, Jefferson went out of his way to see that Henry was remembered as less than he was.[6]

A weakness Henry shared with Hamilton, we read in Jefferson's later correspondence, was an unwillingness to serve the Washington administration in a foreign capacity, as an envoy. But it was his character that Jefferson repeatedly judged: "His self-esteem had never suffered him to act as second to any man on earth." Jefferson finally washed his hands of Patrick Henry with the cruel presumption that this man who had been "the idol of his country ... descended to the grave with less than it's indifference." It was wishful thinking on Jefferson's part, and a sure sign of the extent of his contempt.[7]

With Hamiltonian Federalism, Jefferson's critique, as we shall see, was more complex. Unlike the reputation of a single man, which future generations would be free to debate, an enemy ideology was an essentialist threat. Jefferson's Republican Party could not coexist with its competition as constituted: if the Federalist Party was not revamped, its utter extinction had to be plotted to facilitate the realization of Jefferson's vision. Through a Jeffersonian prism, Hamilton's "monarchism," in the form of a party, was not just wrongheaded but an impairment, a perversion, a transmissible pathology; those who came aboard its antirepublican bandwagon possessed a fundamental weakness of will that prepared them for total dependence.

The political world viewed from Jefferson's position had as its ideal a vision of self-government that came to be called "democracy." The Hamilton sect treated the word "democrat" as a slur, believing that Jefferson was the pied piper of anarchy and misrule: he courted "the mob." Rhetoric aside, what Hamilton championed was national commercial wealth, which he believed attainable by granting exceptional power to trusted insiders, well-heeled "gentlemen," select friends of the central government. As they lined up their forces for battle, both Hamilton and Jefferson identified their opposite as an "intriguer" who would do anything to get his way.

When we address Jefferson's predisposition to deride and degrade his enemies, an important distinction must be made. Despite what modern Americans have come to believe of Jefferson's racism, he does not appear to have felt either contempt or disgust for the Africa-descended, whether free or enslaved. If he allowed himself an emotion in their regard, it was something closer to pity. He convinced himself that the general disparagement of Black persons was owing to "natural" forces; what the modern world views as learned prejudice, he imagined as a scientific principle akin to magnetism: attraction/repulsion. True, he favored the "fair" skin of his own ancestors, rejecting dark complexions and the odor he associated with laboring Blacks; but he presented his thought of cultural pollution in terms of physiology, biochemistry—not a conflict of wills, not a matter of choice. Jefferson did not dislike those he depreciated, even as he imagined their minds as inherently inferior. There is no evidence that he laughed with derision or satirized Black people the way uglier-minded whites did.

Yet in both of these cases, one political, the other anthropological in character, Jefferson held stubbornly to his opinions. He would never come to acknowledge the intellectual or creative power of Blacks, ignoring proof that stared him in the face. His view of Alexander Hamilton was of a different order. Why? Because, again according to the philosopher of culture Miller, a contaminant on the outside is less potent, less critical, than a contaminant inside. Contempt for someone who is your peer, especially in politics, reflects an even more visceral sensation of disgust than what is felt for one you deem "lesser" by nature.[8]

Aaron Burr, without animus, alternately argued alongside and stood in opposition to Hamilton in a number of court cases, all the while knowing his colleague as a troublemaker and a bully. He found his outlet in building a political base by democratic means—by winning elections. That wasn't enough for Jefferson, who clearly loathed Hamilton and who resorted to mocking and belittling the social climber who, unlike Jefferson, never pretended that he lacked ambition. What makes Hamilton a different sort of enemy is Jefferson's schadenfreude. The Caribbean-born New Yorker cornered the Virginian, and it hurt to the point where Jefferson needed to reduce him, to see him fall, to gloat.

His sharing of taunts and barbs with Madison did not help confront the crisis they faced. Once having targeted his antagonist, Jefferson demanded categorical results. He felt certain that the contamination Hamilton threatened America with would lead to a poisoning of the very soul of the republic, which was everything to him. Patrick Henry may have been undeserving of his elevation, in Jefferson's jaundiced view, and forgettable (as he imagined Henry's descent into obscurity at the end of his life); but in representing the martyred Hamilton as a disease of the soul, the clear and present danger was greater than Henry's could ever be.

CABINET RELATIONS

After four months in Virginia, Jefferson arrived in New York. As he took up his position in Washington's cabinet, a vocabulary in favor of social equality was evident in many places, so that some of the more entitled landed elites could be heard grumbling. Skilled writers of the middling sorts fed expectations of greater democracy in hopeful newspaper pieces. There were as yet none who would question the motives of the president.

George Washington had determinedly assembled his executive advisory group—the first cabinet—from geographically diverse parts. They were men he had counted on in critical times. Secretary of War Henry Knox, a Bostonian, was virtually his military protégé, who had proven his mettle from the opening days of the War for Independence. To Jefferson, Knox was merely a shill for Hamilton.

The first attorney general, Edmund Randolph, was well known and well respected within Virginia's legal and political community. Like Washington, Jefferson had always been aware of the extended Randolph lineage, and of Edmund's background. Early in the Revolutionary War, Washington had hired on Edmund (who was ten years Jefferson's junior) as an aide-de-camp and watched the young man grow into a capable legal advocate. Secretary of State Jefferson was the only nonmilitary member of the cabinet, a fact that presented no disadvantage because he was a rich resource with critical European experience.

Treasury Secretary Hamilton had never seen Europe. If he was an outlier in the cabinet, it was a matter of personality only. His intellectual breadth was not to be underestimated and his boastful ego obliged the president to weigh what he said against the views of others. Washington had had an entire decade to accommodate himself to Hamilton's self-regard and establish a successful working relationship with him. He placed Hamilton's practical value to him over any annoyance attending his glaring ambition. Washington was fifty-seven when he took the oath of office; Jefferson was then forty-six, Knox not quite forty; Randolph and

Hamilton were only in their mid-thirties. Age and seniority was felt (and mattered) to a greater degree in early republican society than it does in the present; yet Hamilton did not defer to anyone or show esteem for his elders in the way Jefferson did. His relationship with Washington was one of mutual self-interest, that is, more transactional than rooted in the fond feelings Washington exhibited toward some others among his wartime aides.

At the Constitutional Convention, despite his subsequent collaboration with Madison on the Federalist Papers, Hamilton did not play a meaningful role. His views were singularly his own and he did not compromise easily. He thought the British model of a strong national government in which changes occurred slowly was the best choice for the United States. That's why Jefferson's democratic theory appeared to him as political turbulence. He wanted to ensure that power remained in the hands of an elite class that outthought those who, like Hamilton, aimed to lift themselves from their common roots but who, unlike Hamilton, did so without the elite education he was fortunate to have obtained on the basis of patronage. Hamilton had married his way into social respectability.

From late 1788 though Washington's inauguration on April 30, 1789, the hands-on constitutionalist James Madison had to divide his time: he was forced to vie with his younger friend James Monroe for a House seat after Patrick Henry saw to it that Madison was barred from the U.S. Senate. Between campaign appearances in his district, he did more than anyone else to give structure to the first presidency. Washington felt he could not do without Madison. "I want to write a private & confidential letter to you," the president-elect penned just after New Year's Day 1789, trying to ascertain Madison's whereabouts. Jefferson's recall from France fitted Madison's purposes.[9]

Inauspiciously, Washington spent most of the first several months of his presidency bedridden in the temporary capital, New York City. Congress did not complete the task of establishing the executive departments until summer's end. The slow pace continued with the Bill of Rights debate in Congress and Washington's autumn tour of New England, attempts to unify the states under a federal mantle. The First Congress took a break, reassembling in January 1790, when Hamilton introduced his Report on Public Credit, a plan for retiring the nation's $75 million debt, which Madison immediately reacted against owing to the provision that exclusively rewarded the investor class.

Even before Jefferson arrived in New York in March 1790, the performative features of Washington's presidency were set in place. At the start of his administration, he queried Vice President John Adams and Treasury Secretary Hamilton on how he should preserve presidential dignity "without subjecting himself to the imputation of superciliousness or unnecessary reserve." Washington was all business.

Presidential levees occurred weekly. In her book on the first cabinet, the historian Lindsay Chervinsky says that "any man dressed in respectable attire could enter the president's home every Tuesday afternoon." On these occasions, Washington wore a ceremonial sword as he greeted guests. The first lady hosted her own invitation-only drawing room on Friday evenings, attended by men and women together. Elite families took advantage of the opportunity to be seen.

Private dinners were another regular feature of the first term, meant to provide a sense of conviviality so that the methodical president did not appear stiff and distant. An added advantage was the chance for Washington to soften up legislators as they gave consideration to the administration's policies (something Jefferson would do just as effectively during his presidency). Chervinsky writes: "Washington was a conniving politician who carefully crafted his image." She notes as well that the first president never used the term "cabinet" to refer to the men who comprised the executive departments—it was the press that came up with the now universal term; to Washington, they were uniformly "the gentlemen of my family" or simply "the secretaries." He preferred one-on-one meetings, wherein one suspects Jefferson was somewhat low-key as Hamilton combined factual understanding with aggressive persuasion. A limited number of meetings of the entire cabinet took place in the first years of the administration, more after the Anglo-French War erupted in early 1793, when, as Jefferson reflected in later years, "Hamilton and myself were daily pitted in the cabinet like two cocks."[10]

Four months after his arrival in Virginia, Jefferson finally joined the administration. In the weeks immediately following, he was saddled with one of his infamous "periodical head-achs." Any armchair psychologist can put two and two together: he didn't relish the job and was preoccupied with the unknowns that lay ahead. Until Washington had been in office nearly a year, there was neither a foreign policy establishment nor a definable foreign policy. At least there was as yet no fixed expression of partisanship, either.

In June 1790, Jefferson accompanied Washington on a fishing trip. Two months later, the national capital moved from New York to Philadelphia, where it would remain for the rest of the decade. Whether or not the matter of a permanent federal city was as yet discussed, the two Virginians were equally in favor of positioning the national capital on the Potomac. When Congress adjourned, Jefferson returned to Monticello. He occupied himself with studying such policy assignments as the regulation of commercial shipping and finding means to compete with British dominance on the seas. On his way back to Philadelphia, he stopped at Washington's Mount Vernon. All was well.

The federal government was beginning to jell. It was, for the most part, a honeymoon year in national politics. Relations between Jefferson and Hamilton remained civil. As the astute and vigilant Madison had been at the center of the domestic political debate throughout the 1780s, the earliest opposition to Hamilton came from that direction. Congressman Madison was taken aback by Hamilton's announced plan to relieve the states of their debts. Virginia and its Southern neighbors had dutifully repaid most of what they owed, while Northern states like Massachusetts and New York had not.

But there was more to it. Hamilton would be propping up the speculators in government IOUs who had scooped up securities at a small fraction of their face value and would profit handsomely by being patient with the new government. Madison identified a frightening precedent: unfair advantage being given to the wealthiest while the voiceless were trampled. He took the side of the original owners of the government's debt, unpaid war veterans whose small freeholds required immediate cash. Showing where his allegiance lay, Hamilton left these folks in the lurch while enriching the bigwigs. It was a sign of things to come.

So was Washington's acquiescence to quasiroyal treatment and his comfort in living as he did at home, waited on by people of color whom he owned as well as white servants native to the city. It fell under Hamilton's purview to allocate funds for an accomplished chef, imported wine, and hairdressers: the chief magistrate and his wife entertained lavishly, so they had to look good. In both New York and Philadelphia, the Washingtons enjoyed their privilege.

Secretary Jefferson's situation was different. In the first and second temporary capitals, he lived modestly, though he would not have thought for a minute that the Washingtons should sacrifice ease. He followed Madison's policy agenda, yet continued to treat Hamilton as a man of honor through the end of 1790, sensitive to his new colleague's stated fear that any more dissension over the repayment of outstanding state debts could lead to disunion. Once Jefferson's forbearance evaporated, all he could see was treachery in the heart of his rival. There was no turning back.

"HEAD OF A PARTY"

It was with the constitutionally questionable establishment of a national bank in the early months of 1791 that the knives came out. A matter of public embarrassment added fuel to the fire in Jefferson's belly.

Though Hamilton didn't care much for Vice President John Adams, he took perverse pleasure in Jefferson's predicament when it became public, in May of that year, that he'd called Adams a monarchy-curious "heretic." In this instance, Jefferson was forwarding a borrowed pamphlet to a Philadelphia printer, a stranger to him, and appended a cover note written, as he fretted in a letter to Madison, "currente calamo" (without much reflection—literally, "with running pen"). The quoted insult to Adams became the preface to Thomas Paine's highly controversial, monarchy-bashing *Rights of Man*, which would be banned and burned in Britain. Hamilton was "open mouthed against me," Jefferson told Madison, "unreserved" in telling others of Jefferson's opposition to the administration he served. Though Jefferson and Adams remained cordial, Jefferson gave up on Hamilton and those who slavishly promoted his interests. These men would soon become the "monarchists" and "monocrats" (a term Jefferson invented, synonymous with "aristocrat") who aimed to tear down republican guardrails.

When it came to the Bank of the United States, imitative of the Bank of England, Hamilton thought big. Private investors would own more of the bank than the government did, yet it would collect taxes, manage the national debt, and fund major public projects. It would privilege wealthy citizens of the Northeast over the agrarian South. It would concentrate power in the hands of money men who were beholden to Hamilton.

Disabused of his earlier belief in the value of collegiality, Jefferson made common cause with Madison, providing him with intelligence about policy discussions in the cabinet so that the congressman could lobby legislative allies and prepare a strong response. Jefferson's feud with Hamilton was still just simmering: the hardening of a two-party system would not really occur until 1792, sparked by the rise of an opposition press and a reshuffling in Congress. The self-interestedness of states was temporarily muted, as "Republican" and "Federal" came to denote the Madison-Jefferson and Hamilton positions. Party politics was born.

Hamilton's role in creating the conditions under which parties formed occurred as he shifted his focus from the vigorous "little Madison" to the thinner-skinned Jefferson. He circulated the idea that Jefferson had stolen Madison away from him, that prior to Jefferson's return from France, Madison and he had viewed federalism in compatible terms. They had taken walks together, sharing perspectives on government that Madison suddenly no longer favored. He had been magically seduced away from sensible policy, acquiescing to Jefferson's preference for a weak central government. In a fateful move, Hamilton elevated Jefferson into a republican champion by turning him into a Svengali.

Yet it was decidedly Madison who initiated the most critical challenges to the treasury secretary's agenda. Acting in concert with Jefferson, he proposed that his former college roommate Philip Freneau, "a man of acknowledged genius," be brought to Philadelphia to set up a newspaper that would act as a check on Hamilton's unimpeded aggrandizement of power. The idea was to provide an alternative to the administration mouthpiece, John Fenno's Hamilton-loving *Gazette of the United States*.

After months of wrangling, Madison got his wish. Freneau's *National Gazette* began publishing in the fall of 1791. Its backers hoped to grow it into a truly national paper, its antiaristocratic message disseminated through the post far beyond Philadelphia. Madison and Jefferson worried that most of the country was ignorant of the threat America faced, that monarchy could yet arise on its shores.

It took until the middle of 1792 before the war between the two Philadelphia-based papers came to a head, pitting two cabinet members against each other. In July, it was revealed in the Hamiltonian *Gazette of the United States* that Freneau's newspaper, which had stepped up its attacks on Hamilton, did not spring independently from Freneau's brain, and that the separate salary he received as a translator for the State Department implicated one person only in the message Freneau delivered: Thomas Jefferson.

According to the *Gazette*, the corrupt relationship was forged to amplify "the views of a certain party, of which Mr. Jefferson is the head." Freneau's explicit denial that Jefferson had any stake in, or relationship to, his paper did not erase suspicion. (Madison was not named, though he was cast as "a particular friend" of Freneau and Jefferson, with complicity in the nefarious arrangement.) For his part, Jefferson deceived Washington when he parsed his words so as to deny his role in Freneau's political activities and weakly insisted that the paper was critical of nonrepublican ideas, not of Washington's policies or motives. In fact, Jefferson was directly involved in the outreach to Freneau as early as February 1791. In correspondence, he grew more and more fixated on trends he prophesied, frequently counterposing such phrases as "political heresies" and "pure republicanism" as he laid down a gauntlet in the battle with the increasingly confident Hamilton.

Hamilton did not make concessions. Hoping to get his way, he routinely upped the ante, engaged heatedly, performed in public, spoke off the cuff, battled with words. It was his loose lips that led to affairs of honor and eventually to the dueling ground where he forfeited his life.

In cabinet meetings, President Washington presided—as his title literally prescribed—rather than commanded. He listened, learned, weighed options, and attempted to remain neutral until he had to lean in one direction or another. Owing to his overriding desire to privilege social order over democracy, he generally favored Hamilton. While it is not clear exactly when Jefferson sensed that he could no longer succeed with Washington, when he became convinced that the president was the "dupe" of his rival secretary on critical matters, he relied increasingly on Madison as a counterforce. He finally sounded the alarm (too late) in an exasperated letter to Washington accusing Hamilton of corruption, insisting that he had multiple members of Congress in his pocket after bettering their personal financial condition.[11]

It is instructive to compare an earlier instance where Jefferson reacted to a people being duped into believing those who would deceive them. Writing from Paris of European alignments in his official correspondence with John Jay, then occupying the position equivalent to his own in Washington's cabinet, Jefferson cautioned, in 1787, that the United States should never accept any foreign nation's promise of support as binding. He reported to Jay: "I am satisfied that the king of England beleives the mass of our people to be tired of their independance, and desirous of returning under his government: and that the same opinion prevails in the ministry and nation. They have hired their news-writers to repeat this lie in their gazettes so long that they have become the dupes of it themselves." Fast forward five years: seeing dangers inherent in putting one's trust in newspapers and seemingly earnest aides, Jefferson informed Washington on September 9, 1792, that of the political blunders he had committed in his time in public life, being "duped" by Hamilton was the one that occasioned "the deepest regret."[12]

The letter was written in response to Washington's appeal to his two secretaries to find a way to work together. It amounted to nearly four thousand words. This one letter is of paramount importance in our effort to process Jefferson's recurrence to a language of disgust and contempt when he felt a need to defend his own rational mind, honorable intent, and essential decency against imputations from one who was out to get him.

Without suggesting that Washington was being duped by Hamilton, he admitted to his own failing in that regard. "I was duped into by the Secretary of the treasury," he wrote, "and made a tool for forwarding his schemes, not then sufficiently understood by me; and of all the errors of my political life, this has occasioned me the deepest regret." Referring to his cabinet competor by his military title, "Colo[nel] Hamilton," was ostensibly a way to indicate his own solicitous bearing, respectful even in exasperation, as he affected to speak Washington's language.

In testifying to his personal embarrassment in having been duped, Jefferson was just warming up. The word that mattered now was "intrigue." Only one of the feuding officers of government was an "intriguer," he claimed. And not just that: Hamilton's intrigues literally threatened to bring down the experimental republic. Trusting that the president would take the time to read every word carefully, he would get to the point by the end of the long letter.

But first, Jefferson felt he had to justify himself. He paused in his argument to explain that he'd intended to put off revealing the depth of his disgust until Washington had concluded his service to America, when both of them were "uninterested spectators" of national affairs, retired to their respective farms. Jefferson hoped the president appreciated his reluctance to spill his guts about Hamilton's guile. It was only required that he speak his mind in the moment because Hamilton's charges had been made public, alleging that he, Jefferson, was intriguing against the administration by conniving with *his* friends in Congress.

To Jefferson, "intrigue" meant advancing one's personal influence by using the authority granted to one executive department to manipulate the members of another branch of the government. (He also used the term "intermeddle," and at times paired "intrigue" with "cabal," doubling down on the image of an active conspiracy.) Hamilton had made his accusations in the press, while Jefferson swore that any remarks he made that were critical of Hamilton's management of the Treasury Department consisted in "the mere enunciation of my sentiments in conversation, and chiefly among those who, expressing the same sentiments, drew mine from me."

He wished to assure the president that his method was quite the opposite of Hamilton's. He did not initiate such talk, but merely reaffirmed what like-minded political men were telling him. "I never had the desire to influence the members [of Congress], so neither had I any other means than my friendships, which I valued too highly to risk by usurpations on their freedom of judgment." In short, Jefferson had casually expressed a privately held opinion. He was innocent of every one of Hamilton's charges. As Jefferson would put it most emphatically in a letter to Madison after both he and Hamilton were out of office but still their parties' principals, "Hamilton is really a colossus to the antirepublican party. Without numbers, he is an host within himself." Hamilton was the guilty party, driven by a massive ego to lash out.

In the middle of the unavoidably long letter to the president, Jefferson repeats Washington's core concern back to him: "If the question be By whose fault is it that Colo. Hamilton and myself have not drawn together? the answer will depend on that to two other questions; Whose principles of administration best justify, by their purity, conscientious adherence? and Which of us has, notwithstanding, stepped farthest into the controul of the department of the other?" Claiming purity of motive is standard for Jefferson, as, in this case, he could point to his own hands-off relationship to Treasury matters in contrast with Hamilton's direct communication with senior British diplomats in pushing his own foreign policy agenda.

Without missing a beat, Jefferson reacted next to Hamilton's denigration of him in publicizing Jefferson's reported objections to the federal Constitution, which Jefferson had made, of course, from the remote vantage point of Paris. The charge was patently false, declared Jefferson: "No man in the U.S., I suppose, approved of every tittle in the constitution: no one, I believe approved more of it than I did." Whereas Jefferson liked best its "vitally republican" elements, Hamilton's main objections was that it lacked "a king and house of lords." Even when on the defensive, as he often was, Jefferson knew how to rub it in.

Had he reviewed the first number in the Federalist Papers, authored by Hamilton, he would have seen a preview of that man's conviction that he could spot a government in trouble because of populist trickery. In October 1787, Hamilton accused the Constitution's opponents of a "perverted ambition" to sink the federalist cause in order to retain personal power that they would otherwise be surrendering to national institutions. As if already thinking of Jefferson's "man of the people" pose, he added that "a dangerous ambition more often lurks behind the specious mask of zeal for the rights of the people than under the forbidden appearance of zeal for the firmness and efficiency of government"; that the despotic force responsible for overturning "the liberties of republics" came from demagogic champions who came to the fore "by paying an obsequious court to the people; commencing demagogues, and ending tyrants." Jefferson knew there were historical examples of such developments, but they did not exonerate Hamilton from the charge of abusing the power of his office.

In the letter to Washington, Jefferson goes all out to make the "intriguer" charge stick: "His system flowed from principles adverse to liberty, and was calculated to undermine and demolish the republic, by creating an influence of his department over the members of the legislature. I saw this influence actually produced, and it's first fruits to be the establishment of the great outlines of his project by the votes of the very persons who, having swallowed his bait were laying themselves out to profit by his plans... These were no longer the votes then of the representatives of the people, but of deserters from the rights and interests of the people: and it was impossible to consider their decisions, which had nothing in view but to enrich themselves."

To enrich themselves. As he would routinely depict Patrick Henry—corrupted by a love of money—so he identified the weak spot in the Federalist legislators whom Hamilton was able to exploit from his position as head of the Treasury. They swallowed the bait the secretary had set as a most devious lure.

The latter half of Jefferson's letter is mostly a pained, lawyerly explanation of his ethics in the hiring of Philip Freneau to publish a newspaper that served as an alternative to the Hamilton-friendly organ. It is hard to imagine Washington lapping up its compendious detail. More in keeping with his known yearning for Monticello, Jefferson wound down the letter by reiterating his urgent desire to retire from his cabinet position with dignity intact. And then came the final blow, as he produced on the page the nastiest possible attack on Hamilton's character before signing off with "great & sincere affection and respect."

"I will not suffer my retirement to be clouded," he wrote, "by the slanders of a man whose history, from the moment at which history can stoop to notice him, is a tissue of machinations against the liberty of the country which has not only recieved and given him bread, but heaped it's honors on his head." The inference to be drawn from Jefferson's words is unmistakable: instead of appreciating the good fortune that plucked the humbly born youth from obscurity and delivered him to the burgeoning city of New York, Hamilton had taken it upon himself to pass summary judgment on a Virginian of respectable lineage whose one "defect" was his ability to recognize Alexander Hamilton as a designing, intriguing, corrupting "enemy to the Republic." Hamilton was beyond redemption, and if Washington could not see that Jefferson had his country's interest at heart and Hamilton did not, they had best not broach the subject further.[13]

Altogether, from 1791 to 1793, in widely shared letters and newspaper attack pieces, Hamilton, without the least restraint, repeatedly hounded Jefferson by name. Claiming for himself (and those who embraced his nation-building project) the mantle of "national union, national respectability, public order," he contrasted himself with Jefferson, "the patron and promoter of national disunion." In

Hamilton's mind, it was Freneau's newspaper that lit the destructive fire, having been established for one purpose: "abusing and traducing the Secretary of the Treasury." The instigator, Jefferson, had acted "to vilify and depreciate the government of the United States—to misrepresent and traduce the administration of it, except in the single department, of which that Gentleman is the head."

It is not wrong to conclude that Hamilton's litany justified Jefferson's pique in the September 9 letter to Washington. In the month prior, Hamilton had accused him of more than malfeasance: Jefferson was disturbing the peace of the country by forming a "party," a term used interchangeably with "faction" at this time and bearing the same pejorative meaning. "Mr. Jefferson is emulous of being the head of a party, whose politics have constantly aimed at elevating State-power, upon the ruins of National Authority." This smacked very much of Hamilton's language in Federalist 1.

Jefferson's tepid support for the federal Constitution at the time of the Federalist Papers was one thing, the man's character something else—deceptive, if not unstable. "Mr. Jefferson has hitherto been distinguished as the quiet[,] modest, retiring philosopher—as the plain simple unambitious republican. He shall not now for the first time be regarded as the intriguing incendiary—the aspiring turbulent competitor." With increasing flippancy, this time writing under the pseudonym "Scourge," Hamilton found an excuse to bring up the decade-old attack on Jefferson's untimely retreat from his governorship during Arnold's invasion, again calling out, in mocking tones, the disguise of "Plain Thomas J—wonderful humility on all occasions—the flimsy veil of inordinate ambition."

The language was contemptuous. It was language he would never have used to criticize Madison. Jefferson alone had the target on his back as that "intriguing incendiary," that "aspiring turbulent competitor" operating behind a "flimsy veil" of "inordinate ambition." Hamilton's reaction to Jefferson's moralistic pose during cabinet meetings mirrored the certainty that Hamilton felt about his own rectitude and justification. As Robert M. S. McDonald, professor of history at West Point, writes of this moment in the history of American politics: "Hamilton's attempt to discredit Jefferson backfired. Instead, by criticizing Jefferson's conduct and character, Hamilton thrust him into the forefront of newspaper readers' political consciousness." Jefferson was now the recognized leader of the Republican Party.[14]

Their temperamental differences only exacerbated their bad chemistry. Each saw the other's manner as distasteful, presumptuous, insolent. They appeared snakelike: one fast, feisty, and outspoken, rearing up to strike; the other slow, studied, and withdrawn, but no less prone to aggressive action. Washington was flummoxed. He heard Hamilton hissing and knew that Jefferson was seething even before he read his September complaint. History does not have a record of their private conversation at Mount Vernon when Jefferson stopped by in early October. But history makes it clear that even when Jefferson was alone with the president, he could not sway him, and in later years he rationalized that Washington had lost his firm grip on decision-making and was permitting "others" to think for him.

As for the impulsive Hamilton, never known for backing down, he, too, had no intention of alleviating Washington's concerns. He'd written the very same day Jefferson did, September 9, opening with "I most sincerely regret the causes of the uneasy sensations you experience." It was Jefferson who caused the rupture, who was somehow predisposed to take on Hamilton from day one: "I *know* that I have been an object of uniform opposition from Mr. Jefferson, from the first moment of his coming to the City of New York to enter upon his present office." While there is a good amount of contrary evidence, one cannot dismiss Hamilton's statement as a bald lie. Jefferson's body language may have been perceived other than as intended, or else Hamilton bought in to what someone told him: "I *know*, from the most authentic sources, that I have been the frequent subject of the most unkind whispers and insinuating from the same quarter. I have long seen a formed party in the Legislature, under his auspices, bent upon my subversion."

Hamilton's charge against Jefferson is somewhat at odds with a long and purposeful letter he'd written a few months earlier, however. The addressee was Edward Carrington, a Virginia planter and acquaintance of Washington's whose credentials included wartime service as a colonel in the southern theater, where, like Hamilton, he took part in the decisive Battle of Yorktown. To this gentleman Hamilton assigned most of the blame for the rise of an opposition to Madison, whom he attacked for "*insidious insinuations*" about Hamilton's coziness with speculators in "public money"; to wit, "The whole manner of this transaction left no doubt in any ones mind that Mr. Madison was actuated by *personal* & political animosity." He held Jefferson to account for wooing Madison away from earlier stances that neatly accorded with Hamilton's. Hamilton failed to understand, or chose to ignore, Madison's independence, his originality as a thinker, and his penchant for changing his mind on observing and weighing new circumstances.

To Carrington, Hamilton framed the Madison-Jefferson alliance as cataclysmic, underscoring his dual indictment: "*Mr. Madison cooperating with Mr. Jefferson is at the head of a faction decidedly hostile to me and my administration.*" Augmenting the charge in the letter to Washington, he insisted he'd been a "silent sufferer" who'd held off until very lately what he admitted to—his printed attacks on Jefferson's moral character. In their September 9 letters, then, Hamilton and Jefferson alike thought it important to convince the president they worked for that a hallmark of their personalities was self-control.[15]

The two-party system in American politics was now firmly in place. It remains to show how such a realization occurred, in light of the fact that the federal Constitution had made no provision for organized parties. John Quincy Adams, who was in the thick of it, describes events succinctly and, for the most part, dispassionately. In *Parties in the United States*, a manuscript he penned that was not published until the twentieth century, he identifies as the first Federalists those who endorsed the Constitution in the years between the Philadelphia convention and Washington's inauguration. After 1790, it became absurd for the Constitution's critics—those who had feared "consolidated" power at the center—to retain the name "Antifederalists," insofar as they were the ones who most obviously embraced the *federative principle*, which sought a clear balance between the "rights and powers" of the states and those of the national government. To designate their sect, they adopted "Republican" and to a lesser degree "Democrats," thereby "recommending them to the special favor of the people, and at the same time, stigmatizing their adversaries by the implication that they were anti-republicans, monarchists and aristocrats." Adams goes on to say that the emotions stirred up by the French Revolution played a critical role in reinforcing party divisions.[16]

As the Republicans coalesced as a national political party, Jefferson and Madison contrived to attract leading citizens of the toss-up state of New York to their existing alliance with agrarians across the South. Hamilton's home state was up for grabs. The Hamiltonians were opposed by two family-led parties, the Livingstons and the Clintons. Jefferson and Madison toured the state in the late spring of 1791, and historians remain uncertain just how much political glad-handing they did during the journey. Hamilton's allies were convinced that they had done a great deal of it. Over the course of that year and, more demonstrably, in 1792, a year of greater divergence, New York became a focal point.

Hamilton was hurt, personally as well as politically, when his father-in-law and patron, Philip Schuyler, lost his U.S. Senate seat. Schuyler was descended from an old and prosperous Dutch family, some of whom had intermarried with Livingstons. Irish-descended George Clinton, the state's five-term governor, was an old friend of Washington's who had diverged from his earlier suspicions about a too-strong central government but who disagreed with Hamilton's economic policies. What happened in 1792 was that alliances shifted: the Livingstons, until recently in the Schuyler camp, feeling that they'd been overlooked by the powerful Treasury secretary when appointments were doled out, threw their support to Hamilton's erstwhile friend Aaron Burr, wartime colonel and astute New York State attorney general, who claimed a socially progressive following among artisans, liberal humanists, and those moderate Federalists willing to at least consider Jefferson's democratically inspired ideas. Schuyler's defeat was deliberately aimed at the power-engrossing Hamilton.

No doubt contributing to Hamilton's ire was the comparison he could not help but draw to a peer whom he preferred to paint as an arriviste with outsized aims. For the first time, he told his New York allies to be wary of Aaron Burr as an "embryo Caesar." It was an ironic statement, insofar as Jefferson reported on an early conversation in which Hamilton identified with the greatness of Julius Caesar, who upended the Roman Republic; the classical scholar John Adams saw Caesar in Hamilton no less than Jefferson did. As for the rising fortunes of Aaron Burr, Hamilton's fixation would bubble up as he witnessed Burr's dynamic advocacy in the courtroom firsthand, ever alert to Burr's visible political skills. They would continue to see each other in court, as often on the same as on the opposing side, through 1800.

The Clintons and Livingstons now stood in opposition to Hamilton. In the spring of 1792, New York's political elite were toasting Jefferson and referring to their affiliation (at this very early stage) as the Republican Party. Jefferson and Madison were open to having Governor Clinton contest John Adams, in the hope of electing a Republican as a second-term vice president to Washington. While falling short of Adams in the electoral college that fall, Clinton made a creditable showing, receiving support from the presidential electors of Virginia, North Carolina, and Georgia in addition to those of his home state. Up to this point, the Federalists, with good cause, treated Congressman Madison as the Virginia-dominated Republican Party leader; but Hamilton's pointed attacks in the press presented his personal nemesis, Jefferson, not Madison, as the more dangerous and disruptive Republican, who could potentially win the presidency and oust the law-and-order Federalists. Hamilton's Jefferson problem was to intensify in 1793, as the French Revolution reached the Jacobin Terror phase.[17]

FRENCH FRENZY

As congressional Republicans (principally Virginians) were demanding to see records relating to Hamilton's official transactions, in hopes of embarrassing him and driving him from office, events across the Atlantic in 1793 put Jefferson on the defensive and made Hamilton's position more, not less, secure. In September 1792, Jefferson's pamphleteer friend Thomas Paine fled to Paris, where he joined its government for a short while before suffering imprisonment under the terrorizing Jacobins and nearly losing his life.

The administration was deeply unsettled by these events. It wasn't enough that King Louis XVI was executed in January 1793, and that the Anglo-French War broke out the following month; the newest diplomatic envoy from France, thirty-year-old Edmond-Charles Genêt, although of a bourgeois background, acted the part of a barn-burning radical. He frustrated Secretary of State Jefferson by parading and blustering up and down the Atlantic coast, inveighing against the British and any who would support them during this time of war. With inflammatory speech and writings, he sought nothing less than to recruit American privateers to join the fight. Genêt was not only bypassing the administration, he also unleashed public criticism of the president.

Jefferson was in a bind. Weeks before news of the king's execution reached him, he had written to William Short a letter, hyperbolic and ill-timed, that lives in infamy. It has been an effective, if all too convenient, piece of circumstantial evidence for dismissing Jefferson as an apologist for bloody murderers. Though he had friends in Paris who were already "martyrs to this cause," he said, he refused to give up on the French. Every war had its martyrs, and so be it: "I would have seen half the Earth desolated. Were there but an Adam and an Eve left in every country, and left free, it would be better than as it now is." Three and a half years since the Bastille, he could not abandon his faith; he remained hopeful that France would stabilize, that Lafayette and his ilk would return. And at this time, Condorcet still lived.

To the more knowledgeable and objective Short, who was on the scene, Jefferson had been away too long to appreciate how the mood had lately turned. Jefferson, being Jefferson, insisted that Short understand that "99 in an hundred of our citizens" agreed with his reading of the situation. More hyperbole. As to the Adam and Eve quote, the historian John Boles writes with conviction about the problem of taking Jefferson's words too literally: it was a manner of expression Jefferson used with the few he trusted most, "almost as if to rid himself of intense emotions." It was indeed that, but at the same time it demonstrates a cold-bloodedness in Jefferson that cannot be ignored.[18]

Washington, buoyed by Hamilton, had reason to fear that French radicalism could infect American minds. Jefferson was the French Revolution's best American friend, yet even he could not get through to "Citizen Genêt." The man's outrageous action placed Jefferson squarely with his Federalist foe; his antipathy toward Genêt rivaled anything he'd ever write about Hamilton. To Madison, he fumed: "Hotheaded, all imagination, no judgment, passionate, disrespectful & even indecent toward the P[resident]." Writing in code, he cried out for help, lest Genêt "sink the republican interest." Genêt had to be recalled to Paris—best if Republicans were seen taking the lead.

The inexperienced envoy had made Hamilton's job much easier. Jefferson complained about Hamilton's long-winded speeches in meetings with Washington in which both secretaries took part. His own influence was obviously weakening. Hamilton intensified his newspaper harangues, and Jefferson, in a panic lest these opinions be swallowed whole, once more leaned on Madison to do what he himself refused to do. "For god's sake, my dear Sir," he cried, "take up your pen, select the most striking heresies, and cut him to peices [sic]."[19]

While sitting on the hot seat, Jefferson stubbornly refused to write. He took pride (as he told Washington) never to publish what he could not, in good conscience, sign his name to; but this was splitting hairs, because he methodically appealed to allies to dish out the dirt.

Eventually, the administration (including Jefferson, in this instance) got what it wanted. Upon his dismissal, the loud-mouthed Genêt, rather ironically, expressed a mortal fear of persecution if he went home; so he sought asylum in the United States. Washington demurred, and the lapsed diplomat settled in upstate New York, married a daughter of Governor George Clinton, and led a mostly quiet existence through the end of Jefferson's presidency, at which time he tried to influence presidential electors to vote for his father-in-law rather than Madison. Strange doings, but then when were national political contests not a roller-coaster ride?

Jefferson did not directly contest George Washington. In spite of the strong suspicions he and Madison shared as to how London would exploit even the slightest shift in America's long-established support of France, Jefferson found a way to accommodate Washington's declaration of American neutrality in the Anglo-French War. With the treaty of 1778 that cemented the French-American alliance now effectively mooted, the British appeared to have gotten their way, and in the

United States, many Republicans saw the administration's decision as a complete capitulation. To the French, it was indisputable: the United States had sold them out. While Hamiltonians transferred the vocabulary they'd used for England in the past to Revolutionary France, Republicans reacted against any suggestion that English government systems were kin to the American. Newspaper readers were constantly reminded of London's commercial restrictions on U.S. shipping and the slew of indignities imposed by the rulers of the seas.[20]

As all this was happening, Jefferson received anecdotal reports that both encouraged him and planted seeds of doubt. Back from a fact-finding tour of their home state, Edmund Randolph reported that Virginians had not turned against Washington, but only the secretary of the Treasury "*personally.*" Madison, at home while Congress was in recess, agreed that the state's leaders were still committed to the cause of France and remained deeply suspicious of Hamilton's machinations. Jefferson craved this kind of intelligence. But his nerves were tested.

Around the president and other cabinet members, he maintained a studied manner. But his pen told a very different story. Immediately after a private conversation with Washington in August 1793, Jefferson jotted down verbatim notes, wanting at his fingertips an extensive private record that he could draw on at any later date in support of whatever historical narrative he might decide to produce. The president feared "fermentation . . . in the minds of the public," Jefferson recorded. "He said he believed the Republican party were perfectly pure, but when men put a machine into motion it is impossible for them to stop it exactly where they would chuse." In this context, Washington said that he wished he'd called it quits after one term, and that he was struggling to find successors to Jefferson and Hamilton, both of whom had separately told him they wanted to leave government. Setting down the precise give-and-take between Washington and himself, Jefferson noted, "Here I interrupted him by saying . . ." All in all, it's a vibrant picture of the two men's interactions, if from the perspective of one of them only.

Accordingly, Jefferson reassured Washington that he could rely on a spirit of moderation among Republicans. He appealed to the president to appreciate the difficulty of his own position, volunteering that his ever increasing "repugnance" for public office was in no small measure conditioned by the personal attacks, by his being battered in print by those who "bear me peculiar hatred"; and here he generalized: "the wealthy Aristocrats, the Merchants connected closely with England," all of which obviously led back to Hamilton. Meanwhile, in his correspondence with Madison and others, Jefferson resorted more and more to the derisive labels he'd come up with for Federalists: "monocrats," "the monarchical party," the "Anglican party."[21]

He lost the battle for the president's ear on policy matters. And as if the disturbance caused by Genêt wasn't enough to threaten peace and political health in Philadelphia, the first wave of deaths from yellow fever occurred there in August 1793, before long shutting down day-to-day government operations. Jefferson and his fifteen-year-old daughter Maria escaped the epidemic, accompanying Washington from Philadelphia to Mount Vernon before proceeding to Madison's Montpelier plantation, where the pair strategized.

Hamilton contracted and survived the "malignant fever," which wiped out ten percent of Philadelphia's population, relying (as he himself willfully disseminated in print) on a West Indian physician's remedy. If the esteemed Dr. Benjamin Rush, who stayed in the city to treat the ill at great personal risk, is to be believed, Hamilton refused to take the remedy Rush favored because it was introduced to the public by "a decided Democrat and a friend to Madison and Jefferson."

On receiving reports that Hamilton was bedridden, Jefferson penned one of his coldest comments. Attributing hypochondriac tendencies to the patient, he expressed doubt to Madison that Hamilton had even contracted the dreaded yellow fever. Ignoring the fact that Madison was deathly afraid of the water, and that he himself was no warrior except on the page, Jefferson charged: "A man as timid as he is on the water, as timid on horseback, as timid in sickness, would be a phaenomenon if the courage of which he has the reputation on military occasions were genuine."[22]

Jefferson was deeply unhappy. He'd already made his desires known to his political friends through a letter to Madison meant to be shared. "To my fellow-citizens the debt of service has been fully and faithfully paid." He expected that his retirement to Monticello would be permanent. Hamilton had exhausted him. The harried statement stands as one of the most poetic of Jefferson's epistolary career:

> There has been a time when ... the esteem of the world was of higher value in my eye than every thing in it. But age, experience, and reflection, preserving to that only it's due value, have set a higher on tranquility. The motion of my blood no longer keeps time with the tumult of the world. It leads me to seek for happiness in the lap and love of my family, in the society of my neighbors and my books, in the wholesome occupations of my farm and my affairs, in an interest or affection in every bud that opens, in every breath

that blows around me, in an entire freedom of rest or motion, of thought or incogitancy, owing account to myself alone of my hours and actions.[23]

It is true that he was writing to Madison in great detail his schedule for planting and how he would divide his fields between corn, peas, potatoes, rye, wheat, and restorative clover. But this statement is so much more than that: the quintessential Jeffersonian embrace of nature and tribute to the tranquil scene atop his private mountain, akin to his "our own dear Monticello, where has nature spread so rich a mantle under the eye?" tribute in the Head and Heart letter of 1786. His definition of inner peace, especially after cabinet confrontations had enfeebled him, was a matter of regaining power as the master of all he saw; and, while he would never admit it, he did not wish to remain beholden to the deference he paid to Washington, as required in his government position. As lord of the manor, Jefferson was no longer subservient to anyone.

At Washington's behest, he agreed to stay on as secretary of state through the end of the year, and so he did. He rejoined the administration in Philadelphia once the fever had run its course. But come January 5, 1794, he departed for home with no intention of ever returning to government service. By that time, almost no member of Congress could deny belonging to one of the two political parties. The Republican Party would be Madison's party, and if Jefferson had his way, he would do no more than cheer on all willing combatants from the sidelines.

Figure 14. "Congressional Pugilists," 1798. Rough etching on paper of a celebrated fight on the House floor between Republican Matthew Lyon and Federalist Roger Griswold at a time of Federalist ascendancy—an extended moment of political strife that a powerless vice president Jefferson dubbed "the reign of witches." (Courtesy Library of Congress)

CHAPTER 9

"The Late Political Paroxysm"
Fever, Delirium, and Calumny

TWO WOMEN OF CHILDBEARING age, approximately one year apart in age, carried their babies to term at or near Monticello on a schedule that almost appeared intentional. Martha Jefferson Randolph bore sons and daughters in 1794, 1796, 1799, 1801, 1803, 1806, and 1808. Sally Hemings bore sons and daughters in 1795, 1798, 1799, 1801, 1805, and 1808. In at least three of those years, the two women were pregnant at the same time.

As to their offspring, history has been able to determine, perhaps not surprisingly, that the difference in their treatment was pronounced. Jefferson's precious grandchildren were the recipients of letters and gifts and social privileges. Sally Hemings's children had far less to show for their distinctive lineage. The two eldest were lost to history once they'd passed for white as young adults and presumably changed their surnames. The Hemingses who stayed on at Monticello, unacknowledged by their father but willed their freedom, remade their lives beyond the limits of Virginia. They left no record of having received any real affection from Thomas Jefferson. He gave them a head start in life, and not a whole lot else.

How could Jefferson have been emotionally disconnected from his mixed-race children when his Randolph grandchildren were cherished? Many Southerners who were similarly classed as "gentlemen" exhibited greater interest in their "natural" children. His Randolph grandchildren stayed in touch in later years with Hemingses who were a significant part of their childhood—they mattered to one another. Annette Gordon-Reed has shown that the generations of Hemingses born after 1790 received names that derived from Jefferson and Randolph lineages; or, in the case of James Madison Hemings—the first Hemings to enter Jefferson historiography by testifying in a public paper—bore the name of Thomas Jefferson's most trusted friend.[1]

As for Jefferson himself, the story of elite men's fascination with the sensuality of lower-class female servants is a very old one. This is one very plausible interpretation of the attraction he felt for Sally Hemings. Though obviously not the whole story, it may well explain the initial allure, whether those feelings arose in Paris, as many scholars now believe, or germinated until she was a bit older. Either way, psychologists recognize that desire has the tendency to diminish one's critical faculties.

Jefferson hadn't exhibited a sexual attraction to young girls prior to Sally Hemings, as far as is known; it was the experienced female who titillated him. Were it not that Sally was his late wife's half sister and, by all accounts, quite attractive, the enslaved house servant who tended to his private rooms would seem an anomalous choice for a widower who deliberately denied himself the standard arrangement: a second wife from an elite background. Had he chosen to ally with someone who offered him financial security, he could have been rescued from the ever mounting debts he had inherited from John Wayles more than two decades before. He chose otherwise, setting the stage for the explanation passed down through generations: that he had promised Patty on her deathbed never to remarry.

As he did not make what would have been the practical choice of a mate, he must have had a different priority. Removing companionate love from the equation, given the lack of any noticeable treatment to suggest it, Sally Hemings was precisely what her son Madison stated of his mother: Jefferson's "concubine"—a woman kept for sex. Perhaps, too, his inability to have sons with his wife left him unsatisfied, and Sally's three sons who lived into adulthood fulfilled a certain need in Jefferson. Of course, this is pure speculation. But if it were so, why did he see to it that they were equipped with only artisanal skills, like their older Hemings half brothers? Why not provide an education in the kinds of books that lined the shelves of his private library? Mysteries persist in trying to explain this side of Thomas Jefferson.

Many of the Hemings males were literate. Letters survive that were exchanged between Jefferson, his Randolph grandchildren, and members of the Hemings family. But those that allude to Sally, or to anything else that might embarrass Jefferson, have been (purposefully, one supposes) destroyed. The record does not indicate whether Sally herself was literate. In any event, she did not accompany Jefferson to Philadelphia, even when he traveled there with Maria. Soon after his return home from the capital in the summer of 1797, Sally became pregnant with the first of her sons to survive to adulthood, who was given the name William Beverley, after a prominent Virginian with a Randolph connection. Both Madison and Eston Hemings, the two youngest sons, would go on to include the name Beverley (as well as Wayles) when their children were born.[2]

There were serious tensions in the early 1790s between Jefferson and two key members of the Hemings clan. The long-trusted Martin, eldest of Sally's half brothers, was known for his courage in standing up to the British when a raiding party threatened the integrity of Monticello in 1781, and he continued to serve as a butler for many years. In 1792, he demanded to be sold, though no reason for their conflict or its final resolution is given in known texts. All that is clear is that Jefferson would have been pleased to be rid of him at that time—Martin was much later recalled by the Randolph granddaughters as a "gloomy" presence. Even more complicated was the bid for freedom from James Hemings, the highly skilled French-trained chef who cooked for Jefferson and his dinner guests in Philadelphia. In his case, Jefferson prepared and signed a document agreeing to "make him free" after James first trained another in the vocation (it would be his and Sally's brother Peter). The phrasing of the document shows Jefferson taking credit for having subsidized James's culinary training; read carefully, there is little to suggest benevolence on Jefferson's part in a legalistic stipulation that he would eventually free this valued contributor to his happiness and his social reputation as a giving host.[3]

HEMINGS BLOOD

Blood is a vital fluid. In literary language, it is a metaphor for human essence, for life itself. In drama, it is copiously shed. Shakespeare uses some form of the word "blood" more than eight hundred times. He tended to repeat the phrase "flesh and blood"; he lavished attention on "noble" or "royal" blood, just as "bloody deeds" are everywhere in the plays. Blood is "mingled with the crime of lust" in *Comedy of Errors*; in *Hamlet*, even thoughts are called "bloody."

For hundreds of years, blood has been a colloquial measure of group identity—hereditary characteristics, family, ancestry, common descent, race. Thinking high and mighty thoughts, the eighteenth century recognized the "lifeblood" of a society or a nation. In eighteenth-century medicine, blood had to be "tempered" to ensure good health. It was part of the legal language of inheritance. In war, "blood and treasure" were expended at a cost that went beyond the pecuniary.

The coupling of "blood and treasure" was an extremely common trope for leading figures of the Revolutionary generation. Though the phrase is missing from Jefferson's correspondence, he did test out "blood and treasure" in his rough draft of the Declaration of Independence before replacing it with more creative language bewailing the forfeiture of "ties of common kindred" as the British viciously turned their backs on the colonies. Here, Jefferson was stipulating that the blood of kinship (whether fictive or biological), when denied by one party, meant abandonment of affectionate ties. That there ran "not a drop of my blood in the veins of any living creature" was the Indian Logan's plaint that so moved the author of *Notes on Virginia*.

Blood and substance, like body and spirit, are synonymous with life itself. In *Notes*, Jefferson coupled "blood and substance" in praising the Revolutionaries' spirit. In one of the most viscerally powerful lines in the Declaration, he indicted the king for having "sent hither swarms of Officers to harrass our people, and eat out their substance." Of the swarms, we may think of killer bees—that's the kind of image he was igniting here. The verb "harass" contributed to the sense of enfeeblement. One can appreciate the impact of Jefferson's sensation-enriched vocabulary, and in this one sentence, he is imagining the unprovoked invader as a bird of prey, a vulture. America is left with only one option: to save itself by preserving its substance, shielding its blood from the external threat.

Jefferson's conceptual framework included an inherited understanding that the English-speaking world was an amalgam of centuries of contacts between the original Celtic Britons and migrating Angle, Saxon, and other Germanic tribes, as well as the Romans. English blood, then, was multiethnic, but nevertheless regarded as pure. In Western tradition, purity was already associated with a woman's sexual innocence, so the relationship between sex and bloodline was hard to separate. With the introduction of lifelong enslavement for the African-blooded, bloodlines were measured through the mother, and the general presumption was that the portion of the man's blood that was Black played a role in corrupting him.[4]

The Caribbean sugar islands, with their massive numbers of African slaves, became a radical experiment in "blood mixing" in the seventeenth century, with a stigmatizing effect on the legal and class structure replicated in Britain's North American colonies. Conditions in Jefferson's Virginia reflected a history of mixed-race reproduction dating back several generations; an entire century had passed since the colony had enacted the matrilineal transmission of slave status in 1662. Long familiar with matters of bastardy or illegitimacy, Jefferson would eventually put on paper his mathematical explanation of Virginia's legal tradition, demonstrating on the basis of animal breeding that "pure negro" was converted into "pure white" by removing the African over three generations of "crossing," thereby "clearing" (or cleansing) tainted blood. Preserving a racialized social order made sense to him.[5]

Sadly, by placing a monetary value on his and other planters' enslaved men and women, he participated in a commodification of the womb. He exposed something terribly unattractive in his character when, in his seventies, he shared a self-interested calculation with his son-in-law: "I know of no error more consuming to an estate than that of stocking farms with men almost exclusively. I consider a woman who brings a child every two years as more profitable than the best man of the farm." The livestock analogy is grotesque, and indicative of a mindset that did not end with Jefferson.[6]

The sexual exploitation of enslaved women could not be denied, and Jefferson did not disguise its ubiquity in Virginia. Yet he was married to a language that associated corrupted bloodlines with natural law, a language that treated Black blood as a contaminant of the Anglo-Saxon American. In the most notorious section of *Notes*, he writes: "Among the Romans, emancipation required but one effort. The slave, when made free, might mix with, without staining[,] the blood of his master. But with us a second is necessary, unknown to history. When freed, he is to be removed beyond the reach of mixture." The historian Robert Pierce Forbes points out that Jefferson was most likely the first public commentator in the United States to propose a massive removal effort.[7]

As an indicator of intimate relations, blood could be socially defining, life-depriving ("spilled" or "shed"), or life-giving. When in 1793, Jefferson wrote that he could no longer abide the fractured condition of Washington's presidential cabinet, it was "the motion of my blood" that put him out of sync with "the tumult of the world." He had to find a state of calm, without obstruction, where the heart (figuratively as well as physiologically) could function properly.[8]

He required a credible justification for quitting when the going got rough. He thought he'd found it in "the motion of my blood." What took place at Monticello next belongs to a narrative lost to Jefferson biography until its recovery in 1974 by Fawn Brodie. The last of John Wayles's twelve children was twenty-one in 1795, when she became pregnant at Monticello. This was the first of Sally Hemings's six conceptions to occur on the mountain. Owing no one an explanation once he'd returned to the "wholesome" life he contrived, the record reveals that Thomas Jefferson was present at the time of conception as well as at the time of birth.

So, how did he adjudge the blood that ran in the veins of the light-skinned, mixed-race people whose presence at Monticello from 1773 he welcomed, whom he knew as his wife's half siblings, all bearing the surname of a long deceased white ship's captain named Hemings? The clearest explanation is the one that emphasizes aesthetic considerations. The reasons for an enforced separation of Black and white were, for Jefferson, a matter of natural attraction / natural repulsion, a matter of essential biochemistry. That was not the case with the Hemingses. They *looked* acceptable.

The "deep rooted prejudices entertained by the whites" and the "ten thousand recollections, by the Blacks, of injuries they have sustained" constituted Jefferson's two-sided coin, his rationale for why interracial "convulsions" would end in the "extermination" of the weaker party. Still stronger rationale for Black removal lay, for him, in Nature itself. "The first difference which strikes us is that of colour.— Whether the black of the negro resides in the reticular membrane between the skin and scarf-skin, or in the scarf-skin itself; whether it proceeds from the colour of the blood, the colour of the bile, or from that of some other secretion, the difference is fixed in nature."

By "nature," Jefferson really means his personal assumptions about beauty. He takes the "fine mixtures of red and white," pleasing "suffusions of color," that comprise variations in European flesh tone, and contrasts this with "that immoveable veil of black which covers the emotions of the other race." An immovable veil does cover the emotions, but it's not what he imagines. The immoveable piece, the protective covering, is Jefferson's narrowly framed system of belief.

His deployment of "body" language as an empirical (anthropological) category is a conceit. He claims he possesses the expertise required to assess the inner dimension of Black life: the impulses, the passions, which he abstracts from his interactions with the enslaved. He reflects what others were saying who used such words as "stain" or "taint," the "corruption" of blood that the Black essence imposed on the white essence. Amalgamation of Indian and white was, for Jefferson, the one means of averting the extinction of the former; but amalgamation of Black and white produced no hereditary advantage at all.

His aesthetic explanation is quite revealing, insofar as the Hemingses, and especially Sally, had straight or nearly straight "flowing hair," the first natural attribute Jefferson refers to after his "immoveable veil" comment in *Notes*. He plainly associates "superior beauty" with flowing hair. We know that preservation of the locks of hair of loved ones, often set in jewelry, was common, and that this practice held a particularly deep meaning for Jefferson. While writing *Notes*, Patty was alive and close by, but by the time of its publication, she lay in the plot beside Dabney Carr. Her grieving husband retained a lock of her hair inside that precious keepsake of their love described earlier: a piece of paper on which their two hands combined in a bidding of adieu ("the eternal separation which we are shortly to make," it read, copying Sterne). Her pen started the adieu and his finished. Over the years, he unfolded and refolded the delicate paper repeatedly.[9]

"Eternal" and "immoveable" are graphic, absolute terms. The "eternal monotony" of black warranted "eternal separation" in Jefferson's mind when he proposed the recolonization of Black Americans abroad, and out of the reach of "mixture"; but "eternal separation" had a second, distinctly passionate, nostalgic implication for him in preserving the memory of love and attachment. The irony should not be lost. And when he wrote to Maria Cosway from Monticello while Sally Hemings was pregnant in 1795, he began his letter by telling her he was ensconced "in the full enjoiment of my farm, my family, and my books, having bidden an eternal Adieu to public life which I always hated." An eternal adieu from political strife— he could only hope.[10]

Jefferson's racism operated on more than the one plane. He openly denied to African Americans a poetic sensibility, insisting that no Black person was capable of an imagination that was more than "dull, tasteless, and anomalous" (here meaning unrelatable to a white-established norm). Deprived of a competent imagination, they were, he deduced, unable to understand love. He claimed for himself the knowledge and authority to certify that Blacks could approach their lovemaking only lustfully (it "kindles the senses only, not the imagination"); that it lacked the "tender, delicate mixture of sentiment and sensation" that occurs in a physical union between whites, who experienced physical desire with greater subtlety and deeper attachment. Surely he did not relegate the Hemingses to such a category, reserved as it was for the fictive, impersonal Black he would not accept.[11]

Interestingly, despite the searing cruelty of his language, there is no indication that he believed any sort of contagion arose from any African-European sexual congress. He makes no allusion to what he and every friend he'd ever made could not but be aware of: the pubescent sons of planters often received their first lessons in sex from the enslaved. It is his philosophic pretense that grates, along with his reduction of Black persons to crude caricature as a race driven more by impulse than by reflection. In Jefferson's construction, Black Americans can't help who they are. An African American deserves the emotion of pity from genteel whites but is unworthy of mixing in polite society or mixing with the "blood" of another.

Furthermore, Jefferson's remarks about sex in the *Notes* are linked to neurochemical sensations. His insistence that a person of African descent was, by his observation, a *slave to sensation* presumes having witnessed the lovemaking of unfree men and women. How else could he claim the knowledge to assert that "they are more ardent after their female" than whites, and that love, as practiced by Blacks, is "more an eager desire" than any higher form of sentiment?

He implies that his voyeuristic behavior was not accidental, but scientifically conducted. He is a man who presumes himself above the Other's level of sexual unrestraint, his own impulses being of no relevance. He poses as a scholar of racial difference, a man of civility and restraint married to one of his own social class and, by the time of the publication of *Notes*, a recent widower learning to navigate the seductive atmosphere of Parisian salons. Whether this is evidence of self-deception, hypocrisy, or something else, Jefferson's words are clearly conflicted.

His advertised purpose in *Notes on Virginia* was to produce an encyclopedic picture for the European intelligentsia, a taxonomic map and history of his native state, the largest and most populous, that he wished to see move in a healthy direction. The *Notes* interprets facts that relate to physical nature and to a social environment. His work is intended to display his erudition and open-mindedness.

His race-specific observations are tentative, he says, leaving it to others to conduct the necessary further study. Interestingly, he uses the word "suppose" more than forty times. Once his "suspicion" of Black inferiority is pronounced, it is followed by a caveat that in fact doubles down on his supposition: "It is not against experience to suppose, that different species of the same genus, or varieties of the same species, may possess different qualifications. Will not a lover of natural history then, one who views the gradations of all the races of animals with the eye of philosophy, excuse the effort to keep those in the department of man as distinct as nature has formed them? The unfortunate difference of colour, and perhaps of faculty, is a powerful obstacle to the emancipation of these people." His logic is that of xenophobic intolerance, not supposition.

He calls skin pigmentation an "unfortunate difference," as if somewhere in the past a mistake was made. When *Notes* was publicized where it most mattered to him, in Europe, there was mounting pushback among his intended readership against the Southern slave economy. Marshaling evidence in favor of his region kept Jefferson on the defensive in Paris. To Chastellux, he stated: "I beleive [sic] the Indian then to be in body and mind equal to the whiteman. I have supposed the blackman, in his present state, might not be so. But it would be hazardous to affirm that, equally cultivated for a few generations, he would not become so." That is, the prejudice he bore with regard to Black intellect might soften if he were catapulted into the future. This was sophistry at best.[12]

Had Jefferson paid closer attention to a discourse occurring within art circles in Paris during his years there, he might have been more open to the ideas of Condorcet and Lafayette, and willing to revisit his essentialist views. Sometime around midcentury, medical studies of skin changed French portraitists' impressions when it came to mixing their colors. (The word "pigment," first entering race-centered vocabularies in Jefferson's lifetime, stemmed from the Latin "to paint.") Visible effects of the circulation of blood entered into the artist's thoughts too. On a microscopic level, science had proved that the skin's structure was alike across the world. Beyond gradations of color, artists altered the touch of the brush in rendering skin types: men, women, the old, the young, white and Black subjects, were more subtly distinguished than earlier in the century. In fact, when painting European and African subjects, the same basic colors were placed on the palette. From the artist's perspective, skin became a less substantive matter than physiognomy in portraying ethnicities.[13]

While Jefferson's profound interest in the Parisian art world does not mean he was privy to these changes in perception, the fact remains that drawing artificial distinctions between African and European types based on a false understanding of anatomy went counter to medical research that other elites followed. He might well have arrived at the same conclusion as they, recognizing how thin the layer of skin was that separated these two races that he found to be incompatible in nature. Standing by what he'd written in *Notes*, he bent over backward to save his own skin (as it were). He contested the new science, new art, and new humanism that came more easily to the French. He insisted on an outdated interpretation: that the blackness of Blacks went deeper inside the body than what European intellectuals were saying. The unwanted passions he read into African bodies was being questioned, and he wasn't listening.

The modern liberal mind struggles to comprehend how one born into the system of slavery could feel as comfortable with it as Jefferson did. He expressed his abhorrence for race enslavement in principle while confessing in print to a level of disgust for an entire people whose numbers in Virginia exceeded those of any other Southern colony.

Had he dug a hole for himself? Yes. But we cannot know for certain that the deceit was rooted in craven self-interest. Psychological distancing is more complex than that. Jefferson could not imagine that he himself was closed-minded on this subject by grossly misinterpreting evidence when he discarded proof of Black ingenuity that challenged his theory.[14] In some ways, his behavior is analogous to twenty-first-century climate change denialism, not to mention the persistence of denialism in some corners of America that racism still exists.[15]

Jefferson had no problem criticizing dogmatism in religion. He perceived a level of arrogance among doctrinaire clerics whose historical knowledge was lacking. Yet he himself was married to a kind of faith by embracing an immutable science of race that took as its basis white superiority and subjective measures of physical beauty. In modern parlance, Jefferson was an expert in "spin," who sought clever ways to corroborate fixed beliefs or otherwise discount the practicality of pursuing moral ends. From the 1780s forward, he feigned alignment with the motives expressed by Condorcet and Lafayette, refusing to reexamine his own presumptions once he'd committed them to paper.

To preserve a rational order (as he saw it), Jefferson found it necessary to hold fast to irrational methods of observation and analysis. How conscious he was of his stubbornness in this regard is something we cannot truly know. He was hoping to thrive on the extensive acreage he'd inherited, spread across several counties, and he could not have continued to do so without a reliable labor force. Barring a legislative solution, by which large planters like himself would be fairly compensated for the loss of their labor through a gradual emancipation process, he could not see his way to a more humane solution than the one he'd realistically adopted: providing food, clothing, and shelter for his human property while training favorites (like the Hemingses) in marketable skills that they could draw on to make a decent living in a post-emancipation world.

With or without the state's intervention, his world was bound to collapse; but like so many other elite Virginians with First Family surnames, Jefferson was mired in his tracks. Even as he was slowly able to rid Monticello of the soil-despoiling tobacco crop, he refused to accept where things were heading. The psychological term for this kind of deficient outlook is "cognitive dissonance," an inability to manage the prospects or accommodate the uncomfortable tensions associated with the feared collapse of one's own long-nourished society.

We must accept our disadvantage and return to where this conversation began. The Hemingses were different. They would not have been in the main house, trained in essential artisanal roles in which both quality and trust mattered, if Jefferson perceived any objectionable trait or lack of capacity where that family was concerned. *Notes on Virginia*, a product of the decade of the 1780s, must be read as an artifact of a particular phase in Jefferson's manifestation of personal ambition and scarcely, if at all, related to anyone at Monticello.

Aside from the Hemingses, there were scores of enslaved persons on his mountain. Passionately building a world that betokened isolation as much as it publicized its architect's elevated vision, he would not have dehumanized those unfree men and women either. In different degrees African, they labored so that he could realize a grand design. Until it became a mere matter of economic survival, he felt a feudal, patriarchal obligation.

There is yet more to reflect on here with regard to Jefferson's continuing focus on health and facial beauty. Having traveled to Philadelphia to be inoculated against smallpox, Jefferson in turn inoculated all who lived and labored at Monticello once it became possible. The enslaved technically lacked any right of choice of the medical treatment they received—as late as 1768, a mob in Norfolk had torched the home of a doctor who was inoculating large numbers of individuals, and the outcry led to the Burgesses' putting a stop to the practice. So, one fact bears noting: before Jefferson had his own family inoculated, he first made sure that the enslaved on his plantation suffered no ill effects from the procedure. They were his guinea pigs.

Which leads to one final observation about Jefferson and the many meanings of blood. The common medical practice of bloodletting was still regarded as curative in the second half of the eighteenth century, simply because few patients died as a result of it; but it was not a method Jefferson ever favored. He forbade the bleeding of the Black people who performed manual labor at Monticello. Living in cabins with less protection from the elements than the manor house afforded, he may have thought they would weaken as a result. But he did frequently call upon doctors and midwives to minister to the enslaved.[16]

The inner Jefferson is a complex read. The mixed-race Hemingses, especially those lightest in skin pigmentation ("bright," in the Southern idiom), were free of blood that "blackened," as far as he was concerned; any residual "blackness" in them was benign. They were untainted. They were not defined by blood but by their dependent position. The Hemingses were daily visible, part of the inner circle on the active plantation from its earliest incarnation. They can be described as a parallel subordinate family, subordinate only to the primary family of Jeffersons.[17]

As much as Monticello served as a visual representation of his ideal, its joys did not immunize Jefferson from the wider world. His daily work and exercise regimen was almost ritualized. Rising early and operating on a schedule, he devoted select hours to his library and writing desk, where he mulled over how he wanted to address an ever increasing number of correspondents. The mood he sought to convey in drafting his letters was a soothing generosity of spirit, the same temperate bearing that he manifested in his patient, seemingly unruffled pose in social situations. Yet when he left the mountain, he was still prone to punishing himself—or his body punished him—with stress-induced "periodical head-achs" that compelled him to desist from communicating with the world for hours in a day and sometimes weeks on end. In Williamsburg, Paris, New York, and Washington, D.C., when the "head-ach" struck, he was forced into darkness (literally, a dark room), requiring an immovable veil, the monotony of black, in order to revive him. Yes, ironies abound.[18]

JOHN ADAMS'S VICE PRESIDENT

The Jefferson-Hamilton controversy came to a head in 1792. Social upheaval wrought by a deadly fever and French politics dominated 1793. If Jefferson escaped controversy when he went into a midcareer retirement, he was not able to ignore the news fed to him by Madison, especially that which secured commercial and political advantage to England.

He struggled to hang on to his rural escapism. As before, he peppered letters with metaphorical expressions on the order of putting his "bark" (sailing vessel) into port, with the design to remain and never venture forth into the political maelstrom again. It was the triad of farm, family, and books that called to him, that brought the most satisfaction. Between 1794 and 1797, he directed much of the work on Monticello renovations, with an emphasis on preserving private spaces for himself. For a length of time, one of the few rooms left with its roof attached was his precious library. The home's massive reconception, inspired by all he'd seen in European architecture, now included its signature dome. He had the assistance of, among others, his son-in-law Tom Randolph and the enslaved man he'd known since birth, Jupiter. Jefferson's younger daughter, Maria, was married to her cousin Jack Eppes in the fall of 1797, amid a debris-ridden house in transition.[19]

In 1796, Monticello received a visit from the duc de La Rochefoucauld-Liancourt. Jefferson barely knew the man, an expert in the science of agriculture, who escaped France with the title he'd inherited from the late duke, who had been Jefferson's good friend. In Liancourt's extensive travel journal, he described his week at Monticello. "Mr. Jefferson's house commands one of the most extensive prospects you can meet with," he wrote. Though more interested in observing the land under cultivation ("his land will never be dunged as much as in Europe"), and Jefferson's system of cultivating it (down to his Scottish threshing machine) he eventually turned to the man himself: "In private life, Mr. Jefferson displays a mild, easy and obliging temper, though he is somewhat cold and reserved." Many others commented similarly who did not know him well.[20]

One who did, George Washington, eventually stopped accepting Jefferson's explanations. The final breach occurred in the late spring of 1797, when a few lines in a letter never meant for publication found their way back to America from its Italian recipient. But even before that, Washington's patience was tried, as partisan attacks on his presidency seemed invariably to lead back to his former secretary of state. In 1793–94, relatively short-lived "democratic societies," loosely modeled on the French Jacobin Club, challenged the administration's political narrative. The clubs, launched in Philadelphia before spreading across the United States, deeply angered Washington. They faded away before he left office, but the memory lingered: as Jefferson's political clout increased, Federalists stepped up their all-encompassing critique of slave-owning Southern aristocrats in the Jefferson mold as "violent" Jacobins.

Jefferson made a weak attempt to rescue his relationship with Washington by professing, in his inimitable way, that, contrary to nasty rumors Washington may have heard, he was not "engaged in the bustle of politics," and certainly not "in turbulence and intrigue against the government." Hearing that a conversation over dinner at Monticello had lately found its way to Washington's ear, in language that made him appear to be bad-mouthing the president, Jefferson wrote (all too formalistically) of his trust that Washington's personal knowledge of his character would ensure that he gave no credibility to secondhand reports, and that their past dealings would "overweigh the slander of an intriguer, dirtily employed in sifting the conversations of my table."

All Jefferson could ever do was to rely on his skill as a letter writer to minimize injury to a wobbly relationship. "Political conversation I really dislike," he professed in the same letter, saying he avoided talking politics whenever possible. To this he added a tepid request to see a policy document from the first term—he pretended it was what had prompted the letter—and reiterated, this time more colorfully: "I put away this disgusting dish of old fragments [government matters], and talk to you of my peas and clover." Comparing notes as farmers was one way he softened his language as he affected less interest in potentially divisive issues than he actually felt. He did this quite self-consciously when he wrote to Washington.[21]

Philip Mazzei was an Italian friend of Jefferson's, his former Albemarle neighbor. Together, he and Madison were involved in managing Mazzei's continuing financial interests in Virginia. Washington had met and corresponded with Mazzei during the Revolutionary War, aware of his mission to obtain loans in Europe. It would not have been odd for Jefferson to have an ongoing correspondence with the Italian. In April 1796, he wrote to Mazzei on the subject of the Hamiltonians' political triumphs, and said, "It would give you a fever were I to name to you the apostates who have gone over to these heresies." Without directly naming him, he implicated Washington when he diminished and damned the "Samsons in the field and Solomons in the council, but who have had their heads shorn by the harlot England."

Mazzei had erred in letting Jefferson's letter leave his hands. It was twice translated, circulating first in Italian, then in French. By the time it was republished in the American press, Washington was retired to Mount Vernon and Jefferson was serving as John Adams's vice president. Jefferson was once again in hot water. This time he would not be able to wiggle free, because Washington wasn't listening anymore. It is not too strong a statement: at the end of his life, George Washington felt nothing but disgust for Jefferson. Much later, after Jefferson's death, and with reference to this trying time in their long careers, Madison wrote of his friend's "habit ... of expressing in strong and round terms, impressions of the moment." That was one way of putting it.[22]

This was Jefferson's fate. At the hands of Hamilton, he'd become fair game. Yet he was eminently capable of making things worse for himself when his clever wordsmithing backfired. The *Rights of Man* controversy was nothing compared to the Mazzei letter. It was not a good thing to be on the wrong side of Washington. Even when Jefferson's language was not so sharply drawn as it was in this case, his metaphors and alliteration set in stone a number of memorable positions that made the rounds. He was a political moralist who converted knowledge into feeling. He couldn't help himself.

In 1794, after Jefferson retired to Monticello, Hamilton opted to remain at Washington's side for another year. The only Republican he felt any need to watch was the generally accommodating Edmund Randolph, late attorney general of the United States, and now Jefferson's successor at the State Department. Hamilton's machinations that year involved an ultimately pointless military campaign he led against rural Pennsylvania whiskey distillers who fought the tax he'd seen fit to levy on them. Remaining as Treasury secretary, he added the War Department to his portfolio when Henry Knox resigned.

Once Hamilton left the cabinet, he made sure his people were ensconced. He may have taken a back seat to the prime mover in Edmund Randolph's ouster, but he wasn't exactly an innocent bystander either. His handpicked successor at Treasury, Oliver Wolcott, seized on an intercepted letter and made it appear that Secretary of State Randolph wanted money from France in exchange for a favorable policy. Hamilton voiced his doubts about Randolph to Washington at an early opportunity. "I never had confidence in Mr. Randolph," he wrote artfully after Randolph resigned, adding pugnaciously: "Rendered desperate himself he meditates as much mischief as he can." Washington begged Hamilton to recommend someone to be his next secretary of state—having already asked Patrick Henry and several others, all of whom had turned him down.[23]

Jefferson went back to farming, believing the Republicans could get along without him. Hamilton went home to his wife and five children and restarted his law practice in Manhattan after having too long relied on his father-in-law's wealth to keep him afloat. The truth is that neither of them, despite whatever protestations they might have made, resisted involvement from outside the government. While Jefferson was kept abreast by Madison and others, Hamilton continued to work through congressional allies, particularly when it became clear that Jefferson would be put up by Republicans to succeed Washington after 1796. In a letter to daughter Maria in the second year of his presidency, reflecting back on his time away, Jefferson said, "I remained closely at home, saw none but those who came there, and at length became very sensible to the ill effect it had on my own mind, and of it's direct & irresistible tendency to render me unfit for society, & uneasy when necessarily engaged in it. I felt enough of the effect of withdrawing from the world then, to see that it led to an antisocial & misanthropic state of mind." This perfect encapsulation of his contradictory impulses—to commit to the world and to flee contention—has him concluding, "it will be a lesson I shall never forget."[24]

It was easy for him to say this to his apolitical daughter in the middle of his successful first term as president, when Washington society appealed and he himself dictated the makeup of his dinner guest list. But it does not entirely explain his decision to cut short his retirement. In all probability, his political alter ego Madison nudged him in the direction he himself refused to admit that his controlling ambition had led him.[25]

The message Federalists would send, which Hamilton deemed the best strategy for sinking Jefferson's chances in 1796, was twofold: there was the candidate's "want of firmness" dating to his flight from the governorship in 1781, along with his boasted Enlightenment credentials that could be turned on their head. According to the historian Jeffrey L. Pasley, in the calculations of Hamilton and his associates, Jefferson's soft spot was the effete intellectual's disrespect for Christianity (which upheld social order) and the dilettantism that separated him from the real world. His bookishness, his studied, philosophic demeanor, would be used against him.[26]

Indeed, Jefferson left himself vulnerable. Because of the wide publication of comments he intended solely for the eyes of the recipient, his recourse to letter writing gave him a reputation for stealth and political intrigue as well as a smooth style that could be construed as disingenuous. Hamilton kept Jefferson in his sights more than he ever worried about activist congressman Madison, having rationalized early on that Jefferson had obliged Madison through cunning to publicly oppose Hamilton's policy. He charged that Jefferson gave a false impression of being mellow when he refused to go on the warpath in newspapers, as Hamilton and Madison did.

Hamilton's interpretation was not all wrong. As a legislative leader, Madison was open and aboveboard—that would remain *his* reputation. It was no less true that Jefferson's correspondents were numerous and spread wide, and the constancy, length, and cleverness of his letters to them were, sometimes subtly, sometimes undisguisedly, attempts to defend his frequently assailed character.

A letter to Edward Rutledge of South Carolina is the quintessence of this Jefferson, the peace-seeking, unwilling political combatant, misjudged by many, compelled by circumstances almost beyond his control to stand for the highest executive office. Rutledge was the youngest signer of the Declaration of Independence and, in 1796, a presidential elector who, though Federalist-friendly, chose Jefferson over Adams. He was also the intimate of the South Carolina power brokers

Thomas Pinckney (the current U.S. minister to Great Britain) and Major General Charles Cotesworth Pinckney, all three of them London-educated Charleston natives. Hamilton, after he'd left office, had suggested the elder brother, C. C. Pinckney, to Washington as a proper minister to France at this critical, uncertain moment, because, while a Federalist, Pinckney's discomfort with the French Revolution was muted compared to that of others more closely identified with Hamilton. Washington took the advice.

Jefferson and Rutledge had exchanged letters periodically over the years, so he had reason to feel comfortable in reaching out to a supportive former colleague. Rutledge's twenty-one-year-old son Henry had visited Jefferson at Monticello late in 1795, finding the fifty-three-year-old patriarch, as Jefferson described himself, "in a retirement I doat on," hoping, like an old soldier (which he wasn't, and which Rutledge had been, to the point of having been captured, imprisoned, and exchanged), to "claim my discharge" from public service. The younger Rutledge was shortly to see foreign affairs in a stark new light when he accompanied C. C. Pinckney to France as his private secretary. There, the new U.S. minister would receive a snub that enlarged into the infamous XYZ Affair, which then steered these Charleston aristocrats away from Jefferson's Republicans. While that had not yet happened, Jefferson was cognizant of the Rutledge-Pinckney connection.[27]

In the letter Jefferson wrote after young Henry had visited him, he knew enough of Rutledge's dissatisfaction with the Federalists' willing subordination to British power that he could directly take aim at the "Anglomen" in America. But how much liberty could he take, how far to press his politics? In late 1796, when he wrote again to Rutledge, he was colloquial, without assuming too much. The first paragraph dealt with cowpea, wheat, and rice, and then, the main event: "You have seen my name lately tacked to so much of eulogy and of abuse, that I dare say you hardly thought it meant for your old acquaintance of 76."

This was Jefferson establishing his fundamental lack of control over how he was treated in the press. "In truth I did not know myself under the pens either of my friends or foes. It is unfortunate for our peace that unmerited abuse wounds, while unmerited praise has not the power to heal." His "I don't recognize myself" in excessive acclaim or unrestrained invective is part of his oft-repeated protest that he wanted nothing more than to be left alone, a perennial farmer at heart. "I have no ambition to govern men, no passion which would lead me to delight to ride in a storm." Equating political disputes with tempest conditions was an epistolary staple of Jefferson's.

For emphasis, he tacked on a quote from the great Roman poet Virgil on the superiority of rural life over the fame of a recognized name. Before adding his signature to the letter, he acknowledged the departure of Pinckney for France, wishing only that Rutledge himself (who did not care to stray far from home) had been added to the delegation: "I love to see honest men and honorable men at the helm, men who will not bend their politics to their purses, nor pursue measures by which they may profit, and then profit by their measures." Even here, Jefferson could not exit without a jab at those in political office whom Hamilton had corrupted.[28]

At the time he wrote this letter, Jefferson knew that he would finish behind Adams and become the second president's successor as V.P. and president of the Senate. (Until 1804, when the Twelfth Amendment passed and party tickets were recognized, the second-highest vote getter, even if he were politically opposed, became vice president.) Jefferson and Adams had diverged in a major way when Jefferson interpreted Adams's deeply researched historical treatment, *Discourses on Davila*, as unrepublican, reading into it the supposed "heresies" that Paine's *Rights of Man* was meant to have answered. Jefferson quickly patched things up with Adams in 1791, only to lose that gentleman's respect, six years later, as a dissenting vice president.

The Adams family retreated from Jefferson en masse. "How loth I have been to give him up," Abigail Adams admitted to their son John Quincy. "I am obliged to look upon him as a Man whose Mind is warped by prejudice and so Blinded by Ignorance as to be unfit for the office he holds. However wise and scientific as a Phylosopher, as a politician he is a Child, and the dupe of party!" The childishness she perceived compares to how, in the present century, we would take less seriously a politician who reacted giddily to flattering press coverage and the glare of celebrity. Jefferson was a party leader in an era when that meant being a turbulent character who was open to destroying the existing order. John Adams was an independent, a Federalist in name only.

With respect to Jefferson, Adams was a forgiving man. It took the urgings of protective others, his wife and some non-Hamiltonian Federalists, to convince him he should view his vice president as two-faced. The last straw was a Jefferson letter dated June 4, 1797, that upset Adams as much as the Mazzei letter, circulating at nearly the same time, upset Washington. This other letter, though, was leaked, not to the press, but to John Adams directly (and to him alone). It showed Jefferson angling for a conciliatory posture toward a hostile French government while aiming to empower the states relative to what he saw as an overbearing central government—of which Jefferson himself was an officer. It appeared that he sought to arrest President Adams's initiatives as the administration was just getting under way. Adams recognized that he had reason to be "upon my Guard." He now saw in Jefferson "evidence of a Mind Sowered, yet Seeking for Popularity, and eaten to an honeycomb with ambition." These were strong words to use in speaking about a once-trusted friend.[29]

John Adams was as cautious as he was candid. Like Jefferson, he was eminently capable of making amends when he believed the other was a man of reason and conviction. But at this moment, Jefferson was not playing politics as cautiously as he imagined he was, and he was probably unaware that the contents of the letter had been communicated to Adams.

A flurry of political letters presents Vice President Jefferson feeling a sense of urgency. To Aaron Burr, he wrote that he was left blind to what the Adams administration was planning and doing. Hamilton was elsewhere, and yet "the same secrecy and mystery is affected to be observed by the present, which marked the former administration." Republican members of the House were not doing enough, and Madison had opted to leave Congress. Jefferson thought that many New Yorkers had been "duped" into supporting antirepublican measures, and that Republicans were losing their hold on the people at large. "Indeed, my dear Sir," he told Burr, "we have been but as a sturdy fish on the hook of a dexterous angler, who letting us flounce till we have spent our force, brings us up at last." Picking up on Jefferson's worried message, Burr replied directly: "The Moment requires free communication among those who adhere to the principles of our Revolution." He suggested to Jefferson that it was safer for them to hold a strategy session in person than to conduct important political business through the mails. It made good sense, and Jefferson wrote to Edmund Randolph just after: "The interception of letters is becoming so notorious, that I am forming a resolution of declining correspondence with my friends through the channel of the post altogether."[30]

He was scrambling for allies, for others to lighten his load. "I am tired of the scene," he told Burr, as he made arrangements to return to Monticello between congressional sessions. On the eve of departure from the capital, he unleashed a flurry of similarly drawn letters, writing to Edward Rutledge: "You and I have formerly seen warm debates and high political passions. But gentlemen of different politics would then speak to each other, and separate the business of the senate from that of society. It is not so now. Men who have been intimate all their lives cross the streets to avoid meeting."

The tone and temper of his prose had shifted somewhat. This man who routinely denied his own passion with rhetorical prowess was exploiting the passion he observed, thinking it would bring advantage to his cause. He appeals to Rutledge as one incorruptible man to another, claiming he is doing everything possible to escape the ill humor of the moment: "Tranquility is the old man's milk. I go to enjoy it in a few days, and to exchange the roar and tumult of bulls and bears for the prattle of my grandchildren and senile rest." At fifty-four, unconvincingly affecting the fatigue that attends age and the lessening of personal ambition that is meant to go along with it, he refuses to name the "bulls and bears," while inferring that they are all younger than he and Rutledge.

The way a letter ends is often telling. The unusually sentimental sign-off that follows the "bulls and bears" allusion almost suggests inevitability, that Jefferson is seeing into his own political future and recognizing that this would be their final exchange of letters before partisanship separated them for good. He wishes for Rutledge the same quiet retirement amid family and friends he says he craves: "Be these yours, my dear friend, through long years, with every other blessing, and the attachment of friends as warm and sincere as, your's affectionately...." (The first draft was even more extravagant, wishing "the affection of a thousand friends" instead of mere "attachment of friends"). When Edward Rutledge died in office as election year 1800 commenced, he was the sitting governor of South Carolina, and entirely comfortable with President Adams at the helm.[31]

Vice President Jefferson remained in Philadelphia until the Fourth of July 1797, welcoming his protégé James Monroe back to American shores after a diplomatic stint in France. That assignment had been set in motion by the now disgraced Edmund Randolph, after he'd succeeded Jefferson as secretary of state but before the Hamiltonians arranged for him to be falsely accused of a treasonous feint toward the French. Monroe, in turn, was recalled once he was seen as too fawning toward the latest in tumultuous Revolutionary governments; a dependable Federalist (C. C. Pinckney) was tapped as his successor. Back home, Monroe would proceed to muddy the political waters by publishing a long pamphlet in his own defense, critical of Federalist anti-Gallicism. Ever more reliant on Madison and Monroe these days, Jefferson rode south from Philadelphia, not to return north until the end of the year. Distance left John Adams to imagine the worst about Jefferson. Who knew what he would be doing behind the scenes, what the opposition party he "led" was cooking up between sessions of Congress?[32]

"MR. JEFFERSON IS AN INFINITELY BETTER MAN"

True to form, Jefferson spent those next several months inhaling the politics of personal destruction. He saw the retranslated Mazzei letter in the press on July 8, 1797, when south of Baltimore en route to Virginia. He stewed about it for a time, conferred with others for the next month, and wondered whether saying nothing was better than confessing and explaining what he *really* meant. He recognized that there was no upside in either case.

Did it mitigate his situation when he saw a damning pamphlet by a freelance journalist, the Scottish immigrant James Thomson Callender? It couldn't have hurt. *The History of the United States for the Year 1796* contained an explosive charge: that Alexander Hamilton had been involved in an adulterous relationship with one Maria Reynolds in Philadelphia in 1791–92, during his time as Treasury secretary, and that he used government funds to pay off the blackmailing husband (whom she'd married when she was only fifteen). On July 24, Jefferson wrote to Madison from Monticello: "I see Hamilton has put a short piece into the papers in answer to Callender's publication, and promises shortly something more elaborate." That "something" was a long, discursive, ultimately self-immolating pamphlet, though Hamilton evidently saw it as a compelling defense of his public character.

Callender's charges were accompanied by documents previously in the safe-keeping of James Monroe, who did not—at least not directly—provide them to the scandalmonger. The first of two key chapters opens, somewhat innocuously, with an elaborate report on the Treasury Department's excise tax on snuff makers, before moving on to a tawdry tale of seduction and blackmail. Attempting to extricate himself, Hamilton allegedly had Mrs. Reynolds burn all letters with his signature on them, especially those implicating him in financial arrangements with her unscrupulous husband. Though Jefferson does not appear to have left any trace of his involvement in or knowledge of these things, he looks less convincing in having preordered a number of copies of the pamphlet—for selective distribution, one imagines. And he continued (modestly, anyway) to support Callender's career. Hamilton's rather pitiful thirty-seven-page apologia, printed shortly after, placed the fault squarely upon the "spirit of Jacobinism" (alternately, the "Jacobin Scandal-Club"), which relied on the weapon of "calumny" to "wound the public character and stab the private felicity" of an honorable man. He denied all "improper pecuniary speculation" while confessing to the affair, which he claimed the blackmailing husband ("an obscure, unimportant and profligate man") knew all about and encouraged.

Hamilton appended to his statement fifty-two letters, starting with one signed "Maria" that announced her husband's intention to write to Hamilton's wife. Maria pleaded for Hamilton to see her right away: "I am a Lone I think you had better come here." The last grouping of letters in the Appendix recounts a demand-filled correspondence Hamilton initiated with James Monroe *after* the publication of Callender's pamphlet that would have led to a duel were it not for Monroe's accepting the intercession of "my friend Aaron Burr," who had been, it should be noted, Maria Reynolds's attorney in her successful 1793 divorce suit. Burr, privy to the details of her liaison with Hamilton since 1792, had kept the matter under wraps these five years.[33]

The only mention Hamilton made of Jefferson in his counter-pamphlet was to suggest impropriety in Jefferson's corresponding with a former employee at Treasury who had been critical of Hamilton. It was a gratuitous association that didn't mean much. Madison borrowed Jefferson's copy of the Hamilton pamphlet from Monroe, and after reading it wrote to Jefferson of this "masterpiece of folly," adding what he knew would corroborate Jefferson's thinking: "Next to the error of publishing at all, is that of forgetting that simplicity & candor are the only dress which prudence would put on innocence." Madison delighted in the damage done to Hamilton's reputation, at the same time mocking this haughty man's sudden persecution complex. As for Hamilton's "malignant insinuations" against Republicans, none was, Madison assured, quite so pointless as the one aimed at Jefferson: "its impotence is in exact proportion to its venom."[34]

Madison's edginess, ironic wit, and enjoyment of a certain kind of political farce eluded those who were not close friends. His public writing was invariably direct, prudently argued, and carefully wrought, which is how he descends through history. True, he did not take the kinds of chances his bosom friend did. Jefferson was known for committed positions and the lengths he would go to in order to enlist others in assisting him. He *claimed* the "simplicity & candor" that Madison actually applied in letters and publications. Jefferson's delegation of responsibility may have allowed him to affect a disinterested posture, but it too frequently backfired and showed him to be secretive. He seemed more devious than he was. In the minds of wary Federalists, he was the misguided philosopher—if not presumptive mastermind—behind the raucous, disorderly forces challenging Federalist rule.

As the supreme symbol of the Republicans, with well-publicized marks against him (*Rights of Man* embarrassment, Mazzei letter), Jefferson struggled to represent himself as friendly to moderate, quasi-, and former Federalists. He wished it to appear that he did not see party politics as a zero-sum game. Indeed, in the years after Hamilton's death, it pleased him to reconstruct his memory so that the two secretaries' extended argument could be seen as less emotionally involved than it really was, that it was a philosophical debate between the pure, principled republican and the chief "monocrat," for whom the dangers inherent in popular democracy had to be avoided at all costs.

The Reynolds affair was a dramatic preview of Jefferson's sex scandals to come, though he could not have known that. Exposure of his private life did not stop Hamilton—if anything, he turned up the volume. Having hounded Jefferson from office, next enjoying the ruin of his successor, Randolph, he was sitting pretty. He had installed a cabinet to his liking, entirely shorn of Virginians. He had buttressed Washington's authority. His smugness showed.

Focusing less attention on Jefferson during this Federalist upsurge, Hamilton turned his puppeteering purpose toward replacing the unmanageable President Adams with a friendlier Federalist. Adams was decidedly his own man, one who thought individual character and independent judgment should matter more than strict party affiliation. Standing apart from the political party that claimed him, he created a space for himself where Hamilton lacked the wherewithal to influence him. He eventually fired his Hamilton-stamped cabinet advisers, actions that made Adams more, not less, vulnerable.[35]

Anglo-French hostilities dominated the last years of the century. Since their war began in 1793, the French had been capturing American merchant vessels that were ostensibly conducting trade with Britain. Of the U.S. delegation in Paris in 1798, only Elbridge Gerry, Adams's personal friend, remained in an effort to stave off war. Staunch Southern Federalists Pinckney (South Carolina) and John Marshall (Virginia) had sailed home in consequence of the outrageous demand that they pay up front before any treaty could be negotiated. From the French perspective, all the government wanted was a good-faith loan to the nation they'd rescued from the British military colossus. Pinckney and Marshall, greeted in Philadelphia as patriot heroes, viewed Gerry as an appeaser. In years to come, as the recipient of solicitous letters from Jefferson (in the Rutledge mode), Gerry would become a Republican. In this most consequential year, 1798, Vice President Jefferson agonized as anti-French fervor seeped into Virginia and the Carolinas. He conferred with Madison on legislative means of stalling the executive, knowing how a war with France would bolster the Federalists at all levels of government.[36]

Republican newspapers, meanwhile, attempted to find new ways to explain French behavior. They reminded readers that it wasn't an either/or choice. The British had been resorting to bribery and worse over the years, and three unnamed officials implicated in the snub (X, Y, and Z) did not constitute the French government, nor sufficient cause for war. Citizens were urged to steel themselves when "orders from the Hamilton Club" were sent out to sway the gullible. Under the pseudonym Anti-Machiavel, a writer for the *Aurora*, the chief Republican organ in Philadelphia, looked disapprovingly at the one-sidedness of the spurned envoys' story and questioned the sincerity of Pinckney and Marshall.

Fortunately for Jefferson, President Adams kept his head and persisted with diplomacy until the end of his term. On the other hand, Adams did acquiesce to the Federalist-dominated Congress when he signed the obnoxious Alien and Sedition Acts that shut down editorial criticism of the government by arresting and imprisoning those whose power in print the most determined Federalists sought to deny; even the prominent Federalist John Marshall, soon to be named chief justice, regarded the Alien and Sedition Acts as excessive.

The gap between the striving parties was unbridgeable. There was never a chance that a French force would attack the U.S. mainland, yet rumors flew. At a private dinner in February 1798, the cordial if blunt-speaking Adams alarmed his vice president with a remark Jefferson felt impelled to record (the same as he'd done to preserve unrepublican ideas expressed by Hamilton in cabinet meetings or Washington in their private conversation). "In France," Adams observed, "anarchy had done more harm in one night than all the despotism of their kings had ever done in 20. or 30. Years." Could despotism ever be rationalized? Hamilton, for his part, had little quarrel with the arbitrary method of excluding entry to French troublemakers or deporting recent immigrants whose patriotism was doubted. Among those put on trial was the Hamilton accuser James Callender.[37]

The state of national affairs verged on hysteria. A good many Republican opinion pieces touted liberty's earlier triumph against pressure politics out of London and upped their references to 1776: Federalists were just like former Tories. As passions ran high, the situation became dire enough in the mind of Vice President Jefferson that he worked quietly behind the scenes to undercut the Federalist Congress by feeding a piece of legislation to an ally in Kentucky (formerly part of Virginia, now its sister state). The Kentucky Resolutions, followed by Madison's comparable, if less radical, Virginia Resolutions, broached the dangerous subject of nullification, of granting a state veto power over an objectionable act of Congress that it deemed harmful to itself. In emotional language, Jefferson described this vexing time as "the reign of witches" and optimistically prepared for his own possible presidency, which, a decade into retirement, he would proudly, memorably brand the "Revolution of 1800."[38]

Victory for Jefferson was far from certain, though Hamilton had begun shopping for a different Federalist to out-tally Adams in the Electoral College. Not even Virginia was secure in the Republican column, because George Washington had his own alternative in mind, a spoiler candidate: Patrick Henry.

A resurgent Henry stood for state office in the spring of 1799, not as a party man but in support of federal law. He remained broadly popular, and threatened to upset the Jeffersonian position in the Virginia Assembly. He was not someone who, in opposition, could be classed with "monarchists," "monocrats," "Anglo-monocrats," and "tories," to mention just some of the names Jefferson was using for the worst of the Federalists. Henry did not explicitly agree with the hated Sedition Acts, though he contested a state's power to arbitrarily dismiss what Congress had enacted. Jefferson shook in the knowledge that Henry's "intriguing & cajoleing talents" would likely damage his own political brand. But the Assembly showdown never occurred, because Henry died in early June. There was no one left to take up his cause.[39]

The year 1800 began with a string of eulogies and somber processions flowing from the death of the beloved Washington on December 14, 1799. Shortly after this intelligence reached him, Jefferson left Monticello for Philadelphia. He was still Adams's vice president. He passed by Mount Vernon on Christmas Day without stopping to pay his respects, which was probably the right choice. He resided in Philadelphia through mid-May, spending the summer and early autumn in Virginia. The next time he left home to resume his official duties, he needed go only as far as Washington, D.C., the new, if undeveloped, federal city.

During his final months in Philadelphia, conscious of a responsibility to the institution of the Senate, he put the finishing touches on the enduring parliamentary manual that describes the rules and procedures governing Congress. Meanwhile, another part of his methodical mind was preoccupied with the Northern states, whose votes were critical to his election prospects. "The Republican spirit is beginning to preponderate in Pennsa, Jersey, and N.Y.," he informed Madison, thankful especially to George Clinton and Aaron Burr for their efforts. In determining "the complexion of that legislature," New York's electors would be named by Republicans: it was not as yet the popular vote count that awarded states' electoral votes, though that is what Hamilton tried to put into effect after being blindsided by Burr. He appealed to John Jay, the ethical Federalist governor, who flatly refused to use his executive authority in this way. It was not to be Hamilton's last defeat.[40]

Until Burr became a national candidate, Adams and Jefferson were the two in Hamilton's sights. Almost single-handedly, he split the Federalist Party into Adams and Hamilton factions, banking on the Southern Federalist Charles Cotesworth Pinckney to squeeze past both Adams and Jefferson and into the presidential chair.

It was a flawed plan. Hamilton was the one pulling the strings, not Pinckney's people. He publicized his reasons for urging Federalists to abandon Adams, which included the president's "disgusting egotism"—the irony here evidently lost on the accuser—and Adams's "rage" at Hamilton personally: "There are intrinsic defects in his character which unfit him for the office." Adams's dismissal of Hamilton's favorites from the cabinet clearly went far in motivating him to unleash this scathing publication, in which he cast himself as an open-minded person who had long given Adams his support in the interest of "preserving harmony in the Federal Party."

What Hamilton says about Adams in 1800 is crueler than any of his attacks on Jefferson. His gambit involved one charge only: making Adams appear a pariah, a mentally unhealthy individual, scary, unpredictable, woefully out of step with the Federalist message. He did all he could to contrast the "respectable man" (anyone pro-Hamilton) with the "imperious chief" (Adams), whose unsafe behavior was revealed in every one of his uncontrolled "gusts of passion."[41]

Hamilton's conceit was that he was a fit judge of character—including moral character—and deserved to dictate what was best for the party going forward. His pique had to do with himself, his need to wield influence, his will to power. His audacity was off the charts.

As an able, energetic administrator of the nation's finances, he had exercised power through Washington, influencing foreign policy in the process. Recognizing that he himself was not electable, he thought he could repeat the earlier performance as adjunct to a President Pinckney. Nothing so neatly explains Hamilton's petulance and the naked self-promotion that courses through his open letter on Adams. Hamilton held that the current political mess existed for one reason only: "the ungovernable temper of Mr. ADAMS. It is a fact that he is often liable to paroxisms [sic] of anger, which deprive him of self command . . . Members of the two Houses of Congress have been humiliated by the effects of these gusts of passion."

The desperation Hamilton felt caused him to press the people who had orbited him when he was at the height of his power. In the idiom of the 1790s, he needed to have "confidential friends" on whom he could rely to back him up, to verify the accuracy of his prognosis regarding Adams. While complaining of the manner in which Adams had treated him, he sought help from the cabinet members Adams had recently dismissed from office. In a shouting match with his Hamiltonian secretary of war, Adams had called Hamilton "the greatest intriguant in the World—a man devoid of every moral principle," rubbing it in with "Mr. Jefferson is an infinitely better man." For any straight-shooting Federalist, that documented comment should have been enough.[42]

When Hamilton wrote, his words registered. Momentum quickly built around the sudden candidacy of Charles Cotesworth Pinckney—who, it must be mentioned, resolutely refused to disavow Adams. Jefferson was as artful a political operator as Hamilton. Not to be outdone, he had his own election worker in South Carolina: another Charles Pinckney, the Republican cousin of the Federalist Pinckneys, whom Jefferson would later reward with a diplomatic appointment.

AN APOLITICAL HAMILTON

On the other side of the political divide, Republicans were united. Jefferson was their man. In his fifty-seventh year, without the prodding from friends he'd previously needed when he swore a hatred for electoral politics, the dissatisfied vice president was reenergized. Even to his domesticated elder daughter, he minced no words as election season neared, setting his hopes in 1800 against "the XYZ paroxysms." Before 1796, he probably harbored no desire to be president and was not exhibiting false modesty when he asked Madison to stand for the office. He had since become convinced that it was destiny: "Our opponents perceive the decay of their power," he boasted to Martha, who was no longer the teenage Patsy, but the mother of three daughters and a son. He could not rest, because sedition prosecutions continued apace: "Still they are pressing it, and trying to pass laws to keep themselves in power." He'd accepted the leadership of his party.[43]

On that same day, April 22, 1800, he penned a letter to William Hamilton (no relation) that is rarely mentioned in Jefferson scholarship, though it neatly reflects his state of mind at a critical juncture in his life. This Hamilton was the grandson of one colonial Pennsylvania executive and nephew of another, but was not the least political himself. During the Revolution, he'd maintained an ambiguous stance ("I keep myself for the most part out of the way ... I have other Fish to fry"); in 1784, when Jefferson went to France, he spent two years in England studying English homes and gardens. He wrote to a friend from London: "Every Hour I exist I find myself more attached to America." There was never a doubt as to Hamilton's true allegiance. Returning to the property he'd inherited just outside Philadelphia, the Woodlands, he created an astonishingly diverse, scientifically advanced, neatly designed arboretum that he proudly opened to "the genteel public." The large greenhouse was a remarked-upon feature.

In April 1800, though they shared the same passion for horticulture, Jefferson barely knew the man. He'd just inspected what he called the "botanical curiosities" on Hamilton's property, so moved that he initiated a plant and seed exchange that would continue through his presidency, depositing with Hamilton precious seeds collected on the Lewis and Clark Expedition. In this, his earliest extant letter to the apolitical Hamilton, Jefferson could not arrest his recent impulse to see everything through a political lens.[44]

The key section of the letter starts: "I never considered a difference of opinion in politics, in religion, in philosophy, as cause for withdrawing from a friend. During the whole of the last war, which was trying enough, I never deserted a friend because he had taken an opposite side." Convinced he had put the past to bed, Jefferson moved to the present state of affairs: "However I have seen during the late political paroxysm here, numbers whom I had highly esteemed draw off from me, insomuch as to cross the street to avoid meeting me. The fever is abating, & doubtless some of them will correct the momentary wanderings of their heart, & return again. If they do, they will meet the constancy of my esteem, & the same oblivion of this as of any other delirium which might happen to them." After this, Jefferson went from the general to the specific, presenting a picture of his own blamelessness: "I am happy to find you as clear of political antipathies as I am ... The circumstances of our early acquaintance I have ever felt as binding me in morality as well as in affection: and there are so many agreeable points in which we are in perfect unison, but I am at no loss to find a justification of my constant esteem."[45]

What makes the letter especially interesting is that its charged political passages were cribbed from a letter Jefferson had written to his former cabinet colleague Henry Knox two weeks before. The repetition of language directed at two very different individuals seems a clear indication that Jefferson was bending over backward to convince moderate men that he was without guile.

Knox wrote from Boston, in March 1800, for the first time in five years. "No person has a higher respect & esteem for your Character, any shades of a difference in political opinions notwithstanding." Then, the once celebrated general, intimate of Washington's, updated Jefferson on his personal predicament: the downturn in his personal finances coupled with the Senate's refusal to appoint his admittedly flawed son, known as an incorrigible drinker and gambler, to a lieutenancy in the Navy. Knox hoped that Vice President Jefferson, as president of the Senate, might be able to reverse the decision.

He replied to Knox that he was powerless in such cases. But the paragraph in his letter that says the most reads as follows: "I recieve great pleasure from the continuance of your friendly dispositions. I can with truth reciprocate the assurances that differences of political opinions excited in me no unfriendliness." Then: "Were we to deny our esteem & society to all but those who think with us, every man would be an insulated being, and social relations would be dissolved."

The beauty of this sentiment would be hard for anyone to reject as insincere or deceptive, the way the Federalist press had cast him. Jefferson certainly knew how to strike a pose, continuing in the same bright spirit: "I can say with truth, and with great comfort to my own heart, that I never deserted a friend for difference of opinion in politics, in religion, in physics [probably meaning knowledge of natural science]. But great numbers have deserted me."

He is protesting that he did nothing to deserve the hatred that filled so many newspapers. As if the "desertion" comment had been accidental, his optimism returns. He says he hopes for a better, less angry politics, should he be elected president: The "paroxysm" afflicting his detractors was now "rapidly passing away"; those returning to the fold could rest assured they would "meet again the constancy of my esteem." *He* was constant. *He* was incorruptible. The inconstant ones, the deserters, would see that they were wrong to demonize Thomas Jefferson.[46]

Now, what does this all mean to the "body politic" that has suffered? Paroxysm, fever, delirium—three words specific to disease (to "physic") describe virulent partisanship as a state of sickness. For Jefferson, the "fever" must dissipate, the "delirium" must end with a return to reason. A political disease is temporary and not terminal if one believes in the future.

To be clear, in imagining himself wholly innocent of responsibility for bringing on the infection and contributing to its propagation, Jefferson the rhetorician is not the patient seized by delusion—it's the other guy. His superiority comes from his immunity, which lies in character. Reason is acquired through a good heart and sound judgment. In a way, this is "My Head and My Heart" all over again. The

Head builds things, the Heart makes sure a generosity of spirit prevails... both within him and in the republic he strives to improve.

When he redefines his election as the Revolution of 1800, he means a revolution in the semantic sense that he has guided the body politic through the revolving course of disease, from infection to remission and recovery.

Figure 15. Engraving by Cornelius Tiebout, in honor of Jefferson's election in 1801. A bust of Benjamin Franklin sits on the table, as the new president points to a copy of the Declaration of Independence. Engraving is based on the 1800 portrait of Jefferson by Rembrandt Peale. (Courtesy Library of Congress)

CHAPTER 10

"The Campaign of Slander Is Opening"
Adams vs. Jefferson vs. Burr

THERE CAN BE NO doubt that Thomas Jefferson zealously oversaw his presidential campaign. He was totally hands-on. No affectation of passivity and calm would succeed anymore, because, having worked out the particulars with Madison and others ahead of time, Jefferson saw the political situation in 1800 as dire, and he regarded himself as, in essence, America's savior.

By 1800, John Adams knew Jefferson in many different contexts. Their friendship had been a classic case of opposites attracting, as they sat in the Continental Congress and on the committee to frame the Declaration of Independence. During their collaboration in Paris, in 1784–85, the two families had been genuinely close. Jefferson was new to international diplomacy, and Adams helped him obtain surer footing. They traveled for pleasure in England, in 1786; together again in 1788, they managed delicate negotiations in Amsterdam, over America's unpaid loans. In their years abroad, Jefferson shopped for Abigail Adams; they talked art and history. All that started to cool not long after Jefferson came to Philadelphia in 1790.

As the senior partner in financial negotiations, Adams had had every reason to believe that his learned friend was capable of changing his mind on encountering a different perspective. He came to see a previously hidden side of Jefferson. The long-limbed Virginian maintained his familiar good-natured pose; but as the fractious decade of the 1790s rolled by, his less admirable qualities became known: a resistance to correction and a tendency to see only in black and white.

By 1794, as Jefferson packed up and left Philadelphia, he expressed a desire to abandon politics altogether. It was still two and a half years before he and Adams would be pitted against each another in the first contested presidential election. Adams was not ready to give up on their friendship, but he knew too much about his future opponent to delude himself, writing to his son John Quincy: "The Motives to Mr Jeffersons Resignation are not assigned, and are left open to the Conjectures of a Speculating World. I also am a Speculator in the Principles and Motives of Mens Actions and may guess as well as others." He went on to list seven "speculations." The first was: "Mr. Jefferson has an habit as well as a disposition to expensive Living, and as his Salary was not Adequate to his Luxury, he could not Subdue his Pride and Vanity as I have done, and proportion his Style of Life to his Revenue." Adams, it should be said, was known to work his modest New England farm alongside his hired laborers; his wife was an excellent money manager. Jefferson, of course, lived splendidly and died deeply in debt.

Of Adams's seven enumerated tidbits of speculation about Jefferson in 1794, the most condemning concerned political ambition—an element of his character Jefferson strenuously denied. "Ambition is the Subtlest Beast of the Intellectual and Moral Field," Adams wrote. "It is wonderfully adroit in concealing itself from its owner, I had almost said from itself. Jefferson thinks he shall by this step [resigning his office] get a Reputation of an humble, modest, meek Man, wholly without ambition or Vanity. He may even have deceived himself into this Belief." And the kicker: "But if a Prospect opens, The World will see and he will feel, that he is as ambitious as Oliver Cromwell though no soldier." Cromwell, of course, took part in the English Civil War in the 1640s, fighting against the Royalists before becoming the reformist "Lord Protector" at the head of Parliament. To early American students of English history, he was the personification of ambition.

Adams was wry, but not nasty. In 1794, he thought of Jefferson as a "Wise Man" capable of reflection. Aside from the question of imperfectly disguised ambition, he compared him, not entirely lightheartedly, to Numa, the second king of Rome, who "was called from the Forrests," the mountains where the Sabines dwelled (read: pastoral Albemarle). Numa succeeded the warrior king Romulus as a humble, pacifistic ruler. This could be Jefferson too. Yet Adams was not quite done spinning a web for his now twenty-six-year-old son, who had been an eager companion to Jefferson back when they strolled about Paris. Above his signature, the then vice president returned to the subject of Jefferson's departure from

Philadelphia: "Tho his Desertion may be a Loss to Us, of some Talents[,] I am not sorry for it on the whole, because his soul is poisoned with Ambition and his Temper imbittered against the Constitution and Administration." And finally, for obvious reasons: "All this is confidential."[1]

One thing to be said about John Adams is that he did not disguise who he was at any point in his public career. He did not even try. Though his wit was sharp, his attempts at conviviality were not so smoothly conveyed. He was a keen student of human psychology throughout life, and, to his credit, he acknowledged the prickly temperament for which he was known. Seeing how ill-suited he was to electoral politics, he did not try to court popularity. But neither, he knew, did George Washington, whose heroic reputation was an adequate substitute for conventional warmth. It took the rise in anti-French sentiment in 1798, a nationalist surge after XYZ, for Adams, as commander in chief, to acquire a little of that Washingtonian aura.

It was then that Jefferson's reputation as "friend of the people" gained the most ground. With the Alien and Sedition prosecutions underway and Jefferson's pursuit of the presidency becoming more intense, supporters highlighted his authorship of the Declaration of Independence, the phraseology of which was cherished long before his personal pen was credited with its composition. In 1800, Fourth of July orations in New York and Charleston praised the mind that conceived the document, that gave it a "Manly and energetic" phrasing that moved hearts, and the "perspicacious and energetic language" that made the text sublime.

The more Jefferson's authorship was heralded, the more Federalists grumbled that it was a "weapon," a cheap election ploy. The partisan press went into overdrive that year, drawing the contrast between Jefferson as "a republican in manners" and Adams as a "monarchist." With Burr's electoral coup in the New York legislature in the months before the presidential vote, the *Republican Watch Tower* crowed: "The Goddess of Liberty has put to flight the demon of Aristocracy... Huzza for the *Constitution*, Huzza for *Jefferson*!" Between 1795 and 1800, the advantage Federalists had in the partisan newspaper environment was lost, as more and more Republican presses began operation.[2]

In contrast to the dictates of the modern campaign environment, Jefferson's public appearances were few; it was his reputation on the page that his allies communicated, that political editors dressed up in order to portray him as a protector of rights. His values—all that separated him from the Hamiltonian Federalists—were impressed in newsprint and traveled distances. That was how he was known.

When away from home, Jefferson refused to send letters through the postal service, relying always on private messengers. He did not lose sight of politics for a minute, taking in the opinion writers of newspapers far and wide. He was privy to the worst of what was being said of him, routinely flagging newspapers as organs of "slander." To William Short, still in Europe, he used a diplomatic channel to write of what he was seeing in March 1800: "tho' our quadrennial election is still 9. months distant, the public mind begins already to be agitated. The campaign of slander is opening... Defamation has been carried in our papers to so licentious and revolting a length, that it has lost all it's effect. It does not even give pain to those at whom it is levelled." The imagery of disturbance and dysfunction, in a tone meant to express an absence of concern on his part, denied what he had to have felt, what impelled him to exhort allies to coalesce in support of his key positions: it was the "public mind" that experienced "agitation," not Jefferson.

Calmly stating that he was unable to predict whether he or Adams would prevail, he expressed a faith in his country that no one else in American politics could be sure of at this time of exaggerated emotion: "Our people have so innate a spirit of order & obedience to the law," he told Short, "so religious an acquiescence in the will of the majority, ... that a majority of a single vote, as at the last election, produces as absolute & quiet a submission as an unanimous vote." The "spirit of order & obedience" was a settled part of his political ideology, so much so that he applied it to those like the tax resisters, who, after expressing their pain out of doors, reached out to their governors, and once heard, returned to their peaceful, ordinary lives. Democracy in action. Reason prevailing. Unpopular governors voted out of office.[3]

This language of majority will and minority rights was baked into Jefferson's vision for the American republic. He would invoke it again, more beautifully, in his Inaugural Address the following March, when he spoke of "the sacred principle, that though the will of the majority is in all cases to prevail, that will to be rightful must be reasonable; that the minority possess their equal rights, which equal law must protect, and to violate would be oppression." Even to someone like Short, whom he could not fool and need not spin dreams to, he could not stop himself from celebrating the innate wisdom of the people, knowing all the while that it would be a small number of electors, their names decided on in state legislatures, who determined the outcome of the presidential contest. Those were the men he and his allies had to reach, whose "reasonableness" he banked on, who would know him for the fair-minded man of principle he was constantly selling to the body politic.

The difference in outlook between Thomas Jefferson and John Adams was the latter's equally certain conviction that "Differences and Divisions," "parties and factions," were unavoidable in any republic, and that as much as power and ambition were natural to men, so was the electorate prone to voting into office the less than honorable as often as the good and noble of purpose. Politics would not do without celebrity, he lamented, implicitly skeptical of Jefferson's wishful and wistful thinking.[4]

1800: JEFFERSON IS TESTED

On the home front, the year 1800 began in despondency as two deaths rocked Jefferson's dreamworld. Daughter Maria gave birth to her first child on the last day of December 1799, but any delight he felt turned to grief when the infant died less than a month later. Maria, the less resilient of the Jeffersons' surviving daughters, did not recover her health for several months—no doubt triggering thoughts of how her mother had languished before her own early death. While Jefferson would know twelve grandchildren (though only one of Maria's three children survived childhood) and live to greet thirteen great-grandchildren, he would bury Maria beside her mother before the end of his first term as president.[5]

Before the end of January, Jupiter Evans died as well. Jefferson's reaction was a combination of sorrow and exasperation, because Jupiter was hands-on and known to take chances in his execution of duties for his master. Ailing for some time, he apparently entrusted his life to a doctor steeped in uncertain African medical lore, collapsed into convulsions, and paid the ultimate price. "He leaves a void in my household administration which I cannot fill up," Jefferson wrote. What reads as transactional no doubt conceals the greater emotion he felt in losing his old and steady mate. The four stately limestone columns at the entrance to Monticello are the work of Jupiter, his enslaved stonecutter and his companion on the road for the better part of fifty years.[6]

Along with human tragedies, Jefferson faced greater and greater financial difficulties as he looked at the prospect of the presidency, where his official salary might or might not cover the cost of entertaining. Son-in-law Tom Randolph approached him for assistance in paying the debts he owed, and Jefferson had no choice but to refuse him. He himself had borrowed from William Short, whose Virginia accounts Jefferson was managing during Short's extended stay in Europe. While utilizing the labor of close to a hundred enslaved men and women, his Albemarle farms were not turning a profit. Shortly before he assumed the presidency, the Philadelphia buyer of the tobacco crop from Jefferson's most distant farm (some ninety miles southwest of Monticello) expressed dissatisfaction with the way it was packed; the overseer there lost his job after twelve years of service.

Over the next eight years, as president, Jefferson honored his commitment to reduce the nation's debt, but his own economy did not prosper. There was little he could do to improve the situation in the face of drought and other disincentives. In 1801, he made a striking statement: as widely read as he was on the subject of agricultural science and as attentive as he was to the gardening and landscaping work at Monticello, he admitted (if it was in fact true) that he'd never actually observed his own tobacco being picked. After his presidency ended, he was to try again to get out of debt by expanding the acreage producing tobacco and wheat. It was a losing battle, because tobacco prices fluctuated, and this cash crop, long a substitute for hard currency, did irreparable harm to the soil.

As offensive as his words may strike a modern reader, Jefferson could hardly have found a way to end his reliance on enslaved labor in these years. Absent from home half the year, he couldn't always count on the men he hired as overseers to do a creditable job. And until there were a sufficient number of free laborers to draw from, an existing Virginia plantation could not operate without those already there, born into bondage. Could Jefferson have converted the enslaved into tenants? Perhaps. He clearly lacked the imagination, the will, and the financial cushion to try the experiment. His longing for a healthy pastoral republic met his troubled financial condition and reliance on slavery head-on. He was too accepting of that world, but by no means alone in refusing to take personal risks for the sake of the enslaved.[7]

Until their final rupture, Washington and Jefferson regularly shared detailed information about their crop yields, rotation cycles, and condition of the soil on their respective properties. It bears more than cursory scrutiny that, both before and after they assumed the presidency, the two larger-than-life founders were frequently urged by European friends like Lafayette to serve as examples to their nation by emancipating their oppressed workforce and fulfilling the enlightened principles of the American Revolution. They did not feel the shame we wish they had.

Washington proved no less impotent than Jefferson on this score. Both sought to avoid disciplining enslaved people, providing adequate food and basic medical care and relying on incentives instead of the whip. They kept families together as much as possible—a rather minimal expression of humanity. But that appears to have been the extent of any embarrassment they felt. There is simply no way to cover up the ugliness in how they lived. Washington and Jefferson gave the same kind of attention to the neat appearance of the landscape on approach to the mansion, so that visitors would focus their eye on the verdant scene rather than the "hoe people," as Washington referred to his (mostly female) enslaved labor force. In the 1790s, he consulted Jefferson when the well-known British agricultural writer Arthur Young pressed him on the relative cost-effectiveness in hiring versus purchasing a slave, comparing both to the cost of a white laborer. In response, Jefferson calculated that hiring ultimately worked against the planter, adding gratuitously that "the negro does not perform quite as much work, nor with as much intelligence."[8]

One finds with both Jefferson and Washington a number of conflicting statements over several decades, and historians of slavery have little positive to say about their efforts to remediate the problem. Jefferson was disgusted with the multigenerational degradation of both the enslaved and the enslaver (in principle), and he deplored the lifetime of debt that it incurred on him. It was not out of character for Jefferson to write, as he did from France to his brother-in-law Francis Eppes, on the subject of his debts: "I am decided against selling my lands. They are the only sure provision for my children, and I have sold too much of them already. I am also unwilling to sell negroes, if the debts can be paid without... My debts once cleared off, I shall try some plan of making their situation happier, determined to content myself with a small portion of their labour."

He sounds sincere and compassionate. Until, in the one sentence that follows, he is a cruelly calculating aristocrat: "I think it better for them therefore to be submitted to harder conditions for a while in order that they may afterwards be put into a better situation." In other words, he would look better if, while he was in Europe, his enslaved labor force was worked to the bone so that after his return, he could seize credit by making a noble gesture toward them. There is only one conclusion to draw from this order of thinking.[9]

In the late summer and autumn of 1800, with the national election pending, Governor James Monroe faced what became known as Gabriel's Rebellion. Had it not been for the warnings given by some enslaved people to their master, significant numbers of unfree Virginians would likely have resorted to acts of violence in and around the capital of Richmond. The plot allegedly involved the kidnapping of Monroe himself. Should the state exhibit mercy, Monroe asked his mentor, or display its overpowering strength?

"Where to stay the hand of the executioner is an important question," Jefferson rejoined, and offered a cautious course of action: Don't let your emotions exert undue influence over your decision. In the neighborhood of Monticello, he said, "there is a strong sentiment that there has been hanging enough. The other states & the world at large will for ever condemn us if we indulge a principle of revenge, or go one step beyond absolute necessity." And that was how the state government, more or less, proceeded, hanging a number of the would-be insurrectionists, while transporting many others beyond state lines. What makes Jefferson's recommendation interesting is that he felt the eyes of the world were watching.

There was more than meets the eye in this unrealized rebellion. First, Gabriel escaped capture only to be turned in to authorities by another enslaved man. Second, at least a few white men were in on the plot, which shows that interracial friendships mattered in this environment. Rare though they were, Virginia's political elite took such events to be reminders that anger was simmering on plantations. While free Blacks were not prominent within Gabriel's group, that fact did not move slave owners who saw mass removal as the only safe solution. In *Notes on Virginia*, acknowledging Black self-determination as a right and Black anger as justified, Jefferson was the first to put into print a proposal to pair emancipation with colonization of the enslaved and freeborn alike beyond the reach of white society. After Gabriel, attention turned to Haiti, a republic of former slaves just beginning to take form. As the Haitian Revolution unfolded, Virginia would continue to make and remake manumission laws.

Jefferson held to his original prescription. The faster emancipation-to-removal occurred, he thought, the less drastic the transition would be. He remarked to Monroe that in Albemarle County, "where every thing has been perfectly tranquil," an undercurrent existed among whites who weighed their options amid talk of the "negro conspiracy." Nevertheless, Jefferson saw his home turf, by and large, as a place where free mixed-race people felt secure and well enough respected by their white neighbors. He professed to understand the root cause of rebellion and felt that people of color had every right to live where they could govern themselves, free from white prejudice. As such, he was among those who looked to Haiti as the most practicable destination for the feared, the unwanted, in a society made by and made for people with English surnames.[10]

WHAT THE ELECTION TIE REALLY MEANT

Well before the presidential contest was decided, as local election returns became known, Republicans saw their impressive gains and celebrated. Jefferson wrote to a congressional ally who represented Baltimore: "The spirit of 76. had never left the people of our country. But artificial panics of rawhead & bloody bones had put it to sleep for a while." (Here was the "reign of witches" in another form.) "Whatever may be the event of the Executive election," Jefferson continued, "the Legislative one will give us a majority in the H. of R." A bold majority in the popularly elected part of Congress was enough, he held, to minimize the "mischief" a perverse president could do. He did not allow himself to prophesy the totality of his coming victory.[11]

Because president and vice president could not be from the same state, the Virginia–New York alliance cast Aaron Burr as Jefferson's prospective running mate. It was the astute and loyal Pennsylvania Republican congressman Albert Gallatin, soon to be named Jefferson's secretary of the treasury, who did the most to assure the Virginians that Burr should be favored over the experienced but far less clever George Clinton. Gallatin's intimate connections to New York politicos through the family of his dynamic wife Hannah gave him perspective. When Burr was subsequently iced out of the administration, Gallatin was the one cabinet member who truly understood what Burr had to be feeling, and that he was justified in feeling it.[12]

The events occurring between 1800 and 1804 have a certain poignancy to them. No one anticipated that Jefferson and Burr would end up with the same number of electoral votes. Burr was meant to come in second place to Jefferson in the election of 1800, and never pretended otherwise. But that wasn't enough. He got caught up in a matter of political skulduggery that was not of his own making but that nevertheless, slowly but surely, soured a president on his vice president.

With his usual invisible hand, Jefferson told his Randolph son-in-law that South Carolina and Georgia intended to waste their second vote, so that he would end up with two or three more votes than Burr, and Burr with five more than Adams. It was enough of a cushion to ensure Republican victory all around. In fact, Hamiltonians in South Carolina seemed inclined to split their electoral votes between C. C. Pinckney and Jefferson, dispensing with Adams altogether. In the end, there was insufficient coordination within either party, and the result was chaos.[13]

The conventional telling of the election tie of 1800–01 focuses on the horse race and faulty math. As the Constitution laid out, each elector cast two votes of equal weight; this is, of course, how as the second-place finisher Jefferson became Adams's vice president. This time, while Adams received one more electoral vote than Pinckney (65–64), Jefferson and Burr each ended up with 73. The tie became apparent in the third week of December. It meant that the election was to be decided in the House of Representatives—not the incoming Republican-dominated House, but the outgoing Federalist-dominated House. The final result of the election would be determined by the majority vote tally within each state delegation: one state, one vote. Could the Federalists secure concessions from Jefferson? Or, if not, from Burr? What could be gained by pitting one against the other?

There are additional layers to peel back if one is to appreciate the interplay of personalities. For one, Jefferson amped up his correspondence with Burr. Two questions arise: How much did he worry about the New Yorker, that he felt the need to sound him out? Did he trust Burr's sense of honor, as he claimed he did?

In late January 1801, William Munford, a prized student of George Wythe's and now a young state legislator, arrived in Washington from New York, and he informed Jefferson that yet another letter of his had been making the rounds, this time in Burr's neighborhood. Unlike the Mazzei letter, this one was, Jefferson avowed, a nefarious forgery, though Munford said the handwriting was a credible match to Jefferson's.

The designated head of the ticket wrote with a sense of urgency to his ostensible running mate on February 1, avowing his innocence. "It was to be expected that the enemy would endeavor to sow tares between us," he began his letter, advising Burr to prepare to catch wind of "sentiments highly injurious to you" that Jefferson had never uttered. He himself had grown accustomed to "the common trash of slander," and expressed confidence that Burr would see through all such "contrivances" by their political enemies.[14]

Covering all bases, Jefferson enclosed a copy of the actual letter, which had been subsequently forged or otherwise doctored. It was from Jefferson to Judge Hugh Henry Brackenridge of Pennsylvania, an early and well-rounded resident of the young city of Pittsburgh who had distinguished himself as a satirical novelist as well as a jurist. The letter, which Jefferson had composed on December 18, 1800, was fairly brief and referred to the presumptive tie, but without discrediting Burr. It said: "We are brought into dilemma by the probable equality of the two republican candidates." Jefferson wanted the judge to appreciate that "the federalists in Congress mean to take advantage of this, and either to prevent an election altogether, or reverse what has been understood to have been the wishes of the people as to their President & Vice-president." And that was the sum of it.[15]

So, what motivated Jefferson to write to Burr when he did, on February 1, 1801? He did not tell Burr that he'd received a letter from Judge Brackenridge at the end of January—it is noted in his "Summary Journal of Letters," a meticulous record now housed in the Library of Congress. That letter is explicit in weighing the legal and constitutional questions embedded in Jefferson's December 18 letter, along with what the judge termed "hints, or indicia of the public mind." Brackenridge recognized this moment as "the opening abyss of a probable suspension of the federal government, from the nonelection of a President." The election tie said to him, based on what politically connected Pennsylvanians were informing him, that "violent" Federalists were bent on spiting the Republicans at any cost. This must have alarmed Jefferson, as he thought about what he should and should not say to Burr. The judge anticipated that the Federalists would do "all the mischief in their power," either conspiring to annul the election or else wreaking havoc with the vote so that Burr leapfrogged past Jefferson.[16]

As the new year opened, Jefferson had written from Washington to his daughter Maria, assuring the family that he harbored no doubts about the integrity of Colonel Burr. "The Federalists were confident at first they could debauch Colo. B. from his good faith by offering him their vote to be President, and have seriously proposed it to him. His conduct has been honorable & decisive, and greatly embarrasses them." By the end of January, however, with reason to suspect more foul play, he was stirred to write Burr once more to sound him out and receive further reassurances.[17]

What may have flummoxed candidate Jefferson most was Judge Brackenridge's perception that the Virginian's reputation for reserve would cause "the more strenuous of the republicans . . . to declare themselves for Burr" by reasoning that Burr was made "of sterner stuff" than Jefferson, and inured to political controversy in the rough-and-tumble of New York politics. The logic went that Burr would show his mettle by acting "with double rigor, and sweep from office every individual of the preceding [Federalist/Adams] administration." Jefferson must have been disheartened. His reassuring language of bipartisanship, his rhetorical refrain about the wisdom of the people, could all come back to bite him if Republicans wanted more toughness than his persona suggested.

Burr wrote to him from Albany on February 12, a short letter that Jefferson received eight days later. It contained every assurance Jefferson could have desired. If his residence in Albany, rather than anywhere close to Washington, didn't prove his innocence, Burr acknowledged the lies that were circulating and dismissed "the most malignant spirit of slander and intrigue" as being of no consequence. He had received Jefferson's letter of the first with William Munford's warning about a forgery meant to shake their alliance, and insisted that Jefferson's concern was unwarranted. He signed off with the words, "Continue to believe in the very Great Respect & Esteem, with which I am, your friend..."[18]

On February 14, before he'd received the latest of Burr's reassuring letters, Jefferson jotted notes of Washington gossip that had reached his ears. It was a remark made by Jefferson's successor as minister to France, Gouverneur Morris, a good friend to Hamilton and no fan of Jefferson, who was counseling that Burr could not be trusted. "How comes it," Morris told another, "that Burr who is four hundred miles off (at Albany) has agents here at work with great activity, while Jefferson, who is on the spot, does nothing?"[19]

Three days later, the tie was broken, and the Virginian secured the presidency. Allowing that Jefferson, a prodigious notetaker, was something of a pack rat, one still wonders whether he held on to this particular scrap because he was still unsure of Burr or because he wished to record what Federalists were cooking up, simply for the sake of seeing his history told to his advantage at some future date. It is also plausible to imagine Jefferson seizing on Morris's assessment of Burr's alleged hypocrisy and intrigue so as to justify his own turn against Burr after coming into office. The question becomes whether, at this early date, Jefferson was already manufacturing a rationalization for the disempowerment of his own vice president; for he would grant Burr no more authority than John Adams had shown to him.

∼

How the tie was broken is a story in itself, one that cannot be related without naming Alexander Hamilton as a major irritant. Out of office for several years but integrally involved in everything his party was contriving, he went to great lengths to stop the staunchest Federalists (notably in Massachusetts and Rhode Island) from choosing Burr over Jefferson, which they were preparing to do.[20]

His January 16, 1801, letter to Federalist James A. Bayard is deservedly famous. The Delaware congressman was the man who ultimately voted Jefferson into office in February by casting the deciding vote in the House of Representatives. The letter he received from Hamilton, extremely long, is a calculated argument in favor of the lesser of two evils. What the writer doesn't reveal, however, and what history has overlooked, is that the scariest potential result in Hamilton's thinking was this: if elected, Aaron Burr would effectively become head of the *Federalist* Party.

Having heard that Bayard, unlike many other Federalists, had not made up his mind to support Burr and embarrass Jefferson, Hamilton tried to work his magic. If the unfit Burr were chosen by the Federalists, he said, he would have no choice but to resign from the party—that's how strongly he felt. Jefferson's badness should not be minimized: "I admit that his politics are tinctured with fanaticism," he wrote, that he is "crafty & persevering in his objects," and "not scrupulous about the means of success, nor very mindful of truth." Jefferson was "a contemptible hypocrite," but he could be counted on to abide by the structure of the Constitution, doing nothing that might "contravene his popularity." He would work within the system. And besides, his pro-French sympathies had lately "abated."

Burr, on the other hand, lacked principles and did not care whether he was popular or not. He would capitalize on any and every opportunity to advance his "*extreme & irregular ambition.*" He was "*selfish* to a degree which excludes all social affections." He was "decidedly *profligate.*" The insults cascaded from Hamilton's pen, as he summed up his view that "the force of Mr Burrs understanding is much overrated. He is far more *cunning* than *wise*, far more *dexterous* than *able*. In my opinion he is inferior in real ability to Jefferson."

The language Hamilton used was language Bayard understood all too well, and is not difficult for us to parse either. In the vernacular of their day, "irregular" ambition was another way of saying abnormal and unstable; a lack in social affections implied that one could not form dependable (normal) friendships; "profligate" connoted both extravagance with money and dissipation in sexual life. (Like Jefferson, Burr became a widower while still in his thirties and had a healthy libido.) Jefferson might be "crafty & persevering"; but his friendships were real and sustained. He was knowable. Burr, in this construction, acted upon a base, hidden instinct. "I think it almost certain he will attempt usurpation," Hamilton added ominously.

A certain blindness attached to Hamilton at moments such as these. Did he not see how his own desires and observable ambition (a cabinet secretary leading a federal army in 1794) could be interpreted as immoderate? Couldn't "profligacy" apply to his own admitted sexual transgressions? Nor could he explain away Burr's unquestioned competence as New York's attorney general and a U.S. senator. Burr's popularity among rank-and-file New Yorkers was equally undeniable. What in this character portrait suggested a crime brewing? Burr acquitted himself extremely well during the Revolutionary War, demonstrating outstanding courage, rising in the ranks. Hamilton presented no evidence for the charges he was spewing.

He sent versions of the letter to several other prominent Federalists. To John Rutledge Jr., congressman from South Carolina and nephew of Edward Rutledge, he wrote in confidence that Federalists should not be taken in by Burr, because "there being no prospect that the respectable and sober fœderalists will countenance the projects of an irregular Ambition or prodigal Cupidity, he will not long lean upon them;" rather, he would use them for a time before making his bed with "the most unprincipled of the opposite party to accomplish his ends." Hamilton compared Burr directly to the despised demagogue and notorious conspirator of ancient Rome, Catiline. Each of Hamilton's charges was a precise replica of the historical biography of Catiline, as though he'd lazily transferred the old to the new.[21]

A major misconception, even among scholars, is the general acceptance of Hamilton's argument as to Burr's moral deficiencies. Reading back from the so-called Burr conspiracy, when a murderer vice president was deemed guilty of treason by the president who had just driven him from office, Hamilton's appraisal has a greater ring of credibility. But this, too, as we shall learn, is painting in very broad brushstrokes. Hamilton's active involvement in the election tie story was blatant. His motivation, however, has not been thoroughly evaluated.

Hamilton always portrayed himself as the ultimate insider who knew what others didn't. Anticipating all possibilities, he planted the idea that Burr was willing to *say* he'd govern in a way that would permit the Federalists greater access than Jefferson would allow. But don't be fooled, he warned. Federalists would be made to suffer if they put him in the president's chair.

The truth is more complicated. In fact, the issue wasn't Burr at all. There is no credible evidence that Burr told anyone that he was thinking about undermining the process, countering the wishes of the Republican principals who fully intended to throw away a few Burr votes so that Jefferson outpolled him by one or more electors. Burr knew perfectly well how the Republican-voting states were expected to manage in their state legislatures; their error was logistical, a result of miscommunication over great distances in a five-mile-an-hour world.

Jefferson's initial confidence in his running mate was not misplaced. Burr himself instructed Rhode Island that the state should withhold one of its two votes *from him*. During the transitional months, December through February, he wasn't politicking. And when, in mid-January, Madison proposed that Jefferson and Burr issue a joint statement calling for the *incoming* (Republican-led) Congress to meet to settle the matter of the tie, Burr agreed.

No one worked harder than Hamilton to get Jefferson elected. He knew Burr firsthand as a vigorous New York attorney and astute politician who had gotten the better of him more than once in their state. So he decided to paint Burr as a projector. In the political vocabulary of this era, "projector" could refer either to an ingenious, entrepreneurial type or to an evil genius, one with treacherous intent. By making Burr into a monster, Hamilton acted purely out of pique and for his own political advantage.[22]

Because where would Hamilton be when, in consequence of a manipulation of the vote in the House, Burr became president? If Federalists thought they could gain favor with President Burr, Hamilton would lose his iron grip on the party. Without any help from Hamilton, and whether they succeeded or not with President Burr, they could at least try to pressure him. Hamilton's private logic was simple. Everyone agreed that Jefferson was the avowed enemy of the Federalist Party. With Jefferson at the helm, Hamilton would remain chief planner and plotter, directing the party's efforts in contesting, embarrassing, and unseating the Republican.

One sees a pattern. What was true when Hamilton decided he could not stomach Adams, a Federalist who would not give him the time of day, so it was with Aaron Burr: "If we must have an *enemy* at the head of the government," he'd written a Massachusetts Federalist when his enmity toward the independence of President Adams rankled even more than the prospect of a Jefferson victory, "let it be one whom we can oppose." That was why Hamilton, in his slyest, most underhanded way, was urging his fellow Federalists in 1800–01 to allow the Republicans the "President Jefferson" they so fervently desired.[23]

To make his message as strong as possible, Hamilton had to cast Burr as someone who, if unchecked, might make himself a dictator. In truth, Burr was not that person at all. He refused to play ball with the Federalists. They approached him; he balked. Rather than position himself where he could exert influence, he spent the most critical weeks of the election season in Albany, New York, where he attended his only daughter's wedding on February 2, 1801. On the eleventh, the ballots were counted and the tie confirmed. Six mostly unproductive days later, on the thirty-sixth ballot, Jefferson was declared the victor. His vice president arrived in Washington two full weeks after this, just three days before the inauguration.

A usurper would have behaved quite differently. No one said it better than the Federalist tie breaker from Delaware, Representative Bayard: "The means existed of electing Burr, but they required his cooperation." They tried. They failed to get Burr to go along. He proved himself, in Bayard's words, "a Democrat."[24]

There is no way to know whether Jefferson would have treated his vice president any better had the tie not occurred. The fact remains that the newspapers would not let the issue die, and that the anarchic scenario Judge Hugh Brackenridge presented to Jefferson during the third week of January, while plausible and well argued, never came to pass: the "violent" Federalists failed to unleash chaos. Republicans took both houses of Congress along with the executive.

The conduct of partisan politics was as brutal in 1800 as it would ever be, and Jefferson was no innocent bystander. Virginians, who dominated the governing party, could not claim that Burr had done anything to warrant being ignored post-inauguration. Yes, he was a spry forty-five when he became vice president, and decidedly ambitious. But he was no more ambitious than Jefferson was in the interest of his intended successor and best friend, James Madison.

Without wrecking the Virginia–New York axis, the third president would need to be certain that no New Yorker could use the vice presidency as a springboard to the presidency. That was why, in 1804, he made the switch to George Clinton, sixty-five when he accepted the position, and sixty-nine in 1808, when Jefferson retired after two terms. A Federalist U.S. senator saw exactly what was going on, noting that in his constitutional role as president of the Senate, Burr spoke with eloquence and effectiveness. Once Clinton took his chair, the contrast could not have been more obvious: "He is an old feeble man—he appears altogether unacquainted with our rules—his voice is very weak & feeble—I cannot hear the one half of what he says—he has a clumsey awkward way of putting a question—Preserves little or no order—What a vast difference between him & Aaron Burr!"[25]

In the opening days of 1804, a logical time to be working out reelection strategy, Jefferson knew precisely what he had to do. It was six months before the duel with Hamilton. To justify replacing Burr with Clinton, he composed a personal note, which he deliberately retained and would use to make his case to posterity. It expanded on what a sympathetic New Englander named Hitchburn wanted him to know about Burr's behavior back when the election tie of 1801 was still unresolved. Jefferson did not know Hitchburn very well, but in 1804, he chose to believe the man's recollection of a three-year-old conversation.

The following was overheard: "We must have a president and a constitutional one," said Burr (allegedly). "How is it to be done?" asked the New Englander. "Mr. Jefferson's friends will not quit him." Burr: "Our friends must join the federalist vote." The New Englander: "Who is to be our Vice-President?" Burr: "Mr. Jefferson."[26]

Jefferson believed what he wanted to believe. He had the very human tendency of drawing conclusions by selecting evidence that provided an immediate benefit to him or ratified an earlier preconception. To protect Virginia and Virginians, he tended to equate the national interest with Virginia's interest, and he was always looking after his two closest political friends, Madison and Monroe. Such feelings only intensified over the course of eight years in office. The point is, justifications came easily to him.

Whispers about Burr continued to circulate. Hamilton may have slow-walked him into their memorable duel in 1804, but the vice president's political adversaries in the years 1801–04 encompassed not just Hamiltonian Federalists but also Republican Livingstons and, especially, the Clintonians. The editor of New York's *American Citizen*, Clinton supporter James Cheetham, made waves right and left, prompting Jeffersonians and Hamiltonians alike to revisit the circumstances surrounding the election tie. Gouverneur Morris noted in his diary in the fall of 1802 that he'd read in Cheetham's paper "a long Story about Burr's supposed Negotiation with the Federalists." Jefferson read the papers.[27]

Figure 16. The President's House, before it became known as the White House, 1807. Architectural drawing by Benjamin Henry Latrobe (1764–1820). After arriving from England in 1796, the inspired architect designed buildings in Virginia and Philadelphia before Jefferson hired him to complete construction of the U.S. Capitol. (Courtesy Library of Congress)

CHAPTER 11

"Bloody Teeth & Fangs"

Sentimental Rage, Presidential Power

O N MARCH 4, 1801, AFTER being sworn in as president by John Marshall, the new chief justice, Thomas Jefferson made the most important political speech of his life. His First Inaugural Address has yet to be improved upon as a moral declaration, attesting to America's unsullied, incorruptible self-image. Because of its patriotic value, it outranks the 1786 Head and Heart letter and the 1793 declaration of his retirement from Washington's cabinet ("The motion of my blood no longer keeps time with the tumult of the world") in presenting Jefferson as a man at peace, tolerant of difference, rhapsodically engaging with the natural world. A fertile land unleashes fertile imaginations. Young and vigorous, the United States will only get bigger and better.

The call for a return to civility in political life is the most often quoted section of the address, but the closest to Jefferson's heart is that which nationalizes his personal temperament as a son of the Virginia Piedmont. As "our own dear Monticello, where has nature spread so rich a mantle under the eye" treated Maria Cosway to a vision of nature at its most sublime, the First Inaugural pays tribute to "a rising nation, spread over a wide and fruitful land, traversing all the seas with the rich productions of their industry, . . . advancing rapidly to destinies beyond the reach of mortal eye." It was this style of writing that even his Federalist enemies acknowledged for its excellence, while at the same time perceiving in it the breezy, philosophical abstraction that suggested a less than practical-minded man.

The externalization of sentiment Jefferson so excelled at fed a narrative that promised humane government. He publicized the sort of linguistic expression ordinarily used in private, which is not to say it exposed Jefferson's actual world of feelings. This is important to understand. His rhetorical objective was to convey sincerity, but not quite as the concept is understood today. "Sincerity" belonged to an impressionistic vocabulary with sensory associations, alongside "natural simplicity," "unadorned sentiment," "unfeigned attachment," etc. "Sincerity" served to distinguish eloquence from pandering.

If he were to be believed, the sincerity of the speaker or writer had to be detected in grace and dignity of expression. When in 1783, Jefferson wrote to honor George Washington at the successful conclusion of the Revolutionary War, he recognized the slipperiness of the meaning of the word by affecting to struggle with how he might prove his own sincerity: "Were I to indulge myself in those warm effusions which this subject for ever prompts, they would wear an appearance of adulation very foreign to my nature: for such is become the prostitution of language that sincerity has no longer distinct terms in which to express her own truths." Today, one might judge Jefferson's cleverness as semantic nonsense, a courtier pretending not to be one; but he was simply addressing the ambiguity one faced in adjudging private character on the basis of prevailing standards. Washington would have received Jefferson's epistolary stylization as a magnanimous gesture.[1]

What his critics failed to appreciate in 1801 was that, for Jefferson, nothing could express his love of country so well as his adoration for the sublimity of nature, as it coincided, in a very practical way, with his republican philosophy. He held that the United States, "a chosen country," "the world's best hope," should grow its territory and exploit its agrarian potential, rather than consolidate its wealth in smaller spaces, which would only invite European-style urban squalor. The words he uses throughout the Inaugural Address in referring to the Old World's inheritance are negative and hyperbolic—"throes and convulsions," "exterminating havoc." His republic was to be healthful, dotted with small, independent farms. If all went the way he wanted, America would resist urban concentration for generations to come.

This was partially about healthy versus unhealthy air. He was asked by a French scientist to explain differences in climate across Virginia. In response, he characterized the effects of sea breezes at different times of day, in different seasons, from Williamsburg inland to the mountains. He went on at considerable length: "And of course the air over a country covered by forest must be colder than that over cultivated grounds. The sea being pellucid, the sun's rays penetrate it to a considerable depth. Being also fluid, and in perpetual agitation, it's parts are constantly mixed together...," and so on. Jefferson ruminated on the possible effects of sea breezes all the way west, from the Atlantic to the Mississippi, illustrating his theory by graphing sea level and mountain altitudes along the route. Indulging in this thinking and communicating with scientists was how Jefferson sustained his loving fascination with America's prospects.[2]

Though he held unassailable opinions on political subjects, when it came to the study of agriculture Jefferson was a lifelong learner. He joined agricultural societies, collected books on the science of farming, and especially valued his correspondence with cultivation experts on two continents. Those who visited him at Monticello marveled at the view he enjoyed. William Strickland was one of these. A member of the British Board of Agriculture, he made a series of recommendations of crops to improve agricultural prospects across America. After his visit, he sent what Jefferson described unconventionally as a "charming treatise on manures," saying, "Science never appears so beautiful as when applied to the uses of human life."

Strickland saw through the same lens as his host, writing in the warmest terms a year after his visit: "Where the improvement of the agriculture of a country can go hand in hand, with the improvement of the morals of a people, and the increase of their happiness, there it must stand in its most exalted state,... so is it at present circumstanced in your country." The Englishman possessed a thorough knowledge of the encyclopedic lists sprinkled about *Notes on Virginia*, wherein Jefferson gathered all that was known of geographic formations, varieties of wildlife, native trees, average temperatures and wind speeds for each month of the year. Accordingly, Strickland made observations on air circulation and temperature fluctuation that he experienced as he toured other parts of Virginia.[3]

This was a language that Jefferson spoke with fluency. He was someone different from Washington and Adams, not just in his political leanings, but scholastically in his commitment to the study of natural history as a source of power and the American landscape as a gold mine awaiting excavation. He was as serious about his figurative "chosen country" as he was in *Notes on Virginia* in declaring with dramatic resolve that "the mobs of great cities add just so much to the support of pure government, as sores do to the strength of the human body"; or that "corruption of morals in the mass of cultivators is a phaenomenon of which no age nor nation has furnished an example."

This was his creed. If, in *Notes*, it is "the manners and spirit of a people which preserve a republic in vigor," then, fifteen years after that book's initial publication, entering the presidency without having altered his conception of the country's path forward, he confidently pronounced in his Inaugural Address that the "encouragement of agriculture, and of commerce as its handmaid" will protect the "beloved country." (Designating commerce as a "handmaid" serves to feminize and subordinate it to agriculture.) Jefferson continued seeing the Virginia that nurtured him as a desirable template in embarking the entire nation on a westward-directed future. He invited fresh blood from northern Europe to help grow America's population.[4]

He unquestionably intended his accession to the presidency to mark the commencement of a new political era. His inauguration, the first to take place in Washington, D.C., and the least invested with pomp and ceremony, betokened a major transition. Approximately one thousand people were present in the Senate chamber to hear the political message he delivered in his inaugural address, spoken in his naturally soft voice. A harmonizing appeal (famously, "We are all republicans, we are all federalists") was meant to set America apart from the Old World's patterns of religious intolerance and internecine warfare.

It had been a full decade since his return from Europe. Generalizing its history, he launched into a veritable philippic against the "bitter and bloody persecutions," the "agonizing spasms of infuriated man," that left millions struggling toward a recovery of that "long-lost liberty" that Jefferson associated with a better, if primitive, time in Europe. He would have his rhetorically uplifted Americans forget that their nation was marred by the enslavement of the dark-skinned and the forced removal of Indigenous tribes. He cast the youthful republic as a barely settled continent belonging, in effect, to the freethinking descendants of the Greek polis, the Roman republic, and the mighty Ossianic and Saxon sagas.

Europe's indelible history, the "throes and convulsions of the ancient world," could not infect Jefferson's storied America, now that its birth pangs were nearly ended. Jefferson envisioned birth and rebirth, a place where recent antagonisms could be channeled in a healthy direction, where elections mattered. "The voice of the nation" has been heard, he affirmed with hardly a backward glance at the excruciating months when all were wallowing in a sea of uncertainty, an election stalemated. No more of that. He spirited the audience to acceptance: its good citizens had resolved to "arrange themselves under the will of the law, and unite in common efforts for the common good." (Here is Jefferson putting in motion the same axiom modern leaders turn to in reassuring the public during times of partisan strain that we are still "a nation of laws.")

He thus took the message embodied in Condorcet's *Esquisse* and stamped it American. The U.S. president and the late philosophe saw history through the same lens. "Condorcet took what one might call the polemical psychology of the philosophes to absurd lengths," says Peter Gay in his compendious study of the Enlightenment. Condorcet called out as frauds and powermongers those of the Old World, from tribal chiefs to popes, who did not even believe in the "mysteries" (the word Jefferson attaches to unreasoning clerics) that they "retail to the credulous." These were the same "tyrants, bigots, persecutors, frigid cynics" whom Jefferson held responsible for the "throes and convulsions" that ended only when the reasoning Enlightenment stepped in and pointed the way forward. "The *Esquisse*," writes Gay, "is as much a caricature of the Enlightenment as its testament; it is rationalism run riot, dominated by a simple-minded faith in science that confuses, over and over again, the improvement of techniques with advances in virtue and happiness." Jefferson and Condorcet were true believers in the science of man, unusual in their belief even among their enlightened peers. For them, "the misery of the past" was to be succeeded by a future in which "rational forces" would be enlisted to maximize good, social benefits accruing alongside improvements in education. The optimism of these two thinkers lay in an uncommon faith in progress.[5]

The optimism is laid on thick in Jefferson's Inaugural Address. He is confident that the American people, in accepting the election results and abiding by the rule of law, would "bear in mind this sacred principle, that though the will of the majority is in all cases to prevail, that will to be rightful must be reasonable." The "common good" commanded that. He wants it understood that Federalists and Republicans are "brethren of the same principle." That is, they embrace differing perspectives on policy but are equally attached to the republican form—never mind that the opinions he privately conveyed to his friends show him on guard against misguided High Federalists of the Hamilton mold who remained perversely attached to monarchy, and who would rear their ugly heads in the future if not held back by the controlling voice of the people.

Showing only his public face, Jefferson pretended not to harbor any such fear going forward. An Inaugural Address had to be uplifting. It didn't take him long to pronounce his unsubtle appeal for national reconciliation, "We are all republicans, we are all federalists." This was his way of asking for a modicum of trust in his determination to govern with moderation, that he was not a "Jacobin" as the opposition press branded him.

There is every reason to accept as genuine the new president's good intentions. He explained himself to an ardent Republican, the sitting governor of Pennsylvania: "Between the Monarchist & the Federalist I draw a clear line. The latter is a sect of republicanism. The former it's implacable enemy." And yet his semantics were self-serving: a Federalist was a Republican who had yet to identify himself as such. The idea was that once Federalists recognized him as a man of reasoning and good character, any residual partisan fervor would cool. This was close to what Jefferson would later rationalize with respect to George Washington: that if he'd had more time and greater proximity to the first president, he could have won him back. In Jefferson's recalculation, Washington the tried-and-true republican lost direction when he succumbed to Hamiltonian cynicism.

The section of the First Inaugural that contains Jefferson's momentous appeal for party concord begins with the some of the most humane language of the text: "Let us, then, fellow citizens, unite with one heart and one mind. Let us restore to social intercourse that harmony and affection without which liberty and even life itself are but dreary things." He prepares his hearers (more numerously, readers) for a grand, sermonic gesture. Projecting a future in which political rivals contend respectfully, he recurs to the familiar coupling of head and heart/heart and mind. And recognizing the multiplicity of sects that assemble in houses of worship across the country, he allowed that Americans practiced a "benign religion," "acknowledging and adoring and overruling Providence" (he does not use the word "Christianity"). Jefferson, labeled an atheist by his detractors, wishes only to celebrate the common message of all religious denominations: "honesty, truth, temperance, gratitude, and the love of man." A social people needed only a "wise and frugal Government" to "close the circle of our felicities." That, in sum, was his promise.[6]

Critic by nature, Gouverneur Morris was present for this historic moment. His reaction, as recorded in his diary: "Our new President makes his inaugural Speech—Too long by Half."[7]

THE PRESIDENT'S HOUSE

Jefferson did what he could, at first anyway, to uphold the promise of fairness in government appointments. But he quickly realized that Federalist recriminations would not let up no matter how he behaved in office. The great majority of personnel decisions were to be made in the Treasury Department, which fell under the leadership of the dogged and dutiful, Swiss-born Albert Gallatin, an early

Hamilton critic who would stay in office through Madison's presidency. Jefferson's idea was to win over moderate Federalists by ousting only his most rabid detractors. That was what he proceeded to do, and when challenged, he argued that Federalist fanaticism had denied jobs to Republicans, so it was only right that remunerative offices such as customs collectors should go to deserving Republicans to correct the imbalance. Outspoken Republicans were angry that Jefferson and Gallatin didn't go far enough.[8]

Throughout his two terms, he made it a habit to invite congressmen from both parties to dinner at the President's House, eight or so at a time. Jefferson paid for these out of his salary, and he was known to appear at dinner in worn clothes and flat slippers. French fare was prepared and served by a multiethnic kitchen staff, which included three apprentice cooks from among the enslaved families of Monticello. One of them was the fair-skinned Edith ("Edy") Hern Fossett, whose culinary art was especially prized both in Washington and at Monticello. James Hemings, having earlier been freed, was employed at a Baltimore tavern. He refused to work for his former master as a chef in the President's House, which led Jefferson to bring back President Washington's French chef, Honoré Julien. Jefferson's maître d'hôtel was French as well.

The kitchen was run smoothly. No dinner guest ever complained, save for a British diplomat and his wife who took particular offense at the host's shabby attire and his egalitarian treatment of his guests, be they aristocrats or democrats. A round or oval table tended to support relaxed conversation. The same Briton took umbrage when at one gala the U.S. president chatted but briefly with him, only to move on to Native American guests who apparently held greater interest for him.

Save for the quality of the imported wine he stocked (some twenty thousand bottles over his two terms as president), Jefferson's overall preference for simplicity over pomp extended to his choice of transportation about the capital. His Irish coachman, Joseph Dougherty, did not have a lot of work to do, because Jefferson most often chose to ride out alone, on horseback. This president believed in republican simplicity, a frank informality.[9]

Jefferson's combining of gentrified and democratic manners comes across in his regard for horseflesh. From his entrance into society as a student in Williamsburg, he understood the breeding and trading of quality horses to be both a medium of exchange among peers and a way of establishing one's appreciation of differences in pedigree as a means of demonstrating superior taste. Just as he became a connoisseur of fine wine, honing his skill by traveling to vineyards across France and

Germany, and just as he experimented with and traded in seeds, so did he pay close attention to the blood lineage of his horses. Their nobility mattered in a gentleman's self-presentation, even as he (as the nation's chief magistrate) shunned the stately carriage.[10]

Not surprisingly, when it came to his personal outfits, the opposition party mocked Jefferson's manner as an insincere performance, showiness in reverse. In fact, though, Jefferson is not being two-faced here, nor opaque. His lack of ceremony, combined with an aversion to British sartorial display, expressed a long-held concern lest urban elegance and overrefined manners become America's future. To him, these were un-American traits. As in his invention of the word "monocrat" to denote regressive Federalists, he perceived a threat to his nation's distinctiveness, the homespun (largely agrarian) simplicity that promoted honesty and directness.

It is not that he refused to own a decent suit of clothes either; he had these when he felt they were called for. Critics, past and present, find it all too easy to charge the horseman and wine connoisseur with hypocrisy in his acquisition of fine art and chinaware at Monticello while dressing down in the President's House. As the Jefferson scholar Maurizio Valsania has noted, Jefferson "cracked the code of French casual elegance and added a personal American flavor to it." He accented his domestic world with useful objects that complemented an architectural aesthetic; but as a nationalist, he saw the danger in conformity to foreign tastes. If others succumbed to the temptation, if they learned to admire British manners, to shamelessly worship the pomp of aristocrats, they would begin to put on airs themselves. Falling prey to a moribund concept of luxury, they would come to revile their own commonness.[11]

The President's House, as the White House was first known, was less than glamorous and an insecure place for a head of state to sleep unprotected. On arrival, Jefferson got busy as one might expect of an eager architectural designer. Health- and privacy-conscious, he had the outhouse removed and an indoor water closet installed to his specifications, "so as to be cleansed constantly by a Pipe, throwing Water ... at command." The first occupants, the Adamses, had not been concerned with ornamentation.

Jefferson spared no expense in adding classically styled molding in the areas of the Executive Mansion where he entertained. He installed glass doors and made a series of changes that would resemble a stately pre-Revolutionary French salon, in keeping with the French culinary staff he relied upon to impress guests. Ordering improvements to achieve the style he admired, he created the social environment he desired, while neatly separating his large office from the visiting areas so he could enjoy a degree of privacy. He invited a native of Albemarle, the twenty-six-year-old army veteran Meriwether Lewis, to live with him and serve as presidential secretary. Lewis slept downstairs, Jefferson upstairs, without security.[12]

The early presidents spent no more than half the year in the capital, as congressional sessions were separated by months. An added factor was Washington City's unwholesome environment. Before Pennsylvania Avenue was made permanent, the immediate environs were undistinguished and hardly lush. Roads were as often dusty as muddy. Still, Jefferson spent more time in the capital than his predecessor, who was often content to manage the federal government from distant Boston. A man of habit, Jefferson rose before the sun and was at his desk a good ten hours each day that first year, with a two-hour break in the middle to ride or walk for exercise. Tall and "rawboned," as he was described in his lifetime, he maintained a health regimen peculiar to himself, occasionally comparing notes with physicians. He regarded moderate physical exercise as a good way to reinforce one's mental energy.[13]

His stated commitment to "mild government" did not deter Jefferson from pursuing a strong agenda. He wrote in bold strokes, without boasting, to Republican allies and friends abroad, expressing a sense of himself as the instrument of enlightened popular government. He rode roughshod over the Hamiltonians, at the same time professing (and on some level believing) that his executive actions were taken in an entirely selfless manner. But that could not possibly be true. True believers have plans they keep secret. Jefferson was a true believer.

After the convolutions of the drawn-out election tie, he entered the presidency in an enviable position. He would enjoy a Republican majority in both houses of Congress throughout his two terms. While ostracizing his vice president, he took immense pride in the harmonious relations that subsisted within the cabinet, as he determinedly paved the way for what would come to be known as the Virginia Dynasty of presidents. For twenty-four consecutive years, three two-term Virginians—Jefferson and his two closest associates, Madison and Monroe—ruled the executive branch of government. During these years, the numbers of Federalists in Congress steadily receded until the party collapsed.

Thrust into the kill-or-be-killed arena of partisan politics, Jefferson readily adapted. If the "motion of his blood" still rebelled against public office, one could not tell. He held the same power George Washington once held; his judgment meant what Washington's had. Still, he could hardly have managed without the devotion of Madison and Monroe, the debt management of the astute and tolerant Albert Gallatin, and the dutiful, deferential posture taken by his battle-hardened, two-term secretary of war, the New Hampshirite Henry Dearborn. Day by day, the president was buoyed by supportive letters from Jeffersonians in every part of the country.

He was a consequential president, and not, as a host of newspapers portrayed him, meek and unpretentious. He was very much in charge. Nor did "philosophy" govern his politics. He knew what he wanted to achieve, and knew not to expect instant gratification. In short, he had developed a thicker skin. It showed when, early on, he invited Thomas Paine to travel to America in a U.S. warship, raising the hackles of the religious establishment of Federalist New England for whom Paine was the very embodiment of infidelity. Jefferson couldn't care less, telling Paine he would always stand up to "federal [i.e., Federalist] calumny."[14]

Jefferson had always demonstrated his need for emotional reinforcement in familiar letters. Beautiful writing had the effect of revitalizing him, and the presidency did not put an end to that. Just as he thrived on his daughters' love, and on expressing his heart in correspondence with women who shared his sensitivity to art and nature, there were men who understood these feelings too. John Page was one to whom Jefferson could unburden himself, though he could not exchange his political realism for buoyant confidence with Page the way he did with an exiled English chemist and Unitarian thinker whom he greatly admired, Dr. Joseph Priestley.

Two letters, a year apart, capture Jefferson in this mode. Shortly after inauguration, he cried up the moment in precious words: "We can no longer say there is nothing new under the sun. For this whole chapter in the history of man is new. The great extent of our republic is new... The order & good sense displayed in this recovery from delusion, and in the momentous crisis which lately arose, really bespeak a strength of character in our nation which augurs well for the duration of our republic." Writing to Priestley again in the later spring of 1802, he doubled down on his faith in American citizens' capacity for self-government: "Our people in a body are wise, because they are under the unrestrained and unperverted operation of their own understandings." America would serve as a lesson for the world: "It is impossible not to be sensible that we are acting for all mankind."[15]

Priestley had been driven from England and subsequently persecuted by Jefferson's political enemies in America. As a resident of Pennsylvania since 1794, he was a warm admirer of Paine's *Rights of Man* and sportively identified himself with all "democrats" from the day he stepped ashore. Like Paine, he'd held citizenship in Revolutionary France, and he knew some, like the tragic duc de La Rochefoucauld, who were of Jefferson's circle. And just like Jefferson, the scientist protested an abhorrence for political controversy, though his penchant for writing kept getting him into trouble.

Priestley's friendship with John Adams, begun years earlier in England, fell apart after the passage of the Alien and Sedition Acts, when Priestley became a particular target of Federalists. Jefferson took notice. He made it a habit to reach out to many who fell afoul of ostentatious royalists and religious traditionalists. Castigating "bigotry in Politics & Religion," he gushed in the March 1801 letter to Priestley: "Yours is one of the few lives precious to mankind." In letters to friends, Priestley, in turn, praised the president's vision, applauding his faith in the human spirit. Jefferson deployed an emotional script that provided reassurance for both of them.

Jefferson grew his critique of the teachings of orthodox religious figures ("priestcraft") out of Priestley's 1782 *History of the Corruptions of Christianity*, which he touted often. After finding a copy in Washington, he sent it to a Methodist with Albemarle roots, Henry Fry, whose father Joshua had been a superior mathematician and the surveying partner of Peter Jefferson. To Fry, Jefferson wrote quintessentially: "I consider the doctrines of Jesus as delivered by himself to contain the outlines of the sublimest system of morality that has ever been taught but I hold in the most profound detestation and execration the corruptions of it which have been invented by priestcraft and established by kingcraft constituting a conspiracy of church and state against the civil and religious liberties of mankind." This one complex sentence captures Jefferson's sensibility perfectly.[16]

The priestcraft-kingcraft pairing is more than a little interesting. The language bears a dismissive tone, yet Jefferson is studiously channeling an older meaning when he comes up with such a favored insult. "Craft," here, does not imply artisanal skill so much as artifice; craft as in craftiness, which involves mystery and cunning. Whether it's the wave of a magician's wand or a king's scepter, the idea is the same: a perversion of nature's law.

Entering office, Jefferson maintained exacting standards. He altered the immediate physical environment, as he did at Monticello, by making the President's House into his working world. Margaret Bayard Smith was a native of Pennsylvania who moved to Washington with her newspaper editor husband late in 1800, and immediately came to adore Jefferson. She penned a detailed description of his private quarters: "Around the walls were maps, globes, charts, books &c... Among his roses and geraniums was suspended the cage of his favorite mocking-bird, which he cherished with peculiar fondness, not only for its melodious powers, but for its uncommon intelligence and affectionate disposition... It was the constant companion of his solitary and studious hours... It would perch on his shoulder and takes its food from his lips... He could not live without something to love." She described Jefferson as "fastidious," his outward restraint as "quiet dignity." His was a countenance, she said, "beaming with benevolence and intelligence." While hers is a deeply biased portrait, one can yet imagine how his outward lack of excitability combined with an indefinite spark that enabled him to neutralize many men who disagreed with him on public matters. The image of him in the hostile press convinced all who already disliked what he stood for; but in person, he seemed to know how to put others at ease.[17]

As much as he disparaged the lack of substance behind the admittedly persuasive verbal stylings of Patrick Henry, his own way with words cleverly disguised a rigid belief system at the core of his unspoken ambition. The gorgeous language of Jefferson's First Inaugural Address deserves history's attention as a text that promotes the best possible America, but it was not his complete blueprint for governing.

An emboldened President Jefferson began to nudge America in the direction of what he saw as its destined place in the world. His unapologetic agenda intuited the wishes of his friends in politics, which, to him, equated to the popular will. He found contentment in certainty, especially on subjects where he openly communicated love or loathing. What his literary style did, when advancing a dreamlike American destiny, was to provide grounds for novel policies.

"A TREMENDIOUS ROARING"

An unmitigated expression of moral justification lay behind America's ultimately successful prosecution of a war against the Barbary States and in the windfall acquisition of the Louisiana Territory. Neither policy would have been "front-loaded" were it not for Jefferson's remarkable initiative. Despite his well-articulated republican theory in favor of a small central government, which Federalists had criticized him for in the 1790s, he was a stronger, more determined, more activist executive than Washington (and, arguably, Adams) in the conduct of foreign affairs. On the one hand, Jefferson scaled back on military expenditures, as expected; on the other, from the day he took office, he made it clear to his cabinet that he would adopt a hard stance against demands for tribute from the Barbary powers.

Several European states had regularly acquiesced to a series of North African despots, offering protection money to stop the pirates sailing out of Tripoli, Tunis, Algiers, and Moroccan ports. In a cabinet meeting held two months into his presidency, Jefferson ordered a squadron of frigates to depart for the Mediterranean, with instructions to safeguard U.S. commerce. The navy might have call to punish individual attack vessels; in the event one of the Barbary states made war on the United States, the captain was granted latitude to sink as many of that enemy's vessels as could be found.

The possibility of war was merely hypothetical in the spring of 1801, when the cabinet addressed the Barbary threat and decided on proactive measures. Jefferson proved prophetic, and in his First Annual Message to Congress that December reported that "the least considerable" of the offending states, Tripoli, had already declared war on the United States out of its dissatisfaction with previous tribute arrangements. "The style of the demand admitted but one answer," Jefferson explained. The "small squadron" gave "assurances to that power [Tripoli] of our sincere desire to remain in peace." It hadn't worked.

The practical-minded President Adams had weighed the cost-effectiveness of tribute, but refrained from the action President Jefferson was inclined to take. In fact, Adams and Jefferson first debated this very matter in Paris, in 1785, after Algiers had captured two American vessels. Jefferson staunchly opposed the purchase of peace, even then. In his First Annual Message (the equivalent of today's State of the Union), he defended his captain's bold actions: "Our commerce in the Mediterranean was blockaded; and that of the Atlantic in peril. The arrival of our squadron dispelled the danger." No American lives were lost in the process. And this was just the first deployment.

The administration relentlessly pursued its contemptuous enemy for four years, racking up victories while generating stories of American naval heroics. Jefferson persisted until he was satisfied that U.S. warships had wreaked damage enough to force the Tripolitan pasha (bashaw) to come to terms. Even at a low point in the war, Jefferson was adamant that he would accept no assistance from any European state. When in 1804, Robert Livingston, U.S. minister to France, reached out to allies after the capture of the thirty-eight-gun *Philadelphia*, "begging alms at every court in Europe"—for Jefferson a "self-degradation" beyond pardon—he ordered Livingston's recall. If the Tripolitan War was not a subconscious means of erasing the stain of the invasion of Virginia during Jefferson's wartime governorship, it was an opportunity to display the flag of an ambitious commercial republic and demonstrate a militarism Jefferson was otherwise not known for. With something to prove to the wider world, Jefferson came off looking tough-minded, clearly not one to back down.[18]

His approach to Napoleon showed equal commitment and had far greater implications. In the spring of 1802, wary of what future plans the allied nations of France and Spain might contrive in North America, Jefferson sought to learn whether the French would sell the strategic port city of New Orleans, through which nearly one-third of the nation's commerce passed (his primary aim) and whether Spanish Florida could be had (a long shot).

The president called on the trusted James Monroe to sail to France and bolster the position of Livingston, who, at this point, had yet to embarrass him. Conducting diplomacy at so slow a pace left plenty of room for misunderstandings. Pleasantly shocked on learning that a financially stressed Napoleon had added on to his offer the incomprehensibly vast territory extending from the Mississippi River to the Rocky Mountains, Jefferson agreed to the price without first seeking authorization from Congress. Monroe and Livingston both urged speed. Livingston wrote separate letters to Secretary of State Madison and President Jefferson that the First Consul's ways were mercurial, that the "youthful Conqueror" might change his mind "on the slightest pretence."

Taking these words to heart, Jefferson acted without delay. Under the circumstances, he was happy to have critical suggestions from political allies: "no apologies for writing or speaking to me freely are necessary," he told one; "nothing my friends can do, is so dear to me . . . as the information they give me of their sentiments & those of others on interesting points where I am to act." He faced challenges on constitutional grounds and expected to meet resistance from those in Congress who thought the United States already big enough: it had more federal land for sale than there were buyers, particularly in the Great Lakes region. Why add territory where disunionist sentiment would likely arise, threatening the integrity of the Union?[19]

Congress approved the treaty in October 1803. Before he'd even heard of Napoleon's offer, Jefferson had already begun plotting a westward course. As naturalist, geographer, and the son of a mapmaking surveyor, he thought of national greatness in terms of an ever-expanding agrarian empire, a landscape freer and more productive than anything the long-quarreling Europeans knew. He actively encouraged his proxy, presidential secretary Meriwether Lewis, setting him up with an education in botany, geology, and surveying, before assuring him of the inspiring message his travels would send across the eastern states.[20]

The Lewis and Clark Expedition spanned the years 1804–06. Responsive to Jefferson's desire for a recognizable language of natural beauty, beyond the science he'd come to learn at Jefferson's behest, Lewis, in his extensive journals, tried to echo Jefferson's passages in *Notes* on the sublime landscapes of Virginia. Lewis came upon the Great Falls of Montana unexpectedly and, in his unique orthography, wrote what he felt: "Hearing a tremendous roaring above me I continued my rout across the point of a hill, ... and was again presented by one of the most beatifull objects of nature, a cascade of about fifty feet perpendicular stretching at rightangles ... the water descends in one even an uninterupted sheet wher dashing against the rocky bottom rises into foaming billows of great hight and rappidly glides away, hising flashing, and sparkling."

Explorer Lewis, like Jefferson, admired the unpredictability as well as the ruggedness of Nature. The delight and torment he evokes recalls the description of Monticello Jefferson gave to Mrs. Cosway ("With what majesty do we there ride above the storms!") For both Albemarle natives, the unknown world becomes known to the open-eyed venturer, an uncontained expanse not incompatible with the civilizing aims of future settlers. In a Jeffersonian mode of thought, new energies burst forth in words that bless America as a place of transcendent possibilities.[21]

NEOPHOBIA

When he spoke the line "We are all republicans, we are all federalists," Jefferson did in fact wish to minimize the number of Federalists he dismissed from office. He'd told George Clinton that he aimed to "restore harmony by avoiding everything harsh"; by the start of election year 1804, when it came time to appoint officials to administer the newly acquired Louisiana Territory, he informed William Short that the Federalists only cared to make trouble for him: "They spurned every overture of conciliation. I have therefore long since given up the idea, and proceed in all things without caring what they will think, say or do." In 1802, former Treasury secretary Oliver Wolcott (Hamilton's successor) complained that Jefferson never really had his heart in retaining inoffensive, capable Federalist appointees: "He has incited a spirit of rivalship, passion and resentment, which is utterly uncontrollable."

Understandably, Jefferson was sensitive to injustices that Republicans, at any level, had been subjected to. During his first weeks in office, emotional appeals came to his desk from men whose opinions he honored. One was Thomas Cooper, an English-born chemist who'd joined Joseph Priestley in American exile, only to face persecution for publicizing views that the Federalists despised. Jefferson offered him reassurances by attaching a word he coined—"neophobia"—to Federalists who rebelled against new ideas while "fattening on the labour & ignorance of their fellowmen. Darkness is their delight, & the harbingers of day their dread." Jefferson let Cooper know he'd gotten the message.

To his attorney general, Levi Lincoln, who hailed from the Federalist stronghold of Massachusetts, he calculated in the late summer of 1801 that "the heaping of abuse on me personally has been with the design & the hope of provoking me to make a general sweep of all federalists out of office." He thought he could outsmart the hardcore Federalists and deny them the fodder they needed to rebel en masse by showing "great moderation" in Massachusetts. Then, "the measures we shall pursue & propose for the amelioration of the public affairs will be so confessedly salutary as to unite all men not monarchists in principle." How much this moderating Jefferson was led to the opposite conclusion after pressures were applied by Republican state governors and others is hard to say, but the longer he was in office, the more the party out of power made Jefferson's retrenchment inevitable. In autumn 1802, again to Attorney General Lincoln, he complained that the Federalists were "trying slander now which nothing could prompt but a gall which blinds their judgments as well as their consciences." Their hatred for him had no bounds; he felt it and was responding in kind.[22]

One thing did not change throughout his time in political life. He played politics by feeding information to his allies and urging them to do with it as they saw fit—which, more often than not, led to Jefferson's seeing his will enacted. An instance in the late fall of 1803 is typical of his presidential style. Surreptitiously seeking to influence Senate discussion on Louisiana's territorial government organization, he wrote in confidence to a close ally in the Senate. Virginia native John Breckinridge grew up west of Albemarle, attended the College of William and Mary in the early 1780s, and studied with George Wythe before moving to Kentucky in 1793. His earliest participation in politics was in 1781, when, as a twenty-one-year-old, he fled with fellow legislators to Charlottesville at the time of outgoing Governor Jefferson's ominous final days in office. After the war, when Jefferson was in Paris, Breckinridge married into a prosperous Albemarle family and practiced law in Charlottesville for a time. Once established in the vicinity of Lexington, Kentucky, he became a prominent state legislator in 1798, when then Vice President Jefferson secretly funneled through him the Kentucky Resolutions.[23]

With parallels to Jefferson's upbringing and a record of critical support for Jefferson's pet issues, John Breckinridge was once more a willing channel, this time for a president, and this time as a U.S. senator. Jefferson underscored the delicacy of what they were doing: "You will never let any person know that I have put pen to paper on the subject."

Breckinridge was completely dependable. He went to his grave protecting Jefferson's authorship of the Kentucky Resolutions. Here, in one caustic sentence, we see Jefferson, in real time, giving his uncensored take on the congressional opposition: "You know with what bloody teeth & fangs the federalists will attack any sentiment or principle known to come from me, & what blackguardisms & personalities they make it the occasion of vomiting forth." As Jefferson was painting the opposition in monstrous imagery of this sort, he was seeing himself as a veritable dragon slayer. Once again, without Jefferson's contribution becoming known, the Breckinridge plan for Louisiana passed the Senate.[24]

Because Breckinridge, like Joseph Priestley, was a kindred spirit, Jefferson once more peppered his correspondence with hopeful, even extravagant, thoughts about the future of the republic. Thinking of the additional territory, its extent still unknown and mostly unmapped (the fruits of the Lewis and Clark Expedition were not known until 1806), he projected "a new confederacy" west of the Mississippi that only Federalists would fear as a potential threat to the Atlantic-facing original states. If distance from Washington should impel the creation of sister republics, Jefferson ruminated, what cause for "dread" was there? "I do not view it as an Englishman would the procuring future blessings for the French nation with whom he has no relations of blood or affection . . . It is the elder & the younger son differing. God bless them both, & keep them in union if it be for their good, but separate them if it be better."[25]

The familial metaphor loomed large in Jefferson's script. He imagined the "harmony and affection" motif that he associated with the patriarchal family as a model, on some level, for a republic that pursued peace—or what he once styled "tranquil permanent felicity." Thomas Paine's line in *Common Sense* may have predated, but it nicely tapped into, Jefferson's familial metaphor. Paine: "Youth is the seed time of good habits, as well in nations as in individuals." Jefferson, more didactically: "It is while we are young that the habit of industry is formed. If not then, it never is afterwards. The fortune of our lives therefore depends on employing well the short period of youth."

He looked back on his own early commitment to a wholesome education and grafted it onto a prescription for the American body politic: "Exercise and application produce order in our affairs, health of body, chearfulness of mind, and these make us precious to our friends," he'd told his elder daughter. He lived by these precepts. Onto them he tied another, even more discernibly republican trait: *independence*.

As Northerners and Southerners alike began spreading out and moving west, the frontier ethos embedded itself in the American self-image. The Daniel Boone story, first popularized in the 1780s, became a prototype of literary adventuring, readily associated with conceptions of land and nation. Boone's story of survival found its way into poetry and description across the Atlantic. Now Lewis and Clark and their "Corps of Discovery" could be held up as nervy visionaries in the Jefferson mold whose determination presented fair prospects for the next round of pathfinding, then permanent settlements. With an ever expanding circulation of newspapers, "internal improvements" (roads, canals, and river traffic) marked the next phase of growth and a rhetoric of democratic uplift: forging connections, reducing time, conquering distance.

Jefferson's America didn't need Europe. The new geographic reality, post–Louisiana Purchase, contributed psychically to the sensation that more land meant more strength for the American identity. Again, Paine's *Common Sense* provides a "Jeffersonian" line that became axiomatic: "In no instance hath nature made the satellite larger than its primary planet." America belonged to itself, no longer a satellite of Britain. At least some of this was Jefferson's doing.[26]

His faith in the industriousness of those who came into possession of farms seemed unbounded. Their "affection" for the land and their unbroken connections to the people from whom they had separated was veritable romance. Despite the pettiness he witnessed in political circles, his wait-and-see approach and faith in social experimentation remained strong.

He thought big and thought small at the same time. Few were as certain about the educability of ordinary citizens. He had a remarkably unwavering commitment to the narrative he'd constructed earlier, which crystallized in *Notes on Virginia*, where one locates Jefferson's "chosen people" among independent farmers. No less remarkable is his long acceptance of Ossianic lore as part of history and his unique nostalgia for the primitive Saxon/Scottish Highlands, spiritual forerunners to colonial American settlement. There is an Ossianic quality in his reshaping of reality when applying the view, nourished at Monticello, of a physically and morally healthful pastoral republic of self-governing husbandmen.[27]

As he saw it, in the trans-Mississippi West, white males would all become freeholders. At every level of social organization, as inequality gradually diminished, a solid sense of belonging would naturally materialize. He understood that it would take time for Louisiana's French identity to homogenize with the influx of Americans (especially Virginians); but here as elsewhere in the underpopulated West, even if separate republics formed, they would be kin to the eastern states—effectively one people. Westerners were to be history's latest incarnation of his Saxon model of determined migrants, the difference being that this people would retain strong, affective ties to the original states. It was the best of both worlds, in theory.[28]

The one element Jefferson intentionally distorted in this scenario concerns treatment of Indigenous nations. He leaned on Meriwether Lewis to add to the catalog of Indian vocabularies that Jefferson, as a protoanthropologist, was compiling. He pressed Congress on the idea that the Louisiana Territory would repeat patterns of "lawful" dispossession of Indian land that had evolved in the existing states. He composed an amendment to the Constitution for that purpose: "The legislature of the union shall have authority to exchange the right of occupancy in portions where the US have full right, for lands possessed by Indians within the US on the East Side of the Missisipi." Not unlike his notion of recolonizing free Blacks on lands (in the Americas or in West Africa) where there were no whites, he now conceived a separation of white and Indian peoples whereby Indians in the southern half of Louisiana (below the 31st parallel) would find it desirable to exchange eastern-facing lands that white settlers wanted for lands beyond, where game was still abundant.[29]

He assumed the cultural identity crisis that would befall Indians to be an inevitable part of the civilizing process: in a landscape depleted of game, some would willingly adopt white ways, while the remainder would have to be moved farther from impinging white settlements. Just prior to the acquisition of Louisiana, Jefferson outlined his aggressive reasoning in a letter to General William Henry Harrison, then the governor of Indiana Territory. He feigned an honest desire "to live in perpetual peace with the Indians, to cultivate an affectionate attachment from them." Note that the "affectionate attachment" was expected *from* the Indians, and on an unequal basis. Harrison was meant to do all he could "within the bounds of reason" to protect them from white violence. "We wish to draw them to agriculture, to spinning & weaving,"

Jefferson elaborated, allowing that Indians regarded these labors as women's work; and then, he added coldly, "when they withdraw themselves to the culture of a small piece of land, they will percieve how useless to them are their extensive forests, and will be willing to pare them off from time to time in exchange for necessaries for their farms & families." This was the solution Jefferson wanted: "We shall push our trading houses, and be glad to see the good & influential individuals among them run in debt, because we observe that when these debts get beyond what the individuals can pay, they become willing to lop th[em off] by a cession of lands." To the cabinet official most directly concerned with Indian policy, Secretary of War Henry Dearborn, he was blunt: "Instead of inviting Indians to come within our limits, our object is to tempt them to evacuate them." The cruelty was intentional.[30]

MISCARRIAGE OF JUSTICE

To shape government in his own political image, Jefferson turned his attention to the one branch that stymied him, that was still dominated by Federalists: the Supreme Court. His problem began with the "midnight judges" whom John Adams appointed in the waning days of his administration, the most notable being Chief Justice Marshall, solidly Federalist, who, in Jefferson's first term, showed that his word was all it took to overturn an act of Congress.[31]

With no grounds on which to impeach Marshall or even chip away at his power, Jefferson went with the second best option and urged the impeachment of a vulnerable associate justice. A member of the Supreme Court since 1796, the arch-Federalist Samuel Chase of Maryland had a long-standing reputation for bluster and bullying and delivering politically tinged lectures from the bench when he rode the circuit, as High Court justices in the early republic were obliged to do. That wasn't all that Jefferson had to go on. During the "reign of witches," the outspoken judge presided over the sedition trial of Jefferson's scientific friend Thomas Cooper for defaming President Adams (1799); he also rendered a guilty verdict when the volatile Scottish columnist James Callender came before him (1800), though by 1803, Jefferson would have been reflecting on Callender in a different way, for the newspaperman had let loose in September 1802 with his Jefferson-Hemings exposé (which Jefferson kept silent on), along with the more distant Betsy Walker seduction attempt that the president did not deny. Ironically, part of the Republicans' case against Chase involved his treatment of Callender, who met an untimely death in July 1803, drowning in the James River, reportedly drunk.[32]

Theirs was a small world, with strange bedfellows and awkward connections. The fact should not be lost that Samuel Chase was himself a signer of the Declaration of Independence. Yet as an unrepentant Federalist in 1803, few in high office detested Jefferson as much or as vocally. That spring, in the course of lecturing a Baltimore grand jury, Justice Chase attacked Jefferson's plans to seize back the judiciary from the Federalists who dominated it; he likened Jeffersonian democracy to "mobocracy" that threatened the social order. That is when Jefferson, as an avid consumer of regional newspapers (not to mention party gossip), floated a suggestion to a Maryland congressman who had recently brought impeachment charges against a hard-drinking New Hampshire judge believed insane.[33]

Representative Joseph H. Nicholson was barely thirty at the time of the election tie, when he cast his vote for Jefferson, going to heroic lengths to do so. He had a dangerously high fever in mid-February 1801, and he lay on a stretcher in the Capitol through vote after vote in the knowledge that if he didn't, Maryland's vote would be assigned to Burr. Once the Republican was restored to sound health, Jefferson figured he could count on his support again, and coaxed: "You must have heard of the extraordinary charge of Chace to the grand jury at Baltimore. Ought this seditious & official attack on the principles of our constitution, and on the proceedings of a state, to go unpunished?" To which the president appended his non-denial denial: "I ask these questions for your consideration, for myself it is better that I should not interfere."[34]

President Thomas Jefferson, self-styled champion of republican methods, was putting his finger on the scale here. It is hard to pretend otherwise. With an unwarranted exercise of power aimed at weakening the Supreme Court, he was acting from a private need to humiliate a man who treated a nonelective position as a partisan platform. While the emotion is quite understandable, Jefferson's justice was purely retributive.

The Chase impeachment trial did not get under way until early in 1805. It was presided over by none other than Aaron Burr, as President of the Senate, who, six months post-Hamilton duel, was still a wanted man in New York and New Jersey. The Senate trial amounted to his final act while he remained first in line to the presidency, and his impartiality impressed even the worried Federalists in attendance. What is still more striking is what occurred in advance of the trial: after the House had voted 73–32 to impeach, bringing eight articles, and as the upper chamber readied itself to stage a grand trial, Burr suddenly found himself a much appreciated member of the administration. Jefferson included his outgoing vice president in dinner parties at the President's House. Though he said nothing that was publicly revealed, this was a clear indication that he was unperturbed either by Hamilton's demise or Burr's culpability, and unmoved by Federalist sensibilities. Madison and Gallatin, who had never really disliked Burr, rediscovered him. Burr's subsequent handling of the impeachment process, maintaining decorum against the odds, caused many politicos to wonder what the future held for this controversial figure. They would soon find out.[35]

As the party of unapologetic elitism, the Federalists were able to draw on some of the nation's sharpest lawyers for the Chase trial. Representative Nicholson, under the impression that he might be appointed to the High Court if Chase was convicted, yielded the lead position to the oratorically colorful John Randolph of Roanoke, a physically odd-looking Virginia planter with a high-pitched voice and a reputation for rhetorical excess. Despite their obvious political differences, Randolph was a great fan of John Marshall's—theirs was, in fact, a mutual admiration society that lasted a lifetime.

But Randolph was not nearly as good a prosecutor as he was a showman. He called Chase "a man whose violent temper and arbitrary disposition perpetually drives him into acts of tyranny." But could the justice be impeached for what was not an indictable act? Jefferson had let his feelings get the better of him, and in the end, the law bested partisanship. Republicans held a clear majority of Senate seats (24 to 10), yet six Republicans voted to acquit and the two-thirds majority needed did not materialize.

Because Samuel Chase survived, Jefferson lost his bid to reduce the power of the Marshall court. Marshall, who was himself called to the witness stand in his colleague's defense, took his cue from the verdict and would prove even more of a thorn in Jefferson's side going forward. To make matters worse, the ever-contentious Republican John Randolph would become a vocal critic of President Jefferson as the second term unfolded.[36]

Figure 17. "Thomas Jefferson, the Pride of America." An 1809 engraving by French-born Thomas Gimbrede (1781–1832), who emigrated to America in 1802 and became drawing master at the U.S. Military Academy, West Point. (Courtesy National Portrait Gallery, Smithsonian Institution)

CHAPTER 12

"I Feel No Passion, I Take No Part"
Second Term Schisms

H E'D ACQUIRED A HABIT of command. He appeared unshakable. In addition to his prosecution of the Barbary War and his management of the Louisiana Purchase, President Jefferson established the United States Military Academy at West Point and the Library of Congress in Washington—all of this in his first term.

The election of 1804 was a blowout. Jeffersonian Republicans were the majority even in Massachusetts now, losing only the electoral votes of Connecticut and Delaware. Jefferson did not have a bad word to say about his Federalist opponent, Charles Cotesworth Pinckney, who did not so much as campaign. The great names of Washington, Henry, and Hamilton could not deter him anymore. All were in their graves. Isolated Federalists spoke out, but their power in the national legislature was fast receding.

At Monticello, a grave was dug a few feet from where Patty Jefferson lay, leaving space in between for the casket of Thomas Jefferson. The Jeffersons' second daughter, Maria Eppes, died on the morning of April 17, 1804. Her father was at her bedside, having come down from Washington two weeks before, as Maria was fading. Though one can do no more than speculate, the calendar suggests that during that month, Jefferson took solace of a kind in sharing intimacy with Patty's enslaved half sister. Nine months (almost to the day) after his daughter's death and burial,

Sally Hemings—who had been "Maria's maid" from the time they were both children—gave birth to a son. He received the name James Madison Hemings. Called Jim-Mad by family members, he had light gray eyes, the same hue as those of his biological father, who would grant him freedom in his final will.

One year (almost to the day) after the birth of Madison Hemings, Jefferson's surviving daughter, Martha Jefferson Randolph, bore a son at the President's House and named him James Madison Randolph. The two James Madisons grew up in the immediate neighborhood of Monticello. The first married a mixed-race woman, left Albemarle for Chillicothe, Ohio, raised a large family, and lived to be seventy-two. The second never married and died at twenty-eight, in 1834. He is buried at Monticello.[1]

Understanding what the loss of his daughter meant, Abigail Adams, who had come to despise Jefferson for what she regarded as politically driven meanness, wrote to the grieving father in May. "The powerfull feelings of my heart, have . . . called upon me to shed the tear of sorrow over the departed remains, of Your beloved and deserving Daughter." Reading of Maria's passing in a Boston paper, she recalled her fondness for the nine-year-old who arrived at her doorstep in London in 1787. "The tender Scene of her Seperation from me, rose to my recollection, when She clung around my neck and wet my Bosom with her tears, Saying, 'o! now I have learnt to Love You. Why will they tear me from You.'" It would be another seven years before Thomas Jefferson and John Adams reconciled, but the occasion of a loved one's death did serve as a reminder that politics was too often the cause for dissolution of a friendship. The so-called Revolution of 1800 did not end in a palace coup or the guillotine, and yet there were emotional costs.[2]

Jefferson's actions and writings since 1797 provide no evidence that he devoted any time to reexamining his own motives. His political course was set when President Adams indulged the Hamiltonians he'd inherited, then made his bed with the obnoxious Alien and Sedition Acts. Nor was Jefferson questioning his own personal choices. The mischief-maker James Callender was dead, but the public accusations he instigated lived on. When Madison Hemings was a few months old, a newspaper in Boston mentioned his brother Beverley, the eldest son of Jefferson and Hemings, by name. Word escaped the mountaintop, yet Jefferson did nothing to alter his patterns, nor did he, as far as is known, express any agitation in that regard.[3]

To add one more wrinkle, Jefferson's congressman son-in-law Jack Eppes turns out to have taken after the president in his personal, not just his political, choices. When he and Maria Jefferson married in 1797, Jefferson would not allow Sally

Hemings to leave Monticello and go with the newlyweds, but he "gave" to the couple the teenage Betsy Hemings, a granddaughter of Sally's mother, Elizabeth (Betty) Hemings. Betsy was in all likelihood as light-skinned as Sally. Within a short time after Jack Eppes became a widower, while serving in Congress, he took his late wife's maid, now in her early twenties, to his bed and they had two children together. Jack Eppes remarried in 1809, but is widely thought to have continued intimate relations with Betsy Hemings; she, and not his second wife, was eventually buried beside him, which is more than a little suggestive. It is highly unlikely that President Jefferson was kept in the dark about a relationship with which he would surely have empathized.

He did what he could, where he had influence, to see that Callender's revelations did not resurface in any public record. In 1806, he quietly persuaded Connecticut Republicans to drop the charges against a prominent preacher who was set to stand trial for seditious libel after calling the president a "liar, whoremaster, debaucher, drunkard, gambler, and infidel." The sitting president would not risk more exposure.[4]

When Jefferson had qualms, when he had doubts, the one person he turned to was his secretary of state, James Madison, who now had two namesakes in the Jefferson and Randolph households. Madison accepted Jefferson for who he was, as friends are wont to do. Madison knew all his secrets, as a frequent visitor to Monticello, where Jefferson's private pleasure mattered most, where he sought to shield himself from whatever caused unhappiness, pain, and fear. But of course the American president could not shield himself entirely. He was in his sixties, past the average lifespan of his time. He slept a few hundred yards from the cemetery where those people lay forever whose connection to him existed only in his memories of them. They were the ones he could scarcely do without, but he had to do without them nonetheless.

Did Jefferson feel unluckier in love than others? When John Page wrote a letter of condolence after learning of Maria's death, the grieving parent's heart poured forth its meek acceptance while his head did the math: "The part you take in my loss marks an affectionate concern for the greatness of it. It is great indeed. Others may lose of their abundance; but, I, of my want, have lost, even the half of all I had." With one surviving child, the only living proof of his life with Patty, he tempted fate: "My evening prospects now hang on the slender thread of a single life. Perhaps I may be destined to see even this last cord of parental affection broken!" Any prospect of a quiet retirement was now "fearfully blighted."

In this moment of reflection, he left his oldest friend with a rhetorical question. "When you and I look back on the country over which we have passed, what a field of slaughter does it exhibit! Where are all the friends who entered it with us under all the inspiring energies of health and hope?" Jefferson turned more and more to his growing grandchildren, on whom he lavished attention. He desired to have them close whenever he was back from Washington, and required their presence even more once he finally retired in 1809.[5]

There was never any question but that he would serve out a second term, as Washington had done, and then ease Madison into the office. He framed a letter for several state legislatures, stating that he would adhere to "the admonitions of Nature," and bow to the dictates of age: "I am sensible of that decline which advancing years bring on; and feeling their physical, I ought not to doubt their Mental effect."[6]

Things did not go at all the way he hoped in the second term. A series of events arose that challenged his optimism to an alarming degree. While less in decline than he pretended, he faced the twin ills of British aggression and Republican "schism."

The British could not be talked out of harassing U.S. shipping. A simmering conflict was to drag the United States into a second, ultimately pointless Anglo-American war. As if that wasn't bad enough, Jefferson's hold on his political base was not as strong as he once thought. As early as 1801, writing to the Republican governor of Pennsylvania of "incurable monocrats" whom he would never be able to sway with his talk of conciliation, he noted an emergent danger within his own party: "There is a rock ahead, far more dangerous than that of monarchism. It is the discord shewing itself among the republicans. In no place is it so threatening as in Delaware. The republicans there are fallen into open schism." By 1805, tiny Delaware was not the only state he worried about: "How deeply to be regretted, my dear Sir, is the bitter schism which has lately split the friends of republicanism into two adverse sections in Pensylvania!" He made similar remarks about divisions in New York.[7]

In a Jeffersonian lexicon, "schism" was the exact opposite of "harmony and affection" and "tranquil felicity." The schism that would pain him most personally occurred as his final retirement from political office neared, and that was the falling-out between Madison and Monroe, his two closest Virginia allies, as they vied with each other to succeed him as president.

Then there was the publicity hound John Randolph, the outlandish, unyielding Virginia congressman, seen by some as a comical figure and by others as a public nuisance. Colleagues (and newspaper readers) could not ignore him. In this topsy-turvy moment of undoing, seeing Madison as a proxy for the president he now disfavored, he threw his support to Monroe. His defection from Jefferson's camp in 1805, not entirely unlike the newshound Callender's in 1802, showed the power of publicity and a wavering of presidential prestige that would not end with Jefferson.[8]

The glow of victory over the Tripolitans receded as European jockeying for position revealed weaknesses in the United States' ability to defend its territories. In March 1807, just outside of Norfolk harbor, a British warship fired shots across the bow of the American frigate *Chesapeake*, killing three and wounding eighteen. British officers then boarded the damaged vessel, looking for deserters. This bald act of aggression outraged patriotic Americans and started the slow spiral that would end in a congressional declaration of war five years later. To avoid all-out war, Jefferson opted to squeeze London economically. He proclaimed an embargo, shutting down U.S. exports in order to deprive Britain, the nation's largest trading partner, of all American products. The embargo was a strategic blunder for which Madison was equally responsible. It received scant support from the other members of the cabinet and was unpopular among the president's staunchest friends in Virginia, doing far more harm to U.S. producers and shippers than to the intended target nation. For these reasons, Jefferson left office in March 1809 able to claim only a Pyrrhic victory. New England Federalists saw an opening for them to recover prestige amid the extreme disruption caused by the embargo.[9]

ISSUES OF CONTROL AND SELF-CONTROL

Personality problems plagued Jefferson's presidency. The enmity of John Randolph hit close to home when daughter Martha's husband, Thomas Mann Randolph, as a member of Congress in April 1806, found his Randolph cousin's rant too much to take. He lost his cool and said that "lead and even steel make very proper ingredients in serious quarrels," then rose from his seat and angrily left the building. An affair of honor was initiated. Intermediaries from both parties stepped in and shrewdly acted to avert a duel.

Weeks later, Jefferson received a shock after seeing a story that appeared in two pro-administration newspapers. What he read was enough for him to glean that the ungovernable congressmen were still going at it. To his son-in-law Randolph, he wrote: "It is with an aching heart I take up my pen." He'd heard about the "altercation" and thought it resolved the same day until the press reported otherwise. If the rambunctious Randolphs didn't find a way to cool off, he warned, it would "probably lead to a fatal issue." Jefferson contrasted the two men's position in the community: one was unmarried and unmarriageable (due to physical abnormalities), the other was a father of (so far) seven. "On his side," he told his son-in-law, "unentangled in the affections of the world, a single life, of no value to himself or others. On your's, yourself, a wife, & a family of children, all depending, for all their happiness & protection in this world on you alone." Whether or not this letter was the sole cause of the men's retreat from the precipice, a mutual hatred persisted between them.

Tom Randolph's temper tantrums came and went. After the other son-in-law, the widower Jack Eppes, entered Congress, Jack lived at the President's House, and Tom became convinced that Jefferson favored Jack, the more active and vocal of the two in support of the administration. The allotment of Maria's property was another contributing factor in Tom's jealous outburst: he feared being shortchanged. Slow to accept Jefferson's protestations that he did not favor one over the other, Tom made himself scarce for a time. His absence weighed on Jefferson, until Tom eventually found his way back into the fold.[10]

One has to wonder how Jefferson was able to maintain his reserve in such situations, which he did do. His faith was tested in other ways and with other Virginians, those he knew best and counted on most. So many of these men of inherited privilege displayed the same lack of self-control that the cousins John and Tom Randolph did. Aside from their personal habits—drinking to excess, for instance—planters' lives were subject to such unpredictable factors as weather and the price of tobacco, overseers whose treatment of the enslaved often got them fired, and the creditors whose terms had to be met. Even the best farmers (Tom Randolph was thought to be one) had to deal with soil exhaustion. They prized a life of leisure rather than one of stockpiling money, and they were regularly described in travelers' accounts as courtly, good-natured, and generous. They rationalized the slave economy as the generations before them had; it endowed them with power and lashed them to an odd mix of emotions.

Jefferson trusted these people. He accepted their earthiness, their stubborn independence. He unquestionably understood male ardor. As one whose opinions rarely shifted over time, it is not wrong to repeat a statement Jefferson made in 1785 to his friend the Marquis de Chastellux on reading that gentleman's book in progress about his travels in America. "I have studied their character with attention," he wrote of his fellow Virginians. "I have thought them, as you found them, aristocratical, pompous, clannish, indolent, hospitable." He went on to list, in two columns, the differences between Southerners and Northerners. The Southern gentry were "fiery," "unsteady," and "Voluptuary"—a "voluptuary" being, according to the *Oxford English Dictionary*, "one who is immoderately fond of sensuous pleasures; one who is given up to indulgence in luxury or the gratification of the senses." He contrasted the Southern voluptuary to the "sober" Northerner. Almost tongue in cheek, he went on to say: "An observing traveller, without the aid of the quadrant may always know his latitude by the character of the people among whom he finds himself. It is in Pennsylvania that the two characters seem to meet and blend and to form a people free from the extremes both of vice and virtue."

One wonders, did it not strike him that plantation owners sent their sons north for an education, whereas no Northerners attended college in the South? Of course it did. He himself ordered leather-bound books from Philadelphia publishers, superior clocks and sets of Windsor chairs from Northern makers. He prized the productions of Northern cities without softening his critique of the urban economy.[11]

He retained a strong partiality for his section. Southern representatives did his bidding in Congress, and perhaps that was enough for him. He wanted to replicate the Southern economy (at the expense of Native peoples) by giving incentives to men who relocated to Mississippi Territory, improved the land, and served in the militia. He never revisited his prejudice in favor of the fictive small farmer, his model American. As far back as 1779, when he was working on new state laws for Virginia, he proposed giving land for free. To keep the nation unique meant encouraging mastery of the land. The hyperbolic appeal of his First Inaugural, in which Jefferson declared the United States "a chosen country with room enough for our descendants to the thousandth generation," was meant to celebrate spontaneous growth, aided by just enough incentive from the federal government.[12]

In the emotion-filled second term of his presidency, Jefferson was no longer banking on his talent as a beautiful writer to persuade others. His Second Inaugural Address lacked the harmonious strains of the First. He straightforwardly communicated his legislative agenda, with the only motivational language coming across as formulaic, even lazy: "Contemplating the union of sentiment now manifested so generally, as auguring harmony and happiness to our future course, I offer to our country sincere congratulations." His evocation of sentiment on the subject of Indian policy was delivered in a calculated way. Complimenting his administration for its generous consideration of Native people's material needs, he placed emphasis on the latter's inherent limitations: "They are combated by the habits of their bodies, prejudice of their minds, ignorance, pride, and the influence of interested and crafty individuals among them... These persons inculcate a sanctimonious reverence for the customs of their ancestors." This, of course, is disrespectful and culturally tone-deaf to our ears, but few among his constituency would as yet have disputed his logic. Ironically, too, the words could just as easily describe his fellow Virginians and their habits.[13]

Shuffling papers and juggling issues foreign and domestic subjected him to an inordinate amount of tension. The decision to resort to a belt-tightening embargo ("peaceable coercion"), in response to British depredations on the high seas, looked at first like a way to exhibit strength while avoiding war. But the interruption of trade abroad and the enforcement acts that followed laid responsibility firmly on the chief executive's head. Anglophilic New Englanders spoke openly of disunion. It made no difference when Jefferson doubled down on enforcement; smuggling continued apace. He found himself impotent in attempts to rouse citizens to sacrifice for the nation.[14]

Any remaining zeal to exercise executive authority was on shaky ground now. While residing at the President's House (but not at Monticello), he was afflicted by more of the violent "periodical" headaches that had, since the age of twenty-one, if not longer, pounced on him unexpectedly. They stalled his work schedule for nearly a month in 1807 and again in 1808.[15]

"A MIXTURE OF RUMORS, CONJECTURES, AND SUSPICIONS"

Jefferson's personal demons mingled with his slumping approval as a leader. On the heels on his fruitless attempt to impeach Justice Chase and add Republicans to the Court, he realized that Aaron Burr would not go away quietly. The shunned vice president understood politics all too well. Years of correspondence shows him as a good-humored man, better able than most to rise above resentments. The duel for which he is best known occurred only after Burr ignored or forgave past outbursts for which the hotheaded Hamilton had privately apologized to him.

Burr's surviving correspondence says little about Jefferson's treatment of him, though he was rebuffed repeatedly and knew what it meant. Did he bear a grudge? Anyone would. Was there anything in Burr's past to indicate that he would attempt to bring down the republic? No.

They met on the evening of January 26, 1804, at Burr's request. The New Yorker asked for some public acknowledgment from Jefferson that his replacement by Clinton on the ticket was less meaningful than it appeared, hoping he would "declare to the world" (in Jefferson's rendering) a positive opinion of his erstwhile vice president. The president hedged. When Burr professed that he only sought to avoid a "disadvantageous schism" among Republicans, Jefferson changed the subject. Writing down his recollection of their talk, the president sniped at the other's use of flattery ("Colonel Burr must have thought that I could swallow strong things in my own favor"), adding, with reference to his feelings of four years earlier: "I habitually cautioned Mr. Madison against trusting him too much... There never had been an intimacy between us." By "intimacy" he implied a lack of trust in Burr's word, without allowing that his own trustworthiness might be part of the equation. Secure in his tart observations, Jefferson unquestionably had a future chronicler in mind when he added retrospective commentary to these private notes.[16]

The unwanted vice president's career was in freefall. After an unsuccessful bid to win the governorship of New York in 1804, he slow-walked his way into the Hamilton duel that July, induced by disparaging public comments about his morals in advance of that election. The following year, once he'd made a graceful exit from the Senate at the conclusion of the Chase trial, Burr naturally sought some form of rehabilitation. He had friends in high places, a few of whom wanted him to accept a judgeship in Pennsylvania or enter Congress from a western state.

Burr's road west restarted the rumor mill that eventually ended in a courtroom in Richmond, Virginia. The real villain in the "Burr Conspiracy" (as it has been known since 1806) was the inconstant General James Wilkinson, an experienced soldier who attended the inauguration of Jefferson and Burr in 1801, and sought patronage from the administration. From 1803, he could be found buttering up Burr in New York, his eyes set on the governorship of Louisiana Territory—a post Jefferson soon thereafter awarded him. For his part, Burr generously helped Wilkinson's sons gain admission to Princeton, his alma mater, where his own father had once served as president.[17]

The general did not disguise his ambition to be a part of a greater land grab, and the administration overlooked the credible rumors that he had been, and perhaps still was, on the Spanish payroll. He was telling Jefferson one thing (to go for Texas and the Rio Grande), while telling the Spanish something different (to reclaim lost land that bordered the Mississippi). The truth was, he'd been playing both sides of the street since the 1780s, when he was in Kentucky and flirting with the idea of joining the land to Spain rather than the United States.

> written, which were, indirectly, an answer to his present hints. He left the matter with me for consideration, and the conversation was turned to indifferent subjects. I should here notice, that Colonel Burr must have thought I could swallow strong things in my own favor, when he founded his acquiescence in the nomination as Vice President, to his desire of promoting my honor, the being with me, whose company and conversation had always been fascinating with him, &c. I had never seen Colonel Burr till he came as a member of Senate. His conduct very soon inspired me with distrust. I habitually cautioned Mr. Madison against trusting him too much. I saw afterwards, that under General Washington's and Mr. Adams' administrations, whenever a great military appointment or a diplomatic one was to be made, he came post to Philadelphia to shew himself, and in fact that he was always at market, if they had wanted him. He was indeed told by Dayton in 1800, he might be Secretary at War; but this bid was too late. His election as Vice President was then foreseen. With these impressions of Colonel Burr, there never had been an intimacy between us, and but little association. When I destined him for a high appointment, it was out of respect for the favor he had obtained with the republican party, by his extraordinary exertions and success in the New York election in 1800.

Figure 18. "There never had been an intimacy between us." Excerpt from Jefferson's damning commentary on his personal relations with Aaron Burr, as the words appeared in print for the first time in 1829. Having jotted down these self-serving notes in 1804, Jefferson waited until 1818 to have them bound, along with "secret communications" dating to the Washington administration, in a volume that he made available to his eldest grandson, Thomas Jefferson Randolph, intended for posthumous publication. Knowing that his grandfather was deeply invested in having future historians privilege his interpretation of his life in politics, Randolph exercised due diligence, honoring his elder's wishes. He labeled the late president's collected scraps the *Anas*, a Latin term for anecdotal memoranda.

Westerners in 1805–06 were solid patriots, largely Republican, and looking forward to the conquest of Spain's American territories. Military adventure held an allure for them. Jefferson, as president, openly sought to acquire Florida; he would have his and their wish at least partially granted in 1810, when a private army of Americans took the poorly manned Spanish position and declared West Florida an independent republic. This filibuster, led by a Virginian known to Jefferson, occurred with a wink and a nod from both Jefferson and Madison. Because Burr was not a Virginian, he was less welcome to obtain advantage in the region through filibustering. Non-Virginians were harder for Jefferson to trust.

The displaced vice president was doing nothing that did not comport with the expansionist spirit that prevailed in Republican circles. Aside from perfectly legal land speculation in western Louisiana, Colonel Burr, unable to return to his home state where he was wanted for a capital offense, wished to be in a position, should the anticipated war with Spain occur, to move into Texas/Mexico. The only question is how, in this environment, Jefferson became convinced that Burr was plotting against, rather than with, American interests.[18]

Jefferson made treason out of rumor and innuendo. The primary reason for his believing that Burr was thinking of separating parts of the Louisiana Territory from the United States was that he'd received correspondence from a U.S. district attorney in Kentucky, a Federalist named Joseph Daveiss, who hated Burr for killing Hamilton. Daveiss stated that the resourceful New Yorker was concocting a nefarious disunionist plot in that state.

Kentucky newspapers helped cook up the scandal. Separately, Jefferson's postmaster general, Gideon Granger of Connecticut, repeated a claim he'd been told by General William Eaton, a hero of the offensive against Tripoli who had of late become known as a prodigious drinker. Eaton swore he was on the receiving end of an effort by Burr to recruit talent. His story would evolve to the point of claiming that Burr was planning to assassinate Jefferson.[19]

Burr's situation was awkward, to say the least. As a wanted man in his home state owing to the Hamilton duel, the exile had had to dispose of property there. When newly deprived of office in the spring of 1805, he made an exploratory trip through Kentucky and Tennessee, where he bonded with, among others, fellow duelist and former Republican congressman Andrew Jackson. Kentuckians applauded his slaying of Hamilton, cheering and toasting him along his route, while Federalist newspapers speculated aloud on what Burr's extensive travel might mean. It was already being said that he'd turned revolutionary, gone rogue. From Tennessee, he continued south to New Orleans and reconnected with an old New York ally and new Louisianian, Edward Livingston. As mayor of New York at the start of the Jefferson-Burr administration, this Livingston was caught up in a financial scandal not of his making. Finding a home, a legal practice, and a leadership position in New Orleans, he found love as well, marrying a young and beautiful French woman, a widow.

Livingston and Burr saw the world differently than Jefferson did. Burr's travels were a means to reinvent himself as a public figure, to see what possibilities the West and Southwest held for an agile, adventurous, unattached man on the make, renowned for his political savvy. He returned to Washington from his first western trip in the fall of 1805, dined with Jefferson, and updated him on his activities. They dined together again on February 22, 1806 (which would have been Washington's seventy-fourth birthday), and met once more in mid-March, at which time Burr—who had almost single-handedly placed his state's electoral votes in Jefferson's column in 1800—pressed the president for a diplomatic appointment at a European capital. Jefferson quoted Burr as having said on this occasion that "he could do me much harm" but preferred that their relations should move in a positive direction. According to notes he took on their conversation, Jefferson then told Burr that the American people had lost their confidence in him and he would not lift a finger to help. He had made an enemy of Burr; the break was complete.[20]

It was shortly before the February meeting that Jefferson had heard from the U.S. district attorney in Kentucky that Burr was up to something. The letters from Daveiss kept flowing; he wouldn't let go. Coincident with Burr's second trip west, in the late summer of 1806, new rumblings of Spanish border encroachments produced war fever among westerners. That was when Secretary of War Dearborn ordered General Wilkinson to reinforce New Orleans. Burr had finalized the purchase of Louisiana lands near the Texas border and bought river-worthy boats from Andrew Jackson, who was meant to alert the Tennessee militia to be ready to move south to face the Spanish. Earlier, Burr had engaged a New York land developer and former state legislator to attract young men to make their way to the border region. Preparations for a filibustering expedition were under way, and Jefferson had cut ties with Burr. He was ready to believe just about anything.[21]

He gathered his cabinet in October and urged them to write to western state officials to be on their guard and to arrest Burr if he should attempt anything. Suspicion fell on the grandiose General Wilkinson as well. His checkered past was not to be ignored—and yet it was. He knew the territory all too well, having dealt with Choctaw and Creek Indians on boundary and land sale issues on behalf of the administration prior to the Louisiana Purchase. Postmaster General Granger, having injected the questionable testimony of the hard-drinking General Eaton, also praised Wilkinson at the time of his appointment as "one of the most agreeable, best informed, most genteel, moderate and sensible republicans in the nation." To the administration, James Wilkinson appeared useful and competent.[22]

In November 1806, Daveiss of Kentucky upped the ante, filing criminal charges against Burr for plotting to attack Mexico and sever the western states from the Union. Seeking local counsel, Burr explained to the new U.S. senator from

Kentucky, Henry Clay, that his designs involved only land speculation, that he had as yet made no military preparations, and it was absurd to think he would ever contemplate action against the United States. When asked why he didn't contradict newspaper reports that painted him in a different light, Burr averred that the truth would emerge in due time.

With these explanations, Clay strongly and successfully represented him over a period of weeks. When called to testify in court, newspaper publishers had to admit that there was nothing behind their stories but wild rumors. All charges against Burr were dismissed. But after an interview with Jefferson weeks later, Clay, a twenty-nine-year-old newcomer to Washington, came away believing he had been taken in by his client.[23]

General Wilkinson had been up to his neck in Burr's prospective filibuster from the start. Worried for himself, he wrote to Jefferson, wildly accusing the former vice president of threatening New Orleans with aid from the British navy. He then raised the alarm in New Orleans, urging military preparations against an army of potential plunderers that he estimated at seven thousand men, though Burr was still in Kentucky. It was a total concoction. The dishonorable general went so far as to doctor a letter in order to implicate Burr and exonerate himself.

But Jefferson took Wilkinson's charges at face value and issued a proclamation urging citizens not to join any illegal military campaign against the Spanish. More "evidence" from Wilkinson piled up, and on January 22, 1807, in an address to Congress, the president formally named Burr the head of a conspiracy. He had "seduced" good citizens but could not seduce the "good citizen" General Wilkinson, whom Jefferson now credited with having promptly reported to the president all he knew. Piecing everything together, Jefferson communicated his own interpretation of events: "In Kentucky a premature attempt to bring Burr to justice, without sufficient evidence for his conviction, had produced a popular impression in his favor, and a general disbelief of his guilt. This gave him an unfortunate opportunity of hastening his equipments"—that is to say, following through with logistical preparations. It was Burr alone, the president made clear, who had to be stopped. Yet earlier fears that he was involved with a foreign power were, he had to concede, lately shown to be "without proof or probability." For the little good it did the fugitive Burr, on learning of Wilkinson's manufactured charges, he declared in a letter to the governor of the Mississippi Territory that they were all "vile fabrications."[24]

As a matter of personal psychology, all of the interested parties were exhibiting what drove them to make unusual choices. For Wilkinson, it was the panicky decision to doctor a letter; for Burr, an abortive flight; for Jefferson, the impulse to go public with his fear of a plot against the government. Senator William Plumer of New Hampshire, a dyed-in-the-wool Federalist, felt that all three U.S. presidents had, since 1789, "taken more pains to acquire popularity than to promote the interest of the United States." On January 15, 1807, one week before Jefferson's consequential address to Congress, Plumer penned a curious entry in the Senate diary he'd been keeping as a private record since his arrival in Washington more than three years earlier. The other New Hampshire senator, Nicholas Gilman, a loyal Republican, had reported to him a conversation he'd just had with the president. Jefferson shared with Gilman what his last encounter with Burr was like: he said he'd lost whatever confidence he once lodged in Burr, upon which Burr "intimated to the President, that he would find he had it in his power to do Mr. Jefferson much injury."

Here is what is interesting about that: the comments by Gilman, a member of Congress since 1789, are identical in tenor and a near paraphrase of what Jefferson recorded in private notes of his conversation with Burr *nine* months earlier. Yet in the Message to Congress, he acknowledged that up through the early fall of 1806, all he had to go on was "a mixture of rumors, conjectures, and suspicions as renders it difficult to sift out the real facts"—other than the one fact he'd sifted out: "Neither safety nor justice will permit the exposing names, except that of the principal actor, whose guilt is placed beyond question."

Whatever Burr said or intimated in March 1806, one sees that Jefferson was so taken aback by his forwardness and rattled by his words in their final private meeting that he was prone to believing the worst. As he prepared his January 22, 1807, address to Congress, he was utterly bent on seeing Burr cut down to size, going so far as to declare that Burr intended to "plunder the bank" and "military and naval stores" in New Orleans while pretending to be on a secret mission for Jefferson's administration. Jefferson had finally psyched himself into swallowing the lies of General Wilkinson.[25]

The president had an interpretation of the ex-vice president's spoken threat at their private meeting, and yet Burr did not go after Jefferson's personal life or political behavior from January 1807 through the conclusion of his treason trial the following summer. One must wonder what that means. If Burr had, indeed, threatened to "do much injury" to Jefferson, what prevented him from doing so after Jefferson had leveled a devastating series of accusations against him, doing him harm in the most public way imaginable?

As we have seen before in his reactions to Patrick Henry (perhaps unjustifiably) and Alexander Hamilton (generally with good reason), once a narrative took root in his mind, Jefferson's fixation grew. Over dinner at the end of December 1806, when Senator Plumer sat next to the president, he was told directly that Burr had most likely succeeded in coaxing "large sums" from the Spanish minister in Washington. Plumer declined comment, having heard enough that smacked of nonsense from people who claimed they were solicited by Burr to join his force. He diarized, though, that he thought it impossible that the agile mind of Aaron Burr was capable of such an imprudent choice as to take on so untrustworthy an individual as James Wilkinson as partner in an act of treason. Plumer, for one, was not to be so easily won over to the official line.[26]

Burr was arrested in southwestern Alabama in February 1807, then hauled east a thousand miles, by horseback, to face the music. His sensational trial was held in Richmond, Virginia, and presided over by none other than Chief Justice John Marshall. Burr took an active part in his own defense, and hired on Edmund Randolph, Jefferson's onetime cabinet colleague and immediate successor as secretary of state. By adding Luther Martin, the Jefferson-hating Marylander largely responsible for the acquittal of his friend Justice Chase, the accused had a formidable defense team. "The federalists appear to make Burr's cause their own," Jefferson railed. His frustration was palpable.

The prosecution faced the challenge of proving treason, which required evidence of an overt act of war. It set out to determine, for one, that Burr intended to take over New Orleans. Yet when the flotilla of conscripts for Burr's ostensible army was located, it wasn't arms that were found onboard but books. Nevertheless, Jefferson assured Senator William Branch Giles of Virginia—while still railing at the virtual impossibility of impeaching odious members of the judiciary—that Burr's crimes would be exposed. The testimony of Generals Wilkinson and Eaton, he said, "will satisfy the world, if not the judges," and that "the nation will judge both the offender, & judges for themselves."

That is not what the ornery John Randolph thought. As foreman of the grand jury, he was incensed that Wilkinson was not standing trial at the same time. When the general strode into the courtroom bearing a ceremonial sword, Randolph shouted: "Take that man out and disarm him!" Over the next several days, listening to Wilkinson testify, Randolph had no doubt that the man was a "scoundrel," "from the bark to the very core a villain." He sought an indictment but failed. Wilkinson challenged Randolph to a duel, and the colorful congressman (who would later engage in a duel with Henry Clay) thought so little of Wilkinson's credibility that he refused the general's challenge, writing: "I recognize no right to hold me accountable for my public or private opinion of your character. I cannot descend to your level."[27]

The irregularities and intrigues that punctuate this era in American politics are stunning. Rumormongering, physical threats, sensational duels, newspaper wars, sedition trials, slavery debates, and sexual slurs marked an erratic public discourse. Financial insolvency and persistent health problems rocked private worlds and bled into the postures and positions taken by public men. These factors make Jefferson's faith in the educability and rationality of ordinary people, despite his own aggressiveness in condemning political enemies, seem doubly surprising. The integrity of a system rooted in the essential goodness of citizens was an ideal captured in the Revolutionary propaganda of Thomas Paine, amplified immeasurably by Jefferson's public addresses and other writings. It was unsustainable in a hyperpartisan environment.

"MYSTERIES"

Jefferson used his facility with language as a means to encourage support for his mission to remake America. His refusal to succumb to the fractiousness of the 1790s carried over into his first term, only to be put on hold during his second. Except when writing of Americans' good character in a self-dramatizing effort, that is, in pronouncing on his own embodiment of the national character (which he often did with posterity in mind), he could not sustain the uplifting prose.

In the matter of Burr, the sitting president had no business publicly prejudging the defendant. And yet their personal history almost demanded it. Jefferson's direct involvement in the court proceedings was another matter. Coaching prosecutor George Hay, who was the son-in-law of James Monroe, he opened one of the first in their exchange of letters by announcing his intent: "While Burr's case is depending before the court, I will trouble you, from time to time, with what occurs to me." Two weeks after this, he was on to John Marshall's animus: "The powers given to the Ex[ecuti]ve by the Const[itutio]n are sufficient to protect the other branches from judiciary usurpation of preeminence, & every individual also from judiciary vengeance." Letting Jefferson know who was in charge, the chief justice issued the president a subpoena duces tecum requiring him to turn over Wilkinson's letters to the defense. Jefferson, expressing reluctance, discussed the subject at length in another letter to Hay. Noting for history that even the president was a citizen subject to subpoena, Marshall did not let go. The two men continued to lock horns through the middle months of 1807.[28]

Writing to the Marquis de Lafayette on Bastille Day in July of that year, the president recalled that he'd initially raised the prospect of appointing the beloved Frenchman, a former commander of Continental Army troops, to be Louisiana's first territorial governor. Revealing his pique, he doubled down on a narrative he would never question, of the defendant's total guilt: "Had you been, as I wished, at the head of the government of Orleans, Burr would never have given me one moment's uneasiness. His conspiracy has been one of the most flagitious of which history will ever furnish an example. He meant to separate the Western states from us, to add Mexico to them, place himself at their head, establish what he would deem an energetic government, & thus provide an example & an instrument for the subversion of our freedom." Owing to Marshall's very narrow definition of treason, there was no way a jury could convict Burr.[29]

The trial ended on September 1, 1807. For Jefferson, it was a miscarriage of justice on a massive scale that convicted Marshall in his eyes. He may well have thought that Marshall ruled as he did just to toss the verdict in Jefferson's face. In fact Marshall had never thought much of Jefferson. As a young captain who experienced the rigors of Valley Forge, who attempted, against strong odds, to face Benedict Arnold's invasion force as Governor Jefferson fled Richmond, Marshall felt clear contempt for Jefferson the man.

Resentments went both ways. Jefferson had officially signed Marshall's law license in 1780, upon his passing the bar, and he was likely aware, even then, that the student had attended George Wythe's law lectures for only a matter of weeks and still got through. Just as Jefferson dismissed Patrick Henry's legal erudition on the basis of his scant preparation for the bar, he must have felt something comparable regarding Marshall. Yet on March 4, 1801, Marshall was as bound to administer the oath of office to President Jefferson as Governor Jefferson had been to help launch Marshall's legal career. After that, they probably did their best to avoid face-to-face meetings while engineering each other's defeat.[30]

The Burr decision was a major turning point. Jefferson dropped his moderate façade; whatever was left of it when he pursued Chase was gone now. He was determined to save his legacy. When it came to the press, though there were many more Republican newspapers commencing publication than there were Federalist, he told Senator Plumer, hyperbolically, that he considered no more than one percent of what the newspapers printed to be true. Plumer: "He *darkly* intimated that some restraint ought to be by law imposed upon them."

On this one subject, Jefferson proved fairly consistent. As the Burr trial was gearing up, a young Kentuckian wrote to him, asking the longtime champion of a free press for advice in starting a paper. Jefferson wrote back cynically: "It is a melancholy truth that a suppression of the press could not more compleatly deprive the nation of it's benefits, than is done by it's abandoned prostitution to falsehood. Nothing can now be believed which is seen in a newspaper. Truth itself becomes suspicious by being put into that polluted vehicle." As an embattled president, his reaction to bad press was demonstrably more impassioned than that of his two predecessors in the office; but he appears to have believed all he read about Burr in newspapers—if it was negative.[31]

There is yet more to unpack here. Jefferson knew what John Randolph knew and had good reasons to suspect that Wilkinson was secretly in cahoots with the Spanish enemy. He had known when he appointed him that his general narrowly escaped court-martial in the mid-1790s, falling into some luck when his accuser—his superior in rank—suddenly died. Later, during Madison's first term as president, with Burr out of the way and Jefferson out of office, Wilkinson would be facing court-martial again. At that time, Jefferson would write to James Monroe, contrasting Wilkinson's "Spanish mysteries" to his own "open cherishment of the Western interests." It was an unguardedly self-serving statement, demonstrating Jefferson's weakness for rationalization while glossing over what he ought to have honestly confronted in 1807.

He tried to project consistency in personal letters and presidential addresses, offering assurances that he was bent on proving, through executive action, an unselfish "cherishment" of the open country. He was not a designing speculator, as Washington had been. He did not parade about in a luxurious carriage, as Adams had. He was one of "the people," who dressed down, who rode his own horse around the federal city. "Mystery" was the reverse of who he was.

What "mysteries" meant here, Spanish or otherwise, was secrecy and misdirection. "Mystery" was the resort of the contemptible Wilkinson or the inscrutable Burr, lest their true motives became known. "Mystery" was the label that, years before, Jefferson had tacked onto Patrick Henry, his first political enemy, in attempting to figure out his next move. Addressing Madison in code, he'd written: "Henry as usual is involved in mystery: should the popular tide run strongly in either direction, he will fall in with it." In 1797, dreading the Adams administration as it was unfolding, he wrote to none other than Aaron Burr: "The same secrecy and mystery is affected to be observed by the present, which marked the former administration." Jefferson consistently claimed for himself political purity and personal incorruptibility.³²

In his statement to Congress on January 22, 1807, when he proclaimed Burr the head of a treasonous scheme, Jefferson reported that "the object of the conspiracy" was "so blended, & involved in mystery, that nothing distinct could be singled out for pursuit." This is why the language Jefferson uses in the letter to Monroe in 1812 is so telling. Here he was admitting that the one and only time he took James Wilkinson at his word was on the subject of Burr's guilt: "I have ever & carefully restrained myself from the expression of any opinion respecting Gen¹ Wilkinson, except in the case of Burr's conspiracy, wherein, after he had got over his first agitations, we believed his decision firm, & his conduct zealous for the defeat of the conspiracy." What a capacity to rationalize one's own actions and convictions!³³

It is hard to ignore the contrast here. To suggest that Wilkinson was, shall we say, merely overzealous and not thoroughly corrupt when he doctored a letter from Burr that Burr didn't even write, Jefferson exposes the problem in how he arrived at judgments. Wilkinson was known to act for personal pecuniary gain. Yet, somehow, in this one crucial instance, with so much to lose, Jefferson deemed his general credible. Confirmation bias led Jefferson to drastic interpretations, as it has many times since in presidential history. In their meeting after Burr's first journey west, he somehow did not attempt to tease out of his former ally some idea of his future plans if he could not return to New York without standing trial for shooting Hamilton.³⁴

Could it have gone another way? Probably not. But Jefferson might have permitted himself to see shades of gray, enough to recognize that Burr was not as evil in intent as he assumed, and that Wilkinson was far more guilty than Jefferson allowed himself to believe. As a political operator, Burr had a particular way of cozying up to potential allies and younger men who could be useful to him in advancing his interests. Jefferson had a way of doing that, too: over decades, members of the Virginia legislature and the U.S. Congress were fed ideas from Jefferson on a variety of issues. After Madison became president, Jefferson presented policy suggestions in letters. Madison did not always make the recommended moves, though he invited Jefferson's input.

What many saw as "mystery" about Burr was a preternatural calm, and it was not entirely different from Jefferson's persona. In the courthouse in Lexington,

Kentucky, an observer described Burr's "lofty tranquility." He was not alone in that characterization. Jefferson was eloquent on the page and soft-spoken otherwise, whereas Burr was eloquent in speech (most notably in court and in political assemblies) and wry, even ironic, on the page. He was not generally given to impassioned appeals; he and Jefferson both exhibited gentlemanly self-possession in their outward bearing. That both of these secretive men found Hamilton's pushy manner to be unsettling makes it even more interesting that Jefferson and Burr should be perennially cast in opposition. It would seem that the burden lies more with Jefferson, who, after 1801, was persuaded by individuals he did not know well to see Burr as a mortal threat, not just to Virginia dominance, but to the country.[35]

What lay in Jefferson's heart? It is perhaps understandable that he would have worried about a young, charismatic Burr leaping past the withered-looking Madison to become president. His cold rejection of Burr early in his presidency was probably excessive. Was Burr wrong to expect some patronage power, when the matter of federal appointments was the most urgent business as the new administration was constituting itself? He did not ask much. Jefferson, with insufficient cause, refused to treat him as a partner. The historian Todd Estes succinctly sums up the politician operating here, when he calls Jefferson's method of advancing to party leadership one of flexibility and a certain amount of guile, "marked by engagement and disengagement, of activity and inactivity, by the skillful use of others to work for him." Once these allies became burdensome, or had a negative impact on his larger political vision, he dropped them. "He never confused means and ends."[36]

Of the explanations given by Jefferson after Burr's arrest, the most piquant appears in an impassioned letter to the most active of Jefferson's allies in Congress, the Virginian William Branch Giles. Employing a weighty metaphor without mentioning the duel specifically, Jefferson said that he regarded Burr as a "crooked gun" whose "shot" could not be predicted. This portrait of Burr is classic Jefferson, cleverly phrased, hyperbolic, and replete with rationalizations for his own actions. The passage goes like this: "Against Burr personally I never had one hostile sentiment. I never indeed thought him an honest frank-dealing man, but considered him as a crooked gun or other perverted machine whose aim or stroke you could never be sure of. Still, while he possessed the confidence of the nation, I thought it my duty to respect in him their confidence, & to treat him as if he deserved it." Not one hostile sentiment? As if he had done something unprovoked to warrant Jefferson's hostility? Without Burr he would not have carried the State of New York in 1800. This is the same Jefferson who thought it impossible that he could be wrong in having relied on circumstantial evidence and reports from generals whose motives—either he knew or should have known—were less than pure and other than patriotic.[37]

Thomas Jefferson was, at times, a very angry and frustrated man. The frustrations of his second term resulted in outward-directed actions that proved how feelings of distrust, the fear of schism within *his* party, and a proneness to belief in conspiracy could combine as hatred. He had long focused his hatred on individuals: Patrick Henry, whom he held responsible for the public embarrassments he suffered as wartime governor of Virginia; Alexander Hamilton, whose subversion of his policies goaded him into furious note-taking when his own voice did not prevail in Washington's cabinet; John Marshall, who empowered the Supreme Court, openly challenged the president's will, and remained a thorn that would prick him until the end of his days. And Aaron Burr, who Jefferson believed had it in mind to mobilize a force against him.

So, how did Jefferson react? With the unflinching Colonel Burr, he lost control, vented his anger in ways unbecoming of a chief executive, and failed to get to the bottom of the conspiracy, if that's what it was. He did what he had earlier accused Henry of doing, by bringing serious public charges before pretrial discovery, before the legal process had gotten very far. Burr was just his latest bogeyman.

"WHAT WE HEAR WITH OUR OWN EARS"

The final blow to Jefferson's presidency was the schism between Madison and Monroe. Two old friends both wanted to be president, and Monroe, the younger and thinner-skinned, was unwilling to wait his turn. Having served as the U.S. minister to Great Britain since 1803, he returned to Washington in 1807, after negotiating a treaty that satisfied neither President Jefferson nor Secretary of State Madison; it never even reached Congress for consideration. Monroe felt snubbed. He allowed the Madison-hating congressman John Randolph to persuade him to contest his erstwhile friend in 1808. Jefferson could not stand by and allow a friendship to dissolve that was so critical to the political vision he had nurtured.

In March 1808, he reached out to Monroe, whom he always addressed with something like paternal affection, telling the unappreciated diplomat and former Virginia governor that he was listening to the wrong people and mistaking the state of things. "I cannot indeed judge what falsehoods may have been written or told . . . but you will soon find, my dear Sir, that so inveterate is the rancour of party spirit among us, that nothing ought to be credited but what we hear with our own ears."

Judgment could be clouded by listening to the wrong people, which Jefferson does not seem to have applied to himself (that is, not since he told Washington of his having been "duped" by Hamilton).

In Jefferson's construction, Monroe was allowing himself to be taken in by "the designs of the mischief-makers." He swore that Madison had not said a negative thing about Monroe. "I presume that the most insidious falsehoods are daily carried to you, as they are brought to me, to engage us in the passions of our informers." He didn't believe the gossip, he said, and neither should Monroe. "My knolege of your character is better testimony to me of a negative, than any affirmative which my informant did not hear *from yourself* with his own ears." Here, Jefferson is playing the therapist. "Little is to be believed which interests the prevailing passions, and happens beyond the limits of our own senses. Let us not then, my dear friend, embark our happiness, and our affections, on the ocean of slander, of falsehood & of malice, on which our credulous friends are floating."

Reaching the nub of his appeal to Monroe, he made it even more personal: "If you have been made to believe that I ever did, said, or thought a thing unfriendly to your fame & feelings, you do me injury as causeless as it is afflicting to me." Knowing that only one statement would succeed as a balm, he affected complete neutrality in the presidential contest to come, when in fact he desired the transition that ultimately occurred: Madison, then Monroe. "In the present contest in which you are concerned," he professed, "I feel no passion, I take no part, I express no sentiment. Whichever of my friends is called to the supreme cares of the nation, I know that they will be wisely & faithfully administered." All he wanted was "to pass in tranquility, in the bosom of my family & friends the days which yet remain for me." The retiring president wanted the Albemarle neighbor who took his "partie quarrée" idea most to heart to believe that he wanted to be left out of presidential politicking. It wasn't the whole truth, not even close.[38]

Either Monroe chose to believe, or was satisfied with the effort to assuage. He needed little time before burying whatever dissatisfaction he'd shown toward Jefferson, but he did not fully reconcile with Madison for three years, at which point he accepted an invitation to join the presidential cabinet—and didn't look back.

Jefferson's presidency ended inconclusively, and yet in one sense at least, time had its healing effect. After 1809, his debilitating headaches never returned. In ensuing years, he kept in close communication with his back-to-back Virginia Republican successors as both managed to grow in approval over their two terms—a rare feat among American presidents. Likely because of his two successors' popularity in overseeing the restoration of hopeful patriotism after a second British war, Jefferson's "Revolution of 1800" crystallized in the third president's memory as a hallowed moment in history. In 1819, when he coined the phrase, he anointed himself, on behalf of the citizenry at large, the undeniable victor in a dire struggle for the survival of a beautiful idea. Justice Chase died in 1811. The Republican whose prospects Jefferson (intentionally) and Hamilton (inadvertently) together destroyed, Aaron Burr, spent five long years in European exile before quietly returning to New York in disguise. He reopened his law practice once he received assurances that his own legal woes were over.

Preparing Madison for what he could expect to face in office that might not otherwise be obvious, Jefferson brought up an anonymous letter he'd received from New York. "This is one of the wretched, and dastardly productions, to which the cowards dare not put their names, of which I have recieved, and you will recieve thousands." Without a modern secretarial staff, the president found himself reading mail from strangers, some of which was worthy of a response. But, he cautioned, "of all the anonymous letters which have been constantly pouring in upon me, not more than half a dozen have been written with good views." This was, predictably, an exaggeration, the point nonetheless being that the "ill-tempered and rascally part of our country" took to writing the president "from tavern scenes of drunkenness." And yet, Thomas Jefferson persisted in writing to members of the rising generation that he believed the majority of voting citizens to be sober republicans of a mature disposition.[39]

To judge from the correspondence of his retirement years, he stopped fretting about newspaper editors and others who'd hounded him. There were always exceptions, but with Virginians at peak strength in the executive and legislative branches of government, the Jeffersonian idea of a republic was, in his mind, properly vindicated. There were still Federalists around, and they grumbled; but post–War of 1812 America was the one Jefferson had dreamt of, an expanding empire that had come through crises and appeared unstoppable.[40]

That realization should have been enough. But even his heartening account of the "Revolution of 1800" did not clinch "tranquil permanent felicity" while his obsession with John Marshall persisted. The reigning chief justice only grew in stature, while his Federalist-friendly take on America's post-Revolutionary history stood undefeated. Jefferson had his work cut out for him as he plotted revenge.

PART IV

Imperiled Legacy

Practically, we perceive only the past, the pure present being the invisible progress of the past gnawing into the future.

—HENRI BERGSON, *MATTER AND MEMORY* (1896)

History, True or False, speaks to our passions always.

—LORD BOLINGBROKE, *LETTERS ON THE STUDY AND USE OF HISTORY* (1752)

Figure 19. Monticello, in a popular nineteenth-century engraving by John Chester Buttre (1821–1893).

CHAPTER 13

"Suspicions & Certainties, Rumors & Realities"

Exorcising Washington's Ghost

"Heaven only knows what will become of this poor thoughtless family." The author of these words bore the same name, since marriage, that the mother of Thomas Jefferson was known by before marriage: Jane Randolph. But this Randolph, born Jane Hollins Nicholas, was the wife of Thomas Jefferson's eldest grandson, Thomas Jefferson Randolph, known within the family as Jefferson or Jeff. As an eyewitness to the last days of the family patriarch, Jane Randolph was as helpless as the rest of the Jefferson-Randolph line to stave off the collapse of a dreamworld.

Her husband had traveled many miles, leading up to this moment, in a last ditch attempt to raise funds and rescue his grandfather from total ruin. Back at Monticello in late June 1826, he ministered to the dying man, at the same time tending to his disconsolate mother, Martha Jefferson Randolph. Jane recoiled at each report from her husband. The feeble eighty-three-year-old was refusing medicine and "talks in the most heart breaking way," as she informed her sister. It was not his own life that concerned him anymore, but that of his dear, ever-dutiful daughter. Exacting a promise from Jeff that he'd never leave his mother's side, the fast-declining patient, in Jane's words, "tells him that she is sinking every day under the suffering she endures, and that she is literally dying before his eyes."

Jeff thought otherwise. He judged his mother "more calm & resigned" than expected, though her father had left both of them with an immense burden. The worst of it was his mismanagement of the family's far-flung properties. Monticello itself was likely to be lost. Jane again: "The younger ones look forward to nothing but misery."[1]

What they could not bear was penury. Thomas Jefferson had lived far above his means. The only family member who stood any chance of salvaging their dignity was Jane's husband. At thirty-three, Jeff was the age his grandfather was in 1776. He hoped to keep Monticello in the family through a national lottery, but was close to accepting that the debt was insurmountable. The final straw had been the financial downfall of Wilson Cary Nicholas, Jane's father, a former U.S. senator and Virginia governor, who had been lain to rest in the Monticello graveyard in 1820. Nicholas's death at fifty-nine had occurred not long after Jefferson had cosigned for a loan he'd agreed to, purely out of friendship. They fed off each other's suffering. Now Martha Jefferson Randolph was feeding off the suffering of her world-famous father. Monticello's enslaved would suffer still more.[2]

As he lay helpless, Thomas Jefferson did what he could to control his death, if only symbolically. He scripted his end when he prepared a text for his surviving daughter to find. In his ever careful hand, he titled his final statement to her "A death-bed Adieu." The eight-line verse opens: "Life's visions are vanished, it's dreams are no more." He concludes the touching poem with the promise to convey Martha's love to the "Two Seraphs" who await him, her sister and mother.[3]

Jefferson's unforgotten love for Martha's seraphic mother is most poignantly displayed in his retention of the square scrap of paper on which they shared the lines from Laurence Sterne's *Tristram Shandy*—"time wastes too fast..."—in Patty's hand. The bereaved daughter discovered it just after her father's death in the drawer next to his bed. We have no other specimen of any of the letters from Jefferson to his wife during the weeks and months he was away from her in Revolutionary times. They might have resembled Jeff Randolph's pining letter to Jane from Richmond as he was arranging for legislative approval of the lottery. "For godsake," Jeff pleaded, "write to me twice a week. We have the prospect of affluence and ease the residue of our lives. If you preserve your health I shall be happy. Without you all events will be alike a blank to me. With you only I have known happiness. Your arms have been the haven of all my passions, hopes & fears. Kiss the little ones. God bless you. Your devoted husband." Theirs was a growing family—the sixth daughter, Maria Jefferson Randolph, was born on February 2,

1826, the date this particular letter was likely received. She would live to see the twentieth century.[4]

In a handwritten personal memoir composed after the Civil War, near the end of his own life, Thomas Jefferson Randolph recalled with feeling how devoted he was to his closest relatives: "My grandfather, my mother, and my wife, were my earthly Trinity." Famously—miraculously, it was said—Thomas Jefferson and John Adams made it a point to exit the world on the fiftieth anniversary of American independence, July 4, 1826. Jefferson's heirs were left in dire straits, while the American people were collectively struck dumb by the very improbable, hallowing coincidence of the two long-lived Revolutionaries' "immaculate" deaths.[5]

"WE HAVE BEEN TOO CARELESS OF OUR REPUTATIONS"

In preparing for her father's retirement from the presidency in the spring of 1809, Martha Jefferson Randolph came with her large brood from nearby Edgehill, the twenty-four-hundred-acre plantation of the Randolphs, to assume management of the Monticello household. The emotionally unstable Tom Randolph had the utmost respect for his father-in-law, and so he nodded his agreement in the matter of where he and his wife lived, knowing whose interests always came first.

In the 1810 census, the ex-president indicated that the residents of Monticello included not just Martha, Tom, and nine children, but also Tom's sister and her children (living there only temporarily), as well as Charles Bankhead, husband of Martha's eldest, Anne. Bankhead would be yet another who caused Jefferson profound sorrow, when grandson Jeff defended his sister from spousal abuse and, in 1819, suffered knife wounds at the hands of his bad-tempered, alcoholic brother-in-law. Hearing the near-tragic news as darkness fell, the grandfather promptly rode to his grandson's side. As he knelt beside his namesake, the two cried together. Anne died young, in the sadly familiar fashion, when she failed to recover from childbirth. That was in February 1826, mere months before her grandfather entered his final illness.[6]

Though his closest friends lived in the President's House from 1809 to 1825, Jefferson never once returned to the nation's capital. During the final seventeen years of his life, he reordered his papers, made the case for the version of post-Revolutionary history he wanted posterity to have, and pursued (with little immediate success) potential authors to work with his papers at Monticello and chronicle that history.

In 1829, as literary executor, Thomas Jefferson Randolph published an extensive selection of Jefferson's correspondence, in four volumes. The first opens with a partial "Memoir," which Jefferson composed at the age of seventy-seven, in 1821. It is a disappointing document, written in the first person, yet more like an encyclopedia entry than a personal text. A long section narrates the preparation, drafts, and discussions that surrounded the Declaration of Independence. Explaining the process that resulted in *Notes on Virginia*, Jefferson relates his habit of jotting information "which might be of use to me in any station, public or private . . . on loose papers, bundled up without order." He felt so dishonored by a botched French translation of *Notes*, he says, that he accepted the offer of a London printer to carry forward with the English language original. Even in this enterprise, then, Jefferson desires his reader—historians—to understand that he did not publish his one meaningful book from any giant ambition.

Jefferson does all he can to control the telling of his life story without taking director's credit. He portrays himself as a reluctant hero, giving passive approval to all that brings him notice. He justifies his initial dissent from elements in the Constitution: "I expressed freely, in letters to my friends, and most particularly to Mr. Madison and General Washington, my approbations and objections." Including Washington among "my friends" was not accidental.

Retrospectively, it all makes perfect sense: Jefferson has his position in 1787–1788 neatly align with a progressive narrative, favoring, for example, a single-term presidency of seven years. Though he'd feared "the fierce contentions it might excite," the "practice adopted" by Washington and his three Virginian successors, in retiring after eight years, was evidence of the power of precedent in their sensible republic. Conveniently, the autobiography cuts off upon his return home from France in 1789, in this way avoiding having to address any of the issues that befell him in the Washington administration.

Which is not to say he avoided the difficult decade of the 1790s in all respects. In 1818, he went to lengths to have his contemporaneous notes dating to the Washington administration (known collectively as the *Anas*) bound in three volumes, so they would be published after his death. The *Anas* would serve as damning evidence that Hamilton was a thoroughgoing monarchist, Washington his unfortunate pawn. As a contemporaneous record of privileged conversations, Jefferson's memoranda were meant to be seen as more credible than memories recorded later or secondhand reports by those who might dispute him. He was there, in the room where it happened. Given the right biographer, he figured, *his* view of history would be standardized.[7]

The crucial decade of the 1790s has spawned countless histories over two centuries. Few of their authors go beyond the bitter cabinet contest to take stock of what Jefferson and Hamilton had in common: a commanding sense of their respective roles in the nation's future. They were two self-possessed seekers of influence who thought not of instant gratification, but of long-term, irreversible government solutions. Hamilton was the more open about his ambition. He was fiercely aggressive, with a more reptilian urge to go after what he wanted. Jefferson was just as intense as Hamilton, but passive aggressive. Whenever he could, he had others fight his battles. Hamilton won converts as a force of nature, pushing and prodding and brimming with an overpowering self-confidence. Jefferson tried instead to charm those who were on the receiving end of his effusive letters. It follows that Jefferson was branded by political enemies as sneaky and underhanded. He was able to pitch even his complaints in a way that sounded ungrudging, almost a heartfelt lament. Hamilton's words were decidedly less beautiful, deployed as bludgeons, though he, too, played the victim card.

The two party leaders differed less in their determination than in their styles. Fresh from France in 1790, Jefferson tried a form of state diplomacy in his dealings with President Washington—a honed skill that proved ineffective in a cabinet dynamic. If Patrick Henry won in courtrooms by offering his hearers impassioned and amusing oratory, Hamilton won in the cabinet by clever gamesmanship. Jefferson was not known for, or adept at, theatrical display. And yet, between Hamilton and Jefferson, one cannot easily say which of the two had a greater ambition to reshape the world. As president, Jefferson proved to be more like Hamilton than he could ever admit—not as militant, perhaps, but as intolerant and uncompromising.

Hamilton's premature death obviously made Jefferson's job rewriting their history easier. He could control some things, but he could not control John Marshall, who would continue to dominate the Supreme Court for another six years after Jefferson's death. The chief justice had been granted special access to Washington's private papers. He was able to declare victory over Jefferson with a well-respected five-volume biography of Washington that bore an unmistakably Federalist gloss. The fifth volume, recounting the politics of the 1790s, came out in 1807, the year of the Burr trial and lead-up to the unpopular embargo, when Jefferson was tied up in knots, emotionally wrought, and in no mood for another Marshall takedown.

As an ex-president, he committed himself to overturning Marshall's "five volumed libel" in every way he could. He turned first to the worldly Joel Barlow, a Yale graduate and patriotic poet who came to Jefferson's attention in Paris and went on to collaborate with the politically like-minded Thomas Paine. But Barlow died in 1812, while on a diplomatic mission in Europe for President Madison.

The last of the potential biographers Jefferson pursued was Associate Justice William Johnson, a Jefferson appointee from South Carolina. In 1822–23, Jefferson pitched the project, sending long letters and no doubt thinking how fitting it would be if one Supreme Court justice would undo the damage to Jefferson's reputation done by another. "We have been too careless of our reputations," he appealed to his fellow Republican, "while our tories will omit nothing to place us in the wrong."

While Marshall lived, Jefferson could not entirely avoid the discomfiture wrought by thoughts of politics past. One way to realize his goal was in bringing life to the University of Virginia in his final decade, framing a curriculum in which America's founding principles were taught the "right" way. Yet no matter where he directed his energies, he could not possibly think to abandon the cause of seeing his preferred narrative put into print and disseminated. When a second Adams took the oath of office as the sixth president in 1825, ending the twenty-four-year Virginia dynasty, Jefferson recoiled in the belief that the monarchical seed might soon sprout again. By then, he was virtually alone in such belief, but he just couldn't help himself.[8]

Monarchy was both a literal and symbolic enemy in the Jeffersonian lexicon. His utter abhorrence for the predatory nature of monarchical government, as it was then practiced, triggered the rousing rhetoric he frequently resorted to in his political letters. He'd present two extremes when he was really making a more general point about *tendencies*. One had to know when he was writing for effect and when he was dead serious. An argument he made in a letter home during his residence in France exemplifies the way he framed this sort of argument.

> I am convinced that those societies (as the Indians) which live without government enjoy in their general mass an infinitely greater degree of happiness than those who live under European governments. Among the former, public opinion is in the place of law, and restrains morals as powerfully as laws ever did any where. Among the latter, under pretence of governing they have divided their nations into two classes, wolves and sheep. I do not exaggerate. This is a true picture of Europe.[9]

But he *does* exaggerate to make his point. Jefferson was not claiming that the comparative lack of government authority among Native tribes was to be philosophically balanced against European forms, any more than his description of Indigenous peoples as "merciless Indian Savages" in the Declaration of Independence was a blanket statement about Indians. In that case, he was embellishing the fact that Indian auxiliaries, like Hessian mercenaries, were instruments used in carrying out a brutal policy—just one more damning accusation to be leveled at the unfeeling king.

In later years, Jefferson had a hard time separating "excess government" from a slide into despotism. In charging monarchical regimes with the oppression of their people (wolves vs. sheep), he was saying that Indians' democratic social management practices encouraged moral behavior just as well as, if not better than, a cumbersome body of laws and legal enforcement mechanisms that dictated behavior, undermining freedom. Extreme contrast was how he amplified a message.[10]

As a democratic theorist, Jefferson was quite radical and overly optimistic. Despite having proven himself a strong national executive, he carried into his retirement a prejudice in favor of state and local initiative and the precept that Union could only be held together by asserting equality among the states. As the legal historian Matthew Crow has summarized the Jeffersonian creed: "public liberty cannot survive being subject to a singular and potentially arbitrary will"; democracy required "a fragmenting and diffusion of sovereign judgment across multiple spaces of both legal and political deliberative activity." Diffusion of sovereignty was Jefferson's ultimate resolve as a constitutionalist.

An educated citizenry was the one contingency Jeffersonian democracy could not do without. Exiting the presidency and envisioning his University, he started thinking again about the education package he'd conceived—and failed to convince Virginia's miserly legislature to invest in—during the Revolution. Small-scale "ward republics," as he denoted them, were to provide public-funded education to the very young and select those for continued support beyond the elementary level, whose minds proved most supple. In Jeffersonian theory, the course of morality gleaned from the study of history and government would enable citizens to choose their governors wisely.[11]

The equation of Federalism with monarchy or a monarchist-leaning philosophy of government ("tory" being a stand-in for that) is where Jefferson's emotionalism becomes quite personal. His manipulation of language is disproportionate to the problem he perceives; and his choleric association of Marshall's history of the two parties with a perversion of republicanism is hard to defend. He appears to be saying that his advocacies in the 1790s and beyond preserved, if they did not in fact define, the Spirit of 1776, and that the memory of 1776 would be lost *if the history of his times and Washington's times conflicted.*

Proof of Jefferson's fixation on John Marshall's Washington biography lies in his construction of the *Anas*. In explaining to posterity how he innocently (as a memory aid) began to collect the timely notes that comprised this record of cabinet meetings, he writes: "I made memorandums on loose scraps of paper, taken out of my pocket in the moment, and laid by to be copied fair at leisure, which however they hardly ever were." Thus clarifying why it took him so long to assemble "these scraps, . . . ragged, rubbed, & scribbled as they were," he documented how, years into his retirement, a bookbinder came to Monticello to help him put everything into readable form once Jefferson was in the proper frame to have "given to the whole a calm revisal, when the passions of the time are past [*sic*] away." Explaining that he expunged from the whole those notes he had taken that proved "incorrect, or doubtful, or merely personal or private," he clearly implies that what was left could be seen as the whole truth of who said what, when the fate of the republic hung in the balance.

These were, Jefferson swore, "authentic" documents, belatedly "laid open to the public eye" so as to amend the historical record and prove him guiltless in all things. For his own satisfaction, he had to perform a bit of magic in the *Anas* to reclaim Washington for the Republican brand and in so doing make himself the worthy successor to Washington. It would not be easy to draw a direct line, but that was his objective. Consciously or not, he was grooming history so that he would descend through the ages as an even better republican than Washington, leaving to the general the birth of the republic while elevating himself as its perfector.

In praising the so-called "First among Men" in the reconstructed *Anas*, he finds it necessary to assert: "We are not to suppose that every thing found among Genl Washington's papers is to be taken as gospel truth." As to the gospels, Jefferson cannot resist a squib (citing as an authority his friend Dr. Benjamin Rush, a man of faith), attesting that no clergyman had ever heard George Washington express his belief in Christianity. Jefferson adds a second character witness, Washington's trusted ally Gouverneur Morris—"who pretended to be in his secrets" and who "often told me" that Washington was indeed a nonbeliever. Jefferson balances his criticism of the popular first president by refusing to question his motives, underscoring that they "merit veneration and respect." He wants it known that he never lost any admiration for Washington, "for few men have lived whose opinions were more unbiassed and correct." But he cannot let even this statement stand: "Not that it is pretended he never felt bias. His passions were naturally strong; but his reason, generally, stronger."

And how does Jefferson back up these words? He feels it incumbent on him to include in the *Anas*—and, intuiting his grandfather's desire, Thomas Jefferson Randolph does not edit it out—a raw characterization of a cabinet meeting that took place in August 1793. "The President was much inflamed," the gossipy cabinet officer starts. "Got into one of those passions when he cannot command himself; ran on much on the personal abuse which had been bestowed on him; defied any man on earth to produce one single act of his since he had been in the government, which was not done on the purest motives." Jefferson, feigning subtlety, raises the question of whether some of Washington's papers, as they lay exclusively in Marshall's hands, might have been improperly interpreted; because, as worthy as Washington was of "the love, the veneration, and confidence of all," it was no less true that "with him were deposited suspicions & certainties, rumors & realities, facts & falsehoods." The irony here is that Jefferson, as he emerges in the present study, could just as easily be described as a mix of "suspicions & certainties, rumors & realities, facts & falsehoods." In capturing Washington's humanity, he reconditioned his own.

John Marshall's father and George Washington had been friends from young adulthood. It was obvious to Jefferson—who now wore the garb of a ruthless book critic—that Washington's correspondence had been improperly interpreted: "History may be made to wear any hue, with which the passions of the compiler, royalist or republican, may chuse to tinge it," the *Anas* reads. Next, an even more assertive statement: "Had Gen¹ Washington himself written from these materials a history of the period they embrace, it would have been a conspicuous monument of the integrity of his mind, the soundness of his judgment, and it's powers of discernment between truth & falshood, principles & pretensions."

It is clear what's going on here. Jefferson is reclaiming Washington for himself and his cause by attacking Marshall's prejudicial construction: "The party feelings of his biographer, to whom after his death the collection was confided, have culled from it a composition, as different from what Gen¹ Washington would have offered." Now he goes in for the kill: "Let no man believe that Gen¹ Washington ever intended that his papers should be used for the suicide of the cause, for which he had lived, and for which there never was a moment in which he would not have died." "Suicide" is a pretty strong word—deliberately chosen, of course.

Jefferson will not let up. He allows us to see why he needs for his *Anas* to exist in the world as a counterweight to Marshall. If he, Jefferson, does not amend the historical record (with "scraps" over which his mind and hands exercise control), he assumes no one else will. The "abuse" of Washington's papers was, he says, "chiefly however manifested in the history of the period immediately following the establishment of the present constitution; and nearly with that my memorandums begin." Again, it could not be more plain: Marshall can have the pre-1789 Washington, but cannot be thought credible in portraying the post-1789 Washington.

All that mattered to Jefferson was that posterity should obey *his* pen and cast its lot with *his* contemporaneous record that gave the lie to Federalism's version of history. The *Anas* came at the tail end of the final volume of his grandson's collection. Exposing Jefferson as a partisan warrior, Jefferson's "memorandums," once published, were the genie that could not be put back in the bottle.[12]

Sensing what might come next, editor Jeff Randolph exercised caution. In March 1829, he heard from his younger brother Benjamin Franklin Randolph that Jefferson's set of Marshall's *Washington* had already escaped the family's clutches when their grandfather's possessions were being sold, bit by bit, as part of the effort to save Monticello. It was time for the family to close ranks: "Ben Tells me the Life of Washington by Marshall was filled with notes in my grand fathers hand writing," he informed his brother-in-law Nicholas Trist. "Might there not be some which prudence would require not to be published during Marshalls life?" Trist was thought to have the best chance of succeeding in buying them back, or at least persuading the new owner not to let them out of his hands for the foreseeable future. Were Jefferson's marginalia to be made public, they would provide new fodder for old enemies.[13]

From these revelations, it becomes clearer that Jefferson took deliberate measures over the course of his public life, and into retirement, to fashion a morally secure persona that future generations would adopt and cherish. He wanted to be known to posterity in the precise terms he presented: as a fair-minded man who faced challenges head-on and responded to crises with justice and equanimity, seizing opportunities to strengthen and improve his nation. This became the dominant narrative that established "Jeffersonian democracy" as the essence of what America aspired to be, what freedom was.

What we have seen over the preceding chapters, however, is a rather different story of personality development, and a book without investment in the validation of a moral identity, either for Thomas Jefferson or for the idea of America that he contributed so much to. Intimate history, as biography, finds a firmer basis in the flesh-and-blood individual's turn of mind: his impulses, inclinations, wit, and whims, all that shaped him as a social being. It regards him as a product of his culture.

That complicated person exercised a unique influence over the language of politics, establishing the main attributes of the republican ethos and fashioning a memorable place for himself in the national imagination. Nevertheless, Jefferson's reflections on his own history must remain at least partially suspect, just as his recollection for John Adams of the Williamsburg speech of the Cherokee chief Outassetè was. In writing his life story in the letters and scraps he preserved, he meant for us to accept an autobiographical narrative that he effectively denied being autobiography, professing it as raw, undressed, unrefined evidence, a verbatim recording free of biased commentary. Yet it was handpicked, hand-ordered, a line of bread crumbs for historians to reconstruct as an illuminating account of American history. It was autobiography disguised as others' biographies.[14]

THE ANDROGYNOUS JEFFERSON

His notable and enduring hatreds aside, and as improbable as it seems looking backward from the 1820s, Jefferson believed in friendship as an organizing principle and "harmony and affection" as its political embodiment. The "harmony and affection" he introduces into his First Inaugural, "without which liberty and even life itself are but dreary things," is unabashedly sentimental. It converts the ambiguous conception of American liberty into something said to be intuitively experienced under conditions then existing—"liberty" becomes an almost rapturous form of awareness, a can-do political faith prescribed by an avowed rationalist in religion. Thinking to the future, Jefferson very much intended to spur a nostalgic impulse, wishing that later generations would reawaken a sleeping spirit and imagine the "Spirit of '76" and the "Revolution of 1800" as a golden age. Whether or not Jefferson made it happen, his fantasy of America was often enough repeated that this is how millions of Americans have been taught to regard the founders writ large.

"Harmony and affection" is nothing less than Jefferson preaching his personal gospel. In 1818, to Henry Dearborn, his former secretary of war, he swelled: "In looking back on past life the greatest pleasure I feel, is in recollections of the friends who have been my fellow-laborers, & my greatest happiness in the harmony and affection in which I lived & parted with them." The next year was when Jefferson proclaimed the Revolution of 1800 "as real a revolution in the principles of our government as that of 76. was in it's form." As a hallowed event, it deified him in the republican firmament. George Washington had no such ambition. Nor did the self-aggrandizing Hamilton. Jefferson's commitment to legacy was extraordinary.

To win people's affections was to win the future. He had gone to great lengths to confront Marshall. One carefully crafted letter at a time, he abetted the cause of posthumous vindication. It was on his mind when he solicited help from younger politicians, and when, days before death, he invited a dissenting writer to inspect his papers, hoping for a change of heart. Having taken these steps to curate his own afterlife, he was assured that his grandchildren's generation would pick up where he left off.[15]

Which is precisely what happened. The Randolphs did everything possible to bring the best Jefferson to light. A quarter century after his death, the grandchildren, themselves aging, opened their hearts to Henry S. Randall (1811–1876), an upstate New York Democrat. In 1858, he gave the world *The Life of Thomas Jefferson*, a solid three-volume biography of a man of exquisite character whose words stirred the spirit and who loved his family and his country beyond measure.

On the subject of Jefferson's *Anas*, Randall is quite chatty. He concedes that they were "undoubtedly" brought together in one place so that they could readily be published—but only if the Federalist resurgence Jefferson was afraid of occurred, causing the truth about Hamilton's political perversions to be "concealed from the popular knowledge," in which case Jefferson's memorandums would stand as an "expedient" and be used exclusively for the purpose of preventing the vigorous republic he adored from rumbling its way to monarchy. "But the designs of the Federalists were not successful," Randall sighed. "No minute documentary evidence became necessary to expose and overthrow their projects, whatever they were." The biographer goes on for sixteen pages, justifying the *Anas* while excoriating Marshall's treatment of Jefferson and other Republicans in *Life of Washington*. With malice aforethought, Marshall effectively described Jefferson as a longtime critic of Washington who, as a member of his cabinet, "secretly and sedulously" organized a party against his president. Jefferson in turn felt Marshall's attack as (in Randall's words) "mortal stabs" to "both his reputation as a statesman and a man."

Defending Jefferson as none but his surviving family members could, Randall reprinted an 1808 critique of Marshall's *Washington* extracted from the greatly esteemed *Edinburgh Review*, with such lines as "We look in vain, through these stiff and countless pages, for any sketch or anecdote that might fix a distinguishing feature of private character in the memory." Rendering a verdict on the biography's "pronounced dullness and frigidity," the reviewer complains that heroic biography is vapid when the writer maintains "a most dignified and mortifying silence" about his subject's humanity.[16]

Randall could never be accused of portraying Thomas Jefferson as frigid, let alone depriving him of a soul. The family's authorized biographer was granted access to every Jefferson manuscript remaining in their possession, along with artifacts that Randall took home and treated as sacred relics. In describing the widower's relationship with daughters Martha and Maria, Randall attributed to Jefferson "a feminine general cast of his feelings," saying that he was a man who could be all things to all people, paternal and maternal.

A close family friend, Margaret Bayard Smith, also saw in Jefferson, from their first encounter in 1800, an unruffled demeanor that did not change, which was more or less the feminine ideal of his time and place. She described his voice as "almost femininely soft and gentle." Her description tracks with his intense ("female") response to the death of his wife. According to gender-specific patterns (as they were understood at the time), the feminine character engaged in a lengthy, overly emotional grieving process, sentimentalized the loved one's grave, and nourished memory by keeping the remains physically close. Modern psychologists regard such behavioral tendencies as *personality-based androgyny*, nonconforming to static gender roles. In the modern clinical sense, Jefferson's actions are seen as conducive to a healthy mental outlook. He can be described, in that sense, as a "nurturant," which we also see manifest in his profound love of the garden and the ecstatic joy he experienced watching its flowering alongside his growing grandchildren.[17]

It is important for Randall (no doubt prompted by the grandchildren) to defend the third president at great length against the charge that he was an atheist. This was one of the most troubling of Jeffersonian legacies circulating among Randall's contemporaries that the biographer sought to put to rest. Published at a time when both North and South claimed Jefferson for their cause, Randall's *Life* depicted a moral exemplar and a benevolent slave owner. And, relying on the stated memories of the grandchildren who had at least occasional access to his private spaces, one who could not possibly have been intimate with a woman he owned.[18]

THE INVISIBLE WORLD OF SALLY HEMINGS

Before passing judgment, our century is called upon to accept that what we label as social transgressions might have been classed as regrettable facts of life then; or, as in the case of patriarchy, almost set in stone. Jefferson owned hundreds of human beings. There is scarcely any doubt now that he had sex with a woman he'd inherited as property. He wrote eloquently as he called out the dehumanizing effect of slavery, but he willed freedom to his enslaved flesh and blood while leaving many other individuals to suffer terribly. It is impossible to think of this kind of human tragedy merely as "regrettable facts of life." Because he died over $100,000 in debt (several millions in today's dollars), the majority of those he kept in bondage were sold along with Monticello, a good many separated from the people and places they'd long known. It went beyond poor planning.[19]

Jefferson's most significant statement on slavery after the presidency, showing again the impotency he felt, is the oft-quoted "wolf by the ear" parable associated with the future of slavery in the West. In 1820, he wrote to an incoming senator from the new state of Maine that the wolf could neither be held nor let go safely. He recognized the nation's predicament, but offered nothing different from what he wrote in *Notes on Virginia*: emancipation joined to expatriation. As Peter Onuf has incisively observed, "The anger many Americans now feel toward Jefferson testifies to the difficulty of our ongoing struggle to break the disastrous and destructive link he helped forge between race and nation."[20]

Jefferson was far from unique in his moral culpability. Few of the esteemed founders were financially comfortable at the end of their lives, and by the 1820s, slave breeding had grown into a profit center for landed Virginians whose agricultural output lagged. One planter who had a good head start and died well off, the "virtuous" George Washington, succeeded by exploiting the unearned advantages he had come into at birth, grabbing up choice land and squeezing his tenants for rent. He unashamedly brought enslaved people to serve him in the President's House; when one of them escaped to New Hampshire, he made long efforts to hunt her down and re-enslave her. Washington, Jefferson, and their ilk were conformists: we don't have to "like" them to study the conflicts and personal trials they faced as public figures.[21]

Men like Washington and Jefferson felt an aristocrat's sense of superiority. The essential difference between these two major landowners, aside from one's wealth and the other's debt, is that Washington's mindset more resembled that of a businessman, determinedly looking after his interests, an assertive, hands-on manager, to the extent that his outside responsibilities permitted it. The worldly Jefferson, equally a student of agricultural science, conducted his business more by necessity. In the final year of his life, he admitted to James Monroe, albeit with some false modesty: "To keep a Virginia estate together requires in the owner both skill and attention. Skill I never had and attention I could not have."[22]

If both he and Washington exploited their unfree labor in quest of profit, Jefferson spent more of his energies dreaming up charitable schemes he wasn't able to develop fully, like breeding Spanish Merino sheep for their soft wool. A lifelong experimenter, he learned about varieties of rice from as far away as Southeast Asia, and distributed samples to growers in South Carolina. Hungering for serviceable information to feed his grand plans, eager to share with farmers the world around, Jefferson possessed the expansive mind of a consummate aesthete who felt superior in taste, not just in judgment. He was a pursuer of beauty and the fabricator of an unrealized new world.[23]

Sally Hemings may well have possessed physical beauty. One assumes she did, for he pursued it. Whether she was attracted to him is rather less important, given her position as the daughter of an enslaved domestic servant and a full generation his junior. To the master, she was not a person of gentrified taste, but a person who answered to his needs. How she fitted into the world of his making, his Monticello retreat, can hardly have been a classic love story, though some have sought to imagine it, to ennoble her. In a way, the distinction between the Pocahontas myth (white-adjacent princess bride) and the darker, sexualized, expendable Indian "squaw" in American lore is mirrored in competing renderings of Sally Hemings as Jefferson's "surrogate wife" or the nonconsenting "Black Sal," the representation (or victim) of savage lust.[24]

The only marriage in this story is the connection we can surmise between Thomas Jefferson's inherited position in Virginia society and the lessons of experience—that is, the psychology attaching to a man who could feel and exhibit love, who knew profound loss, who sought to shelter himself from harm as much as his inventive mind could contrive. If he came to love the servant whom he took to his bed, we simply cannot know.

Which brings us back to the presumed start of the relationship: Paris, where so much else of consequence occurred to recast Thomas Jefferson's view of his purpose in life. He was in every respect a "citizen of the world" when the French Revolution broke out, when he sought to return his daughters to the United States, and along with them, James and Sally Hemings. The two Hemingses could have chosen to remain behind, and, under French law, remain free.

It is possible that a pregnant Sally Hemings contemplated having a fatherless child in Europe. But would such a man as Thomas Jefferson have been so cavalier as to give members of his enslaved "family" the power to contest his will, his determination that they accompany him home? How long would it have been before he wore them down? Knowing this master of argument better now, wouldn't he instead have affected to listen considerately, the better to bend to their will on one or another matter as it suited him? He coaxed and flattered others (younger and less experienced in politics than he) to do his bidding in Washington, so it is hardly conceivable that he performed less adroitly with those who were bound to him, to whom he routinely issued instructions.

The notion that Sally Hemings, at sixteen, at the urging of her proud, occasionally insistent older brother James, entered into a negotiation with Jefferson, the senior American diplomat in Paris, by throwing in his face the prospect of her life as a free woman is hard to accept on the face of it. It is quite possible that, as her son Madison Hemings related many decades later, she extracted a promise that the children of Jefferson whom she bore would be freed at twenty-one; but how strenuously these two young Hemingses wrestled with Jefferson to obtain concessions is very much open to question. When Jefferson agreed to free James in 1793, he did so by a written instrument expressing intent, but with no legal force, by which he presented himself as a generous, all-knowing patriarch who had authorized (if with some reluctance) this change in status: "Having been at great expence in having James Hemings taught the art of cookery, desiring to befriend him, and to require from him as little in return as possible, I do hereby promise and declare . . ." These words were followed by a critical contingency: James would first have to train his replacement in Monticello's kitchen.[25]

Would not Jefferson, in a paternalistic tone of voice, have reminded James and Sally at the end of their time in Paris that a man in his position offered them stability and sustenance, while a life in France as a free person offered no such benefits; that they would be living on their own in uncertain conditions amid social turmoil and economic insecurity? What value did freedom have for a young, vulnerable female, even if she did have a brother with culinary skills and a circle of friends?

After all, Patsy Jefferson, who was the same age as her younger sister's maid and who had been attending a fine school in the years preceding Sally and Maria's arrival, did not feel she could cajole rights or greater freedom from her demanding father. To be a dependent woman was to be placed in an unenviable position. To underscore the point, only months after returning to Albemarle, Patsy's father did more than give his blessing to her very early marriage to Tom Randolph; he orchestrated it and made sure she understood what a husband's rights were in a Virginia gentry marriage. The fiction of her consent, as a seventeen-year-old, in the decision to marry should not be removed from consideration.

In the absence of a single written word from Sally Hemings, history has precious little on which to judge her, despite the outstanding work of Annette Gordon-Reed in making the Hemingses historically whole—that is, complex actors with social prospects and enduring ties apart from their experiences as individuals born into slavery. But the fact is inescapable that Jefferson's concubine had emotions we will never have access to, and the question of consent cannot be resolved. Basically, we know that she was invested in her children's happiness, and that she was a dependent member of the Monticello household. No evidence exists that she had the power to resist her master's carnal desire, whether or not it was something she cared for. One cannot even begin to speculate on what she thought about her own position as a subject of local, then national gossip through the years in which she was continuing to bear Jefferson's children.

There is, however, tantalizing evidence from the real world of Sally Hemings that should not be overlooked. When Jefferson died, she removed a few seemingly insignificant items to retain as keepsakes, which later passed to her son Madison. These included an inkwell along with a pair of spectacles Jefferson wore. The inkwell presumably symbolized the writing he did in the privacy of his bedchamber, and the spectacles sat upon the eyes that had looked upon her own face. It is hard to dismiss her retention of such items as meaningless or emotionless.[26]

His feelings for Sally Hemings and the sons and daughters she bore him remain unclear. He must have felt tenderness, though Sally, as she appeared to those who labored in the vicinity, did not transcend her constricted (domestic) position subordinate to the white Jefferson-Randolphs. In psychological terms, to the degree that speculation is warranted, I posit that the catastrophic loss of Patty Jefferson in 1782 lingered with the overwrought widower, who was again obliged to face that kind of loss when his daughter Maria languished and died in 1804—once again at Monticello, once again after postpartum problems. He may well have opted not to remarry and procreate with a second Virginia planter's daughter, so as to avoid exposure to the kind of pain he knew he could not bear. Memory can be a heavy weight. Of course, that would have to imply that he valued Sally Hemings's life less than he would an imagined second wife. Or could it be that he simply wasn't willing to share Monticello with a wife who wasn't Patty, even if she would have brought him the kind of wealth that could alleviate the crushing Wayles debt?

There are many more unresolvable questions than there are likely answers here. His father-in-law, John Wayles, had turned to Sally Hemings's mother, Elizabeth, after losing three wives in succession. Rather than replicate this pattern, Jefferson avoided serial marriage and went directly to the last option for a sexually active Southern man of pronounced social stature: an enslaved woman. The losses she suffered when two (or possibly three) of their children died young were arguably somewhat more manageable for the father who would never have given his name to them. If his enslaved concubine had succumbed after one of those births, in his rationalizing mind the degree of pain and suffering would have been more supportable than the traumatic loss of his wife. It is a cold conclusion to draw, but one that I believe comports with Jefferson's hot-and-cold emotions.

I am suggesting that we should reckon with the "Sally Hemings story" as we do with evidence of Jefferson's personal anxieties as these emerge in all he wrote over the years. He rationalized almost effortlessly. On the basis of his extensive reading and thinking, he was convinced that he knew what was best. He felt morally secure. He doled out advice. He willfully shaped his legacy (or at least tried), and he managed his little mountain as he saw fit.

THE SOUND OF A BELL

When he was not feeling aggrieved by the prospect of influential Federalist voices outlasting his, or dodging creditors, Jefferson was reveling in his life in Nature. In one of his oft-quoted letters to the remarkable portrait painter, museum owner, and inventor Charles Willson Peale of Philadelphia, he wrote, "I have often thought that if heaven had given me choice of my position & calling, it should have been on a rich spot of earth, well watered, and near a good market for the productions of the garden. No occupation is so delightful to me as the culture of the earth, & no culture comparable to that of the garden." Then, preciously, "Tho' an old man, I am but a young gardener." It was Jefferson in his appealingly poetic mode, a naturalist who rhapsodized rural life as well-ordered and tranquil, generating not only real independence but also generosity and good manners.[27]

Peale was one of those talented Philadelphians whom Jefferson esteemed. In the City of Brotherly Love, the Virginian encountered literary wits, scientists, and experts in gardening like William Hamilton, with whom he had formed a strong horticultural bond in 1800. Peale painted Jefferson's portrait when the Virginian was secretary of state; subsequently, one of his artist sons, the aptly named Rembrandt Peale, painted Jefferson both as vice president and as president. All three portraits are detailed and evocative: light and color combine exquisitely.

From the elder Peale, Jefferson ordered two ingenious mechanical polygraphs constructed of mahogany and brass. Nothing else material so delighted him as this useful device: the writer moved the pen with one hand as a second pen replicated the letter. From approximately 1805, one polygraph sat on the desk in his Monticello study, another in the President's House. The more than two hundred letters Jefferson and Peale exchanged occasionally contained diagrams; they were two inveterate worshippers of natural beauty and mechanical invention who in old age conversed about health and diet, alike in their lifelong resort to experiment. Jefferson bathed his feet in cold water each morning, which he said prevented colds; among his books was a history of cold bathing. Peale used cool-water baths to ward off yellow fever. Both did what they thought possible to delay the body's inevitable breakdown.[28]

To another close Philadelphia friend, Dr. Benjamin Rush, Jefferson wrote in 1811 of his daily habit of exercise in the course of the workday: "My present course of life admits less reading than I wish. From breakfast, or noon at latest, to dinner, I am mostly on horseback, attending to my farms or other concerns, which I find healthful to my body, mind, & affairs." Jefferson always associated country living with improved prospects for health. He openly disputed many of the medical claims of his assertive friend Rush, having persuaded himself that Nature was the best healer for most human ills. He visualized Nature's developmental as well as wild character: it was dynamic, continuously changing and refreshing itself, and if only partially knowable, capable of revealing its healing potential to the individual who observed closely. Seeking Nature's counsel, he was skeptical of most forms of medicine (inoculation being a notable exception). This was one area of his daily life in which Jefferson's convictions regularly influenced him in practice.[29]

Peale had so often heard his friend's theories that in his first letter to Jefferson after the third president left Washington for good, the painter signed off with "The improvements of your farms I hope will give you funds of pleasing amusements, and that the exercise you must take in a salubrious air will contribute to good health and long life with a serene mind." It was an era when people braved an ocean voyage in order to cure themselves of serious respiratory ailments, and as early as 1772,

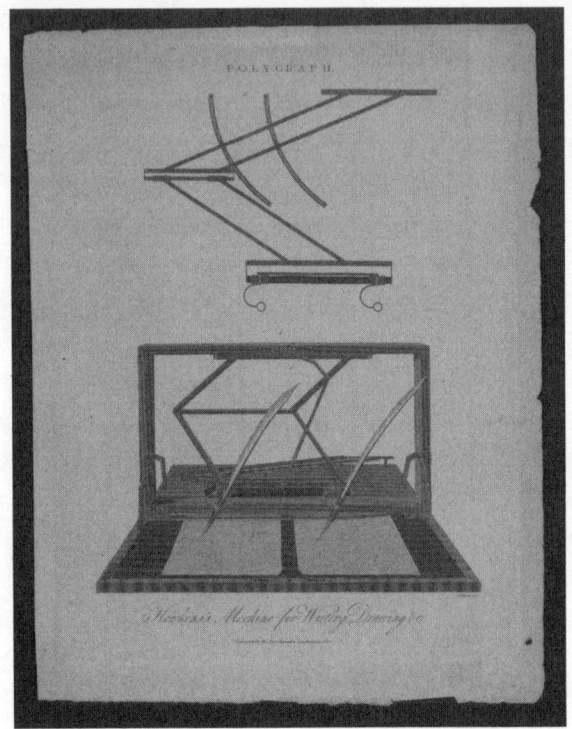

Figure 20. The polygraph, so named by its English inventor, John Isaac Hawkins (1772–1854), who supplied Jefferson through Charles Willson Peale of Philadelphia, the inventor's U.S. representative. During and after his presidency, Jefferson was able to make instantaneous copies of his letters by using this ingenious device. (Courtesy Library of Congress)

in *Experiments and Observations on Different Kinds of Air*, Dr. Joseph Priestley adopted Benjamin Franklin's idea that plants and woods were Nature's purifier, removing "effluvium" (carbon dioxide) from the air. Hence Jefferson had reason to tout the "salubrious air" of his mountain retreat. A Virginia physician of his acquaintance had written Jefferson in the summer of 1801, after learning from the newspaper that the president was taking time away from Washington: "Permit me to congratulate you on your good health & that you have leisure to pay this Visit, to your friends in Virginia & Enjoy for a moment retirement, & the Salubrious air of your Elevated & charming seat in Albemarle."[30]

When Jefferson entertained friends, young and not so young, in his retirement years, their reports combined a universal delight in the view from Monticello and appreciation for the host's entertaining and informative conversation. British lieutenant Francis Hall spent the night and left "with such a feeling as the traveller quits the mouldering remains of a Grecian temple, or the pilgrim a fountain in the desert." For Hall it was a sublime encounter. Madison and Monroe's attorney general, Richard Rush, a son of Benjamin Rush, wrote, "If it had not been called Monticello, I would call it Olympus." On summer days, "Grandpapa" organized footraces for the Randolph grandchildren, rewarding the winner with more pieces of figs, prunes, or dates than the slower ones received. He gazed on the flowerbeds when all was in bloom, gratified that the young ones shared in his enjoyment of the contrasting colors. He retired for the night at eight or nine or ten o'clock, read awhile, and slept anywhere from five to eight hours. "Our grandfather seemed to read our hearts, to see our invisible wishes," wrote one of the girls. Another recalled "how active was his step, how lively, even playful, were his manners." He spent money he didn't have on his grandchildren. He seemed not to want to know how desperate his finances were.[31]

He had fixed ideas about a good many things, manipulating life's complexities to satisfy an inner imperative that the world should conform to the vision he embraced. His will was strong; he could be quite obstinate. On the page, his artful and often seductive gestures describe what the French Romantic Charles Nodier (1780–1844) saw in a "reflective monomaniac," "the faulty logician of the real world," whose future-directed dreams affect how he sees all possibility. There is a proneness to personal tragedy implied in this characterization, for in replacing the emptiness of loss with proud convictions, Jefferson too often married his worldview to improbable outcomes. His intensity, his drive, was near determinative.[32]

As a pre-Romantic, Jefferson could not even match Rousseau's effort toward emotional self-discovery in the *Confessions*, the posthumously published work in which the quarrelsome Genevan sourced the growth of his imagination and acknowledged his many regrets. As a proto-Romantic, Jefferson pretended to dispassionate reasoning when he modeled the republic on a civic form of "harmony and affection." The outward calm everyone saw was entirely natural, but it was also a cruel camouflage for the frustration he felt in losing battles; that half-honest sense of himself as a "son of nature" ineffectively masked the anger he felt toward those whose bad-mouthing was offensive enough to justify his fighting for future honor. The closest Jefferson came to expressing a Romantic sensibility was his Head and Heart letter of 1786, when he revealed his desire for intimate companionship, acknowledged his hidden conflict, and tried to justify his vaunted optimism.

Despite his extreme record keeping, Nature's ungovernability lingered about Jefferson's creatively managed, ever improving mountain estate. Apart from his need for vindication in the public realm, which severely limited his capacity to bend, he remained a student of philosophy, which to him, as to the ancients, meant the art of living. In the privacy of his study, he found structure in a passion for solving intellectual problems—again, the combination of Head and Heart. On his horse, taking his daily exercise, away from the gaze of others, he descended from the top where he'd otherwise "look down into the workhouse of nature," as he told Maria Cosway, following the rustic course he'd laid out when Patty was alive, along "roundabouts" built by enslaved laborers. He circumnavigated the property at different elevations, attuned, observant. When he wasn't thinking about his material life, or the financial hole he'd dug for himself that would jeopardize the lives of his own family and the families he accepted as chattel, he studied Nature for consolation, a respite from pain. This kind of passion was nurturing, not disruptive. It was the welcome unknown. It was as close as he came to "letting go."

~

JEFFERSON OPENS HIS AUTOBIOGRAPHY by stating that his paternal lineage originated in Wales. At the end of the last century, a literary scholar from Cardiff, Wales, who specializes in the early-nineteenth-century imagination, came to Charlottesville to study the world Jefferson inhabited. Malcolm Kelsall experienced the stillness of the Monticello property, from base to summit, when the tourists were absent. He ventured into areas of the Blue Ridge that were visible to Jefferson, where an area comprising "tens of thousands of acres . . . remains as it was in the beginning, without culture, a space of infinite silence and of alien being." After completing research into Jefferson's romantic sensibility, the professor gathered his thoughts: "Monticello was never an achieved and fixed thing," he concluded measuredly. "It was first a projection upon futurity by Jefferson's imagination, then a project in decay." That says it all. With its architect's death, the property suffered egregious disregard over the ensuing decades. But while he lived, Jefferson maintained a strong sense of design: long-range plans for improvement and restoration were unremitting.[33]

In 1817, as construction of the University of Virginia was getting under way, Jefferson delivered a sales pitch to Thomas Cooper, a London-born, Oxford-educated religious skeptic, a victim of the Sedition Act, and a good friend of fellow exile Joseph Priestley. "The situation of Charlottesville is in a mountainous, healthy, fertile country," he prompted the émigré, boasting its combination of "delicious climate, good water, cheap subsistence, an independant yeomanry, many wealthy persons, good society, and free as air in religion and politics." It was, as he had informed Maria Cosway in 1786, a liberal dream in motion.[34]

The design of his university was decidedly health-conscious: low buildings with facing neoclassical pavilions across a generous lawn; covered walkways against the weather. Small, ground-level classrooms supported good air circulation. Six small dining halls were maintained so as to avoid excessive contact. Wholesome air was critical to Jefferson as he imagined a community of hungry minds coming from beyond the borders of Virginia to take in the good air and prescribed nutriment of central Virginia.[35]

True to form, after doing all he could to situate the university in his immediate neighborhood (on land previously owned by James Monroe), he micromanaged his brainchild by crafting its curriculum and seeking faculty who would preserve Enlightenment values and safeguard republicanism. He first dubbed it "an academical village," a coinage that has stuck, before making it into a more personal venture, a legacy project. If no state-sponsored "ward republic" came into being, he would at least make his academic dream come true, writing into reality the promise of an educable citizenry. He put his mark on the "village" with serpentine curves and tended gardens, declaring himself "Father of the University of Virginia" by commanding that his tombstone include those exact words.

Did he imagine it would be smooth sailing? The University of Virginia opened its doors in 1825, the year before Jefferson's death, and not all went according to plan while he yet lived. From the start of operations, students drank, gambled, and made mischief—not at all what the patriarch expected after having ridden five miles from his mountaintop every other day, year after year, overseeing construction. On the other hand, he evidently saw no problem with the fact that students had no responsibility for upkeep of their quarters: enslaved domestics cleaned their rooms, lit their fires, washed their clothes, polished their boots, and ran errands for them.[36]

The historian Andrew O'Shaughnessy recounts George Long's reflections on what it was like to come from England to teach the classical languages at "Mr. Jefferson's University." Mere days after his arrival, he ascended to Monticello and encountered the eighty-two-year-old, as so many before him had reported, "tall and dignified," "grave and rather cold in his manner," and "free from all affectation." As he came to know Jefferson better that year, Professor Long listened to his winsome host tell stories of the Revolutionary era while claiming for himself no more than a modest role. An out-of-control social gathering in the fall of 1825 resulted in one spoiled student's tossing a bottle through the teacher's window. By 1827, George Long had returned to England.[37]

Toward the end of his life, as visits from the doctor increased and "irritability of the bladder" (an enlarged prostate) called for the painful self-application of a bougie, walking became difficult for Jefferson. He was able to ride for exercise only when helped onto his horse. He told Peale that he spent upwards of three hours a day on horseback, "without fatigue." When he was ready to greet a visitor to Monticello, the enfeebled patriarch emerged from his secluded quarters, or "Cabinet." The family knew not to disturb him when he was at his writing desk with his books nearby, set at an angle on a rotating swivel stand that held five books at once. He was so intent on securing privacy that early in his occupancy he installed an indoor privy for himself: waste matter fell to ground level, where one of the enslaved was paid a modest bonus for taking care to cart it away. He had been troubled with diarrhea ("my visceral complaint") from his time as president; the condition worsened in his final years and was most likely the cause of his death.[38]

Daniel Webster, a forty-two-year-old congressman when he visited, gave a precise, close-up description of Jefferson in his final years. Noting the thinning of his hair, "once red, now turning gray," he analyzed the head, "set rather forward on his shoulders," and the chin, "rather long, but not pointed." Jefferson's mouth was unusual in that he'd been able to preserve his teeth, which might be why the mouth bore "an expression of contentment and benevolence." Webster found his subject's limbs to be "uncommonly long," matched by equally impressive hands and feet. "His walk is not precise and military, but easy and swinging." For a man of his advanced age, Thomas Jefferson appeared unusually healthy, his sight and hearing still good. That day, he was in the mood to talk about the Greek and Anglo-Saxon languages; and, for good measure, the American Revolution.[39]

An itinerant bookseller recorded the conversation he had with the mountaintop sage in the spring of 1824, some months before Webster made his way south. According to Samuel Whitcomb, Jefferson did not decline to answer any of his politically sensitive questions, or admittedly personal ones. On the subject of slavery, Jefferson repeated his colonizationist dictate, now looking favorably on the "experiment" of Haiti, a desirable island on which America's emancipated slaves might be resettled. Though he'd refused to recognize Haitian independence during his presidency, he thought the time had come. He restated his deep-seated prejudice against Blacks, denying them a mental capacity equal to that of whites while unconvincingly conceding, "They are possessed of the best hearts of any people in the world."

Regarding Georgia's claims to Indian lands, Jefferson exhibited similar condescension, with one difference: he held to the opinion he'd expressed to Secretary of War Henry Knox in 1791, when he was secretary of state, that "Indians have a right to the occupation of their Lands independent of the States within whose chartered lines they happen to be." It was up to the tribes to decide when it felt right to sell. Whitcomb quotes him as labeling Georgia "the most greedy of land of any State." This is a less calculating Jefferson than the one who, as president, gave William Henry Harrison the idea of manipulating Indians into selling their lands: "We shall push our trading houses, and be glad to see the good & influential individuals among them run in debt." Again, one must exhibit caution before seizing on a single Jefferson quote as the unchanging essence of his character; it appears here that long-assimilated Indian tribes of the Atlantic states were to be given more consideration than those whose encounters with whites had begun more recently.[40]

On the subject of religion, Jefferson broke from his usual posture when he spoke to his visitor. He'd hidden his personal religious views from the public as best he could over the years, always urging correspondents not to publish anything he revealed in a personal letter that touched at all on religion. From the moment his "twenty gods or no god" quip made the rounds after *Notes on Virginia* was put in print, he was plenty exposed and controversial enough without giving more fodder to his critics. In election year 1800, he was viciously attacked as a "French infidel and atheist." When chatting with holier-than-thou Northern Federalists, the faux-Christian Alexander Hamilton peevishly called Jefferson "an atheist and fanatic."

Whitcomb recorded his host firmly declaring his belief in "a Supreme Being," though he disputed the bookseller's conviction that Jesus had declared his divinity. "He never did so," Jefferson interrupted Whitcomb, who countered with "He professed to have Divine Aid in working miracles." Jefferson: "No He did not." The octogenarian philosopher ended their uncomfortable discussion by saying that Dr. Priestley was the one thinker who had the history of Christianity right.[41]

Before dismissing the bookseller, Jefferson insisted, as he had to others, that he adored Jesus the compassionate revolutionary. But he would have nothing to do with the mangling of ancient history that he attributed to those who'd corrupted it in the centuries after Jesus lived, with reports of miracles. "Paul was the first who had perverted the Doctrines of Christ," he informed Whitcomb. This was Priestley's view in *Corruptions of Christianity*. Jefferson held that insofar as Jesus never claimed divinity, he should be perceived as a moral teacher, not a manifestation of Nature's God, the Creator.[42]

Perhaps the best description of Jefferson's intellectualization of religious life is that argued by the classicist Karl Lehmann in his book *Thomas Jefferson: American Humanist*, published in 1947. Lehmann endowed Jefferson with a syncretistic philosophy of life: in seeking happiness, a Christian concept of virtue and goodness harmonized with an Epicurean belief in the communion of spirit and flesh—the art of living well that the Greek meditated on. Jefferson held that sensory pleasure was natural and not to be repressed through ascetic alienation. In the Head and Heart letter, he casts "the gloomy Monk, sequestered from the world" as a foil, and in his opening to the *Anas*, the monk represents "frigid insensibility." In the mind of the Jefferson who accepts the conditions that Epicurus philosophizes, passion is ineradicable—a sign of goodness, and the basis of progress, when channeled into productive fields of action.[43]

Privileging knowledge over faith, Jefferson identified himself as a "rational Christian." He had real doubts about heaven as the abode of souls. In questioning the existence of a nonmaterial plane, he could not imagine a soul's existence outside the living person—the analogy Priestley used was to ask how the sound of a bell could exist absent the physical bell. Jefferson readily admitted ignorance of what became of the soul once corporeal life ended. But when it came to theories of an afterlife, he never gave up questioning.[44]

THE SOUL TAKES ITS DEPARTURE

Before Jefferson takes his leave of us, and we of him, it is worth revisiting the predisposition of each generation to treat its own perspective on human knowledge as wiser and less bound up in false presumptions than what preceded. The cultural historian, as a kind of referee, has to make sense of the emotions, persuasions, and conjectures of a strange world, pausing good and long before imposing judgment upon people whose views were shaped under different conditions than those we face today. All societies are reactive, responding in spasms of momentary fear or puzzlement, and in ways that allow even disreputable beliefs to persist for extended periods. It takes a thoughtful backward glance to deepen the conversation, to see in other than black and white and to replace ideological rigidity with a richer curiosity.

The same rule applies to assumptions about the world that connect to larger mysteries about the purpose of human existence. Eighteenth-century students of nature should not be seen as gullible or blind when we note how many of them became intrigued by observable, or even rumored, phenomena that seem absurd to believe in now. For then we must analogize to the study of "unknowns" that the living generation has pondered: near-death experiences, angels, ESP, extraterrestrials—even Bigfoot. Like those who came before, we lack certain answers, and feed our imagination.

Jefferson reaped pleasure from mechanical invention, tinkering with every new gadget, measuring atmospheric change, monitoring the health of crops, noting the first appearance in spring of swallows and whippoorwills. He also had a pronounced love of archaeology and paleontology, convinced that extinction formed no part of Nature's plan, and that somewhere there still lived woolly mammoths and the giant ground sloth of the Pleistocene period, officially known as *M. jeffersoni* to this day.[45]

Many in Jeffersonian America were convinced that swallows buried themselves in mud and hibernated there for months at a time, flightless and in a deathlike trance. It was first reported in 1785 that rather than migrate, these fork-tailed insectivores burrowed into the bottom of a pond or lake and remained in a "torpid state" through the winter months before reemerging in spring, their wings covered with a sticky substance. They were rarely spotted in either the submerged or recently resurrected state, but there was just enough circumstantial evidence to keep the question alive in scientific journals and newspapers into the following century. Two sturdy factions, the migrationists and the hibernationists, debated this bit of arcana for decades. The natural world was a world of wonders, and inquiring minds wanted to see the mystery of disappearing swallows solved, one way or the other.[46]

The nature of belief is a matter of study for neuroscientists, theologians, and everyone in between. Human curiosity is an inextinguishable force, and the line between rationality and irrationality is not clearly marked. For the polymath Jefferson, who uncharacteristically ran out of patience in dealing with an itinerant bookseller's conventional views, only "rational religion," a historically informed, revelation-free deism (god in Nature), made sense. But even here he found the evidence inadequate.

Hypotheses about a possible afterlife kept him guessing for many years. Honoring the right of conscience that he and Madison co-enshrined in the Statute of Virginia for Religious Freedom in the 1780s, he never tried to impose his deism on the younger members of his family, and he did not entirely dismiss the idea that a well-lived life found its reward in a nonterrestrial form. While he could not find satisfying words for what was unknowable, at various times he did speculate on postcorporeality: what happens when you die.[47]

At twenty-one, while a student in Williamsburg, Jefferson had already begun to express interest in the afterlife. To an unnamed individual—a classmate, most likely—he penned a little letter hazarding an opinion about resurrection (or post-mortem resuscitation) that is relatable to the swallow "torpor" controversy and to the nature of belief more broadly. "Perusing a magazine," the young scholar began, "I met with an account of a person who had been drowned. He had continued underwater 24 hours, and upon being properly treated when taken out he was restored to life." It was not an isolated instance—the point is that Jefferson believed what he'd read. The simplicity of the treatment fascinated him: "Nothing is requisite but to give the vital warmth to the whole body by gentle degrees, and to put the blood in motion by inflating the lungs." In soliciting the friend's position on the matter, he posed a two-part question: "We are generally taught that the soul leaves the body

Figure 21. Jefferson's grave in the Monticello cemetery, ca. 1866. This is the only known photograph of the original obelisk when it still marked Jefferson's grave. It was designed by Jefferson as death approached, erected in 1833, but chipped away at by souvenir hunters as the private cemetery fell into disrepair. In 1883, this obelisk was replaced with the taller obelisk that visitors to Monticello see today. According to descendants, the man pictured is the youngest of Jefferson's grandsons, George Wythe Randolph (1818–1867). (Courtesy Special Collections, University of Virginia Library)

at the instant of death but does not this story contradict this opinion? When then does the soul take it's departure?"[48]

In Jefferson's case, it was on July 4, 1826, the Jubilee of American Independence. At that particular moment in history, many of his fellow Americans were sure that such a remarkable coincidence could not have happened without divine intervention.

APPENDIX A

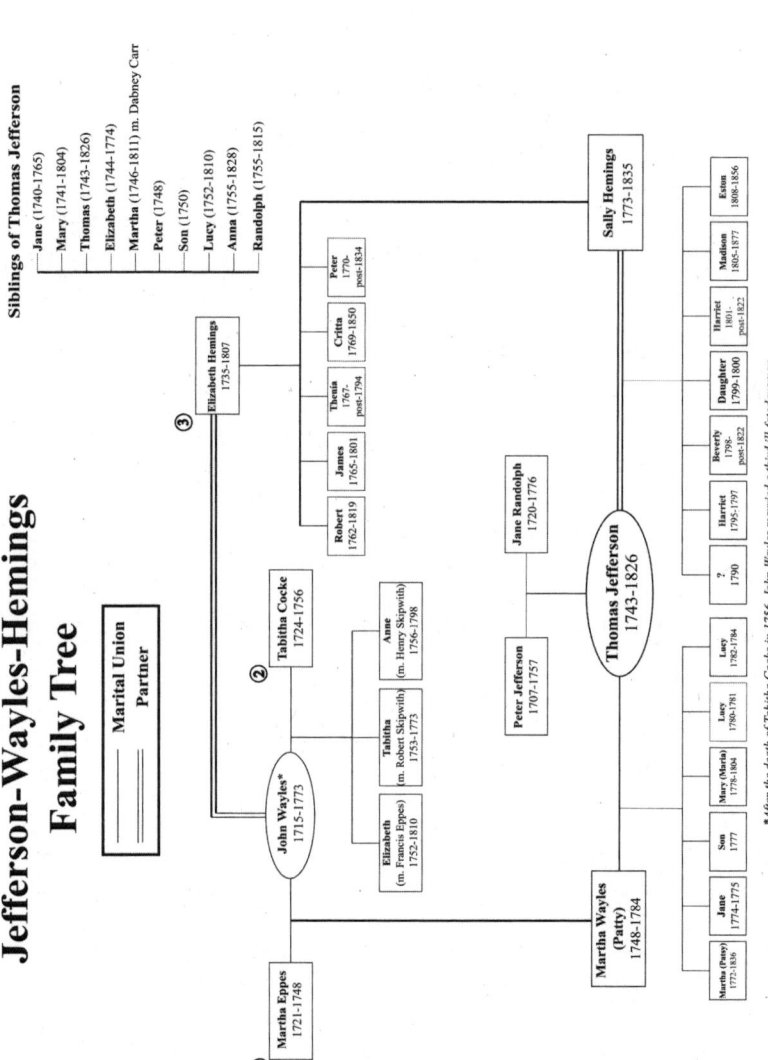

APPENDIX B

A Note on Sources, and Sources of Inspiration

My favorite modern philosopher of history, Paul Ricoeur, likened the historian's journey to the psychodrama of a courtroom: a historian hears testimony, engages in a critical examination of select witnesses, and thinks long and hard. The difference is that a judge's decision is meant to be final, while no historian expects the same. No one, Ricoeur writes, is "the sole tribunal of history." Rather, the scholar "pries open" what a judge has closed with a verdict. In cross-examining Jefferson, I have repaired to the archive (where testimony sits), mindful that all historical work is provisional.[1]

From generation to generation, Jefferson biographies have made their impression and then disappeared. The majority sing his praises; a few shockers paint him as a monster and hold him accountable for the sins of the nation. Specialized treatments are too numerous to count and, for the most part, well developed and discerning; some are decidedly salty, with an ax to grind. You can't not have an opinion about the third president.

Jefferson's place in America's civil religion is huge. His three most prominent twentieth-century defenders were Julian P. Boyd, founding editor of the modern edition of the *Papers of Thomas Jefferson* (1950–); Dumas Malone, who spent more than three decades compiling his six-volume *Jefferson and His Time* (1948–80); and Merrill D. Peterson, a distinguished professor of history at the University of Virginia and the author of, among numerous other books, *The Jefferson Image in the American Mind* (1960) and *Thomas Jefferson and the New Nation* (1970).

Every Jefferson scholar owes a debt to Malone, no matter where he or she comes down on the founder's private character. Impeccable in his research, Malone presents a man who wears a halo as bright as the one that typically envelops George Washington in nineteenth-century political biography. Where the motives of America's "greats" are imagined pure and unselfish, it is because national creation myths have demanded it.

As a graduate student at the University of Virginia in the early 1990s, I found it impossible not to feel the weight of arguments spun from earlier writings. Boyd and

Malone were too big to fail, as the saying goes, and Merrill Peterson, not long retired, was a generous guide who befriended me. My doctoral dissertation, published as *The Inner Jefferson: Portrait of a Grieving Optimist* (1995), was an examination of an expressive letter writer, steeped as he was in a strong epistolary tradition. The subject of Jefferson's possible relationship with Sally Hemings was peripheral to my topic; I took it on from the perspective of all that Jefferson and his white progeny left on the page, minimizing oral histories that spoke to what history was not meant to see. In consequence of the persuasive DNA testing conducted in 1998, I published an apologia—which I contend is good for the scholar's soul. After that piece, "The Seductions of Thomas Jefferson," I went on to study the range of attitudes toward human sexuality that prevailed in the eighteenth century. The result was *Jefferson's Secrets: Death and Desire at Monticello* (2005).

The foregoing is meant to recount, in the briefest way, the path I took to the present project, which I expect will be my final word on Jefferson. One outlier among twentieth-century studies of Jefferson is the popular treatment that spawned this book. Ahead of its publication, Fawn Brodie's *Thomas Jefferson: An Intimate History* (1974) earned its author a permanent banishment from what was then a tight-knit community of mainstream historians of the founding era. She had already been excommunicated from the Mormon Church for her biography of Joseph Smith, in which she branded the religion's founder a fraud. Now the conscientious UCLA professor was insisting that Thomas Jefferson had loved his enslaved domestic, Sally Hemings, thirty years his junior. As the author fully expected (and informed her editor ahead of time), she received at least as many pans as raves in newspaper reviews. Critics dismissed her "psychobiography" or "psychohistory" as an unreliable vehicle for attempting to comprehend historical actors. In delivering the 1973 Jefferson Lecture in the Humanities, the renowned psychoanalyst Erik Erikson explained the issue he had in being described generally as a practitioner of psychohistory: "I have come to use this term only with tacit quotation marks . . . I would not wish to associate myself with all that is done in the name of this term."[2]

I read Brodie's "intimate history" even before I cracked open the first of Malone's six volumes. She runs into trouble with her heavy-handed use of Freudian methodology in framing her portrait of a man of passion. Finding Jefferson to have struggled with inner dissatisfaction, she was bitten by Freud's profound sense of resignation, his belief in an unwavering state of anxiety as the dominant feature of human psychology. While she took too many liberties, Brodie documented a different Jefferson than the head-driven philosophe who wrote America into being. Fawn Brodie broke the mold, in a good way.

Her book sold hundreds of thousands of copies. Yet its success paled in comparison to the number one fiction title of that season, Gore Vidal's *Burr* (1973). I make mention of it because Jefferson's disposition toward Aaron Burr, his frosty treatment of his vice president at critical moments, looms large in the final chapters of this book.

Vidal's novel is awash in creative supposition. As a fictional memoirist, his Aaron Burr shows he does not like Mr. Jefferson in the least. Preempting Brodie's argument in favor of a love match, Vidal's hypersexualized Burr appears to know Jefferson's mind well enough to declare his enslaved concubine an ideal wife for the master of Monticello: "submissive, shy, and rather stupid." As president, Vidal's Jefferson, with "a thin-lipped smile," is a cruel dictator. His horse lives in fear of him and his pet mockingbird cringes when he comes close.[3]

Curiously, Vidal later authored a nonfiction book about the American founding, and it sold but modestly. That book characterized the historical Jefferson not as an obnoxious prig but as a deep thinker. The novel, on the other hand, had a sizable impact on millions of Americans, who took *Burr* as a reliable reflection of history, no less than HBO's well-acted but fanciful John Adams miniseries substituted for legitimate historical scholarship in the early 2000s. Next, Lin-Manuel Miranda's Broadway megahit *Hamilton* induced many who knew better to treat what was a masterful theatrical performance as a legitimate engagement with the historical record. *Hamilton* charmed academics, unfazed that the playwright had converted a manifestly mean-spirited disputant into an immigrant-extolling abolitionist mascot embodying the progressive spirit of the Obama era. Reclaiming history from popularizers is an old problem.

The reason I call back Jefferson treatments of a half century ago, placing Fawn Brodie and Gore Vidal side by side, is to give credit where credit is due and to remind readers that the field of Jefferson studies has a history that relates to the constant reshaping of American cultural identity. Unlike Vidal's in *Burr*, Brodie's skill as a biographer is notable, and her treatment of Jefferson is sensitive. She clearly has a soft spot for him, though her critics mostly failed to recognize that.

In most respects, Brodie captured Jefferson's human qualities with authority. But she may also have invested too much of herself in the narrative. A twentieth-century Utahn who said her childhood home reminded her of Monticello, and who saw her father in Jefferson, may not be a wholly objective psychoanalyst for an eighteenth-century Virginian. And yet she motivated other Jefferson scholars to make the personal matter more. I doubt I would be designating mine an intimate history were it not for her worthy example.[4]

The status of knowledge is ever changing. We let go of Brodie's America when the words "postindustrial" and "postmodern" came into vogue; for better or for worse, biography and memoir are markedly different now. I have always promoted interdisciplinary approaches by historians, looking as widely as possible for insights. And so, in conceiving how, fifty years after its publication, Fawn Brodie's bestselling "intimate history" could be improved on and new avenues opened up for historians to responsibly approach the psychology of personality, I reread her book appreciatively (and, of course, critically). Of major biographers, she was the only one who made a concerted effort to get inside Jefferson's head to the extent that her analysis cannot be called anything but a psychological study. To a somewhat more limited degree, *American Sphinx: The Character of Thomas Jefferson* (1996), by Joseph J. Ellis, delves into Jefferson's psychology, as does the more recent *"Most Blessed of the Patriarchs": Thomas Jefferson and the Empire of the Imagination* (2016), an impressively detached examination of self-image and personal motives co-authored by Annette Gordon-Reed and Peter S. Onuf.

Sensitive to the perspectives these books have adopted, *Being Thomas Jefferson* focuses on episodes and individual relationships that I find particularly informative but that are incidental to the themes pursued by Professors Ellis, Gordon-Reed, and Onuf, all of whom, I should add, are scholars whose conversation I have profited from over the years. I have tried to make it clear to the reader where and why I am departing from the interpretations of others in emphasizing how Jefferson loved and hated, and how he manipulated language in order to rationalize his behavior and attain his goals.

An earlier biographer whose work I deem authoritative and whose objectivity sets him apart was, surprisingly, not a professional historian at all, but a World War I–era chemist who became a practicing attorney. Nathan Schachner (1895–1955) wrote reputable biographies of Aaron Burr and Alexander Hamilton before turning to the Virginian. His two-volume *Thomas Jefferson: A Biography* (1951), long out of print, is still very readable, and I cite it in the endnotes where the research and interpretation commend it. I also cite a cradle-to-grave biography of the current century, John B. Boles's *Jefferson: Architect of American Liberty* (2017), a painstakingly researched, somewhat more sympathetic treatment than is seen in the majority of Jefferson books and articles of late.

APPENDIX B   331

Additional sources of Jefferson material dating from the early years of the republic are sprinkled through the endnotes and deserving of consideration. Not the least of these is Leonard Levy's *Jefferson and Civil Liberties* (1963), which interrogates the "darker side," as the subtitle reads, of America's so-called "apostle of liberty." The book is an early acid test of rhetoric versus reality, and, without treating Jefferson and slavery, prefigures the revisionist literature scholars have produced in the years since.

Since 2000, the number of authors who have written thoughtfully about Jefferson has grown, each one targeting specific aspects of his personal behavior. Kevin J. Hayes covers a life of reading in his unique and perceptive work *The Road to Monticello: The Life and Mind of Thomas Jefferson* (2008); Jon Meacham assesses a canny political operative in *Jefferson: The Art of Power* (2012); Robert M. S. McDonald shows how Jefferson's peers saw him in *Confounding Father: Thomas Jefferson's Image in His Own Time* (2016); Maurizio Valsania does a superior job of recreating eighteenth-century norms for everything from physical presentation and posture to masculine and feminine characteristics in *Jefferson's Body: A Corporeal Biography* (2017); and the literary scholar Fred Kaplan conveys the power and peril embodied in Jefferson's writing in *His Masterly Pen: A Biography of Jefferson the Writer* (2022).

Additionally, I wish to endorse those specialized titles I have recurred to most often in developing my ideas and arguments for this book. The following are all compelling works, representing multiple generations of historical scholarship, that might not otherwise draw the reader's attention: Noble E. Cunningham Jr., *The Jeffersonian Republicans: The Formation of Party Organization, 1789–1801* (1957), and *The Jeffersonian Republicans in Power: Party Operations, 1801–1809* (1963); Alfred F. Young, *The Democratic Republicans of New York* (1967); Garry Wills, *Inventing America: Jefferson's Declaration of Independence* (1978); Charles A. Miller, *Jefferson and Nature: An Interpretation* (1988); Jack McLaughlin, *Jefferson and Monticello: The Biography of a Builder* (1988); Jay Fliegelman, *Declaring Independence: Jefferson, Natural Language, and the Culture of Performance* (1993); Peter S. Onuf, *Jefferson's Empire: The Language of American Nationhood* (2000) and *Jefferson and the Virginians: Democracy, Constitutions, and Empire* (2018); Eva Sheppard Wolf, *Race and Liberty in the New Nation* (2006); Hannah Spahn, *Thomas Jefferson, Time, and History* (2011); Michal Jan Rozbicki, *Culture and Liberty in the Age of the American Revolution* (2011); Brian Steele, *Thomas Jefferson and American Nationhood* (2012); John Ferling, *Jefferson and Hamilton: The Rivalry That Forged a Nation* (2013); Maurizio Valsania, *Nature's Man: Thomas Jefferson's Philosophical Anthropology*

(2013); and Francis D. Cogliano, *A Revolutionary Friendship: Washington, Jefferson, and the American Republic* (2024).

I accept that this book will succeed best if the reader's conclusions about Jefferson as a likable or unlikable figure are not traceable to its author's perceived investment in that question. Yet I confess my admiration for two campaigns Jefferson formulated at the time of the Revolution and continued to advance, which I see as evidence of a laudable humanity: the right of conscience ("It does me no injury for my neighbor to say there are twenty gods, or no god. It neither picks my pocket nor breaks my leg"); and his endorsement of public education as a means to encourage good citizenship ("Those persons whom nature hath endowed with genius and virtue, should be rendered by liberal education worthy to receive, and able to guard the sacred deposit of the rights and liberties of their fellow citizens"). In 1816, at age seventy-three, he compressed these ideas into a single sentence: "Bigotry is the disease of ignorance, of morbid minds," he wrote to John Adams. Of course, he meant something different than we do in decrying bigotry, which explains, in part, why he often disappoints. Suffice it to say that Jefferson regarded the mind's idleness as the greatest threat to any human being.[5]

It is a truism that every attempt at history writing and biography is an improvisation, including this one. Improvisation describes Jefferson, too. His capacious mind blended with an attraction to creative wordplay—often the very sound of words—as he willfully sought to exercise an effect on mind and spirit, and move a nation.

ACKNOWLEDGMENTS

When I was in graduate school at the University of Virginia in the early 1990s, I had the good fortune to commune with two elders in the profession, Daniel P. Jordan and Merrill D. Peterson, and a witty, effervescent scholar, new to UVA, Peter S. Onuf. All three opened doors and helped shape my approach to Jefferson scholarship. Their intellectual honesty and professionalism continue to remind me of my good fortune in warranting their friendship as I once more give my energies to understanding one of history's most problematic political actors.

Dan was the inspired director of Monticello, a UVA PhD who hired an amazing team of experts and transformed the mountaintop estate into a site that lured world leaders and millions of visitors. Reminiscing one day over lunch during the Obama years, he told me stories of the presidents, governors, and foreign dignitaries he'd hosted. He was deeply impressed by how much ex-president Jimmy Carter had read about Jefferson; and how George H. W. Bush staged a command performance on national education policy on the mountain, with cabinet members and most of the state governors on hand for a dinner that featured an outlandish dessert: a replica of Monticello constructed entirely of chocolate. Dan was moved when Caroline Kennedy told him that her father, while residing in the White House, kept Jefferson's *Garden Book* on his nightstand.

While casting a light on Jefferson's humanity, Dan Jordan ignited efforts to restore to historical memory the long-undervalued African Americans who labored in Monticello's neighborhood. Until the mid-1980s, tour guides used the word "servant" exclusively, mitigating the indignities suffered. Dan made sure that historical truths were no longer hidden, that the reality of life on a racially mixed working plantation was properly conveyed. He was proud to have brought into better focus the lives of Monticello's enslaved families, a project that continues strong to this day.

When we met, Merrill Peterson was the age I am now, retired, still immersed in writing new books. By that time, though, he decided that he'd said all he wanted to about the founding generation and had passed the torch to a rising generation of scholars. In the opening pages of his thousand-page biography, *Thomas Jefferson and the New Nation*, he made the "mortifying confession" that he had come to consider Jefferson "the least self-revealing" of those who were present at the creation. Merrill was a bit like that himself: generous, judicious, yet also watchful and discreet.

His successor as Thomas Jefferson Foundation Professor of History, Peter Onuf, is a giant of a thinker with an infectious enthusiasm for historical analysis and a stage presence words cannot do justice to. I hold the distinction of being the first of his many grateful PhD students. Aside from Peter's memorable books and incisive articles on Jeffersonian America, he embodies the highest ethic of intellectual engagement.

Special thanks to Bruce Brodie, Fawn Brodie's son and a psychologist by profession, for indulging me in candid conversation. He provided me with a picture of what it was like growing up in a household with two academic parents who both used psychoanalytic theory in their work and who were socially active in that community. Even after her stunning success with *Thomas Jefferson: An Intimate History*, and while remarking that he, too, came to consider the book "overly Freudian," Bruce Brodie assured me that Fawn Brodie had the humility to regard her treatment as *an* alternative to standard biographies, not *the* alternative.

The scholars I've turned to as I've committed myself to one more "go" at Jefferson need to be properly thanked. Monticello's president, Jane Kamensky, herself a distinguished historian, has kept me up to speed during planning for the 250th anniversary of Jefferson's Declaration, and all that lies beyond. Of those who have read my work in depth and offered critical assistance, I acknowledge, with deep gratitude, Meg Kennedy and Ben Blohowiak, Matt Dennis and Lizzie Reis, Newell Bringhurst, Frank Cogliano, Greg May, Peter Onuf, Andrew O'Shaughnessy, Susan Stein, Maurizio Valsania, David Waldstreicher, and Phil Wurtz. These individuals have all provided unabashed advice. At the *Papers of Thomas Jefferson*, Jim McClure has proven himself an exemplary successor to the astute, generous Barbara Oberg, and I sincerely appreciate his input as well.

At Monticello's International Center for Jefferson Studies and the attractive, well-stocked Jefferson Library, I have enjoyed fruitful conversations with Frank Cogliano, John Ragosta, Andrew Davenport, and indispensable ICJS veterans Anna Berkes and Endrina Tay. At UVA Special Collections, expert advisers Regina Rush and Ervin Jordan were generous with their time, while the skillful designer Evelyn Garey worked with me to get the graveyard and genealogy charts done right. The Condorcet scholar Iain McLean provided necessary clarifications on the mind of that major Enlightenment figure. An appreciative nod as well to Chip Stokes, whose commitment to Jeffersonian educational ideals warrants notice. I am always grateful for (and proud of) my long-ago students Spencer McBride and Andrew Wegmann, accomplished historians in their own right, who provide valuable insights whenever called upon.

My literary agent, Laura Gross, is a bringer of light and provider of excellent counsel. My thanks as well to her associate Lauren Scovel. At Bloomsbury, I could not have had a more enthusiastic editor than Anton Mueller, whose prodding helped me reshape the manuscript in beneficial ways. Added thanks to Sage Gilbert and Suzanne Keller for diligently shepherding the manuscript through production, and to copyeditor Emily DeHuff for her many remedial suggestions.

And then there's Josh Burstein, who as a child considered Monticello a second home. He has a vantage point these days that allows him to offer editorial advice in service of those who aren't necessarily compelled to rummage through endnotes. In the end, no editorial assistance surpasses what I receive every day from my partner and all-time favorite co-author, Nancy Gale Isenberg.

NOTES

ABBREVIATIONS

BRODIE   Fawn Brodie, *Thomas Jefferson: An Intimate History* (New York: W. W. Norton, 1974)

FOL   Founders Online, https://founders.archives.gov/ (National Archives)

MALONE   Dumas Malone, *Jefferson in His Time*, 6 vols. (Boston: Little, Brown, 1948–80)

JMB   *Jefferson's Memorandum Books*, James A. Bear Jr. and Lucia C. Stanton, eds. (Princeton, NJ: Princeton University Press, 1997)

PTJ   *Papers of Thomas Jefferson*, Julian P. Boyd et al., eds. (Princeton, NJ: Princeton University Press, 1950–)

PTJ-R   *Papers of Thomas Jefferson, Retirement Series*, J. Jefferson Looney, ed. (Princeton, NJ: Princeton University Press, 2004–)

RANDALL   Henry S. Randall, *Life of Thomas Jefferson*, 3 vols. (New York: Derby & Jackson, 1858)

SOWERBY   E. Millicent Sowerby, comp., *Catalogue of the Library of Thomas Jefferson*, 5 vols. (Charlottesville: University Press of Virginia, 1983)

INTRODUCTION

1. In the extraordinary "Dialogue between Head and Heart" that he penned to a love interest, Jefferson engaged one of the nautical metaphors he favored: "The art of life is the art of avoiding pain: and he is the best pilot who steers clearest of the rocks and shoals with which it is beset." TJ to Maria Cosway, October 12, 1786, *PTJ*,

10:443–55. Charles A. Miller conducted an exhaustive study of such appearances in *Ship of State: The Nautical Metaphors of Thomas Jefferson* (Lanham, MD: University Press of America, 2003).

2. Many excellent works tackle these subjects. I draw especially on George Makari, *Soul Machine: The Invention of the Modern Mind* (New York: W. W. Norton, 2015); Roy Porter's remarkable *Flesh in the Age of Reason: The Modern Foundations of Body and Soul* (New York: W. W. Norton, 2003); Ritchie Robertson, *The Enlightenment: The Pursuit of Happiness, 1680–1790* (New York: HarperCollins, 2021); Ernst Cassirer, *The Philosophy of the Enlightenment* (Princeton, NJ: Princeton University Press, 1951); and Peter Gay, *The Enlightenment, An Interpretation: The Rise of Modern Paganism* and *The Enlightenment, An Interpretation: The Science of Freedom* (New York: W. W. Norton, 1979 [New York: Knopf, 1966 and 1969]). One of the best-known medical theorists of the day, Samuel Auguste Tissot, asserted that diseases of the nerves had become increasingly widespread and frequent in the eighteenth century; see Tissot, *De la Santé des Gens de Lettres* (Lausanne, Switzerland: Franç. Grasset & Co., 1775), quote at 185n.

3. William Seale, *The President's House: A History* (Baltimore: Johns Hopkins University Press, 1986), 1:88–89.

4. A trenchant example of his intimate language in a public document appears in Jefferson's original rough framing of the Declaration of Independence, where he wrote that Americans had fruitlessly appealed to British "justice & magnanimity" and "the ties of our common kindred to disavow . . . usurpations"; yet "the disturbers of our harmony" remained unmoved, "permitting their chief magistrate to send over not only soldiers of our common blood, but Scotch & foreign mercenaries to invade & deluge us in blood." It is immediately after he invokes "the last stab," etc., and concludes: "We must endeavor to forget our former love for them." The combination of loving commitment and ultimate betrayal are devastating. (*PTJ*, 1:243–47).

5. Among the many significant works relating to Jefferson's attitudes, the larger racial environment he was privy to and conversant in, and the nature of slavery in his native Virginia, I have found, for the purposes of this book, particular value in the following titles: David Brion Davis, *The Problem of Slavery in the Age of Revolution, 1770–1823* (Ithaca, NY: Cornell University Press, 1975); John Chester Miller, *The Wolf by the Ears: Thomas Jefferson and Slavery* (New York: Free Press, 1977); Peter S. Onuf, *Jefferson's Empire: The Language of American Nationhood* (Charlottesville: University Press of Virginia, 2000), esp. chap. 5; Joshua D. Rothman, *Notorious in the Neighborhood: Sex and Families across the Color Line in Virginia, 1787–1861* (Chapel Hill: University of North Carolina Press, 2003); Eva Sheppard

Wolf, *Race and Liberty in the New Nation: Emancipation in Virginia from the Revolution to Nat Turner's Rebellion* (Baton Rouge: Louisiana State University Press, 2006); David Waldstreicher, *Slavery's Constitution: From Revolution to Ratification* (New York: Hill & Wang, 2009); Andrew S. Curran, *The Anatomy of Blackness: Science and Slavery in the Age of Enlightenment* (Baltimore: Johns Hopkins University Press, 2011); Nicholas Guyatt, *Bind Us Apart: How Enlightened Americans Invented Racial Segregation* (New York: Basic Books, 2016); Padraig Riley, *Slavery and the Democratic Conscience: Political Life in Jefferson's Virginia* (Philadelphia: University of Pennsylvania Press, 2016); Arthur Scherr, *Rightful Liberty: Slavery, Morality, and Thomas Jefferson's World* (Macon, GA: Mercer University Press, 2021); Cara Rogers Stevens, *Thomas Jefferson and the Fight Against Slavery* (Lawrence: University Press of Kansas, 2024).

6. TJ to Benjamin Rush, September 23, 1800, *PTJ*, 32:166–69.
7. Clearly, the relative weight of seeing, hearing, smelling, and touching has registered differently in individual lives as technologies change, and it should not be ignored. For a guide to contextualizing emotions past, see in particular Mark M. Smith, *A Sensory History Manifesto* (University Park, PA: Penn State University Press, 2021), chap. 1; Peter Charles Hoffer, *Sensory Worlds in Early America* (Baltimore: Johns Hopkins University Press, 2003), Introduction; Carolyn Purnell, *The Sensational Past: How the Enlightenment Changed the Way We Use Our Senses* (New York: W. W. Norton, 2017). On interiority in this context, see Brad Pasanek, *Metaphors of Mind: An Eighteenth-Century Dictionary* (Baltimore: Johns Hopkins University Press, 2015), chap. 10; also instructive is the methodology used by G. J. Barker-Benfield, especially in *The Culture of Sensibility: Sex and Society in Eighteenth-Century Britain* (Chicago: University of Chicago Press, 1992), and the work of the philosopher Robert C. Solomon in clarifying the false dichotomy between reason and passion, most notably in his book *The Passions: The Emotions of Life* (Garden City, NY: Doubleday, 1976).
8. Merrill D. Peterson, *Thomas Jefferson and the New Nation* (New York: Oxford University Press, 1970), viii; Andrew Burstein, "The Problem of Jefferson Biography," *Virginia Quarterly Review*, 70, 3 (Summer 1994): 403–20. Complicating the question of Jefferson and his racial prejudices, it is useful to note that his historical reputation among Black Americans has not been constant. Before the DNA study conducted in the late 1990s, indeed, before Fawn Brodie's "intimate history" appeared, historically informed African Americans long accepted the oral history account of Jefferson's unacknowledged relationship with Sally Hemings and understood him to be hypocritical; yet it is just as true that up to the civil rights movement, newspapers serving Black communities praised the antislavery credentials

of Jefferson and the democratic ideals he inspired. Because his legacy was as easily applied to social morality and justice as to Southern-style racism, present-day convictions do not tell the whole story.

9. The reader will find that the present book engages with Brodie's "intimate history" without replicating its themes. As to the interdisciplinary elements I pursue, literary scholarship is the closest to my own discipline, though the work of cognitive psychologists has proven instrumental as well. Renouncing Brodie's Freudianism yet acknowledging the restraint she also exhibited, I take my cue from psychologists who see mind and actions, awareness and judgment, emotion and culture, as working parts that function together. A cultural historian abides by similar principles, which makes me wary about issuing any grand rulings on Jefferson's psyche, though I would be remiss if, after presenting evidence, I were to shy from drawing conclusions about Jefferson's motives and predilections.

10. Inasmuch as intimacy must be taken up in the proper historical context, emotions have a social and cultural dimension as well as a sexual one, as I laid out in my most recent book, *Longing for Connection: Entangled Memories and Emotional Loss in Early America* (Baltimore: Johns Hopkins University Press, 2024). In any life, formative experiences are generally as critical as mature apprehensions, and in Jefferson's case, the metaphorical concept of "life as a journey" is to be seen in combination with literal moves taken from one neighborhood to another. Meaningful exchanges of social circles occurred as he exchanged the emotional comfort and personal power experienced at Monticello for Philadelphia, Paris, and elsewhere. These are just some of the elements that conditioned emotional life, and did so with an intensity that has not been fully explored in historical biography. As to sexual currents involving the American founders and the way their actual attitudes were cleaned up when they were enshrined in patriotic lore, see Thomas A. Foster, *Sex and the Founding Fathers: The American Quest for a Relatable Past* (Philadelphia, PA: Temple University Press, 2014).

11. The classic vignette describing Jefferson's delicacy of manner is provided by Margaret Bayard Smith in *The First Forty Years of Washington Society*, ed. Gaillard Hunt (New York: Scribner's, 1906); see also Merrill D. Peterson, ed., *Visitors to Monticello* (Charlottesville: University Press of Virginia, 1989), 45–54; for analysis of intimate conversation in an elite all-male Anglo-American social environment, see, notably, Kate Davison, "Occasional Politeness and Gentlemen's Laughter in 18th-Century England," *Historical Journal* 57, 4 (December 2014): 921–45; and for the satirical edge in such conversation, see Vic Gatrell, *City of Laughter: Sex and Satire in Eighteenth-Century London* (New York: Walker, 2006). Although an emphasis may be placed on Britain, early America imported its cultural forms, no less than

its material products, far more than the rhetorical construction of "Independence" acknowledges.

12. Jefferson's disapproving comments as an adult were generally no more obnoxious than terming the wife of the British ambassador a "virago," and vaguely alluding to streetwise "harpies"; such comments were similar, for instance, to expressions found in letters from purportedly prim members, male and female, of the Adams family (e.g., calling out a "shrew" or a "harpy"). Jefferson's more sustained misogynistic comments are found in quotations derived from giants of Western literature, which were included in his Literary Commonplace Book and never intended for publication. The ubiquity of misogynistic expressions in colloquial speech in the eighteenth century led to the publication of multiple editions of Francis Grose, *A Classical Dictionary of the Vulgar Tongue* (London: S. Hooper, 1788). In this vast collection of vernacular words and phrases, a woman was "baggage"; sexualized, she could be "laced mutton," her "privities" given euphemistic names like "man trap," "money," "notch," "cock alley," or "old hat" (because "frequently felt"). Loose imagery made a midwife into a "groper," an ungovernable woman into a "hellcat," etc.

13. In elite circles, the operative definition of enlightened morals did not necessarily extend to marital fidelity—at least, it was not the first component of a known code that could not be compromised without dire consequences. Ritchie Robertson writes: "When sexual activity was released from religious constraints, the resulting freedom tended to benefit men, especially upper-class men, more than women. It was generally agreed that since a woman was in an important sense the property of her husband, and since men did not wish to be saddled with other men's illegitimate children, women's sexuality had to be strictly confined" (Robertson, *The Enlightenment*, 293–305, quote at 305). Enlightenment-era figures, notably John Locke and Jean-Jacques Rousseau, saw sex as a building block of the social order, of family, law, and the nation state, Adam and Eve having forged the first social contract. As a traditionalist in matters of sex, Rousseau believed, like Jefferson, that women were, by nature, intended to remain weak and passive by comparison; see Mary Severance, "Sex and the Social Contract," *ELH* 67, 2 (Summer 2000): 453–513; Daniel Juan Gil, "Before Intimacy: Modernity and Emotion in the Early Modern Discourse of Sexuality," *ELH* 69, 4 (Winter 2002): 861–87; Porter, *Flesh in the Age of Reason*, chap. 15; Jenny Davidson, *Breeding: A Partial History of the Eighteenth Century* (New York: Columbia University Press, 2009), 118–23; in addition to Brodie, works that engage with Jefferson's women problems include Jan Ellen Lewis, "Jefferson and Women," in John B. Boles and Randal Hall, eds., *Seeing Jefferson Anew* (Charlottesville: University of Virginia Press, 2010), 152–171; Virginia Scharff, *The Women Jefferson Loved* (New York: HarperCollins, 2010),

esp. chap. 7; Cynthia A. Kierner, *Martha Jefferson Randolph, Daughter of Monticello* (Chapel Hill: University of North Carolina Press, 2012), esp. 110–15; Catherine Kerrison, *Jefferson's Daughters: Three Sisters, White and Black, in a Young America* (New York: Ballantine, 2019); Jon Kukla, *Mr. Jefferson's Women* (New York: Knopf, 2007); Maurizio Valsania, *Jefferson's Body: A Corporeal Biography* (Charlottesville: University of Virginia Press, 2017), 163–88; and my own *Jefferson's Secrets: Death and Desire at Monticello* (New York: Basic Books, 2005), esp. chap. 4. By way of contrast, it is worth noting that Jefferson's diplomatic successor in Paris, New York's amorously inclined Gouverneur Morris, took the opposite tack, untroubled by politicized females and open to their sexual forwardness; see William Howard Adams, *Gouverneur Morris* (New Haven, CT: Yale University Press, 2003), 180–86.

14. Burstein, *Jefferson's Secrets*, 166–69; Nancy Isenberg and Andrew Burstein, *The Problem of Democracy: The Presidents Adams Confront the Cult of Personality* (New York: Viking, 2019), 509n37; Porter, *Flesh in the Age of Reason*, 144–47; and Roy Porter, "Mixed Feelings: The Enlightenment and Sexuality in 18th-Century Britain," in Paul-Gabriel Boucé, ed., *Sexuality in Eighteenth-Century Britain* (Manchester, England: Manchester University Press, 1982). On the class element in evolving understandings of sexual opportunity and restriction, see Michel Foucault, *The History of Sexuality: Volume 1, An Introduction* (New York: Vintage, 1978), 116–26. Mark Silk, a scholar of early religion, delved into an obscure reference to Roman mythology in a John Adams letter of 1794, raising the possibility that he had an inkling about Jefferson's relationship with Hemings. I cannot completely dismiss the possibility, though no evidence exists that Adams was, at that time, privy to any possible gossip emanating from Jefferson's Virginia neighbors about private life at Monticello; nor did Sally Hemings bear a child in the years 1791–94, and the author even acknowledges that "a political eon passed" between the date of the letter and any known suggestion of the relationship; see Mark Silk, "Did John Adams Out Thomas Jefferson and Sally Hemings?," *Smithsonian Magazine* (November 2016).

15. Nicholas Guyatt cites the Revolutionary physician David Ramsay of South Carolina, author of the first history of the American Revolution, as perhaps the earliest among his peers to castigate Jefferson for his published debasement of African Americans: "You have depressed the negroes too low," he charged in 1786. An example of the kind of reaction Jefferson's opinions received when he was president is the Irish-born reformer Thomas Branagan, whose 1804 *Preliminary Essay on the Oppression of the Exiled Sons of Africa* reflected his earlier experience working on slave ships. Branagan refuted Jefferson's assumption that Blacks were

"an inferior order of beings" on the basis of what he'd seen with his own eyes in West Africa: "sensible, ingenious, hospitable and generous as any people"; and yet, indicative of conflicts to come in America, by 1805, the Irish American had turned pessimistic, projecting violence emanating from free Blacks in the North once Southern Blacks left that benighted culture and relocated north; see Guyatt, *Bind Us Apart*, 26–27, 81–84. On the tradition of unauthorized sexual histories, Peter Burke shows that the appearance in the seventeenth and eighteenth centuries of the "secret history" as a familiar form was invariably a reaction against whitewashed official histories that bathed in encomiums for leaders; see Burke, "Publicizing the Private: The Rise of 'Secret History,'" in Christian J. Emden and David Midgley, eds., *Changing Perceptions of the Public Sphere* (New York: Berghahn Books, 2012), chap. 3.

16. During Jefferson's lifetime, the Sally Hemings "scandal" did not go beyond ribald gossip, nor rise to the level where it threatened his reputation. Whatever prominent Virginians might have said privately, they would not have gone public with any comment about his private behavior.

17. Curiously, whereas John Adams's intellectual struggle with a quest for "fame" has been a subject of interest among historians, the same is not the case with Jefferson; see Peter Shaw, *The Character of John Adams* (Chapel Hill: University of North Carolina Press, 1976); and Douglass Adair, *Fame and the Founding Fathers* (New York: W. W. Norton, 1974).

18. It is probable that Jefferson was aware that Fama, the Roman personification of Fame (Pheme in Greek), was a spreader of gossip. On the phenomenon of fame in its larger historical context, see Leo Braudy, *The Frenzy of Renown: Fame and Its History* (New York: Vintage, 1997). Jefferson did not suffer from public (visual) recognition until he found himself gawked at later in life when it became necessary to guard his privacy by screening in his study and bedroom against those who intruded on his retirement by ascending Monticello just to catch a glimpse of him. On his habit of dress, see Valsania, *Jefferson's Body*, 48–68, and Gaye Wilson, *Jefferson on Display: Attire, Etiquette, and the Art of Presentation* (Charlottesville: University of Virginia Press, 2018); for a strong analysis of Jefferson's brush with fame, see McDonald, *Confounding Father*, chap. 1.

19. The only other manmade structure in the United States so designated by the United Nations Educational, Scientific, and Cultural Organization (UNESCO) is Independence Hall in Philadelphia, which, of course, also figures prominently in Thomas Jefferson's personal history.

20. TJ to Joseph Priestley, June 19, 1802, *PTJ*, 37:625–26. Leonard W. Levy found in this statement the key to what he termed Jefferson's "messianic nationalism"; see Levy,

Jefferson and Civil Liberties: The Darker Side (Cambridge, MA: Harvard University Press, 1963), 21.

21. Daniel J. Boorstin, *The Lost World of Thomas Jefferson* (Chicago: University of Chicago Press, 1948 [repr. 1981]), 173.
22. TJ to John Breckinridge, January 29, 1800, *PTJ*, 31:344–45.
23. The immense number of books, popular articles, poems, and honors accorded to Jefferson from the time of his death is nowhere better cataloged than in Merrill D. Peterson's "Guide to Sources," in *The Jefferson Image in the American Mind* (New York: Oxford University Press, 1960), 459ff; see also Frank Shuffelton, *Thomas Jefferson: A Comprehensive, Annotated Bibliography of Writings About Him* (New York: Garland, 1983), and Shuffelton, *Thomas Jefferson, 1981–1990: An Annotated Bibliography* (New York: Garland, 1992). On the nature of historical revisionism, and the power of contemporary political culture on history and biography, see James M. Banner Jr., *The Ever-Changing Past: Why All History Is Revisionist History* (New Haven, CT: Yale University Press, 2021); Prof. Banner's analysis of "conceptual revisionism," the "most immediately disruptive" form of revisionism, makes it clear that Jefferson's changing reputation has been, to a considerable degree, occasioned by the relatively recent contributions of work on race, class, gender, sexuality, and the natural world, ending the long reign of what had been the "master narrative," in which politically ascendant white males were the driving force behind all that mattered to the founding era; see esp. 152–55, and 163–72 for his treatment of the Jefferson-Hemings DNA results and the overturning of assumptions by scholarly consensus.
24. Humanism as a philosophic system is generally understood as one that embraces the autonomy, integrity, and political rights of individuals. In the eighteenth-century Enlightenment, it embraced freethinking with respect to religion and religious authority.
25. See Rev. Francis Allen, *A Complete English Dictionary* (London: J. Wilson & J. Fell, 1765); similarly, in *Oxford English Dictionary*.
26. "First Inaugural Address," March 4, 1801; TJ to Mme de Tessé, March 20, 1787, *PTJ*, 11:226, 33:148–52; Jay Fliegelman, *Declaring Independence: Jefferson, Natural Language, and the Culture of Performance* (Stanford, CA: Stanford University Press, 1993), 102–107, 114–19. At the risk of overgeneralizing, one might speculate that the effect Jefferson aims for through the work of his pen is a kind of seductiveness that represses the desire to seize center stage. The popularity he achieves is attributable to a number of factors, but I do wish to suggest that the combination of an absence of ostentation in person and his extraordinary performance on the page distinguished him in his time.

27. See especially Susan R. Stein, *The Worlds of Thomas Jefferson at Monticello* (New York: Harry N. Abrams, 1993), in which Jefferson's workstation is pictured at 103–105. The bookstand held up to five books and could fold shut when not in use.
28. Constance Classen, *The Deepest Sense: A Cultural History of Touch* (Urbana: University of Illinois Press, 2012), esp. chap. 6, "Tactile Arts"; Peterson, ed., *Visitors to Monticello*.
29. The *Papers of Thomas Jefferson* were published at Princeton University exclusively, beginning in 1950, until the *Retirement Series* (covering the years 1809 to 1826) was launched at Monticello and began publishing in 2004. The *Retirement Series*, under the editorial leadership of J. Jefferson Looney since its inception, is scheduled to reach the end of Jefferson's life by 2027; the original series will not reach 1809 until after 2030. On Jefferson's inventive shelving and filing systems for books and letters, see Diane Ehrenpreis and Endrina Tay, "Enlightened Networks: Thomas Jefferson's System for Working from Home," *Transactions of the American Philosophical Society* 110, 2 (2022): 197–218.
30. His dinner table at Monticello was the site of intellectual performance, where he related anecdotes concerning his own history. During his presidency, Jefferson's dinner parties in Washington were typically designed to seduce members of Congress into favoring his agenda. These were held regularly, orchestrated by Jefferson directly, and more often than not segregated by party affiliation, absent of ladies whom he did not intend to be privy to political conversation; see Merry Ellen Scofield, "The Fatigues of His Table: The Politics of Presidential Dining During the Jefferson Administration," *Journal of the Early Republic* 26, 3 (Fall 2006): 449–69.
31. *Jefferson's Memorandum Books*, James A. Bear Jr. and Lucia C. Stanton, eds. (Princeton, NJ: Princeton University Press, 1997), abbreviated in this book as *JMB*.
32. See Peterson, *Jefferson Image in the American Mind*; Francis D. Cogliano, *Thomas Jefferson: Reputation and Legacy* (Charlottesville: University of Virginia Press, 2006); and Andrew Burstein, *Democracy's Muse: How Thomas Jefferson Became an FDR Liberal, a Reagan Republican, and a Tea Party Fanatic, All the While Being Dead* (Charlottesville: University of Virginia Press, 2015).
33. For a concise yet thorough treatment of Jefferson's conception of democracy, individually and collectively, as an antimonarchical and antiaristocratic expression of the oneness of the American people, see Peter S. Onuf, "Jefferson and American Democracy," in Francis D. Cogliano, ed., *A Companion to Thomas Jefferson* (Malden, MA: Wiley-Blackwell, 2012), 397–418. History shows that democracy is disorderly and does not necessarily bring out the best in people; this was the Adamsian view in the 1790s and beyond. My point is that the Jeffersonian rhetoric of democratic individualism is subverted when the cause of human dignity it is meant to serve suffers in

areas of equality of educational opportunity, legal rights in practice, and the central role corporations have come to play in exercising political pressure. For a good analysis of these issues, connecting soft authoritarianism and democratic individualism, see Nadia Urbinati, *The Tyranny of the Moderns* (New Haven, CT: Yale University Press, 2015), 12–27; on FDR's conversion of Jefferson's political image, see Burstein, *Democracy's Muse*, 3–26.

34. The obnoxious use of the Confederate battle flag and removal of Confederate statues from the U.S. Capitol and various cities sparked considerable discussion and debate from 2015, leading to acts of violence, most notably over the Robert E. Lee statue in Charlottesville that brought white nationalists to the city in August 2017. Jefferson's symbolism became part of a media-fueled conversation during these years; see, pointedly, Michael Signer, *Cry Havoc: Charlottesville and American Democracy Under Siege* (New York: Public Affairs, 2020); "Thomas Jefferson Statue Removed from City Hall After Complaints That It Honored an Enslaver," *Washington Post*, November 23, 2021; Sarah Smart, "Statue of Thomas Jefferson Is Removed from New York City Hall After 187 Years," CNN, November 24, 2021, www.cnn.com/2021/11/24/us/thomas-jefferson-statue-removed/index.html.

35. I am guided by such works as *The Knowledge Illusion: Why We Never Think Alone* (New York: Riverhead, 2017), in which cognitive scientists Steven Sloman and Philip Fernbach detail frailties in the human mind that cause even outwardly intelligent people to deny the complexity of the truth, instead assigning singular credit for historical change where many others, sometimes many thousands, bring their passion and expertise to any movement. "Human memory is finite and human reasoning is limited," they assert (p. 200), noting that Susan B. Anthony was not singularly responsible for the Nineteenth Amendment, and Martin Luther King Jr. did not make civil rights legislation happen on the strength of his ideas alone. We know that Thomas Jefferson did not democratize America. Hero worship is natural, resistant to correction, an oversimplification that is almost always wrong.

CHAPTER 1: "SAVAGE ENOUGH"

1. On the pact between Jefferson and Carr, see Randall, 1:83.
2. TJ to Madison, December 8, 1784, *PTJ*, 7:558–59. The word *carré(e)* means simply "square."
3. TJ's sketch, ca. March 1826, Manuscripts Division, Library of Congress. The taller obelisk that stands there now was installed after the version Jefferson sketched (set in place in 1833) was carved up by souvenir-hunting visitors to Monticello over succeeding years, after Monticello was sold to offset Jefferson's debts. The protective

iron gate preventing entry today was installed later in the middle decades of the nineteenth century; prior to that, a brick wall was all that bounded the cemetery. The original obelisk was given to the University of Missouri (Columbia) by Jefferson's heirs in 1883 (see http://www.monticello-assoc.org/1826-to-civil-war.html).

4. The text of Jefferson's will is given in Nathan Schachner, *Thomas Jefferson: A Biography* (New York: Appleton-Century-Crofts, 1951), 1:20–21, and Brodie, 38. Projecting the Freudian interpretation that persists throughout the biography, Brodie follows directly with "A father's death always means release from a certain parental despotism, benevolent though it may be. But when the liberation comes too young, and is accompanied by sudden responsibility without real power—for Jefferson inherited no property or slaves till twenty-one—there is likely to be disconcerting experience of inadequacy if not outright youthful failure."

5. Susan Kern, *The Jeffersons at Shadwell* (New Haven, CT: Yale University Press, 2010), 59–62; Thomas Jefferson Randolph's Memoirs, ca. 1874, Papers of the Randolph Family of Edgehill, MSS 1397, Special Collections, University of Virginia Library, Charlottesville, Box 11, folder 35.

6. K. Edward Lay and Nathaniel Mason Pawlett, "Architectural Surveys Associated with Early Road Systems," *Bulletin of the Association for Preservation Technology* 12 (1980): 3–36. The name "Secretary's" derives from the first purchaser of land in the area, John Carter, who served as secretary of the Council of the Colony of Virginia.

7. Randall, 1:9n.

8. *The Garden and Farm Books of Thomas Jefferson*, Robert C. Baron, ed. (Golden, CO: 1987), 32; Frederick Doveton Nichols and Ralph E. Griswold, *Thomas Jefferson, Landscape Architect* (Charlottesville: University Press of Virginia, 1978), 2–6.

9. Jefferson's reluctance to disinter his father and sister may have had to do with the taboo of removing the bones of those long deceased. We don't know enough to speculate as to when or how the two grave markers came to disappear.

10. Randall remarks on the resemblance and calls Peter Jefferson's penmanship, of which there are few extant examples, "beautiful" (1:15); Abigail Adams to Cotton Tufts, September 8, 1784, *Adams Family Correspondence*, Richard Alan Ryerson, ed. (Cambridge, MA: Harvard University Press, 1993), 5:456–59.

11. The last of the signers was Charles Carroll of Carrollton, Maryland (1737–1832), who was no fan of Jefferson's. Before the election of 1800, fearing a Jefferson presidency, he said the Virginian lacked "steadiness & prudence" and "would dissolve this Union." See Carroll to Alexander Hamilton, April 18, 1800, *Papers of Alexander Hamilton*, Harold C. Syrett, ed. (New York: Columbia University Press, 1976), 12:412–13.

12. Malone, 1:426–31; TJ to John Page, September 6, 1808, FOL. Jefferson's lifelong friend Page, a conscientious Anglican, was near death; whether or not Jefferson was

thinking of it at the time, September 6 was the anniversary of his own wife's death. The lines from Job appear in the section of the *Book of Common Prayer* titled "The Order for the Burial of the Dead."

13. The Fry-Jefferson map was quite reliable, and Jefferson drew on it at length when he produced his own Virginia map in 1786 for inclusion in *Notes on the State of Virginia*, published in London and Paris while he resided in France as the U.S. minister. See Coolie Verner, "Mr. Jefferson Makes a Map," *Imago Mundi* 14 (1959): 96–108.

14. Kern, *The Jeffersons at Shadwell*, 183–99; Jeffrey L. Hantman, *Monacan Millennium: A Collaborative Archaeology and History of a Virginia Indian People* (Charlottesville: University of Virginia Press, 2018), chap. 2; how often Jefferson encountered Indians is not easy to pinpoint, but in a letter of 1792, from Philadelphia, he reminded his daughter of a chief from the Mississippi region who visited them at the time of the British invasion of central Virginia, and was moved to name his son Jefferson: "One of the Indian chiefs now here, whom you may remember to have seen at Monticello a day or two before Tarlton drove us of [*sic* for "off"], remembers you and enquired after you. He is of the Pioria nation. Perhaps you may recollect that he gave our name to an infant son he then had with him and who, he now tells me, is a fine lad" (TJ to Martha Jefferson Randolph, December 31, 1792, *PTJ*, 24:806).

15. Nancy Shoemaker, *A Strange Likeness: Becoming Red and White in Eighteenth-Century North America* (New York: Oxford University Press, 2004), 129–39; on the social composition of the Virginia backcountry west of Albemarle, see Warren R. Hofstra, "'The Extention of His Majesties Dominions': The Virginia Backcountry and the Reconfiguration of Imperial Frontiers," *Journal of American History* 84 (March 1998): 1281–1312; and Hofstra, "The Virginia Backcountry in the Eighteenth Century: The Question of Origins and the Issue of Outcomes," *Virginia Magazine of History and Biography* 101 (October 1993): 485–508.

16. Dating of *Notes on Virginia* tends to be imprecise. Jefferson considered his book complete as of late 1782/early 1783, though it first appeared in Europe while he resided in Paris. There was a 1785 edition published in Paris (a small print run of two hundred copies), and a larger number produced in London by John Stockdale and published in 1787. See *Notes on the State of Virginia*, Robert Pierce Forbes, ed., (New Haven, CT: Yale University Press, 2022), xix–xxi.

17. *Notes on the State of Virginia*, ed. Forbes, Query VI, esp. 99–105. The speech was first printed in the *Virginia Gazette*, February 4, 1775. Jefferson's rendering of the tragedy he sets forth in the Logan episode reveals an acute sensibility that attaches to his taste in literature before the Revolution, in which tales of distress predominate.

One can argue that his draft of the Declaration of Independence is of a piece with sentimental fiction. There is sublimity written into the upheaval in the tragic character's life. For a pertinent study of this phenomenon, see Paul Goring, *The Rhetoric of Sensibility in Eighteenth-Century Culture* (New York: Cambridge University Press, 2005).

18. The context in which Jefferson reexamined his memories was the imminence of a second war with Great Britain. Congress was in the very process of declaring war, and Anglo-Indian alliances in the Great Lakes region were of preeminent concern. Praising the peaceful Cherokees, who, though no longer a presence in Virginia, were by Jefferson's accounting "far advanced in civilisation," with agricultural self-sufficiency, improving literacy, and representative government, he deplored the tribes of the Northwest that fell under England's sway. Not all would be seduced, he averred, but "the backward will yield, & be thrown further back. These will relapse into barbarism & misery, lose numbers by war & want, and we shall be obliged to drive them, with the beasts of the forest into the Stony [i.e., Rocky] mountains." Jefferson to Adams, June 11, 1812, *PTJ-R*, 5:123–25; TJ to the Marquis de Chastellux, June 7, 1785, *PTJ*, 8:184–86.

19. Jefferson's chief aim here was to illustrate the uncontested power of language. Though he was struck dumb, he meant to separate himself, and his knowledge, from less discerning writers who drew their conclusions about Indians from conversations colonial British, French, and Americans transcribed at treaty councils. These accounts, whether focused on trade, religion, or cultural practices, rarely approximated a balanced narrative. Jefferson wished to show sensitivity to an ancient culture that most whites considered "strange" and did not do justice to.

20. The renowned psychologist Daniel Kahneman writes about the mind's difficulty in separating memories from experience. "The remembering self is sometimes wrong, but it is the one that keeps score and governs what we learn from living, and it is the one that makes decisions... This is the tyranny of the remembering self." See Kahneman, *Thinking, Fast and Slow* (New York: Farrar, Straus & Giroux, 2011), chap. 35, quote at 381; see also Daniel L. Schachter, *Searching for Memory: The Brain, the Mind, and the Past* (New York: Basic Books, 1996), especially on "flashbulb memories" (pp. 195–201), which could explain the power of Jefferson's long-held image of the Cherokee chief.

21. Douglas McClure Wood, "'I Have Now Made a Path to Virginia': Outacite Ostenaco and the Cherokee-Virginia Alliance in the French and Indian War," *West Virginia History*, New Series 2 (Fall 2008): 31–60; Colin G. Calloway, *The American Revolution in Indian Country: Crisis and Diversity in Native American Communities* (New York: Cambridge University Press, 1995), 7–32 and chap. 7.

22. What seems remarkable is how little oral history about Peter and Jane has been obtained from this family, given that Jefferson forged an especially strong bond with his numerous grandchildren and shared anecdotes with them relating to lessons learned as he grew older. When left in the hands of subsequent generations, Shadwell is a blur and Peter Jefferson's personality is gleaned mainly through accounts of his activities outside the family. Thomas failed to pass down stories that would point to father and son forming any kind of emotional connection. See variously the interpretations given by Randall, 1:6–19; Schachner, *Thomas Jefferson*, chaps. 1 and 2; Merrill D. Peterson, *Thomas Jefferson and the New Nation* (New York: Oxford University Press, 1970), 5–9; Brodie, 40–44; and Jack McLaughlin, *Jefferson and Monticello: The Biography of a Builder* (New York: Henry Holt, 1988), 46–49. Peterson doubted that father and son were able to enjoy an affectionate relationship owing to the lengthy separations. Susan Kern provides the most detail about life at Shadwell and paints a thorough, appreciative portrait of Jane Randolph Jefferson as a competent individual warranting her son's respect, noting, too, that the name Jane was passed down within the Jefferson-Randolph genealogy; see Kern, *The Jeffersons at Shadwell*, 68–71.

23. Jefferson's great-granddaughter wrote of the family account of Peter's "remarkable powers of endurance," of his wary eye in confronting ravenous animals in the wilderness, rising above episodes of hunger when others in his party fainted. Peter is quoted saying, "It is the strong in body who are both the strong and free in mind." See Sarah N. Randolph, *The Domestic Life of Thomas Jefferson* (Charlottesville: University Press of Virginia, 1978), 19–20. Fed material from Jefferson's grandchildren, Henry S. Randall writes of Peter as a man of "gigantic stature and strength" and states that his son told the family of an incident in which Peter had by himself "pulled down a ruinous shed" with a rope, after "three able-bodied slaves" could not do so. "He was one of those calmly and almost sternly self-relying men, who lean on none, who desire help from none. And he certainly had both muscles and mind which could be trusted!" Curiously, the biographer goes on to say that Jefferson's "aversion" to discussing his mother was "unquestionably" owing to "shyness." See Randall, 1:13–14.

24. By comparison, population in rural areas outside Philadelphia around midcentury did not exceed five households per square mile, and in such places the average landholding was smaller than in rural Virginia. See Duane E. Ball, "Dynamics of Population and Wealth in Eighteenth-Century Chester County, Pennsylvania," *Journal of Interdisciplinary History* 6 (Spring 1976): 621–44; on the importance of smithing and geographical distribution of other kinds of artisan activity in the colonial period, see Christine Daniels, "'WANTED: A Blacksmith Who Understands

Plantation Work': Artisans in Maryland, 1700–1810," *The William and Mary Quarterly* 50 (October 1993): 743–67.

25. "Letter of Rev. James Maury to Philip Ludwell, on the Defence of the Frontiers of Virginia, 1756," *Virginia Magazine of History and Biography* 19 (July 1911): 292–304.

26. Brodie, 54–55. Malone credits Maury with an Enlightenment sensibility but gives more attention to his embitterment from being in poor health, financially burdened, and constantly arguing with other clerics; Malone, 1:43–45. Kevin J. Hayes, a superior researcher, provides the most insightful and nuanced portrait of Maury, interpolating a course of study from the scholar's books and his known writings on education; contrary to the depictions of Brodie and Malone, Hayes notes that "Maury's erudition rests lightly on his words, which remain playful and unassuming." See Hayes, *The Road to Monticello: The Life and Mind of Thomas Jefferson* (New York: Oxford, 2008), 32–42, quote at 40.

27. Land acquisition was ever on the lips of the Albemarle gentry. Once the French and Indian War ended, the attention of Virginians returned to Kentucky's settlement potential. All adopted the Indian word for the region they had their sights set on, and when the Revolution came, "Kentucke" still lay mostly in Indigenous hands. So, in 1776, Virginians promptly determined it to be a separate county within their state, which, based upon the charter issued in 1609 by James I, extended to the Mississippi River. Some claim that the word for Kentucky is of Cherokee origin and means "land of tomorrow," while other linguists believe it derives from a different Iroquois tongue, Wyandot or Seneca, and means "meadowland." See William Bright, *Native American Place Names of the United States* (Norman: University of Oklahoma Press, 2004), 213.

28. TJ to Elizabeth Blair Thompson, January 19, 1787; to John Page, June 25, 1804; to William Blount, March 19, 1796, *PTJ*, 11:58, 29:34, 43:652-53; to Benjamin Rush, August 17, 1811; to Maury Jr., April 25, 1812, *PTJ-R*, 4:87-88, 669–71; Randall, 1:18. "The happiest moments [my heart] knows are those in which it is pouring forth it's affections to a few esteemed characters," he wrote quintessentially to his Philadelphia landlady and lifelong friend Eliza House Trist; TJ to Trist, December 15, 1786, *PTJ*-10:601.

29. Edgar Wallace, "Dabney Carr," *Louisa County Historical Magazine* 2 (December 1970): 8–15; TJ to John Page, February 21, 1770, *PTJ*, 1:36.

30. Nancy Isenberg and Andrew Burstein, *The Problem of Democracy: The Presidents Adams Confront the Cult of Personality* (New York: Viking, 2019), 258–59.

31. *The Memoirs of Lieut. Henry Timberlake* (London: printed for the author, 1765), quote at 125; Stephanie Pratt, "Reynolds' 'King of the Cherokees' and Other Mistaken Identities in the Portraiture of Native American Delegations, 1710–1762," *Oxford Art*

Journal 21 (1998): 133–50. Timberlake generally used the name Ostenaco for the Cherokee chief, occasionally invoking the alternative names Man Killer and Judd's Friend (referring to an early trader). In England the name was written as Outacity; elsewhere he has been designated Outacite Ostenaco. As to the fallibility of memory, I have consulted many works in cognitive neuroscience on episodic memory, or "constructive memory," as it's also known, and point to Daniel L. Schacter as one of the most influential scholars in the field.

32. TJ to Baron Geismar, September 6, 1785; to Charles Bellini, September 30, 1785, *PTJ*, 8:499–500, 568.
33. The sketch has been dated to May 1768 or earlier; Persian jasmine had only been recently introduced to the American South a short time before this, by the aptly named Alexander Garden, a South Carolinian of Scottish origin, after whom the gardenia was named; see "Monticello: mountaintop layout plan," in the Coolidge Collection at the Massachusetts Historical Society, image N61; K34.
34. Everett E. Edwards, *Jefferson and Agriculture* (Washington, D.C.: United States Department of Agriculture, 1943); Barbara McEwan, *Thomas Jefferson: Farmer* (Jefferson, NC: McFarland, 1991), viii–xii, 86–89; Lucia Stanton, "Better Tools for a New and Better World: Jefferson Perfects the Plow," in Leonard Sadowsky et al., eds., *Old World, New World: American and Europe in the Age of Jefferson* (Charlottesville: University of Virginia Press, 2010), 200–222; Philip Tabb to TJ, April 7, 1809; TJ to Tabb, June 1, 1809, *PTJ-R*, 1:111, 252. Tabb had an interest in versions of moldboard plows. Jefferson's Philadelphia friend, the celebrated portrait painter and technology enthusiast Charles Willson Peale, told him: "Your Mould-board ought to be studied by every Man that makes a Plow"; see Peale to TJ, September 9, 1811, *PTJ-R*, 4:137.

CHAPTER 2: "SUKEY AT SMITH"

1. Mark R. Wenger, "Thomas Jefferson, the College of William and Mary, and the University of Virginia," *Virginia Magazine of History and Biography* 103, 3 (July 1995): 339–74; Merrill D. Peterson, *Thomas Jefferson and the New Nation* (New York: Oxford University Press, 1970), 10–18; Alan Taylor, *Thomas Jefferson's Education* (New York: W. W. Norton, 2019), 19–28.
2. Randall, 1:20–21; on Jefferson's reportedly "easy and natural" conversational style with visitors, and the contrast in his familiar style with that of Henry, see Annette Gordon-Reed and Peter S. Onuf, *"Most Blessed of the Patriarchs": Thomas Jefferson and the Empire of the Imagination* (New York: W. W. Norton, 2016), 238–47, 254–61; on Henry's diction, see Kevin J. Hayes, *The Mind of a Patriot: Patrick Henry*

and the World of Ideas (Charlottesville: University of Virginia Press, 2008), 57–58; for a strong synthesis of the Jefferson-Henry relationship over time, and Jefferson's refusal to respond to Henry's attempts to repair their broken ties after they'd parted ways politically, see John A. Ragosta, "Thomas Jefferson v. Patrick Henry," *Virginia Magazine of History and Biography* 132, 3 (2024): 207–44.

3. In a patriotic application, Jefferson and others frequently credited someone, male or female, as an "ornament of their country"; on pronatalism, see Jenny Davidson, *Breeding: A Partial History of the Eighteenth Century* (New York; Columbia University Press, 2009).

4. Similarly, "Yea, men should have begotten children from some other source, no female race existing; thus would no evil ever have fallen on mankind." (Euripides); *Jefferson's Literary Commonplace Book*, ed. Douglas L. Wilson (Princeton, NJ: Princeton University Press, 1989), 73, 76, 81; Kenneth A. Lockridge, *On the Sources of Patriarchal Rage: The Commonplace Books of William Byrd and Thomas Jefferson and the Gendering of Power in the Eighteenth Century* (New York: New York University Press, 1992). Senior scholars reviewing Lockridge's fascinating, controversial interpretation of Jeffersonian misogyny (rooted in hostility toward his mother) overall tended to praise the work; for a more nuanced critique, see Frank Shuffelton, "Presenting Jefferson," *Early American Literature*, 30, 3 (1995): 275–85; and Nancy Isenberg, "Boys to Men," *American Quarterly* 48, 2 (June 1996): 367–74.

5. *Jefferson's Literary Commonplace Book*, 126–27.

6. John D. Battle Jr., "The 'Periodical Head-achs' of Thomas Jefferson," *Cleveland Clinic Journal of Medicine* 51 (Fall 1984): 531–39. Recent studies indicate that the onset of migraines in men typically starts between age fifteen and nineteen, and that they disproportionately affect women worldwide (18 percent to 6 percent). Migraine is most often brought on by mood disorders, anxiety, and stress, especially in its chronic form; see Aimen Vanood et al., "Migraine and the Gender Divide," *Neurologic Clinics*, 41, 2 (May 2023): 2321–47; Francesca Pistoia et al., "Behavioral and Psychological Factors in Individuals with Migraine Without Psychiatric Comorbidities," *Journal of Headache and Pain*, 23 (August 26, 2022), n.p.

7. Kevin J. Hayes, *The Road to Monticello: The Life and Mind of Thomas Jefferson* (New York: Oxford, 2008), 50–57; TJ to William Duane, October 1, 1812, *PTJ-R*, 5:366. To his friend Dr. Benjamin Rush, Jefferson had written a year earlier: "Having to conduct my grandson through his course in Mathematics, I have resumed that study with great avidity"; see TJ to Rush, August 17, 1811, *PTJ-R*, 4:87.

8. *Autobiography*, https://www.loc.gov/resource/mtj1.052_0517_0609/; Malone, 1:80.

9. W. Edwin Hemphill, "George Wythe Courts the Muses," *William and Mary Quarterly* 9 (July 1952): 338–45.

10. In 1774, Jefferson yielded to Wythe's broad-mindedness when he included in his recommendations to the Virginia delegation to the Continental Congress the possibility, after slavery's abolition, "the infranchisement of the slaves we have." His efforts continued into 1783, though abolition was never a cause Jefferson would stick his neck out for, and there is no evidence that he ever believed that free Blacks held a stake in American society; see Richard D. Brown, *Self-Evident Truths: Contesting Equal Rights from the Revolution to the Civil War* (New Haven, CT: Yale University Press, 2017), 12–13; and Paul Finkelman, "Jefferson and Slavery: 'Treason against the Hopes of the World,'" Peter S. Onuf, ed., *Jeffersonian Legacies* (Charlottesville: University Press of Virginia, 1994), 181–221.
11. Imogene E. Brown, *American Aristides: A Biography of George Wythe* (Rutherford, NJ: Fairleigh Dickinson University Press, 1981), esp. chap. 16; Brown, *Self-Evident Truths*, 13–14; Bruce Chadwick, *I Am Murdered: George Wythe, Thomas Jefferson, and the Killing that Shocked a New Nation* (Hoboken, NJ: John Wiley & Sons, 2009); W. Edwin Hemphill, "Examinations of George Wythe Sweeney for Forgery and Murder," *William and Mary Quarterly* 12 (October 1955): 543–74; William DuVal to TJ, June 4, 1806; TJ to DuVal, June 14, 1806, FOL; Angela Onwuachi-Willig, "Multiracialism and the Social Construction of Race: The Story of *Hudgins v. Wrights*," in *Race Law Stories*, ed. Rachel F. Moran and Devon Wayne Carbado (St. Paul, MN: Foundation Press, 2008), 147–73; *Hudgins v. Wrights*, 11 Va. 134 (1806).
12. Here I am thinking of the lack of constraint Jefferson felt when he gave chase to the state religion or applied his pen to the task of confronting imperial preconceptions about colonial subservience. Once the yoke of British dominion was eliminated, he worked to overturn what he saw as a seizure of the free mind by the religious establishment. He became a more proactive version of Wythe in this early period of his political career.
13. Linda K. Tesar, "Forensic Bibliography: Reconstructing the Library of George Wythe," *Law Library Journal* 105 (Winter 2013): 57–73; Tesar, "The Library Reveals the Man: George Wythe, Legal and Classical Scholar," in *"Esteemed Bookes of Lawe" and the Legal Culture of Early Virginia*, ed. Warren M. Billings and Brent Tarter (Charlottesville: University of Virginia Press, 2017), 115–36; Wythe bookplate at the Colonial Williamsburg Foundation, translation courtesy of Encyclopedia Virginia (https://encyclopediavirginia.org). Compared to most bibliophiles of the time, Wythe's taste in books did not extend to religious texts. The history of thought dominated.
14. TJ to Wythe, October 23, 1794, *PTJ*, 28:181; Randall, 1:31–32; Schachner, *Thomas Jefferson*: 1:32–33.
15. TJ to Robert Skipwith, August 3, 1771, *PTJ*, 1:74–77.

16. *JMB*, 1:265, 346. He first mentions Belinda by name in his accounts of 1771; she and her several children became his property on his mother's death.
17. TJ to Page, December 25, 1762, and January 20, 1763, *PTJ*, 1:3–9.
18. Science has determined that adult brains are cognitively better formed to respond to rejection with positive views of oneself (i.e., self-protective biases). In modern psychological studies, heightened sensitivity to rejection is found among younger people; this is one area in which the distance between Jefferson's time and ours is less critical. Wary of generalizing, I am accepting of the validity of conclusions in a combined psychology/brain science study at Harvard University in which physiology of the brain is as important a factor as social behavior; see Alexandra M. Rodman, Katherine E. Powers, and Leah H. Somerville, "Development of Self-Protective Biases in Response to Social Evaluative Feedback," *Proceedings of the National Academy of Sciences* 114, 50 (December 12, 2017): 13158–63.
19. TJ to Page, April 9, 1764, *PTJ*, 1:17–18.
20. Charles Hobson, "An Enduring Political Rivalry: Thomas Jefferson and John Marshall," in Dustin Gish and Andrew Bibby, eds., *Rival Visions: How Jefferson and His Contemporaries Defined the Early American Republic* (Charlottesville: University of Virginia Press, 2021), 300–301.
21. Ronald Hatzenbuehler, "Growing Weary in Well-Doing: Thomas Jefferson's Life among the Virginia Gentry," *Virginia Magazine of History and Biography* 101, 1 (January 1993): 5–36; Cynthia Kierner, "'The Dark and Dense Cloud Perpetually Lowering over Us': Gender and the Decline of the Gentry in Postrevolutionary Virginia," *Journal of the Early Republic* 20, 2 (2000): 185–217; Christopher Michael Curtis, *Jefferson's Freeholders and the Politics of Ownership in the Old Dominion* (New York: Cambridge University Press, 2012), 35–36; on the eventual impact of Virginia's decline on the psychology of elite Virginians, see Robert P. Sutton, "Nostalgia, Pessimism, and Malaise: The Doomed Aristocrat in Late Jeffersonian Virginia," *Virginia Magazine of History and Biography*, 76, 1 (January 1968): 41–55.
22. Randall, 1:40–41.
23. The "Walker Affair" is a staple of every modern Jefferson biography, routinely paired in press commentaries with allusions to his relationship with Sally Hemings; TJ to John Walker, April 13, 1803, *PTJ*, 40:187–89.
24. Thomas Shelton, *Tachygraphy, or Short-Writing the Most Easie Exact and Speedie* (London: E. Tracy, 1710); TJ to Page, January 23, 1764, *PTJ*, 1:14–15; *JMB*, 1:207–208.
25. Brodie, 73.
26. *JMB*, 1:209–10, 253. The editors of *Jefferson's Memorandum Books* note that there was a Smith's boardinghouse Jefferson later visited and that his father-in-law-to-be owned a property called Stith's.

27. Malone, 1:153–55, 447–51; TJ to Page, July 15, 1763, *PTJ*, 1:11.
28. While it has been erroneously reported that he rode the circuit and practiced law in a number of county courts, he frequently provided legal services to distant county attorneys when filings were made in the General Court in Williamsburg. From 1761, county court lawyers were proscribed from practicing in the General Court, and vice versa; see Frank L. Dewey, *Thomas Jefferson, Lawyer* (Charlottesville: University Press of Virginia, 1986), Appendix B.
29. Susan Dunn, *Dominion of Memories: Jefferson, Madison, and the Decline of Virginia* (New York: Basic Books, 2007); Charles A. Miller, *Jefferson and Nature: An Interpretation* (Baltimore: Johns Hopkins University Press, 1988), esp. 219–22.
30. TJ to Thomas Mann Randolph, May 30, 1790, *PTJ*, 16:448–50.
31. TJ to Adams, June 10, 1815, *PTJ-R*, 8:523.
32. *Jefferson's Literary Commonplace Book*, Introduction, Appendix B; statistics regarding Greek entries at 230.
33. Matthew Stewart, *Nature's God: The Heretical Origins of the American Republic* (New York: Norton, 2014), 274–87. Jefferson's precepts, his rules for life that borrow from the aforementioned authors, are repeated most often in his instructive letters to young men first acquiring a reading habit.
34. John Bernard, *Retrospections of America, 1797–1811* (New York: Harper & Brothers, 1887), 238–39.
35. For an analysis of the appeal of *Tristram Shandy* that speaks as well to the interiority contained in it that Jefferson would have responded to, see Stephen Toulmin, "The Inwardness of Mental Life," *Critical Inquiry* 6, 1 (1979): 1–16. Both Jefferson and Sterne refused to be tied down by confining conventions for the written word; for examples that promote comparisons with Jefferson's creative neology and figures of speech, see especially Marshall Brown, *Preromanticism* (Stanford, CA: Stanford University Press, 1991), chap. 11. Rarely is the film version of a book near as satisfying as the original, but in the case of *Tristram Shandy: A Cock and Bull Story*, the 2005 movie written by Frank Cottrell Boyce, directed by Michael Winterbottom, and starring Steve Coogan, is a brilliant exercise in capturing for a modern audience the anarchic genius of Sterne's original.
36. David Thomas Konig and Michael P. Zuckert, eds., *Jefferson's Legal Commonplace Book* (Princeton, NJ: Princeton University Press, 2019), Introduction. When establishing a curriculum for the University of Virginia in advance of its 1825 opening, Jefferson stated that "from an early period of my studies indeed, I have been sensible of the importance of making [Anglo-Saxon] a part of the regular education of our youth; and at different times, as leisure permitted, I applied myself to the study of

it, with some degree of attention." See "An Essay or Introductory Lecture towards Facilitating Instruction in the Anglo-Saxon . . . ," FOL.

37. Only at the end of his life, with hindsight, could Jefferson look upon the ancient Anglo-Saxon language as a common cultural inheritance, spiritually linking the United States and Britain: "How much would contribute to the happiness of these two nations a brotherly emulation in doing good to each other, rather than the mutual vituperations so unwisely and unjustifiably sometimes indulged in by both," he wrote nostalgically in 1825. "No two people on earth can so much help, or hurt each other." Invoking "the kind affections of kindred blood," the abandonment of which marked the crescendo of his Declaration in 1776, he advanced his plan to join linguistic forces: "Let us then . . . vie in common efforts to do each other all the good we can . . . to reform and republish, in forms more advantageous, what we already possess, and theirs to add to the common stock the inedited treasures which have been too long buried in their despositories [sic]" (ibid., FOL).

CHAPTER 3: "TILL HARMONY ROUSE EV'RY GENTLE PASSION"

1. *Jefferson's Literary Commonplace Book*, ed. Douglas L. Wilson (Princeton, NJ: Princeton University Press, 1989), Appendix A.
2. Peterson, *Thomas Jefferson and the New Nation* (New York: Oxford University Press), 13; *JMB*, 1:3–23, 50–53; Dewey, *Thomas Jefferson, Lawyer*, chap. 4.
3. Jefferson's disparagement of Henry's studiousness and legal erudition stem from his understanding (probably confirmed for him by George Wythe, who examined Henry for the bar in 1760) that Henry scarcely had any interactions with legal scholars, relied on a few key texts, and learned mostly on his own. On Jefferson's pique and the facts of the matter, see Dewey, *Thomas Jefferson, Lawyer*, 124–25; Jon Kukla, *Patrick Henry: Champion of Liberty* (New York: Simon & Schuster, 2017), 32–37; Peter S. Onuf, *Jefferson and the Virginians: Democracy, Constitutions, and Empire* (Baton Rouge: Louisiana State University Press, 2018), 53–54.
4. Malone, 1:121–23; Randall, 1:50; John B. Boles, *Jefferson: Architect of American Liberty* (New York: Basic Books, 2017), 28.
5. Lucia Stanton, *"Those Who Labor for My Happiness": Slavery at Thomas Jefferson's Monticello* (Charlottesville: University of Virginia Press, 2012), 107–109; *JMB*, 1:209–210 and passim. In *JMB*, there are more than a hundred instances of Jefferson's allocating funds for Jupiter to spend, or borrowing from him when he himself lacked petty cash; material on T. J. Randolph and Phil Evans is in Papers of the Randolph Family of Edgehill, Special Collections, University of Virginia Library,

MSS 1397, Box 11, folder 35. It should also be noted, however, that after the Civil War Randolph became increasingly attached to white supremacist groups.

6. Malone, 1:156; Brodie, 86, 505n26. *Virginia Gazette*, January 2, 1772. Bathurst Skelton's death was reported in the *Virginia Gazette* in October 1768, without its cause being named.

7. Ronald L. Giese, *Tobacco Cultivation in Virginia, 1610–1863, and Patterns of Thought and Management Related to Thomas Jefferson* (Lynchburg, VA: Thomas Jefferson's Poplar Forest, 2016).

8. *JMB*, xxxviii, 245–49; Frederick Doveton Nichols and Ralph E. Griswold, *Thomas Jefferson, Landscape Architect* (Charlottesville: University Press of Virginia, 1978), 90–96, 100. Both Rowe's and Shenstone's Works are included in the 1771 library recommendations Jefferson made to Robert Skipwith; two excerpts from *The Fair Penitent* are included in the Literary Commonplace Book as well, likely written down during the same period. See also Jack McLaughlin, *Jefferson and Monticello: The Biography of a Builder* (New York: Henry Holt, 1988), 340–41; McLaughlin notes that Shenstone ended up more or less as Jefferson did (if not precisely for the same reasons), his expenditures in beautifying his farm causing grave financial distress. Touring English gardens in 1786, Jefferson commented on Shenstone, "It is said that he died of the heartaches which his debts occasioned him" (344).

9. *Jefferson's Literary Commonplace Book*, ed. Douglas L. Wilson (Princeton, NJ: Princeton University Press, 1989), 115, 179–80; N. Rowe, *The Fair Penitent: A Tragedy* (Dublin: George Risk, 1723), Act I, scene 1; Act II, scene 1; Act III, scene 1, quotes at 5–7, 14, 26, 30. "The World shou'd learn to love by Virtuous Rules, and Marriage be no more the Jest of Fools," says Horatio (Act I, scene 1, 12); later, confronting Lothario, he expresses his disgust with the rake's savage nature as an unmarriageable man: "Rather than make you bles't they wou'd die Virgins, and stop the Propagation of Mankind" (Act II, scene 2, 20). A survey of newspapers from the 1760s through the 1780s indicates that the play was performed in cities like New York, Philadelphia, and Savannah and widely sold in bookstores.

10. Skipwith to TJ, July 17, 1771; TJ to Robert Skipwith, August 3, 1771, *PTJ*, 1:74–77. Tabitha Wayles Skipwith appears to have died no later than 1773, when she would have been nineteen; almost nothing is known of the later life of Robert Skipwith (1748–?), though he may have remarried, because he was later referred to as "my grandfather" by an unnamed grandson; see also Malone, 1:432–33.

11. *JMB*, 1:297, 343; Andrew Burstein, *The Inner Jefferson: Portrait of a Grieving Optimist* (Charlottesville: University Press of Virginia, 1995), 40, 65–66; Matthew R. Halley, "Jefferson's Ornithology Reconsidered," *Proceedings of the American Philosophical Society* 162, 3 (September 2018): 231–58; other than the mockingbird, goldfinches

and cardinals were commonly kept by early Americans; see Christal G. Pollock, "Companion Birds in Early America," *Journal of Avian Medicine and Surgery* 27, 2 (June 2013): 148–51.

12. Sarah N. Randolph, *The Domestic Life of Thomas Jefferson* (Charlottesville: University Press of Virginia, 1978), 44–45.
13. Randall, 1:63, Randolph, *Domestic Life*, 342–44.
14. *JMB*, 1:36–37, 249, 252; McLaughlin, *Jefferson and Monticello*, 34–35; Nichols and Griswold, *Thomas Jefferson, Landscape Architect*, 102; James M. Gabler, *Passions: The Wines and Travels of Thomas Jefferson* (Baltimore: Bacchus Press, 1995), 3.
15. TJ to Fleming, May 19, 1773, *PTJ*, 1:97–98.
16. *JMB*, 1:340; TJ to Dabney Carr (the son), January 9, 1816, *PTJ-R*, 9:367–69, referencing Jefferson's correspondence with William Wirt that became part of the latter's Patrick Henry biography.
17. Barbara McEwen, *Thomas Jefferson: Farmer* (Jefferson, NC: McFarland, 1991), 2, 42–43, 198n8; Herbert E. Sloan, *Principle and Interest: Thomas Jefferson and the Problem of Debt* (Charlottesville: University Press of Virginia, 1995), 14–18, 55, 254n15; *Autobiography*, handwritten text digitally retrievable at https://www.loc.gov/resource/mtj1.052_0517_0609/; Randall, 1:65–66. Unlike Monticello, Poplar Forest was the property's name a good many years before Jefferson inherited it.
18. Lucia Stanton, *"Those Who Labor for My Happiness,"* 108, 168; Annette Gordon-Reed, *The Hemingses of Monticello: An American Family* (New York: W. W. Norton, 2008), 496–503; Lucia Stanton, "Jefferson's People: Slavery at Monticello," in Frank Shuffelton, ed., *The Cambridge Companion to Thomas Jefferson* (New York: Cambridge University Press, 2009), 83–86. When forced by his inherited debt to sell land and slaves in 1785, 1792, and 1793, Jefferson kept the families who lived and labored at Monticello intact.
19. *JMB*, 1:372, 406. The child, of course, received the name of Jefferson's still-living mother, whose burial placement in 1776 has been discussed in chapter 1. The naming follows tradition, though it also suggests a dutiful son, not one with conflicted feelings toward his parent. Another way to look at the naming is to recall how deeply Jefferson cherished his older sister Jane, who died at the age of twenty-five, in 1765.

CHAPTER 4: "THROWN INTO A REVERIE"

1. Modern philosophy links perceptual experience such as that which intensive reading produces to creativity, free will, and consciousness itself; for a concise explanation of the phenomenon, see Mark Sadoski, "Imagination, Cognition, and Persona," *Rhetoric Review* 10, 2 (Spring 1992): 266–78; on emotive response

and the cultural mind, see Antonio Damasio, *The Strange Order of Things: Life, Feeling, and the Making of Cultures* (New York: Pantheon, 2018); on reading and socialization, see esp. Abigail Williams, *The Social Life of Books: Reading Together in the Eighteenth-Century Home* (New Haven, CT: Yale University Press, 2017).

2. *JMB*, 1:370–75; Merrill D. Peterson, *Thomas Jefferson and the New Nation* (New York: Oxford University Press, 1970), 33–45; Malone, 1:128–42, 169–73; Brodie, 94–97.

3. TJ to Charles McPherson, February 27, 1773; James Macpherson to Charles McPherson, August 7, 1773; Charles McPherson to TJ, August 12, 1773, *PTJ*, 1:96–97, 100–102. It is worth noting that when Robert Skipwith requested of Jefferson a list of books for his starter library, he specifically mentioned *Fingal* as one he wished to own, possibly because when they met at the Wayles home, Jefferson had talked it up; see Skipwith to TJ, July 17, 1771, *PTJ*, 1:74–75.

4. *Jefferson's Literary Commonplace Book*, 172. "The death of the youth was dark in his soul," went a typical line from *Fingal* (Book III).

5. *Fingal: An Ancient Epic Poem . . . Translated from the Gallic Language by James Macpherson* (Dublin: Richard Fitzsimons, 1762), Books I–III, 14n, 16, 50n, 54n, 58, 119n, 164n. Modern Irish and Scottish both descended from the Celts, and Fingal was meant to be the Scottish version of the Irish figure Finn mac Cumhal (Finn MacCool)—predating the latter's appearance in literature in order to separate and privilege the abused Scottish Highlands over the colorful traditions of Ireland.

6. Hugh Trevor-Roper, *The Invention of Scotland: Myth and History* (New Haven, CT: Yale University Press, 2008), chap. 4; for a worthwhile comparison to the Homeric effect, see Joel P. Christensen, *The Many-Minded Man: The Odyssey, Psychology, and the Therapy of Epic* (Ithaca, NY: Cornell University Press, 2020).

7. Trevor-Roper, *Invention of Scotland*, chaps. 5 and 6; Sowerby, 4:464–66; Paul J. deGategno, *James Macpherson* (Boston: Twayne Publishers, 1989). Celtic Ireland was a more literate place than the Scottish Highlands, yet its poems and songs did not find their way to Scotland until the second millennium. Without being publicly vocal, Scotsman David Hume was one who considered *Fingal* a forgery. Trevor-Roper cites chapter and verse, showing that James Macpherson had a close cousin named Lachlan Macpherson of Strathmashie, a well-heeled wit and poet whose Gaelic was excellent and whose social connections across the Scottish Highlands were broad-based. Another of their surname, Ewen Macpherson, was a schoolmaster who knew old Gaelic well and had a relationship with his kinsman. Ambitious young James, lacking wealth, and probably egged on by his Strathmashie relation, took verses of Ossian known to some Highlanders and creatively embellished. Upon publication of *Fingal*, he could or would not recant once it brought fame to him. So he "found" more old Gaelic writings and patched them together to extend the saga (and his career).

It is more than a little ironic that Trevor-Roper was himself caught up in the initial enthusiasm of the so-called Hitler Diaries when these came to light in 1983. As the author of *The Last Days of Hitler* (1947), he authenticated what later proved to be forgeries. Note, too, that *The Invention of Scotland* was published posthumously.

8. Trevor-Roper, *Invention of Scotland*, 114, 137–38. Calling Jefferson a romantic in this context is meant to connect to his enjoyment of ancient myth, which, as Northrop Frye noted long ago, are "fictions and metaphors that identify aspects of human personality with the natural environment." The Ossianic environment is a sublime one in which positive passions are acted out in raw nature, much in the way that the Homeric epics were regarded at the time Jefferson was exposed to both. Again, Frye says that "locating the sublime in mountains and oceans and wildernesses, where a solitary traveler confronts it" does not restrict either the idea that "the reasonable may be associated with the natural"—that romantics can be conservative—or that "nature is a moral riddle," all of which corresponds to Jefferson's appreciation of the genre; see Frye, *A Study of English Romanticism* (New York: Random House, 1968), 4–5, 26–30. For a nuanced study of Dr. Johnson's search for literary truth, see Thomas M. Curley, *Samuel Johnson, the Ossian Fraud, and the Celtic Revival in Great Britain and Ireland* (New York: Cambridge University Press, 2009).

9. Andrew Burstein, *The Inner Jefferson: Portrait of a Grieving Optimist* (Charlottesville: University Press of Virginia, 1995), 31–34, 297n49; Sowerby, 4:497; Kevin J. Hayes, *The Road to Monticello: The Life and Mind of Thomas Jefferson* (New York: Oxford University Press, 2008), chap. 10; Amanda Louise Johnson draws a fascinating connection between the Ossianic revenge plot and the Indian Logan whose passions Jefferson celebrates in *Notes on Virginia*: Johnson, "Thomas Jefferson's Ossianic Romance," *Studies in Eighteenth-Century Culture* 45 (2016): 26–29; TJ to Peter Carr, August 10, 1787, *PTJ*, 12:14–19; "Statement of Account with John March," July 10, 1803, *PTJ*, 40:712. Hugh Blair's 1783 *Lectures on Rhetoric and Belles Lettres* was to become a standard college text in the U.S. through to the Civil War. Soon after its appearance, Jefferson enthusiastically acquired copies and favored James Madison with one. The copy of Ossian he presented to granddaughter Septimia Randolph (1814–1887) was a 1783 Paris edition that survives and is at Monticello. Other correspondence indicates that his erudite, worldly older granddaughter, Ellen Wayles Randolph (Coolidge), was well versed in Ossian.

10. Preface to *Fingal: An Ancient Epic Poem* (Dublin, 1762 edition). At the age of eighty, in 1823, Jefferson finally admitted in an aside that Macpherson was likely a fraud: "Ossian, if not antient, is equal to the best morsels of antiquity." (TJ to Lafayette, November 4, 1823, FOL.)

11. He did not regard his own inherited privilege as necessarily productive of haughty indifference, though it is easy to imagine how others might see hypocrisy in his pose.
12. Hannah Spahn observes in this context that Jefferson "did not see a fundamental difference in the ways historical and fictional writings represented the idealized nature of an ordered universe." He "even considered it rather impractical that historical lessons were 'confined to real life.'" See Spahn, *Thomas Jefferson, Time, and History* (Charlottesville: University of Virginia Press, 2011), 129; TJ to Robert Skipwith, August 3, 1771, *PTJ*, 1:76–81.
13. Marquis de Chastellux, *Travels in North America in the Years 1780, 1781, and 1782*, 2 vols., trans. and ed. Howard C. Rice Jr. (Chapel Hill: University of North Carolina Press, 1963), 2:389–95; Burstein, *Inner Jefferson*, 32–33; John B. Boles, *Jefferson: Architect of American Liberty* (New York: Basic Books, 2017), 105–106. Macpherson's Ossian stimulated a taste for pathos then current.
14. *Jefferson's Legal Commonplace Book*, 329–47, quote at 333. The Celts had formed into "cantons," Pelloutier writes, using the word by which the Swiss have designated their political-administrative subdivisions going back many centuries. To Pelloutier, these Celtic cantons effectively constituted nations (340–41); Sowerby, 1:105. On Jefferson's Anglo-Saxon emphasis as a kind of romance, see Amanda Louise Johnson, "Thomas Jefferson's Anglo-Saxon Genesis," *Modern Philology* 114, 3 (February 2017): 680–701.
15. Jack P. Greene, "State Identities and National Identity in the Era of the American Revolution," in *Creating the British Atlantic: Essays on Transplantation, Adaptation, and Continuity* (Charlottesville: University of Virginia Press, 2013), chap. 15.
16. Nathan Schachner, *Thomas Jefferson: A Biography* (New York: Appleton-Century-Crofts, 1951), 1:103; Peterson, *Thomas Jefferson and the New Nation*, 71; Imogene E. Brown, *American Aristides: A Biography of George Wythe* (Rutherford, NJ: Fairleigh Dickinson University Press, 1981), 67–69; John Kukla, *Patrick Henry: Champion of Liberty* (New York: Simon & Schuster, 2017), 147–57; John Ferling, *Independence: The Struggle to Set America Free* (New York: Bloomsbury, 2011), 60–93; and John Ferling, *Whirlwind: The American Revolution and the War That Won It* (New York: Bloomsbury, 2015), 91–98; on Pendleton's personal and political style in relation to his Revolutionary peers, see Jack P. Greene, "Character, Persona, and Authority: A Study in Alternative Styles of Political Leadership in Revolutionary Virginia," in W. Robert Higgins, ed., *The Revolutionary War in the South: Power, Conflict, and Leadership* (Durham, NC: Duke University Press, 1979), 3-42. Jefferson was no doubt eager to impress his mother's first cousin Peyton Randolph with the argument advanced in *A Summary View*. It was a Virginia-level version of what he would inject two years later into the Declaration. In both texts, he sought to encompass the views

of a large body of men rather than to impose the views of a singular thinker; yet his particular imprint remains.

17. *A Summary View of the Rights of British America* (Williamsburg, VA: Clementina Rind, [1774]), 6. This was Jefferson's personal, annotated copy, now preserved in the Library of Congress and available in digital form: https://www.loc.gov/item/08016823/

18. Richard B. Sher, *The Enlightenment and the Book* (Chicago: University of Chicago Press, 2009), 528; *The Rights of Great Britain Asserted against the Claims of America* (Philadelphia: R. Bell, 1776), quotes at 56–57, 65, 73, 88.

19. On Germaine, see Andrew Jackson O'Shaughnessy, *The Men Who Lost America: British Leadership, the American Revolution, and the Fate of the Empire* (New Haven, CT: Yale University Press, 2013), 170–75; "Fragment of the Composition Draft of the Declaration of Independence," *PTJ*, 1:420–23.

20. *Jefferson's Legal Commonplace Book*, 227–39; Hayes, *The Road to Monticello*, 89–92. In addition to a historical understanding of how barbarism was succeeded by royalism, some of Kames that Jefferson copied down concerned how the impulse to avenge injuries and perceived wrongs was translated into legislation as societies matured, how "the practice of converting punishment into money" was altered once crime was "reckoned too atrocious to admit of a pecuniary conversion."

21. Sher, *The Enlightenment and the Book*, 504–505; Andrew H. Browning, *Schools for Statesmen: The Divergent Educations of the Constitution's Framers* (Lawrence: University Press of Kansas, 2022).

22. On the origins and character of the Scots-Irish who migrated to America, see Judith A. Ridner, *The Scots Irish of Early Pennsylvania: A Varied People* (Philadelphia: Pennsylvania Historical Association, 2018).

23. Thomas Reid, *An Inquiry into the Human Mind* (London: Thomas Tegg, 1823), chap. 1, sections II–IV. Reasoning and the moral faculties "unfold themselves by degrees" as a person ages from infancy, he writes, "inspired with the various principles of common sense, as with the passions of love and resentment." Reid, chap. 5 ("Touch"), section VII ("Of the Existence of a Material World"). Gilman M. Ostrander argued that Jefferson was of the Scottish school without consciously knowing it; see Ostrander, "Jefferson and Scottish Culture," *Historical Reflections* 5, 2 (Winter 1978): 233–49.

24. TJ to William G. Munford, December 5, 1798, *PTJ*, 30:594–97; Randall, 1:54.

25. Henry Home, Lord Kames, *Essays on the Principles of Morality and Natural Religion* (Edinburgh: R. Fleming, 1751), Part II, Essay 6 and Conclusion.

26. TJ to Thomas Law, June 13, 1814, *PTJ-R*, 7:415. The British-born Law was, for a time, married to Martha Washington's granddaughter, separating in 1804 and suing for divorce in 1810.

27. Kames, *Essays on the Principles of Morality and Natural Religion*, Part II, Essay 7; Adam Smith, *The Theory of Moral Sentiments* (Amherst, NY: Prometheus Books, 2000), Part III, sect. 3. In Smith, a hierarchy of sympathies extended from self-care to family members to friends to the world at large. While "affection gradually diminishes as the relation grows more and more remote," and loss of physical proximity tends to reduce the quality of these feelings, that does not mean "indifference" will follow, because the power of sympathy is connected to the innate desire to extend beyond oneself, and be regarded as virtuous: "Sensibility to the feelings of others, so far from being inconsistent, with the manhood of self-command, is the very principle upon which that manhood is founded" (Part VI, sect. 2).
28. Smith, *Theory of Moral Sentiments*, Part III, sect. 5.
29. Smith, *Theory of Moral Sentiments*, Part I, sect. 2.
30. Francis Hutcheson, *An Inquiry into the Original of Our Ideas of Beauty and Virtue* (London: D. Midwinter, 1738), Treatise 1, Sections 1 and 4.
31. TJ to Carr, August 10, 1787, *PTJ*, 12:14–19. Similarly, in a philosophic letter to John Adams many years later, contesting the Hobbesian view: "I believe, on the contrary, that it is instinct, and innate, that the moral sense is as much a part of our constitution as that of feeling, seeing, or hearing; as a wise creator must have seen to be necessary in an animal destined to live in society: that every human mind feels pleasure in doing good to another." TJ to Adams, October 14, 1816, *The Adams-Jefferson Letters: The Complete Correspondence Between Thomas Jefferson and Abigail and John Adams*, ed. Lester J. Cappon (Chapel Hill: University of North Carolina Press, 1987), 492.
32. Sher, *The Enlightenment and the Book*, 506–515. Until the final third of the eighteenth century, Boston was prominent in American book publishing, only to be eclipsed by Philadelphia; in the nineteenth century, New York emerged as America's publishing center. Throughout these years, many of the entrepreneurs in the print trade were Scottish- or Irish-born.
33. Randall, 1:98–101.
34. Woody Holton, *Liberty Is Sweet: The Hidden History of the American Revolution* (New York: Simon & Schuster, 2021), 202–203; John Kukla, *Patrick Henry: Champion of Liberty* (New York: Simon & Schuster, 2017), 186.
35. Malone, 1:193–99; Kukla, *Patrick Henry*, 165–76; *JMB*, 1:391–99. On the hiring of Richard, see Douglas R. Egerton, *Death or Liberty: African Americans and Revolutionary America* (New York: Oxford University Press, 2009), 41–42; Egerton speculates that in this instance, Jefferson hesitated about bringing one of the enslaved from Monticello because he thought the time spent in the North might expose the man to "dangerous dreams of autonomy."

36. Malone, 1:204; *JMB*, 1:399–403.
37. *JMB*, 1:406–11; TJ to Page, October 31, 1775; to Eppes, November 7 and 21, 1775; Eppes to TJ, November 10, 1775 and June 3, 1776, *PTJ*, 1:250–52, 264, 15:572–75. During absences in 1775 and 1776, outside of Patty herself, Jefferson relied most on Francis Eppes for news of her and their children's health.
38. Malone, 1:159, 209–10.
39. TJ to John Randolph, November 29, 1775; Randolph to TJ, October 25, 1779, *PTJ*, 1:268–70, 3:114–21.
40. *JMB*, 1:412–19; Brodie, 114–15.

CHAPTER 5: "EVERY FIBRE OF THAT PASSION"

1. Garry Wills, *Inventing America: Jefferson's Declaration of Independence* (New York: Vintage, 1978), chap. 11, quote at 209.
2. Jefferson's debt to John Locke's *Essay Concerning Human Understanding* and *Two Treatises on Government* (including his acceptance of the king as a mere man) is well known. When asked by his Italian friend Philip Mazzei to explain the common law, Jefferson wrote: "The Common law is a *written law* the text of which is preserved from the beginning of the 13th. century downwards, but what preceded that is lost. It's substance however has been retained in the memory of the people and committed to writing from time to time in the decisions of the judges and treatises of the jurists, insomuch that it is still considered as a lex scripta, the letter of which is sufficiently known to guide the decisions of the courts." From here, Jefferson combines his understanding of the law's history with Scottish ideas of the moral sense: "When commerce began to make progress, when the transfer of property came into daily use, when the modifications of these transfers were infinitely diversified, when with the improvement of other faculties that of the moral sense became also improved, and learnt to respect justice in a variety of cases which it had not formerly discriminated." TJ to Mazzei, November (?), 1785, *PTJ*, 9:67–72. Note, too, that Mazzei helped Jefferson acquire Italian Renaissance and later Italian titles that privileged natural law and self-governance; see Linda L. Carroll, *Thomas Jefferson's Italian and Italian-Related Books in the History of Universal Personal Rights* (New York: Bordighera Press, 2019).
3. Regarding the Greeks and Romans, one could argue that, in addition to the Roman example (here mentioning Tacitus) and the Greek (Epicurus), Jefferson's Declaration partakes of the ethical concept of equity (*Epieikeia*) in Aristotle, sometimes translated as "justice" or "decency" in the *Nicomachean Ethics*.
4. The phrase "pursuit of happiness" was openly borrowed from John Locke's *Essay Concerning the Human Understanding*. Jefferson never professed that the

Declaration as he wrote it was an original work; rather, it was meant to reflect ideas held in common by the members of Congress. On the obsession with "happiness" among high-minded individuals of this generation, see Henry Steele Commager's essay "The Pursuit of Happiness" in Commager, *Jefferson, Nationalism, and the Enlightenment* (New York: George Braziller, 1975), 93–121; on the Lockean element, see, among other interpretive works, Carl L. Becker, *The Declaration of Independence: A Study in the History of Political Ideas* (New York: Vintage, 1922), chap. 2.

5. Matthew Stewart, *Nature's God: The Heretical Origins of the American Republic* (New York: Norton, 2014), 171–80, 188–94; on Pope's preeminence in America, see Andrew Burstein, *Longing for Connection: Entangled Memories and Emotional Loss in Early America* (Baltimore: Johns Hopkins University Press, 2024).

6. The choice of "self-evident" has served to feed an idealism that masks the social reality. It was meant at the time as justification of America's *self*-founding, the righteous breakaway from Britain ostensibly necessary to rescue natural rights from those who would deny them.

7. "Nonsectarian monotheism" was how America got "In God We Trust" on its currency. See Andrew Koppelman, *Defending American Religious Neutrality* (Cambridge, MA: Harvard University Press, 2013).

8. TJ to R. H. Lee, July 29, 1776; to Madison, December 8, 1784, *PTJ*, 1:477, 7:557–60.

9. *Notes on the State of Virginia*, ed. Robert Pierce Forbes (New Haven, CT: Yale University Press, 2022), Query XVII, 244; TJ to Rush, 1800, September 23, 1800, *PTJ*, 32:166–69.

10. A considerable amount of excellent scholarship exists on Jefferson's activism with respect to religious freedom, including Charles B. Sanford, *The Religious Life of Thomas Jefferson* (Charlottesville: University Press of Virginia, 1984); Merrill D. Peterson and Robert C. Vaughan, eds., *The Virginia Statute for Religious Freedom: Its Evolution and Consequences in American History* (New York: Cambridge University Press, 1988); John A. Ragosta, *Religious Freedom: Jefferson's Legacy, America's Creed* (Charlottesville: University of Virginia Press, 2013); M. Andrew Holowchak, *Thomas Jefferson's* Notes on the State of Virginia: *A Prolegomena* (Wilmington, DE: Vernon Press, 2023), chap. 8; Richard Samuelson, "Jefferson and Religion: Private Belief, Public Policy," in Frank Shuffelton, ed., *The Cambridge Companion to Thomas Jefferson* (New York: Cambridge University Press, 2009), chap. 10.

11. The point here is that Jefferson would not justify slavery as antebellum Southern elites did—a sentiment that might otherwise have helped rescue his reputation

among modern liberals were it not for his and others' foot-dragging during and after his presidency.

12. During the war, "mother country" was rarely evoked by supporters of independence, while on July 3, 1779, in a speech before Parliament, King George III hoped Americans would come to prefer "peace and re-union with their mother country" to an "unnatural and dangerous connection" with France; after the peace, correspondents began referring to the "former mother country." On the inherited Anglo-American understanding of consent and the marriage contract that undergirds Jefferson's logic, see Mary Lyndon Shanley, "Marriage Contract and Social Contract in Seventeenth Century English Political Thought," *Western Political Quarterly* 32, 1 (March 1979): 79–91, writing, "In Locke's view, the marriage contract was revocable, and its terms were negotiable" (90).

13. In eighteenth-century Britain, there were three possible avenues to divorce: (1) "absolute divorce" by act of Parliament, (2) annulment by an ecclesiastical court, proclaiming that there had never been a marriage, (3) also by an ecclesiastical court, a "divorce from bed and board," which resulted in a legal separation. The only practical course of action tended to be for a separate maintenance arrangement to be legislatively ordered, so that spouses lived apart and neither could remarry. In Virginia, an absolute divorce was unknown until after the Revolution. See Frank L. Dewey, *Thomas Jefferson, Lawyer* (Charlottesville: University Press of Virginia, 1986), chap. 7.

14. See especially Frank L. Dewey, "Thomas Jefferson's Notes on Divorce," *William and Mary Quarterly* 39, 1 (January 1982): 212–23; Glenda Riley, "Legislative Divorce in Virginia, 1803–1850," *Journal of the Early Republic* 11, 1 (Spring 1991): 51–67; Riley says of Jefferson that "because he was writing during the early 1770s, he was affected by a trend that had been developing for over seventy years: a gradual broadening of American divorce attitudes and laws. Since the early 1700s, the number of divorce petitions filed in colonies that permitted divorce had increased," though Virginia lagged behind several other colonies (quote at 54). On emotions involved in family inheritance matters, see Jan Lewis, "Domestic Tranquillity and the Management of Emotion Among the Gentry of Pre Revolutionary Virginia," *William and Mary Quarterly* 39, 1 (January 1982): 135–49; *JMB*, 1:277–78.

15. Samuel von Pufendorf, *Of the Law of Nature and Nations* (Oxford, England: L. Litchfield, 1710), Contents and Book 1. Another relevant title Jefferson owned that addressed conjugal relations in various contexts is a 1732 edition denoted "Ochino on Polygamy," which bore the subtitle "The Cases of Polygamy, Concubinage, Adultery, Divorce, &c. Seriously and Learnedly Discussed." Ochino was an

Italian cleric of the sixteenth century who emigrated to Switzerland; see Carroll, *Thomas Jefferson's Italian and Italian-Related Books*, 37–38; Sowerby, 2:51.

16. Matthew Crow, "Thomas Jefferson and the Uses of Equity," *Law and History Review* 33, 1 (February 2015): 151–80; Dewey, *Thomas Jefferson, Lawyer*; Andrew Burstein and Nancy Isenberg, *Madison and Jefferson* (New York: Random House, 2010), 38–41.

17. An earlier, related usage of "desolation" to stir up war fever comes from Lieutenant Colonel Adam Steven, who served under George Washington in two wars. Here, in writing to Washington at the outset of the French-American War, the enemy are Indians: "They go about and Commit their Outrages at all hours of the day and nothing is to be seen or heard of, but Desolation and murders heightened with all Barbarous Circumstances, and unheard of Instances of Cruelty. They Spare the Lives of the Young Women, and Carry them away to gratify the Brutal passions of Lawless Savages." See Steven to Washington, October 4, 1755, *Papers of George Washington, Colonial Series*, ed. W. W. Abbott (Charlottesville: University Press of Virginia, 1983), 2:72–73.

18. Pufendorf repeatedly brings up fidelity to the marriage bed and the dangers resulting from one or the other party's defection, to wit: "In Marriage, the Parties acquire a *Right* over the *Bodies* of each other, which ought not, on either side, to be taken from them against their Will"; Pufendorf, *Of the Law of Nature and Nations*, Book 6, chap. 1; among the Greeks, it was an understood privilege of the well-to-do to engage in sexual frivolity; see James N. Davidson, *Courtesans and Fishcakes: The Consuming Passions of Classical Athens* (New York: St. Martin's, 1997).

19. TJ to R. H. Lee, July 29, 1776, *PTJ*, 1:477–78.

20. Pendleton to TJ, August 10, 1776, *PTJ*, 1:488–89.

21. *JMB*, 1:431.

22. TJ to Hancock, October 11, 1776, *PTJ*, 1:524.

23. *JMB*, 1:432–46, 771n; Susan R. Stein, *The Worlds of Thomas Jefferson at Monticello* (New York: Harry N. Abrams, 1993), 362–63; Charles A. Miller, *Jefferson and Nature: An Interpretation* (Baltimore: Johns Hopkins University Press, 1988), 41–42.

24. TJ to Adams, May 16, 1777; Adams to TJ, May 26, 1777, Lester J. Cappon, ed., *The Adams-Jefferson Letters: The Complete Correspondence between Thomas Jefferson and Abigail and John Adams* (Chapel Hill: University of North Carolina Press, 1987), 4–6; Boles, *Jefferson*, 85–86.

25. TJ to Wythe, August 13, 1786, *PTJ*, 10:243–45; Richard D. Brown, *The Strength of a People: The Idea of an Informed Citizenry in America, 1650–1870* (Chapel Hill: University of North Carolina Press, 1996), 75–77.

26. Malone, 1:252–55, 264; Schachner, *Thomas Jefferson: A Biography*, 175–77; TJ to William Short, April 9, 1788, Thomas Jefferson Papers, Swem Library, College of William Mary.
27. Clark to TJ, February 20, 1782; TJ to Clark, November 26, 1782, *PTJ*, 6:159–60, 204–205. There is evidence that Jefferson spoke contemptuously of Henry's intellect as early as 1776, when his friend Francis Eppes reacted without self-censorship to Henry's becoming Virginia's first governor: "At a time when men of known integrity and sound understanding are most necessary they are rejected and men of shallow understandings fill the most important posts." Eppes to TJ, July 3, 1776, *PTJ*, 15:576.
28. Francis D. Cogliano offers the most detailed analysis of Jefferson's vindictive treatment of Hamilton and Washington's more focused practical-mindedness, in Cogliano, *A Revolutionary Friendship: Washington, Jefferson, and the American Republic* (Cambridge, MA: Harvard University Press, 2024), 128–34; see also Peterson, *Thomas Jefferson and the New Nation*, 174–81; Schachner, *Thomas Jefferson*, 1:182–84. A similar attitude on Jefferson's part would attach to his treatment of Aaron Burr, his own vice president, a quarter century later, when he helped mastermind his prisoner's prosecution and refused to see shades of gray or question his own ethics.
29. Peter McQuilkin Mitchell, "Loyalist Property and the Revolution in Virginia," PhD diss., (Dept. of History, University of Colorado, 1965), chap. 3; TJ to Fleming, June 8, 1779, *PTJ*, 2:288–89.
30. John Ferling, *Whirlwind: The American Revolution and the War That Won It* (New York: Bloomsbury, 2015), 254–61, 281–84; Schachner, *Thomas Jefferson*, 1:186–87; Peterson, *Thomas Jefferson and the New Nation*, 187–92.
31. Harry Ammon, *James Monroe* (New York: McGraw-Hill, 1971); Peter Thompson, *Heir through Hope: Thomas Jefferson's Lifelong Investment in William Short* (New York: Oxford University Press, 2023); George Green Shackelford, *Jefferson's Adoptive Son: A Biography of William Short, 1759–1849* (Lexington: University Press of Kentucky, 1993).
32. Malone, 1:314–15; Page to TJ, December 9, 1780, *PTJ*, 4:191–93.
33. TJ to Lafayette, March 10, 1781, *PTJ*, 5:113–14; Randall, 1:287–90.
34. Peterson, *Thomas Jefferson and the New Nation*, 215–42; Malone, 1:330–69; Boles, *Jefferson*, 101–102; Peter S. Onuf, *Jefferson and the Virginians: Democracy, Constitutions, and Empire* (Baton Rouge: Louisiana State University Press, 2018), 58–59; Kukla, *Patrick Henry*, 257–60, stating that Henry was actually less instrumental in Nicholas's action than Jefferson thought; TJ to Nicholas, July 28, 1781; Nicholas to TJ, July 31, 1781, *PTJ*, 6:104–106. The British effort to capture Jefferson at Monticello is related by Lieutenant-Colonel Banastre Tarleton in his memoir: "The attempt to

secure Mr. Jefferson was ineffectual; he discovered the British dragoons from his house, which stands on the point of a mountain, before they could approach him, and he provided for his personal liberty by a precipitate retreat"; see Tarleton, *A History of the Campaigns of 1780 and 1781 in the Southern Provinces of North America* (London: T. Cadell, 1787), 297.

35. TJ to Monroe, May 20, 1782; to Francis Hopkinson, March 13, 1789, *PTJ*, 6:184–87, 14:650–51.
36. [Louis Hue Girardin], *The History of Virginia*, vol. 4 (Petersburg, VA: M. W. Dunnavant, 1816), chap. 19. Girardin notes that another target of kidnap by the British attackers was Jefferson's neighbor Jack Walker.
37. Autobiography, https://www.loc.gov/resource/mtj1.052_0517_0609/.
38. *JMB*, 1:521.
39. TJ to Benjamin Harrison, September 22, 1782; to Elizabeth Wayles Eppes, October 3[?], 1782, Massachusetts Historical Society and *PTJ*, 6:197–200. Jefferson's draft of the Eppes letter has an unusual number of cross-outs and changes, suggesting the difficulty he had in finding the right language while under emotional strain.
40. Contemporaneous descriptions of Jefferson's process in the weeks and months following Patty's death, and his textualization of his loss, resemble the patterns ascribed more to female than to male eighteenth-century mourners. See, for an overview, Peter Marris, *The Politics of Uncertainty: Attachment in Public and Private Life* (New York: Routledge, 1996), chap. 9; and with particular relevance, Susan M. Stabile, *Memory's Daughters: The Material Culture of Remembrance in Eighteenth-Century America* (Ithaca, NY: Cornell University Press, 2004), 184–88; analyzing the Pennsylvania poet Hannah Griffitts (1727–1817), Stabile writes: "Fancy and imagination inscribe the loss, affection and sensibility transform blood and tears into ink," adding that grief was "part of the larger mistrust of female sensibility as potentially pathological," viewed as "neurotic, disorderly, excessive." Jefferson's behavior, and remarks he made to others, fit this model.
41. Sarah N. Randolph, *The Domestic Life of Thomas Jefferson* (Charlottesville: University Press of Virginia, 1978), 62–64; Andrew Burstein, *The Inner Jefferson: Portrait of a Grieving Optimist* (Charlottesville: University Press of Virginia, 1995), 60–63; *Literary Commonplace Book*, ed. Douglas L. Wilson (Princeton, NJ: Princeton University Press, 1989), 62, 182, 200–201. Jefferson slightly altered Sterne's original, deleting some words, and the exclamation marks are Jefferson's, not Sterne's.
42. Cynthia A. Kierner, *Beyond the Household: Women's Place in the Early South, 1700–1835* (Ithaca, NY: Cornell University Press, 1998); *The Poetical Works of Isaac Watts*, vol. 7 (London: Apollo Press, 1802), 140; Jan Lewis and Kenneth A. Lockridge, " 'Sally Has Been Sick': Pregnancy and Family Limitation Among Virginia Gentry

Women, 1780–1830," *Journal of Social History* 22 (Autumn 1988): 5–19; Susan E. Klepp, "Revolutionary Bodies: Women and the Fertility Transition in the Mid-Atlantic Region, 1760–1820," *Journal of American History* 85, 3 (December 1998): 910–45; Elaine G. Breslaw, *Lotions, Potions, Pills, and Magic: Health Care in Early America* (New York: New York University Press, 2012), 127–28; TJ to William Stephens Smith, October 22, 1786, *PTJ*, 10:478–79. Statistics suggest a degree of self-regulation in family size in American cities, at least after 1800.

43. Randolph to Madison, September 20, 1782, in Andrew Burstein and Nancy Isenberg, *Madison and Jefferson* (New York: Random House, 2010), 93–94.

CHAPTER 6: "GAZING LIKE A LOVER AT HIS MISTRESS"

1. Malone, 1:364–67; TJ to Elizabeth Blair Thompson, January 19, 1787, *PTJ*, 11:56–58.
2. On the use of ciphers by U.S. envoys abroad during this period, see Martin Clagett, *Scientific Jefferson Revealed* (Charlottesville: University of Virginia Endowment, 2009), chap. 5.
3. Nathan Schachner, *Thomas Jefferson: A Biography* (New York: Appleton-Century-Crofts, 1951), 1:247–55; Merrill D. Peterson, *Thomas Jefferson and the New Nation*, 274–85.
4. Peter S. Onuf, *The Origins of the Federal Republic* (Philadelphia: University of Pennsylvania Press, 1983).
5. G. K. Van Hogendorp to TJ, ca. April 6, 1784, and notes recorded later, *PTJ*, 7:80–83; Brodie, 180–81; Andrew Burstein, *The Inner Jefferson: Portrait of a Grieving Optimist* (Charlottesville: University Press of Virginia, 1995), 14–47. "I pitied Your Situation, for I thought you unhappy," Van Hogendorp opened up in the letter to Jefferson, which he sent in anticipation of their meeting again. The Dutch visitor observed Jefferson in Annapolis to be so bookish as to be entirely uninterested in public amusements.
6. Cynthia A. Kierner, *Martha Jefferson Randolph, Daughter of Monticello* (Chapel Hill: University of North Carolina Press, 2012), 42–50; TJ to Martha Jefferson, November 28, December 11, and December 22, 1783, in Randall, 1:389–91. As the family's legacy protector in the 1850s, Randall presented such letters as evidence of the family's openness, while showing Jefferson revealing how he "was wont to habitually address those he most loved and from whom he had the fewest personal reserves."
7. Randall, 1:412.
8. TJ to Monroe, March 18, 1785, *PTJ*, 8:42–45.

9. TJ to Monroe, June 17, 1785, *PTJ*, 8:227–34.
10. TJ to Abigail Adams, June 21, 1785, *The Adams-Jefferson Letters: The Complete Correspondence between Thomas Jefferson and Abigail and John Adams*, ed. Lester J. Cappon (Chapel Hill: University of North Carolina Press, 1987), 35. Rousseau characterized the d'Houdetots' marriage as loveless, the count "a gambler and a chicaner"; see Jean-Jacques Rousseau, *The Confessions* (New York: Penguin, 1953 [1781]), 408–409; Gilbert Chinard, *Les Amitiés américaines de Madame d'Houdetot d'après sa correspondence inédite avec Benjamin Franklin et Thomas Jefferson* (Paris: Librairie Ancienne Édouard Champion, 1924), 44–48.
11. TJ to Mme de Tott, November 28, 1786, February 28, 1787, and April 5, 1787; Mme de Tott to TJ, November 28, 1786, *PTJ*, 10:553–54, 11:187–88, 270–73.
12. Gilbert Chinard, *Thomas Jefferson: The Apostle of Americanism* (Ann Arbor: University of Michigan Press, 1957 [1929]), 161–62; Gilbert Chinard, *Trois amitiés françaises de Jefferson d'après sa correspondance inédite avec Madame de Bréhan, Madame de Tessé et Madame de Corny* (Paris: Société d'édition, 1927), 150–54; Élisabeth Vigée Le Brun was a favorite of the royal court, and completed portraits of Marie Antoinette; her 1785 portrait of Mme de Tott, titled *Bacchante* (a follower of the wine god Bacchus), is owned by the Clark Art Institute, Williamstown, MA; Madame de Corny to TJ, November 25, 1789 and May 19, 1801, *PTJ*, 15:554–55, 34:141–43; TJ to Martha Jefferson, June 14, 1787, *PTJ*, 11:472.
13. Chinard, *Trois amitiés françaises de Jefferson*, 65–76; William Howard Adams, *The Paris Years of Thomas Jefferson* (New Haven, CT: Yale University Press, 1997), 227–32; TJ to Mme de Tessé, March 20, 1787, *PTJ*, 11:226–28.
14. Lafayette to TJ, August 14, 1814, *PTJ-R*, 7:536–37; George Green Shackelford, *Jefferson's Adoptive Son: The Life of William Short, 1759–1849* (Lexington: University Press of Kentucky, 1993).
15. Hume quoted in Peter Gay, *The Enlightenment: The Science of Freedom* (New York: W. W. Norton, 1969), 33–34.
16. Maurizio Valsania, *Jefferson's Body: A Corporeal Biography* (Charlottesville: University of Virginia Press, 2017), 170. A recent study of patterns in European familiar letter writing of the eighteenth century demonstrates how literate women came to vie with male correspondents in expressing wit, drawing on sentimental fiction, and exhibiting increasing ease in just "letting go" on the page; see "The Triumph of the Familiar Letter," chapter 3 in Clare Monagle, Carolyn James, David Garrioch, and Barbara Caine, *European Women's Letter-writing from the Eleventh to the Twentieth Centuries* (Amsterdam: Amsterdam University Press, 2023), 129–194.
17. Anne C. Vila, *Enlightenment and Pathology: Sensibility in the Literature and Medicine of Eighteenth-Century France* (Baltimore: Johns Hopkins University

Press, 1998); G. J. Barker-Benfield, *The Culture of Sensibility: Sex and Society in Eighteenth-Century Britain* (Chicago: University of Chicago Press, 1987); Barker-Benfield explains that the novels that featured sensational psychology were predominantly written by women, and that Austen, for one, saw the genre as empowering for self-assertive women.

18. Roy Porter, *Flesh in the Age of Reason* (New York: W. W. Norton, 2003), chap. 15; Ritchie Robertson, *The Enlightenment: The Pursuit of Happiness, 1690–1790* (New York: Harper, 2021), 301–307; Malone, 2:143–44; TJ to Charles Bellini, September 30, 1785; to John Banister Jr., October 15, 1785; *PTJ*, 8:568–70, 635–38; *JMB*, 1:637. Despite the ocean air and change of venue, Jack died in 1788, soon after he returned to Virginia. Jefferson's friendly but combative argument on female fashion with the wealthy and beautiful Anne Willing Bingham, a Philadelphian he came to know in Paris, underscored his refusal to change his views about female empowerment; again, he cast Americans' relative simplicity as a virtue. Mrs. Bingham politely informed him that his contrasts were "rather overcharged." TJ to Bingham, February 7, 1787, *PTJ*, 11:122–23; Burstein *Inner Jefferson*, 113–14; Valsania, *Jefferson's Body*, 174–75; Annette Gordon-Reed and Peter S. Onuf, *"Most Blessed of the Patriarchs": Thomas Jefferson and the Empire of the Imagination* (New York: W. W. Norton, 2016), 108–12; see also Brian Steele, *Thomas Jefferson and American Nationhood* (New York: Cambridge University Press, 2012), chap. 2.

19. "Quobna Ottobah Cuguono," in Vincent Carretta, ed., *Unchained Voices: An Anthology of Black Authors in the English-Speaking World of the Eighteenth Century* (Lexington: University Press of Kentucky, 1996), 145–84; Jeffrey Gunn, "Creating a Paradox: Quobna Ottobah Cuguono and the Slave Trade's Violation of the Principles of Christianity, Reason, and Property Ownership," *Journal of World History* 21, 4 (December 2010): 629–56; Peter Fryer, *Staying Power: The History of Black People in Britain* (London: Pluto Press, 2018), 100–104. No image of Cuguono exists, though it is believed that he posed for a 1784 etching by Richard Cosway titled "The Artist and His Wife in a Garden, with a Black Servant"; see Edlie L. Wong, *Neither Fugitive nor Free: Atlantic Slavery, Freedom Suits, and the Legal Culture of Travel* (New York: New York University Press, 2009), 33–36.

20. *Jefferson in Paris* (1995), directed by James Ivory, starring a horribly miscast Nick Nolte as Jefferson. Well matched to her role as Maria Cosway was the actress Greta Scacchi, Italian-born daughter of an art dealer and painter. imdb.com/name/nm0000627.

21. Adams, *Paris Years of Thomas Jefferson*, 224–25; Brodie, 200; *Maria Hadfield Cosway* (museum exhibition catalog curated by Monja Faraoni and Laura Facchin,

Fondazione Maria Cosway, Lodi, Italy, 2022); she is shown in a 1787 portrait with her arms folded self-protectively and is wearing a cross.

22. Philippe Bordes, "Richard and Maria Cosway," *Burlington Magazine* 137 (October 1995): 700–702; Brodie, 200–201, 204.

23. Helen Duprey Bullock, *My Head and My Heart: A Little History of Thomas Jefferson and Maria Cosway* (New York: G. P. Putnam, 1945), 14–17; Adams, *Paris Years of Thomas Jefferson*, 225–27.

24. There are several theories about the wrist fracture, from an unsuccessful attempt to vault a fence to a preventable fall from a horse; see *JMB*, 1:639; Malone, 2:72–74; Merrill D. Peterson, *Thomas Jefferson and the New Nation* (New York: Oxford University Press, 1970), 349; Brodie, 207–208; L. H. Butterfield and Howard C. Rice Jr., "Jefferson's Earliest Note to Maria Cosway with Some New Facts and Conjectures on His Broken Wrist," *William and Mary Quarterly* 5, 1 (January 1948): 26–33; and TJ to William S. Smith, October 22, 1786, *PTJ*, 10:478. While it has not been absolutely proved that he was on an outing with Mrs. Cosway when the accident occurred, Malone, for one, says it's "a good guess." Protective of Jefferson's legacy, Malone characterized their relationship this way: "Like other deep intimacies of his life, this one remains obscure and mysterious" (2:72).

25. Sir William Parsons (1745–1817) was a composer of minuets who gave musical instruction to members of King George III's family from 1786. According to the Fondazione Maria Cosway in Lodi, Italy, he "was probably Maria's lover from 1790 to 1795."

26. Diane Boucher, "Maria Cosway (1760–1838): A Commentator on Modern Life," *British Art Journal* 18, 3 (Winter 2017/2018): 78–86; Elizabeth Cometti, "Maria Cosway's Rediscovered Miniature of Jefferson," *William and Mary Quarterly* 9 (April 1952): 152–55; and Susan R. Stein, *The Worlds of Thomas Jefferson at Monticello* (New York: Harry N. Abrams, 1993), 176. It should not escape notice that Trumbull himself already had experience with a sex scandal of his own making, having fathered a child out of wedlock; see Brodie, 213.

27. TJ to Maria Cosway, October 12, 1786, *PTJ*, 10:443–55; Andrew Burstein, *The Inner Jefferson*, 76–99; Jonathan Haidt, "'Dialogue Between My Head and My Heart': Affective Influences on Moral Judgment," *Psychological Inquiry* 13, 1 (2002): 54–56.

28. TJ to Maria Cosway, July 27, 1788, Special Collections, University of Virginia Library, University of Virginia, MSS 1683.

29. The most authoritative treatment of the course their relationship took is in Thompson, *Heir Through Hope: Thomas Jefferson's Lifelong Investment in William Short* (New York: Oxford University Press, 2023).

30. Lafayette to Washington, May 25, 1788, FOL.

31. TJ to Maria Cosway, July 1, 1787, Special Collections, University of Virginia Library, University of Virginia, MSS 1683, and *PTJ*, 11:519.
32. TJ to Monroe, August 9, 1788, *PTJ*, 13:490.
33. TJ to William Short, March 4, 1789, *PTJ*, 14:695–97; Thompson offers a cogent analysis of Jefferson's opinions on marriage in reaction to the ways of the French in *Heir Through Hope*, 56–57.
34. TJ to Maria Cosway, November 29, 1786; and December 27, 1820, *PTJ*, 10:555, *PTJ-R*, 16:497–99. He used the French adage fairly often in his correspondence, especially with William Short.
35. Adams, *Paris Years of Thomas Jefferson*, 225; Brodie, 222–25, 254; for an uncensored look at sexual culture in the artistic circles of London that the Cosways inhabited, see Vic Gatrell, *City of Laughter: Sex and Satire in Eighteenth-Century London* (New York: Walker, 2006).

CHAPTER 7: "AN ABUSE OF STRENGTH"

1. Ruth Mack, "D'Hancarville's Useful History," *Word and Image* 33, 3 (2017): 292–302; Caroline Winterer, "Classical Taste at Monticello," in Peter S. Onuf and Nicholas P. Cole, eds., *Thomas Jefferson, the Classical World, and Early America* (Charlottesville: University of Virginia Press, 2011), 84–85; Andrew Burstein, *The Inner Jefferson: Portrait of a Grieving Optimist* (Charlottesville: University Press of Virginia, 1995), 79; Adams, *Paris Years of Thomas Jefferson*, 107–108, 224–25, citing Francis Haskell, *Past and Present in Art and Taste* (New Haven, CT: Yale University Press, 1987), 31–45, on Hancarville's Italian friend. Hancarville specialized in ancient art, beginning with the Etruscans who ruled central Italy in the sixth century B.C. The remains of the Greeks and later Romans came under his study as well, and he compiled an illustrated history based on the collection he helped the British diplomat William Hamilton to acquire, which Hamilton sold to the British Museum.
2. Claude Quétel, *Escape from the Bastille* (New York: St. Martin's, 1990), first published in French as *Les Évasions de Latude* (1986); Andrew S. Curran, *Diderot and the Art of Thinking Freely* (New York: Other Press, 2019), 83–99. Diderot's incarceration lasted 102 days, during which time he received a visit from Jean-Jacques Rousseau.
3. Sowerby, 1:96; Elbridge Gerry to TJ, November 12, 1798; Fulwar Skipwith to TJ, January 15, 1805, *PTJ*, 30:577–78, 45:343–45.
4. Darren Staloff recently contributed a superior analysis of Jefferson's intellectual association with others who fell into Condorcet's circle, Parisian salon regulars like

the younger Pierre Jean George Cabanis (b. 1757) and Antoine Destutt de Tracy (b. 1754), the latter of whose work relating perception and sensation to the social sciences, *Éléments d'idéologie*, Jefferson helped bring to an American audience; see Staloff, "The Philosophical Politics of Jefferson and Adams," in Dustin Gish and Andrew Bibby, eds., *Rival Visions: How Jefferson and His Contemporaries Defined the Early American Republic* (Charlottesville: University of Virginia Press, 2021), 38–73. For more on the common effort among those in Condorcet's circle to apply their notions of socio-economic health to national policy during Jefferson's years in Paris, see Lynn Hunt, *The Revolutionary Self: Social Change and the Emergence of the Modern individual, 1770-1800* (New York: W. W. Norton, 2025).

5. David Williams, "Biography and the Philosophic Mission: Condorcet's *Vie de Voltaire*," *Eighteenth-Century Studies* 18 (Autumn 1985): 494–502; Ian Davidson, *Voltaire in Exile* (New York: Grove Press, 2004), 270–72, 290–91.

6. Iain McLean and Arnold B. Urken, "Did Jefferson or Madison Understand Condorcet's Theory of Social Choice?" *Public Choice* 73, 4 (June 1992): 445–57; in recent communication with the author, Professor McLean cites Condorcet's precise language in demonstrating Jefferson's direct borrowing from him: "Les bornes de la durée des lois constitutionnelles ne doivent pas s'étendre au delà d'une génération" (The limits placed on the duration of constitutional laws must not extend beyond one generation). See also Herbert L. Sloan, *Principle and Interest: Thomas Jefferson and the Problem of Debt* (Charlottesville: University Press of Virginia, 1995), Appendix A. Sloan prefers to leave open the possibility that they derived the theory in concert with each other, whereas McLean and Urken have no doubt that Condorcet was the greater theorist, the one individual from whom Jefferson derived his argument; Sowerby, 4:52–59.

7. David Williams, *Condorcet and Modernity* (New York: Cambridge University Press, 2004), 250–52.

8. Sowerby, 3:54, 63, 72, 86; TJ to Madison, January 12, 1789, *PTJ*, 14:436–38.

9. Williams, *Condorcet and Modernity*, 223–24, 253–56; TJ to Stiles, December 24, 1786, *PTJ*, 10:629.

10. From a forthcoming study by Iain McLean, shared with the author. TJ to Smith, November 13, 1787, *PTJ*, 12:355–57. Jefferson was telling Smith, a Princeton-educated Revolutionary War military officer, that popular misconceptions that lead to contained acts of violence are supported in a republic, where the rebellious are brought to justice, shown the error of their ways, and restored to civil society.

11. He is most explicit in a letter to a member of Congress from central Virginia: "I am persuaded myself that the good sense of the people will always be found to be the best army. They may be led astray for a moment, but will soon correct themselves.

The people are the only censors of their governors: and even their errors will tend to keep these to the true principles of their institution. To punish these errors too severely would be to suppress the only safeguard of the public liberty... Cherish therefore the spirit of our people, and keep alive their attention. Do not be too severe upon their errors, but reclaim them by enlightening them" (TJ to Edward Carrington, January 16, 1787, *PTJ*, 11:48–50).

12. Williams, *Condorcet and Modernity*, 139–71, quote at 146. He also proposed, during the intermediary period before across-the-board emancipation, that government-appointed doctors would check up on plantations to confirm that the enslaved were kept healthy and safe (151).

13. "Jefferson's Notes from Condorcet on Slavery (1788–89)"; TJ to Condorcet, August 30, 1791, *PTJ*, 14:494–98, 22:98–99.

14. Joel Barlow, *Letter to Henri Gregoire*... (Washington, DC: Roger Chew Weightman, 1809); TJ to Barlow, October 8, 1809, *PTJ-R*, 1:588–90; *Notes on the State of Virginia*, ed. Robert Pierce Forbes (New Haven, CT: Yale University Press, 2022), Query XIV. The historian Alan Taylor trenchantly exposes Jefferson's willful blindness in the same period, in opposing education for the enslaved beyond what encouraged good work habits; in 1808, an anonymous African American wrote to him in mocking tones of his reliance on the unfree, those "sweating in the fields," and asked rhetorically: "Is this the fruits of your education, Sir?" Years later, in conversation with the Marquis de Lafayette at Monticello, Jefferson was overheard protesting that to enlighten unfree Blacks of school age by teaching them to write would only encourage them to forge papers and find their way to freedom; see Taylor, *Thomas Jefferson's Education* (New York: W. W. Norton, 2019), 150–54.

15. Williams, *Condorcet and Modernity*, 158–70, quote at 166; Guillaume Ansart, "Condorcet, Social Mathematics, and Women's Rights," *Eighteenth-Century Studies* 42 (Spring 2009): 347–62; Adams, *Paris Years of Thomas Jefferson*, 136–39.

16. Williams, *Condorcet and Modernity*, 31, 267–68; Amelia Gere Mason, *The Women of the French Salons* (1891), chap. 17, via Project Gutenberg Literary Archive; for an excellent analysis of Jefferson's relationship with Paine from this time forward, see Gaye Wilson, "Thomas Jefferson's Portrait of Thomas Paine," in Simon P. Newman and Peter S. Onuf, eds., *Paine and Jefferson in the Age of Revolutions* (Charlottesville: University of Virginia Press, 2013), 229–51. Mrs. Mazzei died in 1788, while Jefferson and Mazzei were both in Europe; her grave is unmarked, its precise location at Monticello not known. Like Condorcet, Mazzei was an early feminist who believed women capable of holding public office.

17. Antoine-Nicolas de Condorcet, *Sketch for a Historical Picture of the Progress of the Human Mind* (London: Weidenfeld and Nicolson, 1955), 144.

18. Ibid., 34, 45, 129.
19. Ibid., 142. It was Benjamin Franklin who opened doors for Jefferson in England, as in France, by introducing those radicals who took part in elite clubs to which Franklin belonged that were both political and deist-based; see Nicholas Hans, "Franklin, Jefferson, and the English Radicals at the End of the Eighteenth Century," *Proceedings of the American Philosophical Society* 98, 6 (December 1954): 406–26; on Priestley's experiences, see the excellent study by Jenny Graham, *Revolutionary in Exile: The Emigration of Joseph Priestley to America, 1794–1804* (Philadelphia: American Philosophical Society, 1995).
20. Price to TJ, July 2, 1785, *PTJ*, 8:258–59.
21. [Richard Price], *Observations on the Importance of the American Revolution; and the Means of Making It a Benefit to the World* (London: T. Cadell, 1785), 83; TJ to Price, February 1, 1785, *PTJ*, 7:630–31.
22. TJ to Price, August 7, 1785, *PTJ*, 8:356–57. Note, too, that Price and Priestley were dissenters who brought Unitarianism to America; Jefferson eagerly embraced Unitarianism, acknowledging his debt to Priestley in particular. See Ritchie Robertson, *The Enlightenment: The Pursuit of Happiness* (New York: Harper, 2021), 735–36; and Andrew Burstein, *Jefferson's Secrets: Death and Desire at Monticello* (New York: Basic Books, 2005), chap. 9.
23. Williams, *Condorcet and Modernity*, 146, 193; for a sophisticated analysis of his projection of a peaceful and productive future, see Hanna Roman, "Conjecturing a New World in Condorcet's *Esquisse d'un tableau historique des progrès de l'esprit humain*," *MLN* 129 (September 2014): 780–95.
24. Condorcet, *Sketch for a Historical Picture of the Progress of the Human Mind*, 181.
25. Alexandre Koyré, "Condorcet," *Journal of the History of Ideas* 9 (April 1948): 131–52, esp. 138–39; Emma Rothschild, "Condorcet and the Conflict of Values," *Historical Journal* 39 (September 1996): 677–701, quote at 689.
26. Arthur Scherr introduces an interesting fact: a Virginia marriage law passed in 1788, and renewed four years later, disallowed marriage to either a deceased wife's sister or a deceased brother's wife; see Scherr, *Rightful Liberty: Slavery, Morality, and Thomas Jefferson's World* (Macon, GA: Mercer University Press, 2021), 374. Thus, Jefferson was constrained by law even if he wanted to make his relationship with Sally Hemings legitimate—which is highly doubtful for a variety of reasons, among them the lack of affection he showed to the children who bore the surname Hemings.
27. Brodie, 228–32; Isaac Jefferson, "Memoirs of a Monticello Slave," in James A. Bear Jr., ed., *Jefferson at Monticello* (Charlottesville: University Press of Virginia, 1967); Andrew Burstein, *Jefferson's Secrets: Death and Desire at Monticello* (New

York: Basic Books, 2005), 148–49. In her nuanced study of the evidence of Sally Hemings's skin pigmentation, and by interpolating from descriptions of her two youngest sons, Annette Gordon-Reed has concluded that she was "a light-skinned, very obviously black woman," light-skinned enough to blush; see Gordon-Reed, *Hemingses of Monticello*, 271–72; TJ to Maria Cosway, April 24, 1788, *PTJ*, 13:103–104; the only evidence of sexual innuendo in this letter comes with Jefferson's reference to Laurence Sterne on noses, from an episode in *Tristram Shandy* in which "nose" stands in for "phallus" and indicates that Jefferson was not shy in transgressing a Virginia gentleman's sense of propriety in broaching the topic of sexual arousal with her in particular. In her next letter, Maria appears not to have understood the double entendre joke. Yet Brodie is presuming a subconscious thought of Jefferson's that reveals lustful thoughts directed at his biracial household servant.

28. Abigail Adams to TJ, February 11, 1786, June 26 and 27, 1787, *Adams-Jefferson Letters*, 119, 178–79; Gordon-Reed, *Hemingses of Monticello*, 197–201; Lucia Stanton, *"Those Who Labor for My Happiness": Slavery at Thomas Jefferson's Monticello* (Charlottesville: University of Virginia Press, 2012), 168, 173–74, 184–86; John B. Boles, *Jefferson: Architect of American Liberty* (New York: Basic Books, 2017), 148–53.

29. Abigail Adams to TJ, July 6 and September 10, 1787; TJ to Abigail Adams, July 1, 1787, *Adams-Jefferson Letters*, 179–84, 197; Madame de Corny to TJ, August 4, 1787, in Chinard, *Trois amitiés françaises de Jefferson*, 181–82; *JMB*, 1:660. On Jefferson's reaction to the death of his daughter Lucy in this context, see Randall, 1:415, 3:588–89; Randolph, *Domestic Life of Thomas Jefferson*, 101–107; Peterson, *Thomas Jefferson and the New Nation*, 300–301; Brodie, 190–91.

30. Brodie, 234; Boles, *Jefferson*, 154; on the insignificance of Jefferson's clothing purchases for Hemings, see Valsania, *Jefferson's Body*, 192, 241n178. Annette Gordon-Reed interprets this episode in a fuller context, drawing forth different possibilities of what Jefferson's attentiveness to Hemings's appearance might mean as intimacy develops between a patriarchal figure and his young charge, while living under the same roof; see *Hemingses of Monticello*, 259–60, 276–81, 294–307, 718–19n. Records of clothing purchases in Jefferson's *Farm Book* during the years when Madison and his younger brother Eston Hemings were growing indicate that neither they nor Sally Hemings were provided with shirts or other garments of a better quality than those given to others at Monticello. However, Valsania also identifies an 1807 letter Jefferson wrote to Monticello's overseer, indicating that daughter Martha specifically directed clothing purchases for several of the Hemingses (ibid., 153).

After spending years with Short's correspondence, the author of *Heir through Hope*, Peter Thompson, is of the opinion that Short, a lifelong intimate of Jefferson's who helped arrange the departing party's voyage to America, at no time interfered or offered Jefferson advice on his relations with Sally Hemings. Virginia Scharff, in *The Women Jefferson Loved* (New York: Harper, 2010), takes a dim view of Jefferson's treatment of Hemings at this time, emphasizing the manipulative and exploitative elements.

31. On sexual satire of upper-class men in Anglo-American culture, see the copiously illustrated Vic Gatrell, *City of Laughter: Sex and Satire in Eighteenth-Century London* (New York: Walker & Co., 2006), quotes at 297, 299. Americans accepted the sexualization of young females of the working class. John Wood Sweet writes that an unmarried free woman who made her living as a seamstress either lived with her parents or supplemented her wages by becoming a domestic servant in another household; in cities, where brothels abounded, some turned to prostitution in order to retain a measure of autonomy; see Sweet, *A Sewing Girl's Tale: A Story of Crime and Consequences in Revolutionary America* (New York: Henry Holt, 2022), 40–41.

32. In accepting Jefferson's paternity of Sally Hemings's children, though the evidence is not absolute, my reasoning falls into several categories. Statistically, he is the likeliest partner because, counting back from the six confirmed births between 1795 and 1808, Hemings never conceived when Jefferson was not present at Monticello, yet he was often away for several months at a time; his grandchildren's claim that their promiscuous, since deceased, Carr cousin confessed to having had regular relations with Sally Hemings has been shown by DNA to be impossible. The only other plausible father, because he carried the same Y chromosome, was Jefferson's brother Randolph, whose visits to Monticello were few and little remarked upon—not enough for reasonable doubt.

Additional reasoning concerns the sexualized culture in which Jefferson lived as a man of privilege, and a personal history that makes it difficult to accept the thirty-nine-year-old widower's neglect of his sexual needs over the next four decades on a private mountain where his desires, his passions, came first. Further, Madison Hemings's recorded testimony, given when he was in his sixties, reads soberly. In referring to Jefferson as "father," he noted (nonjudgmentally) an absence of emotional commitment, even as Jefferson uniquely granted freedom to this entire nuclear family, privileging them above all other human beings he owned. Finally, a frequent visitor to Monticello, a planter associated with Jefferson's work in establishing the University of Virginia, twice recorded in a private diary his deep disappointment that Jefferson's sexual relationship with Hemings was being used by other Virginia planters who fathered children with enslaved women to excuse their own actions; for more detail, see Burstein, *Jefferson's Secrets*, chap. 6.

33. William H. Gaines Jr., *Thomas Mann Randolph: Jefferson's Son-in-Law* (Baton Rouge: Louisiana State University Press, 1966), chaps. 2 and 3; Jonathan Daniels, *The Randolphs of Virginia* (Garden City, NY: Doubleday, 1972), 129–33; Kierner, *Martha Jefferson Randolph*, 81–92, 133–35; Scharff, *Women Jefferson Loved*, 265–69; Joseph J. Ellis, *American Sphinx: The Character of Thomas Jefferson* (New York: Knopf, 1997), 134–36; Gordon-Reed, *Hemingses of Monticello*, 418; Brodie, 250–51; Boles, *Jefferson*, 208–209. Distant cousins, in the case of Martha Jefferson and Tom Randolph, meant that the newly wedded couple's great-grandfathers were brothers. Martha and her sister Maria were the half nieces of Sally Hemings because their mother was Sally's half sister.
34. Gordon-Reed, *Hemingses of Monticello*, 120–21. The other Jefferson males include nephews and cousins.
35. Malone, 2:203–37; Peterson, *Thomas Jefferson and the New Nation*, 385–86.
36. TJ to Geismar, September 6, 1785, *PTJ*, 8:499–500. It was subsequent to this letter that Jefferson visited Germany (1788), and met with Geismar.
37. Chinard, *Trois amitiés françaises de Jefferson*, 153–54. He had paid a call on her before leaving the city and she was not at home, so he left a short note.
38. Adams, *Paris Years of Thomas Jefferson*, 296; Williams, *Condorcet and Modernity*, 42–43.

CHAPTER 8: "OPEN MOUTHED AGAINST ME"

1. The book that explicitly draws historical connections between Niccolò Machiavelli and Hamilton (the superior) and Jefferson (inferior) Machiavellians is John Lamberton Harper, *American Machiavelli: Alexander Hamilton and the Origins of U.S. Foreign Policy* (New York: Cambridge University Press, 2004). My characterization recognizes certain of the parallels Harper brings up—political realism as a necessity in a struggling young republic—but is otherwise intended to express the commonly held perception of a "Machiavellian" as one who will at times use a devious stratagem to obtain political advantage. Both Hamilton and Jefferson used Machiavellian cunning: Hamilton more openly engaged in forceful speech when and where he could do so practically, resorting as well to newspaper opinion pieces; Jefferson acted more subtly in strategically argued letters that circulated.
2. William Ian Miller, *The Anatomy of Disgust* (Cambridge, MA: Harvard University Press, 1997), 32, 50; Andrew Burstein, *Jefferson's Secrets: Death and Desire at Monticello* (New York: Basic Books, 2005), chap. 2.
3. See for example, the sensational case of Richard and Nancy Randolph in 1792, as described in John Kukla, *Patrick Henry: Champion of Liberty* (New York: Simon & Schuster, 2017), 376–78.

4. Herbert E. Sloan, *Principle and Interest: Thomas Jefferson and the Problem of Debt* (Charlottesville: University Press of Virginia, 1995), chap. 1, quote at 25.
5. John A. Ragosta, *For the People, for the Country: Patrick Henry's Final Political Battle* (Charlottesville: University of Virginia Press, 2023), 78–87, 96–102; Peter S. Onuf, *Jefferson and the Virginians: Democracy, Constitutions, and Empire* (Baton Rouge: Louisiana State University Press, 2018), 60–63, 68–76.
6. TJ to Wirt, April 12, 1812, *PTJ-R*, 4:597, 602–603.
7. TJ to Wirt, April 12, 1812, *PTJ-R*, 4:597, 602–604.
8. Miller, *Anatomy of Disgust*, 58. Here, he explains that the inside is where "soul and character and virtue" are located, "where the undulating flesh of the heart muscle is also the metaphorical seat of courage; where the convolutions of the brain are the seat of mind and thought. The inside, while disgusting in its physicality, is somehow honest by not alluring us with false fronts."
9. Gerald Stourzh, *Alexander Hamilton and the Idea of Republican Government* (Stanford, CA: Stanford University Press, 1970); Francis D. Cogliano, *A Revolutionary Friendship: Washington, Jefferson, and the American Republic* (Cambridge, MA: Harvard University Press, 2024), 207–14; Washington to Madison, January 2, 1789, FOL.
10. Lindsay Chervinsky, *The Cabinet: George Washington and the Creation of an American Institution* (Cambridge, MA: Harvard University Press, 2020), 142–45, 183; Chervinsky, "George Washington and the Cabinet: The Unlikely Development of an Unintended Institution," in Max M. Edling and Peter J. Kastor, eds., *Washington's Government: Charting the Origins of the Federal Administration* (Charlottesville: University of Virginia Press, 2021), 29–56; TJ to Walter Jones, March 5, 1810, *PTJ-R*, 2:272–74.
11. The preceding paragraphs synthesize events that many historians have covered; see Randall, 2:68–91; Malone, 2:423–56; Boles, *Jefferson*, 214–28; Lance Banning, *The Jeffersonian Persuasion: Evolution of a Party Ideology* (Ithaca, NY: Cornell University Press, 1978), chaps. 5 and 6; Noble E. Cunningham Jr., *The Jeffersonian Republicans: The Formation of Party Organization, 1789–1801* (Chapel Hill: University of North Carolina Press, 1957), chap. 1; Merrill D. Peterson, *Thomas Jefferson and the New Nation* (New York: Oxford University Press, 1970), 432–71; Nathan Schachner, *Thomas Jefferson: A Biography* (New York: Appleton-Century-Crofts, 1951), chaps. 32 and 33; Schachner, *Alexander Hamilton* (New York: A. S. Barnes, 1946), chaps. 18 and 19; John E. Ferling, *Jefferson and Hamilton: The Rivalry That Forged a Nation* (New York: Bloomsbury, 2013), 214–33; Ferling, *The First of Men: A Life of George Washington* (Knoxville: University of Tennessee Press, 1988), chap. 15; Andrew Burstein and Nancy Isenberg, *Madison and Jefferson* (New York: Random House, 2010), 212–17; TJ to Madison, May 9, 1791, *PTJ*, 20:293–94.

12. Leonard D. White, *The Federalists: A Study in Administrative History* (New York: Macmillan, 1956), chap. 19; TJ to John Jay, November 3, 1787; to Washington, September 9, 1792, *PTJ*, 12:309–13; 24:351–53; TJ to John Norvell, June 11, 1807, FOL.
13. TJ to Washington, September 9, 1792, *PTJ*, 24:351–60; TJ to Madison, September 21, 1795, *PTJ*, 28:475-76.
14. Hamilton essays, "An American, I," August 4, 1792, "Catullus, I, II, & III," September 15–29, 1792; Philip M. Marsh, *Monroe's Defense of Jefferson and Freneau Against Hamilton* (Oxford, OH: self-published, 1948); Marsh, "Randolph and Hamilton: 'Aristides' Replied to 'An American,' 'Catullus' and 'Scourge,'" *Pennsylvania Magazine of History and Biography* 72, 3 (July 1948): 247–52; *JMB*, 2:879; Cogliano, *Revolutionary Friendship*, 219–23; Andrew Burstein, *The Inner Jefferson: Portrait of a Grieving Optimist* (Charlottesville: University Press of Virginia, 1995), 206–22; Malone, 2:448–77; Robert M. S. McDonald, *Confounding Father: Thomas Jefferson's Image in His Own Time* (Charlottesville: University of Virginia Press, 2016), 39–40.
15. As proof of his forbearance, Hamilton told Washington that he'd directly prevented an attack on Jefferson at the time of the *Rights of Man* controversy: "I can even assure you, that I was instrumental in preventing a very severe and systematic attack upon Mr. Jefferson, by an association of two or three individuals, in consequence of the persecution, which he brought upon the Vice President, by his indiscreet and light letter to the Printer, transmitting *Paine's* pamphlet." One is hard-pressed to read this one instance as a compelling example of Hamiltonian moderation and self-control. See Hamilton to Carrington, May 26, 1792; to Washington, September 9, 1792; *Papers of Alexander Hamilton*, ed. Harold C. Syrett (New York: Columbia University Press, 1966), 11:426–45, 12:347–50; Andrew Burstein and Nancy Isenberg, *Madison and Jefferson* (New York: Random House, 2010), 246–49; Ferling, *Jefferson and Hamilton*, 227–38.
16. John Quincy Adams, *Parties in the United States* (New York: Greenberg, 1941), 10–13; for another well-reasoned explanation, see Russell L. Hanson, "'Commons' and 'Commonwealth' at the American Founding: Democratic Republicanism as the New American Hybrid," in Terence Ball and J. G. A. Pocock, eds., *Conceptual Change and the Constitution* (Lawrence: University Press of Kansas, 1988), 165–93.
17. Malone, 2:359–62; Schachner, *Alexander Hamilton*, 290–92; Cunningham, *Jeffersonian Republicans*, chap. 2; Eran Shalev, *Rome Reborn on Western Shores: Historical Imagination and the Creation of the American Republic* (Charlottesville: University of Virginia Press, 2009), 223–34; Alfred F. Young, *The Democratic Republicans of New York* (Chapel Hill: University of North Carolina Press, 1967), 197–98, 209–11, 279–83, 314, 317, 324–30. For a time, Burr's name was mentioned as a better V.P. candidate than Clinton, though Madison and Monroe favored the governor.

18. TJ to Short, January 3, 1793, *PTJ*, 25:14–17; Boles, *Jefferson*, 242–43.
19. Marco Sioli, "Citizen Genêt and Political Struggle in the Early American Republic," *Revue française d'études américaines* 64 (May 1995): 259–67; Christopher J. Young, "Connecting the President and the People: Washington's Neutrality, Genêt's Challenge, and Hamilton's Fight for Public Support," *Journal of the Early Republic* 31, 3 (Fall 2011): 435–66; Malone, 3:114–31; Burstein and Isenberg, *Madison and Jefferson*, 261–63; TJ to JM, July 7 and August 3, 1793, *PTJ*, 26:443–44, 545, 548–49, 606–607.
20. Donald H. Stewart, *The Opposition Press of the Federalist Period* (Albany: State University of New York Press, 1969), 137–41; Cogliano, *Revolutionary Friendship*, 224-32; Malone, 3:68-81. In cabinet discussions, Hamilton had argued for a complete abandonment of the French, as he and Jefferson tussled over their differing interpretations of international law. In its final form, the proclamation was a watered-down version of what it might have been if Hamilton had gotten his way.
21. TJ to Madison, July 21 and August 11, 1793, with transcript of conversation dated August 6, *PTJ*, 26:649–51; Madison to TJ, July 22, 1793.
22. *JMB*, 2:901–902; Benjamin Rush to Julia Stockton Rush, October 3, 1793, in L. H. Butterfield, ed., *Letters of Benjamin Rush* (Princeton, NJ: Princeton University Press, 1951), 2:701. Rush believed that Hamilton's having publicly promoted the treatment he received from the St. Croix doctor was responsible for hundreds of needless deaths. See Rush to Elias Boudinot, September 25, 1793, in ibid., 681; TJ to Madison, September 8, 1793, *PTJ*, 27:61–63.
23. TJ to Madison, June 9, 1793, *PTJ*, 26:239–42. Hamilton had raised the prospect of his own imminent retirement to Washington that same month. Curiously, a Google Ngram search shows that the words "tranquil" and "tranquillity" reached a peak in their usage in the years 1790–1800.

CHAPTER 9: "THE LATE POLITICAL PAROXYSM"

1. Annette Gordon-Reed, *The Hemingses of Monticello: An American Family* (New York: W. W. Norton, 2008), 620–21.
2. Gordon-Reed, *Hemingses of Monticello*, 530–35.
3. Lucia Stanton, *"Those Who Labor for My Happiness": Slavery at Thomas Jefferson's Monticello* (Charlottesville: University of Virginia Press, 2012), 180, 185–86; Gordon-Reed, *Hemingses of Monticello*, 402–403, 486–92, 504–505. Correspondence from Bob Hemings to Jefferson after he was granted his freedom in the mid–1790s are noted in Jefferson's "Summary Journal of Letters" as having been received, but they were not retained, one presumes because they make mention of his sister Sally.

4. In the Williamsburg-based *Virginia Gazette* (September 29, 1775), publishing as resistance to British officialdom was reaching fever pitch, the activities of a Caribbean-based merchant of means were singled out. William Priddis, a supplier of the redcoats in Boston, was overheard growling, "As for the Americans, they might starve and be d——d." The columnist explained that "said rascal Priddis (who by the bye, it seems has some *negro blood* in him)" lacked a moral compass in some way because of that "negro blood."
5. Brooke N. Newman, "Blood Fictions, Maternal Inheritance, and the Legacies of Colonial Slavery," *Women's Studies Quarterly* 48 (Spring/Summer 2020): 27–44; TJ to Francis Gray, March 4, 1815, *PTJ-R*, 8:310–12; Burstein, *Jefferson's Secrets*, chap. 5; Maurizio Valsania, *Jefferson's Body: A Corporeal Biography* (Charlottesville: University of Virginia Press, 2017), 158–60.
6. TJ to John W. Eppes, June 20, 1820, *PTJ-R*, 16:66–67. Curiously, Jefferson demeaned hereditary rulers of Europe with analogies to animals of prey; see Arthur Scherr, *Rightful Liberty: Slavery, Morality, and Thomas Jefferson's World* (Macon, GA: Mercer University Press, 2021), 142.
7. *Notes on the State of Virginia*, ed. Robert Pierce Forbes (New Haven, CT: Yale University Press, 2022), Query XIV, reference at 223n.
8. TJ to Madison, June 9, 1793, *PTJ*, 26:239–42. Today, we continue to invoke the metaphor positively in "blood brother," "blood ties," and "bleeding heart," and negatively in "blood feud," "blood diamond," and "blood money."
9. Andrew Burstein, *The Inner Jefferson: Portrait of a Grieving Optimist* (Charlottesville: University Press of Virginia, 1995), 60–63. The latest scholarly work on hair and racial identity is Sarah Gold McBride, *Whiskerology: The Culture of Hair in Nineteenth-Century America* (Cambridge, MA: Harvard University Press, 2025).
10. TJ to Cosway, September 8, 1795, *PTJ*, 28:455.
11. See the insightful arguments offered by Maurizio Valsania regarding these subjects and Jefferson's willful refusal to acknowledge subtleties in pressing his points, in *Jefferson's Body*, esp. 146–57.
12. TJ to Chastellux, June 7, 1785, *PTJ*, 8:184–86.
13. Mechthild Fend, *Fleshing Out Surfaces: Skin in French Art and Medicine, 1650–1850* (Manchester, UK: Manchester University Press, 2016), 146–67; compare Andrew S. Curran, *The Anatomy of Blackness: Science and Slavery in an Age of Enlightenment* (Baltimore: Johns Hopkins University Press, 2011), chap. 3.
14. "Among the blacks is misery enough, God knows, but no poetry... Their love is ardent, but in kindles the senses only, not the imagination." In Query XIV, he abjectly dismisses the celebrated African-born poet-prodigy Phillis Wheatley ("The compositions under her name are beneath the dignity of criticism...") and the multitalented

writer Ignatius Sancho; for a stinging analysis of Jefferson's racism in Query XIV, see Hannah Spahn, *Black Reason, White Feeling: The Jeffersonian Enlightenment in the African American Tradition* (Charlottesville: University of Virginia Press, 2024), 124–33.

15. Modern studies focus on strategies of denial and remediation, how the complaint that "affirmative action has gone too far" matches up against artificial forms of correction, rectifying past inequalities in symbolic, sometimes shortsighted, ways that can be interpreted as tokenism, such as giving a higher percentage of Oscars or book awards to people of color in a given year. A useful Australian study establishes divisions into which rationalization among racists has been expressed: "temporal deflection" (less racism now compared to the past), "spatial deflection" (it's worse in other countries), "deflection from mainstream" (it's only prevalent among certain groups of people), and "absence discourse" (racism no longer exists); see Jacqueline K. Nelson, "Denial of Racism and Its Implications for Local Action," *Discourse & Society* 24, 1 (January 2013): 89–109.

16. Elaine G. Breslaw, *Lotions, Potions, Pills, and Magic: Health Care in Early America* (New York: New York University Press, 2012), 36, 56, 103. Jefferson championed inoculation in the broadest sense, as part of his philosophy of medicine and advocacy of health education; he also promoted vaccination among Indian tribes, even equipping Lewis and Clark with vaccine materials; see Robert S. Gibson, *Thomas Jefferson and Early American Healthcare* (Savannah, GA: Frederic C. Beil, 2023), 33–38.

17. I use the phrase "parallel subordinate family" in my earlier *Jefferson's Secrets: Death and Desire at Monticello* (New York: Basic Books, 2005), chap. 6. On Black and white blood in context of Jefferson's regard for the Hemingses as his wife's close relatives, see Annette Gordon-Reed, *The Hemingses of Monticello: An American Family* (New York: W. W. Norton, 2008), esp. 285–87.

18. John D. Battle Jr., "The 'Periodical Head-achs' of Thomas Jefferson," *Cleveland Clinic Journal of Medicine* 51 (Fall 1984): 531–39. Jefferson reports experiencing the "head-ach" almost exclusively when he is outside Virginia; the absence of reports while at Monticello does not necessarily indicate that he did not suffer from them at home, though it is certainly suggestive.

19. Jack McLaughlin, *Jefferson and Monticello: The Biography of a Builder* (New York: Henry Holt, 1988), 248–64. Maria's mother-in-law, Elizabeth Wayles Eppes, was the half sister of Maria's mother, Martha (Patty) Wayles Jefferson, which means Maria and Jack were effectively first cousins. Additionally, her father-in-law, Francis Eppes, was her mother's first cousin, as Patty's mother and Francis's father were brother and sister.

20. Merrill D. Peterson, ed., *Visitors to Monticello* (Charlottesville: University Press of Virginia, 1989), 18–30.
21. TJ to Washington, June 19, 1796, *PTJ*, 29:127–30; on the Federalist association of Southern planters with Jacobinism, see Rachel Hope Cleves, *The Reign of Terror in America: Visions of Violence from Anti-Jacobinism to Antislavery* (New York: Cambridge University Press, 2009), chap. 3.
22. TJ to Mazzei, April 4, 1796; JM to Nicholas Trist, May 15, 1832, FOL; Cogliano, *Revolutionary Friendship*, 250–51; Burstein and Isenberg, *Madison and Jefferson*, 323–25. Still smarting in the 1820s, eager to see his history written more sympathetically, Jefferson wrote at great length to New York Democrat Martin Van Buren that Washington definitely understood the Mazzei letter to have referred strictly to the Revolutionary veteran officers' elitist Society of the Cincinnati. Jefferson went so far as to set forth every detail dating to their 1784 conversation, initiated by Washington: "He called on me at Annapolis. It was a little after candle-light, and he sat with me till after midnight, conversing, almost exclusively on that subject. While he was feelingly indulgent to the motives which might induce the officers to promote it, he concurred with me entirely in condemning it." TJ to Van Buren, June 29, 1824, FOL.
23. Hamilton to Washington, October 16, 1795; Washington to Hamilton, October 29, 1795, *Papers of Alexander Hamilton*, 19:324–28, 355–63, regarding Edmund Randolph. The Whiskey Rebellion proved a black mark on Washington's second term. Going back to 1786, when distressed farmers in western Massachusetts shut down the courts to avoid being foreclosed upon, Washington looked upon such people as "desperate characters." An aggressive landowner whose properties extended west to the Ohio River, he was less sensitive to the concerns of hardscrabble farmers than he ought to have been; they did not have it easy, wanted protection from the state, and were willing to take up arms to save themselves from financial ruin. However, Washington was not as eager as Hamilton to stage a military show of force against those who resisted the tax on the whiskey they produced. Hamilton saw the protest as part of a coordinated "Jacobin" movement against his administration and convinced Washington to allow him to lead the federal troops. In *The Whiskey Rebellion: Frontier Epilogue to the American Revolution* (New York: Oxford University Press, 1986), Thomas P. Slaughter observes that Hamilton addressed the needs of large, successful New York distillers but "discriminated most harshly against frontier regions," because, as Jefferson's opposite, he had no sympathy for rural life (p. 147).
24. TJ to Maria Jefferson Eppes, March 3, 1802, *PTJ*, 36:676–77.

25. Madison had not held executive office to this point. He was a highly successful floor manager in the national legislature, though he had lately faced setbacks in rallying his troops against the Federalists. Also, he was Jefferson's junior by eight years and no doubt regarded his friend as the best suited to seek the presidency after the two-and-a-half-year hiatus. For his part, Jefferson would have perceived John Adams's vulnerabilities as a candidate, as well as being aware that the Federalist press did not buy in to Jefferson's retiring persona. Washington was leaving office while conflicts abroad remained volatile, and Jefferson feared where they were heading. Aware that the Federalists still had strength in numbers where electoral votes were concerned, he may have looked upon himself already as a republican savior-in-waiting, the one who could arrest what he saw as the increasingly obnoxious course of elite Federalism; see Burstein and Isenberg, *Madison and Jefferson*, 305–17.

26. Jeffrey L. Pasley, *The First Presidential Contest: 1796 and the Founding of American Democracy* (Lawrence: University Press of Kansas, 2013), 230–31; on "want of firmness," see Nathaniel C. Green, *The Man of the People: Political Dissent and the Making of the American Presidency* (Lawrence: University Press of Kansas, 2020), chap. 4.

27. Marvin R. Zahniser, "Edward Rutledge to His Son, August 2, 1796," *South Carolina Historical Magazine* 64, 2 (April 1963): 65–72; James Haw, *John and Edward Rutledge of South Carolina* (Athens: University of Georgia Press, 1997); TJ to Rutledge, November 30, 1795, *PTJ*, 28:541–42.

28. TJ to Rutledge, December 27, 1796, *PTJ*, 29:229–33. Mimicking Jefferson's style, Rutledge offered his own Virgil reference in a later letter, by comparing Charles Cotesworth Pinckney, negotiator in Paris, to the Greek hero Aeneas. If negotiations stalled, he wrote, "we have one consolation in knowing that, if Palinurus should be asleep, my friend Æneas is on the watch." Palinurus was the pilot of Aeneas's vessel in Virgil's *Aeneid*. Rutledge to TJ, May 19, 1797, *PTJ*, 29:386–87.

29. Abigail Adams to John Quincy Adams, November 3, 1797, *Adams Family Correspondence*, ed. Sara Martin et al. (Cambridge, MA: Harvard University Press, 2015), 12:276–80; TJ to Peregrine Fitzhugh, June 4, 1797, *PTJ*, 29:415–19. Fitzhugh was a Marylander with a decided interest in political gossip; the leaker was his nephew by marriage.

30. TJ to Burr, June 17, 1797; to Randolph, June 27, 1797; Burr to TJ, June 24, 1797, *PTJ*, 29:437–40, 447–48, 459–60.

31. TJ to Rutledge, June 24, 1797, *PTJ*, 29:455–57.

32. *JMB*, 2:964, 974; on Randolph's case, see Burstein and Isenberg, *Madison and Jefferson*, 297–300.

33. TJ to Madison, July 24, 1797, *PTJ*, 29:483–84; *JMB*, 2:963; Jacob Katz Cogan, "The Reynolds Affair and the Politics of Character," *Journal of the Early Republic* 16, 3

(Autumn 1996): 389–417; Nancy Isenberg, *Fallen Founder: The Life of Aaron Burr* (New York: Viking, 2007), 120–21. As to Hamilton's sexual nature, imagined and debated, see Caroline V. Hamilton, "The Erotic Charisma of Alexander Hamilton," *Journal of American Studies* 45, 1 (February 2011): 1–19; [Alexander Hamilton], *Observations on Certain Documents . . . in Which the Charge of Speculation Against Alexander Hamilton, Late Secretary of the Treasury, Is Fully Refuted* (Philadelphia: John Fenno, 1797); and [James Thomson Callender], *The History of the United States for 1796; Including a Variety of Interesting Particulars . . .* (Philadelphia: Snowden & McCorkle, 1797), chaps. 6 and 7. Callender contrasts the Federalists' treatment of Monroe as "guilty of corruption by foreign influence" with Hamilton's actual corruption and Monroe's "lenity" and "solicitude" in burying the charges, largely on the basis of Hamilton's assurances.

34. Madison to Jefferson, October 20, 1797, *PTJ*, 29:562.
35. Joseph J. Ellis, *Passionate Sage: the Character and the Legacy of John Adams* (New York: W. W. Norton, 1993), 61–62; Burstein and Isenberg, *Madison and Jefferson*, 320; Isenberg and Burstein, *The Problem of Democracy: The Presidents Adams Confront the Cult of Personality* (New York: Viking, 2019), chap. 8; James H. Read, "Alexander Hamilton's View of Thomas Jefferson's Ideology and Character," in Douglas Ambrose and Robert W. T. Martin, eds., *The Many Faces of Alexander Hamilton* (New York: New York University Press, 2006), 77–106.
36. In 1797, Adams wanted to dispatch Jefferson to Paris, but Jefferson thought it unwise, for both political and constitutional reasons, to return to France. The open-minded Adams asked him to query Madison as well. Even Hamilton, who worked through allies in Congress to commit to a stronger U.S. military, would have accepted a bipartisan negotiating team then. In general, see Alexander DeConde, *The Quasi-War: The Politics and Diplomacy of the Undeclared Naval War with France, 1797–1801* (New York: Scribner, 1966).
37. Stewart, *The Opposition Press of the Federalist Period*, chap. 8, quotes at 296, 298; Malone, 3:376–93; "Notes on a Conversation with John Adams," February 15, 1798, *PTJ*, 30:113. In his inimitable fashion, marking the differences in outlook and temperament between the president and vice president, Madison took notes of his own, sprung from his head, in advance of the Fourth of July, composing a mock toast: "May [Jefferson] never feel the passion of J.A. nor [Adams be] forsaken by the philosophy of T.J." (see Burstein and Isenberg, *Madison and Jefferson*, 336.)
38. Stewart, *The Opposition Press of the Federalist Period*, 423–24; Francis D. Cogliano, *Emperor of Liberty: Thomas Jefferson's Foreign Policy* (New Haven, CT: Yale University Press, 2014), 138–43; Burstein and Isenberg, *Madison and Jefferson*, 337–41; Cunningham, *Jeffersonian Republicans*, 126–29.

39. John A. Ragosta, *For the People, for the Country: Patrick Henry's Final Political Battle* (Charlottesville: University of Virginia Press, 2023), 152–60, quote at 158.
40. TJ to Madison, March 25, 1800, *PTJ*, 31:455–56; Malone, 3:453–57; *JMB*, 2:1011, 1019, 1031.
41. "Gusts of passion" was not a throwaway line. In the eighteenth century, "passion" was paired with desire, heat, affections, fits, ebullition (violent outpouring), resentments, cruelty, etc. Hamilton claimed the insight to identify "strong sensations" that others surely felt who perceived that same lack of judgment he saw in the "fortuitous emanations of momentary impulses." In emotion-driven correspondence of this period, "strong sensations" were "excited," with "paroxysms" and "convulsions" resulting. Hamilton's open letter about Adams's unfitness contained the prevailing buzzwords that alluded to disturbances in psychological balance (the same vocabulary Jefferson more routinely drew upon), in which human beings were found to be rational or irrational as a consequence of healthy or unhealthy nerves. The nervous system was a governing system of social and personal behavior alike.
42. Alexander Hamilton, *Letter from Alexander Hamilton concerning the Public Conduct and Character of John Adams* (New York: John Furman, 1800), quotes at 4, 8–12, 38; Isenberg and Burstein, *Problem of Democracy*, 224–30; John Ferling, *Adams vs. Jefferson: The Tumultuous Election of 1800* (New York: Oxford University Press, 2004), 140–47.
43. TJ to Martha Jefferson Randolph, April 22, 1800, *PTJ*, 31:535–36.
44. Sarah P. Stetson, "William Hamilton and His 'Woodlands,'" *Pennsylvania Magazine of History and Biography* 73, 1 (January 1949): 26–33; James A. Jacobs, "William Hamilton and the Woodlands: A Construction of Refinement in Philadelphia," *Pennsylvania Magazine of History and Biography* 130, 2 (April 2006): 181–209, letters of 1779 and 1784 at 183, 186; *JMB*, 2:1018.
45. TJ to William Hamilton, April 22, 1800, *PTJ*, 31:533–55. In an uncommonly pained piece of writing, Jefferson reassessed the circumstances under which they had met three years before, when he first arrived in town to assume the vice presidency. He explained now that he'd meant no offense by failing to observe the ritual of reciprocating in-person visits, having felt obliged, given the fracturing of political society, to adjust his previously looser habit when it came to social calls: "I owe it to the opportunity of placing myself justly before you, and of assuring you there was no person here to whom I had less disposition of shewing neglect than to yourself." This letter succeeded in correcting a mistaken impression.
46. Knox to TJ, March 9, 1800; TJ to Knox, April 8, 1800, *PTJ*, 31:423–24, 487–88.

CHAPTER 10: "THE CAMPAIGN OF SLANDER IS OPENING"

1. John Adams to John Quincy Adams, January 3, 1794, FOL; *Adams Family Correspondence*, vol. 10, ed. Margaret A. Hogan et. al. (Cambridge, MA: Harvard University Press, 2011), 3–4. "The Life of Numa" is recounted in Plutarch.
2. Robert M. S. McDonald, "Thomas Jefferson's Changing Reputation as Author of the Declaration of Independence: the First Fifty Years," *Journal of the Early Republic* 19, 2 (Summer 1999): 169–95, quotes at 181–82; Donald H. Stewart, *The Opposition Press of the Federalist Period* (Albany: State University of New York Press, 1969), 572–74, 583–84; Jeffrey L. Pasley, *"The Tyranny of Printers": Newspaper Politics in the Early American Republic* (Charlottesville: University Press of Virginia, 2001), esp. Appendix 1.
3. TJ to Short, March 26, 1800, *PTJ*, 31:463–66. Similarly, to staunch ally John Taylor of Caroline, he wrote a few months earlier: "I cease from this time during the ensuing twelve-month to write political letters, knowing that a campaign of slander is now to open upon me, & believing that the postmasters will lend their inquisitorial aid to fish out any new matter of slander they can, to gratify the powers that be." (TJ to Taylor, November 26, 1799, *PTJ*, 31:244–45.) This was nothing new. To John Page: "I sincerely thank you for your kind interest in the injurious slanders against me in the public papers." (June 6, 1798, *PTJ*, 30:392) John B. Boles also notes Jefferson's reluctance to write on political matters in 1800, while obviously campaigning; he had James Monroe subscribe to two newspapers so that Jefferson's name did not appear on subscription lists; see Boles, *Jefferson: Architect of American Liberty* (New York: Basic Books, 2017), 306.
4. These ideas are drawn, in large part, from Adams's *Discourses on Davila* (1790), which Jefferson construed as somehow friendly to monarchy; see Nancy Isenberg and Andrew Burstein, *The Problem of Democracy: The Presidents Adams Confront the Cult of Personality* (New York: Viking, 2019), 138–39.
5. TJ to Thomas Mann Randolph, February 4, 1800, *PTJ*, 31:359–61; see Malone, vol. 6, Appendix 1 for genealogy.
6. Lucia Stanton, *"Those Who Labor for My Happiness": Slavery at Thomas Jefferson's Monticello* (Charlottesville: University of Virginia Press, 2012), 107–113.
7. Nathan Schachner, *Thomas Jefferson: A Biography* (New York: Appleton-Century-Crofts, 1951), 2:643; Herbert E. Sloan, *Principle and Interest: Thomas Jefferson and the Problem of Debt* (Charlottesville: University Press of Virginia, 1995), 196–97; Barbara McEwan, *Thomas Jefferson: Farmer* (Jefferson, NC: McFarland, 1991), 47–48, 142–43; Susan Dunn, *Dominion of Memories: Jefferson, Madison, and the Decline of Virginia* (New York: Basic Books, 2007), 23–29.

8. Bruce A. Ragsdale, *Washington at the Plow: The Founding Farmer and the Question of Slavery* (Cambridge, MA: Harvard University Press, 2021), quotes at 132, 211; "Notes on Arthur Young's Letter to George Washington," June 18, 1792, *PTJ*, 24:95–99.
9. TJ to Eppes, July 30, 1787, *PTJ*, 11:650–54.
10. Monroe to TJ, September 9 and 15, 1800; TJ to Monroe, September 20, 1800, *PTJ*, 32:131–32, 144–45, 160–61; Arthur Scherr, *Rightful Liberty: Slavery, Morality, and Thomas Jefferson's World* (Macon, GA: Mercer University Press, 2021), chap. 4; Douglas R. Egerton, *Gabriel's Rebellion: The Virginia Slave Conspiracies of 1800 and 1802* (Chapel Hill: University of North Carolina Press, 1993); Eva Sheppard Wolf, *Race and Liberty in the New Nation: Emancipation in Virginia from the Revolution to Nat Turner's Rebellion* (Baton Rouge: Louisiana State University Press, 2006), 104–23.
11. TJ to Samuel Smith, October 17, 1800, *PTJ*, 32:227–28. The OED explains that "raw head and bloody bones" harks back to English folklore, at least two centuries before this, referring to a fearful figure whose skin had eroded from his face, with a skull for a head. His appearance was invoked to scare children.
12. Gregory May, *Jefferson's Treasure: How Albert Gallatin Saved the New Nation from Debt* (New York: Regnery History, 2018), 89–95, 123–24. Hannah Gallatin was a daughter of Commodore James Nicholson, formerly of the Continental Navy, who was a staunch New York Republican and on the receiving end of a challenge to duel from Alexander Hamilton in 1795.
13. TJ to Thomas Mann Randolph, December 12, 1800, *PTJ*, 32:300.
14. TJ to Burr, February 1, 1801, *PTJ*, 32:528–29.
15. TJ to Brackenridge, December 18, 1800, *PTJ*, 32:318–19.
16. Brackenridge to TJ, January 19, 1801, *PTJ*, 32:483–88; "Summary Journal of Letters," Library of Congress.
17. TJ to Maria Jefferson Eppes, January 4, 1801, *PTJ*, 32:391–92.
18. Burr to TJ, February 12, 1801, *PTJ*, 32:577.
19. Jefferson's gossipy political scrapbooks are known collectively as the *Anas*. They were reassembled and published early in the twentieth century. Morris's remark was conveyed to Jefferson by John Armstrong Jr., who had married into the powerful New York Livingston clan that maintained ties with Burr. On the structure of the *Anas*, see Kevin J. Hayes, *The Road to Monticello: The Life and Mind of Thomas Jefferson* (New York: Oxford University Press, 2008), chap. 28. At Christmastime 1800, Washington City was abuzz with the expectation that Jefferson haters would elevate Burr to the presidency. Morris captured this talk in his diary, observing that Virginia Federalist Henry Lee and Hamilton's successor at Treasury, Oliver

Wolcott, both adjudged the states'-rights Jefferson "dangerous" and "a theoretic man who would bring the national Government back to Something like the old Confederation." Robert Goodloe Harper of South Carolina, another Jefferson hater, told Morris that he considered Burr an "intimate" friend and guaranteed that "he thinks Mr. B's Temper and Disposition give ample Security for a Conduct hostile to the democratic Spirit." (Here, "democratic" meant pro-French and hostile to Federalist principles of good order.) Morris looked upon a "wounded," dispirited Jefferson surrogate, Wilson Cary Nicholas, senator from Virginia and Albemarle County resident, after warning him that "serious and considered Men" would see that Burr came into office. Also among Morris's visitors in this period was Virginia Federalist Thomas Evans, on February 1, another possible rumor spreader; see entries of December 25, 26, and 27, 1800, in *The Diaries of Gouverneur Morris*, ed. Melanie Randolph Miller (Charlottesville: University of Virginia Press, 2018), 2:151, 155, 158.

20. Out of desperation, on December 22, 1800, Hamilton wrote of Burr's unprincipled ambition to Theodore Sedgwick, Federalist of Massachusetts and Speaker of the House at the time: "His ambition aims at nothing short of permanent power and wealth in his own person. For heaven's sake let not the Fœderal party be responsible for the elevation of this Man." Nonetheless, Sedgwick wavered between casting his vote for Burr or for Jefferson, and Hamilton wrote him again on January 21, 1801: "I beg you as you love your country, your friends and yourself to reconsider dispassionately the opinion you have expressed in favour of Burr." Only three of the fourteen members of the Massachusetts congressional delegation ended up voting for Jefferson over Burr. *Papers of Alexander Hamilton*, 25:269, 328–29.

21. Hamilton to Bayard, January 16, 1801; to Rutledge, January 4, 1801, *Papers of Alexander Hamilton*, 25:293–95, 319–24.

22. Hamilton was aware of articles in the Federalist press praising Burr: he had escaped with his life after accompanying General Richard Montgomery on the risky march to Quebec in 1775; he was a distinguished Revolutionary officer before Hamilton had even come to General Washington's attention. Burr's "urbanity of manners" contrasted with the portrait Hamilton painted of a reprobate, and many Federalists understood this; see Nancy Isenberg, *Fallen Founder: The Life of Aaron Burr* (New York: Viking, 2007), 196–220; Nathan Schachner, *Alexander Hamilton* (New York: A. S. Barnes, 1946), chap. 46; John Ferling, *Adams vs. Jefferson: The Tumultuous Election of 1800* (New York: Oxford University Press, 2004), 175–81.

23. Hamilton to Theodore Sedgwick, May 10, 1800, *Papers of Alexander Hamilton*, 24:474–75.

24. Isenberg, *Fallen Founder*, 220.

25. Everett Somerville Brown, ed., *William Plumer's Memorandum of Proceedings in the United States Senate* (New York: Macmillan, 1923), 352–53.
26. Entry of January 1804, in the *Anas*.
27. Entry of October 13, 1802, *Diaries of Gouverneur Morris*, 2:252.

CHAPTER 11: "BLOODY TEETH & FANGS"

1. TJ to Washington, January 22, 1783, *PTJ*, 6:222; with reference to the determination of public character in this period, through the *apparent* exposure of inner decency, sincerity, and moral conscience, Jay Fliegelman writes: "Jefferson's oratorical anxieties are less that his private self will be penetrated than that he will be unable and unwilling to surrender stoical self-possession for sentimental externalization, unable, that is, to deliver, in the wished-for transparencies of public behavior, the kind of private self, or endless narrative and revelation of a private self, demanded of him." See Fliegelman, *Declaring Independence: Jefferson, Natural Language, and the Culture of Performance* (Stanford, CA: Stanford University Press, 1993), 125.
2. TJ to Jean Baptiste Le Roy, November 13, 1786, *PTJ*, 10:524–30.
3. Strickland to TJ, May 20 and 28, 1796, *PTJ*, 29:102–106, 115–19; TJ to Strickland, March 23, 1798, Sowerby, 1:335.
4. *Notes on Virginia*, ed. Robert Pierce Forbes (New Haven, CT: Yale University Press, 2022), Query XIX, 252–53. Jefferson does not regard a manufacturing economy as unneeded; he recognized in 1809 "a due balance between agriculture, manufactures, and commerce" as what sustained a nation's economic health, and by 1816, he admitted: "Experience has taught me that manufacturers are now as necessary to our independence as to our comfort"; see Richard K. Matthews, *The Radical Politics of Thomas Jefferson: A Revisionist View* (Lawrence: University Press of Kansas, 1984), 48–49; on the literature affecting Jefferson's thinking in regard to agrarianism, see especially Caroline Winterer, *American Enlightenments* (New Haven, CT: Yale University Press, 2016), chap. 7; Joyce Appleby, "Commercial Farming and the Agrarian Myth in the Early Republic," *Journal of American History* 68, 4 (March 1982): 833–49; on commerce and agriculture in relation to the Jefferson-Madison synthesis, see Drew R. McCoy, *The Elusive Republic: Political Economy in Jeffersonian America* (Chapel Hill: University of North Carolina Press, 1980).
5. Peter Gay, *The Enlightenment: The Science of Freedom* (New York: W. W. Norton, 1969), 121–22.
6. First Inaugural Address, March 4, 1801, *PTJ*, 33:148–52; for a useful rhetorical analysis of the text, see Stephen Howard Browne, "'The Circle of Our Felicities':

Thomas Jefferson's First Inaugural Address and the Rhetoric of Nationhood," *Rhetoric and Public Affairs* 5, 3 (Fall 2002): 409–38.
7. Entry of March 4, 1801, *Diaries of Gouverneur Morris*, 2:163.
8. Gregory May, *Jefferson's Treasure: How Albert Gallatin Saved the New Nation from Debt* (New York: Regnery, 2018), 116–21; Malone, 4:69–89. Of particular note is Jefferson's refusal to appoint Vice President Burr's close associate Matthew Livingston Davis to any federal office, despite Burr's urging; Davis went so far as to pay Jefferson a visit at Monticello to plead for a job; see Noble E. Cunningham, *The Jeffersonian Republicans in Power: Party Operations, 1801–1809* (Chapel Hill: University of North Carolina Press, 1963), 38–43.
9. Stanton, "Those Who Labor for My Happiness," 41–46; G. S. Wilson, *Jefferson on Display: Attire, Etiquette, and the Arts of Presentation* (Charlottesville: University of Virginia Press, 2018), 160–67; James M. Gabler, *Passions: The Wines and Travels of Thomas Jefferson* (Baltimore: Bacchus Press, 1995), 197–200; Merry Ellen Scofield, "The Fatigues of His Table: The Politics of Presidential Dining During the Jefferson Administration," *Journal of the Early Republic* 26, 3 (Fall 2006): 449–69; Annette Gordon-Reed, *The Hemingses of Monticello: An American Family* (New York: W. W. Norton, 2008), 570, 607; Kelley Fanto Deetz, *Bound to the Fire: How Virginia's Enslaved Cooks Helped Invent American Cuisine* (Lexington: University Press of Kentucky, 2017), chap. 3. It is worth noting that as president, George Washington was informed by Attorney General Edmund Randolph that Pennsylvania law automatically made free an enslaved person who resided in the state for six consecutive months, so he conspired to send his enslaved chef Hercules back to Mount Vernon temporarily. Eventually, Hercules took advantage of the law and escaped slavery (Deetz, 78–87). For his part, Jefferson separated Edy Fossett from her partner, Joe, for so long that Joe disobeyed Jefferson and went on his own to see her (Stanton, 16–17); on Joseph Dougherty's various roles in Jefferson's Washington household, see James B. Conroy, *Jefferson's White House: Monticello on the Potomac* (Lanham, MD: Rowman & Littlefield, 2019), 64–67, 189–91.
10. Carrie B. Douglass, "Breeding and Buying Horses, Connecting Family, Friends, and Neighbors," in David T. Gies and Cynthia Wall, eds., *The Eighteenth Centuries: Global Networks of the Enlightenment* (Charlottesville: University of Virginia Press, 2018): 95–109.
11. Maurizio Valsania, *Jefferson's Body: A Corporeal Biography* (Charlottesville: University of Virginia Press, 2017), 51–64, quote at 57. Brian Steele offers an excellent short lesson in the fine line between Jefferson's constant criticism of aristocratic manners and the concept of a "natural aristocracy" he embraced, through which he hoped to

provide leadership opportunities for talented young men born without social position; in their philosophical debate on this issue, the realist John Adams tried to put a damper on Jefferson's enthusiasm, challenging him to see that all people craved distinction, glared at celebrity with envy, and were less discerning than he imagined. On their debate and Jefferson's views regarding citizen participation in government, see Steele, *Thomas Jefferson and American Nationhood* (New York: Cambridge University Press, 2012), 142–57. Michal Jan Rozbicki delivers a particularly profound analysis of class structure and elite identity in Revolution-era America, cataloging the axiomatic recurrence to a rhetoric of liberty and equality, and contrasting it to the reality of social privilege; see Rozbicki, *Culture and Liberty in the Age of the American Revolution* (Charlottesville: University of Virginia Press, 2011).

12. William Seale, *The President's House: A History* (Baltimore: Johns Hopkins University Press, 1986), 1:88–93.
13. John B. Boles, *Jefferson: Architect of American Liberty* (New York: Basic Books, 2017), 334–35; Valsania, *Jefferson's Body*, 11–14.
14. Merrill D. Peterson, *Thomas Jefferson and the New Nation* (New York: Oxford University Press, 1970), 681–82; Malone, 4:192–99, quote at 198.
15. TJ to Priestley, March 21, 1801, and June 19, 1802, *PTJ*, 33:393–95, 37:325–27.
16. Jenny Graham, *Revolutionary in Exile: The Emigration of Joseph Priestley to America, 1794–1804* (Philadelphia: American Philosophical Society, 1995), 97–149; TJ to Priestley, March 21, 1801; to Fry, June 17, 1804, *PTJ*, 33:393, 43:611. Priestley's book spoke directly to Jefferson's disbelief in the Trinity and the divinity of Jesus.
17. Margaret Bayard Smith, *The First Forty Years of Washington Society*, ed. Gaillard Hunt (New York: C. Scribner's Sons, 1906), 385–86.
18. "Notes on Cabinet Meeting," May 15, 1801, *PTJ*, 34:114–15; First Annual Message, December 8, 1801, *PTJ*, 36:58–67; for quote regarding Livingston, see TJ to Secretary of the Navy Robert Smith, April 27, 1804, *PTJ*, 43:328–29; Malone, 4:97–99; Francis D. Cogliano, *Emperor of Liberty: Thomas Jefferson's Foreign Policy* (New Haven, CT: Yale University Press, 2014), chap. 5; Robert J. Allison, *The Crescent Obscured: The United States and the Muslim World, 1776–1815* (New York: Oxford University Press, 1995), chap. 1; Andrew Burstein and Nancy Isenberg, *Madison and Jefferson* (New York: Random House, 2010), 403–407; Nathan Schachner, *Thomas Jefferson: A Biography* (New York: Appleton-Century-Crofts, 1951), 2:781–83.
19. Livingston to Madison, April 13, 1803, *Papers of James Madison, Secretary of State Series*, ed. J. C. A. Stagg et al. (Charlottesville: University Press of Virginia, 1998), 4:511–15; Livingston to TJ, June 2, 1803; TJ to Wilson Cary Nicholas, September 7, 1803, *PTJ*, 40:470–74, 41:346–48. Jefferson's initial scheme was to purchase the port of New Orleans (to ensure U.S. control over the entire Mississippi), as well as

Spanish Florida; Napoleon did not include Florida in his counteroffer. Jefferson's decision to bypass Congress factored in the length of time required to pass a constitutional amendment permitting the executive to negotiate a treaty with a foreign nation for the purpose of purchasing territory, though Madison assured him he was on firm constitutional ground. For a reliable synthesis, see Schachner, *Thomas Jefferson*, 2:727–57; on conflicted positions in the acquisition of the Louisiana Territory, see Peter S. Onuf, "The Revolution of 1803," in Onuf, *The Mind of Thomas Jefferson* (Charlottesville: University of Virginia Press, 2007), 99–108.

20. Writing of Jefferson's idealization of agrarian political economy, the political theorist Richard K. Matthews stated emblematically: "The rural experience is unique. It allows the individual to have control over his destiny while pursuing happiness in a bucolic aesthetic locale. So great are the chances of men finding human fulfillment in a farm environment that Jefferson believes that no effort ought to be spared in providing all men with the opportunity for such a life." See Matthews, *The Radical Politics of Thomas Jefferson*, 39. For a good analysis of the evolution of Jefferson's convictions regarding land management and expansion, preventing large land companies from controlling the process, see Mark Sturges, "Enclosing the Commons: Thomas Jefferson, Agrarian Independence, and Early American Land Policy, 1774–1789," *Virginia Magazine of History and Biography* 119, 1 (2011): 42–74.

21. Albert Furtwangler, *Acts of Discovery: Visions of America in the Lewis and Clark Journals* (Urbana: University of Illinois Press, 1993), 25–32; Boles, *Jefferson*, 359–60.

22. Cunningham, *The Jeffersonian Republicans in Power*, 18, 52–62; TJ to Cooper, April 17, 1801; to Lincoln, August 26, 1801, and October 25, 1802, *PTJ*, 33:600; 35:145–47; 38:565. The *OED* does not take note of Jefferson's coining of "neophobia," showing its first use to have occurred only in the 1870s in French and 1880s in English.

23. Lowell H. Harrison, *John Breckinridge: Jeffersonian Republican* (Lexington, KY: Filson Club, 1969); Peterson, *Thomas Jefferson and the New Nation*, 612–13, 780–82; Cunningham, *The Jeffersonian Republicans in Power*, 96–97.

24. TJ to Breckinridge, November 24, 1803, *PTJ*, 42:37. Jefferson named Breckinridge to the cabinet in 1805, but he served as U.S. attorney general for only a short time, dying of tuberculosis in December 1806. Consistent with his cultivation of Breckinridge, when Jefferson identified an ambitious younger man he wanted to help advance (because it aided his cause), he appealed for utter discretion; here he is suggesting that William Wirt run for Congress: "I pray you that this letter may be sacredly secret; because it meddles in a line wherein I should myself think it wrong to intermeddle." TJ to Wirt, January 10, 1808, FOL.

25. TJ to Breckinridge, August 12, 1803, *PTJ*, 41:184–86; Peter S. Onuf, *Jefferson's Empire: The Language of American Nationhood* (Charlottesville: University Press

of Virginia, 2000), 117–19; more broadly, see Peter J. Kastor, *The Nation's Crucible: The Louisiana Purchase and the Creation of America* (New Haven, CT: Yale University Press, 2004). Just after assuming office, well before there was the prospect of adding on new territories, Jefferson had written to a former Vermont congressman of "the falsehood of Montesquieu's doctrine that a republic can be preserved only in a small territory." (TJ to Nathaniel Niles, March 21, 1801, *PTJ*, 33:403–404.)

26. Furtwangler, *Acts of Discovery*, 212–14; *Selected Writings of Thomas Paine*, ed. Ian Shapiro and Jane E. Calvert (New Haven, CT: Yale University Press, 2014), 26, 38; TJ to Martha Jefferson Randolph, March 28, 1787, *PTJ*, 11:250–52.

27. Amanda Louise Johnson, "Thomas Jefferson's Ossianic Romance," *Studies in Eighteenth-Century Culture* 45 (2016): 19–35. I am adapting her tart observation: "Rewriting the settler as indigene would also occlude the various forms of colonial violence . . . Jefferson's romance of America, as evidenced in writings such as *Notes on the State of Virginia*, shows an Ossian-like quality to his reshaping of reality" (24). Andrew Trees captures Jefferson's broad interpretation of the Enlightenment in his mixing of the natural world with his faith in political progress in a country that upholds pastoral traditions; see Trees, "Apocalypse Now: Thomas Jefferson's Radical Enlightenment," in Joanne B. Freeman and Johann N. Neem, eds., *Jeffersonians in Power: The Rhetoric of Opposition Meets the Realities of Governing* (Charlottesville: University of Virginia Press, 2019), 199–221.

28. For the origins of Jefferson's thinking as it applies to the politically healthy results of allodial land ownership, an inheritance of the ancient Saxons, see Christopher Michael Curtis, *Jefferson's Freeholders and the Politics of Ownership in the Old Dominion* (New York: Cambridge University Press, 2012), chap. 2. Jefferson allowed for the possible establishment of independent republics in the West as early as his proposed Virginia state constitution in 1776.

29. Bernard W. Sheehan, *Seeds of Extinction: Jeffersonian Philanthropy and the American Indian* (New York: W. W. Norton, 1973), 171, 245–47; "Draft Amendment," approx. July 9, 1803; "Jefferson's Draft of Queries," *PTJ*, 40:685–86, 694–95. Among Jefferson's queries about the geographical boundaries of Louisiana and its existing laws, he asked: "9. What is the population of the province, distinguishing between white & black but excluding Indians, on the East side of the Missisipi? of the settlement on the West side next the mouth? of each distinct settlement in the other parts of the province? and what the geographical position and extent of each of these settlements? 10. What are the foundations of their land-titles? and what their tenure?"

30. TJ to Harrison, February 27, 1803; to Dearborn, December 2, 1804, *PTJ*, 39:589–93, 45:122–23. A more thorough case for the surrender to Anglo-American culture was

made to Indian agent Benjamin Hawkins in a more inviting tone: "[You] have it peculiarly in your power to promote among the Indians a sense of the superior value of a little land well-cultivated over a great deal unimproved... In truth the ultimate point of rest & happiness for them is to let our settlements and theirs meet and blend together, to intermix and become one people, incorporating themselves with us as citizens of the US... Surely it will be better for them to be identified with us, and preserved in the occupation of their lands, than be exposed to the many casualties which may endanger them while a separate people" (TJ to Hawkins, February 18, 1803, *PTJ*, 39:546–49); Peterson, *Thomas Jefferson and the New Nation*, 773–74.

31. This was the famous case of *Marbury v. Madison*, which historians highlight as the case that established judicial review (although in fact a 1792 case, *Hayburn*, when John Jay was chief justice, effectively voided an act of Congress). Upon entering office, Jefferson saw that a number of justices of the peace appointed by Adams at the end of his term had not received their commissions. He reappointed all the Republicans on Adams's list, and some of the Federalists, but he declined to appoint eleven of the men. One, William Marbury, sued for his commission. Marshall ruled that the incoming administration could not be compelled to deliver Marbury's commission, because the act of Congress Marbury relied on (the Judiciary Act of 1789) was unconstitutional. This was good for Jefferson, in the one instance, except that Marshall had just demonstrated the Court's power and emboldened Chief Justice Marshall, who wrote the opinion. See also Richard E. Ellis, *The Jeffersonian Crisis: Courts and Politics in the Young Republic* (New York: Oxford University Press, 1971), chap. 3; for a short synthesis of the tension brewing between the president and the new chief justice, see Joseph J. Ellis, *American Sphinx: The Character of Thomas Jefferson* (New York: Knopf, 1997), 221–27.

32. On press coverage of the conjoined Hemings and Walker issues during Jefferson's presidency, see Robert M. S. McDonald, *Confounding Father: Thomas Jefferson's Image in His Own Time* (Charlottesville: University of Virginia Press, 2016), 144–49. Gouverneur Morris dined at the President's House when the Walker revelation was in the press and recorded in his diary that Jefferson seemed "terribly out of Spirits"; *The Diaries of Gouverneur Morris*, ed. Melanie Randolph Miller (Charlottesville: University of Virginia Press, 2018), entry of January 3, 1803, 2:263.

33. For a clear understanding of the newspapers Jefferson bought, typically from third parties when they were opposition papers he wished to track, see *JMB*, 2:1122–23.

34. TJ to Nicholson, May 13, 1803, *PTJ*, 40:371–73; Schachner, *Thomas Jefferson*, 657, 778; Malone, 4:458–85.

35. Merry Ellen Scofield, "The Fatigues of His Table: The Politics of Presidential Dining During the Jefferson Administration," *Journal of the Early Republic* 26, 3

(Fall 2006): 466–67; Isenberg, *Fallen Founder*, 272–80. "Dinner Guest Records," Appendix II, *PTJ*, 48:724-49.

36. David Johnson, *John Randolph of Roanoke* (Baton Rouge: Louisiana State University Press, 2012), 88–97, quote at 95; see also John M. Grammer, *Pastoral Politics and the Old South* (Baton Rouge: Louisiana State University Press, 1996), chap. 2. A turning point came in the spring of 1806, when Randolph's rants alarmed Jefferson's firmest supporters in Pennsylvania, who foresaw a third political party emerging as the abusive congressman (a "madman") built a base; to old friend James Monroe, the ever-optimistic leader expressed scant concern: "The sudden defection of such a man, could not but produce momentary astonishment & even dismay. But for a moment only." See Thomas Leiper to TJ, March 23, 1806; TJ to Monroe, May 4, 1806, *PTJ*, 49:124-27, 370.

CHAPTER 12: "I FEEL NO PASSION, I TAKE NO PART"

1. Maurizio Valsania, *Jefferson's Body: A Corporeal Biography* (Charlottesville: University of Virginia Press, 2017), 103–105; Gordon-Reed, *Hemingses of Monticello*, 271, 373, 530, 589–93; *JMB*, 2:1124–25. Jefferson was not present at Monticello for the birth of Madison Hemings.
2. Abigail Adams to TJ, May 20, 1804, *PTJ*, 43:458–59.
3. Gordon-Reed, *Hemingses of Monticello*, 592–93, 731n12.
4. Robert M. S. McDonald, "Race, Sex, and Reputation: Thomas Jefferson and the Sally Hemings Story," *Southern Cultures* 4, 2 (Summer 1998): 46–63, quote at 58; the clergyman in question was Azel Backus, first president of Hamilton College, and the rationale Jefferson gave for his reluctance to see Backus tried was to spare the Walker family embarrassment when their part in the Callender exposé was introduced into evidence; Gordon-Reed, *Hemingses of Monticello*, 120, 676n3, "Hemings Family Tree–1." Betsy's mother was Mary Hemings, eldest daughter of Elizabeth Hemings (that is, Sally Hemings's half sister); Betsy's father was reportedly white or of mixed race.
5. TJ to Page, June 25, 1804, *PTJ*, 43:652–53.
6. See, for example, TJ to New York Legislature, December 10, 1807, FOL.
7. TJ to Thomas McKean, July 24, 1801, *PTJ*, 34:625–27; to George Logan, May 11, 1805, and to Caesar Augustus Rodney, October 25, 1805, FOL; Burstein and Isenberg, *Madison and Jefferson*, 439–40.
8. One of Virginia's most respected Jeffersonian politicians, John Taylor of Caroline, wrote that the defectors who supported Monroe over Madison were a strange, eclectic bunch that included aggrieved individuals ("some complication of

enmities & disappointments") who'd expected personal favors from the administration, as well as longtime Federalists with a particular aversion to Madison; see Taylor to Wilson Cary Nicholas, February 4, 1808, Papers of the Randolph Family of Edgehill, MSS 1397, Box 2, folder 66, Special Collections, University of Virginia Library.

9. On the *Chesapeake* incident and embargo, see, among others, Malone, 5:415–38, 469–90, 574–608, 655–57; Schachner, *Thomas Jefferson*, 839–50, 862–86; Boles, *Jefferson*, 413–22.

10. William H. Gaines Jr., *Thomas Mann Randolph: Jefferson's Son-in-Law* (Baton Rouge: Louisiana State University Press, 1966), 60–64; Johnson, *John Randolph of Roanoke*, 112–15; TJ to Thomas Mann Randolph, June 23, 1806, FOL.

11. TJ to Chastellux, September 2, 1785, *PTJ*, 8:467–70; similarly, to his Philadelphia landlady and lifelong friend Eliza House Trist, he called his fellow Virginians "lazy and hospitable . . . their character has some good traits mixed with some feeble ones" (December 15, 1786, *PTJ*, 10:599–601); Ronald L. Hatzenbuehler, *"I Tremble for My Country": Thomas Jefferson and the Virginia Gentry* (Gainesville: University Press of Florida, 2006); Susan Dunn, *Dominion of Memories: Jefferson, Madison, and the Decline of Virginia* (New York: Basic Books, 2007); Erin Austin Dwyer, *Mastering Emotions: Feelings, Power, and Slavery in the United States* (Philadelphia: University of Pennsylvania Press, 2021); Susan R. Stein, *The Worlds of Thomas Jefferson at Monticello* (New York: Harry N. Abrams, 1993), 262–67, 275–77, 368, 375, 378–80. Beautiful pieces of wooden furniture came out of the joinery at Monticello, especially those crafted by John Hemings; yet Jefferson consistently sought furniture from the North.

12. Peter S. Onuf, *Jefferson's Empire: The Language of American Nationhood* (Charlottesville: University Press of Virginia, 2000), 12–17; Boles, *Jefferson*, 77–78; on Jefferson's land reform proposal of 1806, see Steele, *Thomas Jefferson and American Nationhood*, 135.

13. "Second Inaugural Address," March 4, 1805, *PTJ*, 45:652–57.

14. Boles, *Jefferson*, 417–27.

15. John D. Battle Jr., "The 'Periodical Head-achs' of Thomas Jefferson," *Cleveland Clinic Journal of Medicine* 51 (Fall 1984): 535–36.

16. *Anas*, 224–28.

17. *New York Herald*, December 17, 1806; Isenberg, *Fallen Founder*, 286–87.

18. The idea of a filibuster was very much alive in the early years of the republic. William Eaton's desert campaign in Libya, in 1804, involved the arming of Greeks, Italians, and Arabs to restore a fallen pasha to power, and could be viewed as a filibuster. A better-known example of a successful filibuster is the one that announced the

independent Republic of Texas, which remained independent from 1836 to 1845, when it entered the Union. See Isenberg, *Fallen Founder*, 282–91, 307, 330–31; Robert E. May, *Manifest Destiny's Underworld: Filibustering in Antebellum America* (Chapel Hill: University of North Carolina Press, 2002).

19. Isenberg, *Fallen Founder*, 301, 307, 310–11, 330–33. Back in 1775, Henry Dearborn was an intimate of Burr's when they fought side by side in Canada; he'd assessed Burr's character at the time of that shared experience, but as secretary of war in 1805–1807, he did not challenge the president's opinions or question the treatment of Burr.

20. "Notes on a Conversation with Aaron Burr," April 15, 1806, *PTJ*, 49:247.

21. Isenberg, *Fallen Founder*, 304–307; Andrew Burstein, *The Passions of Andrew Jackson* (New York: Knopf, 2003), 71–74. Uncertain whether Burr had Jefferson's blessing to engage the Spanish, Jackson wrote the president alerting him to his activities while volunteering his militia if needed in a conflict with the Spanish. For a key example of Daveiss's impassioned letters of warning, see Daveiss to TJ, January 10, 1806, *PTJ*, 48:347-48.

22. Granger quote in Malone, 5:222; Wilkinson's activities with southern Indian tribes as gleaned from his extensive correspondence with Jefferson and others, in FOL.

23. David S. Heidler and Jeanne T. Heidler, *Henry Clay: The Essential American* (New York: Random House, 2010), 56–64; Brown, ed., *Plumer's Memorandum*, 547–50.

24. Jefferson's Address to U.S. Congress, January 22, 1807, Library of Congress; Isenberg, *Fallen Founder*, 311–16, 319–20.

25. Jefferson recorded his recollection of the mid-March conversation at great length on April 15, 1806, when he'd become aware of a lawsuit in New York where a pro-Jefferson newspaper that routinely excoriated Burr was charged with lying about Burr's intent to undermine Jefferson during the election tie by cooperating with Federalists; contrary evidence was also to be presented at trial that Jefferson, through an intermediary, had in fact expressed a willingness to do the same. Both Burr and Jefferson vehemently denied the charges. That questions should linger in the public with respect to the election of 1800 is indicative of the continuing suspicions entertained by Jefferson.

26. Brown, ed., *Plumer's Memorandum*, 542–43, 574–75.

27. Isenberg, *Fallen Founder*, 324–25, 328; Johnson, *John Randolph of Roanoke*, 121–24; TJ to George Morgan, March 26, 1807; to Giles, April 20, 1807, Library of Congress.

28. TJ to Hay, June 2 and 17, 1807, FOL. On the question of Jefferson's ethics throughout Burr's trial, with particular emphasis on the chief justice and the prosecution,

see Leonard W. Levy, *Jefferson and Civil Liberties: The Darker Side* (Cambridge, MA: Harvard University Press, 1963), 73–89.
29. TJ to Lafayette, July 14, 1807, FOL.
30. Albert J. Beveridge, *Life of John Marshall* (Boston: Houghton-Mifflin, 1929), 1:143-45, 154–61; John B. Boles, *Seven Virginians: The Men Who Shaped Our Republic* (Charlottesville: University of Virginia Press, 2023), 282-83. The year 1780 was the year Marshall was first smitten by his future wife, Mary Ambler, the teenage daughter of Rebecca Burwell and Jaquelin Ambler. The Amblers, as very early residents of Richmond when Jefferson made it the state capital, were greatly disturbed by Jefferson's flight at the time of Arnold's invasion, feelings no doubt shared with Marshall.
31. Brown, ed., *Plumer's Memorandum*, 545; TJ to John Norvell, June 11, 1807, FOL. In 1803, Jefferson told Governor Thomas McKean of Pennsylvania that select prosecutions of newspaper editors for seditious libel—by the states—would be a good thing. Of course, he did not want his suggestion to escape McKean's desk, given his vehemence about federal government prosecutions of Republican editors before 1801: "On the subject of prosecutions, what I say must be entirely confidential," he stressed, "for you know the passion for torturing every sentiment & word which comes from me." Joseph Dennie, editor of the Philadelphia journal *Port-Folio*, mocked Jefferson endlessly, becoming a test case after writing (among other critical opinions) that "democracy is scarcely tolerable . . . It is intolerable here, and the issue will be civil war, desolation, and anarchy." He stood trial in 1803, and was acquitted. Yet another defeat for Jefferson. (TJ to McKean, February 19, 1803, *PTJ*, 39:552–55; Burstein and Isenberg, *Madison and Jefferson*, 412, 419–20.)
32. James Parton, *The Life and Times of Aaron Burr* (Boston: Houghton, Mifflin, 1892), 2:50–52; TJ to Monroe, January 11, 1812, *PTJ-R*, 4:412–13; TJ to Madison, May 7, 1783; to Burr, June 17, 1797, *PTJ*, 6:265–67, 29:438–39.
33. Jefferson's Address to U.S. Congress, January 22, 1807, Library of Congress.
34. Nancy Isenberg poses questions along these lines: "Why did Jefferson not intimate to Burr that some were accusing him of treason?" "Why did Burr not let Jefferson know that he was considering a filibuster?" See *Fallen Founder*, 364–65.
35. Parton, *Life and Times of Aaron Burr*, 2:68–69.
36. Todd Estes, "Jefferson as Party Leader," in Francis D. Cogliano, ed., *A Companion to Thomas Jefferson* (Malden, MA: Wiley-Blackwell, 2012), 128–44, quote at 141–42.
37. TJ to Giles, April 20, 1807, Library of Congress.
38. TJ to Monroe, March 10, 1808, FOL.

39. TJ to Madison, August 5, 1808, *The Republic of Letters: The Correspondence Between Thomas Jefferson and James Madison, 1776–1826*, ed. James Morton Smith (New York: W. W. Norton, 1995), 3:1529–30.
40. On the Federalists during this period, see especially Linda K. Kerber, *Federalists in Dissent: Imagery and Ideology in Jeffersonian America* (Ithaca, NY: Cornell University Press, 1980), and James H. Broussard, *The Southern Federalists, 1800–1816* (Baton Rouge: Louisiana State University Press, 1978).

CHAPTER 13: "SUSPICIONS & CERTAINTIES, RUMORS & REALITIES"

1. Jane Nicholas Randolph to Cary Ann Nicholas Smith, June 27, 1826; Thomas Jefferson Randolph to Jane Nicholas Randolph, undated letters of the same period, in Papers of the Randolph Family of Edgehill, MSS 1397, Special Collections, University of Virginia Library, Box 5, folders 26–28.
2. Malone, 5:313–14, 473–79. Crediting decades of research conducted by Lucia Stanton at Monticello, Arthur Scherr compiles evidence of alternate kindness and coldness toward the enslaved community there, holding that Martha, mirroring her father, protested slave owning when young, but increasingly accommodated herself to it, and even took a hard line on recalcitrant slaves; see Scherr, *Rightful Liberty: Slavery, Morality, and Thomas Jefferson's World* (Macon, GA: Mercer University Press, 2021), 377–81; two of Martha's daughters, Mary and Ellen (the latter of whom married at Monticello and moved with her husband to Boston in 1825), decried the system of slavery, especially the slave auction; see Susan Dunn, *Dominion of Memories: Jefferson, Madison, and the Decline of Virginia* (New York: Basic Books, 2007), 42. For an engrossing analysis of the breakup of Monticello's enslaved families and all that followed in their lives, see Andrew Davenport, "We Were Scattered: The African American Diaspora from Monticello, 1826-1900," PhD diss., (Dept. of History, Georgetown University, 2024).
3. Andrew Burstein, *America's Jubilee: How in 1826 a Generation Remembered Fifty Years of Independence* (New York: Knopf, 2001), chap. 11; Andrew Burstein, *The Inner Jefferson: Portrait of a Grieving Optimist* (Charlottesville: University Press of Virginia, 1995), 265–66.
4. Thomas Jefferson Randolph to Jane Nicholas Randolph, January 30, 1826, Papers of the Randolph Family of Edgehill, MSS 1397, Special Collections, University of Virginia Library, Box 5, folder 19. Registering similar emotion, he wrote to Jane from New York that fall, while bringing his mother to live with her daughter Ellen in Boston:

"God grant that I was fairly settled at home never again to leave my own dear wife and children... and with what delight I look forward to the moment of my return." (November 2, 1826, Papers of the Randolph Family of Edgehill, Box 5, folder 53).
5. Thomas Jefferson Randolph's Memoirs, ca. 1874, Papers of the Randolph Family of Edgehill, MSS 1397, Special Collections, University of Virginia Library, Box 11, folder 35.
6. Cynthia A. Kierner, *Martha Jefferson Randolph, Daughter of Monticello* (Chapel Hill: University of North Carolina Press, 2012), 142–48, 174; Andrew Burstein, *Jefferson's Secrets: Death and Desire at Monticello* (New York: Basic Books, 2005), 71.
7. [Thomas Jefferson Randolph], *Memoir, Correspondence, and Miscellanies, from the Papers of Thomas Jefferson*, 4 vols. (Charlottesville, VA: F. Carr & Co., 1829), text is at the end of the final volume; the collection was named *Anas* by T. J. Randolph, not his grandfather, according to John Van Horne in his "3 Volume" database, https://jefferson3volumes.org; see also "Editorial Note," *PTJ*, 22:33–38; for a critical approach to Jefferson's self-presentation in the Autobiography and *Anas*, see Hannah Spahn, *Thomas Jefferson, Time, and History* (Charlottesville: University of Virginia Press, 2011), 160–61, 194–99; Joseph J. Ellis considers the *Anas* less successful than Jefferson hoped; see Ellis, *American Sphinx: The Character of Thomas Jefferson* (New York: Knopf, 1997), 256–57.
8. I provide an elaborate examination of Jefferson's efforts to write his own history, without literally composing it, in chapter 8 of *Jefferson's Secrets* (quote at 231).
9. TJ to Edward Carrington, January 16, 1787, *PTJ*, 11:49–50.
10. As president, he proved himself quite capable of taming his rhetoric and practicing moderation (retention of some Federalists in lucrative offices, a temporizing response to the Chesapeake Affair), and he could just as easily act with speed and resolve in foreign affairs (the Barbary War, the Louisiana Purchase) without contradiction. His operative principle of mild, decentralized government applied to what "the people" felt in relation to the national authority; the unpopularity of his embargo policy called that principle into question.
11. Matthew Crow, "Thomas Jefferson and the Uses of Equity," *Law and History Review* 33, 1 (February 2015): 179; diffusion of sovereignty, or "layered authorities," as Peter S. Onuf has framed it, marked Jefferson's "comprehensive theory linking individual rights to a federal constitutional design"; see Onuf, *Jefferson's Empire: The Language of American Nationhood* (Charlottesville: University Press of Virginia, 2000), 116–21, quote at 120; Merrill D. Peterson, *Thomas Jefferson and the New Nation* (New York: Oxford University Press, 1970), 146–50, 961–62; David N. Mayer, *The Constitutional Thought of Thomas Jefferson* (Charlottesville: University Press of Virginia, 1994), 320–29. To see how Jefferson's optimistic

prescription is applied in the context of our modern politics, see Anthony Pratkanis, "Good Propaganda or Propaganda for Good," in Nancy Snow, ed., *Propaganda and American Democracy* (Baton Rouge: Louisiana State University Press, 2014), 29–74.

12. *Memoir, Correspondence, and Miscellanies, from the Papers of Thomas Jefferson*, 443–527; "Thomas Jefferson's Explanations of the Three Volumes Bound in Marbled Paper (the so-called 'Anas')," *PTJ-R*, 12:417–20.

13. T. J. Randolph to N. P. Trist, March 6, 1829, transcript available at tjrs.monticello.org. For a strong narrative about the post-1826 experiences of Jeff Randolph, his accomplished sister Ellen Coolidge, Nicholas Trist, and Madison Hemings, see Christa Dierksheide, *Beyond Jefferson: The Hemingses, the Randolphs, and the Making of Nineteenth-Century America* (New Haven, CT: Yale University Press, 2024).

14. Carolyn A. Barros, "Figura, Persona, Dynamis: Autobiography and Change," *Biography* 15, 1 (Winter 1992): 1–28; Scott E. Casper, *Constructing American Lives: Biography and Culture in Nineteenth-Century America* (Chapel Hill: University of North Carolina Press, 1999); as a counterpoint to Jefferson's self-promoting project, see Elizabeth M. Renker, "'Declaration-Men' and the Rhetoric of Self-Presentation," *Early American Literature* 24, 2 (1989): 120–34, which includes a trenchant analysis of Benjamin Rush's autobiographical writings that call into question the vaunted superiority of Revolutionary leaders.

15. TJ to Dearborn, May 17, 1818; to Spencer Roane, September 6, 1819, *PTJ-R*, 13:49–50, 15:16. Judge Roane (1762–1822) was long a favorite of Jefferson's, an outspoken critic of Chief Justice John Marshall and a devoted Republican with a proslavery agenda. His first wife, who died in 1799, was a daughter of Patrick Henry. On Roane and Marshall, see Charles Hobson, "An Enduring Political Rivalry: Thomas Jefferson and John Marshall," in Dustin Gish and Andrew Bibby, eds., *Rival Visions: How Jefferson and His Contemporaries Defined the Early American Republic* (Charlottesville: University of Virginia Press, 2021), 308–311. The dissenting writer was Henry Lee IV (1787–1837), half brother of future General Robert E. Lee, whose father, the Revolutionary War general "Light Horse Harry" Lee, had authored a critical account of Jefferson's wartime governorship that the son was in the process of revising in 1826; see Burstein, *Jefferson's Secrets*, 271–74.

16. Randall, 2:27–44, quotes at 27 and 39–40.

17. Margaret Bayard Smith, *The First Forty Years of Washington Society*, ed. Gaillard Hunt (New York: Charles Scribner's Sons, 1906), 6–7; Susan M. Stabile, *Memory's Daughters: The Material Culture of Remembrance in Eighteenth-Century America* (Ithaca, NY: Cornell University Press, 2004), 184–88. Androgyny does not imply bisexuality, though it should be said that the psychological community is uncertain

to what degree androgynous expression ("complementarity") is innate vs. a function of socialization; see Kathryn Pauly Morgan, "Androgyny: A Conceptual Critique," *Social Theory and Practice* 8, 3 (Fall 1982): 245–83; Graeme Russell, "The Father Role and Its Relation to Masculinity, Femininity, and Androgyny," *Child Development* 49, 4 (December 1978): 1174–81. Another indication of androgynous patterns is the "periodical head ach" Jefferson experienced, and his undeniable proneness to gossip with allies regarding his suspicions about those who wished him ill: twice as many migraine sufferers are female, and all migraine sufferers exhibit a susceptibility to experiencing negative affect. As a non-psychologist, I am hesitant about suggesting a direct correlation in these matters, though recent literature is quite explicit about behavior patterns in migraine sufferers; see, for example, Rachel E. Davis et al., "Personality Traits, Personality Disorders, and Migraine: A Review," *Neurological Science* 34 (2013), Supplement S7–S10. Any attempt to explain how this "nurturing" Jefferson expended so little of his emotional regard for his children with Sally Hemings is purely a matter of speculation; so I will advance, as a suspicion only, that the Virginia aristocrat's emotional distance is some form of the inherited British model of the patriarch of the manor who sends away the female servant and his mixed-class offspring to avoid scandal.

18. Andrew Burstein, "'Dexterity and Delicacy of Manipulation': Biographers Henry S. Randall and James Parton," and Annette Gordon-Reed, "'That Woman': Fawn Brodie and Thomas Jefferson's Intimate History," in Robert M. S. McDonald, ed., *Thomas Jefferson's Lives: Biographers and the Battle for History* (Charlottesville: University of Virginia Press, 2019), 62–76, 265–68.

19. Lucia Stanton, *"Those Who Labor for My Happiness": Slavery at Thomas Jefferson's Monticello* (Charlottesville: University of Virginia Press, 2012), 195–98. Monticello's enslaved were sold at auction in 1827 and 1829, and Monticello itself sold in 1831. The Jefferson-Randolphs, overall, took solace in their belief that enslaved families were distributed among white planters in Albemarle, or if not, at a navigable distance from other family members. Yet, a number of the children of those closest to the Jefferson-Randolphs were separated from their kin on the auction block as their parents watched in horror. For a complete accounting of the two auctions and the numbers of Monticello residents sold and dispersed, see Davenport, "We Were Scattered." At the first auction alone, he writes, the stampede of buyers did lasting damage to the hardwood floors in Monticello's entrance hall (p. 46). It is not hard to imagine the rank inhumanity exhibited on those days, two years apart, while Jefferson's white heirs still retained control of the property.

20. Peter S. Onuf, "Thomas Jefferson, Race, and National Identity," in Onuf, *The Mind of Thomas Jefferson* (Charlottesville: University of Virginia Press, 2007), 212. Ever

attuned to ideas emanating from his home state, Jefferson saw how, from 1797, the Virginia legislature refused to entertain the prospect of gradual abolition, subsequently bearing down on voluntary manumissions. Meanwhile, the prominent Virginia judge St. George Tucker, with allies beyond the South, made a concerted effort to find a solution, yet he forcefully opposed Jefferson's colonization thinking for its impracticality; see George William Van Cleve, *A Slaveholders' Union: Slavery, Politics, and the Constitution in the Early American Republic* (Chicago: University of Chicago Press, 1010), 206–11; TJ to John Holmes, April 22, 1820, Library of Congress. On the Missouri crisis and 1820 Compromise that elicited Jefferson's letter, many have written on this subject; see Robert Pierce Forbes, *The Missouri Compromise and Its Aftermath: Slavery and the Meaning of America* (Chapel Hill: University of North Carolina Press, 2007); John R. Van Atta, *Wolf by the Ears: The Missouri Crisis, 1819–1821* (Baltimore: Johns Hopkins University Press, 2015). There is no indication that Jefferson imagined his own human property finding new lives abroad, post-emancipation.

21. Erica Armstrong Dunbar, *Never Caught: The Washingtons' Relentless Pursuit of Their Runaway Slave, Ona Judge* (New York: Atria, 2017). The adjective "virtuous" was used to describe Washington in every nineteenth-century biography of him; see Andrew Burstein, *Longing for Connection: Entangled Memories and Emotional Loss in Early America* (Baltimore: Johns Hopkins University Press, 2024), 25, 302n2.

22. Washington's activities over the years are scrupulously covered in Bruce A. Ragsdale, *Washington at the Plow: The Founding Farmer and the Question of Slavery* (Cambridge, MA: Harvard University Press, 2021); Jefferson to Monroe, March 8, 1826, cited in Barbara McEwan, *Thomas Jefferson, Farmer* (Jefferson, NC: McFarland, 1991), 22.

23. On merinos, see *JMB*, 2:1259, and Madison to TJ, June 22, 1810; TJ to Caleb Kirk, February 13, 1809; to James Mease, February 27, 1809; to Madison, July 13, 1810, FOL. On Jefferson's abiding interest in experiments with rice and other plants, see McEwan, *Thomas Jefferson, Farmer*, chap. 4.

24. For an engrossing analysis, see Samantha Pinto, *Infamous Bodies: Early Black Women's Celebrity and the Afterlives of Rights* (Durham, NC: Duke University Press, 2020), chap. 2; Rayna Green, "The Pocahontas Perplex: The Image of Indian Women in American Culture," *Massachusetts Review* 16, 4 (Autumn 1975): 698–714.

25. Annette Gordon-Reed, *The Hemingses of Monticello* (New York: W. W. Norton, 2008), 489–90; Douglas R. Egerton, "Thomas Jefferson and the Hemings Family: A Matter of Blood," *Historian* 59, 2 (Winter 1997): 341.

26. Gordon-Reed, *Hemingses of Monticello*, 374-75, 711n35.

27. TJ to Peale, August 20, 1811, *PTJ-R*, 4:93–94; in an undated text listing his own accomplishments in public life, probably written during his presidency, Jefferson noted: "The greatest service which can be rendered any country is to add an useful plant to it's culture; especially a bread grain. next in value to bread is oil."; see "Summary of Public Service," *PTJ*, 32:122–25.
28. Sidney Hart, "'To Encrease the Comforts of Life': Charles Willson Peale and the Mechanical Arts," in Lillian B. Miller and David C. Ward, eds., *New Perspectives on Charles Willson Peale* (Pittsburgh: University of Pittsburgh Press, 1991), 237–65; Susan R. Stein, *The Worlds of Thomas Jefferson at Monticello* (New York: Harry N. Abrams, 1993), 368; "Baynard on Cold Bathing," Sowerby, 1:417. For the most profound analysis of Jefferson's habits, see Maurizio Valsania, *Jefferson's Body: A Corporeal Biography* (Charlottesville: University of Virginia Press, 2017), Part 1; on Jefferson's strong attention to disease prevention throughout his adult life and theory of yellow fever transmission, see also Robert S. Gibson, *Thomas Jefferson and Early American Healthcare* (Savannah, GA: Frederic C. Beil, 2023), 50–55.
29. TJ to Rush, January 16, 1811, *PTJ-R*, 3:304–305; Richard Harrison Shryock, *Medicine and Society in America, 1660–1860* (Ithaca, NY: Cornell University Press, 1960), 72–74; Maurizio Valsania, *Nature's Man: Thomas Jefferson's Philosophical Anthropology* (Charlottesville: University of Virginia Press, 2013); Charles A. Miller, *Jefferson and Nature: An Interpretation* (Baltimore: John Hopkins University Press, 1988), esp. 244–47.
30. Peale to TJ, April 3, 1809, *PTJ-R*, 1:103–104; James Currie to TJ, August 16, 1801, *PTJ*, 35:93; Joseph Priestley, *Experiments and Observations on Different Kinds of Air* (London: J. Johnson, 1775), 95; Benjamin Franklin to Joseph Priestley, July 1772, FOL; in 1784, writing to Madison, Jefferson expressed interest in Priestley's book, as well as Carl Wilhelm Scheele's *Chemical Observations and Experiments on Air and Fire*.
31. Merrill D. Peterson, *Visitors to Monticello* (Charlottesville: University Press of Virginia, 1989), 72, 78, 92; Sarah N. Randolph, *The Domestic Life of Thomas Jefferson* (Charlottesville: University Press of Virginia, 1978), 342–46; Kevin J. Hayes, *The Road to Monticello: The Life and Mind of Thomas Jefferson* (New York: Oxford University Press, 2008), 524–25.
32. Marina van Zuylen, *Monomania: The Flight from Everyday Life in Literature and Art* (Ithaca, NY: Cornell University Press, 2005), chap. 3, quote at 65.
33. Malcolm Kelsall, *Jefferson and the Iconography of Romanticism: Folk, Land, Culture and the Romantic Nation* (New York: St. Martin's Press, 1999), quotes at 105, 173. Monticello's long decay was not remedied until after 1923, when the Thomas Jefferson Foundation was formed and began its preservation activities.

34. TJ to Cooper, September 1, 1817, *PTJ-R*, 12:3–5. Jefferson wanted to appoint Cooper as professor of chemistry at the university, but the radical polymath's combined reputation for personal combativeness and religious skepticism ultimately made it impossible for Jefferson to get his way; see Alan Taylor, *Thomas Jefferson's Education* (New York: W. W. Norton, 2019), 226–28.

35. In 1805, Jefferson sent the U.S. Capitol architect and physician William Thornton a book in French on means of disinfecting air to prevent contagion. Thornton was eager to avoid future yellow fever outbreaks, and he praised the book for its reported success in eliminating "putrid and noxious Effluvia." He agreed with Jefferson that "unwholesome Diet, relaxation by excessive heat, moisture, and the want of exercise" contributed, along with noxious air, to the spread of disease; see Thornton to TJ, January 1, 1806, *PTJ*, 48:295-300; also Burstein, *Jefferson's Secrets*, 59–61.

36. Andrew J. O'Shaughnessy, *The Illimitable Freedom of the Human Mind: Thomas Jefferson's Idea of a University* (Charlottesville: University of Virginia Press, 2021), 117–25; Taylor, *Thomas Jefferson's Education*, 262–90, describing students' mistreatment of enslaved people, drunkenness, and raucous behavior.

37. O'Shaughnessy, *The Illimitable Freedom of the Human Mind*, 135–37; Malone, 6:464–65.

38. TJ to Peale, July 18, 1824, Library of Congress; Stein, *The Worlds of Thomas Jefferson at Monticello*, 290; Burstein, *Jefferson's Secrets*, 22–23, 32–33; Annette Gordon-Reed and Peter S. Onuf, *"Most Blessed of the Patriarchs": Thomas Jefferson and the Empire of the Imagination* (New York: W. W. Norton, 2016), 262–71; Jack McLaughlin, *Jefferson and Monticello: The Biography of a Builder* (New York: Henry Holt, 1988), 195, 323, stating that in later years, to shield himself from unwanted visitors peering in, he had shutters installed on the windows of his private quarters.

39. Peterson, ed., *Visitors to Monticello*, 97–99. It is curious that Webster should have taken pains to describe Jefferson's head (adding "the habitual protrusion" of his long neck), because Webster himself was renowned for his own head, which was described by portraitists and others as massive and which they associated with his outsized intellect. In another of his books, Peterson writes: "Artists and sculptors clamored to paint and sculpt Webster not just because he was famous but because atop his undistinguished frame reposed one of the most extraordinary heads known to creation"; see Merrill D. Peterson, *The Great Triumvirate: Webster, Clay, and Calhoun* (New York: Oxford University Press, 1987), 390.

40. TJ to Knox, August 10, 1791, *PTJ*, 22:27–28; Bernard W. Sheehan, *Seeds of Extinction: Jeffersonian Philanthropy and the American Indian* (Chapel Hill: University of North Carolina Press, 1973), 256–58; Peterson, ed., *Visitors to Monticello*, 94.

41. TJ to Rush, September 23, 1800, *PTJ*, 32:166–69; Charles B. Sanford, *The Religious Life of Thomas Jefferson* (Charlottesville: University Press of Virginia, 1984), 1; Peterson, ed., *Visitors to Monticello*, 94–95. Whitcomb's portrait of Jefferson's character is mixed: while he says that Jefferson looks twenty years younger than his actual age, he also says, "I should not take him for a generous man"—a singularly odd impression—and "less of a philosopher than a partisan."

42. *Jefferson's Extracts from the Gospels: "The Philosophy of Jesus" and "The Life and Morals of Jesus"* (Princeton, NJ: Princeton University Press, 1983); Sanford, *The Religious Life of Thomas Jefferson*. One might also describe Jefferson as a militant humanist, for he saw fanaticism in forms of religious authority that kept believers in a kind of intellectual infancy. He sought to counteract this enfeeblement by promoting secular knowledge as an instrument of self-responsibility and self-advancement, delivering courage to the reasoning mind. This was how he understood "natural rights." While a champion of choice, an advocate for the private self, he was not modern enough to question the patriarchal convention that the man of the home should be the public voice of the women.

   Jefferson refers here to Paul having held that Jesus and God the Father can be one and separate at the same time: he called Jesus both "Lord" and "Son of God." Priestley and Jefferson differed on small points, mainly that Priestley was convinced that Jesus had supernatural powers, and Jefferson disagreed. Tongue in cheek, Daniel J. Boorstin said of Jefferson's treatment of the Gospels: "He came close to making Jesus a Son of Liberty, and a member of the American Philosophical Society"; see Boorstin, *The Lost World of Thomas Jefferson* (Chicago: University of Chicago Press, 1993 [1948]), 245.

43. Karl Lehmann, *Thomas Jefferson: American Humanist* (Charlottesville: University Press of Virginia, 1985 [1947]), esp. 139–42.

44. Burstein, *Jefferson's Secrets*, 258–62.

45. Charles A. Miller, *Jefferson and Nature: An Interpretation* (Baltimore: Johns Hopkins University Press, 1988), 50–53; Martin Clagett, *Scientific Jefferson Revealed* (Charlottesville: University of Virginia Press, 2009), 95–99; TJ to Maria Jefferson, June 13, 1790, *PTJ*, 16:491–92.

46. Andrew J. Lewis, *A Democracy of Facts: Natural History in the Early Republic* (Philadelphia: University of Pennsylvania Press, 2011), chap. 1; the swallow debate was magnified in the *Medical Repository*, a periodical to which Jefferson had access.

47. While it is not to be taken literally as an expression of religious conviction, writing from France to South Carolinian Edward Rutledge, Jefferson assigned to heavenly reward a measure of moral action against the slave trade: "I congratulate you, my dear friend, on the law of your state for suspending the importation of slaves, and for the

glory you have justly acquired by endeavoring to prevent it for ever. This abomination must have an end, and there is a superior bench reserved in heaven for those who hasten it." He invoked heaven in nonreligious contexts, employing wit in the process, especially with female correspondents. A good example: "I never blame heaven so much as for having clogged the etherial spirit of friendship with a body which ties it to time and place. I am with you always in spirit." To fellow deist John Adams, in their retirement years, he had a habit of writing "heaven" into ambiguous suggestions about the America they would not live to see, as in "You and I shall look down from another world on these glorious atchievements to man, which will add to the joys even of heaven" (TJ to Rutledge, July 14, 1787; to Angelica Schuyler Church, August 17, 1788, *PTJ*, 11:589, 13:520; to Adams, September 4, 1823, FOL); for a concise explanation of the deism of the founders, see Donald Wayne Viney, "American Deism, Christianity, and the Age of Reason," *American Journal of Theology & Philosophy* 31, 2 (May 2010): 83–107.
48. TJ to unknown, July 26, 1764, *PTJ*, 27:665–66.

APPENDIX B: A NOTE ON SOURCES, AND SOURCES OF INSPIRATION

1. Paul Ricoeur, *Memory, History, Forgetting* (Chicago: University of Chicago Press, 2004), 314–26.
2. Jennifer Jensen Wallach, "The Vindication of Fawn Brodie," *Massachusetts Review* 43, 2 (Summer 2002): 277–95; Erik H. Erikson, *Dimensions of a New Identity: The 1973 Jefferson Lectures in the Humanities* (New York: W. W. Norton, 1974), 12–13; Lois W. Banner, "Biography as History," *American Historical Review* 114, 3 (June 2009): 579–86. Erikson made the same cautionary comment to Brodie's editor at W. W. Norton before publication, and urged that her psychoanalytic speculations be less overt.
3. Nancy Isenberg, "'I Come to Bury Caesar': Burr Biographers on Jefferson," in Robert M. S. McDonald, ed., *Thomas Jefferson's Lives: Biographers and the Battle for History* (Charlottesville: University of Virginia Press, 2019), 127–48. Twenty-five years after Vidal's *Burr*, the literary scholar Max Byrd published a clever historical novel titled *Jefferson*, which focuses on the Paris years and casts Jefferson's personal secretary, William Short, instead of Burr, as his narrator.
4. Newell G. Bringhurst, *Fawn McKay Brodie: A Biographer's Life* (Norman: University of Oklahoma Press, 1999). Newell Bringhurst, "My 'Affair' with Fawn McKay Brodie: Motives, Pain, and Pleasure," *Dialogue Journal* 35, 3 (Fall 2002); Newell Bringhurst, "Fawn Brodie's Thomas Jefferson: The Making of a Popular and

Controversial Biography," *Pacific Historical Review* 62, 4 (November 1993): 433-54; Newell Bringhurst, "Fawn M. Brodie: Her Biographies as Autobiography," *Pacific Historical Review* 59, 2 (May 1990): 203-29, especially 225-26. Bringhurst's quote about her Utah home and Monticello, of seeing her father in Jefferson, is from a *New York Post Magazine* interview published on April 27, 1974. Bringhurst bolsters the evidence by quoting another interview around the same time, in which Brodie compared the two men's strict self-control and shared desire for "adoring, deferential" daughters. In a conversation on March 2, 2025, Fawn Brodie's son Bruce, a practicing psychologist for decades, informed me that to grow up in the Brodie household was to imbibe, on a regular basis, psychoanalytic theory. It was "like a religion" at home, he said.

5. Jennings L. Wagoner Jr., *Jefferson and Education* (Charlottesville: Monticello Monograph series, 2004), 33–37. The quotes are from *Notes on the State of Virginia*, Query XVII, and Jefferson's 1779 "Bill for the More General Diffusion of Knowledge," no. 79, respectively; TJ to John Adams, August 1, 1816, *PTJ-R*, 10:285–86.

INDEX

Adams, Abigail
    fondness for Maria Jefferson,
        161, 270
    and Sally Hemings, 160
    sours on TJ, 212
    TJ confides in, 9, 127, 131, 227
Adams, John,
    in Continental Congress, 91, 105
    conversation/letters with TJ, 13–16,
        23, 26, 48, 105, 270, 305, 332
    death, 10, 297
    as diplomat in Europe, 123,
        126–27, 160, 227
    disappointed in TJ, 212–14, 228
    and election of 1800, 229,
        231, 235
    and Hamilton, 169, 187, 217,
        219–21, 241, 270
    as president, 169, 212–14,
        217–21, 237, 238, 241,
        252, 255, 256, 257, 264,
        270, 286
    and *Rights of Man* controversy,
        178, 212
    as vice president, 176, 178,
        187, 228
Adams, John Quincy
    associates with TJ in Paris,
        70, 228
    doubts TJ's veracity, 24, 212–213
    and Indians, 23
    political career of, 186, 300
Adams, Nabby, 119
Adams, Samuel, 34

Adventures of Peregrine Pickle
    (1751), 39
Adventures of Roderick Random
    (1748), 39
African Americans
    and colonization, 98, 152, 201, 234,
        263, 318, 407n20
    cultural conditioning and,
        163–64, 234
    laws affecting, 198–99
    TJ's scientific racism and, xix,
        xxxiv–xxxv, 153–54, 173,
        198–206
    See also slavery
d'Alembert, Jean le Rond, 159
Alien and Sedition Acts, 218, 229,
    255, 270
Ambler, Jacquelin, 41, 43
American Citizen (newspaper), 243
American Philosophical Society, xxix,
    411n42
American Revolution
    Cherokees and, 11, 20
    Condorcet on, 149, 155, 158
    and TJ's legacy, 22, 25, 36, 50, 61,
        68, 79–82, 86, 95–98, 103–115,
        133, 149, 155–58, 198, 301,
        317–18, 332
    Virginia and, 13–14, 42, 46, 62, 68,
        77, 96, 103–114
    Washington as leader in, 108, 111,
        208, 246
Anas, 278, 298, 302–304, 306, 320,
    392n19

antislavery
    Condorcet and, xxxiv,
        151–52, 154
    Cosways and, 135
    Price and, 156–57
    TJ's mixed legacy regarding, 106,
        125, 157, 354n10
    Wythe and, 36–37, 54, 157, 354n10
Arendt, Hannah, 1
Arnold, Benedict, 111–12, 123,
    184, 285
Aurora (Philadelphia newspaper), 218

Banister, John, Jr., 132–33
Bankhead, Anne Randolph, 297
Bankhead, Charles, 297
Banneker, Benjamin, 152, 154
Barbary States, 256–57, 269
Barbé-Marbois, François, 14
Barlow, Joel, 153–54, 300
Bartolozzi, Francesco, 137, 138
Bayard, James, 238–39, 241
Belinda (Shadwell slave), 39
Bell, Robert, 80
Bergson, Henri, 293
Bernard, John, 49
Beverley, William, 197
Blair, Hugh, 71–72, 361n9
Blair, Dr. John, 99
blood, as measure of identity and
    belonging, 197–200
Boles, John, 188
Bolingbroke, Henry St. John,
    48, 50, 293
Bonaparte, Napoleon, 73, 128,
    170, 258
Boone, Daniel, 21, 262
Boorstin, Daniel, xxviii, 411n42
Boston Tea Party, 79

Boyd, Julian P., 327
Brackenridge, Hugh Henry, 236–37,
    241
Breckinridge, John, 260–61, 397n24
Brodie, Fawn M., xiii, xx, xxii, xxxv, 20,
    44, 130, 134, 135, 159–61, 199,
    328–30, 340n9, 347n4, 412n4
Buchan, William, 83
Burr, Aaron
    and Chase trial, 265–66
    and election of 1800, 219, 229,
        235–43, 265, 392n19, 393n20,
        402n25
    letters to/from TJ, 213, 236–38
    and Hamilton, 173, 187, 216, 220,
        238–41
    and novel by Vidal, 329
    and Princeton, 82, 277
    in TJ's *Anas*, 278
    TJ's refusal to back in 1804,
        276–77
    treason trial of, 283–89, 291, 299
    western "conspiracy" of, 277,
        279–83
Burwell, Rebecca, 39–41, 43, 45
Buttre, John Chester, 294

Caesar, Julius, 187
Callender, James T., 215–16, 218, 264,
    270, 271, 273
Carr, Dabney (TJ's friend), 4, 17,
    21–23, 41, 46, 60–61, 68, 70, 72,
    115, 116, 201
Carr, Dabney (son, judge), 61
Carr, Martha Jefferson, 4, 10, 22,
    63, 115
Carr, Peter, 72, 86–87
Carrington, Edward, 185
de Céspedes, Alba, 1

Chase, Samuel, 264–66, 276, 277, 283, 285, 291
Chastellux, Marquis de, 74, 115, 127, 203, 274
Cheetham, James, 243
Chastellux, Marquis de, 74, 115, 127, 203, 274
Chervinsky, Lindsay, 176
Chesapeake Affair, 273
Chinard, Gilbert, 127, 129
Christianity, 10, 95, 210, 250, 255, 302, 319–20, 411*n*42
Cicero, 12, 48, 88
Clark, George Rogers, 107–108, 114, 170
Clay, Henry, 23, 34, 36, 281, 284
Clinton, George, 186–87, 189, 219, 235, 242–43, 259, 277
College of William and Mary, 22, 23, 26, 29, 30, 33–34, 41, 61, 132, 260
Common Sense (1776), 80, 90, 261–62
"Common Sense" school of thought, 83, 87, 363*n*23
Condorcet, Marie-Jean-Antoine-Nicolas Caritat, Marquis de
  antislavery writing of, xxxiv, 151–52, 154, 156–57
  compatibility with TJ, 147–50, 156, 158
  contrasted with TJ, xxxiv, 150–52
  death of, 151
  Esquisse of, 155, 158–59, 165, 249
  feminism of, 154, 158
Continental Congress, xix, 8, 34, 63, 77, 80, 81, 87, 88, 98, 104, 123, 227
Cornwallis, Lord Charles, 107, 109, 110, 112–13, 124
de Corny, Louis-Éthis, 127

de Corny, Madame Marguérite, 127–28, 161, 164–65
Cosway, Maria Luisa Caterina Cecilia Hadfield
  appearance, 122, 135
  career and paintings of, 135, 137, 143
  founds convent college, 136
  friendship with Hanquerville, 145–46
  introduced to TJ, 134
  marriage, 135, 137–38, 143
  relationship with TJ, 136, 138–43, 147, 154, 159, 160, 163, 201, 316, 317
Cosway, Richard, 135–37, 143, 146
Cugoano, Quobna Ottobah (aka John Stuart), 135

Danry, Jean. *See* Latude
Daveiss, Joseph, 279–80
Deane, Silas, 104, 105
Dearborn, Henry, 254, 264, 280, 305
Declaration of Independence
  250th anniversary of, xxxii
  as divorce instrument, 98–102
  influence of Scottish moral philosophy on, 93–94
  Macpherson's critique of, 80
  removal of slave trade clause from, 79, 151
  signers of, 9, 33, 35, 53, 82, 102, 210, 265
  symbolism of, xix, xxxvi, 226, 229
  TJ's rhetorical skill exhibited in, xvii, xxx–xxxi, 3, 5, 13, 14, 19, 70, 73, 76, 79–82, 86, 89–102, 104, 106, 113–14, 198, 298

Demosthenes, 12, 24, 88
Domestic Medicine (1769), 83
Don Quixote (1605), 39
Dennie, Joseph, 403*n*31
Diderot, Denis, 65, 146
Discourses on Davila (1790–91), 212
Dougherty, Joseph, 251
Douglas, William, 17, 19
Dudley, George, 44–45
Dudley, Molly, 44–45
Dunmore, Lord, 68, 74, 87–88, 104, 105

Eaton, General William, 279, 280, 283, 401*n*18
election of 1796, 209–210, 221
election of 1800, 214, 219, 221, 224, 229, 233, 235–41
election of 1804, 242, 259, 269
election of 1808, 289–90
Ellis, Joseph J., 330
Embargo policy, 273, 276
England. *See* Great Britain
Enlightenment, Age of
    Condorcet and, 148–49, 151, 155–56, 158, 249
    nervous sensation and, xvi
    Scottish moral philosophy and, 80–87
    as taught at the College of William and Mary, 29
    TJ seen to embody, xxix, xxxiv, 26, 95–96, 148–49, 156, 210, 249, 317
Epicurus, 48, 94, 126, 320
Eppes, Elizabeth Wayles, 89, 117
Eppes, Francis, 89, 233
Eppes, Jack (TJ's son-in-law), 207, 270–71, 274

Eppes, Mary (Maria) Jefferson (TJ's daughter)
    birth and early childhood, 106, 116
    death of, 4, 231, 269–71, 274, 311
    married life, 207, 231
    and Sally Hemings, 159, 164, 270–71, 310
Erikson, Erik, 328
Esquisse d'un tableau historique des progrès de l'esprit humain (1795), 155, 158, 165, 249
Essay on the Application of Analysis to the Probability of Majority Decisions (1785), 148
Essay on Man (1733), 48, 95
Essays on the Principles of Morality and Natural Religion (1751), 82–84
Estes, Todd, 285
Euripides, 31, 48, 104
Evans, Jupiter, 55, 60, 74, 207, 231
Evans, Phil, 55

Fair Penitent (1703), 57–58
Fauquier, Francis, 47
Federalist Papers, 175, 182, 184
Federalist Party, 97, 172, 178–79, 183, 186–87, 191, 194, 207, 210–12, 214, 216–21, 229, 236–43, 248–56, 259–61, 264–66, 269, 273, 283, 285, 291, 299, 301, 306
Fenno, John, 179
Fielding, Henry, 39
filibusters, 278, 280–81, 401*n*18
Fleming, Will, 61, 109
Fossett, Edith Hern, 251
Franklin, Benjamin, 26, 89, 91, 104, 105, 123, 126–27, 130, 156, 157, 226, 314

France
- sexual attitudes in, 131–33, 162
- support during American Revolution, 13–14, 104, 109, 111–13
- TJ's feelings for/friendships in, 127–34
- war with England, 183, 189, 217

French and Indian War, 9, 11, 19, 21, 24

French Revolution
- character of and impact on U.S. politics, 186–91, 211
- TJ's thoughts on, 134, 149, 164–65, 309

Freneau, Philip, 179, 183–84
Freud, Sigmund, xx, xxii, 131, 328, 340n9
Fry, Henry, 255
Fry, Joshua, 10, 255

Gabriel's Rebellion, 233–34
Gallatin, Albert, 235, 250–51, 254, 266
Gallatin, Hannah Nicholson, 235
Gatrell, Vic, 162
Gay, Peter, 249
Gazette of the United States, 179
Geismar, Baron von, 106, 164
Genêt, Edmond-Charles, 188–89, 191
Gentleman Farmer (1772), 83
George III, King, xxxi, 26, 180
Germaine, Lord George, 81
Gerry, Elbridge, 53, 217
Gil Blas (1715), 39
Giles, William Branch, 283, 288
Gilman, Nicolas, 282
Gimbrede, Thomas, 268
Girardin, Louis, 114

Gordon-Reed, Annette, 133, 163, 196, 311, 330
Granger, Gideon, 279–80
Great Britain
- and American Revolution, xxxi, 62, 80–81, 83, 87, 90, 124
- and common law, 82, 93, 105, 365n2
- and TJ's presidency, 273, 276, 289
- war with France, 183, 189, 217

Grégoire, Abbé Henri, 153
de Grouchy, Sophie, 154

Haiti, 151, 234, 318
Hamilton, Alexander
- drives TJ into retirement, 191
- economic plan of, 172, 175, 177–78, 187
- involvement in 1800 election, 219–20, 235, 240–41
- personality, 174–76, 185, 276, 288, 299, 306
- perspective of, in Federalist Papers, 175, 182
- political tactics of, 169–70, 171, 180–81, 190, 206, 209–210, 217, 219–20, 241, 299
- relations with Washington, 174, 180, 185–86, 209, 211
- and Reynolds Affair, 215–17
- rivalry with Burr, 187, 216, 238–43, 265–66, 276, 291
- TJ's denigration of, 172–75, 177–78, 180–83, 191, 206, 212, 213, 289–90, 298, 306
- writes critically of TJ, 6, 181, 183–85, 187, 189, 208, 210, 319

Hamilton, Henry, 108, 111
Hamilton, William, 221–22, 313

Hancock, John, 88, 104
d'Hancarville, Pierre-François Hugues, 145–46, 162, 375*n*1
Harrison, William Henry, 263, 319
Harvie, John, 8
Hawkins, John Isaac, 314
Hay, George, 284–85
Herodotus, 48
Hemings, Betsy, 271
Hemings, Beverley, 197, 270
Hemings, Elizabeth (Betty), 56, 271, 312
Hemings, Eston, 197
Hemings, James (chef), 160, 197, 251, 310
Hemings, (James) Madison, 161, 196–97, 270, 310
Hemings, Martin, 197
Hemings, Peter, 197
Hemings, Robert, 62
Hemings, Sally
  appearance, 159, 201, 271, 309, 379*n*27
  DNA paternity test (1998) and, xx, 63, 134, 328, 339*n*8, 380*n*32
  in France, 161–62
  as Mrs. Jefferson's half sister, xxiii, 159, 161, 162, 196, 269
  pregnancies, 161, 195, 197, 199–201, 310
  question of literacy, 196–97
  as TJ's enslaved "concubine," xxiii, 56, 62–63, 162–64, 196, 309–312, 329, 380*n*32
Henry, Patrick
  as governor, 105, 107–108, 113, 175
  land speculation of, 42
  popularity of, 31, 54, 170–72
  as practicing attorney, 99, 170, 299

  role in American Revolution, 68, 77, 78, 88
  TJ disparages, 30, 97, 108, 114, 170–72, 174, 183, 256, 283, 285, 289
  TJ first encounters, 30
  Washington tries to recruit for high office, 209, 219
  Wirt's biography of, 108, 170
Herodotus, 48
Historical Law Tracts (1758), 82
History of the Corruptions of Christianity (1782), 255, 319
History of England (1754), 82
History of the United States for the Year 1796 (1797)
Home, Henry. *See* Kames, Lord
Homer, 31, 48, 70–72, 128
Horace, 31
d'Houdetot, Comtesse, 127–28
House of Burgesses, 18, 22, 38, 63, 68, 88, 107, 124
Hume, David, 82, 86, 100, 131
Hutcheson, Francis, 86

Iliad, 48, 71, 116
Indians
  Cherokee, 2, 10, 14–16, 19, 23, 25–26, 305
  Choctaw, 280
  Creek, 280
  Monacan, 10, 24
  as portrayed in Declaration of Independence, 20, 301
  as portrayed in *Notes on Virginia*, 12–13, 16
  TJ claims compassion for, 13, 14, 23, 26, 300
  TJ's treatment of, as president, 14, 23, 263–64

Inquiry into the Human Mind (1764), 82
Inquiry into the Origin of Our Ideas of Beauty and Virtue (1725), 86
intimacy (in historical relief), xx–xxiii, 43, 55, 56, 67, 98, 127, 160–61, 277–78, 305
intrigue (as watchword in amours or politics), 132–33, 173, 181–83, 207, 210, 219, 221, 237–38, 284

Jackson, Andrew, 279, 280
Jay, John, 126, 180, 220
Jefferson, Elizabeth, 68
Jefferson, Isaac, 159
Jefferson, Jane Randolph (TJ's mother), 3, 6–9, 17–18, 60, 91
Jefferson, Jane Randolph (TJ's infant daughter), 63
Jefferson, Jane (TJ's sister), 9, 57
Jefferson, Lucy (TJ's daughter), 115, 124, 161
Jefferson, Maria ("Polly"). *See* Eppes, Mary (Maria) Jefferson
Jefferson, Martha ("Patsy"). *See* Randolph, Martha Jefferson
Jefferson, Martha ("Patty") Wayles Skelton (TJ's wife)
    causes anxiety for TJ, 89
    courtship and marriage, 55–57, 59–60, 132, 137, 163
    character of, 60, 154
    death of, xxiii, 4, 18, 116–18, 123, 139, 196, 201, 269, 311
    pregnancies and births, 60, 62, 104, 106, 112, 115, 119
Jefferson, Peter (TJ's father), 6–10, 14, 17–18, 20, 42, 43, 56, 69, 255
Jefferson, Randolph (TJ's brother), 10, 103

Jefferson, Thomas
    accused of atheism, 97, 153, 210, 250, 307
    accused of cowardice, xxix, 67, 110–14
    agrarianism of, 6, 27, 83, 206–207, 232, 247–48, 262–63, 309
    Anas (desultory political notes) of, 278, 298, 302–304, 306, 320, 392n19
    androgynous qualities of, 136, 307, 370n40, 406n17
    animosity toward Hamilton, 41, 172–75, 177–78, 180–83
    animosity toward Henry, 30, 97, 107–108, 114, 170–72, 174, 183, 256, 283, 285, 289
    animosity toward/frustrated by Marshall, 41–42, 291, 264, 266, 284–85, 289, 291, 299–304, 306
    anxiety evidenced by, xvi, xxii, 31–32, 40, 68, 89, 103, 132–33, 171, 282, 312, 353n6, 394n1
    as architect, 8, 26–29, 49
    attachment to the garden, 7, 27, 47, 106–107, 130, 192, 222, 232, 307, 312–13, 317
    attacked by Federalists as "Jacobin" radical, 207, 215, 249
    attacks on private character, xxv–xxvi, 43, 67, 113, 260
    characterizes Southern gentry traits, 274–75
    coded correspondence of, 44, 124, 189, 286
    cognitive dissonance and, 204–205
    at the College of William and Mary, 22, 23, 26, 29, 30, 33–34

Jefferson, Thomas (*continued*)
   and colonization of Blacks, 98, 152, 201, 234, 263, 318, 407*n*20
   in Confederation Congress, 124–25
   in Continental Congress, 88–89, 91, 98, 101–105
   death of, 5, 10, 296
   and deaths of family members, xxiii, xxv, 3–4, 9, 18, 43, 57, 116–18, 139, 196, 201, 269, 271, 311
   and Declaration of Independence, xix, xxx–xxxi, 3, 19, 33, 35, 53, 70, 73, 76, 79–82, 86, 89, 102, 104, 106, 113–14, 151, 158, 198, 210, 226, 227, 229, 265, 298, 301
   DNA paternity test (1998) and, xx, 63, 134, 328, 339*n*8, 380*n*32
   education of, 17, 19–23, 29–30, 33–38
   education reform proposed by, 105–106, 301
   effort to establish/maintain control, xv, xviii, xxxi, 30, 40–41, 53, 55, 69, 78, 104–105, 108, 115–16, 125, 129, 161, 163, 204, 211, 289, 296–300, 304, 309, 312
   and election of 1796, 209–210, 221
   and election of 1800, 214, 219, 221, 224, 229, 233, 235–41
   and election of 1804, 242, 259, 269
   and election of 1808, 289–90
   emotional distance from mixed-race children, 159, 195
   faith in democracy, xviii, xxv, xxxvii, 172, 230, 235, 249, 254, 262–63, 301, 304
   feints toward antislavery thinking, 125, 152–53, 157
   financial woes of, 30, 36, 42, 46–47, 62, 232, 309, 315
   and French Revolutionary politics, 134, 149, 164–65, 191, 309
   as governor, 91, 107–114, 257, 289
   handwriting of, 9, 44, 53, 138, 236
   hardened opinions of, xxviii, xxxiv, xxxv, 134, 203–204, 227, 256, 300, 312
   "harmony and affection" evoked by, xxv, 101, 250, 261, 272, 305–306, 315
   "Head and Heart" letter of, 138–39, 143, 145, 160, 192, 245, 315–16, 320
   health-consciousness of, xxvi, 45–46, 53, 126, 205, 252, 262, 313–15, 317, 318, 410*n*35
   in House of Burgesses, 22, 63, 68, 107
   humanism of, xxvii, xxxvii, 48–49, 96, 158
   hyperbole in writings of, xxxii, 12, 14, 22, 26, 49, 69, 133, 150, 188, 246, 275, 285–86, 288, 300–301
   Inaugural Address (1801), xxxi, 230, 245–46, 248–50, 256, 275, 305
   Inaugural Address (1805), 23, 275–76
   and Indians, 10–17, 19–20, 23–24, 263–64, 300–301
   and Kentucky Resolutions, 218, 260–61
   law career and legal acumen of, 37, 47–50, 53–54, 59, 62, 81–82, 93–94, 99–101, 109–10

Legal Commonplace Book of, 47, 49, 74, 81
library of, xv, xxxi, 32, 35, 37, 41, 47–49, 52, 55, 57–58, 82, 90, 99, 105, 124, 196, 206
Literary Commonplace Book of, 47–49, 69, 118, 167, 341*n*12
longs for "partie quarrée" with intimates, 4–5, 22, 24, 34, 41, 142, 290
and Louisiana Purchase, 262–63, 269, 280
manners and personality, xxxiii, 30, 39, 68, 85, 105, 125–26, 136, 147, 153, 208, 227, 251–52, 256
married life of, 4, 59–60, 68, 119, 137
as mathematician, 17, 33–34, 148, 199
at Maury's school, 19–24
meaning of friendship to, xxix, 5, 21–22, 29, 41, 46, 68, 106–107, 127–28
meaning of Monticello to, xxvi, 26, 45, 56–59, 136
meaning of the word "intrigue" to, 132–33, 173, 181–83, 207, 219
meaning of the word "mystery" to, 286–87
Memorandum Books of, xxxv
mockingbirds of, xxxv, 59, 105, 329
as music afficionado, 59, 89, 103, 106, 125, 135
misogyny attributed to, xxii, 31–32, 341*n*12, 353*n*4
muted ambition/pursuit of celebrity by, xvi, xvii, xix, xxvi, xxx, 13, 30, 33, 38, 68, 82, 90, 105, 107, 113, 173, 184, 205, 210, 211, 214, 221, 228–29, 256, 288, 298–99, 304–306
on "Nature's God," 94–98, 320
"neophobia" described by, 260
and *Notes on Virginia*, 12–13, 16, 114, 151–53, 162, 198, 202–203, 205, 234, 247, 259, 262, 298, 308, 319
opposition to slave trade, 79, 151, 157
optimism of, xvi, xxv, xxviii–xxix, xxxvi, 149, 230, 248–49, 259, 261, 301
and Ossian, 53, 69–74, 115, 118
and party "schism," 272, 277, 289
"periodical" headaches suffered by, xxvi, 33, 38, 85, 176, 206, 276, 290, 353*n*6
pet mockingbirds, xxxv, 59, 105, 329
physical descriptions of, 9, 32–33, 60, 253, 270, 318
privacy/private life valued by, xxxi, 113, 206–207, 253, 318
and "pursuit of happiness," xxv, xxvi, 31, 95, 320, 365–66*n*4
on recolonization of Blacks, 98, 152, 200–203, 234, 263, 318, 407*n*20
relationship with parents, 6–9, 17–18, 37
relationship with Sally Hemings, xxiii, 56, 62–63, 159, 162–64, 196, 311–12, 329, 380*n*32
religious views of, 48, 83–84, 94–98, 105, 150, 158, 204, 222, 223, 250, 255, 305, 319–23
as republican savior, xxviii, xxx, 227, 253, 304, 387*n*25

Jefferson, Thomas (*continued*)
   and revisal of Virginia's laws, xxvii, 36
   and "Revolution of 1800," 219, 224, 270, 291, 305–306
   and Saxon precedent, 74–75, 78, 94, 198, 248, 262, 263
   scientific racism of, 153–54, 200–206
   sexual (extramarital) activity of, 43–46, 63, 119, 137–38, 162, 196, 311
   sexuality, as understood or conveyed by, xxi, 57–58, 99–100, 102, 104, 128–33, 136, 142–43, 154, 161–63, 196, 198–202, 368*n*18
   and slave ownership, xviii, xxv, xxviii, xxxiv–xxxv, 24, 27, 36, 55, 57, 59, 62–63, 88, 103, 106, 132, 157, 159–64, 173, 200–205, 231–34, 248, 296, 307–308, 316–18, 377*n*14
   spelling choices of, xxxi
   statue of removed, xxxvi
   and Sterne's writings, 49, 118, 128–29, 139, 201, 296
   and *Summary View of the Rights of British America*, 74–75, 78–80, 90, 94, 99, 148
   "Summary Journal of Letters" maintained by, xxxiii, 47, 129, 237
   and University of Virginia, 136, 300, 309, 317
   and value placed on letter writing, xxv, xxxiii, xxxiv, 21, 47, 63, 86, 89, 107, 126, 140–42, 206, 208, 214, 254, 328
   in Virginia legislature, 105–106
   Virginia-centered outlook of, 4, 5, 18, 82, 106, 133, 242, 247, 259, 288
   and Walker Affair, 43–46, 74, 102, 132
   on women's prescribed roles, xxii, 31, 118–19, 125–26, 154
   writing faculty of, xxx, 33, 79–80, 86, 90, 91, 101, 113, 128–29, 138–39, 208–209, 245–46, 254, 256
   See also specific individuals for TJ's personal relations with each
Johnson, Samuel, 72, 73
Johnson, William, 300
Jouett, Jack, 112
Julien, Honoré, 251

Kames, Lord (Henry Home), 81–85
Kauffman, Angelica, 138
Knox, Henry, 174, 209, 222–23, 319

La Rochefoucauld, Louis Alexandre, Duc de, 130, 140, 164, 165
La Rochefoucauld Liancourt, Duc de, 207
Lafayette, Marquis de,
   in American Revolution, 111, 112, 114, 127
   compares TJ and Short, 140
   in French Revolution, 128, 148, 149, 164–65, 188, 203–204
   presses TJ on slavery, 152, 232
   socializes with TJ in France, 129, 130
   and TJ preference for Louisiana governorship, 285
Latrobe, Benjamin Henry, 244

Latude (Jean Danry), 145–47
de Latude, Vissec, 146
Le Brun, Élisabeth Vigée, 130
Lee, Richard Henry, 88, 96, 103
Lehmann, Karl, 320
Lesage, Alain-René, 39
Lettres d'un citoyen des États-Unis (1788), 149
Lewis, Meriwether, 253, 258, 263
Lewis and Clark Expedition, 21, 222, 259, 261, 262
Lincoln, Levi, 260
Livingston, Edward, 279
Livingston, Robert, 91, 257–58
Locke, John, xxix, 93, 100, 156, 365–66n4
Logan (Indian), 12–13, 25, 198
Lomax, Judith, 72
Long, George, 317–18
Looney, J. Jefferson, xxxiii
Louis XVI, King, 151, 188
Louisiana Purchase, 258–62, 269, 280, 396n19
Loyal Land Company, 7–8, 19, 21, 42

Machiavelli, Niccolò, 169, 218, 381n1
Mackenzie, Henry, 83
Macpherson, James, 69–73, 75, 360n7
Madison, Dolley Payne Todd, 132
Madison, James
  contests Hamilton, 175, 177–80, 184–87, 190, 216
  and death of Mrs. Jefferson, 120
  falling out with Monroe, 289–90
  friendship and communication with TJ, xxix, 4, 109, 123, 124, 132, 142, 148, 149–50, 157, 164, 173, 178, 180, 181, 185, 186, 189, 191–92, 206, 208, 214, 215, 221, 242, 254, 271, 272, 277, 298
  political activity, 41, 157, 189, 192, 206, 210, 218, 227, 240, 258, 266, 271–73, 321
  presidency, 24, 251, 253, 286, 291, 300, 315
  at Princeton, 82
  and TJ's distancing from Burr, 277, 278, 288
Malone, Dumas, 20, 34, 327–28
Man of Feeling, The (1771), 83
Marshall, John
  as chief justice, 264, 266, 283–85, 289, 299, 399n31
  legal training, 36, 285
  TJ's hatred for/frustration with, 41–42, 291, 264, 266, 284–85, 289, 291, 299–304, 306
  as Washington's biographer, 299–304, 306–307
  and XYZ Affair, 217–18
Marshall, Mary, 41
Martin, Luther, 283
Mason, George, 42
Maury, James (Reverend), 19–24, 27, 33, 47, 351n26
Maury, James, Jr., 22,
Mazzei, Philip, 107, 155, 208, 212, 215, 216, 236, 377n16
McDonald, Robert M. S., 184
McLean, Iain, 150
McPherson, Charles, 69, 72, 81
Memorandum Books (accounts maintained by TJ), xxxv, 57
Miller, William Ian, 169, 173
Milton, John, 32, 100
Miranda, Lin-Manuel, 329

Monroe, James
  as diplomat, 214, 258
  falling out with Madison, 272, 289–90
  Governor Henry subverts, 175
  as president, 253, 315
  and Reynolds Affair, 215–16
  as Virginia governor, 233
  TJ as patron/ally of, xxix, 4–5, 41, 109, 111, 142, 242, 254, 284, 317
  TJ's letters to, 113–15, 123, 126–27, 142, 286–87, 309
de Montaigne, Michel, 64
Montesquieu, Charles Louis de Secondat, 47
Monticello
  cemetery at, 3–5, 24, 57, 322
  design and construction of, xv, xxxi, 8, 27–28, 45, 56–57, 206–207
  gardens, 8, 27, 47, 56, 106, 130, 222, 232, 312–13
  library at, xv, xxxi, 32, 35, 37, 41, 47–49, 52, 55, 57–58, 82, 90, 99, 105, 124, 196, 206
  meaning of, to TJ, xxii, xxvi, 6, 26, 45, 56, 106, 123, 136, 206
  slavery at, 60, 63, 202–206, 231–33, 308
  TJ forced to flee, 112
  TJ rhapsodizes, to Mrs. Cosway, 141–42, 192, 245
  on U.S. coin, 8
  visitors to, xxxiii, 49, 62, 69, 74, 115, 207, 211, 247, 271, 318–19, 380*n*32, 395*n*8
  as World Heritage site, xxvii
Morris, Gouverneur, 238, 243, 250, 302, 392*n*19
Morris, Robert, 124
Munford, William, 236–37

Native Americans. *See* Indians
Newton, Isaac, xxix, 95–96
Nicholas, George, 113
Nicholas, Wilson Carey, 296
Nicholson, Joseph H., 265–66
Night-Thoughts (1742), 48
Notes on the State of Virginia (1785, 1787)
  and agrarian ideal, 247, 258–59, 262
  Logan story featured in, 12–13, 198
  passages on Blacks, 151–53, 162, 202–203, 205, 234, 308
  production of, 16, 114, 202, 298
  and right of conscience, 97, 319

Observations on the Importance of the American Revolution (1784), 156
Onuf, Peter S., 133, 308, 330
O'Shaughnessy, Andrew, 317
Ossian, 49, 66, 69–75, 115, 118, 127
Outassetè (Ostenaco), 2, 11, 15, 17, 23–26, 305

Page, Frances, 42
Page, John, 22, 31, 41–46, 61, 89, 97, 107, 109–111, 254
Paine, Thomas, 80, 155, 158, 188, 212, 254–55, 261, 284, 300
Papers of Thomas Jefferson, xxxiii, xxxv, 327, 345*n*29
Paradise Lost (1667), 48
Parties in the United States (1830s, unpub.), 186
Pasley, Jeffrey L., 210
Peale, Charles Willson, 312–14, 318

Peale, Rembrandt, 226, 313
Pelloutier, Simon, 74
Pendleton, Edmund, 8, 77–78, 103, 105–106
Peterson, Merrill D., 17, 53, 327
Pinckney, Charles Cotesworth (Federalist), 211, 214, 217–18, 220–21, 235, 269
Pinckney, Charles (Republican), 221
Pinckney, Thomas, 211
Plumer, William, 282–83, 285–86
Pocahontas, 8
Pope, Alexander, 48, 95, 103
Poplar Forest, 62, 112, 113, 116
Price, Richard, 156–58
Priestley, Joseph, 156, 158, 254–55, 259, 261, 314, 316, 319–20, 411*n*42
Proclamation Line (1763), 11
Pufendorf, Samuel von, 100, 102, 104, 368*n*18

Randall, Henry S., xiii, 92, 111, 306–307
Randolph, Benjamin Franklin, 304
Randolph, Edmund, 91, 120, 174, 190, 209, 213, 214, 283
Randolph, George Wythe, 322
Randolph, Isham, 8
Randolph, Jane Hollins Nicholas, 295–96
Randolph, John (Loyalist/attorney general), 89–90
Randolph, John (of Roanoke), 266, 272–73, 283, 286, 289
Randolph, Martha ("Patsy") Jefferson (TJ's daughter),
 birth and early childhood, 60, 89, 104, 106, 112
 child-rearing of, 118, 163, 195, 221, 270
 and Monticello cemetery, 4
 and mother's death, 115–16, 120
 in France, 3, 124, 126, 140, 160, 163
 relations with husband, 69, 118, 163, 297
 relations/correspondence with TJ, 106, 125–26, 129, 221, 307, 311
 and Sally Hemings, 164
 and TJ's death, 295–96
 wedding at Monticello, 163, 311
Randolph, Peyton, 77–78, 88–90
Randolph, Thomas Jefferson (TJ's grandson), 4, 30, 34, 278, 295–98, 303–304
Randolph, Thomas Mann, 68
Randolph, Thomas Mann, Jr. (TJ's son-in-law), 4, 163, 207, 231, 273–74, 297, 311
Randolph, William, 8
Raynal, Abbé de, 134–35
Réflexions sur l'esclavage des nègres (1788), 151–52
Reid, Thomas, 83, 86
Republican Party, 153, 178, 186–92, 194, 209, 211–13, 216–19, 221, 229, 234–37, 240, 242–43, 248–51, 253, 259–60, 264–66, 269, 271–72, 277–79, 285, 290, 300, 302, 306
Republican Watch Tower (newspaper), 229
Reynolds, Maria, 215–17
Ricoeur, Paul, 327
Rights of Great Britain Asserted Against the Claims of America (1776), 80
Rights of Man (1791), 178, 208, 212, 216, 254
Robertson, Ritchie, 341*n*13

Robespierre, Maximilien, 159
Roosevelt, Franklin D., xxxvi
Rousseau, Jean-Jacques, 127–28, 315, 341*n*13
Rowe, Nicholas, 57–58
Rush, Dr. Benjamin, 97, 191, 302, 313, 315
Rush, Richard, 315
Rutledge, Edward, 210–14, 217, 239
Rutledge, John, Jr., 239

Sall (sister of Jupiter), 68
Saxon migration
    and Declaration of Independence, 50
    and *A Summary View*, 74–75, 78, 94, 198, 248, 262, 263
Schiavonetti, Luigi, 122
Schuyler, Philip, 186–87
Seasons, The (1748), 48
Sentimental Journey, A (1768), 128, 139, 160
sexual standards/sexual reputations, xxi, 52, 57–58, 63, 102, 104, 119, 128–31, 136, 143, 154, 161–63, 196, 198–202, 239, 284, 341*n*13, 379*n*27, 380*n*31, 380*n*32
Shadwell
    burials at, 9, 57, 60
    destroyed by fire, 18, 55, 59
    Indians visit, 2, 11, 14–17
    situation and resources of, 6–8, 18, 26
    slavery at, 18, 59
Shakespeare, William, xxiii, 17, 38, 48, 71, 73, 167, 197
Shays's Rebellion, 150–51
Shelton, Thomas, 44
Shenstone, William, 57, 63

Sherman, Roger, 91
Short, William
    intimacy with TJ, 4, 110, 112, 139, 142, 162, 259
    letters to/from TJ during French Revolution, 188, 230
    relationship with duchesse Rosalie, 130, 140, 142
    as TJ's personal secretary, 4, 130, 139, 142
Skelton, Bathurst, 55, 68
Skelton, John, 55–56
Skipwith, Robert, 58, 71, 73, 82, 87, 103, 110
slavery
    and artisanal/construction work, 18, 60, 231, 251, 316
    and Declaration of Independence, 79, 98
    and socio-economic conditions in Virginia, 46, 47, 198–99, 207, 233, 274, 296, 308
    TJ's accommodation with, xviii, xxv, xxviii, 24, 27, 36, 55, 57, 59, 62–63, 88, 103, 106, 132, 157, 159–64, 173, 199–205, 231–34, 248, 296, 307–308, 317, 318, 377*n*14
    and TJ's inheritance, 6–7, 36, 39, 47, 62
    Washington and, 77, 232–33, 308–309
    Wythe and, 36–37, 54, 157, 354*n*10
Small, William, 33–34
Smith, Adam, 82, 84, 86, 119, 154
Smith, Margaret Bayard, 255–56, 307
Smith, William Stephens, 119, 150
Smollett, Tobias, 39
Socrates, 156

Spinoza, Baruch, 96
Spirit of the Laws (1748), 47
Sterne, Laurence, 49, 118, 128, 139, 160, 201, 296
Stewart, Matthew, 95
Stiles, Ezra, 150
Strickland, William, 247
Suck (wife of Jupiter Evans), 62
Summary View of the Rights of British America, A (1774), 74–75, 78–80, 90, 94, 99, 148
Sweeney, George Wythe, 37

Tacitus, 94
Tessé, the Comtesse de (Adrienne-Catherine de Noailles), 128–31, 136
Theory of Moral Sentiments (1759), 82
Thompson, James, 48
Thomson, Charles, 53
Thoughts and Sentiments on the Evil and Wicked Traffic of the Slavery and Commerce of the Human Species (1787), 135
Timberlake, Lieut. Henry, 16, 25–26
Tissot, Samuel-Auguste, 52
Tom Jones (1749), 39
de Tott, Sophie, 128–29, 131, 134, 139, 160
Townley, Charles, 136–37, 146
Trevor-Roper, Hugh, 72
Trist, Eliza House, 151
Trist, Nicholas, 304
Tristram Shandy (1759–67), 49, 118, 296, 379n27
Trumbull, John, iii, 134, 138, 168
Turgot, Anne-Robert-Jacques, 150, 156, 159

University of Virginia, 300–301, 316–17

Valsania, Maurizio, 131, 252
Van Buren, Martin, 152, 233, 288
Vindication of the Rights of Women (1792), 154
Virgil, 31–32, 48, 212
Virginia
  colonial government of, 18, 22
  invasion of, 109–113, 257
  land cession by, 125
  and partisan politics, 217–19
  and race mixing, 198–99
  and repayment of war debts, 177
  Revolutionary reconstitution of, 93, 96–98, 103–108
  sexual mores in, 132
  slave rebellion in, 233–34
  and slave economy, 198–99, 232, 234
  TJ as governor of, 107–114
  TJ's particular identification with, 82, 104, 132–33, 163, 245, 247, 288
Virginia Gazette, 12, 87–88
Virginia–New York axis (in electoral politics), 186, 235, 242
Voltaire, xxxiv, 148

Walker, Betsy Moore, 43–46, 102
Walker, John (Jack), 21, 43–46, 74, 87, 102, 109
Walker, Dr. Thomas, 8, 21, 43, 46
Waller, Thomas, 87
Washington, George
  activities during the Revolution, 77, 91, 106, 108, 109, 111–12, 246
  death of, 219

Washington, George (*continued*)
  early career of, 11
  falling out with TJ, 207–208, 212, 219
  land interests of, 42, 286, 308
  and Lafayette, 140, 232
  Marshall's biography of, 299, 302–304, 306–307
  personality and personal habits, xxv, xxx, 229, 302–303, 308
  presidency, xxx, xxxiv, 53, 164, 169, 171–72, 174–76, 180, 187, 190–91, 209, 211, 250, 253, 256, 272, 298
  and slavery, 232–33, 308–309
  supposed virtues of, 127, 303, 306, 327
  and TJ-Hamilton feud, 179–86, 189, 250, 290, 298
  TJ takes notes on conversations with, 190, 218
Watts, Isaac, 119
Wayles, John, 56, 61–62, 68, 112, 171, 196, 312
Wayles, Martha Eppes, 56

Webster, Daniel, 318
Whiskey Rebellion, 209, 387n23
Whitcomb, Samuel, 318–19
Wilkinson, General James, 277, 280–84, 286–87
Wills, Garry, 93
Wirt, William, 108, 170
Witherspoon, John, 82, 86
Wolcott, Oliver, 259
Wollstonecraft, Mary, 154
Wythe, George
  murder of, 37
  on slavery, 36–37, 54, 157
  as TJ's mentor and friend, 33–38, 47, 48, 61, 68, 89, 93, 104–106, 109–110, 132
  uneasy relations with Pendleton, 77–78

XYZ Affair, 211, 221, 229

yellow fever epidemic, 191, 313
Young, Edward, 48

Zoffany, Johan, 136, 146

A NOTE ON THE AUTHOR

ANDREW BURSTEIN recently retired from Louisiana State University, where he was the Charles P. Manship Professor of History. He is the author of twelve previous books, including *The Passions of Andrew Jackson* (Knopf) and *Jefferson's Secrets* (Basic Books), and two coauthored dual biographies: *Madison and Jefferson* (Random House) and *The Problem of Democracy* (Viking), a unique study of the two Presidents Adams. His books have received praise in the *New York Times*, *Washington Post*, *Wall Street Journal*, and various other recognized periodicals. As a noted Jefferson scholar, he serves on the advisory board of the *Papers of Thomas Jefferson*. A consultant on several documentary films, he was prominently featured in the Ken Burns PBS documentary *Thomas Jefferson*. As a frequent opinion writer, he has written extensively for Salon and other national news outlets. He earned a PhD in U.S. history from the University of Virginia after having studied Chinese politics and culture at Columbia University and the University of Michigan. He lives in Charlottesville.